Samuel Johnson
The Lives of the Poets

# SAMUEL JOHNSON

## THE LIVES
## OF THE MOST EMINENT
## ENGLISH POETS; WITH
## CRITICAL OBSERVATIONS
## ON THEIR WORKS

With an Introduction and Notes by

ROGER LONSDALE

Volume II

CLARENDON PRESS · OXFORD

# OXFORD
## UNIVERSITY PRESS

Great Clarendon Street, Oxford OX2 6DP

Oxford University Press is a department of the University of Oxford.
It furthers the University's objective of excellence in research, scholarship,
and education by publishing worldwide in

Oxford New York

Auckland Cape Town Dar es Salaam Hong Kong Karachi
Kuala Lumpur Madrid Melbourne Mexico City Nairobi
New Delhi Shanghai Taipei Toronto

With offices in

Argentina Austria Brazil Chile Czech Republic France Greece
Guatemala Hungary Italy Japan Poland Portugal Singapore
South Korea Switzerland Thailand Turkey Ukraine Vietnam

Oxford is a registered trade mark of Oxford University Press
in the UK and in certain other countries

Published in the United States
by Oxford University Press Inc., New York

British Library Cataloguing in Publication Data

Data available

Library of Congress Cataloguing in Publication Data

Data available

Typeset by SPI Publisher Services, Pondicherry, India
Printed in Great Britain
on acid-free paper by

Biddles Ltd, King's Lynn, Norfolk

ISBN 0-19-927897-0   978-0-19-927897-8 (set)

ISBN 0-19-928479-2   978-0-19-928479-5 (Volume i)

ISBN 0-19-928480-6   978-0-19-928480-1 (Volume ii)

ISBN 0-19-928481-4   978-0-19-928481-8 (Volume iii)

ISBN 0-19-928482-2   978-0-19-928482-5 (Volume iv)

1 3 5 7 9 10 8 6 4 2

# CONTENTS TO VOLUME II

# LIVES OF THE ENGLISH POETS
## IN ALPHABETICAL ORDER

# SHORT TITLES

Place of publication in London unless otherwise stated.

Bate (1978)
W. Jackson Bate, *Samuel Johnson* (1978)
*BB*
William Oldys et al. (eds.), *Biographia Britannica* (7 vols., 1747–66); 2nd edn.,
ed. Andrew Kippis (6 vols., 1778–93)
*Bibliography*
J. D. Fleeman (comp.), *A Bibliography of the Works of Samuel Johnson*, prepared
for publication by James McLaverty (2 vols., Oxford, 2000)
Boswell, *Applause*
*Boswell: The Applause of the Jury 1782–85*, ed. Irma S. Lustig and Frederick
A. Pottle (New York, 1981)
Boswell, *Catalogue*
*Catalogue of the Papers of James Boswell at Yale University*, ed. Marion Pottle
et al. (3 vols., New Haven, 1993)
*Boswell in Extremes*
*Boswell in Extremes 1776–1778*, ed. Charles MCC. Weis and Frederick A. Pottle
(New York, 1970)
Boswell, *Laird of Auchinleck*
*Boswell: Laird of Auchinleck 1778–1782*, ed. Joseph W. Reed and Frederick A.
Pottle (New York, 1977)
Boswell, *Making of the Life*
*The Correspondence and Other Papers of James Boswell Relating to the Making of
the Life of Johnson*, ed. Marshall Waingrow (1969; 2nd edn., Edinburgh, 2001)
Boswell, *Members of the Club*
*The Correspondence of James Boswell with Certain Members of the Club*, ed. Charles
N. Fifer (1976)
Boswell, *Ominous Years*
*Boswell: The Ominous Years 1774–1776*, ed. Charles Ryskamp and Frederick
A. Pottle (New York, 1963)
Brown, *Critical Opinions*
*The Critical Opinions of Samuel Johnson*, ed. Joseph Epes Brown (Princeton,
1926; New York, 1961)
Burke, *Corresp.*
Edmund Burke, *Correspondence*, ed. Thomas W. Copeland et al. (10 vols.,
Cambridge, 1958–78)
Burke, *Enquiry*
Edmund Burke, *A Philosophical Enquiry into our Ideas of the Sublime and
Beautiful* (1757), ed. James T. Boulton (1958)

Burney, *Diary and Letters*
   *The Diary and Letters of Madame d'Arblay*, ed. Austin Dobson (6 vols., 1904–5)
Burney, *Early Journals*
   *The Early Journals and Letters of Fanny Burney*, ed. Lars E. Troide et al., vols. i–
   (Oxford, 1988–  )
Carnie (1956)
   R. H. Carnie, 'Lord Hailes's Notes on Johnson's "Lives of the Poets"', *N & Q*
   201 (1956), 73–5, 106–8, 174–6, 343–6, 486–9
Chesterfield, *Letters*
   Earl of Chesterfield, *Letters*, ed. Bonamy Dobrée (6 vols., 1932)
Clifford (1955)
   James L. Clifford, *Young Sam Johnson* (New York, 1955)
Clifford (1979)
   James L. Clifford, *Dictionary Johnson: Samuel Johnson's Middle Years* (New
   York, 1979)
Clifford, *Mrs. Thrale*
   James L. Clifford, *Hester Lynch Piozzi (Mrs. Thrale)* (Oxford, 1941)
Cokayne
   G. E. Cokayne, *The Complete Peerage* (rev. edn., 13 vols., 1910–59)
Cokayne, *Baronetage*
   G. E. Cokayne, *The Complete Baronetage* (6 vols., Exeter, 1900–9)
Cowper, *Letters*
   William Cowper, *Letters and Prose Writings*, ed. James King and Charles Rys-
   kamp (5 vols., Oxford, 1979–86)
Cunningham, *Lives* (1854)
   *Lives of the Most Eminent English Poets. . . By Samuel Johnson*, ed. Peter Cun-
   ningham (3 vols., 1854)
Damrosch (1976)
   Leopold Damrosch, Jr., *The Uses of Johnson's Criticism* (Charlottesville, Va., 1976)
DeMaria (1986)
   Robert DeMaria, Jr., *Johnson's Dictionary and the Language of Learning* (Oxford, 1986)
Dennis, *Works*
   *The Critical Works of John Dennis*, ed. Edward Niles Hooker (2 vols., Baltimore,
   1939–43)
*Dict.*
   Samuel Johnson, *A Dictionary of the English Language* (2 vols., 1755; 4th edn., 1773)
Doddridge, *Corresp.*
   *Calendar of the Correspondence of Philip Doddridge, D.D. (1702–1751)*, ed. G. F.
   Nuttall (London, 1979)
Dodsley, *Collection*
   *A Collection of Poems by Several Hands*, ed. Robert Dodsley (6 vols., 1748–58)
Dodsley, *Corresp.*
   *The Correspondence of Robert Dodsley 1733–64*, ed. James E. Tierney (Cam-
   bridge, 1988)

*Early Biographies* (1974)
  *The Early Biographies of Samuel Johnson*, ed. O. M. Brack, Jr., and Robert
  E. Kelley (Iowa City, 1974)
*Early Biog. Writings* (1973)
  *Early Biographical Writings of Dr. Johnson*, ed. J. D. Fleeman (Westmead, 1973)
Edinger (1977)
  William Edinger, *Samuel Johnson and Poetic Style* (Chicago, 1977)
*Eng. Poets* (1779)
  *The Works of the English Poets. With Prefaces, Biographical and Critical, By
  Samuel Johnson* (58 vols., 1779; 2nd edn., 75 vols., 1790)
Evelyn, *Diary*
  *The Diary of John Evelyn*, ed. E. S. de Beer (6 vols., Oxford, 1955)
Fleeman, *Handlist* (1967)
  J. D. Fleeman (ed.), *A Preliminary Handlist of Documents & Manuscripts of
  Samuel Johnson* (Oxford, 1967)
Fleeman, *Handlist* (1984)
  J. D. Fleeman, *A Preliminary Handlist of Copies of Books Associated with
  Dr. Samuel Johnson* (Oxford, 1984)
Fleeman (1962)
  J. D. Fleeman, 'Some Proofs of Johnson's *Prefaces to the Poets*', *Library*, 5th ser.
  17 (1962), 213–30
Folkenflik
  Robert Folkenflik, *Samuel Johnson, Biographer* (Ithaca, NY, 1978)
Forster, *Alumni Oxon.*
  Joseph Forster, *Alumni Oxonienses: The Members of the University of Oxford,
  1500–1714* (4 vols., 1891–2); *1715–1886* (4 vols., 1887–8)
Foxon, *English Verse*
  D. F. Foxon, *English Verse, 1701–1750: A Catalogue of Separately Printed Poems*
  (2 vols., Cambridge, 1975)
Garrick, *Letters*
  *The Letters of David Garrick*, ed. David M. Little and George M. Kahrl (3 vols.,
  1963)
*GD*
  Thomas Birch, John Peter Bernard, and John Lockman, *A General Dictionary,
  Historical and Critical* (10 vols., 1734–41)
*Gent. Mag.*
  *Gentleman's Magazine* (1731–  )
*Gleanings*
  A. L. Reade, *Johnsonian Gleanings* (11 vols., 1909–52)
Goldsmith, *Coll. Works*
  Oliver Goldsmith, *Collected Works*, ed. Arthur Friedman (5 vols., Oxford, 1966)
Gray, *Coresp.*
  *The Correspondence of Thomas Gray*, ed. Paget Toynbee and Leonard Whibley
  (3 vols., Oxford, 1935; corrected edn. by H. W. Starr, 1971)

*Guardian*
  *The Guardian*, ed. John Calhoun Stephens (Lexington, Mass., 1982)
Hagstrum (1952)
  Jean H. Hagstrum, *Samuel Johnson's Literary Criticism* (Chicago, 1952)
Hart (1950)
  E. L. Hart, 'Some New Sources of Johnson's *Lives*', *PMLA* 65 (1950), 1088–111
Hawkins, *J's Works* (1787)
  *The Works of Samuel Johnson*, ed. Sir John Hawkins (11 vols., 1787)
Hawkins, *Life*
  *The Life of Samuel Johnson* (1787) (also as vol. i of the preceding)
Hazen
  Allen T. Hazen, *Samuel Johnson's Prefaces and Dedications* (New Haven, 1937)
Henson
  Eithne Henson, *'The Fictions of Romantick Chivalry': Samuel Johnson and Romance* (1992)
Highfill, *Dictionary*
  Philip H. Highfill et al., *A Biographical Dictionary of Actors, Actresses, Musicians. . . 1660–1800* (16 vols., Carbondale, Ill., 1973–93)
Hill (1905)
  *Lives of the English Poets by Samuel Johnson*, ed. George Birkbeck Hill (3 vols., Oxford, 1905)
Jacob
  Giles Jacob, *The Poetical Register: or, The Lives and Characters of the English Dramatick Poets* (1719); *An Historical Account of the Lives and Writings of our Most Considerable English Poets* (1720); 2nd edn. as *The Poetical Register* (1723) 2 vols.
*J. Misc.*
  *Johnsonian Miscellanies*, ed. George Birkbeck Hill (2 vols., Oxford, 1897)
*Journey* (1985)
  Samuel Johnson, *A Journey to the Western Islands of Scotland*, ed. J. D. Fleeman (Oxford, 1985)
Kaminski
  Thomas Kaminski, *The Early Career of Samuel Johnson* (New York, 1987)
*L81–L83*
  Samuel Johnson, *The Lives of the Most Eminent English Poets* (4 vols., 1781; 4 vols., 1783)
*Letters*
  *The Letters of Samuel Johnson*, ed. Bruce Redford (5 vols., Oxford, 1992–94)
*Letters* (1788)
  *Letters to and from the Late Samuel Johnson, LL.D.. . . Published from the Original MSS. in her Possession, by Hester Lynch Piozzi* (2 vols., 1788)
*Letters*, ed. Chapman
  *The Letters of Samuel Johnson, with Mrs. Thrale's Genuine Letters to Him*, ed. R. W. Chapman (3 vols., Oxford, 1952)

*Life*
> Boswell's Life of Johnson, Together with Boswell's Journal of a Tour to the Hebrides, ed. George Birkbeck Hill, rev. L. F. Powell (6 vols., 1934–50; vols. v and vi, 2nd edn., 1964)

Lipking (1970)
> Lawrence Lipking, *The Ordering of the Arts in Eighteenth-Century England* (Princeton, 1970)

Lipking (1998)
> Lawrence Lipking, *Samuel Johnson: The Life of an Author* (Cambridge, Mass., 1998)

Lobban
> J. H. Lobban, *Dr. Johnson's Mrs. Thrale* (Edinburgh, 1910)

*London Stage*
> The London Stage 1660–1800: Pt. i: 1660–1700, ed. W. Van Lennep (Carbondale, Ill., 1965); Pt. ii: 1700–1729, ed. E. L. Avery (1960); Pt. iii: 1729–1747, ed. A. H. Scouten (1961); Pt. iv: 1747–1776, ed. G. W. Stone, Jr. (1962); Pt. v: 1776–1800, ed. C. B. Hogan (1968)

McCarthy
> W. McCarthy, 'The Composition of Johnson's *Lives*: A Calendar', *PQ* 60 (1981), 53–67

McGuffie
> Helen L. McGuffie, *Samuel Johnson in the British Press 1749–84: A Chronological Checklist* (New York, 1976)

*MR*
> *Monthly Review* (1749– )

*NCBEL*
> George Watson (ed.), *The New Cambridge Bibliography of English Literature* (5 vols., Cambridge, 1969–77)

Nichols, *Lit. Anec.*
> John Nichols, *Literary Anecdotes of the Eighteenth Century* (9 vols., 1812–16)

Nichols, *Lit. Ill.*
> John Nichols, *Illustrations of the Literary History of the Eighteenth Century* (8 vols., 1817–58)

Nichols, *Minor Lives*
> Minor Lives: A Collection of Biographies by John Nichols, ed. E. L. Hart (Cambridge, Mass., 1971)

Nichols, *Sel. Collection*
> John Nichols (ed.), *A Select Collection of Poems* (8 vols., 1780–2)

*OASJ*
> Samuel Johnson (The Oxford Authors), ed. Donald Greene (Oxford, 1984); reissued as *The Major Works* (World's Classics, Oxford, 2000).

*P79–P81*
> Samuel Johnson, *Prefaces, Biographical and Critical, to the Works of the English Poets*, vols. i–iv (1779); vols. v–x (1781)

Pepys

*The Diary of Samuel Pepys*, ed. Robert Latham and William Matthews (11 vols., 1970–83)

Percy, *Corresp.*

*The Percy Letters*, ed. David Nichol Smith, Cleanth Brooks and A. F. Falconar (9 vols., Baton Rouge, La., 1944–88), incl. Thomas Percy's *Corresp.* with: i *Edmond Malone*, ed. A. Tillotson (1944); ii *Richard Farmer*, ed. C. Brooks (1946); iii *Thomas Warton*, ed. M. G. Robinson and L. Dennis (1951); iv *David Dalrymple, Lord Hardes*, ed. H. F. Falconer (1954); v *Evar Evans*, ed. A. Lewis (195); vii *William Shenstone*, ed. C. Brooks (1977); ix *Robert Anderson*, ed. W. E. K. Anderson (1988)

*POAS*

George deForest Lord (ed.), *Poems on Affairs of State* (7 vols., New Haven, 1963–75)

*Poems*

*The Poems of Samuel Johnson*, ed. David Nichol Smith and E. L. McAdam, Jr. (1941), rev. J. D. Fleeman (Oxford, 1974)

Pope, *Corresp.*

*The Correspondence of Alexander Pope*, ed. George Sherburn (5 vols., Oxford, 1956)

Pope, *TE*

*The Twickenham Edition of the Poems of Alexander Pope*, ed. John Butt et al. (10 vols., 1938–67)

Potter, *Inquiry*

Robert Potter, *An Inquiry into Some Passages in Dr. Johnson's Lives of the Poets* (1783)

Prior, *Lit. Works*

*The Literary Works of Matthew Prior*, ed. H. Bunker Wright and Monroe K. Spears (2 vols., Oxford, 1959; 2nd edn., 1971)

*Queeney Letters*

*The Queeney Letters: Being Letters Addressed to Hester Maria Thrale by Doctor Johnson, Fanny Burney and Mrs. Thrale-Piozzi*, ed. Marquis of Lansdowne (1934)

Reddick

Allen Reddick, *The Making of Johnson's Dictionary, 1746–73* (Cambridge, 1990)

Reynolds, *Discourses*

Sir Joshua Reynolds, *Discourses*, ed. Pat Rogers (1992)

Reynolds, *Portraits*

Sir Joshua Reynolds, *Portraits*, ed. F. W. Hilles (1952)

Rogers (1980)

Pat Rogers, 'Samuel Johnson and the Biographic Dictionaries', *RES* 31 (1980), 149–71

Rymer, *Critical Works*

Thomas Rymer, *Critical Works*, ed. C. A. Zimansky (New Haven, 1956)

Shenstone, *Letters*

*Letters of William Shenstone*, ed. Marjorie Williams (Oxford, 1939)

Shiels, *Lives*
[Robert Shiels or Shiells], *The Lives of the Poets of Great Britain and Ireland, to the Time of Dean Swift. By Mr. Cibber* (5 vols., 1753)
*Spectator*
Donald F. Bond (ed.), *The Spectator* (5 vols., Oxford, 1965)
Spence
Joseph Spence, *Observations, Anecdotes, and Characters of Books and Men*, ed. James M. Osborn (2 vols., Oxford, 1966)
Spingarn
J. E. Spingarn (ed.), *Critical Essays of the Seventeenth Century* (3 vols., Oxford, 1908)
Swift, *Corresp.*
*The Correspondence of Jonathan Swift*, ed. Harold Williams (5 vols., Oxford, 1963–5)
Swift, *Jnl. to Stella*
Jonathan Swift, *Journal to Stella*, ed. Harold Williams (2 vols., Oxford, 1948; also as vols. xv–xvi of *Prose Writings* below
Swift, *Poems*
Jonathan Swift, *Poems*, ed. H. Williams (3 vols., Oxford, 1937; 2nd edn. Oxford, 1938, cited)
Swift, *PW*
Jonathan Swift, *Prose Writings*, ed. Herbert Davis (14 vols., Oxford, 1939–68)
*Tatler*
Donald F. Bond (ed.), *The Tatler* (3 vols., Oxford, 1987)
Thomson, *Letters*
*James Thomson (1700–1748): Letters and Documents*, ed. A. D. McKillop (Lawrence, Kan. 1958)
Thrale-Piozzi, *Anecdotes*
*Anecdotes of the Late Samuel Johnson* (1786) (cited from *J. Misc.*, i. 144–351)
*Thraliana*
*Thraliana: The Diary of Mrs. Hester Lynch Thrale*, ed. K. C. Balderston (2 vols., Oxford, 1942; rev. edn., 1951, cited)
Venn, *Alumni Cantab.*
*Alumni Cantabrigienses*, Pt. i: *To 1751*, ed. John Venn and J. A. Venn (4 vols., Cambridge, 1922–7); Pt. ii: *1752–1900*, ed. J. A. Venn (6 vols., Cambridge, 1940–54)
Walpole, *Corresp.*
*The Yale Edition of Horace Walpole's Correspondence*, ed. W. S. Lewis et al. (48 vols., New Haven, 1937–83)
Warton, *Essay*
*An Essay on the Writings and Genius of Pope* (1756; 2nd edn., 1762, as *Essay on the Genius and Writings* etc.; vol. ii, 1782; 5th edn., 2 vols., 1806)
Watson
John Dryden, *Of Dramatic Poesy and Other Critical Essays*, ed. George Watson (2 vols., 1962)

Wood

    Anthony Wood, *Athenae Oxonienses... To which are added, the Fasti, or Annals, of the said University* (2 vols., 1691–2; 2nd edn., 2 vols., 1721, cited)

Wordsworth, *Prose Works*

    William Wordsworth, *Prose Works*, ed. W. J. B. Owen and J. W. Smyser (3 vols., Oxford, 1974)

*YW*

    *The Yale Edition of the Works of Samuel Johnson*, general editor, J. H. Middendorf: i: *Diaries, Prayers, and Annals*, ed. E. L. McAdam, Jr., with Donald and Mary Hyde (1958); ii: *The Idler* and *The Adventurer*, ed. W. J. Bate, J. Bullitt, and L. F. Powell (1963); iii–v: *The Rambler*, ed. W. J. Bate and A. B. Strauss (1969); vi: *Poems*, ed. E. L. McAdam, Jr. with G. Milne (1964); vii–viii: *Johnson on Shakespeare*, ed. A. Sherbo (1968); ix: *A Journey to the Western Isles of Scotland*, ed. M. Lascelles (1971); x: *Political Writings*, ed. D. J. Greene (1977); xiv: *Sermons*, ed. J. H. Hagstrum and J. Gray (1978); xv: *A Voyage to Abyssinia*, ed. J. J. Gold (1985); xvi: *Rasselas and Other Tales*, ed. G. J. Kolb (1990)

## PERIODICALS

| | |
|---|---|
| *Age of J* | *Age of Johnson* |
| *BJECS* | *British Journal for Eighteenth-Century Studies* |
| *BLR* | *Bodleian Library Record* |
| *BNYPL* | *Bulletin of the New York Public Library* |
| *BRH* | *Bulletin of Research in the Humanities* |
| *DUJ* | *Durham University Journal* |
| *EC* | *Essays in Criticism* |
| *ECL* | *Eighteenth-Century Life* |
| *ECS* | *Eighteenth-Century Studies* |
| *ELH* | *Journal of English Literary History* |
| *ELN* | *English Language Notes* |
| *ES* | *English Studies* |
| *HLQ* | *Huntington Library Quarterly* |
| *JEGP* | *Journal of English and Germanic Philology* |
| *JNL* | *Johnsonian News Letter* |
| *MLN* | *Modern Language Notes* |
| *MLQ* | *Modern Language Quarterly* |
| *MP* | *Modern Philology* |
| *N & Q* | *Notes and Queries* |
| *PBSA* | *Publications of the Bibliographical Society of America* |
| *PMLA* | *Publications of the Modern Language Association of America* |
| *PQ* | *Philological Quarterly* |
| *RES* | *Review of English Studies* |

| SB | *Studies in Bibliography* |
| SEC | *Studies in Eighteenth-Century Culture* |
| SEL | *Studies in English Literature* |
| SP | *Studies in Philology* |
| TLS | *Times Literary Supplement* |

# BUTLER

OF the great author of Hudibras there is a life prefixed to the later editions   1
of his poem, by an unknown writer, and therefore of disputable authority;
and some account is incidentally given by Wood, who confesses the uncertainty of his own narrative; more however than they knew cannot now be
learned, and nothing remains but to compare and copy them.

SAMUEL BUTLER was born in the parish of Strensham in Worcestershire,   2
according to his biographer, in 1612. This account Dr. Nash finds
confirmed by the register. He was christened Feb. 14.

His father's condition is variously represented. Wood mentions him as   3
competently wealthy; but Mr. Longueville, the son of Butler's principal
friend, says he was an honest farmer with some small estate, who made a
shift to educate his son at the grammar school of Worcester, under
Mr. Henry Bright, from whose care he removed for a short time to
Cambridge; but, for want of money, was never made a member of any
college. Wood leaves us rather doubtful whether he went to Cambridge or
Oxford; but at last makes him pass six or seven years at Cambridge, without
knowing in what hall or college; yet it can hardly be imagined that he lived
so long in either university, but as belonging to one house or another; and it
is still less likely that he could have so long inhabited a place of learning with
so little distinction as to leave his residence uncertain. Dr. Nash has
discovered that his father was owner of a house and a little land, worth
about eight pounds a year, still called *Butler's tenement*.

Wood has his information from his brother, whose narrative placed him   4
at Cambridge, in opposition to that of his neighbours which sent him to
Oxford. The brother's seems the best authority, till, by confessing his
inability to tell his hall or college, he gives reason to suspect that he was
resolved to bestow on him an academical education; but durst not name a
college, for fear of detection.

He was for some time, according to the author of his Life, clerk to   5
Mr. Jefferys of Earl's Croomb in Worcestershire, an eminent justice of
the peace. In his service he had not only leisure for study, but for recreation:
his amusements were musick and painting; and the reward of his pencil was
the friendship of the celebrated Cooper. Some pictures, said to be his, were
shewn to Dr. Nash, at Earl's Croomb; but when he enquired for them some

years afterwards, he found them destroyed, to stop windows, and owns that they hardly deserved a better fate.

6    He was afterwards admitted into the family of the Countess of Kent, where he had the use of a library; and so much recommended himself to Selden, that he was often employed by him in literary business. Selden, as is well known, was steward to the Countess, and is supposed to have gained much of his wealth by managing her estate.

7    In what character Butler was admitted into that Lady's service, how long he continued in it, and why he left it, is, like the other incidents of his life, utterly unknown.

8    The vicissitudes of his condition placed him afterwards in the family of Sir Samuel Luke, one of Cromwell's officers. Here he observed so much of the character of the sectaries, that he is said to have written or begun his poem at this time; and it is likely that such a design would be formed in a place where he saw the principles and practices of the rebels, audacious and undisguised in the confidence of success.

9    At length the King returned, and the time came in which loyalty hoped for its reward. Butler, however, was only made secretary to the Earl of Carbury, president of the principality of Wales; who conferred on him the stewardship of Ludlow Castle, when the Court of the Marches was revived.

10    In this part of his life, he married Mrs. Herbert, a gentlewoman of a good family; and lived, says Wood, upon her fortune, having studied the common law, but never practised it. A fortune she had, says his biographer, but it was lost by bad securities.

11    In 1663 was published the first part, containing three cantos, of the poem of Hudibras, which, as Prior relates, was made known at Court by the taste and influence of the Earl of Dorset. When it was known, it was necessarily admired: the king quoted, the courtiers studied, and the whole party of the royalists applauded it. Every eye watched for the golden shower which was to fall upon the author, who certainly was not without his part in the general expectation.

12    In 1664 the second part appeared; the curiosity of the nation was rekindled, and the writer was again praised and elated. But praise was his whole reward. Clarendon, says Wood, gave him reason to hope for "places and employments of value and credit;" but no such advantages did he ever obtain. It is reported, that the King once gave him three hundred guineas; but of this temporary bounty I find no proof.

13    Wood relates that he was secretary to Villiers Duke of Buckingham, when he was Chancellor of Cambridge: this is doubted by the other writer, who yet allows the Duke to have been his frequent benefactor. That both these accounts are false there is reason to suspect, from a story told by

Packe, in his account of the Life of Wycherley, and from some verses which Mr. Thyer has published in the author's remains.

"Mr. Wycherley," says Packe, "had always laid hold of any opportunity 14 which offered of representing to the Duke of Buckingham how well Mr. Butler had deserved of the royal family, by writing his inimitable Hudibras; and that it was a reproach to the Court, that a person of his loyalty and wit should suffer in obscurity, and under the wants he did. The Duke always seemed to hearken to him with attention enough; and, after some time, undertook to recommend his pretensions to his Majesty. Mr. Wycherley, in hopes to keep him steady to his word, obtained of his Grace to name a day, when he might introduce that modest and unfortunate poet to his new patron. At last an appointment was made, and the place of meeting was agreed to be the Roebuck. Mr. Butler and his friend attended accordingly: the Duke joined them; but, as the d—l would have it, the door of the room where they sat was open, and his Grace, who had seated himself near it, observing a pimp of his acquaintance (the creature too was a knight) trip by with a brace of Ladies, immediately quitted his engagement, to follow another kind of business, at which he was more ready than in doing good offices to men of desert; though no one was better qualified than he, both in regard to his fortune and understanding, to protect them; and, from that time to the day of his death, poor Butler never found the least effect of his promise!"

Such is the story. The verses are written with a degree of acrimony, such 15 as neglect and disappointment might naturally excite; and such as it would be hard to imagine Butler capable of expressing against a man who had any claim to his gratitude.

Notwithstanding this discouragement and neglect, he still prosecuted his 16 design; and in 1678 published the third part, which still leaves the poem imperfect and abrupt. How much more he originally intended, or with what events the action was to be concluded, it is vain to conjecture. Nor can it be thought strange that he should stop here, however unexpectedly. To write without reward is sufficiently unpleasing. He had now arrived at an age when he might think it proper to be in jest no longer, and perhaps his health might now begin to fail.

He died in 1680; and Mr. Longueville, having unsuccessfully solicited a 17 subscription for his interment in Westminster Abbey, buried him at his own cost in the church-yard of Covent Garden. Dr. Simon Patrick read the service.

Granger was informed by Dr. Pearce, who named for his authority 18 Mr. Lowndes of the treasury, that Butler had an yearly pension of an hundred pounds. This is contradicted by all tradition, by the complaints of Oldham, and by the reproaches of Dryden; and I am afraid will never be confirmed.

19  About sixty years afterwards, Mr. Barber, a printer, Mayor of London, and a friend to Butler's principles, bestowed on him a monument in Westminster Abbey, thus inscribed:

M. S.

SAMUELIS BUTLERI,

Qui *Strenshamiæ* in agro *Vigorn*. nat. 1612, obiit *Lond*. 1680.

Vir doctus imprimis, acer, integer;

Operibus Ingenii, non item præmiis, fœlix:

*Satyrici* apud nos Carminis Artifex egregius;

Quo simulatæ Religionis Larvam detraxit,

Et Perduellium scelera liberrime exagitavit:

Scriptorum in suo genere, Primus et Postremus.

Ne, cui vivo deerant ferè omnia,

Deesset etiam mortuo Tumulus,

Hoc tandem posito marmore, curavit

JOHANNES BARBER, Civis *Londinensis*, 1721.

20  After his death were published three small volumes of his posthumous works: I know not by whom collected, or by what authority ascertained; and, lately, two volumes more have been printed by Mr. Thyer of Manchester, indubitably genuine. From none of these pieces can his life be traced, or his character discovered. Some verses, in the last collection, shew him to have been among those who ridiculed the institution of the Royal Society, of which the enemies were for some time very numerous and very acrimonious, for what reason it is hard to conceive, since the philosophers professed not to advance doctrines, but to produce facts; and the most zealous enemy of innovation must admit the gradual progress of experience, however he may oppose hypothetical temerity.

21  In this mist of obscurity passed the life of Butler, a man whose name can only perish with his language. The mode and place of his education are unknown; the events of his life are variously related; and all that can be told with certainty is, that he was poor.

22  THE poem of Hudibras is one of those compositions of which a nation may justly boast; as the images which it exhibits are domestick, the sentiments unborrowed and unexpected, and the strain of diction original and peculiar. We must not, however, suffer the pride, which we assume as the countrymen of Butler, to make any encroachment upon justice, nor appropriate those honours which others have a right to share. The poem of Hudibras is not wholly English; the original idea is to be found in the

History of Don Quixote; a book to which a mind of the greatest powers may be indebted without disgrace.

Cervantes shews a man, who having, by the incessant perusal of incred- 23 ible tales, subjected his understanding to his imagination, and familiarised his mind by pertinacious meditation to trains of incredible events and scenes of impossible existence, goes out in the pride of knighthood, to redress wrongs, and defend virgins, to rescue captive princesses, and tumble usurpers from their thrones; attended by a squire, whose cunning, too low for the suspicion of a generous mind, enables him often to cheat his master.

The hero of Butler is a Presbyterian Justice, who, in the confidence of 24 legal authority, and the rage of zealous ignorance, ranges the country to repress superstition and correct abuses, accompanied by an Independent Clerk, disputatious and obstinate, with whom he often debates, but never conquers him.

Cervantes had so much kindness for Don Quixote, that, however he 25 embarrasses him with absurd distresses, he gives him so much sense and virtue as may preserve our esteem: wherever he is, or whatever he does, he is made by matchless dexterity commonly ridiculous, but never contemptible.

But for poor Hudibras, his poet had no tenderness: he chuses not that any 26 pity should be shewn or respect paid him: he gives him up at once to laughter and contempt, without any quality that can dignify or protect him.

In forming the character of Hudibras, and describing his person and 27 habiliments, the author seems to labour with a tumultuous confusion of dissimilar ideas. He had read the history of the mock knights-errant; he knew the notions and manners of a presbyterian magistrate, and tried to unite the absurdities of both, however distant, in one personage. Thus he gives him that pedantick ostentation of knowledge which has no relation to chivalry, and loads him with martial encumbrances that can add nothing to his civil dignity. He sends him out *a colonelling*, and yet never brings him within sight of war.

If Hudibras be considered as the representative of the presbyterians, it is 28 not easy to say why his weapons should be represented as ridiculous or useless; for, whatever judgement might be passed upon their knowledge or their arguments, experience had sufficiently shown that their swords were not to be despised.

The hero, thus compounded of swaggerer and pedant, of knight and 29 justice, is led forth to action, with his squire Ralpho, an Independant enthusiast.

30     Of the contexture of events planned by the author, which is called the action of the poem, since it is left imperfect, no judgement can be made. It is probable, that the hero was to be led through many luckless adventures, which would give occasion, like his attack upon the *bear and fiddle*, to expose the ridiculous rigour of the sectaries; like his encounter with Sidrophel and Whacum, to make superstition and credulity contemptible; or, like his recourse to the low retailer of the law, discover the fraudulent practices of different professions.

31     What series of events he would have formed, or in what manner he would have rewarded or punished his hero, it is now vain to conjecture. His work must have had, as it seems, the defect which Dryden imputes to Spenser; the action could not have been one; there could only have been a succession of incidents, each of which might have happened without the rest, and which could not all co-operate to any single conclusion.

32     The discontinuity of the action might however have been easily forgiven, if there had been action enough; but I believe every reader regrets the paucity of events, and complains that in the poem of Hudibras, as in the history of Thucydides, there is more said than done. The scenes are too seldom changed, and the attention is tired with long conversation.

33     It is indeed much more easy to form dialogues than to contrive adventures. Every position makes way for an argument, and every objection dictates an answer. When two disputants are engaged upon a complicated and extensive question, the difficulty is not to continue, but to end the controversy. But whether it be that we comprehend but few of the possibilities of life, or that life itself affords little variety, every man who has tried knows how much labour it will cost to form such a combination of circumstances, as shall have at once the grace of novelty and credibility, and delight fancy without violence to reason.

34     Perhaps the Dialogue of this poem is not perfect. Some power of engaging the attention might have been added to it, by quicker reciprocation, by seasonable interruptions, by sudden questions, and by a nearer approach to dramatick spriteliness; without which, fictitious speeches will always tire, however sparkling with sentences, and however variegated with allusions.

35     The great source of pleasure is variety. Uniformity must tire at last, though it be uniformity of excellence. We love to expect; and, when expectation is disappointed or gratified, we want to be again expecting. For this impatience of the present, whoever would please, must make provision. The skilful writer *irritat, mulcet*, makes a due distribution of the still and animated parts. It is for want of this artful intertexture, and those necessary changes, that the whole of a book may be tedious, though all the parts are praised.

If unexhaustible wit could give perpetual pleasure, no eye would ever 36 leave half-read the work of Butler; for what poet has ever brought so many remote images so happily together? It is scarcely possible to peruse a page without finding some association of images that was never found before. By the first paragraph the reader is amused, by the next he is delighted, and by a few more strained to astonishment; but astonishment is a toilsome pleasure; he is soon weary of wondering, and longs to be diverted.

> Omnia vult belle Matho dicere, dic aliquando
> Et bene, dic neutrum, dic aliquando male.

Imagination is useless without knowledge: nature gives in vain the power 37 of combination, unless study and observation supply materials to be combined. Butler's treasures of knowledge appear proportioned to his expence: whatever topick employs his mind, he shews himself qualified to expand and illustrate it with all the accessories that books can furnish: he is found not only to have travelled the beaten road, but the bye-paths of literature; not only to have taken general surveys, but to have examined particulars with minute inspection.

If the French boast the learning of Rabelais, we need not be afraid of 38 confronting them with Butler.

But the most valuable parts of his performance are those which retired 39 study and native wit cannot supply. He that merely makes a book from books may be useful, but can scarcely be great. Butler had not suffered life to glide beside him unseen or unobserved. He had watched with great diligence the operations of human nature, and traced the effects of opinion, humour, interest, and passion. From such remarks proceeded that great number of sententious distichs which have passed into conversation, and are added as proverbial axioms to the general stock of practical knowledge.

When any work has been viewed and admired, the first question of 40 intelligent curiosity is, how was it performed? Hudibras was not a hasty effusion; it was not produced by a sudden tumult of imagination, or a short paroxysm of violent labour. To accumulate such a mass of sentiments at the call of accidental desire, or of sudden necessity, is beyond the reach and power of the most active and comprehensive mind. I am informed by Mr. Thyer of Manchester, the excellent editor of this author's reliques, that he could shew something like Hudibras in prose. He has in his possession the common-place book, in which Butler reposited, not such events or precepts as are gathered by reading; but such remarks, similitudes, allusions, assemblages, or inferences, as occasion prompted, or meditation produced; those thoughts that were generated in his own mind, and might be usefully applied to some future purpose. Such is the labour of those who write for immortality.

41    But human works are not easily found without a perishable part. Of the ancient poets every reader feels the mythology tedious and oppressive. Of Hudibras, the manners, being founded on opinions, are temporary and local, and therefore become every day less intelligible, and less striking. What Cicero says of philosophy is true likewise of wit and humour, that "time effaces the fictions of opinion, and confirms the determinations of Nature." Such manners as depend upon standing relations and general passions are co-extended with the race of man; but those modifications of life, and peculiarities of practice, which are the progeny of error and perverseness, or at best of some accidental influence or transient persuasion, must perish with their parents.

42    Much therefore of that humour which transported the last century with merriment is lost to us, who do not know the sour solemnity, the sullen superstition, the gloomy moroseness, and the stubborn scruples of the ancient Puritans; or, if we knew them, derive our information only from books, or from tradition, have never had them before our eyes, and cannot but by recollection and study understand the lines in which they are satirised. Our grandfathers knew the picture from the life; we judge of the life by contemplating the picture.

43    It is scarcely possible, in the regularity and composure of the present time, to image the tumult of absurdity, and clamour of contradiction, which perplexed doctrine, disordered practice, and disturbed both publick and private quiet, in that age, when subordination was broken, and awe was hissed away; when any unsettled innovator who could hatch a half-formed notion produced it to the publick; when every man might become a preacher, and almost every preacher could collect a congregation.

44    The wisdom of the nation is very reasonably supposed to reside in the parliament. What can be concluded of the lower classes of the people, when in one of the parliaments summoned by Cromwell it was seriously proposed, that all the records in the Tower should be burnt, that all memory of things past should be effaced, and that the whole system of life should commence anew?

45    We have never been witnesses of animosities excited by the use of minced pies and plumb porridge; nor seen with what abhorrence those who could eat them at all other times of the year would shrink from them in December. An old Puritan, who was alive in my childhood, being at one of the feasts of the church invited by a neighbour to partake his cheer, told him, that, if he would treat him at an alehouse with beer, brewed for all times and seasons,

he should accept his kindness, but would have none of his superstitious meats or drinks.

One of the puritanical tenets was the illegality of all games of chance; and he that reads Gataker upon *Lots*, may see how much learning and reason one of the first scholars of his age thought necessary, to prove that it was no crime to throw a die, or play at cards, or to hide a shilling for the reckoning. 46

Astrology, however, against which so much of this satire is directed, was not more the folly of the Puritans than of others. It had in that time a very extensive dominion. Its predictions raised hopes and fears in minds which ought to have rejected it with contempt. In hazardous undertakings, care was taken to begin under the influence of a propitious planet; and when the king was prisoner in Carisbrook Castle, an astrologer was consulted what hour would be found most favourable to an escape. 47

What effect this poem had upon the publick, whether it shamed imposture or reclaimed credulity, is not easily determined. Cheats can seldom stand long against laughter. It is certain that the credit of planetary intelligence wore fast away; though some men of knowledge, and Dryden among them, continued to believe that conjunctions and oppositions had a great part in the distribution of good or evil, and in the government of sublunary things. 48

Poetical Action ought to be probable upon certain suppositions, and such probability as burlesque requires is here violated only by one incident. Nothing can shew more plainly the necessity of doing something, and the difficulty of finding something to do, than that Butler was reduced to transfer to his hero the flagellation of Sancho, not the most agreeable fiction of Cervantes; very suitable indeed to the manners of that age and nation, which ascribed wonderful efficacy to voluntary penances; but so remote from the practice and opinions of the Hudibrastick time, that judgement and imagination are alike offended. 49

The diction of this poem is grossly familiar, and the numbers purposely neglected, except in a few places where the thoughts by their native excellence secure themselves from violation, being such as mean language cannot express. The mode of versification has been blamed by Dryden, who regrets that the heroick measure was not rather chosen. To the critical sentence of Dryden the highest reverence would be due, were not his decisions often precipitate, and his opinions immature. When he wished to change the measure, he probably would have been willing to change more. If he intended that, when the numbers were heroick, the diction should still remain vulgar, he planned a very heterogeneous and unnatural composition. If he preferred a general stateliness both of sound and words, he can be only understood to wish that Butler had undertaken a different work. 50

51    The measure is quick, spritely, and colloquial, suitable to the vulgarity of
the words and the levity of the sentiments. But such numbers and such
diction can gain regard only when they are used by a writer whose vigour of
fancy and copiousness of knowledge entitle him to contempt of ornaments,
and who, in confidence of the novelty and justness of his conceptions, can
afford to throw metaphors and epithets away. To another that conveys
common thoughts in careless versification, it will only be said, "Pauper
videri Cinna vult, & est pauper." The meaning and diction will be worthy
of each other, and criticism may justly doom them to perish together.

52    Nor even though another Butler should arise, would another Hudibras
obtain the same regard. Burlesque consists in a disproportion between the
style and the sentiments, or between the adventitious sentiments and the
fundamental subject. It therefore, like all bodies compounded of heterogeneous parts, contains in it a principle of corruption. All disproportion is
unnatural; and from what is unnatural we can derive only the pleasure
which novelty produces. We admire it awhile as a strange thing; but, when
it is no longer strange, we perceive its deformity. It is a kind of artifice,
which by frequent repetition detects itself; and the reader, learning in time
what he is to expect, lays down his book, as the spectator turns away from a
second exhibition of those tricks, of which the only use is to shew that they
can be played.

# ROCHESTER

JOHN WILMOT, afterwards Earl of Rochester, the son of Henry Earl of Rochester, better known by the title of Lord Wilmot, so often mentioned in Clarendon's History, was born April 10, 1647, at Ditchley in Oxfordshire. After a grammatical education at the school of Burford, he entered a nobleman into Wadham College in 1659, only twelve years old; and in 1661, at fourteen, was, with some other persons of high rank, made master of arts by Lord Clarendon in person. 1

He travelled afterwards into France and Italy; and, at his return, devoted himself to the Court. In 1665 he went to sea with Sandwich, and distinguished himself at Bergen by uncommon interpidity; and the next summer served again on board [the ship commanded by] Sir Edward Spragge, who, in the heat of the engagement, having a message of reproof to send to one of his captains, could find no man ready to carry it but Wilmot, who, in an open boat, went and returned amidst the storm of shot. 2

But his reputation for bravery was not lasting: he was reproached with slinking away in street quarrels, and leaving his companions to shift as they could without him; and Sheffield Duke of Buckingham has left a story of his refusal to fight him. 3

He had very early an inclination to intemperance, which he totally subdued in his travels; but, when he became a courtier, he unhappily addicted himself to dissolute and vitious company, by which his principles were corrupted, and his manners depraved. He lost all sense of religious restraint; and, finding it not convenient to admit the authority of laws which he was resolved not to obey, sheltered his wickedness behind infidelity. 4

As he excelled in that noisy and licentious merriment which wine incites, his companions eagerly encouraged him in excess, and he willingly indulged it; till, as he confessed to Dr. Burnet, he was for five years together continually drunk, or so much inflamed by frequent ebriety, as in no interval to be master of himself. 5

In this state he played many frolicks, which it is not for his honour that we should remember, and which are not now distinctly known. He often pursued low amours in mean disguises, and always acted with great exactness and dexterity the characters which he assumed. 6

7      He once erected a stage on Tower-hill, and harangued the populace as a mountebank; and, having made physick part of his study, is said to have practised it successfully.

8      He was so much in favour with King Charles, that he was made one of the gentlemen of the bedchamber, and comptroller of Woodstock Park.

9      Having an active and inquisitive mind, he never, except in his paroxysms of intemperance, was wholly negligent of study: he read what is considered as polite learning so much, that he is mentioned by Wood as the greatest scholar of all the nobility. Sometimes he retired into the country, and amused himself with writing libels, in which he did not pretend to confine himself to truth.

10     His favourite author in French was Boileau, and in English Cowley.

11     Thus in a course of drunken gaiety, and gross sensuality, with intervals of study perhaps yet more criminal, with an avowed contempt of all decency and order, a total disregard to every moral, and a resolute denial of every religious obligation, he lived worthless and useless, and blazed out his youth and his health in lavish voluptuousness; till, at the age of one and thirty, he had exhausted the fund of life, and reduced himself to a state of weakness and decay.

12     At this time he was led to an acquaintance with Dr. Burnet, to whom he laid open with great freedom the tenour of his opinions, and the course of his life, and from whom he received such conviction of the reasonableness of moral duty, and the truth of Christianity, as produced a total change both of his manners and opinions. The account of those salutary conferences is given by Burnet, in a book intituled, *Some Passages of the Life and Death of* John *Earl of* Rochester; which the critick ought to read for its elegance, the philosopher for its arguments, and the saint for its piety. It were an injury to the reader to offer him an abridgement.

13     He died July 26, 1680, before he had completed his thirty-fourth year; and was so worn away by a long illness, that life went out without a struggle.

14     Lord Rochester was eminent for the vigour of his colloquial wit, and remarkable for many wild pranks and sallies of extravagance. The glare of his general character diffused itself upon his writings; the compositions of a man whose name was heard so often, were certain of attention, and from many readers certain of applause. This blaze of reputation is not yet quite extinguished; and his poetry still retains some splendour beyond that which genius has bestowed.

15     Wood and Burnet give us reason to believe, that much was imputed to him which he did not write. I know not by whom the original collection was made, or by what authority its genuineness was ascertained. The first

edition was published in the year of his death, with an air of concealment, professing in the title page to be printed at *Antwerp*.

Of some of the pieces, however, there is no doubt. The Imitation of 16 Horace's Satire, the Verses to Lord Mulgrave, the Satire against Man, the Verses upon *Nothing*, and perhaps some others, are I believe genuine, and perhaps most of those which the late collection exhibits.

As he cannot be supposed to have found leisure for any course of 17 continued study, his pieces are commonly short, such as one fit of resolution would produce.

His songs have no particular character: they tell, like other songs, in 18 smooth and easy language, of scorn and kindness, dismission and desertion, absence and inconstancy, with the common places of artificial courtship. They are commonly smooth and easy; but have little nature, and little sentiment.

His imitation of Horace on Lucilius is not inelegant or unhappy. In the 19 reign of Charles the Second began that adaptation, which has since been very frequent, of ancient poetry to present times; and perhaps few will be found where the parallelism is better preserved than in this. The versification is indeed sometimes careless, but it is sometimes vigorous and weighty.

The strongest effort of his Muse is his poem upon *Nothing*. He is not the 20 first who has chosen this barren topick for the boast of his fertility. There is a poem called *Nihil* in Latin by *Passerat*, a poet and critick of the sixteenth century in France; who, in his own epitaph, expresses his zeal for good poetry thus:

> —Molliter ossa quiescent
> Sint modo carminibus non onerata malis.

His works are not common, and therefore I shall subjoin his verses. 21

In examining this performance, *Nothing* must be considered as having 22 not only a negative but a kind of positive signification; as I need not fear thieves, I have *nothing*; and *nothing* is a very powerful protector. In the first part of the sentence it is taken negatively; in the second it is taken positively, as an agent. In one of Boileau's lines it was a question, whether he should use *à rien faire*, or *à ne rien faire*; and the first was preferred, because it gave *rien* a sense in some sort positive. *Nothing* can be a subject only in its positive sense, and such a sense is given it in the first line:

> *Nothing*, thou elder brother ev'n to shade.

In this line, I know not whether he does not allude to a curious book *de Umbra*, by Wowerus, which, having told the qualities of *Shade*, concludes with a poem in which are these lines:

Jam primum terram validis circumspice claustris
Suspensam totam, decus admirabile mundi
Terrasque tractusque maris, camposque liquentes
Aeris & vasti laqueata palatia cœli—
Omnibus UMBRA prior.

23    The positive sense is generally preserved, with great skill, through the whole poem; though sometimes, in a subordinate sense, the negative *nothing* is injudiciously mingled. Passerat confounds the two senses.

24    Another of his most vigorous pieces is his Lampoon on Sir Car Scroop, who, in a poem called *The Praise of Satire*, had some lines like these\*;

He who can push into a midnight fray
His brave companion, and then run away,
Leaving him to be murder'd in the street,
Then put it off with some buffoon conceit;
Him, thus dishonour'd, for a wit you own,
And court him as top fidler of the town.

25    This was meant of Rochester, whose *buffoon conceit* was, I suppose, a saying often mentioned, that *every Man would be a Coward if he durst*; and drew from him those furious verses; to which Scroop made in reply an epigram, ending with these lines:

Thou canst hurt no man's fame with thy ill word;
Thy pen is full as harmless as thy sword.

26    Of the satire against *Man*, Rochester can only claim what remains when all Boileau's part is taken away.

27    In all his works there is sprightliness and vigour, and every where may be found tokens of a mind which study might have carried to excellence. What more can be expected from a life spent in ostentatious contempt of regularity, and ended before the abilities of many other men began to be displayed?

28         Poema Cl. V. JOANNIS PASSERATII,

Regii in Academia Parisiensi Professoris.

Ad ornatissimum virum ERRICUM MEMMIUM.

Janus adest, festæ poscunt sua dona Kalendæ,
Munus abest festis quod possim offerre Kalendis.
Siccine Castalius nobis exaruit humor?

---

\* I quote from memory

Usque adeò ingenii nostri est exhausta facultas,
Immunem ut videat redeuntis janitor anni?
Quod nusquam est, potius nova pervestigia quæram.

Ecce autem partes dum sese versat in omnes
Invenit mea Musa NIHIL, ne despice munus.
Nam NIHIL est gemmis, NIHIL est pretiosius auro.
Huc animum, huc igitur vultus adverte benignos:
Res nova narratur quæ nulli audita priorum,
Ausonii & Graii dixerunt cætera vates,
Ausoniæ indictum NIHIL est Græcæque Camœnæ.

E cœlo quacunque Ceres sua prospicit arva,
Aut genitor liquidis orbem complectitur ulnis
Oceanus, NIHIL interitus & originis expers.
Immortale NIHIL, NIHIL omni parte beatum.
Quòd si hinc majestas & vis divina probatur,
Num quid honore deûm, num quid dignabimur aris?
Conspectu lucis NIHIL est jucundius almæ,
Vere NIHIL, NIHIL irriguo formosius horto,
Floridius pratis, Zephyri clementius aura;
In bello sanctum NIHIL est, Martisque tumultu:
Justum in pace NIHIL, NIHIL est in fœdere tutum.
Felix cui NIHIL est, (fuerant hæc vota Tibullo)
Non timet insidias: fures, incendia temnit:
Sollicitas sequitur nullo sub judice lites.
Ille ipse invictis qui subjicit omnia fatis
Zenonis sapiens, NIHIL admiratur & optat.
Socraticique gregis fuit ista scientia quondam,
Scire NIHIL, studio cui nunc incumbitur uni.
Nec quicquam in ludo mavult didicisse juventus,
Ad magnas quia ducit opes, & culmen honorum.
Nosce NIHIL, nosces fertur quod Pythagoreæ
Grano hærere fabæ, cui vox adjuncta negantis.
Multi Mercurio freti duce viscera terræ
Pura liquefaciunt simul, & patrimonia miscent,
Arcano instantes operi, & carbonibus atris,
Qui tandem exhausti damnis, fractique labore,
Inveniunt atque inventum NIHIL usque requirunt.
Hoc dimetiri non ulla decempeda possit:
Nec numeret Libycæ numerum qui callet arenæ:
Et Phœbo ignotum NIHIL est, NIHIL altius astris.
Tuque, tibi licet eximium sit mentis acumen,
Omnem in naturam penetrans, & in abdita rerum,
Pace tua, Memmi, NIHIL ignorare vidêris.

Sole tamen NIHIL est, & puro clarius igne.
Tange NIHIL, dicesque NIHIL sine corpore tangi.
Cerne NIHIL, cerni dices NIHIL absque colore.
Surdum audit loquitúrque NIHIL sine voce, volátque
Absque ope pennarum, & graditur sine cruribus ullis.
Absque loco motuque NIHIL per inane vagatur.
Humano generi utilius NIHIL arte medendi.
Ne rhombos igitur, neu Thessala murmura tentet
Idalia vacuum trajectus arundine pectus,
Neu legat Idæo Dictæum in vertice gramen.
Vulneribus sævi NIHIL auxiliatur amoris.
Vexerit & quemvis trans mœstas portitor undas,
Ad superos imo NIHIL hunc revocabit ab orco.
Inferni NIHIL inflectit præcordia regis,
Parcarúmque colos, & inexorabile pensum.
Obruta Phlegræis campis Titania pubes
Fulmineo sensit NIHIL esse potentius ictu:
Porrigitur magni NIHIL extra mœnia mundi:
Diíque NIHIL metuunt. Quid longo carmine plura
Commemorem? virtute NIHIL præstantius ipsa,
Splendidius NIHIL est; NIHIL est Jove denique majus.
Sed tempus finem argutis imponere nugis:
Ne tibi si multa laudem mea carmina charta,
De NIHILO NIHILI pariant fastidia versus.

# ROSCOMMON

Wentworth Dillon, Earl of Roscommon, was the son of James Dillon 1
and Elizabeth Wentworth, sister to the earl of Strafford. He was born in
Ireland, during the lieutenancy of Strafford, who, being both his uncle and
his godfather, gave him his own surname. His father, the third earl of
Roscommon, had been converted by Usher to the protestant religion; and
when the popish rebellion broke out, Strafford thinking the family in great
danger from the fury of the Irish, sent for his godson, and placed him at his
own seat in Yorkshire, where he was instructed in Latin; which he learned
so as to write it with purity and elegance, though he was never able to retain
the rules of grammar.

Such is the account given by Mr. *Fenton*, from whose notes on Waller 2
most of this account must be borrowed, though I know not whether all that
he relates is certain. The instructer whom he assigns to Roscommon is one
Dr. *Hall*, by whom he cannot mean the famous *Hall*, then an old man and a
bishop.

When the storm broke out upon Strafford, his house was a shelter no 3
longer; and Dillon, by the advice of Usher, was sent to *Caen*, where the
Protestants had then an university, and continued his studies under
*Bochart*.

Young Dillon, who was sent to study under Bochart, and who is repre- 4
sented as having already made great proficiency in literature, could not be
more than nine years old. Strafford went to govern Ireland in 1633, and was
put to death eight years afterwards. That he was sent to Caen, is certain;
that he was a great scholar, may be doubted.

At Caen he is said to have had some preternatural intelligence of his 5
father's death.

"The lord Roscommon, being a boy of ten years of age, at Caen in 6
Normandy, one day was, as it were, madly extravagant in playing, leaping,
getting over the tables, boards, &c. He was wont to be sober enough; they
said, God grant this bodes no ill-luck to him! In the heat of this extravagant
fit, he cries out, *My father is dead*. A fortnight after, news came from Ireland
that his father was dead. This account I had from Mr. Knolles, who was his
governor, and then with him,—since secretary to the earl of Strafford;
and I have: heard his lordship's relations confirm the same." *Aubrey's
Miscellany*.

7      The present age is very little inclined to favour any accounts of this kind, nor will the name of Aubrey much recommend it to credit: it ought not, however, to be omitted, because better evidence of a fact cannot easily be found than is here offered, and it must be by preserving such relations that we may at last judge how much they are to be regarded. If we stay to examine this account, we shall see difficulties on both sides; here is a relation of a fact given by a man who had no interest to deceive, and who could not be deceived himself; and here is, on the other hand, a miracle which produces no effect; the order of nature is interrupted, to discover not a future but only a distant event, the knowledge of which is of no use to him to whom it is revealed. Between these difficulties, what way shall be found? Is reason or testimony to be rejected? I believe what Osborne says of an appearance of sanctity may be applied to such impulses or anticipations as this: *Do not wholly slight them, because they may be true: but do not easily trust them, because they may be false.*

8      The state both of England and Ireland was at this time such, that he who was absent from either country had very little temptation to return: and therefore Roscommon, when he left Caen, travelled into Italy, and amused himself with its antiquities, and particularly with medals, in which he acquired uncommon skill.

9      At the Restoration, with the other friends of monarchy, he came to England, was made captain of the band of pensioners, and learned so much of the dissoluteness of the court, that he addicted himself immoderately to gaming, by which he was engaged in frequent quarrels, and which undoubtedly brought upon him its usual concomitants, extravagance and distress.

10     After some time a dispute about part of his estate forced him into Ireland, where he was made by the duke of Ormond captain of the guards, and met with an adventure thus related by *Fenton*.

11     "He was at Dublin as much as ever distempered with the same fatal affection for play, which engaged him in one adventure that well deserves to be related. As he returned to his lodgings from a gaming-table, he was attacked in the dark by three ruffians, who were employed to assassinate him. The Earl defended himself with so much resolution, that he dispatched one of the aggressors; whilst a gentleman, accidentally passing that way, interposed, and disarmed another: the third secured himself by flight. This generous assistant was a disbanded officer, of a good family and fair reputation; who, by what we call the partiality of fortune, to avoid censuring the iniquities of the times, wanted even a plain suit of cloaths to make a decent appearance at the castle. But his lordship, on this occasion, presenting him to the Duke of Ormond, with great importunity prevailed

with his grace, that he might resign his post of captain of the guards to his friend; which for about three years the gentleman enjoyed, and, upon his death, the duke returned the commission to his generous benefactor."

When he had finished his business, he returned to London; was made 12 Master of the Horse to the Dutchess of York; and married the Lady Frances, daughter of the Earl of Burlington, and widow of Colonel Courteney.

He now busied his mind with literary projects, and formed the plan of a 13 society for refining our language, and fixing its standard; *in imitation*, says Fenton, *of those learned and polite societies with which he had been acquainted abroad.* In this design his friend Dryden is said to have assisted him.

The same design, it is well known, was revived by Dr. Swift in the 14 ministry of Oxford; but it has never since been publickly mentioned, though at that time great expectations were formed by some of its establishment and its effects. Such a society might, perhaps, without much difficulty, be collected; but that it would produce what is expected from it, may be doubted.

The Italian academy seems to have obtained its end. The language was 15 refined, and so fixed that it has changed but little. The French academy thought that they refined their language, and doubtless thought rightly; but the event has not shewn that they fixed it; for the French of the present time is very different from that of the last century.

In this country an academy could be expected to do but little. If an 16 academician's place were profitable, it would be given by interest; if attendance were gratuitous, it would be rarely paid, and no man would endure the least disgust. Unanimity is impossible, and debate would separate the assembly.

But suppose the philological decree made and promulgated, what would 17 be its authority? In absolute governments, there is sometimes a general reverence paid to all that has the sanction of power, and the countenance of greatness. How little this is the state of our country needs not to be told. We live in an age in which it is a kind of publick sport to refuse all respect that cannot be enforced. The edicts of an English academy would probably be read by many, only that they might be sure to disobey them.

That our language is in perpetual danger of corruption cannot be denied; 18 but what prevention can be found? The present manners of the nation would deride authority, and therefore nothing is left but that every writer should criticise himself.

All hopes of new literary institutions were quickly suppressed by the 19 contentious turbulence of King James's reign; and Roscommon, foreseeing that some violent concussion of the State was at hand, purposed to retire to

Rome, alleging, that *it was best to sit near the chimney when the chamber smoaked*; a sentence, of which the application seems not very clear.

20      His departure was delayed by the gout; and he was so impatient either of hinderance or of pain, that he submitted himself to a French empirick, who is said to have repelled the disease into his bowels.

21      At the moment in which he expired, he uttered, with an energy of voice that expressed the most fervent devotion, two lines of his own version of *Dies Iræ*:

> My God, my Father, and my Friend,
> Do not forsake me in my end.

—He died in 1684; and was buried with great pomp in Westminster-Abbey.

22      His poetical character is given by Mr. Fenton:

"In his writings," says Fenton, "we view the image of a mind which was naturally serious and solid; richly furnished and adorned with all the ornaments of learning, unaffectedly disposed in the most regular and elegant order. His imagination might have probably been more fruitful and sprightly, if his judgement had been less severe. But that severity (delivered in a masculine, clear, succinct style) contributed to make him so eminent in the didaetical manner, that no man, with justice, can affirm he was ever equalled by any of our nation, without confessing at the same time that he is inferior to none. In some other kinds of writing his genius seems to have wanted fire to attain the point of perfection; but who can attain it?"

23      From this account of the riches of his mind, who would not imagine that they had been displayed in large volumes and numerous performances? Who would not, after the perusal of this character, be surprised to find that all the proofs of this genius, and knowledge and judgement, are not sufficient to form a single book, or to appear otherwise than in conjunction with the works of some other writer of the same petty size? But thus it is that characters are written: we know somewhat, and we imagine the rest. The observation, that his imagination would probably have been more fruitful and spritely if his judgement had been less severe, may be answered, by a remarker somewhat inclined to cavil, by a contrary supposition, that his judgement would probably have been less severe, if his imagination had been more fruitful. It is ridiculous to oppose judgement to imagination; for it does not appear that men have necessarily less of one as they have more of the other.

24      We must allow of Roscommon, what Fenton has not mentioned so distinctly as he ought, and what is yet very much to his honour, that he is perhaps the only correct writer in verse before Addison; and that, if there

are not so many or so great beauties in his compositions as in those of some contemporaries, there are at least fewer faults. Nor is this his highest praise; for Mr. Pope has celebrated him as the only moral writer of King Charles's reign:

> Unhappy Dryden! in all Charles's days,
> Roscommon only boasts unspotted lays.

His great work is his Essay on Translated Verse; of which Dryden writes  25
thus in the preface to his Miscellanies:

"It was my Lord Roscommon's Essay on Translated Verse," says Dryden, "which made me uneasy, till I tried whether or no I was capable of following his rules, and of reducing the speculation into practice. For many a fair precept in poetry is like a seeming demonstration in mathematicks, very specious in the diagram, but failing in the mechanick operation. I think I have generally observed his instructions; I am sure my reason is sufficiently convinced both of their truth and usefulness; which, in other words, is to confess no less a vanity than to pretend that I have, at least in some places, made examples to his rules."

This declaration of Dryden will, I am afraid, be found little more than  26
one of those cursory civilities which one author pays to another; for when the sum of lord Roscommon's precepts is collected, it will not be easy to discover how they can qualify their reader for a better performance of translation than might have been attained by his own reflections.

He that can abstract his mind from the elegance of the poetry, and  27
confine it to the sense of the precepts, will find no other direction than that the author should be suitable to the translator's genius; that he should be such as may deserve a translation; that he who intends to translate him should endeavour to understand him; that perspicuity should be studied, and unusual and uncouth names sparingly inserted; and that the style of the original should be copied in its elevation and depression. These are the rules that are celebrated as so definite and important; and for the delivery of which to mankind so much honour has been paid. Roscommon has indeed deserved his praises, had they been given with discernment, and bestowed not on the rules themselves, but the art with which they are introduced, and the decorations with which they are adorned.

The Essay, though generally excellent, is not without its faults. The story  28
of the Quack, borrowed from Boileau, was not worth the importation: he has confounded the British and Saxon mythology:

> I grant that from some mossy idol oak,
> In double rhymes, our *Thor and Woden* spoke.

The oak, as I think Gildon has observed, belonged to the British druids, and *Thor* and *Woden* were Saxon deities. Of the *double rhymes*, which he so liberally supposes, he certainly had no knowledge.

29     His interposition of a long paragraph of blank verses is unwarrantably licentious. Latin poets might as well have introduced a series of iambicks among their heroicks.

30     His next work is the translation of the Art of Poetry; which has received, in my opinion, not less praise than it deserves. Blank verse, left merely to its numbers, has little operation either on the ear or mind: it can hardly support itself without bold figures and striking images. A poem frigidly didactick, without rhyme, is so near to prose, that the reader only scorns it for pretending to be verse.

31     Having disentangled himself from the difficulties of rhyme, he may justly be expected to give the sense of Horace with great exactness, and to suppress no subtilty of sentiment for the difficulty of expressing it. This demand, however, his translation will not satisfy; what he found obscure, I do not know that he has ever cleared.

32     Among his smaller works, the Eclogue of Virgil and the *Dies Iræ* are well translated; though the best line in the *Dies Iræ* is borrowed from Dryden. In return, succeeding poets have borrowed from Roscommon.

33     In the verses on the Lap-dog, the pronouns *thou* and *you* are offensively confounded; and the turn at the end is from Waller.

34     His versions of the two odes of Horace are made with great liberty, which is not recompensed by much elegance or vigour.

35     His political verses are spritely, and when they were written must have been very popular.

36     Of the scene of *Guarini*, and the prologue to *Pompey*, Mrs. Phillips, in her letters to Sir Charles Cotterel, has given the history.

"Lord Roscommon," says she, "is certainly one of the most promising young noblemen in Ireland. He has paraphrased a Psalm admirably, and a scene of *Pastor Fido* very finely, in some places much better than Sir Richard Fanshaw. This was undertaken merely in compliment to me, who happened to say that it was the best scene in Italian, and the worst in English. He was only two hours about it. It begins thus:

> Dear happy groves, and you the dark retreat
> Of silent horrour, Rest's eternal seat."

37     From these lines, which are since somewhat mended, it appears that he did not think a work of two hours fit to endure the eye of criticism without revisal.

When Mrs. Phillips was in Ireland, some ladies that had seen her 38
translation of Pompey, resolved to bring it on the stage at Dublin; and, to
promote their design, Lord Roscommon gave them a prologue, and Sir
Edward Dering an Epilogue; "which," says she, "are the best performances
of those kinds I ever saw." If this is not criticism, it is at least gratitude. The
thought of bringing Cæsar and Pompey into Ireland, the only Country over
which Cæsar never had any power, is lucky.

Of Roscommon's works, the judgement of the publick seems to be right. 39
He is elegant, but not great; he never labours after exquisite beauties, and he
seldom falls into gross faults. His versification is smooth, but rarely vigorous, and his rhymes are remarkably exact. He improved taste, if he did not
enlarge knowledge, and may be numbered among the benefactors to English
literature.

# OTWAY

1 OF THOMAS OTWAY, one of the first names in the English drama, little is known; nor is there any part of that little which his biographer can take pleasure in relating.

2 He was born at Trottin in Sussex, March 3, 1651, the son of Mr. Humphry Otway, rector of *Woolbedding*. From Winchester-school, where he was educated, he was entered in 1669 a commoner of Christ-church; but left the university without a degree, whether for want of money, or from impatience of academical restraint, or mere eagerness to mingle with the world, is not known.

3 It seems likely that he was in hope of being busy and conspicuous: for he went to London, and commenced player; but found himself unable to gain any reputation on the stage.

4 This kind of inability he shared with Shakspeare and Jonson, as he shared likewise some of their excellences. It seems reasonable to expect that a great dramatick poet should without difficulty become a great actor; that he who can feel, could express; that he who can excite passion, should exhibit with great readiness its external modes: but since experience has fully proved that of those powers, whatever be their affinity, one may be possessed in a great degree by him who has very little of the other; it must be allowed that they depend upon different faculties, or on different use of the same faculty; that the actor must have a pliancy of mien, a flexibility of countenance, and a variety of tones, which the poet may be easily supposed to want; or that the attention of the poet and the player have been differently employed; the one has been considering thought, and the other action; one has watched the heart, and the other contemplated the face.

5 Though he could not gain much notice as a player, he felt in himself such powers as might qualify for a dramatick author; and in 1675, his twenty-fifth year, produced *Alcibiades*, a tragedy; whether from the *Alcibiade* of *Palaprat*, I have not means to enquire. Langbain, the great detector of plagiarism, is silent.

6 In 1677 he published *Titus and Berenice*, translated from Racine, with the *Cheats of Scapin* from Moliere; and in 1678 *Friendship in Fashion*, a comedy, which, whatever might be its first reception, was, upon its revival at Drury-lane in 1749, hissed off the stage for immorality and obscenity.

Want of morals, or of decency, did not in those days exclude any 7
man from the company of the wealthy and the gay, if he brought with
him any powers of entertainment; and Otway is said to have been at this
time a favourite companion of the dissolute wits. But, as he who desires no
virtue in his companion has no virtue in himself, those whom Otway
frequented had no purpose of doing more for him than to pay his reckoning.
They desired only to drink and laugh; their fondness was without benevolence, and their familiarity without friendship. Men of wit, says one of
Otway's biographers, received at that time no favour from the Great but
to share their riots; *from which they were dismissed again to their own
narrow circumstances. Thus they languished in poverty without the support of
innocence.*

Some exception, however, must be made. The Earl of Plymouth, one of 8
King Charles's natural sons, produced for him a cornet's commission in
some troops then sent into Flanders. But Otway did not prosper in his
military character; for he soon left his commission behind him, whatever
was the reason, and came back to London in extreme indigence; which
Rochester mentions with merciless insolence in the *Session of the Poets*:

> Tom Otway came next, Tom Shadwell's dear zany,
> And swears for heroicks he writes best of any;
> Don Carlos his pockets so amply had fill'd,
> That his mange was quite cured, and his lice were all kill'd.
> But Apollo had seen his face on the stage,
> And prudently did not think fit to engage
> The scum of a play-house, for the prop of an age.

*Don Carlos*, from which he is represented as having received so much 9
benefit, was played in 1675. It appears, by the Lampoon, to have had great
success, and is said to have been played thirty nights together. This
however it is reasonable to doubt, as so long a continuance of one play
upon the stage is a very wide deviation from the practice of that time; when
the ardour for theatrical entertainments was not yet diffused through the
whole people, and the audience, consisting nearly of the same persons,
could be drawn together only by variety.

The *Orphan* was exhibited in 1680. This is one of the few plays that keep 10
possession of the stage, and has pleased for almost a century, through all the
vicissitudes of dramatick fashion. Of this play nothing new can easily be
said. It is a domestick tragedy drawn from middle life. Its whole power is
upon the affections; for it is not written with much comprehension of
thought, or elegance of expression. But if the heart is interested, many
other beauties may be wanting, yet not be missed.

11    The same year produced *The History and Fall of Caius Marius*; much of which is borrowed from the *Romeo and Juliet* of Shakspeare.

12    In 1683 was published the first, and next year the second, parts of *The Soldier's Fortune*, two comedies now forgotten; and in 1685 his last and greatest dramatick work, *Venice preserved*, a tragedy, which still continues to be one of the favourites of the publick, notwithstanding the want of morality in the original design, and the despicable scenes of vile comedy with which he has diversified his tragick action. By comparing this with his *Orphan*, it will appear that his images were by time become stronger, and his language more energetick. The striking passages are in every mouth; and the publick seems to judge rightly of the faults and excellences of this play, that it is the work of a man not attentive to decency, nor zealous for virtue; but of one who conceived forcibly, and drew originally, by consulting nature in his own breast.

13    Together with those plays he wrote the poems which are in the late collection, and translated from the French the *History of the Triumvirate*.

14    All this was performed before he was thirty-four years old; for he died April 14, 1685, in a manner which I am unwilling to mention. Having been compelled by his necessities to contract debts, and hunted, as is supposed, by the terriers of the law, he retired to a publick house on Tower-hill, where he is said to have died of want; or, as it is related by one of his biographers, by swallowing, after a long fast, a piece of bread which charity had supplied. He went out, as is reported, almost naked, in the rage of hunger, and finding a gentleman in a neighbouring coffee-house, asked him for a shilling. The gentleman gave him a guinea; and Otway going away bought a roll, and was choaked with the first mouthful. All this, I hope, is not true; and there is this ground of better hope, that Pope who lived near enough to be well informed, relates in Spence's memorials, that he died of a fever caught by violent pursuit of a thief that had robbed one of his friends. But that indigence, and its concomitants, sorrow and despondency, pressed hard upon him, has never been denied, whatever immediate cause might bring him to the grave.

15    Of the poems which the late collection admits, the longest is the *Poet's Complaint of his Muse*, part of which I do not understand; and in that which is less obscure I find little to commend. The language is often gross, and the numbers are harsh. Otway had not much cultivated versification, nor much replenished his mind with general knowledge. His principal power was in moving the passions, to which Dryden * in his latter years left an illustrious testimony. He appears, by some of his verses, to have been a zealous royalist: and had what was in those times the common reward of loyalty; he lived and died neglected.

---

* In his preface to Fresnoy's *Art of Painting*

# WALLER

EDMUND WALLER was born on the third of March, 1605, at Colshill in  1
Hertfordshire. His father was Robert Waller, Esquire, of Agmondesham in
Buckinghamshire, whose family was originally a branch of the Kentish
Wallers; and his mother was the daughter of John Hampden, of Hampden
in the same county, and sister to Hampden, the zealot of rebellion.

His father died while he was yet an infant, but left him an yearly income  2
of three thousand five hundred pounds; which, rating together the value of
money and the customs of life, we may reckon more than equivalent to ten
thousand at the present time.

He was educated, by the care of his mother, at Eaton; and removed  3
afterwards to King's College in Cambridge. He was sent to parliament in his
eighteenth, if not in his sixteenth year, and frequented the court of James
the First, where he heard a very remarkable conversation, which the writer
of the Life prefixed to his Works, who seems to have been well informed of
facts, though he may sometimes err in chronology, has delivered as indubitably certain.

"He found Dr. Andrews, bishop of Winchester, and Dr. Neale, bishop of  4
Durham, standing behind his Majesty's chair; and there happened something extraordinary," continues this writer, "in the conversation those prelates had with the king, on which Mr. Waller did often reflect. His Majesty
asked the bishops, "My Lords, cannot I take my subjects money, when
I want it, without all this formality of parliament?" The bishop of Durham
readily answered, 'God forbid, Sir, but you should: you are the breath of our
nostrils.' Whereupon the King turned and said to the bishop of Winchester,
"Well, my Lord, what say you?" 'Sir,' replied the bishop, 'I have no skill to
judge of parliamentary cases.' The King answered, "No put-offs, my Lord;
answer me presently." 'Then, Sir,' said he, 'I think it is lawful for you to take
my brother Neale's money; for he offers it.' Mr. Waller said, the company
was pleased with this answer, and the wit of it seemed to affect the King; for,
a certain lord coming in soon after, his Majesty cried out, "Oh, my lord, they
say you lig with my Lady.' 'No, Sir,' says his Lordship in confusion; 'but
I like her company, because she has so much wit.' "Why then," says the
King, "do you not lig with my Lord of Winchester there?"

Waller's political and poetical life began nearly together. In his eight-  5
eenth year he wrote the poem that appears first in his works, on "the

Prince's Escape at St. Andero;" a piece which justifies the observation made by one of his editors, that he attained, by a felicity like instinct, a style which perhaps will never be obsolete; and that, "were we to judge only by the wording, we could not know what was wrote at twenty, and what at fourscore." His versification was, in his first essay, such as it appears in his last performance. By the perusal of Fairfax's translation of Tasso, to which, as* Dryden relates, he confessed himself indebted for the smoothness of his numbers, and by his own nicety of observation, he had already formed such a system of metrical harmony as he never afterwards much needed, or much endeavoured, to improve. Denham corrected his numbers by experience, and gained ground gradually upon the ruggedness of his age; but what was acquired by Denham, was inherited by Waller.

6      The next poem, of which the subject seems to fix the time, is supposed by Mr. Fenton to be the Address to the Queen, which he considers as congratulating her arrival, in Waller's twentieth year. He is apparently mistaken; for the mention of the nation's obligations to her frequent pregnancy, proves that it was written when she had brought many children. We have therefore no date of any other poetical production before that which the murder of the Duke of Buckingham occasioned: the steadiness with which the King received the news in the chapel, deserved indeed to be rescued from oblivion.

7      Neither of these pieces that seem to carry their own dates, could have been the sudden effusion of fancy. In the verses on the Prince's escape, the prediction of his marriage with the princess of France, must have been written after the event; in the other, the promises of the King's kindness to the descendants of Buckingham, which could not be properly praised till it had appeared by its effects, shew that time was taken for revision and improvement. It is not known that they were published till they appeared long afterwards with other poems.

8      Waller was not one of those idolaters of praise who cultivate their minds at the expence of their fortunes. Rich as he was by inheritance, he took care early to grow richer by marrying Mrs. Banks, a great heiress in the city, whom the interest of the court was employed to obtain for Mr. Crofts. Having brought him a son, who died young, and a daughter, who was afterwards married to Mr. Dormer of Oxfordshire, she died in childbed, and left him a widower of about five and twenty, gay and wealthy, to please himself with another marriage.

9      Being too young to resist beauty, and probably too vain to think himself resistible, he fixed his heart, perhaps half fondly and half ambitiously, upon

* Preface to his Fables.

the Lady Dorothea Sidney, eldest daughter of the Earl of Leicester, whom he courted by all the poetry in which Sacharissa is celebrated; the name is derived from the Latin appellation of *sugar*, and implies, if it means any thing, a spiritless mildness, and dull good-nature, such as excites rather tenderness than esteem, and such as, though always treated with kindness, is never honoured or admired.

Yet he describes Sacharissa as a sublime predominating beauty, of lofty 10 charms, and imperious influence, on whom he looks with amazement rather than fondness, whose chains he wishes, though in vain, to break, and whose prefence is *wine* that *inflames to madness*.

His acquaintance with this high-born dame gave wit no opportunity of 11 boasting its influence; she was not to be subdued by the powers of verse, but rejected his addresses, it is said, with disdain, and drove him away to solace his disappointment with Amoret or Phillis. She married in 1639 the Earl of Sunderland, who died at Newberry in the king's cause; and, in her old age, meeting somewhere with Waller, asked him, when he would again write such verses upon her; "When you are as young, Madam," said he, "and as handsome, as you were then."

In this part of his life it was that he was known to Clarendon, among the 12 rest of the men who were eminent in that age for genius and literature; but known so little to his advantage, that they who read his character will not much condemn Sacharissa, that she did not descend from her rank to his embraces, nor think every excellence comprised in wit.

The Lady was, indeed, inexorable; but his uncommon qualifications, 13 though they had no power upon her, recommended him to the scholars and statesmen; and undoubtedly many beauties of that time, however they might receive his love, were proud of his praises. Who they were, whom he dignifies with poetical names, cannot now be known. Amoret, according to Mr. Fenton, was the Lady Sophia Murray. Perhaps by traditions preserved in families more may be discovered.

From the verses written at Penshurst, it has been collected that he 14 diverted his disappointment by a voyage; and his biographers, from his poem on the Whales, think it not improbable that he visited the Bermudas; but it seems much more likely that he should amuse himself with forming an imaginary scene, than that so important an incident, as a visit to America, should have been left floating in conjectural probability.

From his twenty-eighth to his thirty-fifth year, he wrote his pieces on the 15 Reduction of Sallee; on the Reparation of St. Paul's; to the King on his Navy; the panegyrick on the Queen Mother; the two poems to the Earl of Northumberland; and perhaps others, of which the time cannot be discovered.

16    When he had lost all hopes of Sacharissa, he looked round him for an easier conquest, and gained a Lady of the family of Bresse, or Breaux. The time of his marriage is not exactly known. It has not been discovered that this wife was won by his poetry; nor is any thing told of her, but that she brought him many children. He doubtless praised some whom he would have been afraid to marry; and perhaps married one whom he would have been ashamed to praise. Many qualities contribute to domestick happiness, upon which poetry has no colours to bestow; and many airs and sallies may delight imagination, which he who flatters them never can approve. There are charms made only for distant admiration. No spectacle is nobler than a blaze.

17    Of this wife, his biographers have recorded that she gave him five sons and eight daughters.

18    During the long interval of parliament, he is represented as living among those with whom it was most honourable to converse, and enjoying an exuberant fortune with that independence and liberty of speech and conduct which wealth ought always to produce. He was however considered as the kinsman of Hampden, and was therefore supposed by the courtiers not to favour them.

19    When the parliament was called in 1640, it appeared that Waller's political character had not been mistaken. The King's demand of a supply produced one of those noisy speeches which disaffection and discontent regularly dictate; a speech filled with hyperbolical complaints of imaginary grievances. "They," says he, "who think themselves already undone can never apprehend themselves in danger, and they who have nothing left can never give freely." Political truth is equally in danger from the praises of courtiers, and the exclamations of patriots.

20    He then proceeds to rail at the clergy, being sure at that time of a favourable audience. His topick is such as will always serve its purpose; an accusation of acting and preaching only for preferment: and he exhorts the Commons *carefully* to *provide* for their *protection against Pulpit Law.*

21    It always gratifies curiosity to trace a sentiment. Waller has in this speech quoted Hooker in one passage; and in another has copied him, without quoting. "Religion," says Waller, "ought to be the first thing in our purpose and desires; but that which is first in dignity is not always to precede in order of time; for well-being supposes a being; and the first impediment which men naturally endeavour to remove, is the want of those things without which they cannot subsist. God first assigned unto Adam maintenance of life, and gave him a title to the rest of the creatures before he appointed a law to observe."

22    "God first assigned Adam," says Hooker, "maintenance of life, and then appointed him a law to observe.—True it is, that the kingdom of God must

be the first thing in our purpose and desires; but inasmuch as a righteous life presupposeth life, inasmuch as to live virtuously it is impossible, except we live; therefore the first impediment which naturally we endeavour to remove is penury, and want of things without which we cannot live." B. I. sect. 9.

The speech is vehement; but the great position, that grievances ought to 23 be redressed before supplies are granted, is agreeable enough to law and reason: nor was Waller, if his biographer may be credited, such an enemy to the King, as not to wish his distresses lightened; for he relates, "that the King sent particularly to Waller, to second his demand of some subsidies to pay off the army; and Sir Henry Vane objecting against first voting a supply, because the King would not accept unless it came up to his proportion, Mr. Waller spoke earnestly to Sir Thomas Jermyn, comptroller of the household, to save his master from the effects of so bold a falsity; 'for, he said, I am but a country gentleman, and cannot pretend to know the King's mind:' but Sir Thomas durst not contradict the secretary; and his son, the Earl of St. Albans, afterwards told Mr. Waller, that his father's cowardice ruined the King."

In the Long Parliament, which, unhappily for the nation, met Nov. 3, 24 1640, Waller represented Agmondesham the third time; and was considered by the discontented party as a man sufficiently trusty and acrimonious to be employed in managing the prosecution of Judge Crawley, for his opinion in favour of ship-money; and his speech shews that he did not disappoint their expectations. He was probably the more ardent, as his uncle Hampden had been particularly engaged in the dispute, and by a sentence which seems generally to be thought unconstitutional particularly injured.

He was not however a bigot to his party, nor adopted all their opinions. 25 When the great question, whether Episcopacy ought to be abolished, was debated, he spoke against the innovation so coolly, so reasonably, and so firmly, that it is not without great injury to his name that his speech, which was as follows, has been hitherto omitted in his works:

* "There is no doubt but the sense of what this nation hath suffered from 26 the present Bishops, hath produced these complaints; and the apprehensions men have of suffering the like, in time to come, make so many desire the taking away of Episcopacy: but I conceive it is possible that we may not, now, take a right measure of the minds of the people by their petitions; for, when they subscribed them, the Bishops were armed with a dangerous commission of making new canons, imposing new oaths, and the like; but

---

* This speech has been retrieved, from a paper printed at that time, by the writers of the Parliamentary History.

now we have disarmed them of that power. These petitioners, lately, did look upon Episcopacy as a beast armed with horns and claws; but now that we have cut and pared them, (and may, if we see cause, yet reduce it into narrower bounds) it may, perhaps, be more agreeable. Howsoever, if they be still in passion, it becomes us soberly to consider the right use and antiquity thereof; and not to comply further with a general desire, than may stand with a general good.

27    "We have already shewed, that episcopacy, and the evils thereof, are mingled like water, and oil; we have also, in part, severed them; but I believe you will find, that our laws and the present government of the church are mingled like wine and water; so inseparable, that the abrogation of, at least, a hundred of our laws is desired in these petitions. I have often heard a noble answer of the Lords, commended in this house, to a proposition of like nature, but of less consequence; they gave no other reason of their refusal but this, *Nolumus mutare Leges Angliæ*: it was the bishops who so answered then; and it would become the dignity and wisdom of this house to answer the people, now, with a *Nolumus mutare*.

28    I see some are moved with a number of hands against the Bishops; which, I confess, rather inclines me to their defence: for I look upon episcopacy as a counterscarp, or out-work; which, if it be taken by this assault of the people, and, withall, this mystery once revealed, *That we must deny them nothing when they ask it thus in troops*, we may, in the next place, have as hard a task to defend our property, as we have lately had to recover it from the Prerogative. If, by multiplying hands and petitions, they prevail for an equality in things ecclesiastical, the next demand perhaps may be *Lex Agraria*, the like equality in things temporal.

29    "The Roman story tells us, That when the people began to flock about the senate, and were more curious to direct and know what was done, than to obey, that Commonwealth soon came to ruin: their *Legem rogare* grew quickly to be a *Legem ferre*; and after, when their legions had found that they could make a Dictator, they never suffered the senate to have a voice any more in such election.

30    "If these great innovations proceed, I shall expect a flat and level in learning too, as well as in church-preferments: *Honos alit Artes*. And though it be true, that grave and pious men do study for learning-sake, and embrace virtue for itself; yet it is as true, that youth, which is the season when learning is gotten, is not without ambition; nor will ever take pains to excell in any thing, when there is not some hope of excelling others in reward and dignity.

31    "There are two reasons chiefly alleged against our church-government.

32    "First, Scripture, which, as some men think, points out another form.

"Second, The abuses of the present superiors.  33

"For Scripture, I will not dispute it in this place; but I am confident that,  34
whenever an equal division of lands and goods shall be desired, there will be
as many places in Scripture found out, which seem to favour that, as there
are now alleged against the prelacy or preferment in the church. And, as for
abuses, where you are now, in the Remonstrance, told, what this and that
poor man hath suffered by the bishops, you may be presented with a
thousand instances of poor men that have received hard measure from
their landlords; and of worldly goods abused, to the injury of others, and
disadvantage of the owners.

"And therefore, Mr. Speaker, my humble motion is, That we may settle  35
men's minds herein; and, by a question, declare our resolution, *to reform*,
that is *not to abolish, Episcopacy*."

It cannot but be wished that he, who could speak in this manner, had  36
been able to act with spirit and uniformity.

When the Commons began to set the royal authority at open defiance,  37
Waller is said to have withdrawn from the house, and to have returned with
the king's permission; and, when the king set up his standard, he sent him a
thousand broad-pieces. He continued, however, to sit in the rebellious
conventicle; but "spoke," says Clarendon, "with great sharpness and freedom, which, now there was no danger of being outvoted, was not restrained;
and therefore used as an argument against those who were gone upon
pretence that they were not suffered to deliver their opinion freely in the
house, which could not be believed, when all men knew what liberty
Mr. Waller took, and spoke every day with impunity against the sense
and proceedings of the house."

Waller, as he continued to sit, was one of the commissioners nominated  38
by the parliament to treat with the king at Oxford; and when they were
presented, the King said to him, "Though you are the last, you are not the
lowest nor the least in my favour." Whitlock, who, being another of the
commissioners, was witness of this kindness, imputes it to the king's
knowledge of the plot, in which Waller appeared afterwards to have been
engaged against the parliament. Fenton, with equal probability, believes
that his attempt to promote the royal cause arose from his sensibility of the
king's tenderness. Whitlock says nothing of his behaviour at Oxford: he was
sent with several others to add pomp to the commission, but was not one of
those to whom the trust of treating was imparted.

The engagement, known by the name of Waller's plot, was soon after-  39
wards discovered. Waller had a brother-in-law, Tomkyns, who was clerk of
the Queen's council, and at the same time had a very numerous acquaintance, and great influence, in the city. Waller and he, conversing with great

confidence, told both their own secrets and those of their friends; and, surveying the wide extent of their conversation, imagined that they found in the majority of all ranks great disapprobation of the violence of the Commons, and unwillingness to continue the war. They knew that many favoured the king, whose fear concealed their loyalty; and many desired peace, though they durst not oppose the clamour for war; and they imagined that if those who had these good intentions could be informed of their own strength, and enabled by intelligence to act together, they might overpower the fury of sedition, by refusing to comply with the ordinance for the twentieth part, and the other taxes levied for the support of the rebel army, and by uniting great numbers in a petition for peace. They proceeded with great caution. Three only met in one place, and no man was allowed to impart the plot to more than two others, so that if any should be suspected or seized, more than three could not be endangered.

40     Lord Conway joined in the design, and, Clarendon imagines, incidentally mingled, as he was a soldier, some martial hopes or projects, which however were only mentioned, the main design being to bring the loyal inhabitants to the knowledge of each other; for which purpose there was to be appointed one in every district, to distinguish the friends of the king, the adherents to the parliament, and the neutrals. How far they proceeded does not appear; the result of their enquiry, as Pym declared*, was, that within the walls for one that was for the Royalists, there were three against them; but that without the walls for one that was against them, there were five for them. Whether this was said from knowledge or guess, was perhaps never enquired.

41     It is the opinion of Clarendon, that in Waller's plan no violence or sanguinary resistance was comprised; that he intended only to abate the confidence of the rebels by publick declarations, and to weaken their power by an opposition to new supplies. This, in calmer times, and more than this, is done without fear; but such was the acrimony of the commons, that no method of obstructing them was safe.

42     About this time another design was formed by Sir Nicholas Crispe, a man of loyalty that deserves perpetual remembrance; when he was a merchant in the city, he gave and procured the king, in his exigences, an hundred thousand pounds; and, when he was driven from the Exchange, raised a regiment, and commanded it.

43     Sir Nicholas flattered himself with an opinion, that some provocation would so much exasperate, or some opportunity so much encourage, the King's friends in the city, that they would break out in open resistance, and

* Parliamentary History, Vol. XII.

then would want only a lawful standard, and an authorised commander; and extorted from the King, whose judgement too frequently yielded to importunity, a commission of array, directed to such as he thought proper to nominate, which was sent to London by the Lady Aubigney. She knew not what she carried, but was to deliver it on the communication of a certain token which Sir Nicholas imparted.

This commission could be only intended to lie ready till the time should require it. To have attempted to raise any forces, would have been certain destruction; it could be of use only when the forces should appear. This was, however, an act preparatory to martial hostility. Crispe would undoubtedly have put an end to the session of parliament, had his strength been equal to his zeal; and out of the design of Crispe, which involved very little danger, and that of Waller, which was an act purely civil, they compounded a horrid and dreadful plot. 44

The discovery of Waller's design is variously related. In Clarendon's History it is told, that a servant of Tomkyns, lurking behind the hangings when his master was in conference with Waller, heard enough to qualify him for an informer, and carried his intelligence to Pym. A manuscript, quoted in the Life of Waller, relates, that "he was betrayed by his sister Price, and her presbyterian chaplain Mr. Goode, who stole some of his papers; and if he had not strangely dreamed the night before, that his sister had betrayed him, and thereupon burnt the rest of his papers by the fire that was left in his chimney, he had certainly lost his life by it." The question cannot be decided. It is not unreasonable to believe that the men in power, receiving intelligence from the sister, would employ the servant of Tomkyns to listen at the conference, that they might avoid an act so offensive as that of destroying the brother by the sister's testimony. 45

The plot was published in the most terrifick manner. On the 31st of May (1643), at a solemn fast, when they were listening to the sermon, a messenger entered the church, and communicated his errand to Pym, who whispered it to others that were placed near him, and then went with them out of the church, leaving the rest in solicitude and amazement. They immediately sent guards to proper places, and that night apprehended Tomkyns and Waller; having yet traced nothing but that letters had been intercepted, from which it appeared that the parliament and the city were soon to be delivered into the hands of the cavaliers. 46

They perhaps yet knew little themselves, beyond some general and indistinct notices. "But Waller," says Clarendon, "was so confounded with fear, that he confessed whatever he had heard, said, thought, or seen; all that he knew of himself, and all that he suspected of others, without concealing any person, of what degree or quality soever, or any discourse 47 which he had ever upon any occasion entertained with them; what such and such ladies of great honour, to whom, upon the credit of his wit and great reputation, he had been admitted, had spoke to him in their chambers upon the proceedings in the Houses, and how they had encouraged him to oppose them; what correspondence and intercourse they had with some Ministers of State at Oxford, and how they had conveyed all intelligence thither." He accused the Earl of Portland and Lord Conway as co-operating in the transaction; and testified that the Earl of Northumberland had declared himself disposed in favour of any attempt that might check the violence of the Parliament, and reconcile them to the King.

48  He undoubtedly confessed much, which they could never have discovered, and perhaps somewhat which they would wish to have been suppressed; for it is inconvenient, in the conflict of factions, to have that disaffection known which cannot safely be punished.

49  Tomkyns was seized on the same night with Waller, and appears likewise to have partaken of his cowardice; for he gave notice of Crispe's commission of array, of which Clarendon never knew how it was discovered. Tomkyns had been sent with the token appointed, to demand it from Lady Aubigney, and had buried it in his garden, where, by his direction, it was dug up; and thus the rebels obtained, what Clarendon confesses them to have had, the original copy.

50  It can raise no wonder that they formed one plot out of these two designs, however remote from each other, when they saw the same agent employed in both, and found the commission of array in the hands of him who was employed in collecting the opinions and affections of the people.

51  Of the plot, thus combined, they took care to make the most. They sent Pym among the citizens, to tell them of their imminent danger, and happy escape; and inform them, that the design was to seize the "Lord Mayor and all the Committee of Militia, and would not spare one of them." They drew up a vow and covenant, to be taken by every member of either house, by which he declared his detestation of all conspiracies against the parliament, and his resolution to detect and oppose them. They then appointed a day of thanksgiving for this wonderful delivery; which shut out, says Clarendon, all doubts whether there had been such a deliverance, and whether the plot was real or fictitious.

52  On June 11, the Earl of Portland and Lord Conway were committed, one to the custody of the mayor, and the other of the sheriff; but their lands and goods were not seized.

53  Waller was still to immerse himself deeper in ignominy. The Earl of Portland and Lord Conway denied the charge, and there was no evidence against them but the confession of Waller, of which undoubtedly many

would be inclined to question the veracity. With these doubts he was so much terrified, that he endeavoured to persuade Portland to a declaration like his own, by a letter extant in Fenton's edition. "But for me," says he, "you had never known any thing of this business, which was prepared for another; and therefore I cannot imagine why you should hide it so far as to contract your own ruin by concealing it, and persisting unreasonably to hide that truth, which, without you, already is, and will every day be made more, manifest. Can you imagine yourself bound in honour to keep that secret, which is already revealed by another; or possible it should still be a secret, which is known to one of the other sex?—If you persist to be cruel to yourself for their sakes who deserve it not, it will nevertheless be made appear, ere long, I fear, to your ruin. Surely, if I had the happiness to wait on you, I could move you to compassionate both yourself and me, who, desperate as my case is, am desirous to die with the honour of being known to have declared the truth. You have no reason to contend to hide what is already revealed—inconsiderately to throw away yourself, for the interest of others, to whom you are less obliged than you are aware of."

This persuasion seems to have had little effect. Portland sent (June 29) a 54 letter to the Lords, to tell them, that he "is in custody, as he conceives, without any charge; and that, by what Mr. Waller hath threatened him with since he was imprisoned, he doth apprehend a very cruel, long, and ruinous restraint:—He therefore prays, that he may not find the effects of Mr. Waller's threats, by a long and close imprisonment; but may be speedily brought to a legal trial, and then he is confident the vanity and falsehood of those informations which have been given against him will appear."

In consequence of this letter, the Lords ordered Portland and Waller to 55 be confronted; when the one repeated his charge, and the other his denial. The examination of the plot being continued (July 1), Thinn, usher of the house of Lords, deposed, that Mr. Waller having had a conference with the Lord Portland in an upper room, Lord Portland said, when he came down, "Do me the favour to tell my Lord Northumberland, that Mr. Waller has extremely pressed me to save my own life and his, by throwing the blame upon the Lord Conway and the Earl of Northumberland."

Waller, in his letter to Portland, tells him of the reasons which he could 56 urge with resistless efficacy in a personal conference; but he over-rated his own oratory; his vehemence, whether of persuasion or intreaty, was returned with contempt.

One of his arguments with Portland is, that the plot is already known to a 57 woman. This woman was doubtless Lady Aubigney, who, upon this occasion, was committed to custody; but who, in reality, when she delivered the commission, knew not what it was.

58    The parliament then proceeded against the conspirators, and committed their trial to a council of war. Tomkyns and Chaloner were hanged near their own doors. Tomkyns, when he came to die, said it was a *foolish business*; and indeed there seems to have been no hope that it should escape discovery; for though never more than three met at a time, yet a design so extensive must, by necessity, be communicated to many, who could not be expected to be all faithful, and all prudent. Chaloner was attended at his execution by Hugh Peters. His crime was that he had commission to raise money for the King; but, it appears not that the money was to be expended upon the advancement of either Crispe or Waller's plot.

59    The Earl of Northumberland, being too great for prosecution, was only once examined before the Lords. The Earl of Portland and lord Conway persisting to deny the charge, and no testimony but Waller's yet appearing against them, were, after a long imprisonment, admitted to bail. Hassel, the King's messenger, who carried the letters to Oxford, died the night before his trial. Hampden escaped death, perhaps by the interest of his family; but was kept in prison to the end of his life. They whose names were inserted in the commission of array were not capitally punished, as it could not be proved that they had consented to their own nomination; but they were considered as malignants, and their estates were seized.

60    "Waller, though confessedly," says Clarendon, "the most guilty, with incredible dissimulation affected such a remorse of conscience, that his trial was put off, out of Christian compassion, till he might recover his under-standing." What use he made of this interval, with what liberality and success he distributed flattery and money, and how, when he was brought (July 4) before the House, he confessed and lamented, and submitted and implored, may be read in the History of the Rebellion, (B. vii.). The speech, to which Clarendon ascribes the preservation of his *dear-bought life*, is inserted in his works. The great historian, however, seems to have been mistaken in relating that *he prevailed* in the principal part of his supplica-tion, *not to be tried by a Council of War*; for, according to Whitlock, he was by expulsion from the House abandoned to the tribunal which he so much dreaded, and, being tried and condemned, was reprieved by Essex; but after a year's imprisonment, in which time resentment grew less acrimonious, paying a fine of ten thousand pounds, he was permitted *to recollect himself in another country*.

61    Of his behaviour in this part of his life, it is not necessary to direct the reader's opinion. "Let us not," says his last ingenious biographer, "con-demn him with untempered severity, because he was not a prodigy which the world hath seldom seen, because his character included not the poet, the orator, and the hero."

For the place of his exile he chose France, and staid some time at Roan,   62
where his daughter Margaret was born, who was afterwards his favourite,
and his amanuensis. He then removed to Paris, where he lived with great
splendor and hospitality; and from time to time amùsed himself with
poetry, in which he sometimes speaks of the rebels, and their usurpation,
in the natural language of an honest man.

At last it became necessary, for his support, to sell his wife's jewels; and   63
being reduced, as he said, at last *to the rump jewel*, he solicited from
Cromwell permission to return, and obtained it by the interest of colonel
Scroop, to whom his sister was married. Upon the remains of a fortune,
which the danger of his life had very much diminished, he lived at Hall-
barn, a house built by himself, very near to Beaconsfield, where his mother
resided. His mother, though relatéd to Cromwell and Hampden, was
zealous for the royal cause, and, when Cromwell visited her, used to
reproach him; he, in return, would throw a napkin at her, and say he
would not dispute with his aunt; but finding in time that she acted for the
king, as well as talked, he made her a prisoner to her own daughter, in her
own house. If he would do any thing, he could not do less.

Cromwell, now protector, received Waller, as his kinsman, to familiar   64
conversation. Waller, as he used to relate, found him sufficiently versed in
ancient history; and when any of his enthusiastick friends came to advise
or consult him, could sometimes overhear him discoursing in the cant
of the times: but, when he returned, he would say, "Cousin Waller,
I must talk to these men in their own way:" and resumed the common
style of conversation.

He repaid the Protector for his favours (1654) by the famous panegyrick,   65
which has been always considered as the first of his poetical productions.
His choice of encomiastick topicks is very judicious; for he considers
Cromwell in his exaltation, without enquiring how he attained it; there is
consequently no mention of the rebel or the regicide. All the former part of
his hero's life is veiled with shades; and nothing is brought to view but the
chief, the governor, the defender of England's honour, and the enlarger of
her dominion. The act of violence by which he obtained the supreme power
is lightly treated, and decently justified. It was certainly to be desired that
the detestable band should be dissolved, which had destroyed the church,
murdered the King, and filled the nation with tumult and oppression; yet
Cromwell had not the right of dissolving them, for all that he had before
done could be justified only by supposing them invested with lawful
authority. But combinations of wickedness would overwhelm the world
by the advantage which licentious principles afford, did not those who have
long practised perfidy, grow faithless to each other.

66    In the poem on the war with Spain are some passages at least equal to the best parts of the panegyrick; and in the conclusion, the poet ventures yet a higher flight of flattery, by recommending royalty to Cromwell and the nation. Cromwell was very desirous, as appears from his conversation, related by Whitlock, of adding the title to the power of monarchy, and is supposed to have been with-held from it partly by fear of the army, and partly by fear of the laws, which, when he should govern by the name of King, would have restrained his authority. When therefore a deputation was solemnly sent to invite him to the Crown, he, after a long conference, refused it; but is said to have fainted in his coach, when he parted from them.

67    The poem on the death of the Protector seems to have been dictated by real veneration for his memory. Dryden and Sprat wrote on the same occasion; but they were young men, struggling into notice, and hoping for some favour from the ruling party. Waller had little to expect: he had received nothing but his pardon from Cromwell, and was not likely to ask any thing from those who should succeed him.

68    Soon afterwards the Restauration supplied him with another subject; and he exerted his imagination, his elegance, and his melody, with equal alacrity, for Charles the Second. It is not possible to read, without some contempt and indignation, poems of the same author, ascribing the highest degree of *power and piety* to Charles the First, then transferring the same *power and piety* to Oliver Cromwell; now inviting Oliver to take the Crown, and then congratulating Charles the Second on his recovered right. Neither Cromwell nor Charles could value his testimony as the effect of conviction, or receive his praises as effusions of reverence; they could consider them but as the labour of invention, and the tribute of dependence.

69    Poets, indeed, profess fiction; but the legitimate end of fiction is the conveyance of truth; and he that has flattery ready for all whom the vicissitudes of the world happen to exalt, must be scorned as a prostituted mind, that may retain the glitter of wit, but has lost the dignity of virtue.

70    The Congratulation was considered as inferior in poetical merit to the Panegyrick; and it is reported, that when the king told Waller of the disparity, he answered, "Poets, Sir, succeed better in fiction than in truth."

71    The Congratulation is indeed not inferior to the Panegyrick, either by decay of genius, or for want of diligence; but because Cromwell had done much, and Charles had done little. Cromwell wanted nothing to raise him to heroick excellence but virtue; and virtue his poet thought himself at liberty to supply. Charles had yet only the merit of struggling without success, and suffering without despair. A life of escapes and indigence could supply poetry with no splendid images.

In the first parliament summoned by Charles the Second (March 8,   72
1661), Waller sat for Hastings in Sussex, and served for different places
in all the parliaments of that reign. In a time when fancy and gaiety were the
most powerful recommendations to regard, it is not likely that Waller was
forgotten. He passed his time in the company that was highest, both in rank
and wit, from which even his obstinate sobriety did not exclude him.
Though he drank water, he was enabled by his fertility of mind to heighten
the mirth of Bacchanalian assemblies; and Mr. Saville said, that "no man in
England should keep him company without drinking but Ned Waller."

The praise given him by St. Evremond is a proof of his reputation; for it   73
was only by his reputation that he could be known, as a writer, to a man
who, though he lived a great part of a long life upon an English pension,
never condescended to understand the language of the nation that maintained him.

In parliament, "he was," says Burnet, "the delight of the house, and   74
though old said the liveliest things of any among them." This, however, is
said in his account of the year seventy-five, when Waller was only seventy.
His name as a speaker occurs often in Grey's Collections; but I have found
no extracts that can be more quoted as exhibiting sallies of gaiety than
cogency of argument.

He was of such consideration, that his remarks were circulated and   75
recorded. When the duke of York's influence was high, both in Scotland
and England, it drew, says Burnet, a lively reflection from Waller the
celebrated wit. "He said, the house of commons had resolved that the
duke should not reign after the king's death; but the king, in opposition
to them, had resolved that he should reign even in his life." If there appear
no extraordinary *liveliness* in this *remark*, yet its reception proves the
speaker to have been a *celebrated wit*, to have had a name which the men
of wit were proud of mentioning.

He did not suffer his reputation to die gradually away, which may easily   76
happen in a long life, but renewed his claim to poetical distinction from
time to time, as occasions were offered, either by publick events or private
incidents; and, contenting himself with the influence of his muse, or loving
quiet better than influence, he never accepted any office of magistracy.

He was not, however, without some attention to his fortune; for he asked   77
from the King (in 1665) the provostship of Eaton College, and obtained it;
but Clarendon refused to put the seal to the grant, alleging that it could be
held only by a clergyman. It is known that Sir Henry Wotton qualified
himself for it by Deacon's orders.

To this opposition, the *Biographia* imputes the violence and acrimony   78
with which Waller joined Buckingham's faction in the prosecution of

Clarendon. The motive was illiberal and dishonest, and shewed that more than sixty years had not been able to teach him morality. His accusation is such as conscience can hardly be supposed to dictate without the help of malice. "We were to be governed by janizaries instead of parliaments, and are in danger from a worse plot than that of the fifth of November; then, if the Lords and commons had been destroyed, there had been a succession; but here both had been destroyed for ever." This is the language of a man who is glad of an opportunity to rail, and ready to sacrifice truth to interest at one time, and to anger at another.

79     A year after the Chancellor's banishment, another vacancy gave him encouragement for another petition, which the King referred to the council, who, after hearing the question argued by lawyers for three days, determined that the office could be held only by a clergyman, according to the act of uniformity, since the provosts had always received institution, as for a parsonage, from the bishops of Lincoln. The King then said, he could not break the law which he had made; and Dr. Zachary Cradock, famous for a single sermon, at most for two sermons, was chosen by the Fellows.

80     That he asked any thing else is not known; it is certain that he obtained nothing, though he continued obsequious to the court through the rest of Charles's reign.

81     At the accession of King James (in 1685) he was chosen for parliament, being then fourscore, at Saltash in Cornwall; and wrote a *Presage of the Downfall of the Turkish Empire*, which he presented to the King on his birthday. It is remarked, by his commentator Fenton, that in reading Tasso he had early imbibed a veneration for the heroes of the Holy War, and a zealous enmity to the Turks, which never left him. James, however, having soon after begun what he thought a holy war at home, made haste to put all molestation of the Turks out of his power.

82     James treated him with kindness and familiarity, of which instances are given by the writer of his Life. One day, taking him into the closet, the King asked him how he liked one of the pictures: "My eyes," said Waller, "are dim, and I do not know it." The king said, it was the princess of Orange. "She is," said Waller, "like the greatest woman in the world." The King asked who was that? and was answered, Queen Elizabeth. "I wonder," said the King, "you should think so; but I must confess she had a wise council." "And, Sir," said Waller, "did you ever know a fool chuse a wise one?" Such is the story, which I once heard of some other man. Pointed axioms, and acute replies, fly loose about the world, and are assigned successively to those whom it may be the fashion to celebrate.

83     When the King knew that he was about to marry his daughter to Dr. Birch, a clergyman, he ordered a French gentleman to tell him, that

"the King wondered he could think of marrying his daughter to a falling church." "The King," says Waller, "does me great honour, in taking notice of my domestick affairs; but I have lived long enough to observe that this falling church has got a trick of rising again."

He took notice to his friends of the King's conduct; and said, that "he 84 would be left like a whale upon the strand." Whether he was privy to any of the transactions which ended in the Revolution, is not known. His heir joined the prince of Orange.

Having now attained an age beyond which the laws of nature seldom 85 suffer life to be extended, otherwise than by a future state, he seems to have turned his mind upon preparation for the decisive hour, and therefore consecrated his poetry to devotion. It is pleasing to discover that his piety was without weakness; that his intellectual powers continued vigorous; and that the lines which he composed when *he, for age, could neither read nor write*, are not inferior to the effusions of his youth.

Towards the decline of life, he bought a small house, with a little land, at 86 Colshill; and said, "he should be glad to die, like the stag, where he was roused." This, however, did not happen. When he was at Beaconsfield, he found his legs grow tumid: he went to Windsor, where Sir Charles Scarborough then attended the King, and requested him, as both a friend and a physician, to tell him, *what that swelling meant*. "Sir," answered Scarborough, "your blood will run no longer." Waller repeated some lines of Virgil, and went home to die.

As the disease increased upon him, he composed himself for his depart- 87 ure; and calling upon Dr. Birch to give him the holy sacrament, he desired his children to take it with him, and made an earnest declaration of his faith in Christianity. It now appeared, what part of his conversation with the great could be remembered with delight. He related, that being present when the duke of Buckingham talked profanely before King Charles, he said to him, "My Lord, I am a great deal older than your grace, and have, I believe, heard more arguments for atheism than ever your grace did; but I have lived long enough to see there is nothing in them; and so, I hope, your grace will."

He died October 21, 1687, and was buried at Beaconsfield, with a 88 monument erected by his son's executors, for which Rymer wrote the inscription, and which I hope is now rescued from dilapidation.

He left several children by his second wife; of whom, his daughter was 89 married to Dr. Birch. Benjamin, the eldest son, was disinherited, and sent to New Jersey, as wanting common understanding. Edmund, the second son, inherited the estate, and represented Agmondesham in parliament, but at last turned Quaker. William, the third son, was a merchant in London.

Stephen, the fourth, was an eminent Doctor of Laws, and one of the Commissioners for the Union. There is said to have been a fifth, of whom no account has descended.

90    The character of Waller, both moral and intellectual, has been drawn by Clarendon, to whom he was familiarly known, with nicety, which certainly none to whom he was not known can presume to emulate. It is therefore inserted here, with such remarks as others have supplied; after which, nothing remains but a critical examination of his poetry.

91    "Edmund Waller," says Clarendon, "was born to a very fair estate, by the parsimony, or frugality, of a wise father and mother: and he thought it so commendable an advantage, that he resolved to improve it with his utmost care, upon which in his nature he was too much intent; and, in order to that, he was so much reserved and retired, that he was scarce ever heard of, till by his address and dexterity he had gotten a very rich wife in the city, against all the recommendation and countenance and authority of the Court, which was thoroughly engaged on the behalf of Mr. Crofts; and which used to be successful in that age, against any opposition. He had the good fortune to have an alliance and friendship with Dr. Morley, who had assisted and instructed him in the reading many good books, to which his natural parts and promptitude inclined him, especially the poets; and at the age when other men used to give over writing verses (for he was near thirty years when he first engaged himself in that exercise; at least, that he was known to do so), he surprised the town with two or three pieces of that kind; as if a tenth Muse had been newly born, to cherish drooping poetry. The Doctor at that time brought him into that company, which was most celebrated for good conversation; where he was received and esteemed, with great applause and respect. He was a very pleasant discourser, in earnest and in jest, and therefore very grateful to all kind of company, where he was not the less esteemed for being very rich.

92    "He had been even nursed in parliaments, where he sat when he was very young; and so, when they were resumed again (after a long intermission), he appeared in those assemblies with great advantage; having a graceful way of speaking, and by thinking much on several arguments (which his temper and complexion, that had much of melancholic, inclined him to), he seemed often to speak upon the sudden, when the occasion had only administred the opportunity of saying what he had thoroughly considered, which gave a great lustre to all he said; which yet was rather of delight than weight. There needs no more be said to extol the excellence and power of his wit, and pleasantness of his conversation, than that it was of magnitude enough to cover a world of very great faults; that is, so to cover them, that they were not taken notice of to his reproach; viz. a narrowness in his nature to the

lowest degree; an abjectness and want of courage to support him in any virtuous undertaking; an insinuation and servile flattery to the height, the vainest and most imperious nature could be contented with; that it preserved and won his life from those who were most resolved to take it, and in an occasion in which hé ought to have been ambitious to have lost it; and then preserved him again, from the reproach and contempt that was due to him, for so preserving it, and for vindicating it at such a price; that it had power to reconcile him to those, whom he had most offended and provoked; and continued to his age with that rare felicity, that his company was acceptable, where his spirit was odious; and he was at least pitied, where he was most detested."

Such is the account of Clarendon; on which it may not be improper to 93 make some remarks.

"He was very little known till he had obtained a rich wife in the city." 94

He obtained the rich wife about the age of three-and-twenty; an age before which few men are conspicuous much to their advantage. He was known, however, in parliament and at court: and, if he spent part of his time in privacy, it is not unreasonable to suppose that he endeavoured the improvement of his mind as well as of his fortune.

That Clarendon might misjudge the motive of his retirement is the more 95 probable, because he has evidently mistaken the commencement of his poetry, which he supposes him not to have attempted before thirty. As his first pieces were perhaps not printed, the succession of his compositions was not known; and Clarendon, who cannot be imagined to have been very studious of poetry, did not rectify his first opinion by consulting Waller's book.

Clarendon observes, that he was introduced to the wits of the age by 96 Dr. Morley; but the writer of his Life relates that he was already among them, when, hearing a noise in the street, and enquiring the cause, they found a son of Ben Jonson under an arrest. This was Morley, whom Waller set free at the expence of one hundred pounds, took him into the country as director of his studies, and then procured him admission into the company of the friends of literature. Of this fact, Clarendon had a nearer knowledge than the biographer, and is therefore more to be credited.

The account of Waller's parliamentary eloquence is seconded by Burnet, 97 who, though he calls him "the delight of the house," adds, that "he was only concerned to say that, which should make him be applauded, he never laid the business of the House to heart, being a vain and empty though a witty man."

Of his insinuation and flattery it is not unreasonable to believe that the 98 truth is told. Ascham, in his elegant description of those whom in modern

language we term Wits, says, that they are *open flatterers, and privy mockers.*
Waller shewed a little of both, when, upon sight of the Dutchess of Newcastle's verses on the death of a Stag, he declared that he would give all his
own compositions to have written them; and, being charged with the
exorbitance of his adulation, answered, that "nothing was too much to be
given, that a Lady might be saved from the disgrace of such a vile performance." This, however, was no very mischievous or very unusual deviation
from truth: had his hypocrisy been confined to such transactions, he might
have been forgiven, though not praised; for who forbears to flatter an author
or a lady?

99 Of the laxity of his political principles, and the weakness of his resolution,
he experienced the natural effect, by losing the esteem of every party. From
Cromwell he had only his recall; and from Charles the Second, who
delighted in his company, he obtained only the pardon of his relation
Hampden, and the safety of Hampden's son.

100 As far as conjecture can be made from the whole of his writing, and his
conduct, he was habitually and deliberately a friend to monarchy. His
deviation towards democracy proceeded from his connection with Hampden, for whose sake he prosecuted Crawley with great bitterness: and the
invective which he pronounced on that occasion was so popular, that twenty
thousand copies are said by his biographer to have been sold in one day.

101 It is confessed that his faults still left him many friends, at least many
companions. His convivial power of pleasing is universally acknowledged;
but those who conversed with him intimately, found him not only passionate, especially in his old age, but resentful; so that the interposition of
friends was sometimes necessary.

102 His wit and his poetry naturally connected him with the polite writers of
his time: he was joined with Lord Buckhurst in the translation of Corneille's
Pompey; and is said to have added his help to that of Cowley in the original
draught of the Rehearsal.

103 The care of his fortune, which Clarendon imputes to him in a degree
little less than criminal, was either not constant or not successful; for,
having inherited a patrimony of three thousand five hundred a year in the
time of James the First, and augmented it at least by one wealthy marriage,
he left, about the time of the Revolution, an income of not more than twelve
or thirteen hundred; which, when the different value of money is reckoned,
will be found perhaps not more than a fourth part of what he once
possessed.

104 Of this diminution, part was the consequence of the gifts which he was
forced to scatter, and the fine which he was condemned to pay at the
detection of his plot; and if his estate, as is related in his Life, was

sequestered, he had probably contracted debts when he lived in exile; for we are told that at Paris he lived in splendor, and was the only Englishman, except the Lord St. Albans, that kept a table.

His unlucky plot compelled him to sell a thousand a year; of the waste of 105 the rest there is no account, except that he is confessed by his biographer to have been a bad œconomist. He seems to have deviated from the common practice; to have been a hoarder in his first years, and a squanderer in his last.

Of his course of studies, or choice of books, nothing is known more than 106 that he professed himself unable to read Chapman's translation of Homer without rapture. His opinion concerning the duty of a poet is contained in his declaration, that "he would blot from his works any line that did not contain some motive to virtue."

THE characters, by which Waller intended to distinguish his writings, are 107 spriteliness and dignity; in his smaller pieces, he endeavours to be gay; in the larger, to be great. Of his airy and light productions, the chief source is gallantry, that attentive reverence of female excellence, which has descended to us from the Gothic ages. As his poems are commonly occasional, and his addresses personal, he was not so liberally supplied with grand as with soft images; for beauty is more easily found than magnanimity.

The delicacy, which he cultivated, restrains him to a certain nicety and 108 caution, even when he writes upon the slightest matter. He has therefore in his whole volume nothing burlesque, and seldom any thing ludicrous or familiar. He seems always to do his best; though his subjects are often unworthy of his care. It is not easy to think without some contempt on an author, who is growing illustrious in his own opinion by verses, at one time, "To a Lady, who can do any thing, but sleep, when she pleases." At another, "To a Lady, who can sleep, when she pleases." Now, "To a Lady, on her passing through a crowd of people." Then, "On a braid of divers colours woven by four fair Ladies:" "On a tree cut in paper:" or, "To a Lady, from whom he received the copy of verses on the paper-tree, which for many years had been missing."

Genius now and then produces a lucky trifle. We still read the *Dove* of 109 Anacreon, and *Sparrow* of Catullus; and a writer naturally pleases himself with a performance, which owes nothing to the subject. But compositions merely pretty have the fate of other pretty things, and are quitted in time for something useful: they are flowers fragrant and fair, but of short duration; or they are blossoms to be valued only as they foretell fruits.

Among Waller's little poems are some, which their excellency ought to 110 secure from oblivion; as, *To Amoret*, comparing the different modes of regard with which he looks on her and *Sacharissa*; and the verses *On Love*, that begin, *Anger in hasty words or blows*.

111     In others he is not equally successful; sometimes his thoughts are deficient, and sometimes his expression.

112     The numbers are not always musical; as,

> Fair Venus, in thy soft arms
>     The god of rage confine;
> For thy whispers are the charms
>     Which only can divert his fierce design.
> What though he frown, and to tumult do incline;
>     Thou the flame
>     Kindled in his breast canst tame,
> With that snow which unmelted lies on thine.

113     He seldom indeed fetches an amorous sentiment from the depths of science; his thoughts are for the most part easily understood, and his images such as the superficies of nature readily supplies; he has a just claim to popularity, because he writes to common degrees of knowledge, and is free at least from philosophical pedantry, unless perhaps the end of a song *to the Sun* may be excepted, in which he is too much a Copernican. To which may be added, the simile of the *Palm* in the verses *on her passing through a crowd*; and a line in a more serious poem on the *Restoration*, about vipers and treacle, which can only be understood by those who happen to know the composition of the *Theriaca*.

114     His thoughts are sometimes hyperbolical, and his images unnatural:

>                     —The plants admire,
> No less than those of old did Orpheus' lyre;
> If she sit down, with tops all tow'rds her bow'd;
> They round about her into arbours crowd:
> Or if she walks, in even ranks they stand,
> Like some well-marshal'd and obsequious band.

In another place:

> While in the park I sing, the listening deer
> Attend my passion, and forget to fear:
> When to the beeches I report my flame,
> They bow their heads, as if they felt the same:
> To gods appealing, when I reach their bowers,
> With loud complaints they answer me in showers.
> To thee a wild and cruel soul is given,
> More deaf than trees, and prouder than the heaven!

On the head of a Stag:

> O fertile head! which every year
> Could such a crop of wonder bear!
> The teeming earth did never bring
> So soon, so hard, so huge a thing:
> Which might it never have been cast,
> Each year's growth added to the last,
> These lofty branches had supply'd
> The Earth's bold son's prodigious pride:
> Heaven with these engines had been scal'd,
> When mountains heap'd on mountains fail'd.

Sometimes, having succeeded in the first part, he makes a feeble conclu- 115
sion. In the song of "Sacharissa's and Amoret's Friendship," the two last
stanzas ought to have been omitted.

His images of gallantry are not always in the highest degree delicate.     116

> Then shall my love this doubt displace,
>     And gain such trust, that I may come
> And banquet sometimes on thy face,
>     But make my constant meals at home.

Some applications may be thought too remote and unconsequential: as in  117
the verses on the *Lady dancing*:

> The sun in figures such as these,
>     Joys with the moon to play:
>         To the sweet strains they advance,
>     Which do result from their own spheres;
>         As this nymph's dance
> Moves with the numbers which she hears.

Sometimes a thought, which might perhaps fill a distich, is expanded and  118
attenuated till it grows weak and almost evanescent.

> Chloris ! since first our calm of peace
>     Was frighted hence, this good we find,
> Your favours with your fears increase,
>     And growing mischiefs make you kind.
> So the fair tree, which still preferves
>     Her fruit, and state, while no wind blows,
> In storms from that uprightness swerves;
>     And the glad earth about her strows
>     With treasure from her yielding boughs.

119     His images are not always distinct; as, in the following passage, he confounds *Love* as a person with *love* as a passion:

> Some other nymphs, with colours faint,
> And pencil slow, may Cupid paint,
> And a weak heart in time destroy;
> She has a stamp, and prints the Boy:
> Can, with a single look, inflame
> The coldest breast, the rudest tame.

120     His sallies of casual flattery are sometimes elegant and happy, as that *in return for the Silver Pen*; and sometimes empty and trifling, as that *upon the Card torn by the Queen*. There are a few lines *written in the Dutchess's Tasso*, which he is said by Fenton to have kept a summer under correction. It happened to Waller, as to others, that his success was not always in proportion to his labour.

121     Of these petty compositions, neither the beauties nor the faults deserve much attention. The amorous verses have this to recommend them, that they are less hyperbolical than those of some other poets. Waller is not always at the last gasp; he does not die of a frown, nor live upon a smile. There is however too much love, and too many trifles. Little things are made too important; and the Empire of Beauty is represented as exerting its influence further than can be allowed by the multiplicity of human passions, and the variety of human wants. Such books therefore may be considered as shewing the world under a false appearance, and, so far as they obtain credit from the young and unexperienced, as misleading expectation, and misguiding practice.

122     Of his nobler and more weighty performances, the greater part is panegyrical; for of praise he was very lavish, as is observed by his imitator, Lord Lansdown:

> No satyr stalks within the hallow'd ground,
> But queens and heroines, kings and gods abound;
> Glory and arms and love are all the sound.

123     In the first poem, on the danger of the Prince on the coast of Spain, there is a puerile and ridiculous mention of Arion at the beginning; and the last paragraph, on the *Cable*, is in part ridiculously mean, and in part ridiculously tumid. The poem, however, is such as may be justly praised, without much allowance for the state of our poetry and language at that time.

124     The two next poems are upon the King's *behaviour at the death of* Buckingham, and upon his *Navy*.

122a    He has, in the first, used the pagan deities with great propriety:

> 'Twas want of such a precedent as this
> Made the old heathen frame their gods amiss.

In the poem on the Navy, those lines are very noble, which suppose the  *122b*
King's power secure against a second Deluge; so noble, that it were almost
criminal to remark the mistake of *centre* for *surface*, or to say that the empire
of the sea would be worth little if it were not that the waters terminate in
land.

The poem upon Sallee has forcible sentiments; but the conclusion is  *125*
feeble. That on the Repairs of St. Paul's has something vulgar and obvious;
such as the mention of Amphion; and something violent and harsh, as

> So all our minds with his conspire to grace
> The Gentiles' great apostle, and deface
> Those state-obscuring sheds, that like a chain
> Seem'd to confine, and fetter him again:
> Which the glad saint shakes off at his command,
> As once the viper from his sacred hand.
> So joys the aged oak, when we divide
> The creeping ivy from his injur'd side.

Of the two last couplets, the first is extravagant, and the second mean.

His praise of the Queen is too much exaggerated; and the thought, that  *126*
she "saves lovers, by cutting off hope, as gangrenes are cured by lopping the
limb," presents nothing to the mind but disgust and horror.

Of the *Battle of the Summer Islands*, it seems not easy to say whether it is  *127*
intended to raise terror or merriment. The beginning is too splendid for
jest, and the conclusion too light for seriousness. The versification is
studied, the scenes are diligently displayed, and the images artfully
amplified; but as it ends neither in joy nor sorrow, it will scarcely be read
a second time.

The *Panegyrick* upon Cromwell has obtained from the publick a very  *128*
liberal dividend of praise, which however cannot be said to have been
unjustly lavished; for such a series of verses had rarely appeared before in
the English language. Of the lines some are grand, some are graceful, and all
are musical. There is now and then a feeble verse, or a trifling thought; but
its great fault is the choice of its hero.

The poem of *The War with Spain* begins with lines more vigorous and  *129*
striking than Waller is accustomed to produce. The succeeding parts are
variegated with better passages and worse. There is something too far-
fetched in the comparison of the Spaniards drawing the English on, by
saluting St. Lucar with cannon, *to lambs awakening the lion by bleating*. The
fate of the Marquis and his Lady, who were burnt in their ship, would have

moved more, had the poet not made him die like the Phœnix, because he had spices about him, nor expressed their affection and their end by a conceit at once false and vulgar:

> Alive, in equal flames of love they burn'd,
> And now together are to ashes turn'd.

130    The verses to Charles, on his Return, were doubtless intended to counterbalance the panegyric on Cromwell. If it has been thought inferior to that with which it is naturally compared, the cause of its deficience has been already remarked.

131    The remaining pieces it is not necessary to examine singly. They must be supposed to have faults and beauties of the same kind with the rest. The Sacred Poems, however, deserve particular regard; they were the work of Waller's declining life, of those hours in which he looked upon the fame and the folly of the time past with the sentiments which his great predecessor Petrarch bequeathed to posterity, upon his review of that love and poetry which have given him immortality.

132    That natural jealousy which makes every man unwilling to allow much excellence in another, always produces a disposition to believe that the mind grows old with the body; and that he, whom we are now forced to confess superior, is hastening daily to a level with ourselves. By delighting to think this of the living, we learn to think it of the dead; and Fenton, with all his kindness for Waller, has the luck to mark the exact time when his genius passed the zenith, which he places at his fifty-fifth year. This is to allot the mind but a small portion. Intellectual decay is doubtless not uncommon; but it seems not to be universal. Newton was in his eighty-fifth year improving his Chronology, a few days before his death; and Waller appears not, in my opinion, to have lost at eighty-two any part of his poetical power.

133    His Sacred Poems do not please like some of his other works; but before the fatal fifty-five, had he written on the same subjects, his success would hardly have been better.

134    It has been the frequent lamentation of good men, that verse has been too little applied to the purposes of worship, and many attempts have been made to animate devotion by pious poetry; that they have very seldom attained their end is sufficiently known, and it may not be improper to enquire why they have miscarried.

135    Let no pious ear be offended if I advance, in opposition to many authorities, that poetical devotion cannot often please. The doctrines of religion may indeed be defended in a didactick poem; and he who has the happy power of arguing in verse, will not lose it because his subject is

sacred. A poet may describe the beauty and the grandeur of Nature, the flowers of the Spring, and the harvests of Autumn, the vicissitudes of the Tide, and the revolutions of the Sky, and praise the Maker for his works in lines which no reader shall lay aside. The subject of the disputation is not piety, but the motives to piety; that of the description is not God, but the works of God.

Contemplative piety, or the intercourse between God and the human 136 soul, cannot be poetical. Man admitted to implore the mercy of his Creator, and plead the merits of his Redeemer, is already in a higher state than poetry can confer.

The essence of poetry is invention; such invention as, by producing 137 something unexpected, surprises and delights. The topicks of devotion are few, and being few are universally known; but, few as they are, they can be made no more; they can receive no grace from novelty of sentiment, and very little from novelty of expression.

Poetry pleases by exhibiting an idea more grateful to the mind than 138 things themselves afford. This effect proceeds from the display of those parts of nature which attract, and the concealment of those which repel the imagination: but religion must be shewn as it is; suppression and addition equally corrupt it; and such as it is, it is known already.

From poetry the reader justly expects, and from good poetry always 139 obtains, the enlargement of his comprehension and elevation of his fancy; but this is rarely to be hoped by Christians from metrical devotion. Whatever is great, desireable, or tremendous, is comprised in the name of the Supreme Being. Omnipotence cannot be exalted; Infinity cannot be amplified; Perfection cannot be improved.

The employments of pious meditation are Faith, Thanksgiving, Repent- 140 ance, and Supplication. Faith, invariably uniform, cannot be invested by fancy with decorations. Thanksgiving, the most joyful of all holy effusions, yet addressed to a Being without passions, is confined to a few modes, and is to be felt rather than expressed. Repentance, trembling in the presence of the judge, is not at leisure for cadences and epithets. Supplication of man to man may diffuse itself through many topicks of persuasion; but supplication to God can only cry for mercy.

Of sentiments purely religious, it will be found that the most simple 141 expression is the most sublime. Poetry loses its lustre and its power, because it is applied to the decoration of something more excellent than itself. All that pious verse can do is to help the memory, and delight the ear, and for these purposes it may be very useful; but it supplies nothing to the mind. The ideas of Christian Theology are too simple for eloquence, too sacred for fiction, and too majestick for ornament; to recommend them by tropes and figures, is to magnify by a concave mirror the sidereal hemisphere.

142   As much of Waller's reputation was owed to the softness and smoothness of his Numbers; it is proper to consider those minute particulars to which a versifyer must attend.

143   He certainly very much excelled in smoothness most of the writers who were living when his poetry commenced. The Poets of Elizabeth had attained an art of modulation, which was afterwards neglected or forgotten. Fairfax was acknowledged by him as his model; and he might have studied with advantage the poem of Davies, which, though merely philosophical, yet seldom leaves the ear ungratified.

144   But he was rather smooth than strong; of *the full resounding line*, which Pope attributes to Dryden, he has given very few examples. The critical decision has given the praise of strength to Denham, and of sweetness to Waller.

145   His excellence of versification has some abatements. He uses the expletive *do* very frequently; and though he lived to see it almost universally ejected, was not more careful to avoid it in his last compositions than in his first. Praise had given him confidence; and finding the world satisfied, he satisfied himself.

146   His rhymes are sometimes weak words: *so* is found to make the rhyme twice in ten lines, and occurs often as a rhyme through his book.

147   His double rhymes, in heroick verse, have been censured by Mrs. Phillips, who was his rival in the translation of Corneille's Pompey; and more faults might be found, were not the enquiry below attention.

148   He sometimes uses the obsolete termination of verbs, as *waxeth, affecteth*; and sometimes retains the final syllable of the preterite, as *amazed, supposed*; of which I know not whether it is not to the detriment of our language that we have totally rejected them.

149   Of triplets he is sparing; but he did not wholly forbear them: of an Alexandrine he has given no example.

150   The general character of his poetry is elegance and gaiety. He is never pathetick, and very rarely sublime. He seems neither to have had a mind much elevated by nature, nor amplified by learning. His thoughts are such as a liberal conversation and large acquaintance with life would easily supply. They had however then, perhaps, that grace of novelty, which they are now often supposed to want by those who, having already found them in later books, do not know or enquire who produced them first. This treatment is unjust. Let not the original author lose by his imitators.

151   Praise however should be due before it is given. The author of Waller's Life ascribes to him the first practice, of what Erythræus and some late

critics call *Alliteration*, of using in the same verse many words beginning with the same letter. But this knack, whatever be its value, was so frequent among early writers, that Gascoign, a writer of the sixteenth century, warns the young poet against affecting it; Shakspeare in the *Midsummer Night's Dream* is supposed to ridicule it; and in another play the sonnet of Holofernes fully displays it.

He borrows too many of his sentiments and illustrations from the old 152 Mythology, for which it is vain to plead the example of ancient poets: the deities which they introduced so frequently, were considered as realities, so far as to be received by the imagination, whatever sober reason might even then determine. But of these images time has tarnished the splendor. A fiction, not only detected but despised, can never afford a solid basis to any position, though sometimes it may furnish a transient allusion, or slight illustration. No modern monarch can be much exalted by hearing that, as Hercules had had his *club*, he has his *navy*.

But of the praise of Waller, though much may be taken away, much will 153 remain; for it cannot be denied that he added something to our elegance of diction, and something to our propriety of thought; and to him may be applied what Tasso said, with equal spirit and justice of himself and Guarini, when, having perused the *Pastor Fido*, he cried out, "If he had not read *Aminta*, he had not excelled it."

AS Waller professed himself to have learned the art of versification from 154 Fairfax, it has been thought proper to subjoin a specimen of his work, which, after Mr. Hoole's translation, will perhaps not be soon reprinted. By knowing the state in which Waller found our poetry, the reader may judge how much he improved it.

1.

Erminiaes steed (this while) his mistresse bore
Through forrests thicke among the shadie treene,
Her feeble hand the bridle raines forlore,
Halfe in a swoune she was for feare I weene;
But her flit courser spared nere the more,
To beare her through the desart woods unseene
    Of her strong foes, that chas'd her through the plaine,
    And still pursu'd, but still pursu'd in vaine.

2.

Like as the wearie hounds at last retire,
Windlesse, displeased, from the fruitlesse chace,
When the slie beast Tapisht in bush and brire,
No art nor paines can rowse out of his place:

The Christian knights so full of shame and ire
Returned backe, with faint and wearie pace!
   Yet still the fearefull Dame fled, swift as winde,
   Nor euer staid, nor euer lookt behinde.


3.

Through thicke and thinne, all night, all day, she driued,
Withouten comfort, companie or guide,
Her plaints and teares with euery thought reuiued,
She heard and saw her greefes, but nought beside.
But when the sunne his burning chariot diued
In Thetis waue, and wearie teame vntide,
   On Iordans sandie banks her course she staid,
   At last, there downe she light, and downe she laid.


4.

Her teares, her drinke; her food, her sorrowings,
This was her diet that vnhappie night:
But sleepe (that sweet repose and quiet brings)
To ease the greefes of discontented wight,
Spred foorth his tender, soft, and nimble wings,
In his dull armes foulding the virgin bright;
   And loue, his mother, and the graces kept
   Strong watch and warde, while this faire Ladie slept.


5.

The birds awakte her with their morning song,
Their warbling musicke pearst her tender eare,
The murmuring brookes and whistling windes among
The ratling boughes, and leaues, their parts did beare;
Her eies vnclos'd beheld the groues along
Of swaines and shepherd groomes, that dwellings weare;
   And that sweet noise, birds, winds, and waters sent,
   Prouokte againe the virgin to lament.


6.

Her plaints were interrupted with a sound,
That seem'd from thickest bushes to proceed,
Some iolly shepherd sung a lustie round,
And to his voice had tun'd his oaten reed;
Thither she went, an old man there she found,
(At whose right hand his little flocke did feed)
   Sat making baskets, his three sonnes among,
   That learn'd their fathers art, and learn'd his song.

7.

Beholding one in shining armes appeare
The seelie man and his were sore dismaid;
But sweet Erminia comforted their feare,
Her ventall vp, her visage open laid,
You happie folke, of heau'n beloued deare,
Work on (quoth she) vpon your harmlesse traid,
    These dreadfull armes I beare no warfare bring
    To your sweet toile, nor those sweet tunes you sing.

8.

But father, since this land, these townes and towres,
Destroied are with sword, with fire and spoile,
How may it be unhurt, that you and yours
In safetie thus, applie your harmlesse toile?
My sonne (quoth he) this poore estate of ours
Is euer safe from storme of warlike broile;
    This wildernesse doth vs in safetie keepe,
    No thundring drum, no trumpet breakes our sleepe.

9.

Haply iust heau'ns defence and shield of right,
Doth loue the innocence of simple swaines,
The thunderbolts on highest mountains light,
And seld or neuer strike the lower plaines:
So kings haue cause to feare *Bellonaes* might,
Not they whose sweat and toile their dinner gaines,
    Nor ever greedie soldier was entised
    By pouertie, neglected and despised.

10.

O pouertie, chefe of the heau'nly brood,
Dearer to me than wealth or kingly crowne!
No wish for honour; thirst of others good,
Can moue my hart, contented with mine owne:
We quench our thirst with water of this flood,
Nor fear we poison should therein be throwne:
    These little flocks of sheepe and tender goates
    Giue milke for food, and wooll to make us coates.

11.

We little wish, we need but little wealth,
From cold and hunger vs to cloath and feed;
These are my sonnes, their care preserues from stealth

Their fathers flocks, nor servants moe I need:
Amid these groues I walke oft for my health,
And to the fishes, birds and beastes giue heed,
How they are fed, in forrest, spring and lake,
And their contentment for ensample take.

12.

Time was (for each one hath his doting time,
These siluer locks were golden tresses than)
That countrie life I hated as a crime,
And from the forrests sweet contentment ran,
To Memphis stately pallace would I clime,
And there became the mightie Caliphes man,
And though I but a simple gardner weare,
Yet could I marke abuses, see and heare.

13.

Entised on with hope of future gaine,
I suffred long what did my soule displease;
But when my youth was spent, my hope was vaine,
I felt my native strength at last decrease;
I gan my losse of lustie yeeres complaine,
And wisht I had enjoy'd the countries peace;
I bod the court farewell, and with content
My later age here have I quiet spent.

14.

While thus he spake, Erminia husht and still
His wise discourses heard, with great attention,
His speeches graue those idle fancies kill,
Which in her troubled soule bred such dissention;
After much thought reformed was her will,
Within those woods to dwell was her intention,
Till fortune should occasion new afford,
To turne her home to her desired Lord.

15.

She said therefore, O shepherd fortunate!
That troubles some didst whilom feele and proue,
Yet liuest now in this contented state,
Let my mishap thy thoughts to pitie moue,
To entertaine me as a willing mate
In shepherds life, which I admire and loue;
Within these pleasant groues perchance my hart,
Of her discomforts, may vnload some part.

### 16.

If gold or wealth of most esteemed deare,
If iewels rich, thou diddest hold in prise,
Such store thereof, such plentie haue I seen,
As to a greedie minde might well suffice:
With that downe trickled many a siluer teare,
Two christall streames fell from her watrie eies;
    Part of her sad misfortunes than she told,
    And wept, and with her wept that shepherd old.

### 17.

With speeches kinde, he gan the virgin deare
Towards his cottage gently home to guide;
His aged wife there made her homely cheare,
Yet welcomde her, and plast her by her side.
The Princesse dond a poore pastoraes geare,
A kerchiefe course vpon her head she tide;
    But yet her gestures and her lookes (I gesse)
    Were such, as ill beseem'd a shepherdesse.

### 18.

Not those rude garments could obscure, and hide,
The heau'nly beautie of her angels face,
Nor was her princely ofspring damnifide,
Or ought disparag'de, by those labours bace;
Her little flocks to pasture would she guide,
And milke her goates, and in their folds them place,
    Both cheese and butter could she make, and frame
    Her selfe to please the shepherd and his dame.

# POMFRET

1    OF Mr. JOHN POMFRET nothing is known but from a slight and confused account prefixed to his poems by a nameless friend; who relates, that he was the son of the Rev. Mr. Pomfret, rector of Luton in Bedfordshire; that he was bred at Cambridge, entered into orders, and was rector of Malden in Bedfordshire, and might have risen in the Church; but that, when he applied to Dr. Compton, bishop of London, for institution to a living of considerable value, to which he had been presented, he found a troublesome obstruction raised by a malicious interpretation of some passage in his *Choice*; from which it was inferred, that he considered happiness as more likely to be found in the company of a mistress than of a wife.

2    This reproach was easily obliterated: for it had happened to Pomfret as to almost all other men who plan schemes of life; he had departed from his purpose, and was then married.

3    The malice of his enemies had however a very fatal consequence: the delay constrained his attendance in London, where he caught the small-pox, and died in 1703, in the thirty-sixth year of his age.

4    He published his poems in 1699; and has been always the favourite of that class of readers, who, without vanity or criticism, seek only their own amusement.

5    His *Choice* exhibits a system of life adapted to common notions, and equal to common expectations; such a state as affords plenty and tranquillity, without exclusion of intellectual pleasures. Perhaps no composition in our language has been oftener perused than Pomfret's *Choice*.

6    In his other poems there is an easy volubility; the pleasure of smooth metre is afforded to the ear, and the mind is not oppressed with ponderous or entangled with intricate sentiment. He pleases many, and he who pleases many must have some species of merit.

# DORSET

OF the Earl of Dorset the character has been drawn so largely and so 1
elegantly by Prior, to whom he was familiarly known, that nothing can be
added by a casual hand; and, as its authour is so generally read, it would be
useless officiousness to transcribe it.

Charles Sackville was born January 24, 1637. Having been educated 2
under a private tutor, he travelled into Italy, and returned a little before
the Restoration. He was chosen into the first parliament that was called,
for East Grinstead in Sussex, and soon became a favourite of Charles
the Second; but undertook no publick employment, being too eager of
the riotous and licentious pleasures which young men of high rank, who
aspired to be thought wits, at that time imagined themselves intitled
to indulge.

One of these Frolicks has, by the industry of Wood, come down to 3
posterity. Sackville, who was then Lord Buckhurst, with Sir Charles Sedley
and Sir Thomas Ogle, got drunk at the Cock in Bow-street by Covent-
garden, and, going into the balcony, exposed themselves to the populace in
very indecent postures. At last, as they grew warmer, Sedley stood forth
naked, and harangued the populace in such profane language, that the
publick indignation was awakened; the crowd attempted to force the
door, and, being repulsed, drove in the performers with stones, and broke
the windows of the house.

For this misdemeanour they were indicted, and Sedley was fined five 4
hundred pounds: what was the sentence of the others is not known. Sedley
employed Killigrew and another to procure a remission from the king; but
(mark the friendship of the dissolute!) they begged the fine for themselves,
and exacted it to the last groat.

In 1665, Lord Buckhurst attended the Duke of York as a volunteer in the 5
Dutch war; and was in the battle of June 3, when eighteen great Dutch ships
were taken, fourteen others were destroyed, and Opdam the admiral, who
engaged the Duke, was blown up beside him, with all his crew.

On the day before the battle, he is said to have composed the celebrated 6
song, *To all you Ladies now at land*, with equal tranquillity of mind and
promptitude of wit. Seldom any splendid story is wholly true. I have heard
from the late Earl of Orrery, who was likely to have good hereditary
intelligence, that Lord Buckhurst had been a week employed upon it, and

only retouched or finished it on the memorable evening. But even this, whatever it may substract from his facility, leaves him his courage.

7    He was soon after made a gentleman of the bedchamber, and sent on short embassies to France.

8    In 1674, the estate of his uncle James Cranfield, Earl of Middlesex, came to him by its owner's death, and the title was conferred on him the year after. In 1677, he became, by the death of his father, Earl of Dorset, and inherited the estate of his family.

9    In 1684, having buried his first wife, of the family of Bagot, who left him no child, he married a daughter of the Earl of Northampton, celebrated both for beauty and understanding.

10   He received some favourable notice from King James; but soon found it necessary to oppose the violence of his innovations, and with some other Lords appeared in Westminster-hall, to countenance the Bishops at their trial.

11   As enormities grew every day less supportable, he found it necessary to concur in the Revolution. He was one of those Lords who sat every day in council to preserve the publick peace, after the king's departure; and, what is not the most illustrious action of his life, was employed to conduct the Princess Anne to Nottingham with a guard, such as might alarm the populace, as they passed, with false apprehensions of her danger. Whatever end may be designed, there is always something despicable in a trick.

12   He became, as may be easily supposed, a favourite of King William, who, the day after his accession, made him lord chamberlain of the household, and gave him afterwards the garter. He happened to be among those that were tossed with the King in an open boat sixteen hours, in very rough and cold weather, on the coast of Holland. His health afterwards declined; and on Jan. 19, 1705–6, he died at Bath.

13   He was a man whose elegance and judgement were universally confessed, and whose bounty to the learned and witty was generally known. To the indulgent affection of the publick, Lord Rochester bore ample testimony in this remark: *I know not how it is, but* Lord Buckhurst *may do what he will, yet is never in the wrong.*

14   If such a man attempted poetry, we cannot wonder that his works were praised. Dryden, whom, if Prior tells truth, he distinguished by his beneficence, and who lavished his blandishments on those who are not known to have so well deserved them, undertaking to produce authors of our own country superior to those of antiquity, says, *I would instance your Lordship in satire, and Shakspeare in tragedy.* Would it be imagined that, of this rival to antiquity, all the satires were little personal invectives, and that his longest composition was a song of eleven stanzas?

The blame, however, of this exaggerated praise falls on the encomiast, 15
not upon the author; whose performances are, what they pretend to be, the
effusions of a man of wit; gay, vigorous, and airy. His verses to Howard
shew great fertility of mind, and his *Dorinda* has been imitated by Pope.

# STEPNEY

1 GEORGE STEPNEY, descended from the Stepneys of Pendegrast in Pembrokeshire, was born at Westminster in 1663. Of his father's condition or fortune I have no account. Having received the first part of his education at Westminster, where he passed six years in the College, he went at nineteen to Cambridge, where he continued a friendship begun at school with Mr. Montague, afterwards Earl of Halifax. They came to London together, and are said to have been invited into publick life by the Duke of Dorset.

2 His qualifications recommended him to many foreign employments, so that his time seems to have been spent in negotiations. In 1692 he was sent envoy to the Elector of Brandenburgh; in 1693 to the Imperial Court; in 1693 to the Elector of Saxony; in 1696 to the Electors of Mentz and Cologne, and the Congress at Francfort; in 1698 a second time to Brandenburgh; in 1699 to the King of Poland; in 1701 again to the Emperor; and in 1706 to the States General. In 1697 he was made one of the commissioners of trade. His life was busy, and not long. He died in 1707; and is buried in Westminster-Abbey, with this epitaph, which *Jacob* transcribed.

H. S. E.
GEORGIUS STEPNEIUS, Armiger,
Vir
Ob Ingenii acumen,
Literarum Scientiam,
Morum Suavitatem,
Rerum Usum,
Virorum Amplissimorum Consuetudinem,
Linguæ, Styli, ac Vitæ Elegantiam,
Præclara Officia cum Britanniæ tum Europæ
præstita,
Sua ætate multum celebratus,
Apud posteros semper celebrandus;
Plurimas Legationes obiit
Ea Fide, Diligentia, ac Felicitate,
Ut Augustissimorum Principum
Gulielmi & Annæ
Spem in illo repositam
Numquam fefellerit,
Haud raro superaverit.

Post longum honorum Cursum
Brevî Temporis Spatio confectum,
Cum Naturæ parum, Famæ satis vixerat,
Animam ad altiora aspirantem placide efflavit.

On the Left Hand:

G. S.
Ex Equestri Familia Stepneiorum,
De Pendegrast, in Comitatu
Pembrochiensi oriundus,
Westmonasterii natus est, A. D. 1663.
Electus in Collegium
Sancti Petri Westmonast. A. 1676.
Sancti Trinitatis Cantab. 1682.
Consiliariorum quibus Commercii
Cura commissa est 1697.
Chelseiæ mortuus, &, comitante
Magna Procerum
Frequentia, huc elatus, 1707.

It is reported that the juvenile compositions of Stepney *made grey authors* 3 *blush*. I know not whether his poems will appear such wonders to the present age. One cannot always easily find the reason for which the world has sometimes conspired to squander praise. It is not very unlikely that he wrote very early as well as he ever wrote; and the performances of youth have many favourers, because the authors yet lay no claim to publick honours, and are therefore not considered as rivals by the distributors of fame.

He apparently professed himself a poet, and added his name to those of 4 the other wits in the version of Juvenal; but he is a very licentious translator, and does not recompense his neglect of the author by beauties of his own. In his original poems, now and then, a happy line may perhaps be found, and now and then a short composition may give pleasure. But there is in the whole little either of the grace of wit, or the vigour of nature.

# J. PHILIPS

1   JOHN PHILIPS was born on the 30th of December, 1676, at Bampton in Oxfordshire; of which place his father Dr. Stephen Philips, archdeacon of Salop, was minister. The first part of his education was domestick, after which he was sent to Winchester, where, as we are told by Dr. Sewel, his biographer, he was soon distinguished by the superiority of his exercises; and, what is less easily to be credited, so much endeared himself to his school fellows, by his civility and good-nature, that they, without murmur or ill-will, saw him indulged by the master with particular immunities. It is related, that, when he was at school, he seldom mingled in play with the other boys, but retired to his chamber; where his sovereign pleasure was to sit, hour after hour, while his hair was combed by somebody, whose service he found means to procure.

2   At school he became acquainted with the poets ancient and modern, and fixed his attention particularly on Milton.

3   In 1694 he entered himself at Christchurch; a college at that time in the highest reputation, by the transmission of Busby's scholars to the care first of *Fell*, and afterwards of *Aldrich*. Here he was distinguished as a genius eminent among the eminent, and for friendship particularly intimate with Mr. Smith, the author of *Phædra and Hippolytus*. The profession which he intended to follow was that of Physick; and he took much delight in natural history, of which botany was his favourite part.

4   His reputation was confined to his friends and to the university; till about 1703 he extended it to a wider circle by the *Splendid Shilling*, which struck the publick attention with a mode of writing new and unexpected.

5   This performance raised him so high, that when Europe resounded with the victory of Blenheim, he was, probably with an occult opposition to Addison, employed to deliver the acclamation of the Tories. It is said that he would willingly have declined the task, but that his friends urged it upon him. It appears that he wrote this poem at the house of Mr. St. John.

6   *Blenheim* was published in 1705. The next year produced his greatest work, the poem upon *Cider*, in two books; which was received with loud praises, and continued long to be read, as an imitation of Virgil's *Georgic*, which needed not shun the presence of the original.

He then grew probably more confident of his own abilities, and began to ⁊
meditate a poem on the *Last Day*; a subject on which no mind can hope to
equal expectation.

This work he did not live to finish; his diseases, a slow consumption and 8
an asthma, put a stop to his studies; and on Feb. 15, 1708, at the beginning
of his thirty-third year, put an end to his life. He was buried in the cathedral
of Hereford; and Sir *Simon Harcourt*, afterwards Lord Chancellor, gave him
a monument in Westminster Abbey. The inscription at Westminster was
written, as I have heard, by Dr. *Atterbury*, though commonly given to
Dr. *Freind*.

His Epitaph at Hereford:

JOHANNES PHILIPS

Obiit 15 die Feb. Anno $\begin{cases} \text{Dom.1708.} \\ \text{Ætat, suæ32.} \end{cases}$

Cujus
Ossa si requiras, hanc Urnam inspice;
Si Ingenium nescias, ipsius Opera consule;
Si Tumulum desideras,
Templum adi *Westmonasteriense*:
Qualis quantusque Vir fuerit,
Dicat elegans illa & preclara,
Quæ cenotaphium ibi decorat
Inscriptio.
Quam interim erga Cognatos pius & officiosus,
Testetur hoc saxum
A MARIA PHILIPS Matre ipsius pientissimâ,
Dilecti Filli Memoriæ non sine Lacrymis dicatum.

His Epitaph at Westminster:

Herefordiæ conduntur Ossa,
Hoc in Delubro statuitur Imago,
Britanniam omnem pervagatur Fama
JOHANNIS PHILIPS:
Qui Viris bonis doctisque juxta charus,
Immortale suum Ingenium,
Eruditione multiplici excultum,
Miro animi candore,
Eximiâ morum simplicitate,
Honestavit.
Litterarum Amœniorum sitim,
Quam Wintoniæ Puer sentire cœperat,

Inter Ædis Christi Alumnos jugiter explevit,
In illo Musarum Domicilio
Præclaris Æmulorum studiis excitatus,
Optimis scribendi Magistris semper intentus,
Carmina sermone Patrio composuit
A Græcis Latinisque fontibus feliciter deducta,
Atticis Romanisque auribus omnino digna,
Versuum quippe Harmoniam
Rythmo didicerat.
Antiquo illo, libero, multiformi
Ad res ipsas apto prorsus, & attemperato,
Non Numeris in eundem ferè orbem redeuntibus,
Non Clausularum similiter cadentium sono
Metiri:
Uni in hoc laudis genere Miltono secundus,
Primoque pœne Par.
Res seu Tenues, seu Grandes, seu Mediocres
Ornandas sumserat,
Nusquam, non quod decuit,
Et videt, & assecutus est,
Egregius, quocunque Stylum verteret,
Fandi author, & Modorum artifex.
Fas sit Huic,
Auso licèt à tuâ Metrorum Lege discedere
O Poesis Anglicanæ Pater, atqueConditor, Chaucere,
Alterum tibi latus claudere,
Vatum certe Cineres, tuos undique stipantium
Non dedecebit Chorum.
SIMON HARCOURT Miles,
Viri benè de se, de Litteris meriti
Quoad viveret Fautor,
Post Obitum piè memor,
Hoc illi Saxum poni voluit.
J. PHILIPS, STEPHANI, S.T.P. Archidiaconi
Salop, Filius, natus est Bamptoniæ
in agro Oxon. Dec. 30, 1676.
Obiit Herefordiæ, Feb. 15, 1708.

9    Philips has been always praised, without contradiction, as a man modest,
blameless, and pious; who bore narrowness of fortune without discontent,
and tedious and painful maladies without impatience; beloved by those that
knew him, but not ambitious to be known. He was probably not formed for
a wide circle. His conversation is commended for its innocent gaiety, which
seems to have flowed only among his intimates: for I have been told, that he

was in company silent and barren, and employed only upon the pleasures of his pipe. His addiction to tobacco is mentioned by one of his biographers, who remarks that in all his writings, except *Blenheim*, he has found an opportunity of celebrating the fragrant fume. In common life he was probably one of those who please by not offending, and whose person was loved because his writings were admired. He died honoured and lamented, before any part of his reputation had withered, and before his patron St. John had disgraced him.

His works are few. The *Splendid Shilling* has the uncommon merit of an 10 original design, unless it may be thought precluded by the ancient *Centos*. To degrade the sounding words and stately construction of Milton, by an application to the lowest and most trivial things, gratifies the mind with a momentary triumph over that grandeur which hitherto held its captives in admiration; the words and things are presented with a new appearance, and novelty is always grateful where it gives no pain.

But the merit of such performances begins and ends with the first author. 11 He that should again adapt Milton's phrase to the gross incidents of common life, and even adapt it with more art, which would not be difficult, must yet expect but a small part of the praise which Philips has obtained; he can only hope to be considered as the repeater of a jest.

"The parody on Milton," says Gildon, "is the only tolerable production 12 of its author." This is a censure too dogmatical and violent. The poem of *Blenheim* was never denied to be tolerable, even by those who do not allow it supreme excellence. It is indeed the poem of a scholar, *all inexpert of war*; of a man who writes books from books, and studies the world in a college. He seems to have formed his ideas of the field of *Blenheim* from the battles of the heroic ages, or the tales of chivalry, with very little comprehension of the qualities necessary to the composition of a modern hero, which Addison has displayed with so much propriety. He makes *Marlborough* behold at distance the slaughter made by *Tallard*, then haste to encounter and restrain him, and mow his way through ranks made headless by his sword.

He imitates Milton's numbers indeed, but imitates them very injudi- 13 ciously. Deformity is easily copied; and whatever there is in Milton which the reader wishes away, all that is obsolete, peculiar, or licentious, is accumulated with great care by Philips. Milton's verse was harmonious, in proportion to the general state of our metre in Milton's age; and, if he had written after the improvements made by Dryden, it is reasonable to believe that he would have admitted a more pleasing modulation of numbers into his work; but Philips sits down with a resolution to make no more musick than he found; to want all that his master wanted, though he is very far from having what his master had. Those asperities, therefore, that are venerable in the *Paradise Lost*, are contemptible in the *Blenheim*.

14     There is a Latin ode written to his patron St. John, in return for a present of wine and tobacco, which cannot be passed without notice. It is gay and elegant, and exhibits several artful accommodations of classick expressions to new purposes. It seems better turned than the odes of *Hannes**.

15     To the poem on *Cider*, written in imitation of the *Georgicks*, may be given this peculiar praise, that it is grounded in truth; that the precepts which it contains are exact and just; and that it is therefore, at once, a book of entertainment and of science. This I was told by Miller, the great gardener and botanist, whose expression was, that *there were many books written on the same subject in prose, which do not contain so much truth as that poem.*

16     In the disposition of his matter, so as to intersperse precepts relating to the culture of trees, with sentiments more generally alluring, and in easy and graceful transitions from one subject to another, he has very diligently imitated his master; but he unhappily pleased himself with blank verse, and supposed that the numbers of Milton, which impress the mind with veneration, combined as they are with subjects of inconceivable grandeur, could be sustained by images which at most can rise only to elegance. Contending angels may shake the regions of heaven in blank verse; but the flow of equal measures, and the embellishment of rhyme, must recommend to our attention the art of engrafting, and decide the merit of the *redstreak* and *pearmain*.

17     What study could confer, Philips had obtained; but natural deficience cannot be supplied. He seems not born to greatness and elevation. He is never lofty, nor does he often surprise with unexpected excellence; but perhaps to his last poem may be applied what Tully said of the work of Lucretius, that *it is written with much art, though with few blazes of genius.*

18     The following fragment, written by Edmund Smith, upon the works of Philips, has been transcribed from the Bodleian manuscripts.

---

* This ode I am willing to mention, because there seems to be an error in all the printed copies, which is, I find, retained in the last. They all read;

> Quam Gratiarum cura decentium
> O! O! labellis cui Venus insidet.

The author probably wrote,

> Quam Gratiarum cura decentium
> Ornat; labellis cui Venus insidet.

A prefatory Discourse to the Poem on Mr. Philips, with a character of his writings.

IT is altogether as equitable some account should be given of those who have distinguished themselves by their writings, as of those who are renowned for great actions. It is but reasonable they, who contribute so much to the immortality of others, should have some share in it themselves; and since their genius only is discovered by their works, it is just that their virtues should be recorded by their friends. For no modest men (as the person I write of was in perfection) will write their own panegyricks; and it is very hard that they should go without reputation, only because they the more deserve it. The end of writing Lives is for the imitation of the readers. It will be in the power of very few to imitate the duke of Marlborough; we must be content with admiring his great qualities and actions, without hopes of following them. The private and social virtues are more easily transcribed. The Life of Cowley is more instructive, as well as more fine, than any we have in our language. And it is to be wished, since Mr. Philips had so many of the good qualities of that poet, that I had some of the abilities of his historian.

The Grecian philosophers have had their Lives written, their morals 19 commended, and their sayings recorded. Mr. Philips had all the virtues to which most of them only pretended, and all their integrity without any of their affectation.

The French are very just to eminent men in this point; not a learned man 20 nor a poet can die, but all Europe must be acquainted with his accomplishments. They give praise and expect it in their turns: they commend their Patru's and Moliere's as well as their Conde's and Turenne's; their Pellisons and Racines have their elogies as well as the prince whom they celebrate; and their poems, their mercuries, and orations, nay their very gazettes, are filled with the praises of the learned.

I am satisfied, had they a Philips among them, and known how to value 21 him; had they one of his learning, his temper, but above all of that particular turn of humour, that altogether new genius, he had been an example to their poets, and a subject of their panegyricks, and perhaps set in competition with the ancients, to whom only he ought to submit.

I shall therefore endeavour to do justice to his memory, since nobody else 22 undertakes it. And indeed I can assign no cause why so many of his acquaintance (that are as willing and more able than myself to give an account of him) should forbear to celebrate the memory of one so dear to them, but only that they look upon it as a work intirely belonging to me.

I shall content myself with giving only a character of the person and his 23 writings, without meddling with the transactions of his life, which was altogether private: I shall only make this known observation of his family, that there was scarce so many extraordinary men in any one. I have been acquainted with five of his brothers (of which three are still living), all men of fine parts, yet all of a very unlike temper and genius. So that their fruitful mother, like the mother of the gods, seems to have produced a numerous offspring, all of different though uncommon faculties. Of the living, neither their modesty nor the humour of the present age permits me to speak: of the dead, I may say something.

24    One of them had made the greatest progress in the study of the law of nature and nations of any one I know. He had perfectly mastered, and even improved, the notions of Grotius, and the more refined ones of Puffendorf. He could refute Hobbes with as much solidity as some of greater name, and expose him with as much wit as Echard. That noble study, which requires the greatest reach of reason and nicety of distinction, was not at all difficult to him. 'Twas a national loss to be deprived of one who understood a science so necessary, and yet so unknown in England. I shall add only, he had the same honesty and sincerity as the person I write of, but more heat: the former was more inclined to argue, the latter to divert: one employed his reason more; the other his imagination: the former had been well qualified for those posts, which the modesty of the latter made him refuse. His other dead brother would have been an ornament to the college of which he was a member. He had a genius either for poetry or oratory; and, though very young, composed several very agreeable pieces. In all probability he would have wrote as finely, as his brother did nobly. He might have been the Waller, as the other was the Milton of his time. The one might celebrate Marlborough, the other his beautiful offspring. This had not been so fit to describe the actions of heroes as the virtues of private men. In a word, he had been fitter for my place; and while his brother was writing upon the greatest men that any age ever produced, in a style equal to them, he might have served as a panegyrist on him.

25    This is all I think necessary to say of his family. I shall proceed to himself and his writings; which I shall first treat of, because I know they are censured by some out of envy, and more out of ignorance.

26    The *Splendid Shilling*, which is far the least considerable, has the more general reputation, and perhaps hinders the character of the rest. The style agreed so well with the burlesque, that the ignorant thought it could become nothing else. Every body is pleased with that work. But to judge rightly of the other, requires a perfect mastery of poetry and criticism, a just contempt of the little turns and witticisms now in vogue, and, above all, a perfect understanding of poetical diction and description.

All that have any taste of poetry will agree, that the great burlesque 27
is much to be preferred to the low. It is much easier to make a great
thing appear little, than a little one great: Cotton and others of a very low
genius have done the former; but Philips, Garth, and Boileau, only the
latter.

A picture in miniature is every painter's talent; but a piece for a cupola, 28
where all the figures are enlarged, yet proportioned to the eye, requires a
master's hand.

It must still be more acceptable than the low burlesque, because the 29
images of the latter are mean and filthy, and the language itself entirely
unknown to all men of good breeding. The style of Billingsgate would not
make a very agreeable figure at St. James's. A gentleman would take but
little pleasure in language, which he would think it hard to be accosted in, or
in reading words which he could not pronounce without blushing. The
lofty burlesque is the more to be admired, because, to write it, the author
must be master of two of the most different talents in nature. A talent to find
out and expose what is ridiculous, is very different from that which is to
raise and elevate. We must read Virgil and Milton for the one, and Horace
and Hudibras for the other. We know that the authors of excellent comedies
have often failed in the grave style, and the tragedian as often in comedy.
Admiration and Laughter are of such opposite natures, that they are seldom
created by the same person. The man of mirth is always observing the follies
and weaknesses, the serious writer the virtues or crimes of mankind; one is
pleased with contemplating a beau, the other a hero. Even from the same
object they would draw different ideas: Achilles would appear in very
different lights to Thersites and Alexander. The one would admire the
courage and greatness of his soul; the other would ridicule the vanity and
rashness of his temper. As the satyrist says to Hanibal:

> —I curre per Alpes,
> Ut pueris placeas, & declamatio fias.

The contrariety of style to the subject pleases the more strongly, because 30
it is more surprising; the expectation of the reader is pleasantly deceived,
who expects an humble style from the subject, or a great subject from the
style. It pleases the more universally, because it is agreeable to the taste
both of the grave and the merry; but more particularly so to those who
have a relish of the best writers, and the noblest sort of poetry. I shall
produce only one passage out of this poet, which is the misfortune of his
Galligaskins:

> My Galligaskins, which have long withstood
> The winter's fury and encroaching frosts,
> By time subdued (what will not time subdue!)

This is admirably pathetical, and shews very well the vicissitude of sublunary things. The rest goes on to a prodigious height; and a man in Greenland could hardly have made a more pathetick and terrible complaint. Is it not surprising that the subject should be so mean, and the verse so pompous; that the least things in his poetry, as in a microscope, should grow great and formidable to the eye? especially considering that, not understanding French, he had no model for his style? that he should have no writer to imitate, and himself be inimitable? that he should do all this before he was twenty? at an age, which is usually pleased with a glare of false thoughts, little turns, and unnatural fustian? at an age, at which Cowley, Dryden, and I had almost said Virgil, were inconsiderable? So soon was his imagination at its full strength, his judgement ripe, and his humour complete.

31     This poem was written for his own diversion, without any design of publication. It was communicated but to *me*; but soon spread, and fell into the hands of pirates. It was put out, vilely mangled, by Ben. Bragge; *and impudently said to be corrected by the author*. This grievance is now grown more epidemical; and no man now has a right to his own thoughts, or a title to his own writings. Xenophon answered the Persian, who demanded his arms, "We have nothing now left but our arms and our valour; if we surrender the one, how shall we make use of the other?" Poets have nothing but their wits and their writings; and if they are plundered of the latter, I don't see what good the former can do them. To pirate, and publickly own it, to prefix their names to the works they steal, to own and avow the theft, I believe, was never yet heard of but in England. It will sound oddly to posterity, that, in a polite nation, in an enlightened age, under the direction of the most wise, most learned, and most generous encouragers of knowledge in the world, the property of a mechanick should be better secured than that of a scholar; that the poorest manual operations should be more valued than the noblest products of the brain; that it should be felony to rob a cobler of a pair of shoes, and no crime to deprive the best author of his whole subsistence; that nothing should make a man a sure title to his own writings but the stupidity of them; that the works of Dryden should meet with less encouragement than those of his own Flecknoe, or Blackmore; that Tillotson and St. George, Tom Thumb and Temple, should be set on an equal foot. This is the reason why this very paper has been so long delayed; and while the most impudent and scandalous libels are publickly vended by the pirates, this innocent work is forced to steal abroad as if it were a libel.

Our present writers are by these wretches reduced to the same condition 32
Virgil was, when the centurion seized on his estate. But I don't doubt but
I can fix upon the Mæcenas of the present age, that will retrieve them from
it. But, whatever effect this piracy may have upon us, it contributed very
much to the advantage of Mr. Philips; it helped him to a reputation, which
he neither desired nor expected, and to the honour of being put upon a work
of which he did not think himself capable; but the event shewed his
modesty. And it was reasonable to hope, that he, who could raise mean
subjects so high, should still be more elevated on greater themes; that he,
that could draw such noble ideas from a shilling, could not fail upon such a
subject as the duke of Marlborough, *which is capable of heightening even the*
*most low and trifling genius.* And, indeed, most of the great works which have
been produced in the world have been owing less to the poet than the
patron. Men of the greatest genius are sometimes lazy, and want a spur;
often modest, and dare not venture in publick; they certainly know their
faults in the worst things; and even their best things they are not fond of,
because the idea of what they ought to be is far above what they are. This
induced me to believe that Virgil desired his work might be burnt, had not
the same Augustus that desired him to write them, preserved them from
destruction. A scribling beau may imagine a Poet *may* be induced to write,
by the very pleasure he finds in writing; but that is seldom, when people are
necessitated to it. I have known men row, and use very hard labour, for
diversion, which, if they had been tied to, they would have thought
themselves very unhappy.

But to return to *Blenheim*, that work so much admired by some, and 33
censured by others. I have often wished he had wrote it in Latin, that he
might be out of the reach of the empty criticks, who would have as little
understood his meaning in that language as they do his beauties in his own.

False criticks have been the plague of all ages; Milton himself, in a very 34
polite court, has been compared to the rumbling of a wheel-barrow: he had
been on the wrong side, and therefore could not be a good poet. *And this,*
*perhaps, may be Mr. Philips's case.*

But I take generally the ignorance of his readers to be the occasion of their 35
dislike. People that have formed their taste upon the French writers, can
have no relish for Philips: they admire points and turns, and consequently
have no judgement of what is great and majestick; he must look little in their
eyes, when he soars so high as to be almost out of their view. I cannot
therefore allow any admirer of the French to be a judge of Blenheim, nor
any who takes Bouhours for a compleat critick. He generally judges of the
ancients by the moderns, and not the moderns by the ancients; he takes
those passages of their own authors to be really sublime which come the

nearest to it; he often calls that a noble and great thought which is only a pretty and a fine one, and has more instances of the sublime out of Ovid de Tristibus, than he has out of all Virgil.

36    I shall allow, therefore, only those to be judges of Philips, who make the ancients, and particularly Virgil, their standard.

37    But, before I enter on this subject, I shall consider what is particular in the style of Philips, and examine what ought to be the style of heroick poetry, and next inquire how far he is come up to that style.

38    His style is particular, because he lays aside rhyme, and writes in blank verse, and uses old words, and frequently postpones the adjective to the substantive, and the substantive to the verb; and leaves out little particles, *a*, and *the*; *her*, and *his*; and uses frequent appositions. Now let us examine, whether these alterations of style be conformable to the true sublime.

*  *  *  *  *  *

# WALSH

WILLIAM WALSH, the son of Joseph Walsh, Esq; of Abberley in Worces- 1
tershire, was born in 1663, as appears from the account of Wood; who
relates, that at the age of fifteen he became, in 1678, a gentleman commoner
of Wadham College.

He left the university without a degree, and pursued his studies in London 2
and at home; that he studied, in whatever place, is apparent from the effect;
for he became, in Mr. Dryden's opinion, *the best critick in the nation*.

He was not, however, merely a critick or a scholar, but a man of fashion, 3
and, as Dennis remarks, ostentatiously splendid in his dress. He was
likewise a member of parliament and a courtier, knight of the shire for his
native county in several parliaments; in another the representative of
Richmond in Yorkshire; and gentleman of the horse to Queen Anne
under the duke of Somerset.

Some of his verses shew him to have been a zealous friend to the 4
Revolution; but his political ardour did not abate his reverence or kindness
for Dryden, to whom he gave a Dissertation on Virgil's Pastorals, in which,
however studied, he discovers some ignorance of the laws of French
versification.

In 1705, he began to correspond with Mr. Pope, in whom he discovered 5
very early the power of poetry. Their letters are written upon the pastoral
comedy of the Italians, and those pastorals which Pope was then preparing
to publish.

The kindnesses which are first experienced are seldom forgotten. Pope 6
always retained a grateful memory of Walsh's notice, and mentioned him in
one of his latter pieces among those that had encouraged his juvenile studies:

—Granville the polite,
And knowing Walsh, would tell me I could write.

In his Essay on Criticism he had given him more splendid praise, and, in 7
the opinion of his learned commentator sacrificed a little of his judgement to
his gratitude.

The time of his death I have not learned. It must have happened between 8
1707, when he wrote to Pope; and 1711, when Pope praised him in the
Essay. The epitaph makes him forty-six years old: if Wood's account be
right, he died in 1709.

9      He is known more by his familiarity with greater men, than by any thing done or written by himself.

10     His works are not numerous. In prose he wrote *Eugenia, a defence of women*; which Dryden honoured with a Preface.

10a    *Esculapius, or the Hospital of Fools*, published after his death.

10b    *A collection of Letters and Poems, amorous and gallant*, was published in the volumes called Dryden's Miscellany, and some other occasional pieces.

11     To his Poems and Letters is prefixed a very judicious preface upon Epistolary Composition and Amorous Poetry.

12     In his *Golden Age restored*, there was something of humour, while the facts were recent; but it now strikes no longer. In his imitation of Horace, the first stanzas are happily turned; and in all his writings there are pleasing passages. He has however more elegance than vigour, and seldom rises higher than to be pretty.

# DRYDEN

OF the great poet whose life I am about to delineate, the curiosity which his    1
reputation must excite, will require a display more ample than can now be
given. His contemporaries, however they reverenced his genius, left his life
unwritten; and nothing therefore can be known beyond what casual mention and uncertain tradition have supplied.

JOHN DRYDEN was born August 9, 1631, at Aldwincle near Oundle, the    2
son of Erasmus Dryden of Tichmersh; who was the third son of Sir
Erasmus Dryden, Baronet, of Canons Ashby. All these places are in North-
amptonshire; but the original stock of the family was in the county of
Huntingdon.

He is reported by his last biographer, Derrick, to have inherited from his    3
father an estate of two hundred a year, and to have been bred, as was said, an
Anabaptist. For either of these particulars no authority is given. Such a
fortune ought to have secured him from that poverty which seems always
to have oppressed him; or if he had wasted it, to have made him ashamed
of publishing his necessities. But though he had many enemies, who
undoubtedly examined his life with a scrutiny sufficiently malicious,
I do not remember that he is ever charged with waste of his patrimony.
He was indeed sometimes reproached for his first religion. I am therefore
inclined to believe that Derrick's intelligence was partly true, and partly
erroneous.

From Westminster School, where he was instructed as one of the king's    4
scholars by Dr. Busby, whom he long after continued to reverence, he was
in 1650 elected to one of the Westminster scholarships at Cambridge.

Of his school performances has appeared only a poem on the death of    5
Lord Hastings, composed with great ambition of such conceits as, notwithstanding the reformation begun by Waller and Denham, the example of
Cowley still kept in reputation. Lord Hastings died of the small-pox, and
his poet has made of the pustules first rosebuds, and then gems; at last exalts
them into stars; and says,

> No comet need foretell his change drew on,
> Whose corps might seem a constellation.

At the university he does not appear to have been eager of poetical    6
distinction, or to have lavished his early wit either on fictitious subjects or

public occasions. He probably considered that he who purposed to be an author, ought first to be a student. He obtained, whatever was the reason, no fellowship in the College. Why he was excluded cannot now be known, and it is vain to guess; had he thought himself injured, he knew how to complain. In the Life of Plutarch he mentions his education in the College with gratitude; but in a prologue at Oxford, he has these lines:

> Oxford to him a dearer name shall be
> Than his own mother-university;
> Thebes did his rude unknowing youth engage;
> He chooses Athens in his riper age.

7      It was not till the death of Cromwell, in 1658, that he became a public candidate for fame, by publishing *Heroic Stanzas on the late Lord Protector*; which, compared with the verses of Sprat and Waller on the same occasion, were sufficient to raise great expectations of the rising poet.

8      When the king was restored, Dryden, like the other panegyrists of usurpation, changed his opinion, or his profession, and published ASTREA REDUX, *a poem on the happy restoration and return of his most sacred Majesty King Charles the Second*.

9      The reproach of inconstancy was, on this occasion, shared with such numbers, that it produced neither hatred nor disgrace; if he changed, he changed with the nation. It was, however, not totally forgotten when his reputation raised him enemies.

10      The same year he praised the new king in a second poem on his restoration. In the ASTREA was the line,

> An horrid *stillness* first *invades* the *ear*,
> And in that silence we a tempest fear.

for which he was persecuted with perpetual ridicule, perhaps with more than was deserved. *Silence* is indeed mere privation; and, so considered, cannot *invade*; but privation likewise certainly is *darkness*, and probably *cold*; yet poetry has never been refused the right of ascribing effects or agency to them as to positive powers. No man scruples to say that *darkness* hinders him from his work; or that *cold* has killed the plants. Death is also privation, yet who has made any difficulty of assigning to Death a dart and the power of striking?

11      In settling the order of his works, there is some difficulty; for, even when they are important enough to be formally offered to a patron, he does not commonly date his dedication; the time of writing and publishing is not always the same; nor can the first editions be easily found, if even from them could be obtained the necessary information.

The time at which his first play was exhibited is not certainly known, 12 because it was not printed till it was some years afterwards altered and revived; but since the plays are said to be printed in the order in which they were written, from the dates of some, those of others may be inferred; and thus it may be collected that in 1663, in the thirty-second year of his life, he commenced a writer for the stage; compelled undoubtedly by necessity, for he appears never to have loved that exercise of his genius, or to have much pleased himself with his own dramas.

Of the stage, when he had once invaded it, he kept possession for many 13 years; not indeed without the competition of rivals who sometimes prevailed, or the censure of criticks, which was often poignant and often just; but with such a degree of reputation as made him at least secure of being heard, whatever might be the final determination of the public.

His first piece was a comedy called the *Wild Gallant*. He began with no 14 happy auguries; for his performance was so much disapproved, that he was compelled to recall it, and change it from its imperfect state to the form in which is now appears, and which is yet sufficiently defective to vindicate the criticks.

I wish that there were no necessity of following the progress of his 15 theatrical fame, or tracing the meanders of his mind through the whole series of his dramatick performances; it will be fit however to enumerate them, and to take especial notice of those that are distinguished by any peculiarity intrinsick or concomitant; for the composition and fate of eight and twenty dramas include too much of a poetical life to be omitted.

In 1664 he published the *Rival Ladies*, which he dedicated to the Earl of 16 Orrery, a man of high reputation both as a writer and a statesman. In this play he made his essay of dramatick rhyme, which he defends in his dedication, with sufficient certainty of a favourable hearing; for Orrery was himself a writer of rhyming tragedies.

He then joined with Sir Robert Howard in the *Indian Queen*, a tragedy in 17 rhyme. The parts which either of them wrote are not distinguished.

The *Indian Emperor* was published in 1667. It is a tragedy in rhyme, 18 intended for a sequel to *Howard's Indian Queen*. Of this connection notice was given to the audience by printed bills, distributed at the door; an expedient supposed to be ridiculed in the *Rehearsal*, when Bayes tells how many reams he has printed, to instill into the audience some conception of his plot.

In this play is the description of Night, which *Rymer* has made famous by 19 preferring it to those of all other poets.

The practice of making tragedies in rhyme was introduced soon after the 20 Restoration, as it seems, by the earl of Orrery, in compliance with the opinion of Charles the Second, who had formed his taste by the French theatre; and Dryden, who wrote, and made no difficulty of declaring that he wrote, only to please, and who perhaps knew that by his dexterity of versification he was more likely to excel others in rhyme than without it, very readily adopted his master's preference. He therefore made rhyming tragedies, till, by the prevalence of manifest propriety, he seems to have grown ashamed of making them any longer.

21     To this play is prefixed a very vehement defence of dramatick rhyme, in confutation of the preface to the *Duke of Lerma*, in which Sir Robert Howard had censured it.

22     In 1667, he published *Annus Mirabilis*, the *Year of Wonders*, which may be esteemed one of his most elaborate works.

23     It is addressed to Sir Robert Howard by a letter, which is not properly a dedication; and, writing to a poet, he has interspersed many critical observations, of which some are common, and some perhaps ventured without much consideration. He began, even now, to exercise the domination of conscious genius, by recommending his own performance: "I am satisfied that as the Prince and General [Rupert and Monk] are incomparably the best subjects I ever had, so what I have written on them is much better than what I have performed on any other. As I have endeavoured to adorn my poem with noble thoughts, so much more to express those thoughts with elocution."

24     It is written in quatrains, or heroick stanzas of four lines; a measure which he had learned from the *Gondibert* of Davenant, and which he then thought the most majestick that the English language affords. Of this stanza he mentions the encumbrances, encreased as they were by the exactness which the age required. It was, throughout his life, very much his custom to recommend his works, by representation of the difficulties that he had encountered, without appearing to have sufficiently considered, that where there is no difficulty there is no praise.

25     There seems to be in the conduct of Sir Robert Howard and Dryden towards each other, something that is not now easily to be explained. Dryden, in his dedication to the earl of Orrery, had defended dramatick rhyme; and Howard, in the preface to a collection of plays, had censured his opinion. Dryden vindicated himself in his *Dialogue on Dramatick Poetry*; Howard, in his Preface to the *Duke of Lerma*, animadverted on the Vindication; and Dryden, in a Preface to the *Indian Emperor*, replied to the Animadversions with great asperity, and almost with contumely. The dedication to this play is dated the year in which the *Annus Mirabilis* was published. Here appears a strange inconsistency; but Langbaine affords some help, by relating that the answer to Howard was not published in the

first edition of the play, but was added when it was afterwards reprinted; and as the *Duke of Lerma* did not appear till 1668, the same year in which the Dialogue was published, there was time enough for enmity to grow up between authors, who, writing both for the theatre, were naturally rivals.

He was now so much distinguished, that in 1668 he succeeded Sir 26 William Davenant as poet-laureat. The salary of the laureat had been raised in favour of Jonson, by Charles the First, from an hundred marks to one hundred pounds a year, and a tierce of wine; a revenue in those days not inadequate to the conveniencies of life.

The same year he published his Essay on Dramatick Poetry, an elegant 27 and instructive dialogue; in which we are told by Prior, that the principal character is meant to represent the duke of Dorset. This work seems to have given Addison a model for his Dialogues upon Medals.

*Secret Love, or the Maiden Queen*, is a tragi-comedy. In the preface he 28 discusses a curious question, whether a poet can judge well of his own productions: and determines very justly, that, of the plan and disposition, and all that can be reduced to principles of science, the author may depend upon his own opinion; but that, in those parts where fancy predominates, self-love may easily deceive. He might have observed, that what is good only because it pleases, cannot be pronounced good till it has been found to please.

*Sir Martin Marall* is a comedy, published without preface or dedication, 29 and at first without the name of the author. Langbaine charges it, like most of the rest, with plagiarism; and observes that the song is translated from Voiture, allowing however that both the sense and measure are exactly observed.

*The Tempest* is an alteration of Shakspeare's play, made by Dryden in 30 conjunction with Davenant, "whom," says he, "I found of so quick a fancy, that nothing was proposed to him in which he could not suddenly produce a thought extremely pleasant and surprising; and those first thoughts of his, contrary to the Latin proverb, were not always the least happy; and as his fancy was quick, so likewise were the products of it remote and new. He borrowed not of any other, and his imaginations were such as could not easily enter into any other man."

The effect produced by the conjunction of these two powerful minds 31 was, that to Shakspeare's monster Caliban is added a sister-monster Sicorax; and a woman, who, in the original play, had never seen a man, is in this brought acquainted with a man that had never seen a woman.

About this time, in 1673, Dryden seems to have had his quiet much 32 disturbed by the success of the *Empress of Morocco*, a tragedy written in rhyme by *Elkanah Settle*; which was so much applauded, as to make him think his supremacy of reputation in some danger. Settle had not only been prosperous on the stage, but, in the confidence of success, had published his play, with sculptures and a preface of defiance. Here was one offence added to another; and, for the last blast of inflammation, it was acted at Whitehall by the court-ladies.

33    Dryden could not now repress these emotions, which he called indignation, and others jealousy; but wrote upon the play and the dedication such criticism as malignant impatience could pour out in haste.

34    Of Settle he gives this character. "He's an animal of a most deplored understanding, without conversation. His being is in a twilight of sense, and some glimmering of thought, which he can never fashion into wit or English. His style is boisterous and rough-hewn, his rhyme incorrigibly lewd, and his numbers perpetually harsh and ill-sounding. The little talent which he has, is fancy. He sometimes labours with a thought; but, with the pudder he makes to bring it into the world, 'tis commonly still-born; so that, for want of learning and elocution, he will never be able to express any thing either naturally or justly!"

35    This is not very decent; yet this is one of the pages in which criticism prevails most over brutal fury. He proceeds: "He has a heavy hand at fools, and a great felicity in writing nonsense for them. Fools they will be in spite of him. His King, his two Empresses, his villain, and his sub-villain, nay his hero, have all a certain natural cast of the father—their folly was born and bred in them, and something of the Elkanah will be visible."

36    This is Dryden's general declamation; I will not withhold from the reader a particular remark. Having gone through the first act he says, "To conclude this act with the most rumbling piece of nonsense spoken yet,

> To flattering lightning our feign'd smiles conform,
> Which back'd with thunder do but gild a storm.

*Conform a smile to lightning*, make a *smile* imitate *lightning*, and *flattering lightning*: lightning sure is a threatening thing. And this lightning must *gild a storm*. Now if I must conform my smiles to lightning, then my smiles must gild a storm too: to *gild* with *smiles* is a new invention of gilding. And gild a storm by being *backed with thunder*. Thunder is part of the storm; so one part of the storm must help to *gild* another part, and help by *backing*; as if a man would gild a thing the better for being backed, or having a load upon his back. So that here is *gilding* by *conforming, smiling, lightning, backing*, and *thundering*. The whole is as if I should say thus, I will make my counterfeit smiles look like a flattering stone-horse, which, being backed with a trooper, does but gild the battle. I am mistaken if nonsense is not here pretty thick sown. Sure the poet writ these two lines aboard some smack in a storm, and, being sea-sick, spewed up a good lump of clotted nonsense at once."

Here is perhaps a sufficient specimen; but as the pamphlet, though 37 Dryden's, has never been thought worthy of republication, and is not easily to be found, it may gratify curiosity to quote it more largely.

> Whene'er she bleeds,
> He no severer a damnation needs,
> That dares pronounce the sentence of her death,
> Than the infection that attends that breath.

"*That attends that breath.*—The poet is at *breath* again; *breath* can never 'scape him; and here he brings in a *breath* that must be *infectious* with *pronouncing* a sentence; and this sentence is not to be pronounced till the condemned party *bleeds*; that is, she must be executed first, and sentenced after; and the *pronouncing* of this *sentence* will be infectious; that is, others will catch the disease of that sentence, and this infecting of others will torment a man's self. The whole is thus; *when she bleeds, thou needest no greater hell or torment to thyself, than infecting of others by pronouncing a sentence upon her.* What hodge-podge does he make here! Never was Dutch grout such clogging, thick, indigestible stuff. But this is but a taste to stay the stomach; we shall have a more plentiful mess presently.

"Now to dish up the poet's broth, that I promised: 38

> For when we're dead, and our freed souls enlarg'd,
> Of nature's grosser burden we're discharg'd,
> Then gently, as a happy lover's sigh,
> Like wandering meteors through the air we'll fly,
> And in our airy walk, as subtle guests,
> We'll steal into our cruel fathers breasts,
> There read their souls, and track each passion's sphere:
> See how Revenge moves there, Ambition here.
> And in their orbs view the dark characters
> Of sieges, ruins, murders, blood and wars.
> We'll blot out all those hideous draughts, and write
> Pure and white forms; then with a radiant light
> Their breasts encircle, till their passions be
> Gentle as nature in its infancy:
> Till soften'd by our charms their furies cease,
> And their revenge resolves into a peace.
> Thus by our death their quarrel ends,
> Whom living we made foes, dead we'll make friends.

If this be not a very liberal mess, I will refer myself to the stomach of any moderate guest. And a rare mess it is, far excelling any Westminster white-broth. It is a kind of gibblet porridge, made of the gibblets of a couple of young geese, stodged full of *meteors, orbs, spheres, track, hideous draughts, dark characters, white forms,* and *radiant light,* designed not only to please appetite, and indulge luxury; but it is also physical, being an approved medicine to purge choler: for it is propounded by Morena, as a receipt to cure their fathers of their choleric humours: and were it written in characters as barbarous as the words, might very well pass for a doctor's bill. To conclude, it is porridge, 'tis a receipt, 'tis a pig with a pudding in the belly, 'tis I know not what: for, certainly, never any one that pretended to write sense, had the impudence before to put such stuff as this, into the mouths of those that were to speak it before an audience, whom he did not take to be all fools; and after that to print it too, and expose it to the examination of the world. But let us see, what we can make of this stuff:

> For when we're dead, and our freed souls enlarg'd—

Here he tells us what it is to be *dead*; it is to have *our freed souls set free.* Now if to have a soul set free is to be dead, then to have a *freed soul* set free, is to have a dead man die.

> Then gentle, as a happy lover's sigh—

They two like one *sigh,* and that one *sigh* like two wandering meteors,

> —shall flie through the air—

That is, they shall mount above like falling stars, or else they shall skip like two Jacks with lanthorns, or Will with a wisp, and Madge with a candle."

39     *And in their airy walk steal into their cruel fathers breasts, like subtle guests.* So "that their *fathers breasts* must be in an *airy walk,* an airy *walk* of a *flier. And there they will read their souls, and track the spheres of their passions.* That is, these walking fliers, Jack with a lanthorn, &c. will put on his spectacles, and fall a *reading souls,* and put on his pumps and fall a *tracking of spheres;* so that he will read and run, walk and fly at the same time! Oh! Nimble Jack. *Then he will see, how revenge here, how ambition there*—The birds will hop about. *And then view the dark characters of sieges, ruins, murders, blood, and wars, in their orbs: Track the characters to their forms!* Oh! rare sport for Jack. Never was place so full of game as these breasts! You cannot stir but you flush a sphere, start a character, or unkennel an orb!"

40     Settle's is said to have been the first play embellished with sculptures; those ornaments seem to have given poor Dryden great disturbance. He tries however to ease his pain, by venting his malice in a parody.

"The poet has not only been so impudent to expose all this stuff, but so    41
arrogant to defend it with an epistle; like a saucy booth-keeper, that, when
he had put a cheat upon the people, would wrangle and fight with any that
would not like it, or would offer to discover it; for which arrogance our poet
receives this correction; and to jerk him a little the sharper, I will not
transpose his verse, but by the help of his own words trans-non-sense
sense, that, by my stuff, people may judge the better what his is:

> Great Boy, thy tragedy and sculptures done
> From press, and plates in fleets do homeward come:
> And in ridiculous and humble pride,
> Their course in ballad-singers baskets guide,
> Whose greasy twigs do all new beauties take,
> From the gay shews thy dainty sculptures make.
> Thy lines a mess of rhiming nonsense yield,
> A senseless tale, with flattering fustian fill'd.
> No grain of sense does in one line appear,
> Thy words big bulks of boisterous bombast bear.
> With noise they move, and from players mouths rebound,
> When their tongues dance to thy words empty sound.
> By thee inspir'd the rumbling verses roll,
> As if that rhyme and bombast lent a soul:
> And with that soul they seem taught duty too,
> To huffing words does humble nonsense bow,
> As if it would thy worthless worth enhance,
> To th' lowest rank of fops thy praise advance;
> To whom, by instinct, all thy stuff is dear;
> Their loud claps echo to the theatre.
> From breaths of fools thy commendation spreads,
> Fame sings thy praise with mouths of loggerheads.
> With noise and laughing each thy fustian greets,
> 'Tis clapt by quires of empty-headed cits,
> Who have their tribute sent, and homage given,
> As men in whispers send loud noise to heaven.

"Thus I have daubed him with his own puddle: and now we are come from
aboard his dancing, masking, rebounding, breathing fleet; and as if we had
landed at Gotham, we meet nothing but fools and nonsense."

Such was the criticism to which the genius of Dryden could be reduced,    42
between rage and terrour; rage with little provocation, and terrour with
little danger. To see the highest minds thus levelled with the meanest,
may produce some solace to the consciousness of weakness, and some
mortification to the pride of wisdom. But let it be remembered, that
minds are not levelled in their powers but when they are first levelled in

their desires. Dryden and Settle had both placed their happiness in the claps of multitudes.

43    The *Mock Astrologer*, a comedy, is dedicated to the illustrious duke of Newcastle, whom he courts by adding to his praises those of his lady, not only as a lover but a partner of his studies. It is unpleasing to think how many names, once celebrated, are since forgotten. Of Newcastle's works nothing is now known but his treatise on horsemanship.

44    The Preface seems very elaborately written, and contains many just remarks on the Fathers of the English drama. Shakspeare's plots, he says, are in the hundred novels of *Cinthio*; those of Beaumont and Fletcher in Spanish Stories; Jonson only made them for himself. His criticisms upon tragedy, comedy, and farce, are judicious and profound. He endeavours to defend the immorality of some of his comedies by the example of former writers; which is only to say, that he was not the first nor perhaps the greatest offender. Against those that accused him of plagiarism, he alleges a favourable expression of the king: "He only desired that they, who accuse me of thefts, would steal him plays like mine;" and then relates how much labour he spends in fitting for the English stage what he borrows from others.

45    *Tyrannick Love, or the Virgin Martyr*, was another tragedy in rhyme, conspicuous for many passages of strength and elegance, and many of empty noise and ridiculous turbulence. The rants of Maximin have been always the sport of criticism; and were at length, if his own confession may be trusted, the shame of the writer.

46    Of this play he takes care to let the reader know, that it was contrived and written in seven weeks. Want of time was often his excuse, or perhaps shortness of time was his private boast in the form of an apology.

47    It was written before the *Conquest of Granada*, but published after it. The design is to recommend piety. "I considered that pleasure was not the only end of poesy, and that even the instructions of morality were not so wholly the business of a poet, as that precepts and examples of piety were to be omitted; for to leave that employment altogether to the clergy, were to forget that religion was first taught in verse, which the laziness or dulness of succeeding priesthood turned afterwards into prose." Thus foolishly could Dryden write, rather than not shew his malice to the parsons.

48    The two parts of the *Conquest of Granada* are written with a seeming determination to glut the public with dramatick wonders; to exhibit in its highest elevation a theatrical meteor of incredible love and impossible valour, and to leave no room for a wilder flight to the extravagance of posterity. All the rays of romantick heat, whether amorous or warlike, glow

in Almanzor by a kind of concentration. He is above all laws; he is exempt from all restraints; he ranges the world at will, and governs wherever he appears. He fights without enquiring the cause, and loves in spite of the obligations of justice, of rejection by his mistress, and of prohibition from the dead. Yet the scenes are, for the most part, delightful; they exhibit a kind of illustrious depravity, and majestick madness: such as, if it is sometimes despised, is often reverenced, and in which the ridiculous is mingled with the astonishing.

In the Epilogue to the second part of the *Conquest of Granada*, Dryden 49 indulges his favourite pleasure of discrediting his predecessors; and this Epilogue he has defended by a long postscript. He had promised a second dialogue, in which he should more fully treat of the virtues and faults of the English poets, who have written in the dramatick, epick, or lyrick way. This promise was never formally performed; but, with respect to the dramatick writers, he has given us in his prefaces, and in this postscript, something equivalent; but his purpose being to exalt himself by the comparison, he shews faults distinctly, and only praises excellence in general terms.

A play thus written, in professed defiance of probability, naturally drew 50 down upon itself the vultures of the theatre. One of the criticks that attacked it was *Martin Clifford*, to whom *Sprat* addressed the Life of Cowley, with such veneration of his critical powers as might naturally excite great expectations of instruction from his remarks. But let honest credulity beware of receiving characters from contemporary writers. Clifford's remarks, by the favour of Dr. *Percy*, were at last obtained; and, that no man may ever want them more, I will extract enough to satisfy all reasonable desire.

In the first Letter his observation is only general: "You do live," says he, 51 "in as much ignorance and darkness as you did in the womb: your writings are like a Jack-of-all-trades shop; they have variety, but nothing of value; and if thou art not the dullest plant-animal that ever the earth produced, all that I have conversed with are strangely mistaken in thee."

In the second, he tells him that Almanzor is not more copied from 52 Achilles than from Ancient Pistol. "But I am," says he, "strangely mistaken if I have not seen this very *Almanzor* of yours in some disguise about this town, and passing under another name. Pr'ythee tell me true, was not this Huffcap once the *Indian Emperor*, and at another time did he not call himself *Maximin*? Was not *Lyndaraxa* once called *Almeria*? I mean under *Montezuma* the Indian Emperor. I protest and vow they are either the same, or so alike that I cannot, for my heart, distinguish one from the other. You are therefore a strange unconscionable thief; thou art not content to steal from others, but dost rob thy poor wretched self too."

53    Now was *Settle's* time to take his revenge. He wrote a vindication of his own lines; and, if he is forced to yield any thing, makes reprisals upon his enemy. To say that his answer is equal to the censure, is no high commendation. To expose Dryden's method of analysing his expressions, he tries the same experiment upon the description of the ships in the *Indian Emperor*, of which however he does not deny the excellence; but intends to shew, that by studied misconstruction every thing may be equally represented as ridiculous. After so much of Dryden's elegant animadversions, justice requires that something of Settle's should be exhibited. The following observations are therefore extracted from a quarto pamphlet of ninety-five pages:

> "Fate after him below with pain did move,
> And victory could scarce keep pace above.

54    These two lines, if he can shew me any sense or thought in, or any thing but bombast and noise, he shall make me believe every word in his observations on *Morocco* sense.

55    "In the *Empress of Morocco* were these lines:

> I'll travel then to some remoter sphere,
> Till I find out new worlds, and crown you there.

55a    "On which Dryden made this remark:
    "*I believe our learned author takes a sphere for a country: the sphere of Morocco, as if Morocco were the globe of earth and water; but a globe is no sphere neither, by his leave*," &c. So *sphere* must not be sense, unless it relate to a circular motion about a globe, in which sense the astronomers use it. I would desire him to expound those lines in *Granada*:

> I'll to the turrets of the palace go,
> And add new fire to those that fight below.
> Thence, hero-like, with torches by my side,
> (Far be the omen tho') my Love I'll guide.
> No, like his better fortune I'll appear,
> With open arms, loose vail and flowing hair, ⎫
> Just flying forward from my rowling sphere. ⎭

I wonder, if he be so strict, how he dares make so bold with *sphere* himself, and be so critical in other men's writings. Fortune is fancied standing on a globe, not on a *sphere*, as he told us in the first Act.

56    "Because *Elkanah's Similies are the most unlike things to what they are compared in the world*, I'll venture to start a simile in his *Annus Mirabilis*: he gives this poetical description of the ship called the *London*:

> The goodly London in her gallant trim,
> The Phenix-daughter of the vanquisht old,
> Like a rich bride does to the ocean swim,
> And on her shadow rides in floating gold.

> Her flag aloft spread ruffling in the wind,
> And sanguine streamers seem'd the flood to fire:
> The weaver, charm'd with what his loom design'd,
> Goes on to sea, and knows not to retire.

> With roomy decks, her guns of mighty strength,
> Whose low-laid mouths each mounting billow laves,
> Deep in her draught, and warlike in her length,
> She seems a sea-wasp flying on the waves.

What a wonderful pother is here, to make all these poetical beautifications of a ship! that is, a *phenix* in the first stanza, and but a *wasp* in the last: nay, to make his humble comparison of a *wasp* more ridiculous, he does not say it flies upon the waves as nimbly as a wasp, or the like, but it seemed a *wasp*. But our author at the writing of this was not in his altitudes, to compare ships to floating palaces; a comparison to the purpose, was a perfection he did not arrive to, till his *Indian Emperor's* days. But perhaps his similitude has more in it than we imagine; this ship had a great many guns in her, and they, put all together, made the sting in the wasp's tail: for this is all the reason I can guess, why it seem'd a *wasp*. But, because we will allow him all we can to help out, let it be a *phenix sea-wasp*, and the rarity of such an animal may do much towards the heightening the fancy.

"It had been much more to his purpose, if he had designed to render the 57 senseless play little, to have searched for some such pedantry as this:

> Two ifs scarce make one possibility.
> If justice will take all and nothing give,
> Justice, methinks, is not distributive.
> To die or kill you, is the alternative,
> Rather than take your life, I will not live.

"Observe, how prettily our author chops logick in heroick verse. Three 57a such fustian canting words as *distributive, alternative,* and *two ifs,* no man but himself would have come within the noise of. But he's a man of general learning, and all comes into his play.

"'Twould have done well too, if he could have met with a rant or two, 58 worth the observation: such as,

> Move swiftly, Sun, and fly a lover's pace,
> Leave months and weeks behind thee in thy race.

58a    "But surely the Sun, whether he flies a lover's or not a lover's pace, leaves weeks and months, nay years too, behind him in his race.

58b    "Poor Robin, or any other of the Philomathematicks, would have given him satisfaction in the point.

59

> If I could kill thee now, thy fate's so low,
> That I must stoop, ere I can give the blow.
> But mine is fixt so far above thy crown,
> That all thy men,
> Piled on thy back, can never pull it down.

59a    "Now where that is, Almanzor's fate is fixt, I cannot guess; but wherever it is, I believe Almanzor, and think that all Abdalla's subjects, piled upon one another, might not pull down his fate so well as without piling: besides, I think Abdalla so wise a man, that if Almanzor had told him piling his men upon his back might do the feat, he would scarce bear such a weight, for the pleasure of the exploit; but it is a huff, and let Abdalla do it if he dare.

60

> The people like a headlong torrent go,
> And every dam they break or overflow.
> But, unoppos'd, they either lose their force,
> Or wind in volumes to their former course.

A very pretty allusion, contrary to all sense or reason. Torrents, I take it, let them wind never so much, can never return to their former course, unless he can suppose that fountains can go upwards, which is impossible: nay more, in the foregoing page he tells us so too. A trick of a very unfaithful memory.

> But can no more than fountains upward flow.

Which of a *torrent*, which signifies a rapid stream, is much more impossible. Besides, if he goes to quibble, and say that it is possible by art water may be made return, and the same water run twice in one and the same channel: then he quite confutes what he says; for, it is by being opposed, that it runs into its former course: for all engines that make water so return, do it by compulsion and opposition. Or, if he means a headlong torrent for a tide, which would be ridiculous, yet they do not wind in volumes, but come fore-right back (if their upright lies straight to their former course), and that by opposition of the sea-water, that drives them back again.

61    "And for fancy, when he lights of any thing like it, 'tis a wonder if it be not borrowed. As here, for example of, I find this fanciful thought in his *Ann. Mirab*.

> Old father Thames raised up his reverend head;
> But feared the fate of Simoeis would return;

> Deep in his ooze he sought his sedgy bed;
> And shrunk his waters back into his urn.

This is stolen from Cowley's *Davideis*, p. 9.

> Swift Jordan started, and strait backward fled,
> Hiding amongst thick reeds his aged head.

> And when the Spaniards their assault begin,
> At once beat those without and those within.

This Almanzor speaks of himself; and sure for one man to conquer an army within the city, and another without the city, at once, is something difficult; but this flight is pardonable, to some we meet with in *Granada*. Osmin, speaking of Almanzor:

> Who, like a tempest that outrides the wind,
> Made a just battle, ere the bodies join'd.

Pray what does this honourable person mean by a *tempest that outrides the wind!* A tempest that outrides itself. To suppose a tempest without wind, is as bad as supposing a man to walk without feet; for if he supposes the tempest to be something distinct from the wind, yet as being the effect of wind only, to come before the cause is a little preposterous: so that, if he takes it one way, or if he takes it the other, those two *ifs* will scarce make one *possibility*." Enough of Settle.

*Marriage Alamode* is a comedy, dedicated to the Earl of Rochester; whom 62 he acknowledges not only as the defender of his poetry, but the promoter of his fortune. Langbaine places this play in 1673. The earl of Rochester therefore was the famous Wilmot, whom yet tradition always represents as an enemy to Dryden, and who is mentioned by him with some disrespect in the preface to Juvenal.

*The Assignation, or Love in a Nunnery*, a comedy, was driven off the stage, 63 *against the opinion*, as the author says, *of the best judges*. It is dedicated, in a very elegant address, to Sir Charles Sedley; in which he finds an opportunity for his usual complaint of hard treatment and unreasonable censure.

*Amboyna* is a tissue of mingled dialogue in verse and prose, and was 64 perhaps written in less time than *The Virgin Martyr*; though the author thought not fit either ostentatiously or mournfully to tell how little labour it cost him, or at how short a warning he produced it. It was a temporary performance, written in the time of the Dutch war, to inflame the nation against their enemies; to whom he hopes, as he declares in his Epilogue, to make his poetry not less destructive than that by which Tyrtæus of old animated the Spartans. This play was written in the second Dutch war in 1673.

65    *Troilus and Cressida*, is a play altered from Shakspeare; but so altered that even in Langbaine's opinion, *the last scene in the third act is a masterpiece*. It is introduced by a discourse on *the grounds of criticism in tragedy*; to which I suspect that Rymer's book had given occasion.

66    The *Spanish Fryar* is a tragi-comedy, eminent for the happy coincidence and coalition of the two plots. As it was written against the Papists, it would naturally at that time have friends and enemies; and partly by the popularity which it obtained at first, and partly by the real power both of the serious and risible part, it continued long a favourite of the publick.

67    It was Dryden's opinion, at least for some time, and he maintains it in the dedication of this play, that the drama required an alternation of comick and tragick scenes, and that it is necessary to mitigate by alleviations of merriment the pressure of ponderous events, and the fatigue of toilsome passions. "Whoever," says he, "cannot perform both parts, *is but half a writer for the stage*."

68    The *Duke of Guise*, a tragedy written in conjunction with Lee, as *Oedipus* had been before, seems to deserve notice only for the offence which it gave to the remnant of the Covenanters, and in general to the enemies of the court, who attacked him with great violence, and were answered by him; though at last he seems to withdraw from the conflict, by transferring the greater part of the blame or merit to his partner. It happened that a contract had been made between them, by which they were to join in writing a play; and *he happened*, says Dryden, *to claim the promise just upon the finishing of a poem, when I would have been glad of a little respite.*—Two *thirds of it belonged to him; and to me only the first scene of the play, the whole fourth act, and the first half or somewhat more of the fifth.*

69    This was a play written professedly for the party of the duke of York, whose succession was then opposed. A parallel is intended between the Leaguers of France and the Covenanters of England; and this intention produced the controversy.

70    *Albion and Albania* is a musical drama or opera, written, like the *Duke of Guise*, against the Republicans. With what success it was performed, I have not found.

71    *The State of Innocence and Fall of Man* is termed by him an opera: it is rather a tragedy in heroick rhyme, but of which the personages are such as cannot decently be exhibited on the stage. Some such production was foreseen by Marvel, who writes thus to Milton:

> Or if a work so infinite be spann'd,
> Jealous I was least some less skilful hand,
> Such as disquiet always what is well,

And by ill-imitating would excel,
Might hence presume the whole creation's day,
To change in scenes, and show it in a play.

It is another of his hasty productions for the heat of his imagination raised it in a month.

This composition is addressed to the princess of Modena, then dutchess 72 of York, in a strain of flattery which disgraces genius, and which it was wonderful that any man that knew the meaning of his own words, could use without self-detestation. It is an attempt to mingle earth and heaven, by praising human excellence in the language of religion.

The preface contains an apology for heroick verse, and poetick licence; by 73 which is meant not any liberty taken in contracting or extending words, but the use of bold fictions and ambitious figures.

The reason which he gives for printing what was never acted, cannot be 74 overpassed: "I was induced to it in my own defence, many hundred copies of it being dispersed abroad without my knowledge or consent, and every one gathering new faults, it became at length a libel against me." These copies as they gathered faults were apparently manuscript; and he lived in an age very unlike ours, if many hundred copies of fourteen hundred lines were likely to be transcribed. An author has a right to print his own works, and needs not seek an apology in falsehood; but he that could bear to write the dedication felt no pain in writing the preface.

*Aureng Zebe* is a tragedy founded on the actions of a great prince then 75 reigning, but over nations not likely to employ their criticks upon the transactions of the English stage. If he had known and disliked his own character, our trade was not in those times secure from his resentment. His country is at such a distance, that the manners might be safely falsified, and the incidents feigned; for remoteness of place is remarked by Racine, to afford the same conveniencies to a poet as length of time.

This play is written in rhyme; and has the appearance of being the most 76 elaborate of all the dramas. The personages are imperial; but the dialogue is often domestick, and therefore susceptible of sentiments accommodated to familiar incidents. The complaint of life is celebrated, and there are many other passages that may be read with pleasure.

This play is addressed to the earl of Mulgrave, afterwards duke of 77 Buckingham, himself, if not a poet, yet a writer of verses, and a critick. In this address Dryden gave the first hints of his intention to write an epick poem. He mentions his design in terms so obscure, that he seems afraid lest his plan should be purloined, as, he says, happened to him when he told it more plainly in his preface to Juvenal. "The design," says he, "you know is great, the story English, and neither too near the present times, nor too distant from them.''

78    *All for Love, or the World well lost*, a tragedy founded upon the story of Antony and Cleopatra, he tells us, *is the only play which he wrote for himself*; the rest were given to the people. It is by universal consent accounted the work in which he has admitted the fewest improprieties of style or character; but it has one fault equal to many, though rather moral than critical, that by admitting the romantick omnipotence of Love, he has recommended as laudable and worthy of imitation that conduct which, through all ages, the good have censured as vicious, and the bad despised as foolish.

79    Of this play the prologue and the epilogue, though written upon the common topicks of malicious and ignorant criticism, and without any particular relation to the characters or incidents of the drama, are deservedly celebrated for their elegance and spriteliness.

80    *Limberham, or the kind Keeper*, is a comedy, which, after the third night, was prohibited as too indecent for the stage. What gave offence, was in the printing, as the author says, altered or omitted. Dryden confesses that its indecency was objected to; but Langbaine, who yet seldom favours him, imputes its expulsion to resentment, because it *so much exposed the keeping part of the town*.

81    *Oedipus* is a tragedy formed by Dryden and Lee, in conjunction, from the works of Sophocles, Seneca, and Corneille. Dryden planned the scenes, and composed the first and third acts.

82    *Don Sebastian* is commonly esteemed either the first or second of his dramatick performances. It is too long to be all acted, and has many characters and many incidents; and though it is not without sallies of frantick dignity, and more noise than meaning, yet as it makes approaches to the possibilities of real life, and has some sentiments which leave a strong impression, it continued long to attract attention. Amidst the distresses of princes, and the vicissitudes of empire, are inserted several scenes which the writer intended for comick; but which, I suppose, that age did not much commend, and this would not endure. There are, however, passages of excellence universally acknowledged; the dispute and the reconciliation of Dorax and Sebastian has always been admired.

82*a*   This play was first acted in 1690, after Dryden had for some years discontinued dramatick poetry.

83    *Amphitryon* is a comedy derived from Plautus and Moliere. The dedication is dated Oct. 1690. This play seems to have succeeded at its first appearance; and was, I think, long considered as a very diverting entertainment.

*Cleomenes* is a tragedy, only remarkable as it occasioned an incident    84
related in the *Guardian*, and allusively mentioned by Dryden in his preface.
As he came out from the representation, he was accosted thus by some airy
stripling: *Had I been left alone with a young beauty, I would not have spent my
time like your Spartan. That, Sir*, said Dryden, *perhaps is true; but give me
leave to tell you, that you are no hero*.

*King Arthur* is another opera. It was the last work that Dryden performed    85
for King Charles, who did not live to see it exhibited; and it does not seem to
have been ever brought upon the stage. In the dedication to the marquis of
Halifax, there is a very elegant character of Charles, and a pleasing account
of his latter life. When this was first brought upon the stage, news that the
duke of Monmouth had landed was told in the theatre, upon which the
company departed, and *Arthur* was exhibited no more.

His last drama was *Love triumphant*, a tragi-comedy. In his dedication to    86
the earl of Salisbury he mentions *the lowness of fortune to which he has
voluntarily reduced himself, and of which he has no reason to be ashamed*.

This play appeared in 1694. It is said to have been unsuccessful. The    86*a*
catastrophe, proceeding merely from a change of mind, is confessed by the
author to be defective. Thus he began and ended his dramatick labours with
ill success.

From such a number of theatrical pieces it will be supposed, by    87
most readers, that he must have improved his fortune; at least, that such
diligence with such abilities must have set penury at defiance. But in
Dryden's time the drama was very far from that universal approbation
which it has now obtained. The playhouse was abhorred by the Puritans,
and avoided by those who desired the character of seriousness or decency.
A grave lawyer would have debased his dignity, and a young trader would
have impaired his credit, by appearing in those mansions of dissolute
licentiousness. The profits of the theatre, when so many classes of the
people were deducted from the audience, were not great; and the poet
had for a long time but a single night. The first that had two nights was
*Southern*, and the first that had three was *Rowe*. There were however, in
those days, arts of improving a poet's profit, which Dryden forbore to
practise; and a play therefore seldom produced him more than a hundred
pounds, by the accumulated gain of the third night, the dedication, and
the copy.

Almost every piece had a dedication, written with such elegance and    88
luxuriance of praise, as neither haughtiness nor avarice could be imagined
able to resist. But he seems to have made flattery too cheap. That praise is
worth nothing of which the price is known.

89    To increase the value of his copies, he often accompanied his work with a preface of criticism; a kind of learning then almost new in the English language, and which he, who had considered with great accuracy the principles of writing, was able to distribute copiously as occasions arose. By these dissertations the publick judgment must have been much improved; and Swift, who conversed with Dryden, relates that he regretted the success of his own instructions, and found his readers made suddenly too skilful to be easily satisfied.

90    His prologues had such reputation, that for some time a play was considered as less likely to be well received, if some of his verses did not introduce it. The price of a prologue was two guineas, till being asked to write one for Mr. Southern, he demanded three; *Not*, said he, *young man, out of disrespect to you, but the players have had my goods too cheap.*

91    Though he declares, that in his own opinion his genius was not dramatick, he had great confidence in his own fertility; for he is said to have engaged, by contract, to furnish four plays a year.

92    It is certain that in one year, 1678, he published *All for Love, Assignation*, two parts of the *Conquest of Granada, Sir Martin Marall*, and the *State of Innocence*, six complete plays, with a celerity of performance, which, though all Langbaine's charges of plagiarism should be allowed, shews such facility of composition, such readiness of language, and such copiousness of sentiment, as, since the time of Lopez de Vega, perhaps no other author has possessed.

93    He did not enjoy his reputation, however great, nor his profits, however small, without molestation. He had criticks to endure, and rivals to oppose. The two most distinguished wits of the nobility, the duke of Buckingham and earl of Rochester, declared themselves his enemies.

94    Buckingham characterised him in 1671, by the name of *Bayes* in the *Rehearsal*; a farce which he is said to have written with the assistance of Butler the author of *Hudibras*, Martin Clifford of the Charterhouse, and Dr. Sprat, the friend of Cowley, then his chaplain. Dryden and his friends laughed at the length of time, and the number of hands employed upon this performance; in which, though by some artifice of action it yet keeps possession of the stage, it is not possible now to find any thing that might not have been written without so long delay, or a confederacy so numerous.

95    To adjust the minute events of literary history, is tedious and troublesome; it requires indeed no great force of understanding, but often depends upon enquiries which there is no opportunity of making, or is to be fetched from books and pamphlets not always at hand.

The *Rehearsal* was played in 1671, and yet is represented as ridiculing   96
passages in the *Conquest of Granada* and *Assignation*, which were not
published till 1678, in *Marriage Alamode* published in 1673, and in
*Tyrannick Love* of 1677. These contradictions shew how rashly satire is
applied.

It is said that this farce was originally intended against Davenant, who in   97
the first draught was characterised by the name of *Bilboa*. Davenant had
been a soldier and an adventurer.

There is one passage in the *Rehearsal* still remaining, which seems to have   98
related originally to Davenant. *Bayes* hurts his nose, and comes in with
brown paper applied to the bruise; how this affected Dryden, does not
appear. Davenant's nose had suffered such diminution by mishaps among
the women, that a patch upon that part evidently denoted him.

It is said likewise that Sir Robert Howard was once meant. The design   98*a*
was probably to ridicule the reigning poet, whoever he might be.

Much of the personal satire, to which it might owe its first reception, is   99
now lost or obscured. *Bayes* probably imitated the dress, and mimicked the
manner, of Dryden; the cant words which are so often in his mouth may be
supposed to have been Dryden's habitual phrases, or customary exclamations. *Bayes*, when he is to write, is blooded and purged: this, as Lamotte
relates himself to have heard, was the real practice of the poet.

There were other strokes in the *Rehearsal* by which malice was gra-   100
tified: the debate between Love and Honour, which keeps prince *Volscius*
in a single boot, is said to have alluded to the misconduct of the duke
of Ormond, who lost Dublin to the rebels while he was toying with a
mistress.

The earl of Rochester, to suppress the reputation of Dryden, took Settle   101
into his protection, and endeavoured to persuade the publick that its
approbation had been to that time misplaced. Settle was a while in high
reputation: his *Empress of Morocco*, having first delighted the town, was
carried in triumph to Whitehall, and played by the ladies of the court. Now
was the poetical meteor at the highest; the next moment began its fall.
Rochester withdrew his patronage; seeming resolved, says one of his biographers, *to have a judgement contrary to that of the town*. Perhaps being
unable to endure any reputation beyond a certain height, even when he had
himself contributed to raise it.

Neither criticks nor rivals did Dryden much mischief, unless they gained   102
from his own temper the power of vexing him, which his frequent bursts of
resentment give reason to suspect. He is always angry at some past, or afraid
of some future censure; but he lessens the smart of his wounds by the balm

of his own approbation, and endeavours to repel the shafts of criticism by opposing a shield of adamantine confidence.

103    The perpetual accusation produced against him, was that of plagiarism, against which he never attempted any vigorous defence; for, though he was perhaps sometimes injuriously censured, he would by denying part of the charge have confessed the rest; and as his adversaries had the proof in their own hands, he, who knew that wit had little power against facts, wisely left in that perplexity which generality produces a question which it was his interest to suppress, and which, unless provoked by vindication, few were likely to examine.

104    Though the life of a writer, from about thirty-five to sixty-three, may be supposed to have been sufficiently busied by the composition of eight and twenty pieces for the stage, Dryden found room in the same space for many other undertakings.

105    But, how much soever he wrote, he was at least once suspected of writing more; for in 1679 a paper of verses, called *an Essay on Satire*, was shewn about in manuscript, by which the earl of Rochester, the dutchess of Portsmouth, and others, were so much provoked, that, as was supposed, for the actors were never discovered, they procured Dryden, whom they suspected as the author, to be waylaid and beaten. This incident is mentioned by the duke of Buckinghamshire, the true writer, in his Art of Poetry; where he says of Dryden,

> Though prais'd and beaten for another's rhymes,
> His own deserves as great applause sometimes.

106    His reputation in time was such, that his name was thought necessary to the success of every poetical or literary performance, and therefore he was engaged to contribute something, whatever it might be, to many publications. He prefixed the Life of Polybius to the translation of Sir Henry Sheers; and those of Lucian and Plutarch to versions of their works by different hands. Of the English Tacitus he translated the first book; and, if Gordon be credited, translated it from the French. Such a charge can hardly be mentioned without some degree of indignation; but it is not, I suppose, so much to be inferred that Dryden wanted the literature necessary to the perusal of Tacitus, as that, considering himself as hidden in a crowd, he had no awe of the publick; and writing merely for money, was contented to get it by the nearest way.

107    In 1680, the Epistles of Ovid being translated by the poets of the time, among which one was the work of Dryden, and another of Dryden and Lord Mulgrave, it was necessary to introduce them by a preface; and

Dryden, who on such occasions was regularly summoned, prefixed a discourse upon translation, which was then struggling for the liberty that it now enjoys. Why it should find any difficulty in breaking the shackles of verbal interpretation, which must for ever debar it from elegance, it would be difficult to conjecture, were not the power of prejudice every day observed. The authority of Jonson, Sandys, and Holiday, had fixed the judgement of the nation; and it was not easily believed that a better way could be found than they had taken, though Fanshaw, Denham, Waller, and Cowley, had tried to give examples of a different practice.

In 1681, Dryden became yet more conspicuous by uniting politicks with 108 poetry, in the memorable satire called *Absalom and Achitophel*, written against the faction which, by lord Shaftesbury's incitement, set the duke of Monmouth at its head.

Of this poem, in which personal satire was applied to the support of 109 publick principles, and in which therefore every mind was interested, the reception was eager, and the sale so large, that my father, an old bookseller, told me, he had not known it equalled but by *Sacheverell's* trial.

The reason of this general perusal Addison has attempted to derive from 110 the delight which the mind feels in the investigation of secrets; and thinks that curiosity to decypher the names procured readers to the poem. There is no need to enquire why those verses were read, which, to all the attractions of wit, elegance, and harmony, added the co-operation of all the factious passions, and filled every mind with triumph or resentment.

It could not be supposed that all the provocation given by Dryden would 111 be endured without resistance or reply. Both his person and his party were exposed in their turns to the shafts of satire, which, though neither so well pointed nor perhaps so well aimed, undoubtedly drew blood.

One of these poems is called *Dryden's Satire on his Muse*; ascribed; 112 though, as Pope says, falsely, to *Somers*, who was afterwards Chancellor. The poem, whose soever it was, has much virulence, and some spriteliness. The writer tells all the ill that he can collect both of Dryden and his friends.

The poem of *Absalom and Achitophel* had two answers, now both for- 113 gotten; one called *Azaria and Hushai*; the other *Absalom senior*. Of these hostile compositions, Dryden apparently imputes *Absalom senior* to *Settle*, by quoting in his verses against him the second line. *Azaria and Hushai* was, as *Wood* says, imputed to him, though it is somewhat unlikely that he should write twice on the same occasion. This is a difficulty which I cannot remove, for want of a minuter knowledge of poetical transactions.

114    The same year he published the *Medal*, of which the subject is a medal struck on lord Shaftesbury's escape from a prosecution, by the *ignoramus* of a grand jury of Londoners.

115    In both poems he maintains the same principles, and saw them both attacked by the same antagonist. Elkanah Settle, who had answered *Absalom*, appeared with equal courage in opposition to the *Medal*, and published an answer called *The Medal reversed*, with so much success in both encounters, that he left the palm doubtful, and divided the suffrages of the nation. Such are the revolutions of fame, or such is the prevalence of fashion, that the man whose works have not yet been thought to deserve the care of collecting them; who died forgotten in an hospital; and whose latter years were spent in contriving shows for fairs, and carrying an elegy or epithalamium, of which the beginning and end were occasionally varied, but the intermediate parts were always the same, to every house where there was a funeral or a wedding; might, with truth, have had inscribed upon his stone,

Here lies the Rival and Antagonist of Dryden.

116    Settle was, for this rebellion, severely chastised by Dryden under the name of *Doeg*, in the second part of *Absalom and Achitophel*, and was perhaps for his factious audacity made the city poet, whose annual office was to describe the glories of the Mayor's day. Of these bards he was the last, and seems not much to have deserved even this degree of regard, if it was paid to his political opinions; for he afterwards wrote a panegyrick on the virtues of judge Jefferies, and what more could have been done by the meanest zealot for prerogative?

117    Of translated fragments, or occasional poems, to enumerate the titles, or settle the dates would be tedious, with little use. It may be observed, that as Dryden's genius was commonly excited by some personal regard, he rarely writes upon a general topick.

118    Soon after the accession of king James, when the design of reconciling the nation to the church of Rome became apparent, and the religion of the court gave the only efficacious title to its favours, Dryden declared himself a convert to popery. This at any other time might have passed with little censure. Sir *Kenelm Digby* embraced popery; the two *Rainolds* reciprocally converted one another; and *Chillingworth* himself was a while so entangled in the wilds of controversy, as to retire for quiet to an infallible church. If men of argument and study can find such difficulties, or such motives, as may either unite them to the church of Rome, or detain them in uncertainty, there can be no wonder that a man, who perhaps never enquired why he was a protestant, should by an artful and experienced disputant be made a papist, overborn by the sudden violence of new and unexpected

arguments, or deceived by a representation which shews only the doubts on one part, and only the evidence on the other.

That conversion will always be suspected that apparently concurs with   119 interest. He that never finds his error till it hinders his progress towards wealth or honour, will not be thought to love Truth only for herself. Yet it may easily happen that information may come at a commodious time; and as truth and interest are not by any fatal necessity at variance, that one may by accident introduce the other. When opinions are struggling into popularity, the arguments by which they are opposed or defended become more known; and he that changes his profession would perhaps have changed it before, with the like opportunities of instruction. This was then the state of popery; every artifice was used to shew it in its fairest form; and it must be owned to be a religion of external appearance sufficiently attractive.

It is natural to hope that a comprehensive is likewise an elevated soul, and   120 that whoever is wise is also honest. I am willing to believe that Dryden, having employed his mind, active as it was, upon different studies, and filled it, capacious as it was, with other materials, came unprovided to the controversy, and wanted rather skill to discover the right than virtue to maintain it. But enquiries into the heart are not for man; we must now leave him to his Judge.

The priests, having strengthened their cause by so powerful an adherent,   121 were not long before they brought him into action. They engaged him to defend the controversial papers found in the strong-box of Charles the Second, and, what yet was harder, to defend them against Stillingfleet.

With hopes of promoting popery, he was employed to translate Maim-   122 bourg's History of the League; which he published with a large introduc- tion. His name is likewise prefixed to the English Life of Francis Xavier; but I know not that he ever owned himself the translator. Perhaps the use of his name was a pious fraud, which however seems not to have had much effect; for neither of the books, I believe, was ever popular.

The version of Xavier's Life is commended by Brown, in a pamphlet not   123 written to flatter; and the occasion of it is said to have been, that the Queen, when she solicited a son, made vows to him as her tutelary saint.

He was supposed to have undertaken to translate *Varillas's History of*   124 *Heresies*; and when *Burnet* published Remarks upon it, to have written an *Answer*; upon which Burnet makes the following observation:

"I have been informed from England, that a gentleman, who is famous both for poetry and several other things, had spent three months in translating M. Varillas's History; but that, as soon as my Reflections appeared, he discontinued his labour, finding the credit of his author was gone. Now, if he thinks it is recovered by his Answer, he will perhaps go on with his translation; and this may be, for aught I know, as good an entertainment for him as the conversation that he had set on between the Hinds and Panthers, and all the rest of animals, for whom M. Varillas may serve well enough as an author: and this history and that poem are such extraordinary things of their kind, that it will be but suitable to see the author of the worst poem become likewise the translator of the worst history that the age has produced. If his grace and his wit improve both proportionably, he will hardly find that he has gained much by the change he has made, from having no religion to chuse one of the worst. It is true, he had somewhat to sink from in matter of wit; but as for his morals, it is scarce possible for him to grow a worse man than he was. He has lately wreaked his malice on me for spoiling his three months labour; but in it he has done me all the honour that any man can receive from him, which is to be railed at by him. If I had ill-nature enough to prompt me to wish a very bad wish for him, it should be, that he would go on and finish his translation. By that it will appear, whether the English nation, which is the most competent judge in this matter, has, upon the seeing our debate, pronounced in M. Varillas's favour, or in mine. It is true, Mr. D. will suffer a little by it; but at least it will serve to keep him in from other extravagancies; and if he gains little honour by this work, yet he cannot lose so much by it as he has done by his last employment."

125     Having probably felt his own inferiority in theological controversy, he was desirous of trying whether, by bringing poetry to aid his arguments, he might become a more efficacious defender of his new profession. To reason in verse was, indeed, one of his powers; but subtilty and harmony united are still feeble, when opposed to truth.

126     Actuated therefore by zeal for Rome, or hope of fame, he published the *Hind and Panther*, a poem in which the church of Rome, figured by the *milk-white Hind*, defends her tenets against the church of England, represented by the *Panther*, a beast beautiful, but spotted.

127     A fable which exhibits two beasts talking Theology, appears at once full of absurdity; and it was accordingly ridiculed in the *City Mouse* and *Country Mouse*, a parody, written by Montague, afterwards earl of Halifax, and Prior, who then gave the first specimen of his abilities.

128     The conversion of such a man, at such a time, was not likely to pass uncensured. Three dialogues were published by the facetious *Thomas Brown*, of which the two first were called *Reasons of Mr. Bayes's changing his religion*: and the third *The Reasons of Mr. Hains the player's conversion and re-conversion*. The first was printed in 1688, the second not till 1690, the third in 1691. The clamour seems to have been long continued, and the subject to have strongly fixed the publick attention.

In the two first dialogues *Bayes* is brought into the company of *Crites* and  129
*Eugenius*, with whom he had formerly debated on dramatick poetry. The
two talkers in the third are Mr. *Bayes* and Mr. *Hains*.

Brown was a man not deficient in literature, nor destitute of fancy; but he  130
seems to have thought it the pinnacle of excellence to be a *merry fellow*; and
therefore laid out his powers upon small jests or gross buffoonery, so that
his performances have little intrinsick value, and were read only while they
were recommended by the novelty of the event that occasioned them.

These dialogues are like his other works: what sense or knowledge they  131
contain, is disgraced by the garb in which it is exhibited. One great source of
pleasure is to call Dryden *little Bayes*. *Ajax*, who happens to be mentioned,
is *he that wore as many cowhides upon his shield as would have furnished half the
king's army with shoe-leather.*

Being asked whether he has seen the *Hind and Panther*, Crites answers:  132
*Seen it! Mr.* Bayes, *why I can stir no where but it persues me; it haunts me worse
than a pewter-buttoned serjeant does a decayed cit. Sometimes I meet it in a
band-box, when my laundress brings home my linen; sometimes, whether I will or
no, it lights my pipe at a coffee-house; sometimes it surprises me in a trunkmaker's
shop; and sometimes it refreshes my memory for me on the backside of a
Chancery-lane parcel. For your comfort too, Mr. Bayes, I have not only seen
it, as you may perceive, but have read it too, and can quote it as freely upon
occasion as a frugal tradesman can quote that noble treatise the* Worth of a
Penny *to his extravagant 'prentice, that revels in stewed apples, and penny
custards.*

The whole animation of these compositions arises from a profusion of  133
ludicrous and affected comparisons. *To secure one's chastity*, says Bayes, *little
more is necessary than to leave off a correspondence with the other sex, which, to
a wise man, is no greater a punishment than it would be to a fanatic parson to be
forbid* seeing *the* Cheats *and the* Committee; *or for my Lord Mayor and
Aldermen to be interdicted the sight of the* London Cuckold.—This is the
general strain, and therefore I shall be easily excused the labour of more
transcription.

Brown does not wholly forget past transactions: *You began*, says  134
Crites to Bayes, *with a very indifferent religion, and have not mended the
matter in your last choice. It was but reason that your Muse, which appeared first
in a Tyrant's quarrel, should employ her last efforts to justify the usurpations of
the* Hind.

Next year the nation was summoned to celebrate the birth of the Prince.  135
Now was the time for Dryden to rouse his imagination, and strain his voice.
Happy days were at hand, and he was willing to enjoy and diffuse the
anticipated blessings. He published a poem, filled with predictions of

greatness and prosperity; predictions of which it is not necessary to tell how they have been verified.

136    A few months passed after these joyful notes, and every blossom of popish hope was blasted for ever by the Revolution. A papist now could be no longer Laureat. The revenue, which he had enjoyed with so much pride and praise, was transferred to Shadwell, an old enemy, whom he had formerly stigmatised by the name of *Og.* Dryden could not decently complain that he was deposed; but seemed very angry that Shadwell succeeded him, and has therefore celebrated the intruder's inauguration in a poem exquisitely satirical, called *Mac Flecknoe*; of which the *Dunciad*, as Pope himself declares, is an imitation, though more extended in its plan, and more diversified in its incidents.

137    It is related by Prior, that Lord Dorset, when, as chamberlain, he was constrained to eject Dryden from his office, gave him from his own purse an allowance equal to the salary. This is no romantick or incredible act of generosity; an hundred a year is often enough given to claims less cogent, by men less famed for liberality. Yet Dryden always represented himself as suffering under a public infliction; and once particularly demands respect for the patience with which he endured the loss of his little fortune. His patron might, indeed, enjoin him to suppress his bounty; but if he suffered nothing, he should not have complained.

138    During the short reign of king James he had written nothing for the stage, being, in his own opinion, more profitably employed in controversy and flattery. Of praise he might perhaps have been less lavish without inconvenience, for James was never said to have much regard for poetry: he was to be flattered only by adopting his religion.

139    Times were now changed: Dryden was no longer the court-poet, and was to look back for support to his former trade; and having waited about two years, either considering himself as discountenanced by the publick, or perhaps expecting a second revolution, he produced *Don Sebastian* in 1690; and in the next four years four dramas more.

140    In 1693 appeared a new version of Juvenal and Persius. Of Juvenal he translated the first, third, sixth, tenth, and sixteenth satires; and of Persius the whole work. On this occasion he introduced his two sons to the publick, as nurselings of the Muses. The fourteenth of Juvenal was the work of John, and the seventh of Charles Dryden. He prefixed a very ample preface in the form of a dedication to lord Dorset; and there gives an account of the design which he had once formed to write an epic poem on the actions either of Arthur or the Black Prince. He considered the epick as necessarily including some kind of supernatural agency, and had imagined a new kind of contest between the guardian angels of kingdoms, of whom he conceived

that each might be represented zealous for his charge, without any intended opposition to the purposes of the Supreme Being, of which all created minds must in part be ignorant.

This is the most reasonable scheme of celestial interposition that ever was  141 formed. The surprizes and terrors of enchantments, which have succeeded to the intrigues and oppositions of pagan deities, afford very striking scenes, and open a vast extent to the imagination; but, as Boileau observes, and Boileau will be seldom found mistaken, with this incurable defect, that in a contest between heaven and hell we know at the beginning which is to prevail; for this reason we follow Rinaldo to the enchanted wood with more curiosity than terror.

In the scheme of Dryden there is one great difficulty, which yet he would  142 perhaps have had address enough to surmount. In a war justice can be but on one side; and to entitle the hero to the protection of angels, he must fight in the defence of indubitable right. Yet some of the celestial beings, thus opposed to each other, must have been represented as defending guilt.

That this poem was never written, is reasonably to be lamented. It would  143 doubtless have improved our numbers, and enlarged our language, and might perhaps have contributed by pleasing instruction to rectify our opinions, and purify our manners.

What he required as the indispensable condition of such an undertaking,  144 a publick stipend, was not likely in those times to be obtained. Riches were not become familiar to us, nor had the nation yet learned to be liberal.

This plan he charged Blackmore with stealing; only, says he, *the guardian*  145 *angels of kingdoms were machines too ponderous for him to manage.*

In 1694, he began the most laborious and difficult of all his works, the  146 translation of Virgil; from which he borrowed two months, that he might turn Fresnoy's Art of Painting into English prose. The preface, which he boasts to have written in twelve mornings, exhibits a parallel of poetry and painting, with a miscellaneous collection of critical remarks, such as cost a mind stored like his no labour to produce them.

In 1697, he published his version of the works of Virgil; and that no  147 opportunity of profit might be lost, dedicated the Pastorals to the lord Clifford, the Georgics to the earl of Chesterfield, and the Eneid to the earl of Mulgrave. This œconomy of flattery, at once lavish and discreet, did not pass without observation.

This translation was censured by Milbourne, a clergyman, styled by  148 Pope *the fairest of criticks*, because he exhibited his own version to be compared with that which he condemned.

His last work was his Fables, published in 1699, in consequence, as is  149 supposed, of a contract now in the hands of Mr. Tonson; by which he obliged himself, in consideration of three hundred pounds, to finish for the press ten thousand verses.

150      In this volume is comprised the well-known ode on St. Cecilia's day, which, as appeared by a letter communicated to Dr. Birch, he spent a fortnight in composing and correcting. But what is this to the patience and diligence of Boileau, whose *Equivoque*, a poem of only three hundred forty-six lines, took from his life eleven months to write it, and three years to revise it!

151      Part of this book of Fables is the first Iliad in English, intended as a specimen of a version of the whole. Considering into what hands Homer was to fall, the reader cannot but rejoice that this project went no further.

152      The time was now at hand which was to put an end to all his schemes and labours. On the first of May 1701, having been some time, as he tells us, a cripple in his limbs, he died in Gerard-street of a mortification in his leg.

153      There is extant a wild story relating to some vexatious events that happened at his funeral, which, at the end of Congreve's Life, by a writer of I know not what credit, are thus related, as I find the account transferred to a biographical dictionary:

"Mr. Dryden dying on the Wednesday morning, Dr. Thomas Sprat, then bishop of Rochester and dean of Westminster, sent the next day to the lady Elizabeth Howard, Mr. Dryden's widow, that he would make a present of the ground, which was forty pounds, with all the other Abbey-fees. The lord Halifax likewise sent to the lady Elizabeth, and Mr. Charles Dryden her son, that, if they would give him leave to bury Mr. Dryden, he would inter him with a gentleman's private funeral, and afterwards bestow five hundred pounds on a monument in the Abbey; which, as they had no reason to refuse, they accepted. On the Saturday following the company came: the corpse was put into a velvet hearse, and eighteen mourning coaches, filled with company, attended. When they were just ready to move, the lord Jefferies, son of the lord chancellor Jefferies, with some of his rakish companions coming by, asked whose funeral it was: and being told Mr. Dryden's, he said, "What, shall Dryden, the greatest honour and ornament of the nation, be buried after this private manner! No, gentlemen, let all that loved Mr. Dryden, and honour his memory, alight and join with me in gaining my lady's consent to let me have the honour of his interment, which shall be after another manner than this; and I will bestow a thousand pounds on a monument in the Abbey for him." The gentlemen in the coaches, not knowing of the bishop of Rochester's favour, nor of the lord Halifax's generous design (they both having, out of respect to the family, enjoined the lady Elizabeth and her son to keep their favour concealed to the world, and let it pass for their own expence) readily came out of the coaches, and attended lord Jefferies up to the lady's bedside, who was then sick; he repeated the purport of what he had before said; but she absolutely refusing, he fell on his knees, vowing never to rise till his request was granted. The rest of the company by his desire kneeled also; and the lady, being under a sudden surprize, fainted away. As soon as she recovered her speech, she cried, *No, no.* Enough, gentlemen, replied he; my lady is very good, she says, *Go, go.* She repeated her former words with all her strength, but in vain; for her feeble voice was lost in their acclamations of joy; and the lord Jefferies ordered the hearsemen to carry the corpse to Mr. Russel's, an undertaker's in Cheapside, and leave it there till he should send orders for the embalment, which, he added, should be after the royal manner. His directions were obeyed, the company dispersed, and lady Elizabeth and her son remained inconsolable. The next day Mr. Charles Dryden waited on the lord Halifax and the bishop, to excuse his mother and himself, by relating the real truth. But neither his lordship nor the bishop would admit of any plea; especially the latter, who had the Abbey lighted, the ground opened, the choir attending, an anthem ready set, and himself waiting for some time without any corpse to bury. The undertaker, after three days expectance of orders for embalment without receiving any, waited on the lord Jefferies; who pretending ignorance of the matter, turned it off with an ill-natured jest, saying, That those who observed the orders of a drunken frolick deserved no better; that he remembered nothing at all of it; and that he might do what he pleased with the corpse. Upon this, the undertaker waited upon the lady Elizabeth and her son, and threatened to bring the corpse home, and set it before the door. They desired a day's respite, which was granted. Mr. Charles Dryden wrote a handsome letter to the lord Jefferies, who returned it with this cool answer, "That he knew nothing of the matter, and would be troubled no more about it." He then addressed the lord Halifax and the bishop of Rochester, who absolutely refused to do any thing in it. In this distress Dr. Garth sent for the corpse to the College of Physicians, and proposed a funeral by subscription, to which himself set a most noble example. At last a day, about three weeks after Mr. Dryden's decease, was appointed for the interment: Dr. Garth pronounced a fine Latin oration, at the College, over the corpse; which was attended to the Abbey by a numerous train of coaches. When the funeral was over, Mr. Charles Dryden sent a challenge to the lord Jefferies, who refusing to answer it, he sent several others, and went often himself; but could neither get a letter delivered, nor admittance to speak to him: which so incensed him, that he resolved, since his lordship refused to answer him like a gentleman, that he would watch an opportunity to meet, and fight off-hand, though with all the rules of honour; which his lordship hearing, left the town: and Mr. Charles Dryden could never have the satisfaction of meeting him, though he sought it till his death with the utmost application."

154 This story I once intended to omit, as it appears with no great evidence; nor have I met with any confirmation, but in a letter of Farquhar, and he only relates that the funeral of Dryden was tumultuary and confused.

155 Supposing the story true, we may remark that the gradual change of manners, though imperceptible in the process, appears great when different times, and those not very distant, are compared. If at this time a young drunken Lord should interrupt the pompous regularity of a magnificent funeral, what would be the event, but that he would be justled out of the way, and compelled to be quiet? If he should thrust himself into a house, he would be sent roughly away; and what is yet more to the honour of the present time, I believe, that those who had subscribed to the funeral of a man like Dryden, would not, for such an accident, have withdrawn their contributions.

156 He was buried among the poets in Westminster Abbey, where, though the duke of Newcastle had, in a general dedication prefixed by Congreve to his dramatick works, accepted thanks for his intention of erecting him a monument, he lay long without distinction, till the duke of Buckinghamshire gave him a tablet, inscribed only with the name of DRYDEN.

157 He married the lady Elizabeth Howard, daughter of the earl of Berkshire, with circumstances, according to the satire imputed to lord Somers, not very honourable to either party: by her he had three sons, Charles, John, and Henry. Charles was usher of the palace to pope Clement the XIth, and visiting England in 1704, was drowned in an attempt to swim cross the Thames at Windsor.

158 John was author of a comedy called *The Husband his own Cuckold*. He is said to have died at Rome. Henry entered into some religious order. It is some proof of Dryden's sincerity in his second religion, that he taught it to his sons. A man conscious of hypocritical profession in himself, is not likely to convert others; and as his sons were qualified in 1693 to appear among the translators of Juvenal, they must have been taught some religion before their father's change.

159 Of the person of Dryden I know not any account; of his mind, the portrait which has been left by Congreve, who knew him with great familiarity, is such as adds our love of his manners to our admiration of his genius. "He was," we are told, "of a nature exceedingly humane and compassionate, ready to forgive injuries, and capable of a sincere reconciliation with those that had offended him. His friendship, where he professed it, went beyond his professions. He was of a very easy, of very pleasing access; but somewhat

slow, and, as it were, diffident in his advances to others: he had that in his nature which abhorred intrusion into any society whatever. He was therefore less known, and consequently his character became more liable to misapprehensions and misrepresentations: he was very modest, and very easily to be discountenanced in his approaches to his equals or superiors. As his reading had been very extensive, so was he very happy in a memory tenacious of every thing that he had read. He was not more possessed of knowledge than he was communicative of it; but then his communication was by no means pedantick, or imposed upon the conversation, but just such, and went so far as, by the natural turn of the conversation in which he was engaged, it was necessarily promoted or required. He was extreme ready, and gentle in his correction of the errors of any writer who thought fit to consult him, and full as ready and patient to admit of the reprehensions of others, in respect of his own oversights or mistakes."

To this account of Congreve nothing can be objected but the fondness of  160 friendship; and to have excited that fondness in such a mind is no small degree of praise. The disposition of Dryden, however, is shewn in this character rather as it exhibited itself in cursory conversation, than as it operated on the more important parts of life. His placability and his friendship indeed were solid virtues; but courtesy and good-humour are often found with little real worth. Since Congreve, who knew him well, has told us no more, the rest must be collected as it can from other testimonies, and particularly from those notices which Dryden has very liberally given us of himself.

The modesty which made him so slow to advance, and so easy to be  161 repulsed, was certainly no suspicion of deficient merit, or unconsciousness of his own value: he appears to have known, in its whole extent, the dignity of his character, and to have set a very high value on his own powers and performances. He probably did not offer his conversation, because he expected it to be solicited; and he retired from a cold reception, not submissive but indignant, with such reverence of his own greatness as made him unwilling to expose it to neglect or violation.

His modesty was by no means inconsistent with ostentatiousness: he is  162 diligent enough to remind the world of his merit, and expresses with very little scruple his high opinion of his own powers; but his self-commendations are read without scorn or indignation; we allow his claims, and love his frankness.

Tradition, however, has not allowed that his confidence in himself  163 exempted him from jealousy of others. He is accused of envy and insidiousness; and is particularly charged with inciting Creech to translate Horace, that he might lose the reputation which Lucretius had given him.

164     Of this charge we immediately discover that it is merely conjectural; the purpose was such as no man would confess; and a crime that admits no proof, why should we believe?

165     He has been described as magisterially presiding over the younger writers, and assuming the distribution of poetical fame; but he who excels has a right to teach, and he whose judgement is incontestable may, without usurpation, examine and decide.

166     Congreve represents him as ready to advise and instruct; but there is reason to believe that his communication was rather useful than entertaining. He declares of himself that he was saturnine, and not one of those whose spritely sayings diverted company; and one of his censurers makes him say,

> Nor wine nor love could ever see me gay;
> To writing bred, I knew not what to say.

167     There are men whose powers operate only at leisure and in retirement, and whose intellectual vigour deserts them in conversation; whom merriment confuses, and objection disconcerts; whose bashfulness restrains their exertion, and suffers them not to speak till the time of speaking is past; or whose attention to their own character makes them unwilling to utter at hazard what has not been considered, and cannot be recalled.

168     Of Dryden's sluggishness in conversation it is vain to search or to guess the cause. He certainly wanted neither sentiments nor language; his intellectual treasures were great, though they were locked up from his own use. *His thoughts*, when he wrote, *flowed in upon him so fast, that his only care was which to chuse, and which to reject.* Such rapidity of composition naturally promises a flow of talk, yet we must be content to believe what an enemy says of him, when he likewise says it of himself. But whatever was his character as a companion, it appears that he lived in familiarity with the highest persons of his time. It is related by Carte of the duke of Ormond, that he used often to pass a night with Dryden, and those with whom Dryden consorted: who they were, Carte has not told; but certainly the convivial table at which Ormond sat was not surrounded with a plebeian society. He was indeed reproached with boasting of his familiarity with the great; and Horace will support him in the opinion, that to please superiours is not the lowest kind of merit.

169     The merit of pleasing must, however, be estimated by the means. Favour is not always gained by good actions or laudable qualities. Caresses and preferments are often bestowed on the auxiliaries of vice, the procurers of pleasure, or the flatterers of vanity. Dryden has never been charged with any personal agency unworthy of a good character: he abetted vice and vanity only with his pen. One of his enemies has accused him of lewdness in

his conversation; but if accusation without proof be credited, who shall be innocent?

His works afford too many examples of dissolute licentiousness, and 170 abject adulation; but they were probably, like his merriment, artificial and constrained; the effects of study and meditation, and his trade rather than his pleasure.

Of the mind that can trade in corruption, and can deliberately pollute 171 itself with ideal wickedness for the sake of spreading the contagion in society, I wish not to conceal or excuse the depravity.—Such degradation of the dignity of genius, such abuse of superlative abilities, cannot be contemplated but with grief and indignation. What consolation can be had, Dryden has afforded, by living to repent, and to testify his repentance.

Of dramatick immorality he did not want examples among his predeces- 172 sors, or companions among his contemporaries; but in the meanness and servility of hyperbolical adulation, I know not whether, since the days in which the Roman emperors were deified, he has been ever equalled, except by Afra Behn in an address to Eleanor Gwyn. When once he has undertaken the task of praise, he no longer retains shame in himself, nor supposes it in his patron. As many odoriferous bodies are observed to diffuse perfumes from year to year, without sensible diminution of bulk or weight, he appears never to have impoverished his mint of flattery by his expences, however lavish. He had all the forms of excellence, intellectual and moral, combined in his mind, with endless variation; and when he had scattered on the hero of the day the golden shower of wit and virtue, he had ready for him, whom he wished to court on the morrow, new wit and virtue with another stamp. Of this kind of meanness he never seems to decline the practice, or lament the necessity: he considers the great as entitled to encomiastick homage, and brings praise rather as a tribute than a gift, more delighted with the fertility of his invention than mortified by the prostitution of his judgement. It is indeed not certain, that on these occasions his judgement much rebelled against his interest. There are minds which easily sink into submission, that look on grandeur with undistinguishing reverence, and discover no defect where there is elevation of rank and affluence of riches.

With his praises of others and of himself is always intermingled a strain of 173 discontent and lamentation, a sullen growl of resentment, or a querulous murmur of distress. His works are under-valued, his merit is unrewarded, and *he has few thanks to pay his stars that he was born among Englishmen.* To his criticks he is sometimes contemptuous, sometimes resentful, and some-times submissive. The writer who thinks his works formed for duration, mistakes his interest when he mentions his enemies. He degrades his own dignity by shewing that he was affected by their censures, and gives lasting importance to names, which, left to themselves, would vanish from remembrance. From this principle Dryden did not oft depart; his complaints are for the greater part general; he seldom pollutes his page with an adverse name. He condescended indeed to a controversy with Settle, in which he perhaps may be considered rather as assaulting than repelling; and since Settle is sunk into oblivion, his libel remains injurious only to himself.

174       Among answers to criticks, no poetical attacks, or altercations, are to be included; they are, like other poems, effusions of genius, produced as much to obtain praise as to obviate censure. These Dryden practised, and in these he excelled.

175       Of Collier, Blackmore, and Milbourne, he has made mention in the preface to his Fables. To the censure of Collier, whose remarks may be rather termed admonitions than criticisms, he makes little reply; being, at the age of sixty-eight, attentive to better things than the claps of a play-house. He complains of Collier's rudeness, and the *horse-play of his raillery*; and asserts that *in many places he has perverted by his glosses the meaning* of what he censures; but in other things he confesses that he is justly taxed; and says, with great calmness and candour, *I have pleaded guilty to all thoughts or expressions of mine that can be truly accused of obscenity, immorality, or profaneness, and retract them. If he be my enemy, let him triumph; if he be my friend, he will be glad of my repentance.* Yet, as our best dispositions are imperfect, he left standing in the same book a reflection on Collier of great asperity, and indeed of more asperity than wit.

176       Blackmore he represents as made his enemy by the poem of *Absalom and Achitophel*, which *he thinks a little hard upon his fanatick patrons*; and charges him with borrowing the plan of his *Arthur* from the preface to Juvenal, *though he had*, says he, *the baseness not to acknowledge his benefactor, but instead of it to traduçe me in a libel.*

177       The libel in which Blackmore traduced him was a *Satire upon Wit*; in which, having lamented the exuberance of false wit and the deficiency of true, he proposes that all wit should be re-coined before it is current, and appoints masters of assay who shall reject all that is light or debased.

> 'Tis true, that when the coarse and worthless dross
> Is purg'd away, there will be mighty loss;
> Ev'n Congreve, Southern, manly Wycherley,
> When thus refin'd, will grievous sufferers be;
> Into the melting-pot when Dryden comes,
> What horrid stench will rise, what noisome fumes!
> How will he shrink, when all his lewd allay,
> And wicked mixture, shall be purg'd away!

Thus stands the passage in the last edition; but in the original there was an abatement of the censure, beginning thus:

> But what remains will be so pure, 'twill bear
> Th' examination of the most severe.

Blackmore, finding the censure resented, and the civility disregarded, ungenerously omitted the softer part. Such variations discover a writer who consults his passions more than his virtue; and it may be reasonably supposed that Dryden imputes his enmity to its true cause.

Of Milbourne he wrote only in general terms, such as are always ready 178 at the call of anger, whether just or not: a short extract will be sufficient. *He pretends a quarrel to me, that I have fallen foul upon priesthood; if I have, I am only to ask pardon of good priests, and am afraid his share of the reparation will come to little. Let him be satisfied that he shall never be able to force himself upon me for an adversary; I contemn him too much to enter into competition with him.*

*As for the rest of those who have written against me, they are such scoundrels that they deserve not the least notice to be taken of them. Blackmore and Milbourne are only distinguished from the crowd by being remembered to their infamy.*

Dryden indeed discovered, in many of his writings, an affected and 179 absurd malignity to priests and priesthood, which naturally raised him many enemies, and which was sometimes as unseasonably resented as it was exerted. Trapp is angry that he calls the sacrificer in the *Georgicks* the *holy butcher*: the translation is indeed ridiculous; but Trapp's anger arises from his zeal, not for the author, but the priest; as if any reproach of the follies of paganism could be extended to the preachers of truth.

Dryden's dislike of the priesthood is imputed by Langbaine, and I think 180 by Brown, to a repulse which he suffered when he solicited ordination; but he denies, in the preface to his Fables, that he ever designed to enter into the church; and such a denial he would not have hazarded, if he could have been convicted of falsehood.

Malevolence to the clergy is seldom at a great distance from irreverence 181 of religion, and Dryden affords no exception to this observation. His writings exhibit many passages, which, with all the allowance that can be made for characters and occasions, are such as piety would not have admitted, and such as may vitiate light and unprincipled minds. But there is no reason for supposing that he disbelieved the religion which he disobeyed. He forgot his duty rather than disowned it. His tendency to profaneness is the effect of levity, negligence, and loose conversation, with a desire of accommodating himself to the corruption of the times, by venturing to be wicked as far as he durst. When he professed himself a convert to Popery, he did not pretend to have received any new conviction of the fundamental doctrines of Christianity.

182     The persecution of criticks was not the worst of his vexations; he was much more disturbed by the importunities of want. His complaints of poverty are so frequently repeated, either with the dejection of weakness sinking in helpless misery, or the indignation of merit claiming its tribute from mankind, that it is impossible not to detest the age which could impose on such a man the necessity of such solicitations, or not to despise the man who could submit to such solicitations without necessity.

183     Whether by the world's neglect, or his own imprudence, I am afraid that the greatest part of his life was passed in exigences. Such outcries were surely never uttered but in severe pain. Of his supplies or his expences no probable estimate can now be made. Except the salary of the Laureate, to which king James added the office of Historiographer, perhaps with some additional emoluments, his whole revenue seems to have been casual; and it is well known that he seldom lives frugally who lives by chance. Hope is always liberal, and they that trust her promises make little scruple of revelling to-day on the profits of the morrow.

184     Of his plays the profit was not great, and of the produce of his other works very little intelligence can be had. By discoursing with the late amiable Mr. Tonson, I could not find that any memorials of the transactions between his predecessor and Dryden had been preserved, except the following papers:

"I do hereby promise to pay John Dryden, Esq; or order, on the 25th of March 1699, the sum of two hundred and fifty guineas, in consideration of ten thousand verses, which the said John Dryden, Esq; is to deliver to me Jacob Tonson, when finished, whereof seven thousand five hundred verses, more or less, are already in the said Jacob Tonson's possession. And I do hereby farther promise, and engage myself, to make up the said sum of two hundred and fifty guineas three hundred pounds sterling to the said John Dryden, Esq; his executors, administrators, or assigns, at the beginning of the second impression of the said ten thousand verses.

"In witness whereof I have hereunto set my hand and seal, this 20th day of March, 169$\frac{8}{9}$ .

Jacob Tonson.

> Sealed and delivered, being first
> duly stampt, pursuant to the acts
> of parliament for that purpose,
> in the presence of
>   Ben. Portlock.
>   Will. Congreve."

"March 24th, 1698.

"Received then of Mr. Jacob Tonson the sum of two hundred sixty-eight pounds fifteen shillings, in pursuance of an agreement for ten thousand verses, to be delivered by me to the said Jacob Tonson, whereof I have already delivered to him about seven thousand five hundred, more or less; he the said Jacob Tonson being obliged to make up the foresaid sum of two hundred sixty-eight pounds fifteen shillings three hundred pounds, at the beginning of the second impression of the foresaid ten thousand verses;

I say, received by me<br>John Dryden.

Witness Charles Dryden."

Two hundred and fifty guineas, at 1*l*. 1*s*. 6*d*. is 268*l*. 15*s*.

It is manifest from the dates of this contract, that it relates to the volume of Fables, which contains about twelve thousand verses, and for which therefore the payment must have been afterwards enlarged.                    185

I have been told of another letter yet remaining, in which he desires Tonson to bring him money, to pay for a watch which he had ordered for his son, and which the maker would not leave without the price.                    186

The inevitable consequence of poverty is dependence. Dryden had probably no recourse in his exigencies but to his bookseller. The particular character of Tonson I do not know; but the general conduct of traders was much less liberal in those times than in our own; their views were narrower, and their manners grosser. To the mercantile ruggedness of that race, the delicacy of the poet was sometimes exposed. Lord Bolingbroke, who in his youth had cultivated poetry, related to Dr. King of Oxford, that one day, when he visited Dryden, they heard, as they were conversing, another person entering the house. "This," said Dryden, "is Tonson. You will take care not to depart before he goes away; for I have not completed the sheet which I promised him; and if you leave me unprotected, I must suffer all the rudeness to which his resentment can prompt his tongue."                    187

What rewards he obtained for his poems, besides the payment of the bookseller, cannot be known: Mr. Derrick, who consulted some of his relations, was informed that his Fables obtained five hundred pounds from the dutchess of Ormond; a present not unsuitable to the magnificence of that splendid family; and he quotes Moyle, as relating that forty pounds were paid by a musical society for the use of *Alexander's Feast*.                    188

In those days the œconomy of government was yet unsettled, and the payments of the Exchequer were dilatory and uncertain: of this disorder there is reason to believe that the Laureat sometimes felt the effects; for in                    189 one of his prefaces he complains of those, who, being intrusted with the distribution of the Prince's bounty, suffer those that depend upon it to languish in penury.

190    Of his petty habits or slight amusements, tradition has retained little. Of the only two men whom I have found to whom he was personally known, one told me that at the house which he frequented, called Will's Coffee-house, the appeal upon any literary dispute was made to him; and the other related, that his armed chair, which in the winter had a settled and pre-scriptive place by the fire, was in the summer placed in the balcony, and that he called the two places his winter and his summer seat. This is all the intelligence which his two survivors afforded me.

191    One of his opinions will do him no honour in the present age, though in his own time, at least in the beginning of it, he was far from having it confined to himself. He put great confidence in the prognostications of judicial astrology. In the Appendix to the Life of Congreve is a narrative of some of his predictions wonderfully fulfilled; but I know not the writer's means of information, or character of veracity. That he had the configura-tions of the horoscope in his mind, and considered them as influencing the affairs of men, he does not forbear to hint.

> The utmost malice of the stars is past.—
>
> Now frequent *trines* the happier lights among,
> And *high-rais'd Jove*, from his dark prison freed,
> Those weights took off that on his planet hung,
> Will gloriously the new-laid works succeed.

He has elsewhere shewn his attention to the planetary powers; and in the preface to his Fables has endeavoured obliquely to justify his superstition, by attributing the same to some of the Ancients. The letter, added to this narrative, leaves no doubt of his notions or practice.

192    So slight and so scanty is the knowledge which I have been able to collect concerning the private life and domestick manners of a man, whom every English generation must mention with reverence as a critick and a poet.

193    DRYDEN may be properly considered as the father of English criticism, as the writer who first taught us to determine upon principles the merit of composition. Of our former poets, the greatest dramatist wrote without rules, conducted through life and nature by a genius that rarely misled, and rarely deserted him. Of the rest, those who knew the laws of propriety had neglected to teach them.

Two *Arts of English Poetry* were written in the days of Elizabeth by Webb 194
and Puttenham, from which something might be learned, and a few hints
had been given by Jonson and Cowley; but Dryden's *Essay on Dramatick
Poetry* was the first regular and valuable treatise on the art of writing.

He who, having formed his opinions in the present age of English 195
literature, turns back to peruse this dialogue, will not perhaps find much
increase of knowledge, or much novelty of instruction; but he is to remember that critical principles were then in the hands of a few, who had gathered
them partly from the Ancients, and partly from the Italians and French. The
structure of dramatick poems was not then generally understood. Audiences
applauded by instinct, and poets perhaps often pleased by chance.

A writer who obtains his full purpose loses himself in his own lustre. Of 196
an opinion which is no longer doubted, the evidence ceases to be examined.
Of an art universally practised, the first teacher is forgotten. Learning once
made popular is no longer learning; it has the appearance of something
which we have bestowed upon ourselves, as the dew appears to rise from the
field which it refreshes.

To judge rightly of an author, we must transport ourselves to his time, 197
and examine what were the wants of his contemporaries, and what were his
means of supplying them. That which is easy at one time was difficult at
another. Dryden at least imported his science, and gave his country what it
wanted before; or rather, he imported only the materials, and manufactured
them by his own skill.

The dialogue on the Drama was one of his first essays of criticism, 198
written when he was yet a timorous candidate for reputation, and therefore
laboured with that diligence which he might allow himself somewhat to
remit, when his name gave sanction to his positions, and his awe of the
public was abated, partly by custom, and partly by success. It will not be
easy to find, in all the opulence of our language, a treatise so artfully
variegated with successive representations of opposite probabilities, so
enlivened with imagery, so brighened with illustrations. His portraits of
the English dramatists are wrought with great spirit and diligence. The
account of Shakspeare may stand as a perpetual model of encomiastick
criticism; exact without minuteness, and lofty without exaggeration. The
praise lavished by Longinus, on the attestation of the heroes of Marathon,
by Demosthenes, fades away before it. In a few lines is exhibited a character,
so extensive in its comprehension, and so curious in its limitations, that
nothing can be added, diminished, or reformed; nor can the editors and
admirers of Shakspeare, in all their emulation of reverence, boast of much
more than of having diffused and paraphrased this epitome of excellence, of

having changed Dryden's gold for baser metal, of lower value though of greater bulk.

199   In this, and in all his other essays on the same subject, the criticism of Dryden is the criticism of a poet; not a dull collection of theorems, nor a rude detection of faults, which perhaps the censor was not able to have committed; but a gay and vigorous dissertation, where delight is mingled with instruction, and where the author proves his right of judgement, by his power of performance.

200   The different manner and effect with which critical knowledge may be conveyed, was perhaps never more clearly exemplified than in the performances of Rymer and Dryden. It was said of a dispute between two mathematicians, "malim cum Scaligero errare, quam cum Clavio recte sapere;" that *it was more eligible to go wrong with one than right with the other.* A tendency of the same kind every mind must feel at the perusal of Dryden's prefaces and Rymer's discourses. With Dryden we are wandering in quest of Truth; whom we find, if we find her at all, drest in the graces of elegance; and if we miss her, the labour of the pursuit rewards itself; we are led only through fragrance and flowers: Rymer, without taking a nearer, takes a rougher way; every step is to be made through thorns and brambles; and Truth, if we meet her, appears repulsive by her mien, and ungraceful by her habit. Dryden's criticism has the majesty of a queen; Rymer's has the ferocity of a tyrant.

201   As he had studied with great diligence the art of poetry, and enlarged or rectified his notions, by experience perpetually increasing, he had his mind stored with principles and observations; he poured out his knowledge with little labour; for of labour, notwithstanding the multiplicity of his productions, there is sufficient reason to suspect that he was not a lover. To write *con amore*, with fondness for the employment, with perpetual touches and retouches, with unwillingness to take leave of his own idea, and an unwearied pursuit of unattainable perfection, was, I think, no part of his character.

202   His Criticism may be considered as general or occasional. In his general precepts, which depend upon the nature of things, and the structure of the human mind, he may doubtless be safely recommended to the confidence of the reader; but his occasional and particular positions were sometimes interested, sometimes negligent, and sometimes capricious. It is not without reason that Trapp, speaking of the praises which he bestows on Palamon and Arcite, says, "Novimus judicium Drydeni de poemate quodam *Chauceri*, pulchro sane illo, et admodum laudando, nimirum quod non modo vere epicum sit, sed Iliada etiam atque Æneada æquet, imo superet. Sed novimus eodem tempore viri illius maximi non semper accuratissimas esse censuras, nec ad severissimam critices normam exactas: illo judice id

plerumque optimum est, quod nunc præ manibus habet, & in quo nunc occupatur."

He is therefore by no means constant to himself. His defence and 203 desertion of dramatick rhyme is generally known. *Spence*, in his remarks on Pope's Odyssey, produces what he thinks an unconquerable quotation from Dryden's preface to the Eneid, in favour of translating an epic poem into blank verse; but he forgets that when his author attempted the Iliad, some years afterwards, he departed from his own decision, and translated into rhyme.

When he has any objection to obviate, or any license to defend, he is not 204 very scrupulous about what he asserts, nor very cautious, if the present purpose be served, not to entangle himself in his own sophistries. But when all arts are exhausted, like other hunted animals, he sometimes stands at bay; when he cannot disown the grossness of one of his plays, he declares that he knows not any law that prescribes morality to a comick poet.

His remarks on ancient or modern writers are not always to be trusted. 205 His parallel of the versification of Ovid with that of Claudian has been very justly censured by *Sewel**. His comparison of the first line of Virgil with the first of Statius is not happier. Virgil, he says, is soft and gentle, and would have thought Statius mad if he had heard him thundering out

Quæ superimposito moles geminata colosso.

Statius perhaps heats himself, as he proceeds, to exaggerations somewhat 206 hyperbolical; but undoubtedly Virgil would have been too hasty, if he had condemned him to straw for one sounding line. Dryden wanted an instance, and the first that occurred was imprest into the service.

What he wishes to say, he says at hazard; he cited *Gorbuduc*, which he had 207 never seen; gives a false account of *Chapman's* versification; and discovers, in the preface to his Fables, that he translated the first book of the Iliad, without knowing what was in the second.

It will be difficult to prove that Dryden ever made any great advances in 208 literature. As having distinguished himself at Westminster under the tuition of Busby, who advanced his scholars to a height of knowledge very rarely attained in grammar-schools, he resided afterwards at Cambridge, it is not to be supposed, that his skill in the ancient languages was deficient, compared with that of common students; but his scholastick acquisitions seem not proportionate to his opportunities and abilities. He could not, like Milton or Cowley, have made his name illustrious merely by his learning. He mentions but few books, and those such as lie in the beaten track of

* Preface to Ovid's Metamorphoses.

regular study; from which if ever he departs, he is in danger of losing himself in unknown regions.

209    In his Dialogue on the Drama, he pronounces with great confidence that the Latin tragedy of Medea is not Ovid's, because it is not sufficiently interesting and pathetick. He might have determined the question upon surer evidence; for it is quoted by Quintilian as the work of Seneca; and the only line which remains of Ovid's play, for one line is left us, is not there to be found. There was therefore no need of the gravity of conjecture, or the discussion of plot or sentiment, to find what was already known upon higher authority than such discussions can ever reach.

210    His literature, though not always free from ostentation, will be commonly found either obvious, and made his own by the art of dressing it; or superficial, which, by what he gives, shews what he wanted; or erroneous, hastily collected, and negligently scattered.

211    Yet it cannot be said that his genius is ever unprovided of matter, or that his fancy languishes in penury of ideas. His works abound with knowledge, and sparkle with illustrations. There is scarcely any science or faculty that does not supply him with occasional images and lucky similitudes; every page discovers a mind very widely acquainted both with art and nature, and in full possession of great stores of intellectual wealth. Of him that knows much, it is natural to suppose that he has read with diligence; yet I rather believe that the knowledge of Dryden was gleaned from accidental intelligence and various conversation, by a quick apprehension, a judicious selection, and a happy memory, a keen appetite of knowledge, and a powerful digestion; by vigilance that permitted nothing to pass without notice, and a habit of reflection that suffered nothing useful to be lost. A mind like Dryden's, always curious, always active, to which every understanding was proud to be associated, and of which every one solicited the regard, by an ambitious display of himself, had a more pleasant, perhaps a nearer way, to knowledge than by the silent progress of solitary reading. I do not suppose that he despised books, or intentionally neglected them; but that he was carried out, by the impetuosity of his genius, to more vivid and speedy instructors; and that his studies were rather desultory and fortuitous than constant and systematical.

212    It must be confessed that he scarcely ever appears to want book-learning but when he mentions books; and to him may be transferred the praise which he gives his master Charles.

> His conversation, wit, and parts,
> His knowledge in the noblest useful arts,
>     Were such, dead authors could not give,

But habitudes of those that live;
Who, lighting him, did greater lights receive:
He drain'd from all, and all they knew,
His apprehension quick, his judgement true:
That the most learn'd with shame confess
His knowledge more, his reading only less.

Of all this, however, if the proof be demanded, I will not undertake to 213
give it; the atoms of probability, of which my opinion has been formed, lie
scattered over all his works; and by him who thinks the question worth his
notice, his works must be perused with very close attention.

Criticism, either didactick or defensive, occupies almost all his prose, 214
except those pages which he has devoted to his patrons; but none of
his prefaces were ever thought tedious. They have not the formality of a
settled style, in which the first half of the sentence betrays the other. The
clauses are never balanced, nor the periods modelled; every word seems to
drop by chance, though it falls into its proper place. Nothing is cold or
languid; the whole is airy, animated, and vigorous; what is little, is gay; what
is great, is splendid. He may be thought to mention himself too frequently;
but while he forces himself upon our esteem, we cannot refuse him to stand
high in his own. Every thing is excused by the play of images and the
spriteliness of expression. Though all is easy, nothing is feeble; though
all seems careless, there is nothing harsh; and though, since his earlier
works, more than a century has passed, they have nothing yet uncouth or
obsolete.

He who writes much, will not easily escape a manner, such a recurrence 215
of particular modes as may be easily noted. Dryden is always *another and the
same*, he does not exhibit a second time the same elegances in the same form,
nor appears to have any art other than that of expressing with clearness what
he thinks with vigour. His style could not easily be imitated, either seriously
or ludicrously; for, being always equable and always varied, it has no
prominent or discriminative characters. The beauty who is totally free
from disproportion of parts and features, cannot be ridiculed by an over-
charged resemblance.

From his prose, however, Dryden derives only his accidental and sec- 216
ondary praise; the veneration with which his name is pronounced by every
cultivator of English literature, is paid to him as he refined the language,
improved the sentiments, and tuned the numbers of English Poetry.

After about half a century of forced thoughts, and rugged metre, some 217
advances towards nature and harmony had been already made by Waller
and Denham; they had shewn that long discourses in rhyme grew more

pleasing when they were broken into couplets, and that verse consisted not only in the number but the arrangement of syllables.

218    But though they did much, who can deny that they left much to do? Their works were not many, nor were their minds of very ample comprehension. More examples of more modes of composition were necessary for the establishment of regularity, and the introduction of propriety in word and thought.

219    Every language of a learned nation necessarily divides itself into diction scholastick and popular, grave and familiar, elegant and gross; and from a nice distinction of these different parts, arises a great part of the beauty of style. But if we except a few minds, the favourites of nature, to whom their own original rectitude was in the place of rules, this delicacy of selection was little known to our authors; our speech lay before them in a heap of confusion, and every man took for every purpose what chance might offer him.

220    There was therefore before the time of Dryden no poetical diction, no system of words at once refined from the grossness of domestick use, and free from the harshness of terms appropriated to particular arts. Words too familiar, or too remote, defeat the purpose of a poet. From those sounds which we hear on small or on coarse occasions, we do not easily receive strong impressions, or delightful images; and words to which we are nearly strangers, whenever they occur, draw that attention on themselves which they should transmit to things.

221    Those happy combinations of words which distinguish poetry from prose, had been rarely attempted; we had few elegances or flowers of speech, the roses had not yet been plucked from the bramble, or different colours had not been joined to enliven one another.

222    It may be doubted whether Waller and Denham could have over-born the prejudices which had long prevailed, and which even then were sheltered by the protection of Cowley. The new versification, as it was called, may be considered as owing its establishment to Dryden; from whose time it is apparent that English poetry has had no tendency to relapse to its former savageness.

223    The affluence and comprehension of our language is very illustriously displayed in our poetical translations of Ancient Writers; a work which the French seem to relinquish in despair, and which we were long unable to perform with dexterity. Ben Jonson thought it necessary to copy Horace almost word by word; Feltham, his contemporary and adversary, considers it as indispensably requisite in a translation to give line for line. It is said that Sandys, whom Dryden calls the best versifier of the last age, has struggled hard to comprise every book of his English Metamorphoses

in the same number of verses with the original. Holyday had nothing in view but to shew that he understood his author, with so little regard to the grandeur of his diction, or the volubility of his numbers, that his metres can hardly be called verses; they cannot be read without reluctance, nor will the labour always be rewarded by understanding them. Cowley saw that such *copyers* were a *servile race*; he asserted his liberty, and spread his wings so boldly that he left his authors. It was reserved for Dryden to fix the limits of poetical liberty, and give us just rules and examples of translation.

When languages are formed upon different principles, it is impossible  224 that the same modes of expression should always be elegant in both. While they run on together, the closest translation may be considered as the best; but when they divaricate, each must take its natural course. Where correspondence cannot be obtained, it is necessary to be content with something equivalent. *Translation therefore*, says Dryden, *is not so loose as paraphrase, nor so close as metaphrase*.

All polished languages have different styles; the concise, the diffuse, the  225 lofty, and the humble. In the proper choice of style consists the resemblance which Dryden principally exacts from the translator. He is to exhibit his author's thoughts in such a dress of diction as the author would have given them, had his language been English: rugged magnificence is not to be softened: hyperbolical ostentation is not to be repressed, nor sententious affectation to have its points blunted. A translator is to be like his author: it is not his business to excel him.

The reasonableness of these rules seems sufficient for their vindication;  226 and the effects produced by observing them were so happy, that I know not whether they were ever opposed but by Sir Edward Sherburne, a man whose learning was greater than his powers of poetry; and who, being better qualified to give the meaning than the spirit of Seneca, has introduced his version of three tragedies by a defence of close translation. The authority of Horace, which the new translators cited in defence of their practice, he has, by a judicious explanation, taken fairly from them; but reason wants not Horace to support it.

It seldom happens that all the necessary causes concur to any great effect:  227 will is wanting to power, or power to will, or both are impeded by external obstructions. The exigences in which Dryden was condemned to pass his life, are reasonably supposed to have blasted his genius, to have driven out his works in a state of immaturity, and to have intercepted the full-blown elegance which longer growth would have supplied.

Poverty, like other rigid powers, is sometimes too hastily accused. If the  228 excellence of Dryden's works was lessened by his indigence, their number was increased; and I know not how it will be proved, that if he had written less he would have written better; or that indeed he would have undergone the toil of an author, if he had not been solicited by something more pressing than the love of praise.

229     But as is said by his Sebastian,

>           What had been, is unknown; what is, appears.

We know that Dryden's several productions were so many successive expedients for his support; his plays were therefore often borrowed, and his poems were almost all occasional.

230     In an occasional performance no height of excellence can be expected from any mind, however fertile in itself, and however stored with acquisitions. He whose work is general and arbitrary, has the choice of his matter, and takes that which his inclination and his studies have best qualified him to display and decorate. He is at liberty to delay his publication, till he has satisfied his friends and himself; till he has reformed his first thoughts by subsequent examination; and polished away those faults which the precipitance of ardent composition is likely to leave behind it. Virgil is related to have poured out a great number of lines in the morning, and to have passed the day in reducing them to fewer.

231     The occasional poet is circumscribed by the narrowness of his subject. Whatever can happen to man has happened so often, that little remains for fancy or invention. We have been all born; we have most of us been married; and so many have died before us, that our deaths can supply but few materials for a poet. In the fate of princes the publick has an interest; and what happens to them of good or evil, the poets have always considered as business for the Muse. But after so many inauguratory gratulations, nuptial hymns, and funeral dirges, he must be highly favoured by nature, or by fortune, who says any thing not said before. Even war and conquest, however splendid, suggest no new images; the triumphal chariot of a victorious monarch can be decked only with those ornaments that have graced his predecessors.

232     Not only matter but time is wanting. The poem must not be delayed till the occasion is forgotten. The lucky moments of animated imagination cannot be attended; elegances and illustrations cannot be multiplied by gradual accumulation: the composition must be dispatched while conversation is yet busy, and admiration fresh; and haste is to be made, lest some other event should lay hold upon mankind.

233     Occasional compositions may however secure to a writer the praise both of learning and facility; for they cannot be the effect of long study, and must be furnished immediately from the treasures of the mind.

The death of Cromwell was the first publick event which called forth   234
Dryden's poetical powers. His heroick stanzas have beauties and defects;
the thoughts are vigorous, and though not always proper, shew a mind
replete with ideas; the numbers are smooth, and the diction, if not altogether correct, is elegant and easy.

Davenant was perhaps at this time his favourite author, though Gondi-   235
bert never appears to have been popular; and from Davenant he learned to
please his ear with the stanza of four lines alternately rhymed.

Dryden very early formed his versification: there are in this early pro-   236
duction no traces of Donne's or Jonson's ruggedness; but he did not so soon
free his mind from the ambition of forced conceits. In his verses on the
Restoration, he says of the King's exile,

> He, toss'd by Fate—
> Could taste no sweets of youth's desired age,
> But found his life too true a pilgrimage.

And afterwards, to shew how virtue and wisdom are increased by adversity,
he makes this remark:

> Well might the ancient poets then confer
> On Night the honour'd name of *counsellor*,
> Since, struck with rays of prosperous fortune blind,
> We light alone in dark afflictions find.

His praise of Monk's dexterity comprises such a cluster of thoughts   237
unallied to one another, as will not elsewhere be easily found:

> 'Twas Monk, whom Providence design'd to loose
> Those real bonds false freedom did impose.
> The blessed saints that watch'd this turning scene,
> Did from their stars with joyful wonder lean,
> To see small clues draw vastest weights along,
> Not in their bulk, but in their order strong.
> Thus pencils can by one slight touch restore
> Smiles to that changed face that wept before.
> With ease such fond chimæras we pursue,
> As fancy frames for fancy to subdue:
> But, when ourselves to action we betake,
> It shuns the mint like gold that chymists make:
> How hard was then his task, at once to be
> What in the body natural we see!
> Man's Architect distinctly did ordain
> The charge of muscles, nerves, and of the brain,

> Through viewless conduits spirits to dispense
> The springs of motion from the seat of sense.
> 'Twas not the hasty product of a day,
> But the well-ripen'd fruit of wise delay.
> He, like a patient angler, ere he strook,
> Would let them play a-while upon the hook.
> Our healthful food the stomach labours thus,
> At first embracing what it straight doth crush.
> Wise leaches will not vain receipts obtrude,
> While growing pains pronounce the humours crude;
> Deaf to complaints, they wait upon the ill,
> Till some safe crisis authorize their skill.

238     He had not yet learned, indeed he never learned well, to forbear the improper use of mythology. After having rewarded the heathen deities for their care,

> With *Alga* who the sacred altar strows?
> To all the sea-gods Charles an offering owes;
> A bull to thee, Portunus, shall be slain;
> A ram to you, ye Tempests of the Main.

He tells us, in the language of religion,

> Prayer storm'd the skies, and ravish'd Charles from thence,
> As heaven itself is took by violence.

And afterwards mentions one of the most awful passages of Sacred History.
239     Other conceits there are, too curious to be quite omitted; as,

> For by example most we sinn'd before,
> And, glass-like, clearness mix'd with frailty bore.

How far he was yet from thinking it necessary to found his sentiments on Nature, appears from the extravagence of his fictions and hyperboles:

> The winds, that never moderation knew,
> Afraid to blow too much, too faintly blew;
> Or, out of breath with joy, could not enlarge
> Their straiten'd lungs.—
> It is no longer motion cheats your view;
> As you meet it, the land approacheth you;
> The land returns, and in the white it wears
> The marks of penitence and sorrow bears.

I know not whether this fancy, however little be its value, was not borrowed. A French poet read to Malherbe some verses, in which he represents France as moving out of its place to receive the king. "Though this," said Malherbe, "was in my time, I do not remember it."

His poem on the *Coronation* has a more even tenour of thought. Some 240 lines deserve to be quoted:

> You have already quench'd sedition's brand,
> And zeal, that burnt it, only warms the land;
> The jealous sects that durst not trust their cause
> So far from their own will as to the laws,
> Him for their umpire, and their synod take,
> And their appeal alone to Cæsar make.

Here may be found one particle of that old versification, of which, 241 I believe, in all his works, there is not another:

> Nor is it duty, or our hope alone,
> Creates that joy, but full *fruition*.

In the verses to the lord chancellor Clarendon, two years afterwards, is a 242 conceit so hopeless at the first view, that few would have attempted it; and so successfully laboured, that though at last it gives the reader more perplexity than pleasure, and seems hardly worth the study that it costs, yet it must be valued as a proof of a mind at once subtle and comprehensive:

> In open prospect nothing bounds our eye,
> Until the earth seems join'd unto the sky:
> So in this hemisphere our outmost view
> Is only bounded by our king and you:
> Our sight is limited where you are join'd,
> And beyond that no farther heaven can find.
> So well your virtues do with his agree,
> That, though your orbs of different greatness be,
> Yet both are for each other's use dispos'd,
> His to enclose, and yours to be enclos'd.
> Nor could another in your room have been,
> Except an emptiness had come between.

The comparison of the Chancellor to the Indies leaves all resemblance 243 too far behind it:

> And as the Indies were not found before
> Those rich perfumes which from the happy shore
> The winds upon their balmy wings convey'd,
> Whose guilty sweetness first their world betray'd;
> So by your counsels we are brought to view
> A new and undiscover'd world in you.

244     There is another comparison, for there is little else in the poem, of which,
though perhaps it cannot be explained into plain prosaick meaning, the
mind perceives enough to be delighted, and readily forgives its obscurity,
for its magnificence:

> How strangely active are the arts of peace,
> Whose restless motions less than wars do cease:
> Peace is not freed from labour, but from noise;
> And war more force, but not more pains employs:
> Such is the mighty swiftness of your mind,
> That, like the earth's, it leaves our sense behind,
> While you so smoothly turn and rowl our sphere,
> That rapid motion does but rest appear.
> For as in nature's swiftness, with the throng
> Of flying orbs while ours is borne along,
> All seems at rest to the deluded eye,
> Mov'd by the soul of the same harmony:
> So carry'd on by our unwearied care,
> We rest in peace, and yet in motion share.

245     To this succeed four lines, which perhaps afford Dryden's first attempt at
those penetrating remarks on human nature, for which he seems to have
been peculiarly formed:

> Let envy then those crimes within you see,
> From which the happy never must be free;
> Envy that does with misery reside,
> The joy and the revenge of ruin'd pride.

246     Into this poem he seems to have collected all his powers; and after this he
did not often bring upon his anvil such stubborn and unmalleable thoughts;
but, as a specimen of his abilities to unite the most unsociable matter, he has
concluded with lines, of which I think not myself obliged to tell the
meaning:

> Yet unimpair'd with labours, or with time,
> Your age but seems to a new youth to climb.
> Thus heavenly bodies do our time beget,
> And measure change, but share no part of it:
> And still it shall without a weight increase,
> Like this new year, whose motions never cease.
> For since the glorious course you have begun,
> Is led by Charles, as that is by the sun,
> It must both weightless and immortal prove,
> Because the centre of it is above.

In the *Annus Mirabilis* he returned to the quatrain, which from that time 247
he totally quitted, perhaps from this experience of its inconvenience, for he
complains of its difficulty. This is one of his greatest attempts. He had
subjects equal to his abilities, a great naval war, and the Fire of London.
Battles have always been described in heroick poetry; but a sea-fight and
artillery had yet something of novelty. New arts are long in the world before
poets describe them; for they borrow every thing from their predecessors,
and commonly derive very little from nature or from life. Boileau was the
first French writer that had ever hazarded in verse the mention of modern
war, or the effects of gunpowder. We, who are less afraid of novelty, had
already possession of those dreadful images: Waller had described a sea-
fight. Milton had not yet transferred the invention of fire-arms to the
rebellious angels.

This poem is written with great diligence, yet does not fully answer the 248
expectation raised by such subjects and such a writer. With the stanza of
Davenant he has sometimes his vein of parenthesis, and incidental disquisition, and stops his narrative for a wise remark.

The general fault is, that he affords more sentiment than description, and 249
does not so much impress scenes upon the fancy, as deduce consequences
and make comparisons.

The initial stanzas have rather too much resemblance to the first lines of 250
Waller's poem on the war with Spain; perhaps such a beginning is natural,
and could not be avoided without affectation. Both Waller and Dryden
might take their hint from the poem on the civil war of Rome, *Orbem jam
totum*, &c.

Of the king collecting his navy, he says, 251

> It seems as every ship their sovereign knows,
>   His awful summons they so soon obey;
> So hear the scaly herds when Proteus blows,
>   And so to pasture follow through the sea.

It would not be hard to believe that Dryden had written the two first 251*a*
lines seriously, and that some wag had added the two latter in burlesque. Who would expect the lines that immediately follow, which are
indeed perhaps indecently hyperbolical, but certainly in a mode totally
different?

> To see this fleet upon the ocean move,
>   Angels drew wide the curtains of the skies;
> And heaven, as if there wanted lights above,
>   For tapers made two glaring comets rise.

252    The description of the attempt at Bergen will afford a very compleat
specimen of the descriptions in this poem:

>           And now approach'd their fleet from India, fraught
>               With all the riches of the rising sun:
>           And precious sand from southern climates brought,
>               The fatal regions where the war begun.
>
>           Like hunted castors, conscious of their store,
>               Their way-laid wealth to Norway's coast they bring;
>           Then first the North's cold bosom spices bore,
>               And winter brooded on the eastern spring.
>
>           By the rich scent we found our perfum'd prey,
>               Which, flank'd with rocks, did close in covert lie:
>           And round about their murdering cannon lay,
>               At once to threaten and invite the eye.
>
>           Fiercer than cannon, and than rocks more hard,
>               The English undertake th' unequal war:
>           Seven ships alone, by which the port is barr'd,
>               Besiege the Indies, and all Denmark dare.
>
>           These fight like husbands, but like lovers those:
>               These fain would keep, and those more fain enjoy:
>           And to such height their frantic passion grows,
>               That what both love, both hazard to destroy:
>
>           Amidst whole heaps of spices lights a ball,
>               And now their odours arm'd against them fly:
>           Some preciously by shatter'd porcelain fall,
>               And some by aromatic splinters die.
>
>           And though by tempests of the prize bereft,
>               In heaven's inclemency some ease we find:
>           Our foes we vanquish'd by our valour left,
>               And only yielded to the seas and wind.

253    In this manner is the sublime too often mingled with the ridiculous. The
Dutch seek a shelter for a wealthy fleet: this surely needed no illustration;
yet they must fly, not like all the rest of mankind on the same occasion, but
*like hunted castors*; and they might with strict propriety be hunted; for we
winded them by our noses—their *perfumes* betrayed them. The *Husband*
and the *Lover*, though of more dignity than the Castor, are images too
domestick to mingle properly with the horrors of war. The two quatrains
that follow are worthy of the author.

254    The account of the different sensations with which the two fleets retired,
when the night parted them, is one of the fairest flowers of English poetry.

The night comes on, we eager to pursue
    The combat still, and they asham'd to leave:
'Till the last streaks of dying day withdrew,
    And doubtful moon-light did our rage deceive.

In th' English fleet each ship resounds with joy,
    And loud applause of their great leader's fame:
In firy dreams the Dutch they still destroy,
    And, slumbering, smile at the imagin'd flame.

Not so the Holland fleet, who, tir'd and done,
    Stretch'd on their decks like weary oxen lie;
Faint sweats all down their mighty members run,
    (Vast bulks, which little souls but ill supply.)

In dreams they fearful precipices tread,
    Or, shipwreck'd, labour to some distant shore:
Or, in dark churches, walk among the dead;
    They wake with horror, and dare sleep no more.

It is a general rule in poetry, that all appropriated terms of art should 255 be sunk in general expressions, because poetry is to speak an universal language. This rule is still stronger with regard to arts not liberal, or confined to few, and therefore far removed from common knowledge; and of this kind, certainly, is technical navigation. Yet Dryden was of opinion that a sea-fight ought to be described in the nautical language; *and certainly,* says he, *as those who in a logical disputation keep to general terms would hide a fallacy, so those who do it in any poetical description would veil their ignorance.*

Let us then appeal to experience; for by experience at last we learn as well 256 what will please as what will profit. In the battle, his terms seem to have been blown away; but he deals them liberally in the dock:

So here some pick out bullets from the side,
    Some drive old *okum* thro' each *seam* and rift:
Their left-hand does the *calking-iron* guide,
    The rattling *mallet* with the right they lift.

With boiling pitch another near at hand
    (From friendly Sweden brought) the *seams instops*:
Which, well laid o'er, the salt-sea waves withstand,
    And shake them from the rising beak in drops.

Some the *gall'd* ropes with dawby *marling* blind,
    Or sear-cloth masts with strong *tarpawling* coats:
To try new *shrouds* one mounts into the wind,
    And one below, their ease or stiffness notes.

256a    I suppose here is not one term which every reader does not wish away.

257    His digression to the original and progress of navigation, with his prospect of the advancement which it shall receive from the Royal Society, then newly instituted, may be considered as an example seldom equalled of seasonable excursion and artful return.

258    One line, however, leaves me discontented; he says, that by the help of the philosophers,

> Instructed ships shall sail to quick commerce,
> By which remotest regions are allied.—

Which he is constrained to explain in a note, *By a more exact measure of longitude*. It had better become Dryden's learning and genius to have laboured science into poetry, and have shewn, by explaining longitude, that verse did not refuse the ideas of philosophy.

259    His description of the Fire is painted by resolute meditation, out of a mind better formed to reason than to feel. The conflagration of a city, with all its tumults of concomitant distress, is one of the most dreadful spectacles which this world can offer to human eyes; yet it seems to raise little emotion in the breast of the poet; he watches the flame coolly from street to street, with now a reflection, and now a simile, till at last he meets the king, for whom he makes a speech, rather tedious in a time so busy; and then follows again the progress of the fire.

260    There are, however, in this part some passages that deserve attention; as in the beginning:

> The diligence of trades and noiseful gain
> And luxury more late asleep were laid;
> All was the night's, and in her silent reign
> No sound the rest of Nature did invade
>
> In this deep quiet—

260a    The expression *All was the night's* is taken from Seneca, who remarks on Virgil's line.

> *Omnia noctis erant placida composita quiete,*

that he might have concluded better,

> *Omnia noctis erant.*

261    The following quatrain is vigorous and animated:

> The ghosts of traytors from the bridge descend
> With bold fanatick spectres to rejoice;

About the fire into a dance they bend,
And sing their sabbath notes with feeble voice.

His prediction of the improvements which shall be made in the new city,   262
is elegant and poetical, and, with an event which Poets cannot always boast,
has been happily verified. The poem concludes with a simile that might
have better been omitted.

Dryden, when he wrote this poem, seems not yet fully to have formed his   263
versification, or settled his system of propriety.

From this time, he addicted himself almost wholly to the stage, *to which*,   264
says he, *my genius never much inclined me*, merely as the most profitable
market for poetry. By writing tragedies in rhyme, he continued to improve
his diction and his numbers. According to the opinion of *Harte*, who had
studied his works with great attention, he settled his principles of versification in 1676, when he produced the play of *Aureng Zebe*; and according to
his own account of the short time in which he wrote *Tyrannick Love*, and
the *State of Innocence*, he soon obtained the full effect of diligence, and
added facility to exactness.

Rhyme has been so long banished from the theatre, that we know not its   265
effect upon the passions of an audience; but it has this convenience, that
sentences stand more independent on each other, and striking passages
are therefore easily selected and retained. Thus the description of Night in
the *Indian Emperor*, and the rise and fall of empire in the *Conquest of
Granada*, are more frequently repeated than any lines in *All for Love*, or
*Don Sebastian*.

To search his plays for vigorous sallies, and sententious elegances, or to   266
fix the dates of any little pieces which he wrote by chance, or by solicitation,
were labour too tedious and minute.

His dramatic labours did not so wholly absorb his thoughts, but that he   267
promulgated the laws of translation in a preface to the English Epistles of
Ovid; one of which he translated himself, and another in conjunction with
the Earl of Mulgrave.

Absalom and Achitophel is a work so well known, that particular criti-   268
cism is superfluous. If it be considered as a poem political and controversial,
it will be found to comprise all the excellences of which the subject is
susceptible; acrimony of censure, elegance of praise, artful delineation of
characters, variety and vigour of sentiment, happy turns of language, and
pleasing harmony of numbers; and all these raised to such a height as can
scarcely be found in any other English composition.

It is not, however, without faults; some lines are inelegant or improper,   269
and too many are irreligiously licentious. The original structure of the poem

was defective; allegories drawn to great length will always break; Charles could not run continually parallel with David.

270    The subject had likewise another inconvenience: it admitted little imagery or description, and a long poem of mere sentiments easily becomes tedious; though all the parts are forcible, and every line kindles new rapture, the reader, if not relieved by the interposition of something that sooths the fancy, grows weary of admiration, and defers the rest.

271    As an approach to historical truth was necessary, the action and catastrophe were not in the poet's power; there is therefore an unpleasing disproportion between the beginning and the end. We are alarmed by a faction formed out of many sects various in their principles, but agreeing in their purpose of mischief, formidable for their numbers, and strong by their supports, while the king's friends are few and weak. The chiefs on either part are set forth to view; but when expectation is at the height, the king makes a speech, and

Henceforth a series of new times began.

272    Who can forbear to think of an enchanted castle, with a wide moat and lofty battlements, walls of marble and gates of brass, which vanishes at once into air, when the destined knight blows his horn before it?

273    In the second part, written by *Tate*, there is a long insertion, which, for poignancy of satire, exceeds any part of the former. Personal resentment, though no laudable motive to satire, can add great force to general principles. Self-love is a busy prompter.

274    The *Medal*, written upon the same principles with *Absalom and Achitophel*, but upon a narrower plan, gives less pleasure, though it discovers equal abilities in the writer. The superstructure cannot extend beyond the foundation; a single character or incident cannot furnish as many ideas, as a series of events, or multiplicity of agents. This poem therefore, since time has left it to itself, is not much read, nor perhaps generally understood, yet it abounds with touches both of humorous and serious satire. The picture of a man whose propensions to mischief are such, that his best actions are but inability of wickedness, is very skilfully delineated and strongly coloured.

> Power was his aim: but, thrown from that pretence,
> The wretch turn'd loyal in his own defence,
> And malice reconcil'd him to his Prince.
> Him, in the anguish of his soul, he serv'd;
> Rewarded faster still than he deserv'd:
> Behold him now exalted into trust;

His counsels oft convenient, seldom just.
Ev'n in the most sincere advice he gave,
He had a grudging still to be a knave.
The frauds he learnt in his fanatic years,
Made him uneasy in his lawful gears;
At least as little honest as he cou'd:
And, like white witches, mischievously good.
To his first bias, longingly, he leans;
And rather would be great by wicked means.

The *Threnodia*, which, by a term I am afraid neither authorized nor 275
analogical, he calls *Augustalis*, is not among his happiest productions. Its
first and obvious defect is the irregularity of its metre, to which the ears of
that age, however, were accustomed. What is worse, it has neither tenderness nor dignity, it is neither magnificent nor pathetick. He seems to look
round him for images which he cannot find, and what he has he distorts by
endeavouring to enlarge them. He is, he says, *petrified with grief*; but the
marble sometimes relents, and trickles in a joke.

The sons of art all med'cines try'd,
And every noble remedy apply'd;
With emulation each essay'd
His utmost skill; *nay more they pray'd*:
Was never losing game with better conduct play'd.

He had been a little inclined to merriment before upon the prayers of a 276
nation for their dying sovereign, nor was he serious enough to keep heathen
fables out of his religion.

With him th' innumberable croud of armed prayers
Knock'd at the gates of heaven, and knock'd aloud;
*The first well-meaning rude petitioners*,
All for his life assail'd the throne,
All would have brib'd the skies by offering up their own.
So great a throng not heaven itself could bar;
'Twas almost borne by force *as in the giants war*.
The prayers, at least, for his reprieve were heard;
His death, like Hezekiah's, was deferr'd.

There is throughout the composition a desire of splendor without wealth. 277
In the conclusion he seems too much pleased with the prospect of the new
reign to have lamented his old master with much sincerity.

He did not miscarry in this attempt for want of skill either in lyrick or 278
elegiack poetry. His poem *on the death* of Mrs. *Killigrew*, is undoubtedly the

noblest ode that our language ever has produced. The first part flows with a
torrent of enthusiasm. *Fervet immensusque ruit.* All the stanzas indeed are
not equal. An imperial crown cannot be one continued diamond; the gems
must be held together by some less valuable matter.

279    In his first ode for Cecilia's day, which is lost in the splendor of the
second, there are passages which would have dignified any other poet. The
first stanza is vigorous and elegant, though the word *diapason* is too technical, and the rhymes are too remote from one another.

> From harmony, from heavenly harmony,
>   This universal frame began:
> When nature underneath a heap of jarring atoms lay,
>   And could not heave her head,
> The tuneful voice was heard from high,
>   Arise ye more than dead.
> Then cold and hot, and moist and dry,
> In order to their stations leap,
>   And musick's power obey.
> From harmony, from heavenly harmony,
>   This universal frame began:
>   From harmony to harmony
> Through all the compass of the notes it ran,
>   The diapason closing full in man.

280    The conclusion is likewise striking, but it includes an image so awful in
itself, that it can owe little to poetry; and I could wish the antithesis of
*musick untuning* had found some other place.

> As from the power of sacred lays
>   The spheres began to move,
> And sung the great Creator's praise
>   To all the bless'd above.
> So when the last and dreadful hour
> This crumbling pageant shall devour,
> The trumpet shall be heard on high,
> The dead shall live, the living die,
> And musick shall untune the sky.

281    Of his skill in Elegy he has given a specimen in his *Eleonora*, of which the
following lines discover their author.

> Though all these rare endowments of the mind
> Were in a narrow space of life confin'd,
> The figure was with full perfection crown'd;
> Though not so large an orb, as truly round:

As when in glory, through the public place,
The spoils of conquer'd nations were to pass,
And but one day for triumph was allow'd,
The consul was constrain'd his pomp to crowd;
And so the swift procession hurry'd on,
That all, though not distinctly, might be shown:
So in the straiten'd bounds of life confin'd,
She gave but glimpses of her glorious mind:
And multitudes of virtues pass'd along;
Each pressing foremost in the mighty throng,
Ambitious to be seen, and then make room
For greater multitudes that were to come.
Yet unemploy'd no minute slipp'd away;
Moments were precious in so short a stay.
The haste of heaven to have her was so great, ⎫
That some were single acts, though each compleat; ⎬
And every act stood ready to repeat. ⎭

This piece, however, is not without its faults; there is so much likeness in   282
the initial comparison, that there is no illustration. As a king would be
lamented, Eleonora was lamented.

As when some great and gracious monarch dies,
Soft whispers, first, and mournful murmurs rise
Among the sad attendants; then the sound
Soon gathers voice, and spreads the news around,
Through town and country, till the dreadful blast
Is blown to distant colonies at last;
Who, then, perhaps, were offering vows in vain,
For his long life, and for his happy reign:
So slowly by degrees, unwilling fame ⎫
Did matchless Eleonora's fate proclaim, ⎬
Till publick as the loss the news became. ⎭

This is little better than to say in praise of a shrub, that it is as green as a   282a
tree, or of a brook, that it waters a garden, as a river waters a country.

Dryden confesses that he did not know the lady whom he celebrates; the   283
praise being therefore inevitably general, fixes no impression upon the
reader, nor excites any tendency to love, nor much desire of imitation.
Knowledge of the subject is to the poet, what durable materials are to the
architect.

The *Religio Laici*, which borrows its title from the *Religio Medici* of   284
Browne, is almost the only work of Dryden which can be considered as a
voluntary effusion; in this, therefore, it might be hoped, that the full

effulgence of his genius would be found. But unhappily the subject is rather argumentative than poetical: he intended only a specimen of metrical disputation.

> And this unpolish'd rugged verse I chose,
> As fittest for discourse, and nearest prose.

285    This, however, is a composition of great excellence in its kind, in which the familiar is very properly diversified with the solemn, and the grave with the humorous; in which metre has neither weakened the force, nor clouded the perspicuity of argument; nor will it be easy to find another example equally happy of this middle kind of writing, which, though prosaick in some parts, rises to high poetry in others, and neither towers to the skies, nor creeps along the ground.

286    Of the same kind, or not far distant from it, is the *Hind and Panther*, the longest of all Dryden's original poems; an allegory intended to comprize and to decide the controversy between the Romanists and Protestants. The scheme of the work is injudicious and incommodious; for what can be more absurd than that one beast should counsel another to rest her faith upon a pope and council? He seems well enough skilled in the usual topicks of argument, endeavours to shew the necessity of an infallible judge, and reproaches the Reformers with want of unity; but is weak enough to ask, why since we see without knowing how, we may not have an infallible judge without knowing where.

287    The *Hind* at one time is afraid to drink at the common brook, because she may be worried; but walking home with the *Panther*, talks by the way of the *Nicene Fathers*, and at last declares herself to be the Catholic church.

288    This absurdity was very properly ridiculed in the *City Mouse* and *Country Mouse* of *Montague* and *Prior*; and in the detection and censure of the incongruity of the fiction, chiefly consists the value of their performance, which, whatever reputation it might obtain by the help of temporary passions, seems to readers almost a century distant, not very forcible or animated.

289    Pope, whose judgment was perhaps a little bribed by the subject, used to mention this poem as the most correct specimen of Dryden's versification. It was indeed written when he had completely formed his manner, and may be supposed to exhibit, negligence excepted, his deliberate and ultimate scheme of metre.

290    We may therefore reasonably infer, that he did not approve the perpetual uniformity which confines the sense to couplets, since he has broken his lines in the initial paragraph.

A milk-white Hind, immortal and unchang'd,
Fed on the lawns, and in the forest rang'd;
Without unspotted, innocent within,
She fear'd no danger, for she knew no sin.
Yet had she oft been chac'd with horns and hounds
And Scythian shafts, and many winged wounds
Aim'd at her heart; was often forc'd to fly,
And doom'd to death, though fated not to die.

These lines are lofty, elegant, and musical, notwithstanding the inter- 291
ruption of the pause, of which the effect is rather increase of pleasure by
variety, than offence by ruggedness.

To the first part it was his intention, he says, *to give the majestick turn of* 292
*heroick poesy*; and perhaps he might have executed his design not unsuccessfully, had not an opportunity of satire, which he cannot forbear, fallen
sometimes in his way. The character of a Presbyterian, whose emblem is the
*Wolf*, is not very heroically majestick.

More haughty than the rest, the wolfish race ⎫
Appear with belly gaunt and famish'd face: ⎬
Never was so deform'd a beast of grace. ⎭
His ragged tail betwixt his legs he wears, ⎫
Close clapp'd for shame; but his rough crest he rears, ⎬
And pricks up his predestinating ears. ⎭

His general character of the other sorts of beasts that never go to church, 293
though spritely and keen, has, however, not much of heroick poesy.

These are the chief; to number o'er the rest,
And stand like Adam naming every beast,
Were weary work; nor will the Muse describe
A slimy-born, and sun-begotten tribe;
Who, far from steeples and their sacred sound,
In fields their sullen conventicles found.
These gross, half-animated, lumps I leave;
Nor can I think what thoughts they can conceive;
But if they think at all, 'tis sure no higher
Than matter, put in motion, may aspire;
Souls that can scarce ferment their mass of clay; ⎫
So drossy, so divisible are they, ⎬
As would but serve pure bodies for allay: ⎭
Such souls as shards produce, such beetle things
As only buz to heaven with evening wings;
Strike in the dark, offending but by chance;

> Such are the blindfold blows of ignorance.
> They know not beings, and but hate a name;
> To them the Hind and Panther are the same.

294    One more instance, and that taken from the narrative part, where style was more in his choice, will show how steadily he kept his resolution of heroick dignity.

> For when the herd, suffic'd, did late repair
> To ferny heaths, and to their forest laire,
> She made a mannerly excuse to stay,
> Proffering the Hind to wait her half the way:
> That, since the sky was clear, an hour of talk
> Might help her to beguile the tedious walk.
> With much good-will the motion was embrac'd,
> To chat awhile on their adventures past:
> Nor had the grateful Hind so soon forgot
> Her friend and fellow-sufferer in the plot.
> Yet, wondering how of late she grew estrang'd,
> Her forehead cloudy and her count'nance chang'd,
> She thought this hour th' occasion would present
> To learn her secret cause of discontent,
> Which well she hop'd, might be with ease redress'd, ⎫
> Considering her a well-bred civil beast,                    ⎬
> And more a gentlewoman than the rest.                 ⎭
> After some common talk what rumours ran,
> The lady of the spotted muff began.

295    The second and third parts he professes to have reduced to diction more familiar and more suitable to dispute and conversation; the difference is not, however, very easily perceived; the first has familiar, and the two others have sonorous, lines. The original incongruity runs through the whole; the king is now *Cæsar*, and now the *Lyon*; and the name *Pan* is given to the Supreme Being.

296    But when this constitutional absurdity is forgiven, the poem must be confessed to be written with great smoothness of metre, a wide extent of knowledge, and an abundant multiplicity of images; the controversy is embellished with pointed sentences, diversified by illustrations, and enlivened by sallies of invective. Some of the facts to which allusions are made, are now become obscure, and perhaps there may be many satirical passages little understood.

297    As it was by its nature a work of defiance, a composition which would naturally be examined with the utmost acrimony of criticism, it was prob-

ably laboured with uncommon attention; and there are, indeed, few negligences in the subordinate parts. The original impropriety, and the subsequent unpopularity of the subject, added to the ridiculousness of its first
elements, has sunk it into neglect; but it may be usefully studied, as an
example of poetical ratiocination, in which the argument suffers little from
the metre.

In the poem on *the Birth of the Prince of Wales*, nothing is very remarkable   298
but the exorbitant adulation, and that insensibility of the precipice on which
the king was then standing, which the laureate apparently shared with the
rest of the courtiers. A few months cured him of controversy, dismissed him
from court, and made him again a play-wright and translator.

Of Juvenal there had been a translation by Stapylton, and another by   299
Holiday; neither of them is very poetical. Stapylton is more smooth, and
Holiday's is more esteemed for the learning of his notes. A new version was
proposed to the poets of that time, and undertaken by them in conjunction.
The main design was conducted by Dryden, whose reputation was such
that no man was unwilling to serve the Muses under him.

The general character of this translation will be given, when it is said to   300
preserve the wit, but to want the dignity of the original. The peculiarity of
Juvenal is a mixture of gaiety and stateliness, of pointed sentences and
declamatory grandeur. His points have not been neglected; but his grandeur
none of the band seemed to consider as necessary to be imitated, except
*Creech*, who undertook the thirteenth satire. It is therefore perhaps possible
to give a better representation of that great satirist, even in those parts
which Dryden himself has translated, some passages excepted, which will
never be excelled.

With Juvenal was published Persius, translated wholly by Dryden. This   301
work, though like all the other productions of Dryden it may have shining
parts, seems to have been written merely for wages, in an uniform mediocrity, without any eager endeavour after excellence, or laborious effort of
the mind.

There wanders an opinion among the readers of poetry, that one of these   302
satires is an exercise of the school. Dryden says that he once translated it at
school; but not that he preserved or published the juvenile performance.

Not long afterwards he undertook perhaps the most arduous work of its   303
kind, a translation of Virgil, for which he had shewn how well he was
qualified by his version of the Pollio, and two episodes, one of Nisus and
Euryalus, the other of Mezentius and Lausus.

In the comparison of Homer and Virgil, the discriminative excellence   304
of Homer is elevation and comprehension of thought, and that of Virgil

is grace and splendor of diction. The beauties of Homer are therefore difficult to be lost, and those of Virgil difficult to be retained. The massy trunk of sentiment is safe by its solidity, but the blossoms of elocution easily drop away. The author, having the choice of his own images, selects those which he can best adorn: the translator must, at all hazards, follow his original, and express thoughts which perhaps he would not have chosen. When to this primary difficulty is added the inconvenience of a language so much inferior in harmony to the Latin, it cannot be expected that they who read the Georgick and the Eneid should be much delighted with any version.

305     All these obstacles Dryden saw, and all these he determined to encounter. The expectation of his work was undoubtedly great; the nation considered its honour as interested in the event. One gave him the different editions of his author, and another helped him in the subordinate parts. The arguments of the several books were given him by Addison.

306     The hopes of the publick were not disappointed. He produced, says Pope, *the most noble and spirited translation that I know in any language.* It certainly excelled whatever had appeared in English, and appears to have satisfied his friends, and, for the most part, to have silenced his enemies. Milbourne, indeed, a clergyman, attacked it; but his outrages seem to be the ebullitions of a mind agitated by stronger resentment than bad poetry can excite, and previously resolved not to be pleased.

307     His criticism extends only to the Preface, Pastorals, and Georgicks; and, as he professes, to give his antagonist an opportunity of reprisal, he has added his own version of the first and fourth Pastorals, and the first Georgick. The world has forgotten his book; but since his attempt has given him a place in literary history, I will preserve a specimen of his criticism, by inserting his remarks on the invocation before the first Georgick, and of his poetry, by annexing his own version.

Ver. 1. "*What makes a plenteous harvest, when to turn, The fruitful soil, and when to sow the corn*—It's *unlucky*, they say, *to stumble at the threshold*, but what has a *plenteous harvest* to do here? *Virgil* would not pretend to prescribe *rules* for *that* which depends not on the *husbandman's* care, but the *disposition of Heaven* altogether. Indeed, the *plenteous crop* depends somewhat on the *good method of tillage*, and where the *land's* ill manur'd, the *corn*, without a miracle, can be but *indifferent*; but the *harvest* may be *good*, which is its *properest* epithet, tho' the *husbandman's skill* were never so *indifferent*. The next *sentence* is *too literal*, and *when to plough* had been *Virgil's* meaning, and intelligible to every body; and *when to sow the corn*, is a needless *addition*."

Ver. 3. "*The care of sheep, of oxen, and of kine, And when to geld the lambs, and sheer the swine*, would as well have fallen under the *cura boum, qui cultus habendo sit pecori*, as Mr. *D's deduction* of particulars."

Ver. 5. "*The birth and genius of the frugal bee, I sing*, Mæcenas, *and I sing to thee.* —But where did *experientia* ever signify *birth and genius*? or what ground was there for such a *figure* in this place? How much more manly is Mr. *Ogylby's* version!

> What makes rich grounds, in what celestial signs,
> 'Tis good to plough, and marry elms with vines.
> What best fits cattle, what with sheep agrees,
> And several arts improving frugal bees,
> I sing, *Mæcenas*.

Which four lines, tho' faulty enough, are yet much more to the purpose than Mr. *D's* six."

Ver. 22. "*From fields and mountains to my song repair*. For *patrium linquens nemus, saltusque Lycæi*—Very well explained!"

Ver. 23, 24. "*Inventor* Pallas, *of the fattening oil, Thou founder of the plough, and ploughman's toil*! Written as if *these* had been *Pallas's invention. The ploughman's toil's* impertinent."

Ver. 25. "*—The shroud-like cypress*—Why *shroud-like*? Is a *cypress* pulled up by the *roots*, which the *sculpture* in the *last Eclogue* fills *Silvanus's* hand with, so very like a *shroud*? Or did not Mr. *D.* think of that kind of *cypress* us'd often for *scarves and hatbands* at funerals formerly, or for *widow's vails*, &c. if so, 'twas a *deep good thought*."

Ver. 26. "*—That wear the royal honours, and increase the year*—What's meant by *increasing the year*? Did the *gods* or *goddesses* add more *months*, or *days*, or *hours* to it? Or how can *arva tueri*—signify to *wear rural honours*? Is this to *translate*, or *abuse* an *author*? The next *couplet* are borrow'd from *Ogylby*, I suppose, because *less to the purpose* than ordinary."

Ver 33. "*The patron of the world, and* Rome's *peculiar guard—Idle*, and none of *Virgil's*, no more than the sense of the *precedent couplet*; so again, he *interpolates Virgil* with that and *the round circle of the year to guide powerful of blessings, which thou strew'st around*. A ridiculous *Latinism*, and an *impertinent addition*; indeed the whole *period* is but one piece of *absurdity* and *nonsense*, as those who lay it with the *original* must find."

Ver. 42, 43. "*And* Neptune *shall resign the fasces of the sea*. Was he *consul* or *dictator* there? *And watry virgins for thy bed shall strive*. Both absurd *interpolations*."

Ver. 47, 48. "*Where in the void of heaven a place is free.* Ah happy *D—n,* were *that place* for thee! But where is *that void?* Or what does our *translator* mean by it? He knows what *Ovid* says *God* did, to prevent such a *void* in heaven; perhaps, this was then forgotten: but *Virgil* talks more sensibly."

Ver. 49. "*The scorpion ready to receive thy laws.* No, he would not then have *gotten out of his way* so fast."

Ver. 56. "*The Proserpine affects her silent seat*—What made *her* then so *angry* with *Ascalaphus,* for preventing her return? She was now mus'd to *Patience* under the *determinations of Fate,* rather than *fond* of her *residence.*"

Ver. 61, 2, 3. "*Pity the poet's, and the ploughman's cares, Interest thy greatness in our mean affairs. And use thyself betimes to hear our prayers.* Which is such a wretched *perversion* of *Virgil's noble thought* as *Vicars* would have blush'd at; but Mr. *Ogylby* makes us some amends, by his better lines:

> O wheresoe'er thou art, from thence incline,
> And grant assistance to my bold design!
> Pity with me, poor husbandmen's affairs,
> And now, as if translated, hear our prayers.

This is *sense,* and *to the purpose*: the other, poor *mistaken stuff.*"

308    Such were the strictures of Milbourne, who found few abettors; and of whom it may be reasonably imagined, that many who favoured his design were ashamed of his insolence.

309    When admiration had subsided, the translation was more coolly examined, and found like all others, to be sometimes erroneous, and sometimes licentious. Those who could find faults, thought they could avoid them; and Dr. Brady attempted in blank verse a translation of the Eneid, which, when dragged into the world, did not live long enough to cry. I have never seen it; but that such a version there is, or has been, perhaps some old catalogue informed me.

310    With not much better success, Trapp, when his Tragedy and his Prelections had given him reputation, attempted another blank version of the Eneid; to which, notwithstanding the slight regard with which it was treated, he had afterwards perseverance enough to add the Eclogues and Georgicks. His book may continue its existence as long as it is the clandestine refuge of schoolboys.

311    Since the English ear has been accustomed to the mellifluence of Pope's numbers, and the diction of poetry has become more splendid, new attempts have been made to translate Virgil; and all his works have been

attempted by men better qualified to contend with Dryden. I will not engage myself in an invidious comparison by opposing one passage to another; a work of which there would be no end, and which might be often offensive without use.

It is not by comparing line with line that the merit of great works is to be estimated, but by their general effects and ultimate result. It is easy to note a weak line, and write one more vigorous in its place; to find a happiness of expression in the original, and transplant it by force into the version: but what is given to the parts, may be subducted from the whole, and the reader may be weary, though the critick may commend. Works of imagination excel by their allurement and delight; by their power of attracting and detaining the attention. That book is good in vain, which the reader throws away. He only is the master, who keeps the mind in pleasing captivity; whose pages are perused with eagerness, and in hope of new pleasure are perused again; and whose conclusion is perceived with an eye of sorrow, such as the traveller casts upon departing day. 312

By his proportion of this predomination I will consent that Dryden should be tried; of this, which, in opposition to reason, makes Ariosto the darling and the pride of Italy; of this, which, in defiance of criticism, continues Shakspeare the sovereign of the drama. 313

His last work was his *Fables*, in which he gave us the first example of a mode of writing which the Italians call *refaccimento*, a renovation of ancient writers, by modernizing their language. Thus the old poem of *Boiardo* has been new-dressed by *Domenichi* and *Berni*. The works of Chaucer, upon which this kind of rejuvenescence has been bestowed by Dryden, require little criticism. The tale of the Cock seems hardly worth revival; and the story of *Palamon* and *Arcite*, containing an action unsuitable to the times in which it is placed, can hardly be suffered to pass without censure of the hyperbolical commendation which Dryden has given it in the general Preface, and in a poetical Dedidication, a piece where his original fondness of remote conceits seems to have revived. 314

Of the three pieces borrowed from Boccace, *Sigismunda* may be defended by the celebrity of the story. *Theodore* and *Honoria*, though it contains not much moral, yet afforded opportunities of striking description. And *Cymon* was formerly a tale of such reputation, that, at the revival of letters, it was translated into Latin by one of the *Beroalds*. 315

Whatever subjects employed his pen, he was still improving our measures and embellishing our language. 316

In this volume are interspersed some short original poems, which, with his prologues, epilogues, and songs, may be comprised in Congreve's 317 remark, that even those, if he had written nothing else, would have entitled him to the praise of excellence in his kind.

318      One composition must however be distinguished. The ode for *St. Cecilia's* Day, perhaps the last effort of his poetry, has been always considered as exhibiting the highest flight of fancy, and the exactest nicety of art. This is allowed to stand without a rival. If indeed there is any excellence beyond it, in some other of Dryden's works that excellence must be found. Compared with the Ode on *Killigrew*, it may be pronounced perhaps superiour in the whole; but without any single part, equal to the first stanza of the other.

319      It is said to have cost Dryden a fortnight's labour; but it does not want its negligences: some of the lines are without correspondent rhymes; a defect, which I never detected but after an acquaintance of many years, and which the enthusiasm of the writer might hinder him from perceiving.

320      His last stanza has less emotion than the former; but is not less elegant in the diction. The conclusion is vicious; the musick of *Timotheus*, which *raised a mortal to the skies*, had only a metaphorical power; that of *Cecilia*, which *drew an angel down*, had a real effect: the crown therefore could not reasonably be divided.

321      IN a general survey of Dryden's labours, he appears to have had a mind very comprehensive by nature, and much enriched with acquired knowledge. His compositions are the effects of a vigorous genius operating upon large materials.

322      The power that predominated in his intellectual operations, was rather strong reason than quick sensibility. Upon all occasions that were presented, he studied rather than felt, and produced sentiments not such as Nature enforces, but meditation supplies. With the simple and elemental passions, as they spring separate in the mind, he seems not much acquainted; and seldom describes them but as they are complicated by the various relations of society, and confused in the tumults and agitations of life.

323      What he says of love may contribute to the explanation of his character:

> Love various minds does variously inspire;
> It stirs in gentle bosoms gentle fire,
> Like that of incense on the altar laid;
> But raging flames tempestuous souls invade;
> A fire which every windy passion blows,
> With pride it mounts, or with revenge it glows.

Dryden's was not one of the *gentle bosoms*: Love, as it subsists in itself, 324
with no tendency but to the person loved, and wishing only for correspondent kindness; such love as shuts out all other interest; the Love of the
Golden Age, was too soft and subtle to put his faculties in motion. He
hardly conceived it but in its turbulent effervescence with some other
desires; when it was inflamed by rivalry, or obstructed by difficulties:
when it invigorated ambition, or exasperated revenge.

He is therefore, with all his variety of excellence, not often pathetick; and 325
had so little sensibility of the power of effusions purely natural, that he did
not esteem them in others. Simplicity gave him no pleasure; and for the first
part of his life he looked on *Otway* with contempt, though at last, indeed
very late, he confessed that in his play *there* was *Nature, which is the chief
beauty*.

We do not always know our own motives. I am not certain whether it 326
was not rather the difficulty which he found in exhibiting the genuine
operations of the heart, than a servile submission to an injudicious audience,
that filled his plays with false magnificence. It was necessary to fix attention;
and the mind can be captivated only by recollection, or by curiosity; by
reviving natural sentiments, or impressing new appearances of things:
sentences were readier at his call than images; he could more easily fill the
ear with some splendid novelty, than awaken those ideas that slumber in
the heart.

The favourite exercise of his mind was ratiocination; and, that argument 327
might not be too soon at an end, he delighted to talk of liberty and necessity,
destiny and contingence; these he discusses in the language of the school
with so much profundity, that the terms which he uses are not always
understood. It is indeed learning, but learning out of place.

When once he had engaged himself in disputation, thoughts flowed in on 328
either side: he was now no longer at a loss; he had always objections and
solutions at command; *verbaque provisam rem*—give him matter for his
verse, and he finds without difficulty verse for his matter.

In Comedy, for which he professes himself not naturally qualified, the 329
mirth which he excites will perhaps not be found so much to arise from
any original humour, or peculiarity of character nicely distinguished and
diligently pursued, as from incidents and circumstances, artifices and
surprizes; from jests of action rather than of sentiment. What he had of
humorous or passionate, he seems to have had not from nature, but from
other poets; if not always as a plagiary, at least as an imitator.

Next to argument, his delight was in wild and daring sallies of senti- 330
ment, in the irregular and excentrick violence of wit. He delighted to tread

upon the brink of meaning, where light and darkness begin to mingle;
to approach the precipice of absurdity, and hover over the abyss of unideal vacancy. This inclination sometimes produced nonsense, which he
knew; as,

> Move swiftly, sun, and fly a lover's pace,
> Leave weeks and months behind thee in thy race.
>
> Amariel flies
> To guard thee from the demons of the air;
> My flaming sword above them to display,
> All keen, and ground upon the edge of day.

And sometimes it issued in absurdities, of which perhaps he was not
conscious:

> Then we upon our orb's last verge shall go,
>     And see the ocean leaning on the sky;
> From thence our rolling neighbours we shall know,
>     And on the lunar world securely pry.

These lines have no meaning; but may we not say, in imitation of Cowley on
another book,

> 'Tis so like *sense* 'twill serve the turn as well?

331    This endeavour after the grand and the new, produced many sentiments
either great or bulky, and many images either just or splendid:

> I am as free as Nature first made man,
> Ere the base laws of servitude began,
> When wild in woods the noble savage ran.

> —'Tis but because the Living death ne'er knew,
> They fear to prove it as a thing that's new:
> Let me th' experiment before you try,
> I'll show you first how easy 'tis to die.

> —There with a forest of their darts he strove,
> And stood like *Capaneus* defying Jove;
> With his broad sword the boldest beating down,
> While Fate grew pale lest he should win the town,
> And turn'd the iron leaves of his dark book
> To make new dooms, or mend what it mistook.

> —I beg no pity for this mouldering clay;
> For if you give it burial, there it takes
> Possession of your earth;
> If burnt, and scatter'd in the air, the winds
> That strew my dust diffuse my royalty,

> And spread me o'er your clime; for where one atom
> Of mine shall light, know there Sebastian reigns.

Of these quotations the two first may be allowed to be great, the two latter only tumid.

Of such selection there is no end. I will add only a few more passages; of     332
which the first, though it may perhaps not be quite clear in prose, is not too obscure for poetry, as the meaning that it has is noble:

> No, there is a necessity in Fate,
> Why still the brave bold man is fortunate;
> He keeps his object ever full in sight,
> And that assurance holds him firm and right;
> True, 'tis a narrow way that leads to bliss,
> But right before there is no precipice;
> Fear makes men look aside, and so their footing miss.

Of the images which the two following citations afford, the first is elegant,     333
the second magnificent; whether either be just, let the reader judge:

> What precious drops are these,
> Which silently each other's track pursue,
> Bright as young diamonds in their infant dew?
>
>                                    —Resign your castle—
> —Enter, brave Sir; for when you speak the word,
> The gates shall open of their own accord;
> The genius of the place its Lord shall meet,
> And bow its towery forehead at your feet.

These bursts of extravagance, Dryden calls the *Dalilahs* of the Theatre;     334
and owns that many noisy lines of Maximin and Almanzor call out for vengeance upon him; but I *knew*, says he, *that they were bad enough to please, even when I wrote them.* There is surely reason to suspect that he pleased himself as well as his audience; and that these, like the harlots of other men, had his love, though not his approbation.

He had sometimes faults of a less generous and splendid kind. He makes,     335
like almost all other poets, very frequent use of mythology, and sometimes connects religion and fable too closely without distinction.

He descends to display his knowledge with pedantick ostentation; as     336
when, in translating Virgil, he says, *tack to the larboard*—and *veer starboard*; and talks, in another work, of *virtue spooming before the wind.* His vanity now and then betrays his ignorance:

> They Nature's king through Nature's opticks view'd;
> Revers'd they view'd him lessen'd to their eyes.

He had heard of reversing a telescope, and unluckily reverses the object.

337    He is sometimes unexpectedly mean. When he describes the Supreme Being as moved by prayer to stop the Fire of London, what is his expression?

> A hollow crystal pyramid he takes,
>     In firmamental waters dipp'd above,
> Of this a broad *extinguisher* he makes,
>     And *hoods* the flames that to their quarry strove.

When he describes the Last Day, and the decisive tribunal, he intermingles this image:

> When rattling bones together fly,
> From the four quarters of the sky.

338    It was indeed never in his power to resist the temptation of a jest. In his Elegy on Cromwell:

> No sooner was the Frenchman's cause embrac'd,
> Than the *light Monsieur* the *grave Don* outweigh'd;
> His fortune turn'd the scale—

339    He had a vanity, unworthy of his abilities, to shew, as may be suspected, the rank of the company with whom he lived, by the use of French words, which had then crept into conversation; such as *fraicheur* for *coolness, fougue* for *turbulence*, and a few more, none of which the language has incorporated or retained. They continue only where they stood first, perpetual warnings to future innovators.

340    These are his faults of affectation; his faults of negligence are beyond recital. Such is the unevenness of his compositions, that ten lines are seldom found together without something of which the reader is ashamed. Dryden was no rigid judge of his own pages; he seldom struggled after supreme excellence, but snatched in haste what was within his reach; and when he could content others, was himself contented. He did not keep present to his mind, an idea of pure perfection; nor compare his works, such as they were, with what they might be made. He knew to whom he should be opposed. He had more musick than Waller, more vigour than Denham, and more nature than Cowley; and from his contemporaries he was in no danger. Standing therefore in the highest place, he had no care to rise by contending with himself; but while there was no name above his own, was willing to enjoy fame on the easiest terms.

341    He was no lover of labour. What he thought sufficient, he did not stop to make better; and allowed himself to leave many parts unfinished, in confi-

dence that the good lines would overbalance the bad. What he had once written, he dismissed from his thoughts; and, I believe, there is no example to be found of any correction or improvement made by him after publication. The hastiness of his productions might be the effect of necessity; but his subsequent neglect could hardly have any other cause than impatience of study.

What can be said of his versification, will be little more than a dilatation of the praise given it by Pope. 342

> Waller was smooth; but Dryden taught to join  
> The varying verse, the full-resounding line,  
> The long majestick march, and energy divine.

Some improvements had been already made in English numbers; but the full force of our language was not yet felt; the verse that was smooth was commonly feeble. If Cowley had sometimes a finished line, he had it by chance. Dryden knew how to chuse the flowing and the sonorous words; to vary the pauses, and adjust the accents; to diversify the cadence, and yet preserve the smoothness of his metre. 343

Of Triplets and Alexandrines, though he did not introduce the use, he established it. The triplet has long subsisted among us. Dryden seems not to have traced it higher than to Chapman's Homer; but it is to be found in Phaer's Virgil, written in the reign of Mary, and in Hall's Satires, published five years before the death of Elizabeth. 344

The Alexandrine was, I believe, first used by Spenser, for the sake of closing his stanza with a fuller sound. We had a longer measure of fourteen syllables, into which the Eneid was translated by Phaer, and other works of the ancients by other writers; of which Chapman's Iliad was, I believe, the last. 345

The two first lines of *Phaer*'s third Eneid will exemplify this measure: 346

> When Asia's state was overthrown, and Priam's kingdom stout,  
> All giltless, by the power of gods above was rooted out.

As these lines had their break, or *cæsura*, always at the eighth syllable, it was thought, in time, commodious to divide them; and quatrains of lines, alternately consisting of eight and six syllables, make the most soft and pleasing of our lyrick measures; as, 347

> Relentless Time, destroying power,  
> Which stone and brass obey,  
> Who giv'st to every flying hour  
> To work some new decay.

348     In the Alexandrine, when its power was once felt, some poems, as *Drayton's Polyolbion*, were wholly written; and sometimes the measures of twelve and fourteen syllables were interchanged with one another. Cowley was the first that inserted the Alexandrine at pleasure among the heroick lines of ten syllables, and from him Dryden professes to have adopted it.

349     The Triplet and Alexandrine are not universally approved. *Swift* always censured them, and wrote some lines to ridicule them. In examining their propriety, it is to be considered that the essence of verse is regularity, and its ornament is variety. To write verse, is to dispose syllables and sounds harmonically by some known and settled rule; a rule however lax enough to substitute similitude for identity, to admit change without breach of order, and to relieve the ear without disappointing it. Thus a Latin hexameter is formed from dactyls and spondees differently combined; the English heroick admits of acute or grave syllables variously disposed. The Latin never deviates into seven feet, or exceeds the number of seventeen syllables; but the English Alexandrine breaks the lawful bounds, and surprises the reader with two syllables more than he expected.

350     The effect of the Triplet is the same: the ear has been accustomed to expect a new rhyme in every couplet; but is on a sudden surprized with three rhymes together, to which the reader could not accommodate his voice, did he not obtain notice of the change from the braces of the margins. Surely there is something unskilful in the necessity of such mechanical direction.

351     Considering the metrical art simply as a science, and consequently excluding all casualty, we must allow that Triplets and Alexandrines, inserted by caprice, are interruptions of that constancy to which science aspires. And though the variety which they produce may very justly be desired, yet to make our poetry exact, there ought to be some stated mode of admitting them.

352     But till some such regulation can be formed, I wish them still to be retained in their present state. They are sometimes grateful to the reader, and sometimes convenient to the poet. *Fenton* was of opinion that Dryden was too liberal and Pope too sparing in their use.

353     The rhymes of Dryden are commonly just, and he valued himself for his readiness in finding them; but he is sometimes open to objection.

354     It is the common practice of our poets to end the second line with a weak or grave syllable:

>           Together o'er the Alps methinks we fly,
>           Fill'd with ideas of fair *Italy*.

Dryden sometimes puts the weak rhyme in the first:

> Laugh all the powers that favour *tyranny*,
> And all the standing army of the sky.

Sometimes he concludes a period or paragraph with the first line of a 354*a*
couplet, which, though the French seem to do it without irregularity,
always displeases in English poetry.

The Alexandrine, though much his favourite, is not always very dili- 355
gently fabricated by him. It invariably requires a break at the sixth syllable;
a rule which the modern French poets never violate, but which Dryden
sometimes neglected:

> And with paternal thunder vindicates his throne.

Of Dryden's works it was said by Pope, that *he could select from them better* 356
*specimens of every mode of poetry than any other English writer could supply.*
Perhaps no nation ever produced a writer that enriched his language with
such variety of models. To him we owe the improvement, perhaps the
completion of our metre, the refinement of our language, and much of the
correctness of our sentiments. By him we were taught *sapere & fari*, to think
naturally and express forcibly. Though Davis has reasoned in rhyme before
him, it may be perhaps maintained that he was the first who joined
argument with poetry. He shewed us the true bounds of a translator's
liberty. What was said of Rome, adorned by Augustus, may be applied by
an easy metaphor to English poetry embellished by Dryden, *lateritiam*
*invenit, marmoream reliquit*, he found it brick, and he left it marble.

THE invocation before the Georgicks is here inserted from 357
Mr. Milbourne's version, that, according to his own proposal, his verses
may be compared with those which he censures.

> What makes the richest *tilth*, beneath what signs
> To *plough*, and when to match your *elms* and *vines*;
> What care with *flocks* and what with *herds* agrees,
> And all the management of frugal *bees*,
> I sing, *Mæcenas!* Ye immensely clear,
> Vast orbs of light which guide the rolling year;
> *Bacchus*, and mother *Ceres*, if by you
> We fat'ning *corn* for hungry *mast* pursue,
> If, taught by you, we first the *cluster* prest,
> And *thin cold streams* with *spritely juice* refresht.
> Ye *fawns* the present *numens* of the field,
> *Woodnymphs* and *fawns* your kind assistance yield,

Your gifts I sing! and thou, at whose fear'd stroke
From rending earth the fiery *courser* broke,
Great *Neptune*, O assist my artful song!
And thou to whom the woods and groves belong,
Whose snowy heifers on her flow'ry plains
In mighty herds the *Cæan Isle* maintains!
*Pan*, happy shepherd, if thy cares divine,
E'er to improve thy *Mænalus* incline;
Leave thy *Lycæan wood* and *native grove*,
And with thy lucky smiles our work approve!
Be *Pallas* too, sweet oil's inventor, kind;
And he, who first the crooked *plough* design'd!
*Sylvanus*, god of all the woods appear,
Whose hands a new drawn tender *cypress* bear!
Ye *gods* and *goddesses* who e'er with love,
Would guard our pastures, and our fields improve!
You, who new plants from unsown lands supply;
And with condensing clouds obscure the sky,
And drop 'em softly thence in fruitful showers,
Assist my enterprize, ye gentler powers!

And thou, great *Cæsar!* though we know not yet
Among what gods thou'lt fix thy lofty seat,
Whether thou'lt be the kind *tutelar god*
Of thy own *Rome*; or with thy awful nod,
Guide the vast world, while thy great hand shall bear ⎫
The fruits and seasons of the turning year, ⎬
And thy bright brows thy mother's myrtles wear: ⎭
Whether thou'lt all the boundless ocean sway,
And sea-men only to thyself shall pray,
*Thule*, the farthest island, kneel to thee,
And, that thou may'st her son by marriage be,
*Tethys* will for the happy purchase yield
To make a *dowry* of her watry field;
Whether thou'lt add to heaven a *brighter sign*,
And o'er the *summer months* serenely shine;
Where between *Cancer* and *Erigone*,
There yet remains a spacious *room* for thee.
Where the hot *Scorpion* too his arms declines,
And more to thee than half his *arch* resigns;
Whate'er thou'lt be; for sure the realms below
No just pretence to thy command can show:
No such ambition sways thy vast desires,
Though *Greece* her own *Elysian fields* admires.
And now, at last, contented *Proserpine*

Can all her mother's earnest prayers decline.
Whate'er thou'lt be, O guide our gentle course,
And with thy smiles our bold attempts enforce;
With me th' unknowing *rustics'* wants relieve,
And, though on earth, our sacred vows receive!

MR. DRYDEN, having received from Rymer his *Remarks on the Tragedies* 358
*of the last Age,* wrote observations on the blank leaves; which, having been in
the possession of Mr. Garrick, are by his favour communicated to the
publick, that no particle of Dryden may be lost.

"That we may the less wonder why pity and terror are not now the only 359
springs on which our tragedies move, and that Shakspeare may be more
excused, Rapin confesses that the French tragedies now all run on the
*tendre*; and gives the reason, because love is the passion which most
predominates in our souls, and that therefore the passions represented
become insipid, unless they are conformable to the thoughts of the audience. But it is to be concluded that this passion works not now amongst the
French so strongly as the other two did amongst the ancients. Amongst us,
who have a stronger genius for writing, the operations from the writing are
much stronger: for the raising of Shakspeare's passions is more from the
excellency of the words and thoughts, than the justness of the occasion; and
if he has been able to pick single occasions, he has never founded the whole
reasonably: yet, by the genius of poetry in writing, he has succeeded.

"Rapin attributes more to the *dictio*, that is, to the words and discourse of 360
a tragedy, than Aristotle has done, who places them in the last rank of
beauties; perhaps, only last in order, because they are the last product of the
design, of the disposition or connection of its parts; of the characters, of
the manners of those characters, and of the thoughts proceeding from those
manners. Rapin's words are remarkable: 'Tis not the admirable intrigue, the
surprising events, and extraordinary incidents, that make the beauty of a
tragedy; 'tis the discourses, when they are natural and passionate: so are
Shakspeare's.

"The parts of a poem, tragick or heroick, are,                          361

"1. The fable itself.

"2. The order or manner of its contrivance, in relation of the parts to the
whole.

"3. The manners, or decency of the characters, in speaking or acting what
is proper for them, and proper to be shewn by the poet.

"4. The thoughts which express the manners.

"5. The words which express those thoughts.

362 "In the last of these, Homer excels Virgil; Virgil all other ancient poets; and Shakspeare all modern poets.

363 "For the second of these, the order: the meaning is, that a fable ought to have a beginning, middle, and an end, all just and natural: so that that part, e. g. which is the middle, could not naturally be the beginning or end, and so of the rest: all depend on one another, like the links of a curious chain. If terror and pity are only to be raised, certainly this author follows Aristotle's rules, and Sophocles' and Euripides's example: but joy may be raised too, and that doubly; either by seeing a wicked man punished, or a good man at last fortunate; or perhaps indignation, to see wickedness prosperous and goodness depressed: both these may be profitable to the end of tragedy, reformation of manners; but the last improperly, only as it begets pity in the audience: though Aristotle, I confess, places tragedies of this kind in the second form.

364 "He who undertakes to answer this excellent critique of Mr. Rymer, in behalf of our English poets against the Greek, ought to do it in this manner. Either by yielding to him the greatest part of what he contends for, which consists in this, that the μύθος, i. e. the design and conduct of it, is more conducing in the Greeks to those ends of tragedy, which Aristotle and he propose, namely, to cause terror and pity; yet the granting this does not set the Greeks above the English poets.

365 "But the answerer ought to prove two things: first, that the fable is not the greatest master-piece of a tragedy, though it be the foundation of it.

365a "Secondly, That other ends as suitable to the nature of tragedy may be found in the English, which were not in the Greek.

366 "Aristotle places the fable first; not *quoad dignitatem, sed quoad funda-mentum:* for a fable, never so movingly contrived to those ends of his, pity and terror, will operate nothing on our affections, except the characters, manners, thoughts, and words are suitable.

367 "So that it remains for Mr. Rymer to prove, that in all those, or the greatest part of them, we are inferior to Sophocles and Euripides: and this he has offered at, in some measure; but, I think, a little partially to the ancients.

368 "For the fable itself; 'tis in the English more adorned with episodes, and larger than in the Greek poets; consequently more diverting. For, if the action be but one, and that plain, without any counterturn of design or episode, *i.e.* under-plot, how can it be so pleasing as the English, which have both under-plot and a turned design, which keeps the audience in expect-ation of the catastrophe? whereas in the Greek poets we see through the whole design at first.

"For the characters, they are neither so many nor so various in Sophocles 369
and Euripides, as in Shakspeare and Fletcher; only they are more adapted to
those ends of tragedy which Aristotle commends to us, pity and terror.

"The manners flow from the characters, and consequently must partake 370
of their advantages and disadvantages.

"The thoughts and words, which are the fourth and fifth beauties of 371
tragedy, are certainly more noble and more poetical in the English than in
the Greek, which must be proved by comparing them, somewhat more
equitably than Mr. Rymer has done.

"After all, we need not yield that the English way is less conducing to 372
move pity and terror, because they often shew virtue oppressed and vice
punished: where they do not both, or either, they are not to be defended.

"And if we should grant that the Greeks performed this better, perhaps it 373
may admit of dispute, whether pity and terror are either the prime, or at
least the only ends of tragedy.

"'Tis not enough that Aristotle has said so; for Aristotle drew his models 374
of tragedy from Sophocles and Euripides; and, if he had seen ours, might
have changed his mind. And chiefly we have to say (what I hinted on pity
and terror, in the last paragraph save one), that the punishment of vice and
reward of virtue are the most adequate ends of tragedy, because most
conducing to good example of life. Now pity is not so easily raised for a
criminal, and the ancient tragedy always represents its chief person such, as
it is for an innocent man; and the suffering of innocence and punishment of
the offender is of the nature of English tragedy: contrarily, in the Greek,
innocence is unhappy often, and the offender escapes. Then we are not
touched with the sufferings of any sort of men so much as of lovers; and this
was almost unknown to the ancients: so that they neither administered
poetical justice, of which Mr. Rymer boasts, so well as we; neither knew
they the best common-place of pity, which is love.

"He therefore unjustly blames us for not building on what the ancients 375
left us; for it seems, upon consideration of the premises, that we have wholly
finished what they began.

"My judgement on this piece is this, that it is extremely learned; but that 376
the author of it is better read in the Greek than in the English poets: that all
writers ought to study this critique, as the best account I have ever seen of
the ancients: that the model of tragedy he has here given, is excellent, and
extreme correct; but that it is not the only model of all tragedy, because it is
too much circumscribed in plot, characters, &c.; and lastly, that we may be
taught here justly to admire and imitate the ancients, without giving them
the preference with this author, in prejudice to our own country.

377     "Want of method in this excellent treatise, makes the thoughts of the author sometimes obscure.

378     "His meaning, that pity and terror are to be moved, is, that they are to be moved as the means conducing to the ends of tragedy, which are pleasure and instruction.

379     "And these two ends may be thus distinguished. The chief end of the poet is to please; for his immediate reputation depends on it.

380     "The great end of the poem is to instruct, which is performed by making pleasure the vehicle of that instruction; for poesy is an art, and all arts are made to profit. *Rapin.*

381     "The pity, which the poet is to labour for, is for the criminal, not for those or him whom he has murdered, or who have been the occasion of the tragedy. The terror is likewise in the punishment of the same criminal; who, if he be represented too great an offender, will not be pitied: if altogether innocent, his punishment will be unjust.

382     "Another obscurity is, where he says Sophocles perfected tragedy by introducing the third actor; that is, he meant, three kinds of action; one company singing, or another playing on the musick; a third dancing.

383     "To make a true judgement in this competition betwixt the Greek poets and the English, in tragedy:

383a    "Consider, first, how Aristotle has defined a tragedy. Secondly, what he assigns the end of it to be. Thirdly, what he thinks the beauties of it. Fourthly, the means to attain the end proposed.

384     "Compare the Greek and English tragick poets justly, and without partiality, according to those rules.

385     "Then secondly, consider whether Aristotle has made a just definition of tragedy; of its parts, of its ends, and of its beauties; and whether he, having not seen any others but those of Sophocles, Euripides, &c. had or truly could determine what all the excellences of tragedy are, and wherein they consist.

386     "Next shew in what ancient tragedy was deficient: for example, in the narrowness of its plots, and fewness of persons, and try whether that be not a fault in the Greek poets; and whether their excellency was so great, when the variety was visibly so little; or whether what they did was not very easy to do.

387     "Then make a judgement on what the English have added to their beauties: as, for example, not only more plot, but also new passions; as, namely, that of love, scarce touched on by the ancients, except in this one example of Phædra, cited by Mr. Rymer; and in that how short they were of Fletcher!

"Prove also that love, being an heroick passion, is fit for tragedy, which   388
cannot be denied, because of the example alledged of Phædra; and how far
Shakspeare has outdone them in friendship, &c.

"To return to the beginning of this enquiry; consider if pity and terror   389
be enough for tragedy to move: and I believe, upon a true definition of
tragedy, it will be found that its work extends farther, and that it is to
reform manners, by a delightful representation of human life in great
persons, by way of dialogue. If this be true, then not only pity and terror
are to be moved, as the only means to bring us to virtue, but generally
love to virtue and hatred to vice; by shewing the rewards of one, and
punishments of the other; at least, by rendering virtue always amiable,
tho' it be shewn unfortunate; and vice detestable, though it be shewn
triumphant.

"If, then, the encouragement of virtue and discouragement of vice be the   390
proper ends of poetry in tragedy, pity and terror, though good means, are
not the only. For all the passions, in their turns, are to be set in a ferment: as
joy, anger, love, fear, are to be used as the poet's common-places; and a
general concernment for the principal actors is to be raised, by making them
appear such in their characters, their words, and actions, as will interest the
audience in their fortunes.

"And if, after all, in a larger sense, pity comprehends this concernment   391
for the good, and terror includes detestation for the bad, then let us consider
whether the English have not answered this end of tragedy, as well as the
ancients, or perhaps better.

"And here Mr. Rymer's objections against these plays are to be impar-   392
tially weighed, that we may see whether they are of weight enough to turn
the balance against our countrymen.

"'Tis evident those plays, which he arraigns, have moved both those   393
passions in a high degree upon the stage.

"To give the glory of this away from the poet, and to place it upon the   394
actors, seems unjust.

"One reason is, because whatever actors they have found, the event has   395
been the same; that is, the same passions have been always moved: which
shews, that there is something of force and merit in the plays themselves,
conducing to the design of raising these two passions: and suppose them
ever to have been excellently acted, yet action only adds grace, vigour, and
more life, upon the stage; but cannot give it wholly where it is not first. But
secondly, I dare appeal to those who have never seen them acted, if they
have not found these two passions moved within them: and if the general
voice will carry it, Mr. Rymer's prejudice will take off his single testimony.

396     "This, being matter of fact, is reasonably to be established by this appeal;
as if one man says 'tis night, the rest of the world conclude it to be day; there
needs no farther argument against him, that it is so.

397     "If he urge, that the general taste is depraved, his arguments to prove this
can at best but evince that our poets took not the best way to raise those
passions; but experience proves against him, that these means, which they
have used, have been successful, and have produced them.

398     "And one reason of that success is, in my opinion, this, that Shakspeare
and Fletcher have written to the genius of the age and nation in which they
lived; for though nature, as he objects, is the same in all places, and reason
too the same; yet the climate, the age, the disposition of the people, to whom
a poet writes, may be so different, that what pleased the Greeks would not
satisfy an English audience.

399     "And if they proceeded upon a foundation of truer reason to please the
Athenians than Shakspeare and Fletcher to please the English, it only shews
that the Athenians were a more judicious people; but the poet's business is
certainly to please the audience.

400     "Whether our English audience have been pleased hitherto with acorns,
as he calls it, or with bread, is the next question; that is, whether the means
which Shakspeare and Fletcher have used in their plays to raise those
passions before named, be better applied to the ends by the Greek poets
than by them. And perhaps we shall not grant him this wholly: let it be
granted that a writer is not to run down with the stream, or to please the
people by their own usual methods, but rather to reform their judgements,
it still remains to prove that our theatre needs this total reformation.

401     "The faults, which he has found in their designs, are rather wittily
aggravated in many places than reasonably urged; and as much may be
returned on the Greeks, by one who were as witty as himself.

402     "2. They destroy not, if they are granted, the foundation of the fabrick;
only take away from the beauty of the symmetry: for example, the faults in
the character of the King and No-king are not as he makes them, such as
render him detestable, but only imperfections which accompany human
nature, and are for the most part excused by the violence of his love; so that
they destroy not our pity or concernment for him: this answer may be
applied to most of his objections of that kind.

403     "And Rollo committing many murders, when he is answerable but for
one, is too severely arraigned by him; for it adds to our horror and
detestation of the criminal: and poetick justice is not neglected neither;
for we stab him in our minds for every offence which he commits; and the
point, which the poet is to gain on the audience, is not so much in the death
of an offender as the raising an horror of his crimes.

"That the criminal should neither be wholly guilty, nor wholly innocent, 404
but so participating of both as to move both pity and terror, is certainly a
good rule, but not perpetually to be observed; for that were to make all
tragedies too much alike, which objection he foresaw, but has not fully
answered.

"To conclude, therefore; if the plays of the ancients are more correctly 405
plotted; ours are more beautifully written. And if we can raise passions as
high on worse foundations, it shews our genius in tragedy is greater; for, in
all other parts of it, the English have manifestly excelled them."

THE original of the following letter is preserved in the Library at Lam- 406
beth, and was kindly imparted to the publick by the reverend Dr. Vyse.

Copy of an original Letter from John Dryden, Esq; to his sons in Italy, from
a MS in the Lambeth Library, marked N° 933. p. 56.
*(Superscribed)*

Al Illustrissimo Sig<sup>re</sup>
Carlo Dryden Camariere
d'Honore A. S. S.

In Roma.

Franca per Mantoua.
"Sept. the 3d, our style.

"Dear Sons,
"Being now at Sir William Bowyer's in the country, I cannot write at
large, because I find myself somewhat indisposed with a cold, and am thick
of hearing, rather worse than I was in town. I am glad to find, by your letter
of July 26th, your style, that you are both in health; but wonder you should
think me so negligent as to forget to give you an account of the ship in which
your parcel is to come. I have written to you two or three letters concerning
it, which I have sent by safe hands, as I told you, and doubt not but you have
them before this can arrive to you. Being out of town, I have forgotten the
ship's name, which your mother will enquire, and put it into her letter,
which is joined with mine. But the master's name I remember: he is called
Mr. Ralph Thorp; the ship is bound to Leghorn, consigned to Mr. Peter
and Mr. Tho. Ball, merchants. I am of your opinion, that by Tonson's
means almost all our letters have miscarried for this last year. But, however,
he has missed of his design in the Dedication, though he had prepared the
book for it; for in every figure of Eneas he has caused him to be drawn like
King William, with a hooked nose. After my return to town, I intend to alter
a play of Sir Robert Howard's, written long since, and lately put by him into

my hands: 'tis called *The Conquest of China by the Tartars*. It will cost me six weeks study, with the probable benefit of an hundred pounds. In the mean time I am writing a song for St. Cecilia's Feast, who, you know, is the patroness of musick. This is troublesome, and no way beneficial; but I could not deny the Stewards of the Feast, who came in a body to me to desire that kindness, one of them being Mr. Bridgman, whose parents are your mother's friends. I hope to send you thirty guineas between Michaelmass and Christmass, of which I will give you an account when I come to town. I remember the counsel you give me in your letter; but dissembling, though lawful in some cases, is not my talent; yet, for your sake, I will struggle with the plain openness of my nature, and keep-in my just resentments against that degenerate order. In the mean time, I flatter not myself with any manner of hopes, but do my duty, and suffer for God's sake; being assured, beforehand, never to be rewarded, though the times should alter. Towards the latter end of this month, September, Charles will begin to recover his perfect health, according to his nativity, which, casting it myself, I am sure is true, and all things hitherto have happened accordingly to the very time that I predicted them: I hope at the same time to recover more health, according to my age. Remember me to poor Harry, whose prayers I earnestly desire. My Virgil succeeds in the world beyond its desert or my expectation. You know the profits might have been more; but neither my conscience nor my honour would suffer me to take them; but I never can repent of my constancy, since I am thoroughly persuaded of the justice of the cause for which I suffer. It has pleased God to raise up many friends to me amongst my enemies, though they who ought to have been my friends are negligent of me. I am called to dinner, and cannot go on with this letter, which I desire you to excuse; and am

"Your most affectionate father,

"JOHN DRYDEN."

# SMITH

EDMUND SMITH is one of those lucky writers who have, without much ₁
labour, attained high reputation, and who are mentioned with reverence
rather for the possession than the exertion of uncommon abilities.

Of his life little is known; and that little claims no praise but what can be ₂
given to intellectual excellence, seldom employed to any virtuous purpose.
His character, as given by Mr. Oldisworth, with all the partiality of friendship, which is said by Dr. Burton to show *what fine things one man of parts
can say of another*; and which, however, comprises great part of what can
be known of Mr. Smith, it is better to transcribe at once, than to take by
pieces. I shall subjoin such little memorials as accident has enabled me
to collect.

Mr. EDMUND SMITH was the only son of an eminent merchant, one ₃
Mr. Neale, by a daughter of the famous baron Lechmere. Some misfortunes
of his father, which were soon after followed by his death, were the occasion
of the son's being left very young in the hands of a near relation (one who
married Mr. Neale's sister) whose name was Smith.

This gentleman and his lady treated him as their own child, and put him ₄
to Westminster-school under the care of Dr. Busby; whence after the loss of
his faithful and generous guardian (whose name he assumed and retained)
he was removed to Christ-church in Oxford, and there by his aunt hand-
somely maintained till her death; after which he continued a member of that
learned and ingenious society, till within five years of his own; though, some
time before his leaving Christ-church, he was sent for by his mother to
Worcester, and owned and acknowledged as her legitimate son; which had
not been mentioned, but to wipe off the aspersions that were ignorantly cast
by some on his birth. It is to be remembered for our author's honour, that,
when at Westminster election he stood a candidate for one of the universities, he so signally distinguished himself by his conspicuous performances, that there arose no small contention between the representative
electors of Trinity-college in Cambridge and Christ-church in Oxon,
which of those two royal societies should adopt him as their own. But the
electors of Trinity-college having the preference of choice that year, they
resolutely elected him; who yet, being invited at the same time to Christ-
church, chose to accept of a studentship there. Mr. Smith's perfections, as

well natural as acquired, seem to have been formed upon Horace's plan;
who says in his Art of Poetry,

> "—Ego nec studium sine divite venâ,
> Nec rude quid prosit video ingenium: alterius sic
> Altera poscit opem res, & conjurat amice."

5     He was endowed by Nature with all those excellent and necessary
qualifications which are previous to the accomplishment of a great man.
His memory was large and tenacious, yet, by a *curious felicity* chiefly
susceptible of the finest impressions, it received from the best authors he
read, which it always preserved in their primitive strength and amiable
order.

6     He had a quickness of apprehension, and vivacity of understanding,
which easily took in and surmounted the most subtle and knotty parts of
mathematicks and metaphysicks. His wit was prompt and flowing, yet solid
and piercing; his taste delicate, his head clear, and his way of expressing his
thoughts perspicuous and engaging. I shall say nothing of his person, which
yet was so well *turned*, that no neglect of himself in his dress could render it
disagreeable; insomuch that the fair sex, who observed and esteemed him, at
once commended and reproved him by the name of the *handsome* sloven. An
eager but generous and noble emulation grew up with him; which (as it were
a rational sort of instinct) pushed him upon striving to excel in every art and
science that could make him a credit to his college, and that college the
ornament of the most learned and polite university; and it was his happiness
to have several contemporaries and fellow-students who exercised and
excited this virtue in themselves and others, thereby becoming so deservedly in favour with this age, and so good a proof of its nice discernment.
His judgement, naturally good, soon ripened into an exquisite fineness and
distinguishing sagacity, which as it was active and busy, so it was vigorous
and manly, keeping even paces with a rich and strong imagination, always
upon the wing, and never tired with aspiring. Hence it was, that, though he
writ as young as Cowley, he had no puerilities; and his earliest productions
were so far from having any thing in them mean and trifling, that, like the
junior compositions of Mr. Stepney, they may make grey authors blush.
There are many of his first essays in oratory, in epigram, elegy, and epique,
still handed about the university in manuscript, which shew a masterly
hand; and, though maimed and injured by frequent transcribing, make their
way into our most celebrated miscellanies, where they shine with uncommon lustre. Besides those verses in the Oxford books, which he could not
help setting his name to, several of his compositions came abroad under
other names, which his own singular modesty, and faithful silence, strove in

vain to conceal. The Encœnia and public Collections of the University upon State Subjects, were never in such esteem, either for elegy or congratulation, as when he contributed most largely to them; and it was natural for those who knew his peculiar way of writing, to turn to his share in the work, as by far the most relishing part of the entertainment. As his parts were extraordinary, so he well knew how to improve them; and not only to polish the diamond, but enchase it in the most solid and durable metal. Though he was an academick the greatest part of his life, yet he contracted no sourness of temper, no spice of pedantry, no itch of disputation, or obstinate contention for the old or new philosophy, no assuming way of dictating to others; which are faults (though excusable) which some are insensibly led into, who are constrained to dwell long within the walls of a private college. His conversation was pleasant and instructive; and what Horace said of Plotius, Varius, and Virgil, might justly be applied to him:

"Nil ego contulerim jucundo sanus Amico."
                    Sat. v. l. 1.

As correct a writer as he was in his most elaborate pieces, he read the 7 works of other with candor, and reserved his greatest severity for his own compositions; being readier to cherish and advance, than damp or depress a rising genius, and as patient of being excelled himself (if any could excel him) as industrious to excel others.

'Twere to be wished he had confined himself to a particular profession, 8 who was capable of surpassing in any; but in this, his want of application was in a great measure owing to his want of due encouragement.

He passed through the exercises of the college and university with 9 unusual applause; and though he often suffered his friends to call him off from his retirements, and to lengthen out those jovial avocations, yet his return to his studies was so much the more passionate, and his intention upon those refined pleasures of reading and thinking so vehement (to which his facetious and unbended intervals bore no proportion) that the habit grew upon him, and the series of meditation and reflection being kept up whole weeks together, he could better sort his ideas, and take in the sundry parts of a science at one view, without interruption or confusion. Some indeed of his acquaintance, who were pleased to distinguish between the wit and the scholar, extolled him altogether on the account of the first of these titles; but others, who knew him better, could not forbear doing him justice as a prodigy in both kinds. He had signalized himself in the schools, as a philosopher and polemick of extensive knowledge and deep penetration; and went through all the courses with a wise regard to the dignity and importance of each science. I remember him in the Divinity-school responding and disputing with a perspicuous energy, a ready exactness, and commanding force of argument, when Dr. Jane worthily presided in the chair; whose condescending and disinterested commendation of him, gave him such a reputation as silenced the envious malice of his enemies, who durst not contradict the approbation of so profound a master in theology. None of those self-sufficient creatures, who have either trifled with philosophy, by attempting to ridicule it, or have encumbered it with novel terms, and burdensome explanations, understood its real weight and purity half so well as Mr. Smith. He was too discerning to allow of the character of unprofitable, rugged, and abstruse, which some superficial sciolists (so very smooth and polite as to admit of no impression), either out of an unthinking indolence, or an ill-grounded prejudice, had affixed to this sort of studies. He knew the thorny terms of philosophy served well to fence-in the true doctrines of religion; and looked upon school-divinity as upon a rough but well-wrought armour, which might at once adorn and defend the Christian hero, and equip him for the combat.

10 Mr. Smith had a long and perfect intimacy with all the Greek and Latin Classicks; with whom he had carefully compared whatever was worth perusing in the French, Spanish, and Italian (to which languages he was no stranger), and in all the celebrated writers of his own country. But then, according to the curious observation of the late earl of Shaftesbury, he kept the poet in awe by regular criticism, and as it were, married the two arts for their mutual support and improvement. There was not a tract of credit, upon that subject, which he had not diligently examined, from Aristotle down to Hedelin and Bossû; so that, having each rule constantly before him, he could carry the art through every poem, and at once point out the graces and deformities. By this means he seemed to read with a design to correct, as well as imitate.

11 Being thus prepared, he could not but taste every little delicacy that was set before him; though it was impossible for him at the same time to be fed and nourished with any thing but what was substantial and lasting. He considered the ancients and moderns not as parties or rivals for fame, but as architects upon one and the same plan, the Art of Poetry; according to which he judged, approved, and blamed, without flattery or detraction. If he did not always commend the compositions of others, it was not ill-nature (which was not in his temper) but strict justice that would not let him call a few flowers set in ranks, a glib measure, and so many couplets by the name of poetry: he was of Ben Jonson's opinion, who could not admire,

—Verses as smooth and soft as cream,
In which there was neither depth nor stream.

And therefore, though his want of complaisance for some men's over- 12
bearing vanity made him enemies, yet the better part of mankind were
obliged by the freedom of his reflections.

His Bodleian Speech, though taken from a remote and imperfect copy, 13
hath shewn the world how great a master he was of the Ciceronian
eloquence, mixed with the conciseness and force of Demosthenes, the
elegant and moving turns of Pliny, and the acute and wise reflections of
Tacitus.

Since Temple and Roscommon, no man understood Horace better, 14
especially as to his happy diction, rolling numbers, beautiful imagery, and
alternate mixture of the soft and the sublime. This endeared Dr. Hannes's
odes to him, the finest genius for Latin lyrick since the Augustan Age. His
friend Mr. Philips's ode to Mr. St. John (late Lord Bolingbroke) after the
manner of Horace's Lusory or Amatorian Odes, is certainly a master-piece:
but Mr. Smith's Pocockius is of the sublimer kind, though, like Waller's
writings upon Oliver Cromwell, it wants not the most delicate and surprising turns peculiar to the person praised. I do not remember to have seen any
thing like it in Dr. Bathurst, who had made some attempts this way with
applause. He was an excellent judge of humanity; and so good an historian,
that in familiar discourse he would talk over the most memorable facts in
antiquity, the lives, actions, and characters of celebrated men, with amazing
facility and accuracy. As he had thoroughly read and digested Thuanus's
works, so he was able to copy after him: and his talent in this kind was so
well known and allowed, that he had been singled out by some great men to
write a history, which it was for their interest to have done with the utmost
art and dexterity. I shall not mention for what reasons this design was
dropped, though they are very much to Mr. Smith's honour. The truth is,
and I speak it before living witnesses, whilst an agreeable company could fix
him upon a subject of useful literature, nobody shone to greater advantage:
he seemed to be that Memmius whom Lucretius speaks of;

—Quem tu, Dea, tempore in omni
Omnibus ornatum voluisti excellere rebus.

His works are not many, and those scattered up and down in Miscellanies 15
and Collections, being wrested from him by his friends with great difficulty
and reluctance. All of them together make but a small part of that much
greater body which lies dispersed in the possession of numerous acquaintance; and cannot perhaps be made entire, without great injustice to him,
because few of them had his last hand, and the transcriber was often obliged
to take the liberties of a friend. His condolance for the death of Mr. Philips
is full of the noblest beauties, and hath done justice to the ashes of that

second Milton, whose writings will last as long as the English language, generosity, and valour. For him Mr. Smith had contracted a perfect friendship; a passion he was most susceptible of, and whose laws he looked upon as sacred and inviolable.

16      Every subject that passed under his pen had all the life, proportion, and embellishments bestowed on it, which an exquisite skill, a warm imagination, and a cool judgement, could possibly bestow on it. The epique, lyrick, elegiac, every sort of poetry he touched upon (and he had touched upon a great variety), was raised to its proper height, and the differences between each of them observed with a judicious accuracy. We saw the old rules and new beauties placed in admirable order by each other; and there was a predominant fancy and spirit of his own infused, superior to what some draw off from the ancients, or from poesies here and there culled out of the moderns, by a painful industry and servile imitation. His contrivances were adroit and magnificent; his images lively and adequate; his sentiments charming and majestick; his expressions natural and bold; his numbers various and sounding; and that enameled mixture of classical wit, which, without redundance and affectation, sparkled through his writings, and was no less pertinent than agreeable.

17      His *Phædra* is a consummate tragedy, and the success of it was as great as the most sanguine expectations of his friends could promise or foresee. The number of nights, and the common method of filling the house, are not always the surest marks of judging what encouragement a play meets with: but the generosity of all the persons of a refined taste about town was remarkable on this occasion; and it must not be forgotten how zealously Mr. Addison espoused his interest, with all the elegant judgement and diffusive good-nature for which that accomplished gentleman and author is so justly valued by mankind. But as to *Phædra*, she has certainly made a finer figure under Mr. Smith's conduct, upon the English stage, than either Rome or Athens; and if she excels the Greek and Latin *Phædra*, I need not say she surpasses the French one, though embellished with whatever regular beauties and moving softness Racine himself could give her.

18      No man had a juster notion of the difficulty of composing than Mr. Smith, and he sometimes would create greater difficulties than he had reason to apprehend. Writing with ease, what (as Mr. Wycherley speaks) may be easily written, moved his indignation. When he was writing upon a subject, he would seriously consider what Demosthenes, Homer, Virgil, or Horace, if alive, would say upon that occasion, which whetted him to exceed himself as well as others. Nevertheless, he could not, or would not, finish several subjects he undertook; which may be imputed either to

the briskness of his fancy, still hunting after new matter, or to an occasional indolence, which spleen and lassitude brought upon him, which, of all his foibles, the world was least inclined to forgive. That this was not owing to conceit and vanity, or a fulness of himself (a frailty which has been imputed to no less men than Shakspeare and Jonson), is clear from hence; because he left his works to the entire disposal of his friends, whose most rigorous censures he even courted and solicited; submitting to their animadversions, and the freedom they took with them, with an unreserved and prudent resignation.

I have seen sketches and rough draughts of some poems he designed, set out analytically; wherein the fable, structure, and connexion, the images, incidents, moral, episodes, and a great variety of ornaments, were so finely laid out, so well fitted to the rules of art, and squared so exactly to the precedents of the ancients, that I have often looked on these poetical elements with the same concern, with which curious men are affected at the sight of the most entertaining remains and ruins of an antique figure or building. Those fragments of the learned, which some men have been so proud of their pains in collecting, are useless rarities, without form and without life, when compared with these embryo's, which wanted not spirit enough to preserve them; so that I cannot help thinking, that, if some of them were to come abroad, they would be as highly valued by the poets, as the sketches of Julio and Titian are by the painters; though there is nothing in them but a few outlines, as to the design and proportion. 19

It must be confessed, that Mr. Smith had some defects in his conduct, which those are most apt to remember who could imitate him in nothing else. His freedom with himself drew severer acknowledgements from him than all the malice he ever provoked was capable of advancing, and he did not scruple to give even his misfortunes the hard name of faults; but if the world had half his good-nature, all the shady parts would be entirely struck out of his character. 20

A man, who, under poverty, calamities, and disappointments, could make so many friends, and those so truly valuable, must have just and noble ideas of the passion of friendship, in the success of which consisted the greatest, if not the only, happiness of his life. He knew very well what was due to his birth, though Fortune threw him short of it in every other circumstance of life. He avoided making any, though perhaps reasonable, complaints of her dispensations, under which he had honour enough to be easy, without touching the favours she flung in his way when offered to him at the price of a more durable reputation. He took care to have no dealings with mankind, in which he could not be just; and he desired to be at no other expence in his pretensions than that of intrinsick merit, which was the 21 only burthen and reproach he ever brought upon his friends. He could say, as Horace did of himself, what I never yet saw translated;

"—Meo sum pauper in ære."

22      At his coming to town, no man was more surrounded by all those who really had or pretended to wit, or more courted by the great men, who had then a power and opportunity of encouraging arts and sciences, and gave proofs of their fondness for the name of Patron in many instances, which will ever be remembered to their glory. Mr. Smith's character grew upon his friends by intimacy, and outwent the strongest prepossessions, which had been conceived in his favour. Whatever quarrel a few sour creatures, whose obscurity is their happiness, may possibly have to the age; yet amidst a studied neglect, and total disuse of all those ceremonial attendances, fashionable equipments, and external recommendations, which are thought necessary introductions into the *grand monde*, this gentleman was so happy as still to please; and whilst the rich, the gay, the noble, and honourable, saw how much he excelled in wit and learning, they easily forgave him all other differences. Hence it was that both his acquaintance and retirements were his own free choice. What Mr. Prior observes upon a very great character, was true of him; *that most of his faults brought their excuse with them.*

23      Those who blamed him most, understood him least: it being the custom of the vulgar to charge an excess upon the most complaisant, and to form a character by the morals of a few, who have sometimes spoiled an hour or two in good company. Where only fortune is wanting to make a great name, that single exception can never pass upon the best judges and most equitable observers of mankind; and when the time comes for the world to spare their pity, we may justly enlarge our demands upon them for their admiration.

24      Some few years before his death, he had engaged himself in several considerable undertakings; in all which he had prepared the world to expect mighty things from him. I have seen about ten sheets of his *English Pindar,* which exceeded any thing of that kind I could ever hope for in our own language. He had drawn out the plan of a tragedy of the *Lady Jane Grey,* and had gone through several scenes of it. But he could not well have bequeathed that work to better hands than where, I hear, it is at present lodged; and the bare mention of two such names may justify the largest expectations, and is sufficient to make the town an agreeable invitation.

25      His greatest and noblest undertaking was *Longinus.* He had finished an entire translation of the *Sublime,* which he sent to the reverend Mr. Richard Parker, a friend of his, late of Merton College, an exact critick in the Greek tongue, from whom it came to my hands. The French version of Monsieur Boileau, though truly valuable, was far short of it. He proposed a large

addition to this work, of notes and observations of his own, with an entire system of the Art of Poetry, in three books, under the titles of *Thought, Diction*, and *Figure*. I saw the last of these perfect, and in a fair copy, in which he shewed prodigious judgement and reading; and particularly had reformed the Art of Rhetorick, by reducing that vast and confused heap of terms, with which a long succession of pedants had encumbered the world, to a very narrow compass, comprehending all that was useful and ornamental in poetry. Under each head and chapter, he intended to make remarks upon all the ancients and moderns, the Greek, Latin, English, French, Spanish, and Italian poets, and to note their several beauties and defects.

What remains of his works is left, as I am informed, in the hands of men 26 of worth and judgement, who loved him. It cannot be supposed they would suppress any thing that was his, but out of respect to his memory, and for want of proper hands to finish what so great a genius had begun.

SUCH is the declamation of Oldisworth, written while his admiration was 27 yet fresh, and his kindness warm; and therefore such as, without any criminal purpose of deceiving, shews a strong defire to make the most of all favourable truth. I cannot much commend the performance. The praise is often indistinct, and the sentences are loaded with words of more pomp than use. There is little however that can be contradicted, even when a plainer tale comes to be told.

EDMUND NEAL, known by the name of Smith, was born at Handley, the 28 seat of the Lechmeres, in Worcestershire. The year of his birth is uncertain.

He was educated at Westminster. It is known to have been the practice of 29 Dr. Busby to detain those youths long at school, of whom he had formed the highest expectations. Smith took his Master's degree on the 8th of July 1696: he therefore was probably admitted into the university in 1689, when we may suppose him twenty years old.

His reputation for literature in his college was such as has been told; but 30 the indecency and licentiousness of his behaviour drew upon him, Dec. 24, 1694, while he was yet only Batchelor, a publick admonition, entered upon record, in order to his expulsion. Of this reproof the effect is not known. He was probably less notorious. At Oxford, as we all know, much will be forgiven to literary merit; and of that he had exhibited sufficient evidence by his excellent ode on the death of the great Orientalist, Dr. Pocock, who died in 1691, and whose praise must have been written by Smith when he had been yet but two years in the university.

This ode, which closed the second volume of the *Musæ Anglicanæ*, 31 though perhaps some objections may be made to its Latinity, is by far the best Lyrick composition in that collection; nor do I know where to find it equalled among the modern writers. It expresses, with great felicity, images not classical in classical diction: its digressions and returns have been deservedly recommended by Trapp as models for imitation.

32    He has several imitations of Cowley:

> Vestitur hinc tot sermo coloribus
> Quot tu, Pococki, dissimilis tui
> Orator effers, quot vicissim
> Te memores celebrare gaudent.

33    I will not commend the figure which makes the orator *pronounce colours*, or give to *colours memory* and *delight*. I quote it, however, as an imitation of these lines;

> So many languages he had in store,
> That only Fame shall speak of him in more.

34    The simile, by which an old man, retaining the fire of his youth, is compared to Ætna flaming through the snow, which Smith has used with great pomp, is stolen from Cowley, however little worth the labour of conveyance.

35    He proceeded to take his degree of Master of Arts July 8, 1696. Of the exercises which he performed on that occasion, I have not heard any thing memorable.

36    As his years advanced, he advanced in reputation: for he continued to cultivate his mind, though he did not amend his irregularities, by which he gave so much offence, that, April 24, 1700, the Dean and Chapter declared "the place of Mr. Smith void, he having been convicted of riotous misbehaviour in the house of Mr. Cole an apothecary; but it was referred to the Dean when and upon what occasion the sentence should be put in execution."

37    Thus tenderly was he treated: the governors of his college could hardly keep him, and yet wished that he would not force them to drive him away.

38    Some time afterwards he assumed an appearance of decency; in his own phrase, he *whitened* himself, having a desire to obtain the censorship, an office of honour and some profit in the college; but when the election came, the preference was given to Mr. *Foulkes*, his junior; the same, I suppose, that joined with *Freind* in an edition of part of Demosthenes; the censor is a tutor, and it was not thought proper to trust the superintendance of others to a man who took so little care of himself.

39    From this time Smith employed his malice and his wit against the Dean, Dr. Aldrich, whom he considered as the opponent of his claim. Of his lampoon upon him, I once heard a single line too gross to be repeated.

But he was still a genius and a scholar, and Oxford was unwilling to lose  40
him: he was endured, with all his pranks and his vices, two years longer; but
on Dec. 20, 1705, at the instance of all the canons, the sentence declared five
years before was put in execution.

The execution was, I believe, silent and tender; for one of his friends,  41
from whom I learned much of his life, appeared not to know it.

He was now driven to London, where he associated himself with the  42
Whigs, whether because they were in power, or because the Tories had
expelled him, or because he was a Whig by principle, may perhaps be
doubted. He was however caressed by men of great abilities, whatever
were their party, and was supported by the liberality of those who delighted
in his conversation.

There was once a design hinted at by Oldisworth, to have made him  43
useful. One evening, as he was sitting with a friend at a tavern, he was called
down by the waiter; and, having staid some time below, came up thoughtful. After a pause, said he to his friend, "He that wanted me below was
Addison, whose business was to tell me that a History of the Revolution was
intended, and to propose that I should undertake it. I said, what shall I do
with the character of lord Sunderland? and Addison immediately returned,
When, Rag, were you drunk last? and went away."

Captain *Rag* was a name which he got at Oxford by his negligence of  44
dress.

This story I heard from the late Mr. Clark of Lincoln's Inn, to whom it  45
was told by the friend of Smith.

Such scruples might debar him from some profitable employments; but  46
as they could not deprive him of any real esteem, they left him many
friends; and no man was ever better introduced to the theatre than he,
who, in that violent conflict of parties, had a Prologue and Epilogue from
the first wits on either side.

But learning and nature will now and then take different courses. His  47
play pleased the criticks, and the criticks only. It was, as Addison has
recorded, hardly heard the third night. Smith had indeed trusted entirely
to his merit; had ensured no band of applauders, nor used any artifice to
force success, and found that naked excellence was not sufficient for its own
support.

The play, however, was bought by Lintot, who advanced the price from  48
fifty guineas, the current rate, to sixty; and Halifax, the general patron,
accepted the dedication. Smith's indolence kept him from writing the
dedication, till Lintot, after fruitless importunity, gave notice that he
would publish the play without it. Now therefore it was written; and
Halifax expected the author with his book, and had prepared to reward

him with a place of three hundred pounds a year. Smith, by pride, or caprice, or indolence, or bashfulness, neglected to attend him, though doubtless warned and pressed by his friends, and at last missed his reward by not going to solicit it.

49      Addison has, in the *Spectator*, mentioned the neglect of Smith's tragedy as disgraceful to the nation, and imputes it to the fondness for operas then prevailing. The authority of Addison is great; yet the voice of the people, when to please the people is the purpose, deserves regard. In this question, I cannot but think the people in the right. The fable is mythological, a story which we are accustomed to reject as false, and the manners are so distant from our own, that we know them not from sympathy, but by study: the ignorant do not understand the action, the learned reject it as a school-boy's tale; *incredulus odi*. What I cannot for a moment believe, I cannot for a moment behold with interest or anxiety. The sentiments thus remote from life, are removed yet further by the diction, which is too luxuriant and splendid for dialogue, and envelopes the thoughts rather than displays them. It is a scholar's play, such as may please the reader rather than the spectator; the work of a vigorous and elegant mind, accustomed to please itself with its own conceptions, but of little acquaintance with the course of life.

50      Dennis tells, in one of his pieces, that he had once a design to have written the tragedy of *Phædra*; but was convinced that the action was too mythological.

51      In 1709, a year after the exhibition of *Phædra*, died John Philips, the friend and fellow-collegian of Smith, who, on that occasion, wrote a poem, which justice must place among the best elegies which our language can shew, an elegant mixture of fondness and admiration, of dignity and softness. There are some passages too ludicrous; but every human performance has its faults.

52      This elegy it was the mode among his friends to purchase for a guinea; and, as his acquaintance was numerous, it was a very profitable poem.

53      Of his *Pindar*, mentioned by Oldisworth, I have never otherwise heard. His *Longinus* he intended to accompany with some illustrations, and had selected his instances of the false *Sublime* from the works of Blackmore.

54      He resolved to try again the fortune of the Stage, with the story of Lady Jane Grey. It is not unlikely that his experience of the inefficacy and incredibility of a mythological tale, might determine him to choose an action from English History, at no great distance from our own times, which was to end in a real event, produced by the operation of known characters.

55      A subject will not easily occur that can give more opportunities of informing the understanding, for which Smith was unquestionably qua-

lified, or for moving the passions, in which I suspect him to have had less power.

Having formed his plan, and collected materials, he declared that a few 56 months would complete his design; and, that he might pursue his work with less frequent avocations, he was, in June 1710, invited by Mr. George Ducket to his house at Hartham in Wiltshire. Here he found such opportunities of indulgence as did not much forward his studies, and particularly some strong ale, too delicious to be resisted. He eat and drank till he found himself plethorick: and then, resolving to ease himself by evacuation, he wrote to an apothecary in the neighbourhood a prescription of a purge so forcible, that the apothecary thought it his duty to delay it till he had given notice of its danger. Smith, not pleased with the contradiction of a shopman, and boastful of his own knowledge, treated the notice with rude contempt, and swallowed his own medicine, which, in July 1710, brought him to the grave. He was buried at Hartham.

Many years afterwards, Ducket communicated to Oldmixon the histor- 57 ian, an account, pretended to have been received from Smith, that Clarendon's History was, in its publication, corrupted by Aldrich, Smalridge, and Atterbury; and that Smith was employed to forge and insert the alterations.

This story was published triumphantly by Oldmixon, and may be sup- 58 posed to have been eagerly received: but its progress was soon checked; for finding its way into the Journal of Trevoux, it fell under the eye of Atterbury, then an exile in France, who immediately denied the charge, with this remarkable particular, that he never in his whole life had once spoken to Smith; his company being, as must be inferred, not accepted by those who attended to their characters.

The charge was afterwards very diligently refuted by Dr. Burton of 59 Eaton; a man eminent for literature, and, though not of the same party with Aldrich and Atterbury, too studious of truth to leave them burthened with a false charge. The testimonies which he has collected, have convinced mankind that either Smith or Ducket were guilty of wilful and malicious falsehood.

This controversy brought into view those parts of Smith's life, which 60 with more honour to his name might have been concealed.

Of Smith I can yet say a little more. He was a man of such estimation 61 among his companions, that the casual censures or praises which he dropped in conversation were considered, like those of Scaliger, as worthy of preservation.

He had great readiness and exactness of criticism, and by a cursory glance 62 over a new composition would exactly tell all its faults and beauties.

63    He was remarkable for the power of reading with great rapidity, and of retaining with great fidelity what he so easily collected.

64    He therefore always knew what the present question required; and when his friends expressed their wonder at his acquisitions, made in a state of apparent negligence and drunkenness, he never discovered his hours of reading or method of study, but involved himself in affected silence, and fed his own vanity with their admiration and conjectures.

65    One practice he had, which was easily observed: if any thought or image was presented to his mind, that he could use or improve, he did not suffer it to be lost; but, amidst the jollity of a tavern, or in the warmth of conversation, very diligently committed it to paper.

66    Thus it was that he had gathered two quires of hints for his new tragedy; of which Rowe, when they were put into his hands, could make, as he says, very little use, but which the collector considered as a valuable stock of materials.

67    When he came to London, his way of life connected him with the licentious and dissolute; and he affected the airs and gaiety of a man of pleasure; but his dress was always deficient: scholastick cloudiness still hung about him; and his merriment was sure to produce the scorn of his companions.

68    With all his carelessness, and all his vices, he was one of the murmurers at Fortune; and wondered why he was suffered to be poor, when Addison was caressed and preferred: nor would a very little have contented him; for he estimated his wants at six hundred pounds a year.

69    In his course of reading it was particular, that he had diligently perused, and accurately remembered, the old romances of knight errantry.

70    He had a high opinion of his own merit, and something contemptuous in his treatment of those whom he considered as not qualified to oppose or contradict him. He had many frailties; yet it cannot but be supposed that he had great merit, who could obtain to the same play a prologue from Addison, and an epilogue from Prior; and who could have at once the patronage of Halifax, and the praise of Oldisworth.

71    For the power of communicating these minute memorials, I am indebted to my conversation with Gilbert Walmsley, late register of the ecclesiastical court of Litchfield, who was acquainted both with Smith and Ducket; and declared, that, if the tale concerning Clarendon were forged, he should suspect Ducket of the falsehood; *for Rag was a man of great veracity.*

72    Of Gilbert Walmsley, thus presented to my mind, let me indulge myself in the remembrance. I knew him very early; he was one of the first friends that literature procured me, and I hope that at least my gratitude made me worthy of his notice.

He was of an advanced age, and I was only not a boy; yet he never 73
received my notions with contempt. He was a Whig, with all the virulence
and malevolence of his party; yet difference of opinion did not keep us
apart. I honoured him, and he endured me.

He had mingled with the gay world, without exemption from its vices or 74
its follies, but had never neglected the cultivation of his mind; his belief of
Revelation was unshaken; his learning preserved his principles; he grew
first regular, and then pious.

His studies had been so various, that I am not able to name a man of equal 75
knowledge. His acquaintance with books was great; and what he did not
immediately know, he could at least tell where to find. Such was his
amplitude of learning, and such his copiousness of communication, that it
may be doubted whether a day now passes in which I have not some
advantage from his friendship.

At this man's table I enjoyed many chearful and instructive hours, 76
with companions such as are not often found; with one who has lengthened,
and one who has gladdened life; with Dr. James, whose skill in physick will
be long remembered; and with David Garrick, whom I hoped to have
gratified with this character of our common friend: but what are the
hopes of man! I am disappointed by that stroke of death, which has eclipsed
the gaiety of nations, and impoverished the publick stock of harmless
pleasure.

In the Library at Oxford is the following ludicrous Analysis of *Pocockius:* 77

EX AUTOGRAPHO.

[Sent by the Author to Mr. Urry.]

OPUSCULUM hoc, Halberdarie amplissime, in lucem proferre hactenus
distuli, judicii tui acumen subveritus magis quam bipennis. Tandem ali-
quando Oden hanc ad te mitto sublimem, teneram, flebilem, suavem,
qualem demum divinus (si Musis vacaret) scripsisset Gastrellus: adeo
scilicet sublimem ut inter legendum dormire, adeo flebilem ut ridere
velis. Cujus elegantiam ut melius inspicias, versuum ordinem & materiam
breviter referam. $1^{mus}$ versus de duobus præliis decantatis. $2^{dus}$ & $3^{us}$ de
Lotharingio, cuniculis subterraneis, saxis, ponto, hostibus, & Asia. $4^{tus}$ &
$5^{us}$ de catenis, sudibus, uncis, draconibus, tigribus & crocodilis. $6^{us}$, $7^{us}$, $8^{us}$,
$9^{us}$, de Gomorrha, de Babylone, Babele, & quodam domi suæ peregrino.
$10^{us}$, aliquid de quodam Pocockio. $11^{us}$, $12^{us}$, de Syriâ, Solymâ. $13^{us}$, $14^{us}$,
de Hoseâ & quercu, & de juvene quodam valde sene. $15^{us}$, $16^{us}$, de Ætnâ &
quomodo Ætna Pocockio sit valde similis. $17^{us}$, $18^{us}$, de tubâ, astro, umbrâ,
flammis, rotis, Pocockio non neglecto. Cætera de Christianis, Ottomanis,

Babyloniis, Arabibus, & gravissimâ agrorum melancholiâ; de Cæsare *Flacco*\*, Nestore, & miserando juvenis cujusdam florentissimi fato, anno ætatis suæ centesimo præmaturè abrepti. Quæ omnia cum accuratè expenderis, necesse est ut Oden hanc meam admirandâ planè varietate constare fatearis. Subito ad Batavos proficiscor lauro ab illis donandus. Prius vero Pembrochienses voco ad certamen Poeticum. Vale.

Illustrissima tua deosculor crura.

E. Smith.

* Pro *Flacco*, animo paulo attentiore, scripsissem *Marone*.

# DUKE

Of Mr. RICHARD DUKE I can find few memorials. He was bred at West- 1
minster and Cambridge; and Jacob relates, that he was some time tutor to
the duke of Richmond.

He appears from his writings to have been not ill qualified for poetical 2
compositions; and being conscious of his powers, when he left the university he enlisted himself among the wits. He was the familiar friend of
Otway; and was engaged, among other popular names, in the translations
of Ovid and Juvenal. In his *Review*, though unfinished, are some vigorous
lines. His poems are not below mediocrity; nor have I found much in them
to be praised.

With the Wit he seems to have shared the dissoluteness of the times; for 3
some of his compositions are such as he must have reviewed with detestation in his later days, when he published those Sermons which *Felton* has
commended.

Perhaps, like some other foolish young men, he rather talked than lived 4
viciously, in an age when he that would be thought a Wit was afraid to say
his prayers; and whatever might have been bad in the first part of his life,
was surely condemned and reformed by his better judgment.

In 1683, being then master of arts, and fellow of Trinity College in 5
Cambridge, he wrote a poem on the marriage of the Lady Anne with
George Prince of Denmark.

He took orders; and being made prebendary of Gloucester, became a 6
proctor in convocation for that church, and chaplain to Queen Anne.

In 1710, he was presented by the bishop of Winchester to the wealthy 7
living of Witney in Oxfordshire, which he enjoyed but a few months. On
February 10, 1710–11, having returned from an entertainment, he was
found dead the next morning. His death is mentioned in Swift's Journal.

# KING

1 WILLIAM KING was born in London in 1663; the son of Ezekiel King, a gentleman. He was allied to the family of Clarendon.

2 From Westminster-school, where he was a scholar on the foundation under the care of Dr. Busby, he was at eighteen elected to Christ-church, in 1681; where he is said to have prosecuted his studies with so much intenseness and activity, that, before he was eight years standing, he had read over, and made remarks upon, twenty-two thousand odd hundred books and manuscripts. The books were certainly not very long, the manuscripts not very difficult, nor the remarks very large; for the calculator will find that he dispatched seven a-day, for every day of his eight years, with a remnant that more than satisfies most other students. He took his degree in the most expensive manner, as a *grand compounder*; whence it is inferred that he inherited a considerable fortune.

3 In 1688, the same year in which he was made master of arts, he published a confutation of Varillas's account of Wicliffe; and, engaging in the study of the Civil Law, became doctor in 1692, and was admitted advocate at Doctors Commons.

4 He had already made some translations from the French, and written some humorous and satirical pieces; when, in 1694, Molesworth published his *Account of Denmark*, in which he treats the Danes and their monarch with great contempt; and takes the opportunity of insinuating those wild principles, by which he supposes liberty to be established, and by which his adversaries suspect that all subordination and government is endangered.

5 This book offended prince George; and the Danish minister presented a memorial against it. The principles of its author did not please Dr. King, and therefore he undertook to confute part, and laugh at the rest. The controversy is now forgotten; and books of this kind seldom live long, when interest and resentment have ceased.

6 In 1697 he mingled in the controversy between Boyle and Bentley; and was one of those who tried what Wit could perform in opposition to Learning, on a question which Learning only could decide.

7 In 1699 was published by him *A Journey to London*, after the method of Dr. *Martin Lister*, who had published *A Journey to Paris*. And in 1700 he satirised the Royal Society, at least Sir *Hans Sloane* their president, in two dialogues, intituled *The Transactioneer*.

Though he was a regular advocate in the courts of civil and canon law, he 8 did not love his profession, nor indeed any kind of business which interrupted his voluptuary dreams, or forced him to rouse from that indulgence in which only he could find delight. His reputation as a civilian was yet maintained by his judgements in the courts of Delegates, and raised very high by the address and knowledge which he discovered in 1700, when he defended the earl of Anglesea against his lady, afterwards dutchess of Buckinghamshire, who sued for a divorce, and obtained it.

The expence of his pleasures, and neglect of business, had now lessened 9 his revenues; and he was willing to accept of a settlement in Ireland, where, about 1702, he was made judge of the admiralty, commissioner of the prizes, keeper of the records in Birmingham's tower, and vicar-general to Dr. Marsh the primate.

But it is vain to put wealth within the reach of him who will not stretch 10 out his hand to take it. King soon found a friend as idle and thoughtless as himself, in *Upton*, one of the judges, who had a pleasant house called Mountown, near Dublin, to which King frequently retired; delighting to neglect his interest, forget his cares, and desert his duty.

Here he wrote *Mully of Mountown*, a poem; by which, though fanciful 11 readers in the pride of sagacity have given it a political interpretation, was meant originally no more than it expressed, as it was dictated only by the author's delight in the quiet of *Mountown*.

In 1708, when lord Wharton was sent to govern Ireland, King returned to 12 London, with his poverty, his idleness, and his wit; and published some essays called *Useful Transactions*. His *Voyage to the Island of Cajamai* is particularly commended. He then wrote the *Art of Love*, a poem remarkable, notwithstanding its title, for purity of sentiment; and in 1709 imitated Horace in an *Art of Cookery*, which he published, with some letters to Dr. Lister.

In 1710 he appeared, as a lover of the Church, on the side of Sacheverell; 13 and was supposed to have concurred at least in the projection of *The Examiner*. His eyes were open to all the operations of Whiggism; and he bestowed some strictures upon Dr. Kennet's adulatory sermon at the funeral of the duke of Devonshire.

The *History of the Heathen Gods*, a book composed for schools, was 14 written by him in 1711. The work is useful; but might have been produced without the powers of King. The same year he published *Rufinus*, an historical essay, and a poem, intended to dispose the nation to think as he thought of the duke of Marlborough and his adherents.

In 1711, competence, if not plenty, was again put into his power. He was, 15 without the trouble of attendance, or the mortification of a request, made gazetteer. Swift, Freind, Prior, and other men of the same party, brought him the key of the gazetteer's office. He was now again placed in a profitable employment, and again threw the benefit away. An Act of Insolvency made his business at that time particularly troublesome; and he would not wait till hurry should be at an end, but impatiently resigned it, and returned to his wonted indigence and amusements.

16     One of his amusements at Lambeth, where he resided, was to mortify Dr. Tennison, the archbishop, by a publick festivity, on the surrender of Dunkirk to Hill; an event with which Tennison's political bigotry did not suffer him to be delighted. King was resolved to counteract his sullenness, and at the expence of a few barrels of ale filled the neighbourhood with honest merriment.

17     In the Autumn of 1712 his health declined; he grew weaker by degrees, and died on Christmas-day. Though his life had not been without irregularity, his principles were pure and orthodox, and his death was pious.

18     After this relation, it will be naturally supposed that his poems were rather the amusements of idleness than efforts of study; that he endeavoured rather to divert than astonish; that his thoughts seldom aspired to sublimity; and that, if his verse was easy and his images familiar, he attained what he desired. His purpose is to be merry; but perhaps, to enjoy his mirth, it may be sometimes necessary to think well of his opinions.

# SPRAT

THOMAS SPRAT was born in 1636, at Tallaton in Devonshire, the son of a    1
clergyman; and having been educated, as he tells of himself, not at Westminster or Eaton, but at a little school by the churchyard side, became a
commoner of Wadham College in Oxford in 1651; and, being chosen
scholar next year, proceeded through the usual academical course, and in
1657 became master of arts. He obtained a fellowship, and commenced
poet.

In 1659, his poem on the death of Oliver was published, with those of    2
Dryden and Waller. In his dedication to Dr. Wilkins he appears a very
willing and liberal encomiast, both of the living and the dead. He implores
his patron's excuse of his verses, both as falling *so infinitely below the full and
sublime genius of that excellent poet who made this way of writing free of our
nation*, and being *so little equal and proportioned to the renown of the prince on
whom they were written; such great actions and lives deserving to be the subject of
the noblest pens and most divine phansies.* He proceeds: *Having so long
experienced your care and indulgence, and been formed, as it were, by your
own hands, not to entitle you to any thing which my meanness produces, would be
not only injustice, but sacrilege.*

He published the same year a poem on the *Plague of Athens*; a subject of    3
which it is not easy to say what could recommend it. To these he added
afterwards a poem on Mr. Cowley's death.

After the Restoration he took orders, and by Cowley's recommendation    4
was made chaplain to the Duke of Buckingham, whom he is said to have
helped in writing the *Rehearsal*. He was likewise chaplain to the king.

As he was the favourite of Wilkins, at whose house began those philo-    5
sophical conferences and enquiries, which in time produced the Royal
Society, he was consequently engaged in the same studies, and became
one of the fellows; and when, after their incorporation, something seemed
necessary to reconcile the publick to the new institution, he undertook to
write its history, which he published in 1667. This is one of the few books
which selection of sentiment and elegance of diction have been able to
preserve, though written upon a subject flux and transitory. The History
of the Royal Society is now read, not with the wish to know what they were
then doing, but how their transactions are exhibited by Sprat.

6    In the next year he published *Observations on Sorbiere's Voyage into England, in a Letter to Mr. Wren*. This is a work not ill performed; but perhaps rewarded with at least its full proportion of praise.

7    In 1668 he published Cowley's Latin poems, and prefixed in Latin the Life of the Author; which he afterwards amplified, and placed before Cowley's English works, which were by will committed to his care.

8    Ecclesiastical benefices now fell fast upon him. In 1668 he became a prebendary of Westminster, and had afterwards the church of St. Margaret, adjoining to the Abbey. He was in 1680 made canon of Windsor, in 1683 dean of Westminster, and in 1684 bishop of Rochester.

9    The Court having thus a claim to his diligence and gratitude, he was required to write the History of the Ryehouse Plot; and in 1685 published *A true Account and Declaration of the horrid Conspiracy against the late King, his present Majesty, and the present Government*; a performance which he thought convenient, after the Revolution, to extenuate and excuse.

10   The same year, being clerk of the closet to the king, he was made dean of the chapel-royal; and the year afterwards received the last proof of his master's confidence, by being appointed one of the commissioners for ecclesiastical affairs. On the critical day, when the *Declaration* distinguished the true sons of the church of England, he stood neuter, and permitted it to be read at Westminster; but pressed none to violate his conscience; and when the bishop of London was brought before them, gave his voice in his favour.

11   Thus far he suffered interest or obedience to carry him; but further he refused to go. When he found that the powers of the ecclesiastical commission were to be exercised against those who had refused the Declaration, he wrote to the lords, and other commissioners, a formal profession of his unwillingness to exercise that authority any longer, and withdrew himself from them. After they had read his letter, they adjourned for six months, and scarcely ever met afterwards.

12   When king James was frighted away, and a new government was to be settled, Sprat was one of those who considered, in a conference, the great question, whether the crown was vacant; and manfully spoke in favour of his old master.

13   He complied, however, with the new establishment, and was left unmolested; but in 1692 a strange attack was made upon him by one *Robert Young* and *Stephen Blackhead*, both men convicted of infamous crimes, and both, when the scheme was laid, prisoners in Newgate. These men drew up an Association, in which they whose names were subscribed declared their resolution to restore king James; to seize the princess of Orange, dead or alive; and to be ready with thirty thousand men to meet king James when he

should land. To this they put the names of Sancroft, Sprat, Marlborough, Salisbury, and others. The copy of Dr. Sprat's name was obtained by a fictitious request, to which an answer *in his own hand* was desired. His hand was copied so well, that he confessed it might have deceived himself. Blackhead, who had carried the letter, being sent again with a plausible message, was very curious to see the house, and particularly importunate to be let into the study; where, as is supposed, he designed to leave the Association. This however was denied him, and he dropt it in a flower-pot in the parlour.

Young now laid an information before the Privy Council; and May 7, 14 1692, the bishop was arrested, and kept at a messenger's under a strict guard eleven days. His house was searched, and directions were given that the flower-pots should be inspected. The messengers however missed the room in which the paper was left. Blackhead went therefore a third time; and finding his paper where he had left it, brought it away.

The bishop, having been enlarged, was, on June the 10th and 13th, 15 examined again before the Privy Council, and confronted with his accusers. Young persisted with the most obdurate impudence, against the strongest evidence; but the resolution of Blackhead by degrees gave way. There remained at last no doubt of the bishop's innocence, who, with great prudence and diligence, traced the progress, and detected the characters of the two informers, and published an account of his own examination, and deliverance; which made such an impression upon him, that he commemorated it through life by an yearly day of thanksgiving.

With what hope, or what interest, the villains had contrived an accusation 16 which they must know themselves utterly unable to prove, was never discovered.

After this, he passed his days in the quiet exercise of his function. When 17 the cause of Sacheverell put the publick in commotion, he honestly appeared among the friends of the church. He lived to his seventy-ninth year, and died May 20, 1713.

Burnet is not very favourable to his memory; but he and Burnet were old 18 rivals. On some publick occasion they both preached before the house of commons. There prevailed in those days an indecent custom; when the preacher touched any favourite topick in a manner that delighted his audience, their approbation was expressed by a loud *hum*, continued in proportion to their zeal or pleasure. When Burnet preached, part of his congregation *hummed* so loudly and so long, that he sat down to enjoy it, and rubbed his face with his handkerchief. When Sprat preached, he likewise was honoured with the like animating *hum*; but he stretched out his hand to the congregation, and cried, "Peace, peace, I pray you, peace."

19    This I was told in my youth by my father, an old man, who had been no careless observer of the passages of those times.

20    Burnet's sermon, says Salmon, was remarkable for sedition, and Sprat's for loyalty. Burnet had the thanks of the house; Sprat had no thanks, but a good living from the king; which, he said, was of as much value as the thanks of the Commons.

21    The works of Sprat, besides his few poems, are, The History of the Royal Society, The Life of Cowley, The Answer to Sorbiere, The History of the Ryehouse Plot, The Relation of his own Examination, and a volume of Sermons. I have heard it observed, with great justness, that every book is of a different kind, and that each has its distinct and characteristical excellence.

22    My business is only with his poems. He considered Cowley as a model; and supposed that as he was imitated, perfection was approached. Nothing therefore but Pindarick liberty was to be expected. There is in his few productions no want of such conceits as he thought excellent; and of those our judgment may be settled by the first that appears in his praise of Cromwell, where he says that Cromwell's *fame, like man, will grow white as it grows old*.

# HALIFAX

THE life of the Earl of Halifax was properly that of an artful and active    1
statesman, employed in balancing parties, contriving expedients, and combating opposition, and exposed to the vicissitudes of advancement and
degradation: but in this collection, poetical merit is the claim to attention;
and the account which is here to be expected may properly be proportioned
not to his influence in the state, but to his rank among the writers of verse.

Charles Montague was born April 16, 1661, at Horton in Northampton-    2
shire, the son of Mr. George Montague, a younger son of the earl of
Manchester. He was educated first in the country, and then removed to
Westminster; where in 1677 he was chosen a king's scholar, and recommended himself to Busby by his felicity in extemporary epigrams. He
contracted a very intimate friendship with Mr. Stepney; and in 1682,
when Stepney was elected to Cambridge, the election of Montague being
not to proceed till the year following, he was afraid lest by being placed at
Oxford he might be separated from his companion, and therefore solicited
to be removed to Cambridge, without waiting for the advantages of another
year.

It seems indeed time to wish for a removal; for he was already a school-    3
boy of one and twenty.

His relation Dr. Montague was then master of the college in which he    4
was placed a fellow commoner, and took him under his particular care. Here
he commenced an acquaintance with the great Newton, which continued
through his life, and was at last attested by a legacy.

In 1685, his verses on the death of king Charles made such impression on    5
the earl of Dorset, that he was invited to town, and introduced by that
universal patron to the other wits. In 1687, he joined with Prior in the *City
Mouse and Country Mouse*, a burlesque of Dryden's *Hind and Panther*. He
signed the invitation to the Prince of Orange, and sat in the convention. He
about the same time married the countess dowager of Manchester, and
intended to have taken orders; but afterwards altering his purpose, he
purchased for 1500*l.* the place of one of the clerks of the council.

After he had written his epistle on the victory of the *Boyne*, his patron    6
Dorset introduced him to king William with this expression: *Sir, I have
brought a Mouse to wait on your Majesty*. To which the king is said to have
replied, *You do well to put me in the way of making a Man of him*; and ordered

him a pension of five hundred pounds. This story, however current, seems to have been made after the event. The king's answer implies a greater acquaintance with our proverbial and familiar diction than king William could possibly have attained.

7    In 1691, being member in the house of commons, he argued warmly in favour of a law to grant the assistance of counsel in trials for high treason; and in the midst of his speech, falling into some confusion, was for a while silent; but, recovering himself, observed, "how reasonable it was to allow counsel to men called as criminals before a court of justice, when it appeared how much the presence of that assembly could disconcert one of their own body."

8    After this he rose fast into honours and employments, being made one of the commissioners of the treasury, and called to the privy council. In 1694, he became chancellor of the Exchequer; and the next year engaged in the great attempt of the recoinage, which was in two years happily compleated. In 1696, he projected the *general fund*, and raised the credit of the Exchequer; and, after enquiry concerning a grant of Irish crown-lands, it was determined by a vote of the commons, that Charles Montague, esquire, *had deserved his Majesty's favour*. In 1698, being advanced to the first commission of the treasury, he was appointed one of the regency in the king's absence: the next year he was made auditor of the Exchequer; and the year after created *baron Halifax*. He was however impeached by the commons; but the articles were dismissed by the lords.

9    At the accession of queen Anne he was dismissed from the council; and in the first parliament of her reign was again attacked by the commons, and again escaped by the protection of the lords. In 1704, he wrote an answer to Bromley's speech against occasional conformity. He headed the Enquiry into the danger of the Church. In 1706, he proposed and negotiated the Union with Scotland; and when the elector of Hanover received the garter, after the act had passed for securing the Protestant Succession, he was appointed to carry the ensigns of the order to the electoral court. He sat as one of the judges of Sacheverell; but voted for a mild sentence. Being now no longer in favour, he contrived to obtain a writ for summoning the electoral prince to parliament as duke of Cambridge.

10   At the queen's death he was appointed one of the regents; and at the accession of George the First was made earl of Halifax, knight of the garter, and first commissioner of the treasury, with a grant to his nephew of the reversion of the auditorship of the Exchequer. More was not to be had, and this he kept but a little while; for on the 19th of May, 1715, he died of an inflammation of his lungs.

Of him, who from a poet became a patron of poets, it will be readily 11
believed that the works would not miss of celebration. Addison began to
praise him early, and was followed or accompanied by other poets; perhaps
by almost all, except Swift and Pope; who forbore to flatter him in his life,
and after his death spoke of him, Swift with slight censure, and Pope in the
character of Bufo with acrimonious contempt.

He was, as Pope says, *fed with dedications*; for Tickell affirms that no 12
dedicator was unrewarded. To charge all unmerited praise with the guilt of
flattery, and to suppose that the encomiast always knows and feels the
falsehood of his affertions, is surely to discover great ignorance of human
nature and human life. In determinations depending not on rules, but on
experience and comparison, judgement is always in some degree subject to
affection. Very near to admiration is the wish to admire.

Every man willingly gives value to the praise which he receives, and 13
considers the sentence passed in his favour as the sentence of discernment.
We admire in a friend that understanding that selected us for confidence;
we admire more, in a patron, that judgement which, instead of scattering
bounty indiscriminately, directed it to us; and, if the patron be an author,
those performances which gratitude forbids us to blame, affection will easily
dispose us to exalt.

To these prejudices, hardly culpable, interest adds a power always 14
operating, though not always, because not willingly, perceived. The modesty of praise wears gradually away; and perhaps the pride of patronage may
be in time so increased, that modest praise will no longer please.

Many a blandishment was practised upon Halifax, which he would never 15
have known, had he had no other attractions than those of his poetry, of
which a short time has withered the beauties. It would now be esteemed no
honour, by a contributor to the monthly bundles of verses, to be told, that,
in strains either familiar or solemn, he sings like Montague.

# PARNELL

1 THE Life of Dr. PARNELL is a task which I should very willingly decline, since it has been lately written by Goldsmith, a man of such variety of powers, and such felicity of performance, that he always seemed to do best that which he was doing; a man who had the art of being minute without tediousness, and general without confusion; whose language was copious without exuberance, exact without constraint, and easy without weakness.

2 What such an author has told, who would tell again? I have made an abstract from his larger narrative; and have this gratification from my attempt, that it gives me an opportunity of paying due tribute to the memory of Goldsmith.

*Τὸ γὰρ γέρας ἐςὶ ζανόντων.*

3 THOMAS PARNELL was the son of a commonwealthsman of the same name, who at the Restoration left Congleton in Cheshire, where the family had been established for several centuries, and, settling in Ireland, purchased an estate, which, with his lands in Cheshire, descended to the poet, who was born at Dublin in 1679; and, after the usual education at a grammar school, was at the age of thirteen admitted into the College, where, in 1700, he became master of arts; and was the same year ordained a deacon, though under the canonical age, by a dispensation from the bishop of Derry.

4 About three years afterwards he was made a priest; and in 1705 Dr. Ashe, the bishop of Clogher, conferred upon him the archdeaconry of Clogher. About the same time he married Mrs. Anne Minchin, an amiable lady, by whom he had two sons who died young, and a daughter who long survived him.

5 At the ejection of the Whigs, in the end of queen Anne's reign, Parnell was persuaded to change his party, not without much censure from those whom he forsook, and was received by the new ministry as a valuable reinforcement. When the earl of Oxford was told that Dr. Parnell waited among the croud in the outer room, he went, by the persuasion of Swift, with his treasurer's staff in his hand, to enquire for him, and to bid him welcome; and, as may be inferred from Pope's dedication, admitted him as a favourite companion to his convivial hours, but, as it seems often to have happened in those times to the favourites of the great, without attention to his fortune, which however was in no great need of improvement.

Parnell, who did not want ambition or vanity, was desirous to make 6
himself conspicuous, and to shew how worthy he was of high preferment.
As he thought himself qualified to become a popular preacher, he displayed
his elocution with great success in the pulpits of London; but the queen's
death putting an end to his expectations, abated his diligence: and Pope
represents him as falling from that time into intemperance of wine. That in
his latter life he was too much a lover of the bottle, is not denied; but I have
heard it imputed to a cause more likely to obtain forgiveness from mankind,
the untimely death of a darling son; or, as others tell, the loss of his wife,
who died (1712) in the midst of his expectations.

He was now to derive every future addition to his preferments from his 7
personal interest with his private friends, and he was not long unregarded.
He was warmly recommended by Swift to archbishop King, who gave him a
prebend in 1713; and in May 1716 presented him to the vicarage of Finglas
in the diocese of Dublin, worth four hundred pounds a year. Such notice
from such a man, inclines me to believe that the vice of which he has been
accused was not gross, or not notorious.

But his prosperity did not last long. His end, whatever was its cause, was 8
now approaching. He enjoyed his preferment little more than a year; for in
July 1717, in his thirty-eighth year, he died at Chester, on his way to
Ireland.

He seems to have been one of those poets who take delight in writing. He 9
contributed to the papers of that time, and probably published more than he
owned. He left many compositions behind him, of which Pope selected
those which he thought best, and dedicated them to the earl of Oxford. Of
these Goldsmith has given an opinion, and his criticism it is seldom safe to
contradict. He bestows just praise upon the *Rise of Woman*, the *Fairy Tale*,
and the *Pervigilium Veneris*; but has very properly remarked, that in the
*Battle of Mice and Frogs* the Greek names have not in English their original
effect.

He tells us, that the *Bookworm* is borrowed from *Beza*; but he should 10
have added, with modern applications: and when he discovers that *Gay
Bacchus* is translated from *Augurellus*, he ought to have remarked, that the
latter part is purely Parnell's. Another poem, *When Spring comes on*, is, he
says, taken from the French. I would add, that the description of *Barrenness*,
in his verses to Pope, was borrowed from *Secundus*; but lately searching for
the passage which I had formerly read, I could not find it. The *Night-piece
on Death* is indirectly preferred by Goldsmith to Gray's *Church-yard*; but,
in my opinion, Gray has the advantage in dignity, variety, and originality of
sentiment. He observes that the story of the *Hermit* is in *More's Dialogues*
and *Howell's Letters*, and supposes it to have been originally *Arabian*.

11     Goldsmith has not taken any notice of the *Elegy to the old Beauty*, which is perhaps the meanest; nor of the *Allegory on Man*, the happiest of Parnell's performances. The hint of the *Hymn to Contentment* I suspect to have been borrowed from Cleiveland.

12     The general character of Parnell is not great extent of comprehension, or fertility of mind. Of the little that appears still less is his own. His praise must be derived from the easy sweetness of his diction: in his verses there is *more happiness than pains*; he is spritely without effort, and always delights though he never ravishes; every thing is proper, yet every thing seems casual. If there is some appearance of elaboration in the *Hermit*, the narrative, as it is less airy, is less pleasing. Of his other compositions it is impossible to say whether they are the productions of Nature, so excellent as not to want the help of Art, or of Art so refined as to resemble Nature.

13     This criticism relates only to the pieces published by Pope. Of the large appendages which I find in the last edition, I can only say that I know not whence they came, nor have ever enquired whither they are going. They stand upon the faith of the compilers.

# GARTH

SAMUEL GARTH was of a good family in Yorkshire, and from some school in 1
his own country became a student at Peter-house in Cambridge, where he
resided till he commenced doctor of physick on July the 7th, 1691. He was
examined before the College at London on March the 12th, 1691–2, and
admitted fellow July 26th, 1692. He was soon so much distinguished, by his
conversation and accomplishments, as to obtain very extensive practice;
and, if a pamphlet of those times may be credited, had the favour and
confidence of one party, as Ratcliffe had of the other.

He is always mentioned as a man of benevolence; and it is just to suppose 2
that his desire of helping the helpless, disposed him to so much zeal for the
*Dispensary*; an undertaking of which some account, however short, is proper
to be given.

Whether what Temple says be true, that physicians have had more 3
learning than the other faculties, I will not stay to enquire; but, I believe,
every man has found in physicians great liberality, and dignity of sentiment,
very prompt effusion of beneficence, and willingness to exert a lucrative art,
where there is no hope of lucre. Agreeably to this character, the College of
Physicians, in July 1687, published an edict, requiring all the fellows,
candidates, and licentiates, to give gratuitous advice to the neighbouring
poor.

This edict was sent to the Court of Aldermen; and a question being made 4
to whom the appellation of the *poor* should be extended, the College
answered, that it should be sufficient to bring a testimonial from a clergyman officiating in the parish where the patient resided.

After a year's experience, the physicians found their charity frustrated by 5
some malignant opposition, and made to a great degree vain by the high
price of physick; they therefore voted, in August 1688, that the laboratory of
the College should be accommodated to the preparation of medicines, and
another room prepared for their reception; and that the contributors to the
expence should manage the charity.

It was now expected that the Apothecaries would have undertaken the 6
care of providing medicines; but they took another course. Thinking the
whole design pernicious to their interest, they endeavoured to raise a faction
against it in the College, and found some physicians mean enough to solicit
their patronage, by betraying to them the counsels of the College. The

greater part, however, enforced by a new edict in 1694, the former order of 1687, and sent it to the mayor and aldermen, who appointed a committee to treat with the College, and settle the mode of administring the charity.

7    It was desired by the aldermen, that the testimonials of churchwardens and overseers should be admitted; and that all hired servants, and all apprentices to handicraftsmen, should be considered as *poor*. This likewise was granted by the College.

8    It was then considered who should distribute the medicines, and who should settle their prices. The physicians procured some apothecaries to undertake the dispensation, and offered that the warden and company of the apothecaries should adjust the price. This offer was rejected; and the apothecaries who had engaged to assist the charity were considered as traytors to the company, threatened with the imposition of troublesome offices, and deterred from the performance of their engagements. The apothecaries ventured upon public opposition, and presented a kind of remonstrance against the design to the committee of the city, which the physicians condescended to confute: and at last the traders seem to have prevailed among the sons of trade; for the proposal of the college having been considered, a paper of approbation was drawn up, but postponed and forgotten.

9    The physicians still persisted; and in 1696 a subscription was raised by themselves, according to an agreement prefixed to the Dispensary. The poor were for a time supplied with medicines; for how long a time, I know not. The medicinal charity, like others, began with ardour, but soon remitted, and at last died gradually away.

10    About the time of the subscription begins the action of the *Dispensary*. The Poem, as its subject was present and popular, co-operated with passions and prejudices then prevalent, and, with such auxiliaries to its intrinsick merit, was universally and liberally applauded. It was on the side of charity against the intrigues of interest, and of regular learning against licentious usurpation of medical authority, and was therefore naturally favoured by those who read and can judge of poetry.

11    In 1697, Garth spoke that which is now called the *Harveian* Oration; which the authors of the Biographia mention with more praise than the passage quoted in their notes will fully justify. Garth, speaking of the mischiefs done by quacks, has these expressions: "Non tamen telis vulnerat ista agyrtarum colluvies, sed theriacâ quadam magis perniciosa, non pyrio, sed pulvere nescio quo exotico certat, non globulis plumbeis, sed pilulis æque lethalibus interficit." This was certainly thought fine by the author, and is still admired by his biographer. In October 1702 he became one of the censors of the College.

Garth, being an active and zealous Whig, was a member of the Kit-cat 12
club, and by consequence familiarly known to all the great men of that
denomination. In 1710, when the government fell into other hands, he writ
to lord Godolphin, on his dismission, a short poem, which was criticised in
the *Examiner*, and so successfully either defended or excused by
Mr. Addison, that, for the sake of the vindication, it ought to be preserved.

At the accession of the present Family his merits were acknowledged and 13
rewarded. He was knighted with the sword of his hero, Marlborough; and
was made physician in ordinary to the king, and physician-general to the
army.

He then undertook an edition of Ovid's Metamorphoses, translated by 14
several hands; which he recommended by a Preface, written with more
ostentation than ability: his notions are half-formed, and his materials
immethodically confused. This was his last work. He died Jan. 18. 1717–
18, and was buried at Harrow-on-the-Hill.

His personal character seems to have been social and liberal. He com- 15
municated himself through a very wide extent of acquaintance; and though
firm in a party, at a time when firmness included virulence, yet he imparted
his kindness to those who were not supposed to favour his principles. He
was an early encourager of Pope, and was at once the friend of Addison and
of Granville. He is accused of voluptuousness and irreligion; and Pope, who
says that "if ever there was a good Christian, without knowing himself to be
so, it was Dr. Garth," seems not able to deny what he is angry to hear and
loth to confess.

Pope afterwards declared himself convinced that Garth died in the 16
communion of the Church of Rome, having been privately reconciled. It
is observed by Lowth, that there is less distance than is thought between
scepticism and popery, and that a mind wearied with perpetual doubt,
willingly seeks repose in the bosom of an infallible church.

His poetry has been praised at least equally to its merit. In the *Dispensary* 17
there is a strain of smooth and free versification; but few lines are eminently
elegant. No passages fall below mediocrity, and few rise much above it. The
plan seems formed without just proportion to the subject; the means and
end have no necessary connection. *Resnel*, in his Preface to *Pope's* Essay,
remarks, that Garth exhibits no discrimination of characters; and that what
any one says might with equal propriety have been said by another. The
general design is perhaps open to criticism; but the composition can seldom
be charged with inaccuracy or negligence. The author never slumbers in
self-indulgence; his full vigour is always exerted; scarce a line is left unfinished, nor is it easy to find an expression used by constraint, or a thought
imperfectly expressed. It was remarked by Pope, that the *Dispensary* had

been corrected in every edition, and that every change was an improvement. It appears, however, to want something of poetical ardour, and something of general delectation; and therefore, since it has been no longer supported by accidental and extrinsick popularity, it has been scarcely able to support itself.

# ROWE

NICHOLAS ROWE was born at Little Berkford in Bedfordshire, in 1673. His   1
family had long possessed a considerable estate, with a good house, at
Lambertoun* in Devonshire. The ancestor from whom he descended in a
direct line, received the arms borne by his descendants for his bravery in the
Holy War. His father John Rowe, who was the first that quitted his paternal
acres to practise any art of profit, professed the law, and published Benlow's
and Dallison's Reports in the reign of James the Second, when, in opposition to the notions then diligently propagated, of dispensing power, he
ventured to remark how low his authors rated the prerogative. He was
made a serjeant, and died April 30, 1692. He was buried in the Temple
Church.

Nicholas was first sent to a private school at Highgate; and being after-   2
wards removed to Westminster, was at twelve years chosen one of the
King's scholars. His master was Busby, who suffered none of his scholars
to let their powers lie useless; and his exercises in several languages are said
to have been written with uncommon degrees of excellence, and yet to have
cost him very little labour.

At sixteen he had in his father's opinion made advances in learning   3
sufficient to qualify him for the study of law, and was entered a student of
the Middle Temple, where for some time he read statutes and reports with
proficiency proportionate to the force of his mind, which was already such
that he endeavoured to comprehend law, not as a series of precedents, or
collection of positive precepts, but as a system of rational government, and
impartial justice.

When he was nineteen, he was by the death of his father left more to his   4
own direction, and probably from that time suffered law gradually to give
way to poetry. At twenty-five he produced *The Ambitious Stepmother*, which
was received with so much favour, that he devoted himself from that time
wholly to elegant literature.

His next tragedy (1702) was *Tamerlane*, in which, under the name of   5
Tamerlane, he intended to characterise king William, and Lewis the Fourteenth under that of Bajazet. The virtues of Tamerlane seem to have been
arbitrarily assigned him by his poet, for I know not that history gives any

* In the Villare, *Lamerton*.

other qualities than those which make a conqueror. The fashion however of the time was, to accumulate upon Lewis all that can raise horror and detestation; and whatever good was withheld from him, that it might not be thrown away, was bestowed upon king William.

6    This was the tragedy which Rowe valued most, and that which probably, by the help of political auxiliaries, excited most applause; but occasional poetry must often content itself with occasional praise. Tamerlane has for a long time been acted only once a year, on the night when king William landed. Our quarrel with Lewis has been long over, and it now gratifies neither zeal nor malice to see him painted with aggravated features, like a Saracen upon a sign.

7    The *Fair Penitent*, his next production (1703), is one of the most pleasing tragedies on the stage, where it still keeps its turns of appearing, and probably will long keep them, for there is scarcely any work of any poet at once so interesting by the fable, and so delightful by the language. The story is domestick, and therefore easily received by the imagination, and assimilated to common life; the diction is exquisitely harmonious, and soft or spritely as occasion requires.

8    The character of *Lothario* seems to have been expanded by Richardson into *Lovelace*, but he has excelled his original in the moral effect of the fiction. Lothario, with gaiety which cannot be hated, and bravery which cannot be despised, retains too much of the spectator's kindness. It was in the power of Richardson alone to teach us at once esteem and detestation, to make virtuous resentment overpower all the benevolence which wit, elegance, and courage, naturally excite; and to lose at last the hero in the villain.

9    The fifth act is not equal to the former; the events of the drama are exhausted, and little remains but to talk of what is past. It has been observed, that the title of the play does not sufficiently correspond with the behaviour of Calista, who at last shews no evident signs of repentance, but may be reasonably suspected of feeling pain from detection rather than from guilt, and expresses more shame than sorrow, and more rage than shame.

10   His next (1706) was *Ulysses*; which, with the common fate of mythological stories, is now generally neglected. We have been too early acquainted with the poetical heroes, to expect any pleasure from their revival; to shew them as they have already been shewn, is to disgust by repetition; to give them new qualities or new adventures, is to offend by violating received notions.

11   The *Royal Convert* (1708) seems to have a better claim to longevity. The fable is drawn from an obscure and barbarous age, to which fictions are most easily and properly adapted; for when objects are imperfectly seen, they

easily take forms from imagination. The scene lies among our ancestors in our own country, and therefore very easily catches attention. *Rhodogune* is a personage truly tragical, of high spirit, and violent passions, great with tempestuous dignity, and wicked with a soul that would have been heroic if it had been virtuous. The motto seems to tell that this play was not successful.

Rowe does not always remember what his characters require. In *Tamer-* 12 *lane* there is some ridiculous mention of the God of Love; and Rhodogune, a savage Saxon, talks of Venus, and the eagle that bears the thunder of Jupiter.

This play discovers its own date, by a prediction of the *Union*, in 13 imitation of Cranmer's prophetick promises to *Henry the Eighth*. The anticipated blessings of union are not very naturally introduced, nor very happily expressed.

He once (1706) tried to change his hand. He ventured on a comedy, and 14 produced the *Biter*; with which, though it was unfavourably treated by the audience, he was himself delighted; for he is said to have sat in the house, laughing with great vehemence, whenever he had in his own opinion produced a jest. But finding that he and the publick had no sympathy of mirth, he tried at lighter scenes no more.

After the Royal Convert (1714) appeared *Jane Shore*, written, as its 15 author professes, *in imitation of Shakspeare's style*. In what he thought himself an imitator of Shakspeare, it is not easy to conceive. The numbers, the diction, the sentiments, and the conduct, every thing in which imitation can consist, are remote in the utmost degree from the manner of Shak-speare; whose dramas it resembles only as it is an English story, and as some of the persons have their names in history. This play, consisting chiefly of domestick scenes and private distress, lays hold upon the heart. The wife is forgiven because she repents, and the husband is honoured because he forgives. This therefore is one of those pieces which we still welcome on the stage.

His last tragedy (1715) was *Lady Jane Grey*. This subject had been 16 chosen by Mr. Smith, whose papers were put into Rowe's hands such as he describes them in his Preface. This play likewise has sunk into oblivion. From this time he gave nothing more to the stage.

Being by a competent fortune exempted from any necessity of combating 17 his inclination, he never wrote in distress, and therefore does not appear to have ever written in haste. His works were finished to his own approbation, and bear few marks of negligence or hurry. It is remarkable that his prologues and epilogues are all his own, though he sometimes supplied others; he afforded help, but did not solicit it.

18    As his studies necessarily made him acquainted with Shakspeare, and acquaintance produced veneration, he undertook (1709) an edition of his works, from which he neither received much praise, nor seems to have expected it; yet, I believe, those who compare it with former copies, will find that he has done more than he promised; and that, without the pomp of notes or boasts of criticism, many passages are happily restored. He prefixed a life of the author, such as tradition then almost expiring could supply, and a preface, which cannot be said to discover much profundity or penetration. He at least contributed to the popularity of his author.

19    He was willing enough to improve his fortune by other arts than poetry. He was undersecretary for three years when the duke of Queensberry was secretary of state, and afterwards applied to the earl of Oxford for some publick employment*. Oxford enjoined him to study Spanish; and when, some time afterwards, he came again, and said that he had mastered it, dismissed him with this consolation, "Then, Sir, I envy you the pleasure of reading Don Quixot in the original."

20    This story is sufficiently attested; but why Oxford, who desired to be thought a favourer of literature, should thus insult a man of acknowledged merit; or how Rowe, who was so keen a Whig* that he did not willingly converse with men of the opposite party, could ask preferment from Oxford, it is not now possible to discover. Pope, who told the story, did not say on what occasion the advice was given; and though he owned Rowe's disappointment, doubted whether any injury was intended him, but thought it rather lord Oxford's *odd way*.

21    It is likely that he lived on discontented through the rest of queen Anne's reign; but the time came at last when he found kinder friends. At the accession of king George, he was made poet laureat; I am afraid by the ejection of poor Nahum Tate, who (1716) died in the Mint, where he was forced to seek shelter by extreme poverty. He was made likewise one of the land surveyors of the customs of the port of London. The prince of Wales chose him clerk of his council; and the lord chancellor Parker, as soon as he received the seals, appointed him, unasked, secretary of the presentations. Such an accumulation of employments undoubtedly produced a very considerable revenue.

22    Having already translated some parts of *Lucan's Pharsalia*, which had been published in the Miscellanies, and doubtless received many praises, he undertook a version of the whole work, which he lived to finish, but not to publish. It seems to have been printed under the care of Dr. Welwood, who prefixed the author's life, in which is contained the following character:

* Spence.

"As to his person it was graceful and well-made; his face regular, and of a    23
manly beauty. As his soul was well lodged, so its rational and animal
faculties excelled in a high degree. He had a quick and fruitful invention,
a deep penetration, and a large compass of thought, with singular dexterity
and easiness in making his thoughts to be understood. He was master of
most parts of polite learning, especially the classical authors, both Greek
and Latin; understood the French, Italian, and Spanish Languages, and
spoke the first fluently, and the other two tolerably well.

"He had likewise read most of the Greek and Roman histories in their    24
original languages, and most that are wrote in English, French, Italian, and
Spanish. He had a good taste in philosophy; and, having a firm impression
of religion upon his mind, he took great delight in divinity and ecclesiastical
history, in both which he made great advances in the times he retired into
the country, which were frequent. He expressed, on all occasions, his full
persuasion of the truth of Revealed Religion; and being a sincere member of
the established church himself, he pitied, but condemned not, those that
dissented from it. He abhorred the principles of persecuting men upon the
account of their opinions in religion; and being strict in his own, he took it
not upon him to censure those of another persuasion. His conversation was
pleasant, witty, and learned, without the least tincture of affectation or
pedantry; and his inimitable manner of diverting and enlivening the company, made it impossible for any one to be out of humour when he was in it.
Envy and detraction seemed to be entirely foreign to his constitution; and
whatever provocations he met with at any time, he passed them over
without the least thought of resentment or revenge. As Homer had a Zoilus,
so Mr. Rowe had sometimes his; for there were not wanting malevolent
people, and pretenders to poetry too, that would now-and-then bark at his
best performances; but he was so much conscious of his own genius, and
had so much good-nature as to forgive them; nor could he ever be tempted
to return them an answer.

"The love of learning and poetry made him not the less fit for business,    25
and nobody applied himself closer to it, when it required his attendance.
The late duke of Queensberry, when he was secretary of state, made him his
secretary for publick affairs; and when that truly great man came to know
him well, he was never so pleased as when Mr. Rowe was in his company.
After the duke's death, all avenues were stopped to his preferment; and
during the rest of that reign, he passed his time with the Muses and his
books, and sometimes the conversation of his friends.

"When he had just got to be easy in his fortune, and was in a fair way to    26
make it better, death swept him away, and in him deprived the world of one
of the best men as well as one of the best geniuses of the age. He died like a

Christian and a Philosopher, in charity with all mankind, and with an absolute resignation to the will of God. He kept up his good-humour to the last; and took leave of his wife and friends, immediately before his last agony, with the same tranquillity of mind, and the same indifference for life, as though he had been upon taking but a short journey. He was twice married, first to a daughter of Mr. Parsons, one of the auditors of the revenue; and afterwards to a daughter of Mr. Devenish, of a good family in Dorsetshire. By the first he had a son; and by the second a daughter, married afterwards to Mr. Fane. He died the sixth of December, 1718, in the forty-fifth year of his age; and was buried the nineteenth of the same month in Westminster-abbey, in the isle where many of our English poets are interred, over-against Chaucer, his body being attended by a select number of his friends, and the dean and choir officiating at the funeral."

27    To this character, which is apparently given with the fondness of a friend, may be added the testimony of Pope; who says, in a letter to Blount, "Mr. Rowe accompanied me, and passed a week in the Forest. I need not tell you how much a man of his turn entertained me; but I must acquaint you, there is a vivacity and gaiety of disposition, almost peculiar to him, which make it impossible to part from him without that uneasiness which generally succeeds all our pleasures."

28    Pope has left behind him another mention of his companion, less advantageous, which is thus reported by Dr. Warburton:

      "Rowe, in Mr. Pope's opinion, maintained a decent character, but had no heart. Mr. Addison was justly offended with some behaviour which arose from that want, and estranged himself from him; which Rowe felt very severely. Mr. Pope, their common friend, knowing this, took an opportunity, at some juncture of Mr. Addison's advancement, to tell him how poor Rowe was grieved at his displeasure, and what satisfaction he expressed at Mr. Addison's good fortune; which he expressed so naturally, that he (Mr. Pope) could not but think him sincere. Mr. Addison replied, 'I do not suspect that he feigned; but the levity of his heart is such, that he is struck with any new adventure; and it would affect him just in the same manner, if he heard I was going to be hanged.'—Mr. Pope said, he could not deny but Mr. Addison understood Rowe well."

29    This censure time has not left us the power of confirming or refuting; but observation daily shews, that much stress is not to be laid on hyperbolical accusations, and pointed sentences, which even he that utters them desires to be applauded rather than credited. Addison can hardly be supposed to have meant all that he said. Few characters can bear the microscopick

scrutiny of wit quickened by anger; and perhaps the best advice to authors would be, that they should keep out of the way of one another.

Rowe is chiefly to be considered as a tragick writer and a translator. In his 30 attempt at comedy he failed so ignominiously, that his *Biter* is not inserted in his works; and his occasional poems and short compositions are rarely worthy of either praise or censure; for they seem the casual sports of a mind seeking rather to amuse its leisure than to exercise its powers.

In the construction of his dramas, there is not much art; he is not a nice 31 observer of the Unities. He extends time and varies place as his convenience requires. To vary the place is not, in my opinion, any violation of Nature, if the change be made between the acts; for it is no less easy for the spectator to suppose himself at Athens in the second act, than at Thebes in the first; but to change the scene, as is done by Rowe, in the middle of an act, is to add more acts to the play, since an act is so much of the business as is transacted without interruption. Rowe, by this licence, easily extricates himself from difficulties; as in *Jane Grey*, when we have been terrified with all the dreadful pomp of publick execution, and are wondering how the heroine or the poet will proceed, no sooner has *Jane* pronounced some prophetick rhymes, than—pass and be gone—the scene closes, and *Pembroke* and *Gardiner* are turned out upon the stage.

I know not that there can be found in his plays any deep search into 32 nature, any accurate discriminations of kindred qualities, or nice display of passion in its progress; all is general and undefined. Nor does he much interest or affect the auditor, except in *Jane Shore*, who is always seen and heard with pity. *Alicia* is a character of empty noise, with no resemblance to real sorrow or to natural madness.

Whence, then, has Rowe his reputation? From the reasonableness and 33 propriety of some of his scenes, from the elegance of his diction, and the suavity of his verse. He seldom moves either pity or terror, but he often elevates the sentiments; he seldom pierces the breast, but he always delights the ear, and often improves the understanding.

His translation of the *Golden Verses*, and of the first book of *Quillet's* 34 Poem, have nothing in them remarkable. The *Golden Verses* are tedious.

The version of *Lucan* is one of the greatest productions of English poetry; 35 for there is perhaps none that so completely exhibits the genius and spirit of the original. *Lucan* is distinguished by a kind of senatorial or philosophic dignity, rather, as Quintilian observes, declamatory than poetical; full of ambitious morality and pointed sentences, comprised in vigorous and animated lines. This character Rowe has very diligently and successfully preserved. His versification, which is such as his contemporaries practised, without any attempt at innovation or improvement, seldom wants either melody or force. His author's sense is sometimes a little diluted by additional infusions, and sometimes weakened by too much expansion. But such faults are to be expected in all translations, from the constraint of measures and dissimilitude of languages. The *Pharsalia* of Rowe deserves more notice than it obtains, and as it is more read will be more esteemed.

# TEXTUAL NOTES

## BUTLER

1. editions] edition *P79*

2. 1612. This account Dr. Nash... Feb. 14] 1612; but Mr. Longueville, the son of Butler's principal friend, informed the author of the "General Dictionary" that he was born in 1600 *P79*, *L81*, *rev. in Berg, but partly excised*

3. Mr. Longueville... friend,] the other *P79*, *L81*, *rev. in Berg by Nichols (?)*

   want *P79*, *L81 (not rev. in Berg)*] a want *L83*

   Dr. Nash... called *Butler's tenement.*] *added in L83. (The insertion at the foot of the page in Berg has been excised)*

5. Earl's-Croomb] Earl's-Croom *P79*, *L81*, *rev. in Berg*

   Some pictures... a better fate.] *ins. in Berg, L83*

14. any opportunity *Pack, P79*] an opportunity *L81*, *L83*

16. unpleasing. He] unpleasing; and, if his birth be placed right by Mr. Longueville, he *P79*, *L81*, *rev. in Berg without emendation of punctuation*

    think] well think *P79*, *L81*, *rev. in Berg*

    longer... begin to fail] longer *P79*, *L81*, *rev. in Berg*

18. *Added in L83. (The insertion at the foot of the page in Berg has been excised)*

19. Butler's] Mr. Butler's *P79*, *L81*, *rev. in Berg*

21. The mode] The date of his birth is doubtful; the mode *P79*, *L81*, *rev. in Berg*

23. trains of] think of *P79 (with the catchword* on *instead of* of), *L81*, *rev. in Berg*

43. which perplexed... practice] that perplexed doctrine *P79*, *L81*, *rev. in Berg*

47. this satire *P79*, *L81 (not rev. in Berg)*] the satire *L83*


## ROCHESTER

1. April 10, 1647] in April, 1648 *P79 (corr. in Gent. Mag. (1779), 594)*

   twelve] eleven *P79*

   fourteen] thirteen *P79*

2. the Court] a Court *P79*, *L81*, *rev. in Berg*

   [the ship commanded by] *Burnet*] *om. in all edns.*

11. sensuality] sensualty *P79*, *L81*

13. thirty-fourth] thirty-third *P79*, *L81*, *rev. in Berg by Nichols (?)*

14. itself *P79*, *L81*] itself *L83*

16. the late] this *P79*

25. whose *buffoon conceit . . . durst*;] ins. in *Berg, L83*

27. excellence. What] excellence; and what *P79, L81, rev. in Berg*

28. [l. 33] magnas *Passerat, P79, L81 (not rev. in Berg)*] magnus *L83*


# ROSCOMMON

[*Variants from directly comparable passages in the text in Gent. Mag. (1748) have been noted (48). For passages in 1748 later omitted see the Commentary.*]

1. was the son . . . Strafford. He was] was *P79, L81, rev. in Berg*

    both his uncle and his godfather] his godfather *P79, L81, rev. in Berg*

    father . . . Roscommon,] father *P79, L81, rev. in Berg*

3. was sent] went *P79, L81, rev. in Berg*

7. at last] at least *48*

    shall see] shall find *48*

14. some] some at least *P79, L81, rev. in Berg*

21. *Irae*] *Viae P79 (corr. in Gent. Mag. (1779), 594)*

22. learning,] art and science; and those ornaments *48*

23. spritely] sprightly *P79, L81, rev. in Berg*

    judgement to] judgement and *48*

24. compositions] composition *48*

27. unusual and] unusual or *48*

    rules that] rules which *48*

    important] so important *48*

    praises] honours *48*

    discernment *48, P79*] descernment *L81, L83*

30. Poetry *48, P79, L81*] poetry *L83*

35. political *P79, L81 (not rev. in Berg)*] poetical *L83*

38. says she] says he *P79, L81, rev. in Berg (corr. in Gent. Mag. (1779), 594)*


# OTWAY

4. different use] *rev. in proof to* the different use

    faculty; that the] *rev. in proof to* faculty. The

    that the attention] that *del. in proof*

5. qualify] *rev. to* qualify him *in proof*

6. Racine] Rapin *P79, L81, L83*

7. no purpose] *rev. to* not any purpose *in proof*

    innocence *Works (1712)*] imminence *proof, P79, L81, L83 (queried in Gent. Mag. (1779), 595)*

8. some troops] *rev. to* the troops *in proof*

9. time;] *rev. to* time, *in proof*

   consisting . . . could] consisted . . . who could *rev. in proof*

13. the late] this *P79*

14. is said to have died] died *P79, L81, rev. in Berg*

    and there is this ground . . . friends. But] but *P79, L81, rev. in Berg*

    pressed hard upon him . . . to the grave] brought him to the grave has never been denied *P79, L81, rev. in Berg*

15. the late] this *P79*

15 **note.** *Ins. in Berg, L83*


# WALLER

4. lig with my Lord] with my Lord *proof, queried by Nichols (?)*

5. Waller's . . . began] His . . . begun *rev. in proof*

   poem that] poem which *rev. in proof*

   only by] truely by *rev. in proof (Atterbury's text of 1690 has* barely by*)*

5 **note.** *Ins. in Berg, L83*

6. time] date *rev. in proof*

   considers as congratulating] supposes to have been written at *rev. in proof*

7. that seem . . . dates, could] seem to *P79, L81, rev. in Berg*

   In the verses . . . escape,] In one *P79, L81, rev. in Berg*

   his marriage] the marriage *P79, L81, rev. in Berg*

   France, must] France, which must *P79*

   properly praised] known *P79, L81, rev. in Berg*

   known] indeed known *P79, L81, rev. in Berg*

12. genius . . . but] wit . . . and *rev. in proof*

13. scholars] writers *rev. in proof*; most illustrious scholars *P79, L81, rev. in Berg*

    traditions] tradition *corr. in proof*

    more may] that may *corr. in proof*

14. Whales] Whale *corr. in proof*

15. time] dates *proof*

16. gained] married *rev. in proof*

    this wife] his wife *rev. in proof*

    praised some] praised many *P79, L81, rev. in Berg*

    made only] made *rev. in proof*

    No spectacle is] There is no spectacle *rev. in proof*

17. his biographers have recorded] nothing is known, but *rev. in proof*

19. The King's . . . produced] When the king sent for a supply, he made *rev. in proof*
    complaints] complaint *corr. in proof*

20. the Commons] them *rev. in proof*

21. *At the foot of p. 16 of the proofs, SJ has written* Please to send a revise

22. B. I. sect. 9. *P79, L81*] *not rev. in Berg but om. in L83*

25. speech] *SJ added a note in Berg:* This speech is preserved in the *Parliamentary History (forgetting that P79 and L81 already had a similar note to* **26**)

27. episcopacy *P79, L81*; espiscopacy *L83*

30. is as true *Waller, P79, L81 (not rev. in Berg)*] is true *L83*

39. They proceeded . . . endangered.] *added in L83. (The insertion at the foot of the page in Berg has been excised: see note to* **39***)*

40. Clarendon] as Clarendon *P79, L81, rev. in Berg*
    the Royalists] them *P79, L81, rev. in Berg*
    five] three *P79, L81, rev. in Berg*

40 note. *Ins. in Berg, L83.*

41. power *P79, L81 (not rev. in Berg)*] powers *L83*

43. too frequently] *ins. in Berg, L83*

45. that was left *P79*] left *1711*; that was *L81, L83*

46. May (1643)] May *P79, L81, rev. in Berg*

47. admitted] addicted *rev. in proof*
    had conveyed] conveyed *P79, L81*; derived *Clarendon*
    testified] declared *rev. in proof*

48. which cannot . . . punished] it is not safe to punish *rev. in proof*

49. notice] them notice *rev. in proof*
    sent] seen *corr. in proof*
    dug] digged *corr. in proof*

50. they saw] they found *rev. in proof*

51. shut . . . Clarendon] shut out *rev. in proof*

58. his execution] this execution *P79*
    His crime . . . Waller's plot.] *ins. in Berg, L83*

59. being . . . was] was . . . and was *rev. in proof*
    Waller's yet] that of Waller *rev. in proof*
    Hampden . . . his family; but] Hampden *P79, L81, rev. in Berg*
    their own nomination] the insertion of their names *rev. in proof*

60. with what] and with what *rev. in proof*
    implored] confronted *rev. in proof to* supplicated *and* implored
    he was by expulsion from the House] being expelled the house, he was *rev. in proof to* he was expelled the house, and

Essex; but] Essex, and *proof*

paying] after *rev. in proof*

63. at last] in time *rev. in proof*

    and obtained it] which he obtained *rev. in proof*

    married. Upon] married, and upon *rev. in proof*

    Hall-barn] Hillburn *P79*

    built by himself] which he built *rev. in proof*

    resided. His mother, though related] still lived; who, though related both *rev. in proof*

    would throw] used to throw *rev. in proof*

64. conversation. Waller] conversation; and Waller *rev. in proof*

    discoursing] talking *rev. in proof*

    and resumed . . . conversation] then resume . . . talk *rev. in proof*

65. (1654)] (16 ) *proof, with* 54 *ins., perhaps by SJ*

    His choice . . . very judicious] He has made a very judicious choice of encomiastick topicks *rev. in proof*

    part] parts *corr. in proof*

    England's . . . her dominion] English . . . dominion *rev. in proof*

    The act] The last act *rev. in proof*

    band] conclave *rev. in proof*

    yet Cromwell] but Cromwel *proof*

    he had before done] they had done *rev. in proof*

    advantage] advantages *corr. in proof*

    did not those] but that those *rev. in proof*

66. ventures yet] ventures *rev. in proof*

    adding the title to] the dignity, the title and *rev. in proof*

    monarchy, and] monarchy, from which he *proof*

    from it partly] partly *rev. in proof*

    but is said] and is said *rev. in proof*

67. The poem] His poem *proof*

68. his imagination . . . melody] imagination, elegance, and melody *rev. in proof*

    for Charles] in praise of Charles *rev. in proof*

    now inviting . . . then congratulating] inviting . . . congratulating *rev. in proof*

    recovered right] Coronation *rev. in proof*

    effusions] the effusions *rev. in proof*

69. scorned . . . mind, that] confessed to degrade his powers, and he *rev. in proof*

    but has] but he has *rev. in proof*

71. excellence] greatness *rev. in proof*

yet only] got only *corr. in proof*

images] topicks *rev. in proof*

72. Waller sat] he sat *rev. in proof*

73. maintained] protected *rev. in proof*

74. though old] even then he *rev. in proof.* *(Burnet in fact wrote* even at eighty)

more quoted as exhibiting] supposed to exhibit any representation of abilities employed rather in *rev. in proof to* quoted as exhibiting any representation of abilities displayed rather in *P79, L81, rev. in Berg*

75. and recorded] in satire *rev. in proof*

appear] appears *corr. in proof*

remark, yet] *remark rev. in proof*

76. his muse] his wit *proof*

77. Deacon's] *ins. in proof in space left by printer*

78. *Biographia*] *Biographer corr. in proof*

shewed] sheweth *corr. in proof*

His accusation] This charge *rev. in proof*

rail] accuse *proof*

and to anger] to anger *rev. in proof*

81. in reading] by reading *rev. in proof*

82. once heard] have heard *proof*

successively . . . the fashion] by every man . . . he desires *rev. in proof*

83. King knew] king heard *rev. in proof*

84. notice to his friends] notice, on his part, *rev. in proof*

left] lost *proof*

85. seldom suffer] do not suffer *proof*

by a future] to a future *rev. in proof*

86. a physician *P79, L81 (not rev. in Berg)*] physician *L83*

88. *Not a separate para. in proof*

89. eldest son] eldest *rev. in proof*

90. drawn] so diligently drawn *rev. in proof*

known, with nicety, which] known, as *rev. in proof*

presume] attempt *proof*

93. improper *P79, L81*] impropper *L83*

94. the rich wife *P79, L81, not rev. in Berg*] a rich wife *L83*

about the age of three-] at the age of five- *rev. in proof*

privacy] retirement *proof*

endeavoured the improvement of] might improve *rev. in proof to* intended the improvement of *P79, L81, rev. in Berg*

of his fortune] his fortune *rev. in proof*

95. misjudge] mistake *rev. in proof*

    imagined] supposed *proof*

    Waller's book] the book *rev. in proof*

96. observes] relates *rev. in proof*

98. *Followed in proof only by a new para.*: Such was the life of Waller. Let us now consider his poetry. *del., with* Here I shall put an insertion *in the margin*

99–106. *Not present in the proofs*

101. left] lost *P79, corr. in 'Errata'*

104. plot] *SJ ins. a note in Berg, now cropped*, which he w[ ] forced to raise by the sale of one thousand [ ] year; *probably del. when SJ realized this is already stated in* 105 *below*

107. *At the head of this section in the proofs SJ has written in the margin*: Begin *this* with a two line capital

    spriteliness] elegance *rev. in proof*

109. fortell] fetch *corr. in proof*

113. He seldom indeed] It is but seldom that he *rev. in proof*

    readily] easily *rev. in proof*

    *The final sentence is a separate para. in the proofs, but marked to be closed up.*

    be added] perhaps be added *proof*

    *Palm* in the verses *on her*] *Palm in the* [ ] a poem, *on her  rev. in proof* (*the printer having left a space for the illegible text*)

    *Theriaca.*] *Followed in proof by*:

> All winds blow fair, that did the world embroil;
> Your vapours treacle yield, and scorpions oil.

114. His thoughts . . . his images] The thoughts . . . the images *rev. in proof*

    another *P79, L81, not rev. in Berg*] other *L83*

117. Some . . . may be thought] His . . . are sometimes *rev. in proof*

119. not always distinct] sometimes confused *rev. in proof*

121. Empire of Beauty] Empire of Love *rev. in proof*

    Such books . . . they obtain . . . as misleading] The book . . . it obtains . . . of misleading *rev. in proof*

122. nobler] greater *rev. in proof*

    is panegyrical] of them are panegyricks *rev. in proof*

123. that time] the time *rev. in proof*

124*b*. those lines] the lines *rev. in proof*

129. too far-fetched] false and forced *rev. in proof*

131. his review of that love and] that love and that *rev. in proof*

132. allow much] allow much to *rev. in proof*

are now forced] were forced *rev. in proof*

has the luck to mark] thinks himself to have marked *rev. in proof*

power] powers *P79*

133. had he written . . . been better] he had written on the same subjects with more success *rev. in proof*

134. animate devotion by] supply devotion with *rev. in proof*

135. authorities] great authorities *rev. in proof*

poetical devotion cannot] pious poetry will not *rev. in proof*

indeed] *ins. in proof*

Spring *P79*] spring *L81, L83*

Sky] *ins. in space left by the printer in the proof*

disputation . . . description] disputant . . . describer *rev. in proof*

136. Contemplative] But contemplative *rev. in proof*

state] stile *corr. in proof*

139. obtains] obtain *corr. in proof*

rarely . . . by Christians] not to be hoped *rev. in proof*

desireable, or tremendous] whatever is desireable, whatever is tremendous *rev. in proof*

140. Repentance, trembling *P79*] Repentance trembling *L81, L83*

the judge] its Judge *rev. in proof*

141. loses] *rev. to* now loses *in proof*

pious verse] verse *P79, L81, rev. in Berg*

142. As much] Much *rev. in proof*

owed *P79, L81 (not rev. in Berg)*] owing *L83*

proper] therefore proper *rev. in proof*

143. Davies *P79, L81 (not rev. in Berg)*] Davis *L83*

though merely . . . yet seldom] though . . . seldom *rev. in proof*

144. decision has] fashion seems to have *proof*

145. lived *suggested emendation by Nichols in Berg*] used *proofs, P79, L81, L83*

146. as a rhyme] *ins. in proof*

148. totally] generally *rev. in proof*

150. that grace] the grace *rev. in proof*

Let not . . . his imitators] Let the original author have his due praise *rev. in proof to* Let the original author not lose by his imitators

151. early] our early *P79*

Shakspeare] and Shakespeare *P79*; and Shakspeare *L81, rev. in Berg*

ridicule it . . . displays it] ridicule it *P79, L81, rev. in Berg with* the Love's *del. before* another

152. vain] in vain *rev. in proof*

       ancient] the ancient *P79*

       so far] so far at least *rev. in proof*

       might even then] might *rev. in proof*

153. our elegance . . . our propriety] the elegance . . . propriety *rev. in proof*

154. *SJ wrote in the margin of the proofs:* This should be more distinguished. It is not a continuation of what goes before but a preface to what follows. *In Berg Nichols called for* **154** *to begin a new page*

       (*st. 6, l. 6*) flocke *P79, L81*] flock *L83*

       (*st. 6, l. 7*) Sat *P79, L81, L83*] Set *Fairfax*

       (*st. 8, l. 5*) poore *P79, L81*] pore *L83*

       (*st. 9, l. 2*) swaines *P79, L81*] swains *L83*

       (*st. 10, l. 5*) our *Fairfax, P79, L81*] or *L83*

       (*st. 11, l. 3*) preserues *Fairfax, P79, L81*] perserues *L83*

## POMFRET

6. some species of merit] merit *P79, L81, rev. in Berg*

## DORSET

*In the bottom margin of p. 1 of the proofs, Nichols has written:* A Revise directly | Get Otway pulled again

   1. its authour . . . read] it will appear in the subsequent volumes of this collection *P79*; it has appeared in one of the volumes of the late collection *L81, rev. in Berg*

   2. at that time imagined] imagined at that time *rev. in proof*

   3. such profane . . . that] very profane language till *rev. in proof*

   5. fourteen . . . destroyed,] and fourteen others destroyed; *P79, L81, rev. in Berg*

10. with . . . Lords] was one of the lords who *rev. in proof*

11. those Lords] the lords *rev. in proof*

12. became, as] was, what *rev. in proof*

       He happened . . . those] He was one of the lords *rev. in proof*

13. indulgent] general *rev. in proof*

14. little personal] personal *rev. in proof*

15. His . . . to Howard] The . . . Mrs. Howard *rev. in proof*

## STEPNEY

   1. Westminster . . . the College] Westminster *P79, L81, rev. in Berg*

       went at nineteen] went *P79, L81, rev. in Berg*

2. Sua] Suae *P79*

superaverit] superavit *P79, L81, rev. in Berg*

parum, Famae] parvae Fama *P79, L81 (corr. in Gent. Mag. (1779), 595)*

efflavit] effluvit *P79, L81, rev. in Berg*


## JOHN PHILIPS

[*'MS' in* **30–5** *refers to Edmund Smith's original MS*]

3. friendship] a friendship *P79*

5. Mr. St. John] St. John *P79, L81, rev. in Berg*

7. *Last Day P79*] *Last day L81, L83*

8. non quod] quod non *L81, rev. in Berg*

de Litteris] de quo Litteris *P79*

9. narrowness of] a narrow *P79, L81, rev. in Berg*

of celebrating] celebrating *P79*

12. allow it *P79, L81 (not rev. in Berg)*] allow its *L83*

14 **note**. in the last] in this *P79*

16. alluring] pleasing *P79, L81, rev. in Berg*

29. hero. *P79, L81*] hero: *L83*

30. vicissitude *MS, P79*] vicissitudes *L81, L83*

31. Ben. *P79, L81*] Ben *L83*

33. who would *MS, P79, L81*] who could *L83*

35. and great *MS, P79, L81*] and a great *L83*

a fine *MS, P79*] fine *L81, L83*


## WALSH

2. in London] *Nichols wrote* Qy *at* in the margin of Berg but no change was made in *L83*

3. scholar . . . splendid in his dress] scholar *P79, L81, rev. in Berg*

8. 1711 *P79, L81*] 1721 *L83*

the Essay *P79, L81 (not rev. in Berg)*] his Essay *L83*

12. while] when *P79, L81, rev. in Berg*


## DRYDEN

1. about to] now to *rev. in proof*

a display] an account *rev. in proof*

nothing . . . beyond what] no more . . . than *rev. in proof*

**2.** 9] 9th *P79*

the son] was the son *rev. in proof*

**3.** reported] said *rev. in proof*

patrimony ... his first religion] patrimony, or considered as a deserter from another party *proof (with* party *rev. to* religion), *P79, L81*

Derrick's intelligence ... erroneous] Derrick was misinformed *P79, L81*

**6.** vain] in vain *rev. in proof*

**9.** shared] struck *corr. in proof*

**10.** certainly is] is certainly *rev. in proof*

them as to ... No man] them. As to positive power, no man *rev. in proof*

also privation] only privation *rev. in proof*

**11.** not commonly] not always commonly *rev. in proof*

the time] and the time *rev. in proof*

easily found] always found *rev. in proof*

if even] if ever *corr. in proof*

**12.** since ... said to be] if the plays are *P79, L81*

**14.** began] begun *proof*

criticks] critick *rev. in proof*

**15.** dramatick] theatrical *rev. in proof*

performances; it] performances; and indeed there is the less, as they do not appear in the collection to which this narration is to be annexed. It *P79, L81 (with* is annexed *for* is to be annexed)

especial ... of those] particular ... of some *rev. in proof*

eight] four *rev. in proof*

**16.** *Rival*] *Kind corr. in proof*

**20.** made rhyming] wrote rhyming *rev. in proof*

making] writing *rev. in proof*

**21.** confutation of] answer to *rev. in proof*

**22.** may be esteemed] seems to be *P79, L81*

**24.** encumbrances] difficulties *rev. in proof*

representation] representations *rev. in proof*

**33.** criticism] a criticism *P79*

**37.** we shall have *P79, L81, L83*] we share *Notes*

**38.** [*l. 12 of verse:*] light *Notes, P79*] lights *L81, L83*

**39.** you flush *Notes, P79*] flush *L81, L83*

**50.** *Percy*] *Piercey P79*

**51.** Jack-of-all-trades *Clifford, L81*] Jack of all trades *P79;* Jack-of-all trades *L83*

variety *Clifford, P79*] a variety *L81, L83*

**52.** *Almeria Clifford, P79*] *Almeira L81, L83*

**55a.** leave, "&c. *P79, L81*] leave." &c. *L83*

**61.** those within *P79, L81, L83*] these within *Dryden*

**65–70.** *For the possible misplacing of these paras., see commentary to* **65–70**

**68.** writing a] another *rev. in proofs*

to me only] then to me only  *rev. in proof*

**69.** the controversy] a controversy *rev. in proof*

**70.** *Albion and Albania P79*] *Albion* and *Albania L81, L83*

**71.** scenes] sieves *corr. in proof*

*The final sentence of* **71** *is a separate para. in P79 and L81.*

It is] This is *rev. in proof*

**72.** was wonderful] is wonderful *P79*

**73.** is meant] *ins. in proof*

**74.** manuscript] written *rev. in proof*

**75.** over nations . . . criticks upon] at such a distance, that there was no danger of his knowledge of *rev. in proof*

stage. If he had known and] stage, though, if he had *rev. in proof*

disliked] not liked *proof, P79*; liked *L81*

remoteness] distance *rev. in proof*

**76.** often domestick] also domestick *rev. in proof*

**78.** given to] written for *rev. in proof*

the work] that *rev. in proof*

admitted] committed *rev. in proof*

of style] in style *rev. in proof*

good have] good has *corr. in proof*

despised] *ins. in proof*

**80.** is a comedy] a comedy *rev. in proof*

yet seldom] seldom *rev. in proof*

**82.** sallies] passages *rev. in proof*

approaches] some approaches *rev. in proof*

leave] make *rev. in proof*; beam *P79, corr. in 'Errata'*

this would not] which this would not *rev. in proof*

**85.** *The final sentence was added in L83.*

**87.** theatrical] dramatick *rev. in proof*

**89.** almost new . . . as occasions arose *proof (with* able *ins.), L81 (with* as occasions arose *rev. to* without much labour), *L83*] little known, and therefore welcome as a novelty, and of that flexile and applicable kind, that it might be always introduced without apparent violence or affectation *P79 (a cancel: see commentary to* **89**)

too skilful] as skilful *corr. in proof*

**107.** Fanshaw,] *ins. in L83*

110.  derive from] find in *proof (Life, iv. 45–6)*

118.  *Rainholds] Rainholds P79 (corr. in Gent. Mag. (1779), 594)*

134.  Crites to *P79*] Crites *to L81, L83*

138.  his own opinion *P79*] his opinion *L81, L83*

140.  imagined] imaged *P79*

144.  nor . . . nation] and the nation had not *P79, L81*

146.  cost] could cost *rev. in Rothschild copy of P79*

154.  nor have I met . . . tumultuary and confused] but having been since informed that there is in the register of the College of Physicians an order relating to Dryden's funeral, I can doubt its truth no longer *P79, L81; in the Rothschild copy of P79 SJ rev.* but having since been informed *to* I understood for a time *and* I can doubt its truth no longer *to* but further enquiry cannot discover it *with* I have a *del. below*

155.  Supposing . . . remark that the] The *P79, L81*

182.  helpless] endless *L81*

184.  duly stampt] stampt *P79*

187.  he goes away] *rev. to* him *in Rothschild copy of P79*

      not completed] *rev. to* neglected to complete *in Rothschild copy of P79*

191.  One of his opinions] Of one opinion [opinon *L81*] he is very reasonably suspected, which *P79, L81*

      He put great] There is little doubt that he put *P79, L81*

      veracity] veracity; and, without authority, it is useless to mention what is so unlikely to be true *P79, L81*

      horoscope] planets *P79, L81*

      The letter . . . notions or practice.] *added in L83, with* latter *for* letter

194.  regular and valuable] regular *P79, L81*

198.  brightened *P79*] brightned *L81, L83*

      Marathon] Maranthon *P79, L81*

201.  little labour] great liberality, and seldom published any work without a critical dissertation, by which he encreased the book and the price, with little labour to himself *P79, L81*

203.  translated] again translated *P79*

204.  when he cannot] as he cannot *P79*

205  note. *Added in L83*

220.  transmit] convey *P79, L81*

226.  rules seems] rules seem *P79*

235.  was . . . time] seems at this time to have been *P79, L81*

242.  the reader] the mind *P79, L81*

243.  world betray'd;] world *P79, corr. in 'Errata'*

247.  inconvenience . . . difficulty] inconvenience *P79, L81*

256.  side] sides *P79, L81*

**264.** *Zebe*] *Zeb P79, L81, L83 (cf. Aureng Zebe in* **75** *above)*

**271.** numbers] nnmbers *P79*

**274.** inability of] convenient *proof (Life, iv. 46)*

his first *Dryden, P79*] this first *L81, L83*

**282.** in the initial...there] *rev. to* between the things compared, that it *in Rothschild copy of P79*

**283.** durable materials] materials *P79, L81*

**294.** ferny *Dryden, P79*] ferney *L81, L83*

**297.** and there are] an there are *P79*

**298.** that insensibility] the insensibility *P79, L81*

**305.** *After* Addison *SJ noted in the Rothschild copy of P79* He gained about 1200 L.

**307.** his antagonist] this antagonist *P79, L81*

[Ver. 33.] one piece *P79, L81*] once piece *L83*

[Ver. 61–3.] poor *mistaken P79*] poor-*mistaken L81, L83*

**320.** vicious] vitious *P79, L81*

mortal] monarch *P79 (corr. in Gent. Mag. (1779), 594)*

**321.** have had a mind *P79*] have a mind *L81, L83*

**326.** natural sentiments] former thoughts *P79, L81*

new...things] new *P79, L81*

**327.** not always] seldom *P79, L81*

**328.** thoughts] matter *proof (Life, iv. 46)*

objections and solutions] argument *P79, L81*

**330.** vacancy] emptiness *proof (Life, iv. 46)*

**334.** Maximin] Maxamin *L81, L83*

the harlots...men] many other harlots *proof (Life, iv. 46)*

**336.** descends to display] sometimes displays *proof (Life, iv. 46)*

**339.** had then crept into] were then used in *proof (Life, iv. 46)*

**347.** alternately *P79*] alternately, *L81, L83*

**350.** braces of] braces on *P79*

**356.** Though Davis...argument with poetry] He taught us that it was possible to reason in rhyme *P79, L81*

**358.** having been] being now *P79*

**363.** both these may] both these may *P79*


## SMITH

**5.** chiefly *Oldisworth (1719)*] *chiefly Oldisworth (1714), P79, L81, L83*

**9.** Divinity-school *P79, L81*] Divinity-scool *L83*

understood *P79, L81*] understod *L83*

16. than agreeable *Oldisworth, P79, L81*] and agreeable *L83*

22. *grand monde Oldisworth*] *grande monde P79, L81, L83*

30. exhibited] given *P79, L81*

36. mind, though he] mind; but he *P79, L81*

38. the censor . . . it was not] it not being *P79, L81*

49. from sympathy] by sympathy *P79*

56. less frequent] fewer *P79, L81*

   Hartham] Gartham *P79, L81, L83*

77. [Sent by the Author to Mr. Urry.]] Written by the Author. *P79*

   versuum] versum, *P79, L81*

   peregrino] preregrino *P79*

   de Hoseâ] Hoseâ *P79*

   Ætna Pocockio] Pocockio *P79*

   Ottomanis] Ottomanno *P79*

   abrepti] abrepto *P79*

   varietate] varietati *P79, L81*

77 note. *Added in L83.*


## DUKE

1. few memorials. He] no memorial but in the Lives written by *Jacob*; who relates, that he *proof*

   and Jacob relates, that] that *proof*

   Richmond] Richmond; was made chaplain to queen Anne, and in 1713 preferred to the rich living of Witney in Oxfordshire, which he did not enjoy more than two years *proof*

2. not ill] not well *proof*

   His poems . . . to be praised.] *this sentence opens para. 4 in proof, with* but I have not *for* nor have I

4. been bad in] been *P79, L81*

   was surely] it was *proof*

5–7. *Not in the proofs, except for the information about Queen Anne and Witney originally in para.* 1 *(see above)*


## KING

4. by which his adversaries] his adversaries, *P79, L81*

6. Learning, on a question . . . could decide] Learning *P79, L81*

7. *Lister*, who had . . . *Paris*] *Lister P79, L81*

18. but perhaps] though perhaps *P79, L81*

## SPRAT

3. *Plague]* Stages *corr. in proof*

5. began] he began *rev. in proof*
   exhibited] exposed *rev. in proof*

9. having thus . . . he was] had now . . . and he was *rev. in proof*

10. On the critical] In the critical *proof*

11. lords, and] lords with *rev. in proof*
    profession] declaration *proof*

12. manfully] Sprat *rev. in proof*

13. *Young] Jones corr. in proof*
    both men] both now *corr. in proof*
    These men] The men *rev. in proof*

15. an yearly] *rev. in proof to* a yearly

19. my father, an old man] an old man *P79, L81*

21. each has its] all have their *rev. in proof*

22. and of those our] of which *rev. in proof to* of which our
    settled] made *rev. in proof*


## HALIFAX

2. scholar, and] scholar. He *rev. in proof*
   epigrams. He] epigrams, and *rev. in proof*
   Stepney; and in 1682, when] Stepney. In 1682 Stepney *rev. in proof*
   the election] and the election *rev. in proof*
   placed at] elected to *rev. in proof*
   removed] emoved *proof*

7. their own body] their body *rev. in proof*

8. became chancellor] was made chancellor *rev. in proof*
   being advanced to the first commission . . . he was] he was made first commissioner . . . and was *rev. in proof*

13. and, if . . . an author,] and *P79, L81*


## PARNELL

2. have made] shall make *rev. in proof*
   and have] and shall have *proof, P81, L81*
   it gives] has given *rev. in proof*

due] some due *rev. in proof*

Goldsmith] a departed genius *P81, L81*

3. of the same name] *ins. in proof*

left] left his mansion at *rev. in proof*

settling . . . purchased] settled . . . where he purchased *rev. in proof*

dispensation from] dispensation by *proof*

4. afterwards] after *rev. in proof*

long survived him] *Nichols has written in the margin of the proofs* was living in 1770 *del.*

5. much censure from] the censure of *rev. in proof to* censure from

attention] much attention *rev. in proof*

however . . . need of] indeed did not much want *rev. to* indeed was in no great need of *in proof, P81, L81*

6. preferment. As he] preferment, he *proof, with* as *ins., P81*; perferment, as he *L81*

he displayed] and displayed *proof, with* and *del.*

who died . . . expectations] *ins. in proof*

7. every future] any future *rev. in proof*

unregarded. He was . . . 1713; and] unregarded; for *proof, with* He was warmly recommended by Swift to archbishop King, who gave him a prebend in 1713 *ins. in the margin by Nichols*

8. did not last long] was clouded by that which took away all his powers of enjoying either profit or pleasure, the death of his wife, whom he is said to have lamented with such sorrow as hastened his end *rev. in proof*

enjoyed his] enjoyed this *rev. in proof*

in his thirty-eighth year] *ins. in proof*

9. writing. He] writing; he *rev. in proof*

owned. He left many] *rev. in proof to* owned; and left many

Goldsmith] Dr. Goldsmith *rev. in proof*

his criticism] the criticism of Goldsmith *rev. in proof*

*Tale*, and . . . but] *Tale*, the . . . and *rev. in proof*

has very . . . remarked] very . . . remarks *proof*

10. he should have added] *ins. in proof*

he discovers] he tells us *rev. in proof*

Parnell's] parody *rev. in proof*

would add] will add *rev. in proofs*

was borrowed] was taken *rev. in proof*

Howell's] *Howard's corr. in proof*

12. narrative] composition *proof (Life, iv. 54)*

13. the last] this *P81*

## GARTH

**16.** *Added in L83.*


## ROWE

**1.** Berkford *MS*] Beckford *P81, L81, L83*

1673] 1663 *rev. in MS*

had long . . . considerable] was ancient, his ancestors from *rev. in MS*

when, in opposition] when he had *rev. in MS*

**1 note.** *Not in MS*

**2.** Nicholas] The son *rev. in MS*

**3.** was entered] he was entered *MS*

**4.** elegant literature] the more elegant parts of writing *MS, P81, L81*

**5.** (1702)] *Not in MS*

under the name of] by *rev. in MS*

**6.** Tamerlane . . . time] [This?] tragedy has for many years *MS (cropped)*

and it now] and it *MS*

aggravated] a Saracen's head *rev. in MS*

**7.** stage] English stage *MS*

**8.** retains] has, I fear, *rev. in MS to* dies with

teach us . . . detestation] make us at once esteem, and detest *rev. in MS*

elegance] and elegance *MS, P81, L81*

**9.** expresses] who expresses *MS*

**10.** next (1706)] next tragedy *MS*

have been] have *MS*

been shewn] shew *MS*

**11.** (1708)] *Not in MS*

objects] images *MS*

very easily] more easily *MS*

soul that would] sense of virtue *rev. in MS*

if it] *ins. in MS*

The motto . . . successful.] *ins. in MS*

**13.** to *Henry*] in *Henry MS*

union] Rowe *MS*

**14.** He once (1706) . . . hand. He] He once, I know not in what part of his life, *MS*

**15.** (1714)] *Not in MS*

as some] some *MS*

**16.** (1715)] *Not in MS*

gave nothing more to] wrote no more for *MS, where this sentence begins* **17**

16–17. the stage. Being . . . inclination, he] the stage, being . . . inclination. He *MS*

17. supplied] wrote for *MS*

18. *Not in MS but* * D *calls for its insertion from the end of MS where it is headed* insert p. 6 * D

received] derived *MS*

preface, which] preface who *MS*

19. fortune] revenue *MS*

He was undersecretary . . . afterwards] *ins. in MS*

publick employment] employment in the state *MS*

Spanish] the Spanish langu *rev. in MS*

consolation *MS*] congratulation *P81, L81, L83*

"Then, Sir, I envy you] that he might now enjoy *rev. in MS*

20. how Rowe] why Rowe *MS*.

Pope, who . . . *odd way*] *ins. in MS*

21. shelter by] shelter for *MS, P81, L81*

him, unasked,] him *MS*

23–6. *The Welwood quotation is not in MS but insertion is called for by* * E

27. pleasures *Pope, MS*] pleasure *P79, L81, L83*

28. *The Warburton quotation is not in MS but insertion is called for by* * G

29. even he] he *MS*

Addison can . . . said.] *ins. in MS*

authors] writers *MS*

30. are rarely] seem hardly *rev. in MS*

31. the change] it properly *rev. in MS*

*Jane* pronounced] Jane spoken *rev. in MS*

32. search into nature] search *MS*

nice] any nice *MS*

passion] any passion *MS*

natural] real *rev. in MS*

33. from the elegance] and the elegance *rev. in MS*

34. of the first] the first *MS*

*Golden Verses* are] gold verses are *MS*

35. *Not a new para. in MS, P81, and L81*

35. senatorial *MS*] dictatorial *P81, L81, L83*

which is such] without any *rev. in MS*

his contemporaries practised] he would *rev. in MS*

esteemed] adm *rev. in MS*

# COMMENTARY

## SAMUEL BUTLER (1613–1680)

**Composition.** John Nichols stated that, although 'Cowley' (q.v.) was the first of SJ's *Prefaces* to go to press in Dec. 1777, '*Butler* was the life in which the Doctor at that time more particularly prided himself' (*Gent. Mag.* (Jan. 1785), 9 n.). It is unclear whether Nichols's 'at that time' refers merely to the first few months of SJ's work on his biographies, or more precisely to late 1777, when the two men first came into regular contact through the printing of the *Prefaces*. The fact that in *Prefaces*, ii (1779), sig. b1 of 'Butler' is keyed to 'Vol. VI.', i.e. of the *English Poets*, appears to confirm that it went to press at an early stage, when SJ's biographies were still intended literally to preface their subjects' poetry.

Although B was the third of the thirteen poets SJ listed in his diary on 13 Oct. 1777 (*YW*, i. 279), he did not in fact write about some of the names on this list until 1780. Yet he may at least have started work on 'Butler' at Ashbourne in late Oct. 1777, when he was eager to make visible progress before returning to London (see 'Denham' headnote above, and *Letters*, iii. 83). Two features relate 'Butler' to 'Denham': the formal similarity of the opening comment on the available sources in 1 of both biographies, and his apparent use in both of *GD* (see 'Sources' below) rather than *BB*, on which he usually relied when possible after his return to London. While still at Ashbourne, SJ reminded himself in his diary on 20 Oct. 1777 to write to his friend Richard Farmer at Cambridge. No such letter has survived, but SJ may have been intending to consult Farmer about B's connection with Cambridge (see 3 and n. below), since he later requested similar help with Cambridge poets on 23 May 1780 (*Letters*, iii. 257). It is unlikely that Farmer already had in his possession the Butler MSS, which presumably reached him after the death of Robert Thyer in 1781 (see 'Sources' below), and SJ makes no reference to their being in Farmer's custody. (For this material, lent to Isaac Reed in 1788, see Reed's *Diaries*, ed. C. E. Jones (1946), 161, 185.)

'Butler' had at all events been written and printed by 27 July 1778, when SJ asked Nichols to bind it in a pre-publication volume (now in the Hyde Collection) with 'Denham' and 'Waller' to show to his friends: see *Letters*, iii. 122, and Fleeman (1962), 215 n. Early in her acquaintance with SJ, Fanny Burney noted that on 27 Aug. 1778 he talked about his biographies at Streatham: '*Dryden* is now in the Press; & he told us he had been just writing a Dissertation upon Hudibras' (*Early Journals*, iii. 105). Although SJ had written the original 'little' biography several months earlier, he had presumably only recently added or enlarged the discussion of *Hudibras* in 22–52, as his ideas about the critical scope of his biographies became more ambitious. (See the headnotes to 'Cowley' above and 'Waller' below.) This would explain the disparity between SJ's various references to 'the great author of *Hudibras*' as an object of national pride (see 1, 21–2, 38 below) and his actual demonstration of the poem's limitations (27–34) and of the transient interest of its topical subject matter (41–9).

**Sources.** SJ gives the impression in 1 that Wood, ii. 452–3, and an anonymous life of B, often reprinted in later editions of *Hudibras*, were the only available sources. Although

Hill (1905) identified the second source as the 1732 edition, this 'Life' had in fact appeared as early as *Hudibras* (1704), and was later attributed by William Oldys to Sir James Astry (*Hudibras*, ed. J. S. Wilders (Oxford, 1967), p. xiii n.). That SJ in fact refers in 1 only to primary materials and not to his intermediary sources is clear from the original version of 2 below in *Prefaces* (1779) (see Textual Notes), which originally stated that 'Mr. Longueville, the son of Butler's principal friend, informed the author of the "General Dictionary" that he was born in 1600.' When revising 2 in *Lives* (1783), SJ moved the reference to Charles Longueville to 3, but unhelpfully omitted his original citation of *GD*, vi. 289–99, in which Thomas Birch's article had been followed by an appendix of his correspondence about B with Longueville, Thomas Southerne, and others, as well as Longueville's comments on and corrections to Birch's article.

Although SJ may well have relied, at least initially, on *GD*, the same sources, including Charles Longueville's information, were also available in Thomas Brough-ton's more coherent article on B in *BB*, ii (1748), 1077–82. (Anyone consulting *GD* had to be alert enough to look for its article on B under 'Hudibras': for the 'strange fashion' of calling B 'Hudibras' in the period, see Malone, *Prose Works of Dryden* (1800), iii. 206–7 n.) Both cyclopedias give the material and sources cited by SJ in enough detail to have enabled him to 'compare and copy them' (see 1 below) without reference to the originals: see, in particular, 3–4, 10, 13, 14 and nn. below. The accounts of B in Jacob, ii. 19–21, and Shiels, *Lives*, ii. 233–40, appear to have no bearing on SJ's biography. (In view of SJ's frequent reliance on *BB*, it is worth noting that, before his death, that cyclopedia was able in its turn to borrow from him: the revised article on B in *BB*, iii (2nd edn., 1784), 92–3 n., reprinted the whole of SJ's 'capital criticism' of *Hudibras*.)

Although the anonymous 'Life' and Wood are the only sources named by SJ in 1, he in fact had the advantage over *GD* and *BB* of being able to refer to material first printed in Robert Thyer's edition of B's *Genuine Remains in Verse and Prose* (2 vols., 1759): see 15, 20 below, and cf. 40 below, which suggests that SJ had corresponded about B with Thyer. In 1783 he was able to add further new information to 2–3 and 5 from Treadway Russell Nash's *History of Worcestershire*, ii (1782), 391, to which John Nichols, its printer, may have drawn his attention: SJ had already used this source in 1781 in 'Shenstone' (see headnote below) and 'Lyttelton' 12 n. below. In 1783 he revised 18 below in the light of information in James Granger's *Biographical History* (1775), pointed out by a contributor to *Gent. Mag.* in 1779. SJ's references to Simon Patrick and B's epitaph in 17, 19 below seem to derive directly from the 'Life' of B in Zachary Grey's *Hudibras* (2 vols., 1744), which itself repeatedly cites *GD* rather than Wood as its main source.

Although SJ marked a copy of the 1726 edition of *Hudibras* for quotation in the *Dict.*, its location is now unknown: see Fleeman, *Handlist* (1984), 10. There are apparently twenty-eight quotations from the poem in the *Dict*.

**Publication.** In *Prefaces*, vol. ii (31 Mar. 1779). There are no proofs.

**Modern Sources**
(i) Butler
*Complete Works*, ed. A. R. Waller and R. Lamar (3 vols., Cambridge, 1905–28)
*Hudibras*, ed. J. S. Wilders (Oxford, 1967)
*Prose Observations*, ed. H. de Quehen (Oxford, 1979)
*Three Poems*, ed. A. C. Spence, Augustan Reprint Soc. No. 88 (Los Angeles, 1961)

(ii)

E. S. de Beer, 'The Later Life of SB', *RES* 4 (1928), 159–66

R. P. Bond, *English Burlesque Poetry 1700–1750* (Cambridge, Mass., 1932)

M. M. Duggan, *English Literature and Backgrounds 1660–1700* (New York, 1990), i. 315–22

W. C. Horne, 'SB', in *Dictionary of Literary Biography*, ci (1991), 77–87

B. Parker, 'SB and the End of Analogy', in his *The Triumph of Augustan Poetics: English Literary Culture from Butler to Johnson* (Cambridge, 1998), 25–60

D. Parkes, 'Documents Relating to SB (1613–1680)', *N & Q* 238 (1993), 324–5

H. de Quehen, 'An Account of Works Attributed to SB', *RES* 33 (1982), 262–77

R. Quintana, 'The B–Oxenden Correspondence', *MLN* 48 (1933), 1–11

E. A. Richards, *Hudibras in the Burlesque Tradition* (New York, 1937)

J. L. Thomson, 'SB: A Bibliography', *Bulletin of Bibliography*, 30 (1973), 34–9

L. V. Troost, 'SB' in *Dictionary of Literary Biography*, cxxvi (1993), 17–25

G. Wasserman, *S 'Hudibras' B* (Boston, 1976)

G. Wasserman, *SB and the Earl of Rochester: A Reference Guide* (Boston, 1986)

M. Wilding, 'SB at Barbourne', *N & Q* 211 (1966), 15–19

M. Wilding, 'The Date of SB's Baptism', *RES* 17 (1966), 174–7

M. Wilding, 'B and Gray's Inn', *N & Q* 216 (1971), 293–5

1. See 'Sources' above. SJ usually attributes the 'Life' (1704) to 'his biographer' or 'the author of his Life'. Wood's information (mostly from the MSS of John Aubrey) appeared 'incidentally' in a long account of William Prynne.

2. B was in fact born in late 1612 or early 1613, the son of Samuel and Mary Butler, and baptized on 14 Feb. (Wilding, 'Date', 174–7).

   SJ added the second and third sentences in 1783 from Nash, *History* (see 'Sources' above) to replace Longueville's assertion in *GD*, vi. 289 n., that B was born in 1600 (see Textual Notes, and 21 n. below), a much earlier date than in 'Life' (1704), Wood, ii. 452, and *BB*, ii. 1077.

3. B's family was living at Barbourne, near Claines, by *c*.1621. His father died in 1626, when they were leasing a farm at Defford, near Strensham.

   *Mr. Longueville*: SJ originally referred to the divergence between the accounts of Wood and 'Life' (1704), as noted by *GD*, vi. 289 n. In 1783 he substituted the reference to Charles Longueville's evidence (see Textual Notes). According to Roger North in 1742, William Longueville (1639–1721) of the Inner Temple was B's 'last Patron and Friend . . . Otherwise he might have been literally starved.' His son Charles, also a lawyer, inherited some of B's MSS and annotated Birch's account of B in *GD* (see 'Sources' above). These MSS were later owned by John Clark, who permitted Robert Thyer to print a selection in 1759 (see 20 and n. below), and by Richard Farmer: see *Prose Observations* (1979), pp. xvii–xix, Hawkins, *J's Works* (1787), ii. 177–8 n., and A. Sherbo, *Richard Farmer, Master of Emmanuel College, Cambridge* (Newark, Del., 1992), 181–2.

   SJ added the final sentence from Nash in 1783 (see Textual Notes): 'Butler's tenement' was later known as 'Butler's Cot' (Wilders (1967 edn.), p. xv).

4. SJ's apparent weighing of the inconclusive evidence about B's university career in his sources in fact follows *GD*, vi. 289–90 n. According to Wood ii. 452, B's brother claimed that he was at Cambridge for six or seven years, but there is no record of his matriculation at either university. He was, however, later secretary to the Duke of

Buckingham when he was Chancellor of Cambridge (see 13 n. below). *GD*, followed by *BB*, eventually ruled out Oxford.

5. B's employer was probably Thomas Jefferey of Earl's Croom Court, near Strensham (Wilders (1967 edn.), p. xvii). Wood, ii. 452, stated that B did not meet Samuel Cooper (1609–72), who later painted his portrait, until he was employed by the Countess of Kent (see 6 below).

The final sentence from Nash, which SJ added in 1783, refers to two visits to Earl's Croom in 1738 and 1774 (see Textual Notes). Two paintings attributed to B survive in Earl's Croom Church (Wilders (1967 edn.), p. xvii). Horace Walpole had included a short article on B as a painter in his *Anecdotes of Painting*, ii (1762), 126–7.

6. Elizabeth, Dowager Countess of Kent, of Wrest Park, Bedfordshire, was the patron of the antiquary John Selden (1584–1654), formerly the Earl's steward. SJ mentioned Selden's varied knowledge on 28 Mar. 1772, and also admired his *Table-Talk* (1689) (*Life*, ii. 158, v. 311).

8. Sir Samuel Luke of Cople, Bedfordshire, commanded a troop of dragoons in Cromwell's army. Although SJ follows 'Life' (1704), *GD*, and *BB*, in believing that *Hudibras* originated at this period, it is doubtful whether Luke ever employed B, who probably did not start writing *Hudibras* until *c*.1658 (Wilders (1967 edn.), p. xviii). In a letter of 19 Mar. 1663 to Sir George Oxenden, B stated that he had based the poem on a West Country knight, who had been a colonel in the parliamentary army: see Quintana, 'Correspondence', 4, and Wilding, 'Gray's Inn', 293.

9. For SJ's interest elsewhere in 'loyalty' and its rewards, particularly after the Restoration, see 'Cowley' 35 and n. above.

In 1661/2 B became secretary to Richard, Earl of Carbery, President of the revived Court of the Marches, and Steward of Ludlow Castle, while it was under repair (see 'Milton' 21 and n. above). Carbery's account books record payments made by B to craftsmen at this period. He gave up the post at Ludlow in Jan. 1662, but may have continued working for Carbery in other capacities (Wilders (1967 edn.), pp. xviii–xix).

10. SJ follows *GD*, vi. 291 and n., and later *BB*, in noting the divergent accounts of Mrs Herbert's fortune in Wood, ii. 452 (who describes her only as a widow, and states that B lived on her jointure), and 'Life' (1704). John Aubrey refers to her as a widow named Morgan, but, in either case, no record of the marriage has survived (Wilders (1967 edn.), p. xviii). For B's acquaintance with lawyers at Gray's Inn from *c*.1658, see Wilding, 'Gray's Inn', 293–5.

11. *Hudibras*, Pt. I (dated 1663), appeared in late 1662. *GD*, vi. 291 n., followed by *BB*, cited the reference in Prior's dedication to his *Poems* (1709) to the influence of Charles Sackville, Lord Buckhurst, later Earl of Dorset (see 'Dorset' below): 'Butler ow'd it to Him, that the Court tasted his *Hudibras*' (*Lit. Works*, i. 249). SJ's account of the poem's popularity derives ultimately from Wood, ii. 453. For contemporary evidence, see Pepys's *Diary* (26 Dec. 1662, 6 Feb. 1663): the diarist thought *Hudibras* 'silly' and sold the copy he had bought, but eventually obtained another in an attempt to understand the popularity of a poem 'which all the world cries up to be the example of wit'.

12. *Hudibras*, Pt. II (dated 1664), appeared in late 1663: see Pepys (28 Nov., 10 Dec. 1663). For the Earl of Clarendon, see ultimately Wood, ii. 453. According to Charles Longueville in *GD*, vi. 299 (also cited by *BB*), Charles II gave B £300 not 300 guineas.

13–14. *GD*, vi. 291 and n. (followed by *BB*), had contrasted the divergent accounts in Wood and the 'Life' (1704), and then 'contradicted' them with this anecdote from the 'Memoirs' of the dramatist William Wycherley (1641–1716) in Richardson Pack's *Miscellanies in Verse and Prose* (2nd edn., 1719), 183–4, which later appeared in Jacob, i. 277, and Wycherley's *Posthumous Works* (1728), i. 6–7. For an earlier version of the story, see *Les Soupirs de la Grand Britaigne: or, The Groans of Great Britain* (1713), 65–6.

13. B was secretary to George Villiers, Duke of Buckingham, when he was Chancellor of Cambridge University (1670–4). In 1670, B and Thomas Sprat (see 'Sprat' 3 below) accompanied Buckingham to Versailles to negotiate a treaty with Louis XIV (Wilders (1967 edn.), p. xx). For B's supposed collaboration in Buckingham's *The Rehearsal* (1671), see 'Dryden' 94 and n. below.

14. The anecdote in effect confirms what Dryden had written of Buckingham as Zimri in *Absalom and Achitophel*, ll. 559–60: 'In squandring Wealth was his peculiar Art: | Nothing went unrewarded, but Desert.' Hill (1905) suggested that SJ had this story in mind in *Rambler* 27 (1750) on disappointed aspirants to the patronage of great men.

15. There is some confusion about the 'verses', first mentioned in 13 above. The satirical character of 'A Duke of Bucks' in *Genuine Remains* (1759), ii. 72–5, is in prose, not verse. (Thyer quotes in a note Dryden's character of Zimri from *Absalom and Achitophel*, which SJ would not have mistaken for the work of B.) SJ may have had in mind a poem 'On the Duke of Bucks' in *Poems on Affairs of State*, ii (1703), 216, once attributed to Dryden, and later discussed by Malone, *Prose Works of Dryden* (1800), i. 95–7 n.

16. *Hudibras*, Pt. III (dated 1678), appeared late in 1677. SJ defines 'Abrupt' as '1. Broken; craggy', from Latin 'abruptus' ('broken off') (*Dict*).

   B spent his last years in Rose Alley, Covent Garden, where he was confined with gout in the winter of 1679–80 (Wilders (1967 edn.), p. xxi).

   *and perhaps . . . begin to fail*: substituted in 1783 for SJ's original reference to B's date of birth as suggested by Longueville (see Textual Notes and 2 and n. above).

17. B died on 25 Sept. 1680 of consumption, according to Wood. William Longueville arranged B's burial at St Paul's, Covent Garden, where Dr Simon Patrick (1626–1707), later Bishop of Chichester and of Ely, was Rector. Patrick's part in the funeral service is mentioned in a note to the 'Life' of B in Zachary Grey's *Hudibras* (2 vols., Cambridge, 1744), i, p. viii n., which otherwise follows *GD*'s account. John Aubrey and Thomas Shadwell were among the pall-bearers (*Brief Lives* (1898), i. 136).

18. SJ added this paragraph in 1783 (see Textual Notes).

   The information in James Granger's *Biographical History* (1775), iv. 40, was pointed out by 'Scrutator' in *Gent. Mag.* (Dec. 1779), 594, and cited by Nash, *History*, ii. 391: Nichols could have drawn SJ's attention to either of these sources. Joseph Warton's reference to the pension in his *Essay on Pope*, ii (1782), 246 n.,

may have increased SJ's evident scepticism about it. Dr Zachary Pearce (1690–
1774) had his information through an intermediary from William Lowndes, Secretary of the Treasury 1695–1724. Sir Stephen Fox had in fact been ordered on 30
Nov. 1674 to give B £200, and he was awarded a pension of £100 in Nov. 1677 (not
paid before Sept. 1678), and an additional £20 in 1680 (Wilders (1967 edn.), pp.
xx–xxi).

   SJ refers to John Oldham's 'A Satyr. The Person of Spenser . . . Dissuading . . .
from the Study of Poetry', ll. 175–90 (*Poems*, ed. H. Brooks and R. Selden (Oxford,
1987), 243), and to Dryden on 'unpitied Hudibras' in *The Hind and the Panther*
(1687), III. 247–50. B's poverty often featured in complaints about the fate of
neglected genius: e.g. Otway's prologue to Lee's *Constantine the Great* (1683), ll.
35–6 ('Tell' em how *Spencer* starv'd, how *Cowley* mourn'd, | How *Butler*'s Faith
and Service was return'd'); a letter by Dryden of *c*.1683 ('Tis enough for one Age to
have neglected Mr Cowley, and sterv'd Mr Buttler', *Letters*, ed. C. E. Ward (1942),
21); Dennis, *Remarks on Mr. Pope's Homer* (1717) ('BUTLER was suffer'd to die in a
Garret . . . And yet BUTLER was a whole Species of Poets in one, admirable in a
Manner in which no one else has been tolerable', *Works*, ii. 121); Colley Cibber's
dedication to *Ximena; or, The Heroick Daughter* (1719), p. ix (B 'died with the
highest Esteem of the Court—in a Garret'); the prefatory apparatus to Pope's
*Dunciad* (*TE*, v. 44); David Hume, *History of Great Britain*, ii (1757), 454, on
Charles II's lack of 'true generosity' to B, Otway, and Dryden; and Goldsmith,
*Citizen of the World* (1760–1), on the poverty of Spenser, Otway, B, and Dryden as
'a national reproach' (*Coll. Works*, ii. 343 and cf. 376). See also 'Savage' **274** n.
below.

**19.** SJ described John Barber, Lord Mayor of London 1732–3, as 'a man much
distinguished and employed by the tories' in his 'Life of Edward Cave' in *Gent.
Mag.* (1754), 56. He had printed Pope's edition of the *Works* (1723) of John
Sheffield, Duke of Buckinghamshire, which was suppressed on suspicion of Jac-
obite sympathies: see 'Sheffield' **24** n. and 'Swift' **59** n. below, and *The Life and
Character of John Barber, Esq; Late Lord-Mayor of London* (1741).

   Barber in fact erected the monument in 1721 (as stated in the inscription itself),
some forty years after B's death. As 'Scrutator' noted in *Gent. Mag.* (1783), 47, SJ's
'About sixty years afterwards' is unusually vague, and suggests that the inscription
itself was inserted in SJ's text by another hand. In format it resembles Zachary
Grey's *Hudibras* (1744), i, p. xxxiv, rather than *GD* and *BB*. Grey also quoted the
translation in John Dart, *Westmonasterium* [1742], i. 79. The memorial prompted
Samuel Wesley's epigram, 'On the setting up Mr. Butler's Monument in Westminster Abbey', in *Miscellaneous Poems, By Several Hands*, ed. David Lewis (1726),
18: 'The Poet's Fate is here in Emblem shown; | He ask'd for Bread, and he receiv'd
a Stone', ll. 5–6.

**20.** Jacob, ii. 21, and Longueville in *GD*, vi. 292 n., had dismissed B's *Posthumous
Works* (3 vols., 1715–17) as spurious. After B's MSS passed from Charles Longueville to John Clark of Walgherton, Cheshire, Robert Thyer (1709–81), Keeper of
Chetham's Library, Manchester, published a selection in *Genuine Remains* (2 vols.,
1759): see 'Sources' and **3** n. above and **40** and n. below.

   *the Royal Society*: B ridiculed the recently founded Royal Society in verse in 'The
Elephant in the Moon' and 'A Satire on the Royal Society', and in prose in

'Occasional Reflections upon Dr. Charleton's feeling a Dog's Pulse at Gresham-College' (*Genuine Remains*, i. 1–56, 404–10). Although SJ contrasted the 'great expectations' at the founding of the Royal Society with its actual achievements in *Idler* 88 (1759) (*YW*, ii. 273), he usually disliked satire of scientists (cf. 'Gay' 10 and 'Pope' 222–3 below). See R. B. Schwartz, *SJ and the New Science* (Madison, 1971). For other poets involved with the Royal Society, see 'Cowley' 31 and n. above; and for 'innovation', 'Milton' 58 and n. above.

21. Although B's 'name can only perish with his language', SJ will discuss in 41 ff. below the 'perishable part' of *Hudibras*. In 1783 he deleted 'The date of his birth is doubtful': see Textual Notes, and 1, 16 and nn. above.

22. By 'domestick' SJ evidently means '4. Not foreign' rather than '2. Private; done at home' (*Dict.*): cf. 'Otway' 10 n. below. SJ said on 30 Apr. 1773: 'There is more thinking in [Milton] and in Butler, than in any of our poets' (*Life*, ii. 239). With his praise of B's 'Original and peculiar' diction, cf. his objection to Milton's early poems: 'their peculiarity is not excellence' ('Milton' 177 above).

  For English pride in B's 'unrival'd . . . Genius', see 'Of Originals and Writing' by 'M. B.' in the *Daily Gazetteer*, 25 Sept. 1741, reprinted in *Gent. Mag.* (Sept. 1741), 487–9, while SJ was working for the periodical; and James Granger, *A Biographical History of England* (3rd edn., 4 vols., 1779), iv. 39–40: ' "Hudibras," is, in its kind, almost as great an effort of genius as the "Paradise Lost" itself. It abounds with uncommon learning, new rhymes, and original thoughts. Its images are truly and naturally ridiculous: we are never shocked with excessive distortion or grimace; nor is human nature degraded to that of monkies and yahoos.'

  *Cervantes*: in a brief comparison in *Letters Concerning the English Nation* (1733), 212–13 (cf. 36 n. below), Voltaire suggested that B 'just borrowed the hint' of his poem from Cervantes. According to Mrs Thrale, SJ once described *Don Quixote*, *Robinson Crusoe*, and *The Pilgrim's Progress* as the only books their readers ever 'wished longer': 'After Homer's *Iliad* . . . the work of Cervantes was the greatest in the world, speaking of it . . . as a book of entertainment' (*J. Misc.*, i. 332–3). For later references to Cervantes, see 'Addison' 48 and 'Pope' 225 below.

23. For SJ on the deluded imagination, see also 'Cowley' 16 and n. above and 'Collins' 8 and n. below, and for depictions of Quixotic delusion elsewhere in his writings, see Henson, 111–41.

24. Under 'Presbytery' in the *Dict.* SJ quoted the opening lines of John Cleveland's 'The Mixed Assembly', which refer to 'the rude Chaos of Presbyt'ry, where Lay-men guide | With the tame woolpack Clergie by their side' (*Poems*, ed. B. Morris and E. Withington (Oxford, 1967), 26). See also 'Milton' 56 above. Hudibras's squire is Ralpho, 'an Independent enthusiast' (see 29 below), their theological differences and debates contributing to the satire. SJ defined 'Independent' as 'One who in religious affairs holds that every congregation is a complete church, subject to no superior authority' (*Dict.*).

  *GD*, vi. 297, cited Anthony Collins's description of *Hudibras*, in his *Discourse Concerning Ridicule and Irony* (1729), 42, as 'a daily High-Church entertainment, and a pocket and travelling High-Church companion'. Lord Hailes commented *c.*1782, however, that 'Butler by his witty strictures on ye Presbyterian Independents, has been considered as a friend of ye Church, but I much suspect that he was no Churchman, & no friend of ye Christian religion': see Carnie (1956), 489. For an interpretation of the politics of *Hudibras* as 'pragmatic and untraditional' rather than 'specifically Royalist', see Parker, 'End of Analogy', 25–60.

25. Whereas earlier responses to Don Quixote had often been less sympathetic, SJ had already written in *Rambler* 2 (1750) that 'When we pity him, we reflect on our own disappointments; and when we laugh, our hearts inform us that he is not more ridiculous than ourselves, except that he tells what we have only thought' (*YW*, iii. 11). Shenstone admitted to finding little humour in Cervantes: 'it is not so easy to raise a laugh from the wild atchievements of a madman. The natural passion in that case is pity, with some small portion of mirth at most' (*Works* (1764), ii. 205).

27. 'And out he rode a Colonelling', *Hudibras*, I. i. 14.

30–3. SJ defines 'Action' as '4. The series of events represented in a fable' (*Dict.*). Cf. 'Cowley' 165 ('the duration of an unfinished action cannot be known') and 'Milton' 210 above.

30. See *Hudibras*, I. ii. 793 ff., II. iii. 105 ff., 323 ff., III. iii. 577 ff.

31. For the weaknesses of the 'design' of Spenser's *Faerie Queene*, see Dryden's 'A Discourse Concerning Satire' (1693) (Watson, ii. 83). There is a marked break in *Hudibras*, III. ii, which describes events between the death of Cromwell in 1658 and the Restoration.

32. SJ refers to the Greek historian Thucydides, author of an incomplete history of the Peloponnesian War between Athens and Sparta in 431–404 BC.

33. Cf. *Adventurer* 107 (1753): 'As a question becomes more complicated and involved, and extends to a greater number of relations, disagreement of opinion will always be multiplied' (*YW*, ii. 441). For argument, see also 'Dryden' 328 and 'Swift' 39 below. SJ's comment on the difficulty of contriving novel but credible 'adventures' may reflect his own experience with *Rasselas*.

34. SJ's comments on dialogue elsewhere usually refer to drama: see 'Milton' 198, 203, 205, 265 above, and 'Smith' 49, 'Addison' 137, 'Congreve' 10–11, 33, 'Fenton' 12, and 'Thomson' 34 below; *Rambler* 125 (1751) (*YW*, iv. 305) and *Letters*, iv. 251. Cf. also his praise of the 'ease and simplicity' of Shakespeare's dialogue in 1765 (*YW*, vii. 63). For the importance of 'engaging the attention', see 'Dryden' 312 and n. below.

35. *variety*: see 'Milton' 272 above, and 'Prior' 53, 'Shenstone' 21, and 'Gray' 40 below. SJ's similar assertion that 'novelty is the great source of pleasure' in 'Prior' 67 below reflects the relationship between 'variety' and 'novelty' (see 'Cowley' 55 above). See also *Rasselas*, ch. XLVII: 'Such ... is the state of life, that none are happy but by the anticipation of change'; 'Variety ... is so necessary to content, that even the Happy Valley disgusted me' (*YW*, xvi. 164); *Rambler* 78 (1750); the preface and notes to Shakespeare ('upon the whole, all pleasure consists in variety', and the 'praise of variety' is the 'particular excellence' of *Hamlet* (*YW*, iv. 46, viii. 67, and viii. 1010–11).

*uniformity*: for 'uniformity of sentiment' as a positive aspect of poetry, see 'Cowley' 57 and n. above. For the negative sense implying monotony, see 'Dryden' 290, 'Prior' 68, 'Savage' 342, 'Pope' 309, 374, and 'Shenstone' 21 below; and *Rambler* 80 (1750) ('we should soon grow weary of uniformity', were it not for the change of seasons) (*YW*, iv. 57).

*impatience of the present*: for this recurrent theme of SJ's essays, see e.g. *Ramblers* 2 (1750) ('the mind of man . . . is always breaking away from the present moment, and losing itself in schemes of future felicity'), 41 (1750) ('so frequently are we in want of present pleasure or employment, that we are forced to have recourse every moment to the past and future for supplemental satisfactions'), 207 (1752) ('Such is the emptiness of human enjoyment, that we are always impatient of the present'). See also e.g. *Ramblers* 5, 29, 89, 203, and *Rasselas*, ch. XXX: 'The truth is, that no mind is much employed upon the present: recollection and anticipation fill up almost all our moments' (*YW*, iii. 9, 221, v. 310, xvi. 112).

SJ cites Horace, *Epist.*, II. i. 212. For the tedium which even admired works can induce, see also 'Milton' **252** above and 'Dryden' **270, 312** and 'Prior' **66** ('tediousness is the most fatal of all faults') below.

36. The *Dict.* includes 'Unexhausted' but not 'Unexhaustible'. Hill (1905) silently emended to 'inexhaustible'.

For wit as 'a combination of dissimilar images, or discovery of occult resemblances', see 'Cowley' **56** above. In spite of his reservations here, SJ later asserts B's superiority to Prior in 'exuberance of matter and variety of illustration' ('Prior' **64** below). Voltaire stated of *Hudibras* in *Letters Concerning the English Nation* (1733), 212–13: ''Tis *Don Quixot*, 'tis our *Satyre Menippée* [1594] blended together. I never found so much Wit in one single Book as in that, which at the same Time is the most difficult to be translated.'

For SJ's frequent contrast of 'astonishment' and 'delight', see 'Milton' **276** and n. above; and for his impatience with 'wonders', 'Cowley' **5** and n. above. He finally quotes Martial, *Epig.*, X. 46 ('You want all you say to be smart, Matho. Say sometimes what also is good; say what is middling; say sometimes what is bad'). For SJ's early fondness for Martial, quoted again in **51** below, see Kaminski, 11, 209 n.

37–9. *knowledge*: for SJ's frequent distinction between 'knowledge' acquired by 'study' of books and 'knowledge' acquired by 'observation' of life and human nature, see e.g. *Ramblers* 129, 137, 154 (1751), and *Life*, i. 105 ('knowledge of the world, fresh from life, not strained through books'). Mrs Thrale noted in 1777 that he had 'a great Notion of general Knowledge being necessary to a complete Character, and hated at his heart a solitary Scholar who knew nothing but his Books. The Knowledge of Books says he will never do without looking on Life likewise with an observant Eye' (*Thraliana*, i. 171). Discussing 'St. Kilda poetry' in 1773, SJ asserted that 'it must be very poor, because they have very few images . . . a man cannot make fire but in proportion as he has fuel' (*Life*, v. 228–9).

SJ in fact usually invokes both kinds of knowledge when assessing poets he takes seriously: see **51** below, 'Cowley' **175, 202**, 'Milton' **250, 268** and n. above, and 'Otway' **15**, 'Dryden' **321**, 'Addison' **110**, 'Savage' **101, 332–3**, 'Swift' **113**, 'Broome' **2**, 'Pope' **18, 32, 34, 291, 208**, and 'Shenstone' **33** below. In 1765 he wrote of Shakespeare that 'much knowledge is scattered over his works . . . but it is often such knowledge as books did not supply', and later contrasted knowledge of books with 'naked reason' and 'living manners' (*YW*, vii. 86, viii. 1015). For 'knowledge' as reflected in his quotations in the *Dict.*, see DeMaria (1986), 38–60.

37. For 'imagination', see 'Milton' **229** and n. above, and cf. *Idler* 44 (1759): 'Imagination selects ideas from the treasures of remembrance, and produces novelty only by varied combinations' (*YW*, ii. 137).

*combination*: defined in the *Dict.* as '4. Copulation of ideas in the mind' (illustrated from Locke). Cf. 'genius' as 'that energy which collects, combines, amplifies, and animates' in 'Pope' **310** below, and the lack of 'combination' (and hence variety) of ideas in Shenstone's poetry ('Shenstone' **21** below).

38. Voltaire asserted in a note to 'Le Marseillois et le Lion' (1768): 'Rabelais était profondément savant' (*Œuvres*, xii (1819), 178). After acknowledging B's un-rivalled 'strokes of just and inimitable wit', Hume admitted that his 'allusions are often dark and far-fetched', but continued: 'It is surprizing how much erudition Butler has introduced with so good a grace into a work of pleasantry and humor: Hudibras is perhaps one of the most learned compositions, that is to be found in any language' (*History of Great Britain*, ii (1757), 454). Warton, *Essay*, ii (1782), 403–4, observed that 'no work contains more *learning* than *Hudibras*'.

*confronting them*: in the summer of 1778, while SJ was writing or revising these paragraphs, Britain came close to 'confronting' the French navy in battle.

39. *the operations of human nature*: with B's diligent observation, cf. SJ's comment that the Metaphysical poets 'wrote rather as beholders than partakers of human nature' ('Cowley' **57** above).

*proverbial axioms*: Hazlitt, whose discussion of B's strengths and limitations in *Lectures on the English Comic Writers* (1819) was clearly influenced by SJ, stated that 'nearly one half of his lines are got by heart, and quoted for mottos', and that *Hudibras* was still 'equally in the hands of the learned and the vulgar' (*Complete Works*, ed. P. P. Howe, vi (1931), 62–8). *The Oxford Dictionary of Quotations* (3rd edn., 1979), 117–18, included thirty-six citations of *Hudibras*: e.g. 'For every why he had a wherefore', 'He ne'er consider'd it, as loth | To look a gift-horse in the mouth', 'Then spare the rod, and spoil the child', 'For those that fly, may fight again'. B's 'sententious distichs' were in fact often based on existing proverbs. Cf. SJ's praise in 1765 of Shakespeare's 'practical axioms and domestick wisdom' (*YW*, viii. 62).

Alexander Chalmers suggested in *Gent. Mag.* (Apr. 1788), 302, that the last two sentences of this paragraph applied to SJ himself.

40. Cf. *Rasselas*, ch. XXX: 'When the eye or the imagination is struck with any uncommon work the next transition of an active mind is to the means by which it was performed' (*YW*, xvi. 113). For SJ's interest in the origins of literary works, see 'Milton' **91** and n. above.

Although SJ implies that he had communicated with Robert Thyer, who died in 1781 (see 'Sources' and **20** and n. above), he is not mentioned in SJ's *Letters* or the *Life*. When Christopher Smart introduced Thomas Tyers to SJ (*c.*1754), SJ 'understood he called him by the name of Thyer, that eminent scholar, librarian of Manchester, and a Nonjuror. This mistake was rather beneficial than otherwise to the person introduced' (*Gent. Mag.* (1784), 907). For Thyer, see E. Ogden in *Transactions of the Lancashire and Cheshire Antiquarian Soc.* 41 (1924), 90–136; 47 (1930–1), 58–83. Thyer's edition of the *Genuine Remains* (1759) included material from B's MS commonplace books, reprinted in *Eng. Poets* (1779), vii. 141–357. For Goldsmith's enthusiastic review in the *Critical Review* in Sept. 1759, see *Coll. Works*, i. 206–12. See also H. de Quehen's edition of B's *Prose Observations* (1979).

**41.** *mythology*: for SJ's hostility to modern recycling of ancient mythology as tedious, puerile, 'exploded', and useless, see 'Milton' **182, 234** above and 'Waller' **123–4, 152,** 'Dryden' **238, 276, 335,** 'Smith' **49, 54,** 'Rowe' **10,** 'Prior' **56, 59,** 'Gay' **28, 30,** 'Granville' **12, 26,** 'Yalden' **16,** 'Tickell' **17,** 'Pope' **241, 316, 325, 336, 410,** 'Thomson' **29,** and 'Gray' **34–6, 41, 45** below; and see also 'Essay on Epitaphs' (1740) (*OASJ*, 98), *Rambler* 37 (1750), and *Adventurer* 92 (1753) (*YW*, iii. 205, ii. 419). Langton recalled SJ describing mythology as 'the least pleasing or valuable part' of ancient literature: 'The machinery of the Pagans is uninteresting to us: when a Goddess appears in Homer or Virgil, we grow weary; still more so in the Grecian tragedies, as in that kind of composition a nearer approach to Nature is intended . . . no one who writes now can use the Pagan deities and mythology' (*Life*, iv. 16–17).

SJ himself can use classical mythology ironically, as when professing in 1765 to be 'almost frighted at my own temerity' (in disagreeing with eminent critics), 'as Aeneas withdrew from the defence of Troy, when he saw Neptune shaking the wall, and Juno heading the besiegers' (*YW*, vii. 80–1). He admitted that classical mythology 'was desirable to be known for the sake of understanding other parts of ancient authours', even if it is 'the least pleasing or valuable part of their writings' (*Life*, iv. 2). His projected works as listed by both Hawkins, *Life* (1787), 82–3 n., and Boswell, *Life*, iv. 81–2 n., include a 'History of the Heathen Mythology, with an explication of the fables, both allegorical and historical, with references to the poets', and a 'Dictionary of Ancient History and Mythology'. For a facetious reaction to SJ's views, see John Matthews's coarse *Ode to Cloacina* (1782), in which the mock-dedication hopes that, in spite of his aversion to mythology, SJ will be willing to indulge this particular goddess.

*opinions . . . temporary and local*: the inevitable transience of literature, however elegant or subtle, about 'temporary subjects' is a frequent preoccupation of SJ's essays. SJ translates Cicero, *De Natura Deorum*, II. ii. 5 ('Opinionis enim commenta delet dies, naturae iudicia confirmat'), used earlier as epigraph to *Rambler* 106 (1751) on the transience of merely topical writing (*YW*, iv. 199). See also *Adventurer* 58 (1753) on the ephemerality of 'allusions to recent facts, reigning opinions, or present controversies', although SJ here urges the conscientious reader to 'repair by his candour the injuries of time'. From a different angle, SJ argued in *Adventurer* 95 (1753) that, while basic human experience varies little over time, and 'the anatomy of the mind, as that of the body, must perpetually exhibit the same appearances', the very mutability of fashion and manners always gives the writer fresh opportunities of reflecting his own age (*YW*, ii. 373, 427).

*standing relations and general passions*: Imlac in *Rasselas* (1759), ch. X, argued that the poet 'must divest himself of the prejudices of his age or country . . . must disregard present laws and opinions, and rise to general and transcendental truths, which will always be the same' (*YW*, xvi. 44). In 1765 SJ wrote that 'Nothing can please many, and please long, but just representations of general nature. Particular manners can be known to few, and therefore few only can judge how nearly they are copied'; and that 'the accidental compositions of heterogeneous modes are dissolved by the chance which combined them; but the uniform simplicity of primitive qualities neither admits increase, nor suffers decay' (*YW*, vii. 61–2, 69–70). See also *Idler* 59 (1759), quoted in **42** n. below, and 'Cowley' **49** above, and 'Dryden'

**296** and 'Pope' **83** below (for Homer's freedom from 'local or temporary customs'). For this fundamental tenet of neoclassical aesthetics, see also e.g. Reynolds, *Idlers* 79, 82 (1759), and 'Discourse III' (1770), which echoes the passage from *Rasselas* quoted above (*Discourses*, 110–11).

Voltaire stated in *Letters Concerning the English Nation* (1733), 213, that few now understand the particular satire in *Hudibras*: 'To explain this a Commentary would be requisite, and *Humour* when explain'd is no longer Humour.' In 1738, *GD*, vi. 293, agreed that *Hudibras* needed an explanatory commentary, which Zachary Grey partly supplied in his 1744 edition. *Anecdotes of Polite Literature* (1764), ii. 30–1, claimed that, for this reason, *Hudibras* was now 'but seldom read'. James Granger later admitted that 'There are in it many strokes of temporary satire, and some characters and allusions which cannot be discovered at this distance of time' (see **22** n. above).

On 1 July 1763, SJ talked 'very contemptuously' about Churchill's satiric poetry, claiming that 'it had a temporary currency, only from its audacity of abuse, and being filled with living names, and that it would sink into oblivion' (*Life*, i. 418). Discussing the *Spectator* on 3 Apr. 1773, he declared that 'all works which describe manners, require notes in sixty or seventy years' (*Life*, ii. 212), and told William Strahan, 7 Mar. 1774, that 'In fifty years every book begins to require notes ... to explain forgotten allusions and obsolete words' (*Letters*, ii. 131). For other comments on the subsequent neglect of books on 'transitory' subjects, see 'Walsh' **12**, 'King' **5**, 'Sprat' **5**, 'Garth' **10**, **17**, and 'Addison' **77** below.

**42.** Cf. *Rambler* 106 (1751): 'It is not difficult to obtain readers, when we discuss a question which every one is desirous to understand, which is debated in every assembly, and has divided the nation into parties.' The writer best equipped for survival will, however, be one 'who has carefully studied human nature, and can well describe it' (*YW*, iv. 202, 204). In *Idler* 59 (1759) he had explained why *Hudibras* in particular is 'almost forgotten however embellished with sentiments and diversified with allusions, however bright with wit, and however solid with truth. The hypocrisy which it detected, and the folly which it ridiculed, have long vanished from public notice. Those who had felt the mischiefs of discord, and the tyranny of usurpation, read it with rapture, for every line brought back to memory something known, and gratified resentment, by the just censure of something hated.' The poem 'is now seldom mentioned, and even by those that affect to mention it, is seldom read. So vainly is wit lavished upon fugitive topics' (*YW*, ii. 184).

On 18 Apr. 1775 he said: 'There is in Hudibras a great deal of bullion which will always last. But to be sure the brightest strokes of his wit owed their force to the impression of the characters, which was upon men's minds at the time; to their knowing them, at table and in the street; in short, being familiar with them; and above all, to his satire being directed against those whom a little while before they had hated and feared' (*Life*, ii. 369–70).

**43.** For 'subordination', see also 'Swift' **52** and n. below, and for 'innovators', 'Milton' **58** and n. above. In 'Sermon 23', commemorating the death of Charles I, SJ described the Civil War as 'a war of the rabble against their superiors; a war, in which the lowest and basest of the people were encouraged by men a little higher than themselves, to lift their hands against their ecclesiastical and civil governours, and by which those who were grown impatient of obedience, endeavoured to obtain the power of commanding' (*YW*, xiv. 247). In a passage in Sir Robert Chambers's *Lectures on the English Law* (1986), ii. 22–3, he described the Interregnum as 'an interval in which many political experiments were made, and as all reverence of ancient establishment was lost, the law was thrown open to the capricious innovations sometimes of enthusiasm and sometimes of licentiousness'. For 'The Legacy of the Civil War', and its impact on SJ's birthplace Lichfield, see D. J. Greene, *The Politics of SJ* (2nd edn., 1990), 22–34.

See also SJ's ironic 'Life' of Dr Francis Cheynell (1608–65), the parliamentary reformer, in *The Student* (1751), ii. 260–9, 290–4, 331–4, later reprinted in *Gent. Mag.* (Oct. 1775), 117–21, 176–8. (It was attacked in 1775 as embodying SJ's 'avowed principles in religion and politics': see Folkenflik, 96.) For the 'outrages and crimes of the Puritans' and their 'puritanical malignity', see 'Congreve' 18 below, and SJ's references to their 'turbulence and indecency' and 'obstinacy' in his notes to Shakespeare (*YW*, vii. 205, 381), and to the 'ancient rigour of puritanism' in *Journey* (1985), 87. Hannah More recalled that in 1780, 'I was very bold in combatting some of his darling prejudices: nay, I ventured to defend one or two of the Puritans, whom I found him to allow to be good men, and good writers' (*J. Misc.*, ii. 189).

A late marginal comment by Mrs Thrale-Piozzi related SJ's remarks here to the tumult of ideas which acompanied the French Revolution five years after his death: 'How dreadful 'tis to think that I, who saw dear Dr. Johnson write *this* passage ... lived long enough to witness the *truth* of this *passage* likewise' (Lobban, 133).

*disordered practice*: inserted in 1783 (see Textual Notes).

44. As Hill (1905) noted, Hugh Peters proposed that the Records in the Tower be burned as monuments of tyranny in *Good Work for a Good Magistrate* (1651), 33. Although such radical measures were often suggested during the 'Barebones' Parliament of 1653, there is no evidence that implementation of the proposal was seriously considered.

45. Cf. *Hudibras*, I. i. 225–8: 'Rather then faile, they will defie | That which they love most tenderly, | Quarrel with *minc'd Pies*, and disparage | Their best and dearest friend, *Plum-porredge*', referring to the parliamentary ordinance of 1647 condemning traditional celebrations of Christmas. A proclamation of 1652 reaffirmed 'That no Observation shall be had of the Five and twentieth day of *December*, commonly called *Christmas-Day*,; nor any Solemnity used or exercised in Churches upon that Day in respect thereof'. See *Hudibras*, ed. Grey (1744), i. 28–9 n. and Wilders (1967 edn.), 327 n., and Hawkins's story in *J's Works* (1787), ii. 191 n., of a clergyman 'ejected from his living by the parliament visiters for being a scandalous eater of custard'.

For SJ's interest in prejudices surviving from the 'ancient rigours of puritanism' in Scotland, see *Journey* (1985), 87. They did not in fact entirely die out in England, as SJ implies. Edmund Gosse, *Father and Son* (1907), claimed that his father Philip Henry Gosse, the naturalist, who belonged to the Plymouth Brethren, regarded Christmas 'as an act of idolatry' and would 'denounce the horrors of Christmas' (ed. J. Hepburn (Oxford, 1974), 66–7).

46. Thomas Gataker, *Of the Nature and Use of Lots* (1619), devoted some 360 laborious pages to the relationship of decisions or games based on chance to divine provi-

dence, including 203–35 on the use of dice. For SJ's absorption in Gataker's book in the Hebrides in Oct. 1773, seated in a high wind 'with his back against a large fragment of rock', and with 'a most eremetical appearance', see *Life*, v. 302.

47. *Astrology*: SJ defines it as 'an art now generally exploded as irrational and false' (*Dict.*). See also DeMaria (1986), 71–2. Charles I more than once consulted the astrologer William Lilly (1602–81) in 1647–8, but less about when to escape from imprisonment than where to escape safely to: see Lilly's *History of his Life and Times* (1715), 60–2, listed in the sale catalogue (1785) of SJ's library.

48. Cf. SJ's reference in 'Akenside' 6 below to 'Shaftesbury's foolish assertion of the efficacy of ridicule for the discovery of truth', and his assertion in 'Pope' 359 below that 'satirical criticism . . . rectifies error and improves judgement'. For comments elsewhere on the survival of astrological beliefs, see 'Dryden' 191 and n., 'Congreve' 14, and 'Swift' 30 below.

49. For 'probability' in neoclassical literary theory, see D. L. Patey, *Probability and Literary Form* (Cambridge, 1984). SJ invokes it most frequently in his notes to Shakespeare (e.g. *YW*, vii. 168, 222, 241, 403, viii. 956, 1011, 1037), but see 'Milton' 181, 196, 220 above, and 'Dryden' 50, 213 below.

   SJ refers to *Hudibras*, II. i–ii, based on *Don Quixote*, II. xxxv.

50. *grossly familiar . . . purposely neglected*: SJ can tolerate such diction and versification because *Hudibras* hardly challenges his notions of genuine poetry. As he said on 11 Apr. 1776: 'You may find wit and humour in verse, and yet no poetry. "Hudibras" has a profusion of these; yet it is not to be reckoned a poem' (*Life*, iii. 38). After discussing various linguistic barbarisms, solecisms, and improprieties, George Campbell, *The Philosophy of Rhetoric* (1776), i. 470–1, similarly explained that his remarks did not apply to satire and burlesque: 'There indeed a vulgar, or even what is called a cant expression, will sometimes be more emphatical than any proper term whatsoever.' For poetic diction, see also 'Cowley' 181–4 and n. above, and for the 'familiar', 'Cowley' 138 and n. above.

   Dryden discussed B's versification in 'A Discourse Concerning Satire' (1693) (Watson, ii. 147): for his 'sometimes capricious' criticism, see 'Dryden' 202 below. Dennis had disagreed with Dryden (*Works*, i. 6–10, and cf. 432–4). In *Spectator* 249 (1711) Addison mentioned the 'Dispute among the Criticks, whether Burlesque Poetry runs best in Heroic Verse, like that of [Garth's] Dispensary, or in Doggerel, like that of *Hudibras*', concluding that B would have made 'a much more agreeable Figure' in heroic verse, for all the popularity of his 'double Rhimes'. In *Spectator* 60 (1711) he again attributed B's wide appeal to his outrageous 'Doggerel Rhymes'. The *Monthly Review*, 21 (1759), 171–2, described B as a true genius, who should have lived in 'these more polished times, in which accuracy of composition, and neatness of expression, are more attended to'. See also Bond, *English Burlesque Poetry*, 29–41.

51. SJ's warning against the use of *Hudibras* as a precedent by later writers expands Dennis's assertion in 1717 that B 'was a whole Species of Poets in one, admirable in a Manner in which no one else has been tolerable: A Manner which began and ended in him' (*Works*, ii. 121). Zachary Grey, *Hudibras* (1744), i, p.xxii, claimed that B's 'Numberless Imitators' had 'miserably . . . failed in the Attempt', the 'most happy' being Prior (cf. 'Prior' 63 and n. below). James Beattie, *Essays* (Edinburgh,

1776), 688, also stressed B's 'uncommon acquisitions in learning' and 'singular turn of fancy' as the conditions of his success.

SJ quotes Martial, *Epig.*, VIII. 19 ('Cinna wanted to look poor, and so he is'), applied earlier by Dryden to an inferior poet in 'Of Dramatic Poesy' (Watson, i. 22). Cf. **36** and n. above.

Much of this paragraph (and of **45** above) was later paraphrased or quoted without attribution to SJ by a reviewer in *Gent. Mag.* (Dec. 1787), 1099–100.

52. *Burlesque*: SJ defines it as 'Jocular; tending to raise laughter, by unnatural or unsuitable language or images' (adjective) and 'Ludicrous language or ideas; ridicule' (noun) (*Dict.*). For 'burlesque' elsewhere, see 'Cowley' **103**, **111** and 'Denham' **22** above, and 'Waller' **108**, 'Dryden' **251a**, 'Addison' **72**, 'Prior' **58**, 'Pope' **392**, and 'Young' **165** below. For 18th-century discussions of burlesque, including essays on 'Hudibrastics' in the *Grub-Street Journal* (1730–1), nos. 39, 41, 45, 63, and for the popularity of 'Hudibrastic' verse to the end of the 18th century, see Bond, *English Burlesque Poetry*, E. A. Richards, *Hudibras*, and Dennis, *Works*, i. 432 n. For the 'heterogeneous' in wit, see 'Cowley' **56** above. SJ defines 'Corruption' as '1. The principle by which bodies tend to the separation of their parts' (*Dict.*).

*novelty*: in *Journey to the Western Isles* SJ stated that 'Novelty has always some power . . . But the force of novelty is by its own nature soon at an end' (1985, 8). For the ideal combination of the 'natural' and the 'new', see 'Cowley' **55** and n., and for 'admiration', 'Cowley' **58** and n. above.

*lays down his book*: cf. 'Milton' **252** and n. above. SJ states similarly in 'J. Philips' **11** below that an imitator of his mock-Miltonics could 'only hope to be considered as the repeater of a jest'.


# JOHN WILMOT, EARL OF ROCHESTER (1647–1680)

**Composition.** SJ discussed R with Boswell at Ashbourne on 22 Sept. 1777, shortly before starting work on his biographies: 'Talking of Rochester's Poems, he said, he had given them to Mr. Steevens to castrate for the edition of the Poets, to which he was to write Prefaces.' With this usage cf. the claim on the title page of *Poems on Affairs of State* (1697; 5th edn., 1703), which includes poems by R, that it was 'Published without any Castration', and Samuel Dunster's statement in his preface to Horace's *Satires and Epistles* (1709; 5th edn., 1739) that he had 'castrated our Poet, in translating nothing that bordered on Obscenity, or that was contrary to the Rules of Decency and good Manners'. SJ's host, John Taylor, commented that, if R 'had been castrated himself, his exceptionable poems would not have been written'. SJ went on to discuss the adequacy of Gilbert Burnet's account of R (see 'Sources' below) (*Life*, iii. 191).

R is among the thirteen poets SJ listed in his diary on 13 Oct. 1777, but, since they include such figures as Prior and Pope about whom he would not write until 1780, this has limited evidential value (*YW*, i. 279). These scattered references, and the fact that SJ did not mention 'Rochester' later, make it just conceivable that he wrote it soon after returning to London in early Nov. 1777. The fact that he ignores Dryden in his account of R but made several references to his relations with R in 'Dryden' (written *c*.Apr.– Aug. 1778) (see 'Dryden' **62**, **101**, **105** below) might also slightly increase the likelihood that he wrote 'Rochester' first, but may reflect no more than reliance on particular sources. It is much more likely that SJ initially concentrated on a series of substantial biographies, and that 'Rochester' was one of the shorter lives he completed late in 1778 or early in 1779 and collected in *Prefaces*, vol. iv.

Although SJ told Boswell that Steevens was responsible for the censored text of R in *Eng. Poets* (1779), *Gent. Mag.* (1779), 506, stated that 'the judicious hand of Dr. Johnson' had pruned R's poems (already bowdlerized since 1691 in Tonson's editions), preserving only the 'entirely unexceptionable'. John Nichols, always eager to claim that SJ had been actively involved in the contents of *Eng. Poets* (1779) (see i. 61–8 above), also stated in his *Sel. Collection*, iii. 200 n., that SJ had 'very judiciously pruned them'. In his biography, SJ refers only obliquely to R's notoriously obscene writings (see 11 below).

**Sources.** SJ's ultimate source for 1–13 below was *Some Passages of the Life and Death of…John, Earl of Rochester* (1680) by Gilbert Burnet (1643–1715), later Bishop of Salisbury (1689), commended by SJ in 12 below. When Boswell asked SJ on 22 Sept. 1777 'if Burnet had not given a good Life of Rochester', SJ had replied: 'We have a good *Death*: there is not much *Life*' (*Life*, iii. 191–2). Although *GD* ignored R, there had been accounts in Jacob, ii. 230–6, and Shiels, *Lives*, ii. 269–300, but SJ would have found almost all of his factual information, together with quotations from Wood, ii. 654–7, in the anonymous article in *BB*, vi (ii) (1766), Suppl. 195–6, which he seems certainly to have consulted (see 1 n. below). SJ was evidently also aware of *The Works of the Earls of Rochester, Roscomon, and Dorset* (1731) (see 'Roscommon' headnote below), in which R's poems were conveniently preceded by Saint-Évremond's 'Life' of R, Robert Wolseley's 'Preface' to R's *Valentinian* (1685), an extract from Wood, quotations from Robert Parsons's *Sermon* (1680) at R's funeral, as well as Burnet's narrative (i, pp. iii–xliii).

The 'high encomium' of Burnet's *Some Passages* in 12 below prompted SJ's friend Thomas Davies to reprint it in 1782, together with Parsons's *Sermon*, and prefaced by SJ's own account of R. Davies presumably did so with the permission of SJ, who is described in the 'Advertisement' as 'the greatest name in literature'. There were four further editions of this collection between 1787 and 1810 (*Bibliography*, ii. 1501–3).

R is one of the eight poets (of the fifty-two in *Eng. Poets*) not quoted in the *Dict*.

**Publication.** In *Prefaces*, vol. iv (31 Mar. 1779). Although separately paginated, it was printed together with 'Yalden' (q. v.): see Fleeman, *Handlist*, 229 n. There are no proofs.

**Modern Sources:**
(i) Rochester

*Complete Poems*, ed. D. M. Vieth (New Haven, 1968)
*Letters*, ed. J. Treglown (Oxford, 1980)
*Poems*, ed. K. Walker (Oxford, 1984)
*Works*, ed. H. Love (Oxford, 1999)

(ii)

E. Burns (ed.), *Reading R* (Liverpool, 1995)
M. M. Duggan, *English Literature and Backgrounds 1660–1700* (2 vols., New York, 1990), ii. 1032–49
D. Farley-Hills (ed.), *R: The Critical Heritage* (1972) (includes accounts of R by Burnet, 47–91, and Wood, 170–3, and John Aubrey's notes, 177–8)

N. Fisher (ed.), *That Second Bottle: Essays on John Wilmot, Earl of R* (Manchester, 2000)

G. Greene, *Lord R's Monkey* (1974)

G. Greer, *John Wilmot, Earl of R* (2000)

V. de Sola Pinto, *R: Portrait of a Restoration Rake* (1935), revised as *Enthusiast in Wit* (1962)

K. Robinson, 'R's Income from the Crown', *N & Q* 227 (1982), 46–50

G. Roebuck, 'John Wilmot, Earl of R', in *Dictionary of Literary Biography*, cxxxi (1993), 215–35

M. Thormählen, *R: The Poems in Context* (Cambridge, 1993)

J. Treglown (ed.), *Spirit of Wit: Reconsiderations of R* (Oxford, 1982)

G. Wasserman, *Samuel Butler and the Earl of R: A Reference Guide* (Boston, 1986)

1. R was in fact born on 1 Apr. 1647, the son of Henry Wilmot (1612?–58), a Royalist general who was created Earl of Rochester 1652, and his wife Anne St John. See Clarendon, *History of the Rebellion*, ed. W. D. Macray (Oxford, 1888), iii. 345–6, 388–9.

    SJ originally dated R's birth 'April, 1648', but revised this and subsequent estimates of R's age in 1781, with a later change in 13 in 1783 (see Textual Notes). 'April 1648' probably derives from Wood, ii. 654, via *BB*, since Jacob and Shiels give only '1648'. SJ's revised date in 1781 came from James Granger, *Biographical History* (1775), iv. 49 n., cited by 'Scrutator' in *Gent. Mag.* (Dec. 1779), 594.

    Since SJ elsewhere complains when biographers fail to name the schoolmasters of eminent men (see 'Hughes' 1 below), his own failure to mention John Martin, identified as R's teacher at Burford by Wood, ii. 654, but not by *BB*, suggests that he did not consult Wood at first hand. R matriculated from Wadham College, Oxford, on 18 Jan. 1660, and received his MA on 9 Sept. 1661 from Clarendon as Chancellor of the University. According to Wood, ii. 654, as cited by *BB*, Clarendon kissed R on the left cheek as he admitted him to his degree. For verses 'To His Sacred Majesty' attributed to the 13-year-old R in *Brittania Rediviva* (Oxford, 1660), but said by Wood, ii. 656, to be by Robert Whitehall of Merton College, see Love (1999 edn.), 109–10, 435.

2. R travelled abroad with his tutor, Sir Andrew Balfour, between Nov. 1661 and Dec. 1664. His naval exploits with Edward Montagu, Earl of Sandwich, and Sir Edward Spragge in 1665/6 are described by Burnet, *Passages*, 9–11. SJ does not mention his marriage on 29 Jan. 1667 to Elizabeth Malet.

    [*the ship commanded by*]: accidentally omitted in all SJ's editions, and supplied from Burnet, *Passages* (see Textual Notes).

3. See 24 below, and 'Sheffield' 3 and n. below. The incident occurred in Nov. 1669 (Vieth (1968 edn.), p. xxv; *Letters*, 55).

4–5. SJ's ultimate source is Burnet, *Passages*, 11–16.

4. For later references to the 'dissolute and vitious' Restoration court, see 'Roscommon' 9, 'Otway' 7, 'Waller' 72, 'Dryden' 181, 'Duke' 3–4, and 'Dorset' 2–4 below.

7. See Burnet, *Passages*, 27–8. R's notorious impersonation of Alexander Bendo, a mountebank, has been dated *c*.1675/6 (Vieth (1968 edn.), p. xxvii).

8. R became a Gentleman of the Bedchamber on 21 Mar. 1666 (receiving no payment until 18 Nov. 1667), and Ranger and Keeper of Woodstock Park in Feb. 1674 (Wood, ii. 654; Vieth (1968 edn.), pp. xxii, xxviii; *Letters*, 16 and n., 95 n.). For an earlier pension of £500 p.a. granted by Charles II in Feb. 1661, see Vieth (1968 edn.), p. xix, and Robinson, 'Income', 46–50.

9. Wood, ii. 654–5, in fact said only that R 'was a Person of most rare Parts, and his natural Talent was excellent, much improved by Learning and Industry, being throughly acquainted with the Classick Authors, both Greek and Latin; a thing very rare (if not peculiar to him) among those of his Quality'. This again suggests that SJ was not using Wood at first hand. Thomas Hearne dismissed Wood's account of R as 'so great a Master of Classick Learning', in *Remarks and Collections*, ed. C. E. Doble, iii (Oxford, 1889), 263. SJ's second sentence derives ultimately from Burnet, *Passages*, 26.

10. From Burnet, *Passages*, 8. For Boileau see also 26 and n. below, and for other admirers of Cowley, 'Milton' 164 above and 'Sprat' 2, 22 below.

11. SJ's reference to 'intervals of study perhaps yet more criminal' is as close as he comes to referring to R's obscene writings as opposed to his dissolute behaviour. (For SJ's repeated emphasis on the irregularity of his studies, see 9 above and 17, 27 below.) Burnet stated that R's lack of religious conviction and enjoyment of 'Lewd Actions and irregular Mirth' led him 'to bend his Wit, and direct his Studies and Endeavours to support and strengthen these ill Principles both in himself and others' (*Passages*, 15–16).

   Although he usually takes seriously the testimony of those with personal knowledge of his subjects, SJ ignores Robert Wolseley's often quoted preface to *Valentinian* (1685), no doubt because it defended R's obscenity by comparing it to the naked figures esteemed in painting and statuary (Spingarn, iii. 18–31). In *Rambler* 77 (1750) SJ had denounced 'the settled purpose of some writers, whose powers and acquisitions place them high in the rank of literature, to set fashion on the side of wickedness; to recommend' debauchery and lewdness' (*YW*, iv. 42). For his condemnation of obscenity elsewhere, see 'Dryden' 170–1 and n. below.

12. R's 'salutary conferences' with Burnet (see 'Sources' above) began in the autumn of 1679. SJ's refusal even to abridge Burnet's triumphant account of R's 'deathbed conversion', quoted at length by Shiels, *Lives*, ii. 291–4, may reflect some scepticism about it. For his views on 'repentance' elsewhere, see *Rambler* 110 (1751) and 'Sermon 2' (*YW*, iv. 220–6, xiv. 17–27).

13. In 1783 SJ corrected his estimate of R's age at his death (see Textual Notes and cf. 1 n. above).

14. *vigour*: for all his disapproval of R's character, SJ later seems to relate the 'vigour of his colloquial wit' to qualities in R's verse. Cf. his 'vigorous' versification (19), a 'vigorous' lampoon (24), and the general 'sprightliness and vigour' of his works (27). For 'vigour' as involving 'brevity and compression', see 'Shenstone' 31 below; for a more 'correct' and 'elegant' contemporary of R who was 'rarely vigorous', see 'Roscommon' 24, 39 above; and for 'vigour' as a recurrent demand in the *Lives*, see 'Milton' 277 and n. above.

   *wild pranks*: Shiels, *Lives*, ii. 282–91, had related at length at least some of the stories regularly purveyed by R's early biographers.

For R's later reputation, see Hume and Walpole in **27** n. below, and the preface to his (mostly spurious) *Poetical Works* (1761), p. v: 'the very Name of *Rochester* is a sufficient Passport wherever the English language is spoken or understood; And we doubt not but it will give the highest Delight to all those who have Youth, Fire, Wit and Discernment.' James Granger wrote less positively about R's readers in his *Biographical History of England* (3rd edn., 4 vols., 1779), iv. 49: 'Though the earl of Rochester was in the highest repute as a satirist he was but ill entitled to that distinction: his satires are not only unpolite, but grossly indecent. His poem "On Nothing," and his "Satire against Man," are a sufficient proof of his abilities: but... the greatest part of his works are trivial or detestable. He has had a multitude of readers: so have all other writers who have soothed, or fallen in with, the prevailing passions and corruptions of mankind.' SJ himself was not averse to quoting R in conversation. On 10 Apr. 1776 he quoted 'An Allusion to Horace', ll. 34–6, and on 24 Apr. 1779 'A Letter from Artemisia', l. 45, though without attributing it to R (*Life*, iii. 29, 386–7).

**15.** According to Burnet, *Passages*, 14, discussing R's talent for witty libel and satire, 'when any thing extraordinary that way came out, as a Child is fathered sometimes by its Resemblance, so it was laid at his door as its Parent and Author'. Wood, ii. 655, also referred to the obscene writings 'fathered upon the Earl (as most of this kind were, right or wrong, which came out at any time, after he had once obtained the Name of an excellent smooth, but withall a most lewd Poet)'. R's *Poems on Several Occasions* published in the autumn of 1680 shortly after his death, with the false imprint 'Printed at Antwerp', included libertine verse by several other writers. For the problematic canon of his verse, see D. M. Vieth, *Attribution in Restoration Poetry* (1963), Vieth's edition of the *Poems* (1968), and *Works*, ed. H. Love (1999), especially the section of 'Disputed Works' (246–63).

**16.** In recommending that Steevens should 'castrate' R's poems (see 'Composition' above), SJ may also have handed over to him the question of their authenticity. He refers to 'An Allusion to Horace, the Tenth Satyr of the First Book' (Love (1999 edn.), 71–4); 'An Epistolary Essay, from M. G. to O. B. upon their mutuall Poems', later entitled 'An Epistolary Essay from Lord Rochester to Lord Mulgrave' (Love (1999 edn.), 98–101; cf. 'Sheffield' **3** below); 'A Satyre against Reason and Mankind' (Love (1999 edn.), 57–63); and 'Upon Nothinge' (Love (1999 edn.), 46–8).

*the late collection*: *Eng. Poets* (1779).

**18.** For other discussions of love poetry, see 'Cowley' **14** and n.; and for similar derisive lists of the usual topics of 'artificial courtship', 'Cowley' **123** above and 'Sheffield' **22** below.

*smooth and easy*: SJ's repetition of such a phrase in successive sentences is an unusual oversight.

The equation of social and literary skills implicit in SJ's definition of 'Ease' as '5. Unconstraint; freedom from harshness, formality, forced behaviour, or conceits' (*Dict.*) is reinforced by his illustrative quotation from Pope, *Essay on Criticism*, ll. 362–3: 'True Ease in Writing comes from Art, not Chance, | As those move easiest who have learn'd to dance.' ('Easy' is '8. Not constrained; not stiff', again quoting Pope.) *Idler* 77 (1759) defined 'Easy poetry' as 'that in which natural thoughts are expressed without violence to the language. The discriminating character of ease consists principally in the diction... Where any artifice appears in the construction of the verse, that verse is no longer easy' (*YW*, ii. 239). Cf. *Guardians* 12, 15 (1713), probably by Steele ('every Thought which is agreeable to Nature, and exprest in Language suitable to it, is written with Ease'); and Robert Lloyd, 'An Epistle to Mr. Colman. Written in the Year 1756' (*Poetical Works* (1774), i. 165–70).

SJ believed that the 'ease' of Restoration and early 18th-century verse had been succeeded by 'ambition of ornament, and luxuriance of imagery', as in 'Gray' **48** below ('too little appearance of ease and nature'). Elsewhere he distinguishes the true 'ease' usually obtainable only by 'diligence' ('Milton' **178**) from the mere 'ease of a trifler' ('Pope' **354**). For other examples of the term, see 'Dryden' **214**, 'King' **18**, 'Smith' **18** (not by SJ), 'Parnell' **12**, 'Addison' **156, 167**, 'Prior' **55**, 'Blackmore' **29**, 'Swift' **31, 139**, 'Watts' **6, 35**, 'Shenstone' **22, 33**, and 'Akenside' **22**.

19. For 'An Allusion to Horace', see **16** above; and for 'imitation', see 'Pope' **209–10, 372** and n. below, and H. F. Brooks, 'The "Imitation" in English Poetry, Especially in Formal Satire, before the Age of Pope', *RES* 25 (1949), 124–40.

20. For 'Upon Nothing', see **16** above and 'Pope' **18** below.

*this barren topick*: SJ echoes Addison's praise of R's 'admirable Poem upon that barren Subject' in *Spectator* 305 (1712). For recent discussion of the intellectual background to 'Upon Nothing', see the essays by T. Barley and P. Baines in E. Burns (ed.), *Reading R* (Liverpool, 1995), 98–113, 137–65, and for 'Nihil' as a subject for ingenious rhetoric in the Renaissance, see R. Colie, *Paradoxia Epedemica* (Princeton, 1966), ch. VII. *Nihil* (Paris, 1587) by Jean Passerat (1534–1602) was later included in *Argumentorum Ludicrorum* (Leiden, 1623), ii. 107–9. Passerat's lines ('My bones will sleep peacefully, provided they are not burdened with bad songs') had also been quoted from his epitaph in 'l'Eglise des Jacobins de la rue S. Jaques', in *Ménagiana* (3rd edn., Paris, 1715), vi. 255. For another epitaph by Passerat, see SJ's early 'Essay on Epitaphs' in *Gent. Mag.* (1740), 594–5, and his notes on *Hamlet* in 1765 (*YW*, viii. 958).

21. See **28** below.

22. *taken positively, as an agent*: for a comparable discussion of 'poetry . . . ascribing . . . agency' to 'darkness' and 'cold', see 'Dryden' **10** below.

SJ refers to Boileau, *Satires*, II. 62: 'La nuit à bien dormir, et le jour à rien faire.' Boileau consulted the French Academy as to whether his usage was preferable to 'L'une à dormir, et l'autre à ne rien faire' in La Fontaine: see his *Œuvres* (Paris, 1747), i. 47 and n., v. 188–90.

SJ quotes Johann von Wower (Ioan. Wowerus, 1576–1635), *Dis Aestiva, sive de Umbra Paegnion* (1610), 130, which he had earlier cited as 'the Shadow of WOWERUS' in his 'Life of Browne' (1756), p. xxv, and invokes again in 'Yalden' **17** below.

24. SJ refers to 'On the Suppos'd Author of A late Poem in Defence of Satyr' (1677) (Love (1999 edn.), 106–7). For 'In Defence of Satyr' (1677) by Sir Carr Scroope (1649–80), see Love (1999 edn.), 102–5, and *POAS* i. 364–70. While it is impressive that SJ could quote a version of ll. 52–9 'from memory', as his footnote claims, there are inevitable inaccuracies: cf. 'To fatal *Mid-night* quarrels, can betray, | His brave *Companion*, and then run away; | Leaving him to be murder'd in the *Street*, | Then put it off, with some *Buffoone* Conceit; | This, this is he, you shou'd beware of all, | Yet him a pleasant, witty *Man*, you call | To whet your Dull Debauches up, and down, | You seek him as top *Fidler* of the *Town*.' Scroope alluded to an incident which took place in June 1676.

25. SJ added his misquotation of 'For all men would be cowards if they durst' from 'A Satyre against Reason and Mankind', l. 158, in 1783 (see Textual Notes). The 'buffoon conceit' is now usually taken to be R's 'To the Post Boy' (Love (1999 edn.), 42–3). SJ refers to R's 'On the Suppos'd Author of A late Poem in Defense of Satyr' and quotes, with 'hurt' for 'blast', Scroope's 'Answer By way of Epigram', ll. 5–6 (Love (1999 edn.), 106–7).

26. While revising the *Lives* in Aug. and Sept. 1782, SJ systematically read Boileau's works, noting on 30 Aug. that 'I this day finished Boileau's Satires of which I had not read any one through before' (*YW*, i. 327). See **10, 16** above. R's 'Satyr against Reason and Mankind' is partly based on Boileau's *Satire* VIII. ('Timon', unmentioned by SJ and recently consigned to R's 'Disputed Works' by Love (1999 edn.), 259–63, also imitated Boileau, *Satire* III.) Voltaire, who preferred to consider R as 'the Man of Genius, the great Poet' rather than as 'the Man of Pleasure', had compared Boileau and R to the latter's advantage in *Letters Concerning the English Nation* (1733), 197–204. See also J. F. Moore, 'The Originality of R's *Satyr aginst Mankind*', *PMLA* 58 (1943), 393–401, and P. C. Davies, 'R and Boileau: A Reconsideration', *Comparative Lit.* 21 (1969), 348–55. For other references to Boileau as a source or precedent for English poets, see 'Roscommon' **28**, 'Dryden' **247**, and 'Pope' **212, 340, 368** below.

27. SJ agrees here with Hume: 'The very name of Rochester is offensive to modern ears; yet does his poetry discover such energy of style and such poignancy of satyre, as give ground to imagine what so fine a genius, had he fallen in a more happy age and followed better models, was capable of producing. The ancient satyrists often used great liberty in their expressions; but their freedom no more resembles the licence of Rochester than the nakedness of an Indian does that of a common prostitute' (*History of Great Britain*, ii (1757), 453). Horace Walpole was franker than SJ about R's obscenity, describing him as 'A Man, whom the Muses were fond to inspire, and ashamed to avow … Lord Rochester's poems have much more obscenity than wit, more wit than poetry, more poetry than politeness' (*Royal and Noble Authors* (2nd edn., 1759), ii. 43).

28. See **20–1** above. Hawkins later claimed that, 'for the insertion of this poem Johnson had, as it is said, no other aid than his own recollection' (*Life* (1787), 17).

Isobel Grundy, *Scale of Greatness* (1986), 99–100, has suggested that SJ's emphasis on the poems on 'Nothing' by R and Passerat effects 'a most striking association between the brilliant young life thrown away, and the two productions of intellect exercised upon nullity'. One may also note that SJ seems almost sadistically to leave readers who were hoping for the titillation usually offered by accounts of R's career stranded on a bleak expanse of modern Latin verse.


## WENTWORTH DILLON, EARL OF ROSCOMMON (1637–1685)

**Composition.** SJ does not refer to 'Roscommon' and there is no evidence for dating it. The fact that R was one of the thirteen poets he listed in his diary on 13 Oct. 1777 is no indication of his immediate intentions, since he was not to write about several these poets until 1780. 'Roscommon' was probably one of the short biographies written under pressure in late 1778 or early 1779 for vol. iv of the *Prefaces*. It was a special case in that

SJ could make substantial use of his own earlier 'Life' of R and may therefore have been written early in this sub-series.

**Sources.** SJ did not acknowledge his main source, his own early 'LIFE *of the Earl of* ROSCOMMON' in *Gent. Mag.* (May 1748), 214-17. Of 1-28 only **2, 4,** and **14-18** were added to, or differ significantly from, the 1748 text. SJ's main task in 1779 was merely to move most of the lengthy original footnotes into the main narrative. The critical survey of R's verse in **29-39** was, however, mostly added in 1779. Some short passages in the 1748 text omitted in 1779 have been quoted in the notes to **9, 14, 22,** and **26** below, and variants in directly comparable passages included in the Textual Notes.

SJ's acknowledged source in 1748 had been '*Fenton*'s notes on *Waller*', cited again in **2** below. This refers to a long note about R in Elijah Fenton's *Works of Edmund Waller* (1729), pp. lxxv-lxxvii (see 'Fenton' **15** and n. below). C. L. Batten, 'SJ's Sources for "The Life of R"', *MP* 72 (1974), 185-9, argued persuasively, however, that SJ must in fact have relied on the slightly revised version of Fenton's note in *The Works of the Earls of Rochester, Roscomon, and Dorset; The Dukes of Devonshire, Buckinghamshire, &c. With Memoirs of Their Lives* (2 vols., 1731, and later edns.), ii, pp. xi-xvii. In this collection SJ would also find George Sewell's 'Some Memoirs of the Earl of Roscomon' (ii, pp. iii-viii), originally published in 1718, the source for the story related from Aubrey in **5-6** below, which is not in Fenton. Sewell could also have guided SJ to the quotation from Katherine Philips's *Letters* he added in 1779 (see **36** n. below). For other detailed points made by Batten, see also **2** n. and **22** n. below.

The immediate purpose of SJ's 'Life' of R (1748) is uncertain. Uniquely among SJ's biographies, its format imitates that of Pierre Bayle's *Dictionnaire*, which had been adopted by both *GD* and *BB* (see i. 89-90 above): an outline narrative at the head of the page supported by elaborate annotation, in this case mostly quotation from Fenton which SJ would compress and revise in 1779. SJ introduced it in 1748 with the assertion that 'our collections of *English* lives must be considered imperfect, none of them having an account of him' (214 n.). Since an account of R had already appeared in *GD*, viii (1739), 775-6 (which, also relying heavily on Fenton, inevitably resembles SJ's), this assertion raises the possibility that SJ was filling some pages of the *Gent. Mag.* with a biography of R he had originally written much earlier, i.e. before 1739. The Baylean format of the article might even suggest that this could have been for submission to *GD* itself. That R was in SJ's mind in the late 1730s is indicated by several approving references to him in the notes to his translation of Crousaz's *Commentary on Pope's Essay on Man* (1739): see *OASJ*, 84, 89, 95. If SJ's original 'Life' was not in fact written earlier than 1739, the account in *GD* would itself obviously become one of its potential sources. Two of the small pieces of evidence on which Batten argued his case for SJ's reliance on the *Works of the Earls* (1731)—the reference to Bishop Hall in **2** and the citation of Katherine Philips in **36**—apply equally to *GD*, which did not, however, include the story from Aubrey. On the whole, it seems unlikely that SJ relied on it in 1748 (cf. also **1** n., **21** below).

There are other possibilities. The 'Life' (1748) could have been intended for the annotated edition of R which Hawkins claimed that SJ had once projected (*Life* (1787), 82 n.). Alternatively, its compilation could have some unexplained connection with the *Biographia Britannica*, which had begun appearing in 1747 under the editorship of William Oldys, with whom SJ had worked on the Harleian Library earlier in the 1740s (*Life*, i. 175). The short account of R which eventually appeared in *BB*, vi (ii) (1766),

Suppl. 41–2, could derive from either Fenton, *GD*, or SJ's own 1748 narrative. In 1753 Shiels, *Lives*, ii. 344–53, acknowledged SJ's anonymous biography as his source, referring to its 'ingenious author', and introduced into his narrative a compliment to SJ's forthcoming *Dictionary* (see **16–18** n. below).

SJ's silent use in 1779 of his earlier biography was first pointed out in *Gent. Mag.* (1779), 594, by 'Scrutator' (John Loveday), who had noticed the reference to the 'Life' (1748) by Shiels. Since it had not been collected with other early works by SJ in Thomas Davies's *Miscellaneous and Fugitive Pieces* (1773–4), the discovery of his authorship of the early biography and use of it in 1779 was greeted with surprise in an editorial note in *Gent. Mag.*, which claimed that SJ, 'in the new preface, has not servilely copied himself. The facts are unavoidably the same, and many entire passages retained; but the whole is put into a more regular form, and is considerably improved and enlarged' (594 n.). This note may well have been written by Nichols, in an attempt to reassure purchasers of the *Eng. Poets* (1779) that the proprietors were not sanctioning the recycling of old biographies for their series, the current practice in Bell's rival *British Poets*. Isaac Reed was the first editor to collect the original biography of 1748 in SJ's *Works*, xiv (1788), 413–20.

On 31 Oct. 1784, a few weeks before his death, SJ made a cryptic memorandum in some miscellaneous literary notes: 'Roscommon's Life. Bakers papers' (*YW*, i. 408). Tonson's edition of R's *Poems* (1717), sig. A2ᵛ. ('To the Reader'), had already referred to an unpublished 'Account of the Life and Writings of the Earl of *Roscomon* by a Gentleman that was very intimately acquainted with his Lordship'. This was no doubt the MS life of R by Knightley Chetwood (1650–1720) used by Fenton in 1729 and described in Nichols, *Sel. Collection*, vi. 52–4 n., as among the MSS of Thomas Baker at Cambridge (see also **13** n. below). Nichols also supplied some information about R's family (from 'a gentleman whose name I am not at liberty to disclose') which SJ added to **1** below in 1783.

In spite of SJ's somewhat lukewarm final assessment of R's achievement in **39** below, he had included 301 quotations from his verse in *Dict.* (1755), increased to 304 in 1773.

**Publication.** In *Prefaces*, vol. iv (31 Mar. 1779). There are no proofs.

**Modern Sources:**
C. L. Batten, 'SJ's Sources for "The Life of R" ', *MP* 72 (1974), 185–9
M. M. Duggan, *English Literature and Backgrounds 1660–1700* (New York, 1990), i. 400–1
C. Niemeyer, 'The Birth Date of the Earl of R', *RES* 9 (1933), 449–51
C. Niemeyer, 'The Earl of R's Academy', *MLN* 49 (1934), 432–7
C. Niemeyer, 'A R Canon', *SP* 36 (1939), 622–36

1. R was the son of James Dillon (*c.*1605–1649), 3rd Earl of Roscommon (1642), and Elizabeth Wentworth, sister to Thomas Wentworth, Earl of Strafford, Lord Deputy of Ireland (1632) and Lord-Lieutenant (1640), who was executed for high treason in May 1641. SJ added his information about R's parents and his relationship to Strafford in 1783 (see Textual Notes), no doubt from Nichols, *Sel. Collection*, vi. 53 n. Since it had been available in *GD*, viii (1739), 775, it seems clear that *GD* was not SJ's source either in 1748 or 1779 (see 'Sources' above). The fact that in *Lives* (1783), vol. i, sig. U8 (303–4) is a cancel may be related to these revisions.

According to Wood, ii (ii). 223, James Ussher (1581–1656), Primate of Ireland, converted R's father to Protestantism. Although Malone later argued that the convert was in fact Robert Dillon, the 2nd Earl (*J's Works* (1816), ix. 185 n.), Cokayne, xi. 126, accepted Wood's account. For SJ's description of Ussher as 'the great luminary of the Irish church', see *Life*, ii. 132, and see also 'Milton' **46–7** above.

R was born in Ireland in 1637 (Niemeyer, 'Birth Date', 449–51) and styled Lord Kilkenny-West 1642–9. By 1641 he was at Wentworth Woodhouse in Yorkshire. For another youthful poet's problems with the 'rules of grammar', see 'Cowley' **4–5** above.

2. SJ corrects his statement in *Gent. Mag.* (1748), 214, that R's tutor was 'afterwards *Bishop* of *Norwich*' (i.e. Joseph Hall (1574–1656): see 'Milton' **46** above). The error derived from *Works of the Earls* (1731), ii, p. xii, and not from Fenton (ed.), *Waller* (see 'Sources' above), but is also found in *GD*. R's tutor has not been certainly identified.

3. R attended the Calvinist College at Caen. *BB*, VI, Suppl., 41 n., translated the description of Samuel Bochart (1599–1667) in J. B. Ladvocat, *Dictionnaire portatif* (Paris, 1752) as 'one of the most learned men of that age...He was master of Greek, Hebrew, Arabic, Coptic, and several other languages...He was a member of the academy, where he died May 16, 1667, as he was pronouncing the speech.'

4. Since R would have been aged only 4 when Strafford was executed in May 1641, his education at Caen obviously began several years later: **5–6** below indicate that he was there in 1649. Thomas Butler (1634–80), son of the Duke of Ormond and later Earl of Ossory, was also at Caen in 1648 and 1650–2 (*DNB*). For 'literature' as learning, see 'Milton' **4** above.

5–6. R's father died at Bishop Bramhall's lodgings in Limerick on 8 Nov. 1649 after falling down a stone staircase. Since Fenton does not relate the story from John Aubrey's *Miscellanies* (1696), 89, SJ presumably took it from *Works of the Earls* (1731), ii, p. v, which also reprinted George Sewell's brief biography from the original edition of the *Works* (1718): see Batten, 'Sources', 185–6. In 1748 SJ also reproduced the error of 'Stafford' for 'Strafford' in *Works* (1731), which, however, reads (correctly) 'Table-Boards' in the quotation from Aubrey.

7. SJ transferred this paragraph without revision from *Gent. Mag.* (1748), 215 n. Cf. his note to *Othello* in 1765: 'There has always prevailed in the world an opinion, that when any great calamity happens at a distance, notice is given of it to the sufferer by some dejection or perturbation of mind, of which he discovers no external cause. This is ascribed to that general communication of one part of the universe with another, which is called sympathy and antipathy' (*YW*, viii. 1040). For his views on the 'second sight', see *Journey to the Western Islands* (1985), 89–91, and see also 212 n. for Bacon's description in *Sylva Sylvarum* (1627) of a dream anticipating his father's death. For a recent case of 'preternatural intelligence', see 'Lyttelton' **29** n. below and *Life*, iv. 94–5.

SJ finally quotes Francis Osborne (1593–1659), 'Advice to a Son', in *Works* (1673), 103: 'Despise not *a profession of Holiness*, because it may be true; But have a care how you trust it, for fear it should be false.' In 1772 SJ described Osborne as 'A conceited fellow. Were a man to write so now, the boys would throw stones at him' (*Life*, ii. 193).

8. R travelled with William Cavendish, later Duke of Devonshire (*DNB*).

9. R was restored to his ancestral honours and estates by the Act of Settlement of 29 Dec. 1660. He did not in fact become Captain of the Band of Gentlemen Pensioners with £1,000 p.a. until 1674.

   For other references to the dissolute Restoration court, see 'Rochester' 4 and n. above. In *Gent. Mag.* (1748), 215 n., SJ had commented on Fenton's account of R's gambling: 'This was the fate of many other men, whose genius was of no other advantage to them, than that it recommended them to employments, or to distinction, by which the temptations to vice were multiplied, and their parts became soon of no other use than that of enabling them to succeed in wickedness.'

10. R was almost continuously in Ireland 1662–74, partly in dispute over his estates (Niemeyer, 'Academy', 432–3). James Butler, Duke of Ormond, Lord-Lieutenant of Ireland 1662–9, made R captain of a troop of the Regiment of Guards on 29 June 1666.

11. SJ quotes Fenton (ed.), *Waller*, p. lxxvi, replacing 'there' with 'at Dublin' in the first sentence.

12. Wood, ii (ii). 223, mentions R's appointment as Master of the Horse to Mary of Modena, the second Duchess of York. R had married Frances, daughter of Richard Boyle, Earl of Burlington, and widow of Sir Francis Courteney, in Apr. 1662. She died *c.*1672. SJ does not refer to R's second marriage in Nov. 1674 to Isabella Boynton, maid of honour to the Duchess of York, although Nichols, *Sel. Collection*, vi. 53–4 n., noted it.

13. SJ's 'now' suggests that he read Fenton (ed.), *Waller*, pp. lxxvi–lxxvii, as indicating that R's plan for an academy dated from as early as the 1660s. Niemeyer, 'Academy', 433–5, following Knightley Chetwood's MS life of R in Cambridge University Library (see 'Sources' above), believed that it began in about 1682. It was at this period that R received the degrees of LL D from Cambridge in 1680 and of DCL from Oxford in 1683. Members of the 'society' mentioned by Chetwood included Lords Halifax, Maitland, and Cavendish, the Earl of Dorset, Sir Charles Scarborough, Col. Finch, and John Dryden, with others 'of less note & Abilities': 'They aim'd at refining our Language, without abating the force of it, & therefore instead of making a laborious Dictionary, they purposed severally to peruse our best writers, & mark such words, as they thought vulgar, base, improper, or obsolete.' The main outcome of the group's activities seems to have been a number of translations of classical texts: see J. A. Winn, *John Dryden and his World* (1987), 387–8.

   According to Fenton, John Dryden was 'a principal assistant' in the scheme. He had supported the creation of an English Academy to regulate the language on the model of the French Académie in the preface to *The Rival Ladies* (1664), and in Dec. 1664 was appointed to the Royal Society's committee 'for improving the English language'. He returned to the idea in the dedication of *Troilus and Cressida* (1679), the 'Discourse of Satire' (1693), and the dedication of *Examen Poeticum* (1693) (Watson, i. 51, 239 and n., ii. 152; *Works*, ii. 277 n.). See O. F. Emerson, 'John Dryden and a British Academy', *Proceedings of the British Academy*, 10 (1921), 45–58, reprinted in H. T. Swedenborg (ed.), *Essential Articles for the Study of John Dryden* (Hamden, Conn., 1966), 263–80. Defoe later proposed an academy 'to polish and refine the *English* Tongue' in his *Essay upon Projects* (1697), as did Prior in 1701. For a broader view of plans for an English Academy in this period, see A. C. Baugh and T. Cable, *A History of the English Language* (3rd edn., 1978), 253–94, and, for SJ's views, Reddick, 14–15, 20–1, 198 n., 208–9 n.

14–18. With the exception of the opening sentence of **14**, SJ added these views on the feasibility of an English Academy in 1779. This deserves to be emphasized, since at least one authority has interpreted these paragraphs as evidence for the development of SJ's thinking about his *Dictionary* (see also **16–18** n. below), assuming that, as early as May 1748, he 'had apparently begun to have doubts . . . about the ability of any philological authority to set standards for the language and expect them to have any effect': see Reddick, 208–9 n.

14. In *Gent. Mag.* (1748), 216 n., after quoting Fenton's account of R's plan, SJ continued: 'This design was again set on foot, under the ministry of the Earl of *Oxford*, and was again defeated by a conflict of parties, and the necessity of attending only to political disquisitions, of defending the conduct of the administration, and forming parties in the parliament.' Although the next sentence opened with a double quotation mark, it does not derive from Fenton, and may also be SJ's own, since the quotation is not closed, and he echoed the opening in 1779: 'Since that time it has never been mentioned, either because it has been hitherto a sufficient objection, that it was one of the designs of the Earl of *Oxford*, the detestable Earl of *Oxford*, by whom *Godolphin* was defeated, or because the statesmen who succeeded him have not had more leisure for literary schemes.' (The opening quotation mark was omitted when the 1748 text was reprinted in *Works*, xiv. 416 n., in 1788.)

SJ went on in 1748 to refer to Swift's *Proposal for Correcting, Improving and Ascertaining the English Tongue* (1712). Voltaire, *Letters Concerning the English Nation* (1733), 235–7, asserted that the Whigs subverted Swift's scheme after 1714. For the political context of Swift's *Proposal*, see his *PW*, iv, pp. xi–xii, and 'Swift' **40** below, and cf. 'Addison' **91** and 'Prior' **14–15** below.

Although SJ states that the design 'has never since been publickly mentioned', Shiels, one of his assistants on the *Dictionary*, wrote in his own account of R in *Lives* (1753), ii. 348: 'It will, no doubt, surprize many of the present age, and be a just cause of triumph to them, if they find that what Roscommon and Oxford attempted in vain, shall be carried into execution, in the most masterly manner, by a private gentleman, unassisted, and unpensioned. The world has just reason to hope this from the publication of an English Dictionary, long expected, by Mr. Johnson; and no doubt a design of this sort, executed by such a genius, will be a lasting monument of the nation's honour, and that writer's merit.' Joseph Warton also linked R's plans for an academy with SJ's *Dictionary* in his *Essay on Pope* (1756), 199–200, and a contributor to the *London Chronicle* (12–14 Apr. 1757) claimed that the *Dictionary* had 'supplied the Want of an Academy of Belles Lettres'. For continuing interest in such schemes, see A. W. Read, 'Suggestions for an Academy in England in the Latter Half of the Eigheenth Century', *MP* 36 (1938–9), 145–56, and J. G. Basker, 'Minim and the Great Cham: Smollet and J on the Prospect of an English Academy', in J. Engell (ed.), *J and his Age* (Cambridge, Mass., 1984), 137–61, and *Tobias Smollett: Critic and Journalist* (Newark, Del., 1988), 17–28.

15. SJ refers to the Accademia della Crusca established at Florence in 1582, and the Académie Française founded in 1634 by Cardinal Richelieu. SJ had presented his

*Dict.* to these academies in 1755: see J. H. Sledd and G. J. Kolb, *Dr. J's Dictionary* (Chicago, 1955), 146–7.

**16–18.** Although in his original *Plan of a Dictionary* (1747) SJ hoped to contribute to the stability of the English language, his later 'Preface' admitted the impossibility of such an ambition and was sceptical about the notion of an English Academy, hoping, indeed, that 'the spirit of English liberty will hinder or destroy' such a scheme: see *OASJ*, 324–5. Dick Minim in *Idler* 61 (1759) had predictably 'formed a plan for an academy of criticism', because of his 'great admiration of the wisdom and munificence by which the academies of the continent were raised' (*YW*, ii. 190). Goldsmith claimed in 1759 that 'the necessity of such an institution became every day more apparent' (*Coll. Works*, i. 503). Although SJ's cynicism in **16** about the practical workings of such a society ('If an academician's place were profitable, it would be given by interest', etc.) is striking, his friend Arthur Murphy defended the idea of a British 'Academy of Literature' against SJ's objections in his *Essay on Dr. J* (1792), 114–19. See also A. Reddick as cited in **13**, **14–18** nn. above, and DeMaria (1986), ch. VI.

**17–18.** Cf. SJ's 'Sermon 7': 'The prevailing spirit of the present age seems to be the spirit of scepticism and captiousness, of suspicion and distrust, a contempt of all authority, and a presumptuous confidence in private judgement; a dislike of all established forms' (*YW*, xiv. 77). See also his discussion on 10 Apr. 1778, beginning 'Subordination is sadly broken down in this age' (*Life*, iii. 262), and for his views on 'subordination' elsewhere, see 'Swift' **52** and n. below. In a different context SJ could take a more positive view of such lack of respect for authority, as when attributing 'The Bravery of the English Common Soldiers' to 'neglect of subordination': 'The equality of English privileges, the impartiality of our laws, the freedom of our tenures, and the prosperity of our trade dispose us very little to reverence of superiors' (*British Mag.* (Jan. 1760); *OASJ*, 549–50).

**19.** Fenton (ed.), *Waller*, p. lxvii, is the source for R's statement that 'it would be best to sit next the chimney when the chamber smok'd'. Unlike SJ, 'Scrutator' in *Gent. Mag.* (Feb. 1780), 65, found R's meaning 'sufficiently clear': 'in his Lordship's opinion, the troubles in King James's reign proceeded [i.e. would proceed] from the Court of Rome.' R in fact died shortly before the accession of James II (see **21** below).

All SJ's references to James II indicate that he considered his removal to have been necessary. As he wrote in 1756, James 'was not ignorant of the real interest of his country; he desired its power and happiness, and thought rightly, that there is no happiness without religion; but he thought very erroneously and absurdly, that there is no religion without popery'. The 'necessity of self-preservation had impelled the subjects of James to drive him from the throne'. In 1770 SJ referred to James's 'dangerous bigotry' (*YW*, x. 142, 342). He told Bennet Langton that 'It was become impossible for him to reign any longer in this country', and in conversation on 6 Apr. 1775 described him as 'a very good King', who 'unhappily believed that it was necessary for the salvation of his subjects that they should be Roman Catholicks' (*Life*, i. 430, ii. 341; see also Hawkins, *Life* (1787), 504–5). For SJ the preservation of the Church of England was a more fundamental concern than loyalty to the King. For later references to the 'turbulence', violent 'innovations', and 'enormities' of James's reign, see 'Dorset' **10–11** and 'Granville' **5** below, and, for the dilemma faced by other poets in these years, see also 'Dryden' 138, 'Sprat' 10–13, and 'Sheffield' 13 below.

21. R in fact died on 17 Jan. 1685 (Niemeyer, 'Canon', 630). *GD*, viii (1739), 776 and n., dated his death 17 Jan. 1684, following Wood, ii (ii). 223.

22–7. SJ transferred these paragraphs with little alteration from his footnotes in *Gent. Mag.* (1748), 216–17.

22. Except for 5–6 and 14–18, SJ has been heavily dependent to this point on Fenton (ed.), *Waller*, whom he now quotes directly (p. lxxvii), substituting 'In his writings' for 'In them' in the first sentence. In *Gent. Mag.* (1748), 216 n., he had described the passage as 'a character too general to be critically just'.

Batten, 'Sources', 187, detected here a clue to SJ's possible source: Fenton actually wrote 'a mind that was naturally serious' (as in *GD*), whereas SJ, like *Works of the Earls* (1731), ii, p. xvii, has 'a mind which', etc. There are, however, variants from both Fenton (ed.), *Waller* and *Works* (1731) later in SJ's quotation.

23. R's verse had been collected with that of Rochester (q.v. above) in 1707, and with that of Richard Duke (q.v. below) in 1717. Since SJ had already commented on the 'petty size' of R's output in 1748, he could have been referring to R's inclusion in two anthologies published in the next two years: *The Works of the Most Celebrated Minor Poets* (2 vols., 1749) and *The Works of Celebrated Authors* (2 vols., 1750). There had, in fact, been separate editions of R's *Works* at Glasgow in 1749 and 1753. For a similar reaction to the sparse output of another titled poet, see 'Dorset' 14 below.

*imagination . . . judgement*: for the opposition of 'wit' (or 'fancy') to 'judgement', see Hobbes's 'Answer' to Davenant's 'Preface to *Gondibert*' (1650): 'Judgment begets the strength and structure, and Fancy begets the ornaments of a poem' (Spingarn, ii. 59). By 1720 this was something of a cliché: 'The greater the Wit is, and the more Strength and Vigour that the Imagination has to form Ideas in Poetry, the more Discretion and Judgment is requisite to moderate that Heat, and govern its natural Fury' (Jacob, ii, p. xxi). Predictably, Dick Minim in *Idler* 60 (1759) asserted 'that a perfect writer is not to be expected, because genius decays as judgment increases' (*YW*, ii. 186). In SJ's conception of poetic genius imagination and judgement are united: see 'Pope' 373 below, and his argument on the subject with William Robertson in 1773 (*Life*, v. 34–5). Cf. also 'Prior' 72 below, for judgement as hindering faults, but not producing excellence; and 'Young' 154 below for reliance on 'chance' inspiration rather than judgement. For 'imagination' elsewhere, see 'Milton' 229 and n. above.

*spritely*: the *Dict.* also includes the spelling 'Sprightly'. Although SJ revised the spelling here to 'spritely' in 1783 (see Textual Notes and cf. 35 below), 'sprightly' survives in the quotation from Fenton in 22 above.

24. *the only correct writer in verse before Addison*: the first reference to 'correctness' in the *Lives* in fact merely repeats SJ's text of 1748. He defines it as 'Accuracy; exactness; freedom from faults' (*Dict.*). Cf. 'Waller' 5, 'Dryden' 356, 'Addison' 129, 157, 'Prior' 70–2, and 'Pope' 30, 94 below. For the developments in English versification it denotes, see 'Cowley' 185–99 and n. above, and for its limitations, see 39 below. According to Chetwood's MS life, R himself considered Dryden 'as a naturall rather than a correct Poet' (Niemeyer, 'Academy', 434).

By the mid-century 'correctness' was coming to seem old-fashioned (and even unpatriotic) in some quarters, as in Warton's *Essay on Pope* (1756), 202: 'CORRECT-NESS is a vague term, frequently used without meaning and precision. It is perpetually the nauseous cant of the French critics, and of their advocates and pupils, that the English writers are generally INCORRECT.' SJ showed qualified sympathy for this view in 1765 when contrasting Shakespeare as an abundant if entangled forest with the formal garden of 'a correct and regular writer' (*YW*, vii. 84). At times he prefers alternatives such as 'regularity' and 'propriety', as in 'Dryden' **218** ('the establishment of regularity, and the introduction of propriety in word and thought') and **263** ('formed his versification, or settled his system of propriety'): see also 'Waller' **153**, 'Congreve' **16**, 'Yalden' **16**, 'Swift' **85**, and 'Young' **155** below.

SJ quotes Pope's *Imit. Horace, Ep. II. i.* (1737), ll. 213–14. (Pope had already praised R in 17ll in *Essay on Criticism*, ll. 725–8.) R wrote in his *Essay on Translated Verse*, ll. 115–16: '*Immodest words* admit of no defence, | For want of *Decency* is want of *Sense.*'

SJ's reference to 'Mr. Pope' survives from the 1748 text, published four years after the poet's death. Such formality is occasionally found elsewhere (see e.g. 'Mr. Dryden' and 'Mr. Pope' in 'Walsh' **2**, **5** below), but in 'Fenton' **26** below SJ revised 'Mr. Pope' to 'Pope' in the proofs (see Textual Notes).

**25.** For 'great', see 'Milton' **194** n. above. R published *An Essay on Translated Verse* in 1684; for the revised 1685 text, see Spingarn, ii. 297–309.

SJ quotes Dryden's preface to *Sylvae* (1685) (*Works*, iii. 3). Addison later praised the *Essay* in his 'Account of the Greatest English Poets' (1694), ll. 108–11, and in *Spectator* 253 (1711) called it 'a Master-piece in its kind'. Granville also praised the verse-essays by R and Sheffield as pioneering contributions to English criticism in his 'Essay upon Unnatural Flights in Poetry' (1701) (see 'Granville' **30** and n. below). Even Warton, *Essay on Pope* (1756), 199, wrote that R had decorated an apparently 'barren subject' with 'many precepts of utility and taste', and that his *Essay* was 'indisputably better written' than Sheffield's ('Sheffield' **23–5** below).

**26.** For 'cursory civilities' between authors, see 'Milton' **277** above. R had in fact died before Dryden published his preface to *Sylvae*. SJ does not mention that Dryden's 'To the Earl of Roscommon, on his Excellent Essay on Translated Verse' was prefixed to the *Essay*. He had quoted ll. 30–1 in the *Dict.* under 'Essay'.

**27.** In *Gent. Mag.* (1748), 217 n., the passage equivalent to **26** continued with a compilation (beginning 'They are, however, here laid down') of R's precepts in the *Essay*, 'disentangled from the ornaments with which they are embellished', which were then further summarized as in **27**. Shiels, *Lives*, ii. 350–2, had imitated this section in 1753. Given the importance he usually attaches to verse translation in the *Lives*, one might have expected SJ to react more positively to the *Essay*, but he basically adapts what he had written in 1748. For the 'reasonableness' of the rules of translation expounded by Dryden, see 'Dryden' **224–6** below, and for translation elsewhere, see 'Denham' **32** and n. above.

SJ may have reacted here to Charles Gildon's summary of the 'useful lessons' in R's *Essay* in *The Laws of Poetry as Laid Down by the Duke of Buckinghamshire, the Earl of Roscommon and by the Lord Lansdowne* (1721), 338–9, at the end of a 60-page commentary on the poem. A copy of Gildon's *Laws* is listed in the sale catalogue (1785) of SJ's library. *BB*, vi Suppl., 42 n., had also praised R's eminence 'in the didactical manner'. For a later contrast of 'the elegance of the poetry' with 'the sense of the precepts' in the *Essay on Man*, see 'Pope' **365–6** below.

28. Gildon, *Laws of Poetry*, 322, 343, pointed out both R's debt to Boileau's *Art poétique*, IV. 1–24, and the confusion of British and Saxon mythology. For 'confounded . . . mythology', see also 'Rowe' **12** and n. below.

29–39. SJ added most of these concluding paragraphs in 1779.

29. Towards the end of the *Essay on Translated Verse* (2nd edn., 1685), which is otherwise in couplets, R inserted twenty-seven lines of blank verse in praise of Milton (Spingarn, ii. 308–9), whose reputation was about to be boosted by Tonson's elaborate subscription edition of *Paradise Lost* (1688) (see 'Milton' **137** and n. above). Addison approved of R's blank-verse interlude in *Spectator* 333 (1712), and his 'noble encomium' and 'rational recommendation of blank verse' led Warton, *Essay* (1756), 200, to praise him as 'the first critic who had taste and spirit enough publicly to praise the Paradise Lost'. See **30** and n. below.

30. R's *The Art of Poetry* (dated 1680 for 1679), a version of Horace's *Ars Poetica*, in fact preceded his *Essay on Translated Verse*. (Wood, ii (ii). 223, had dated both poems 1680.) Although SJ's objections to blank verse in **29–30** are predictable (see 'Milton' **274** n. above), he had quoted *The Art of Poetry* frequently in the *Dict*.

R's version of Horace was generally less admired than his *Essay*. Leonard Welsted, *Epistles, Odes, &c.* (2nd edn., 1725), pp. xxvii–xxviii, described it as 'low and prosaic', with 'nothing of that spirit of poetry, or beauty of language, which alone makes the original pleasing'. Shiels, *Lives*, ii. 353, later stated: 'Amongst the MSS. of Mr. Coxeter, we found Lord Roscommon's translation of Horace's Art of Poetry, with some sketches of alterations he intended to make; but they are not great improvements; and this translation, of all his lordship's pieces, is the most unpoetical.' For Thomas Coxeter (1689–1747), collector and antiquarian, see *Life*, iii. 158, and i. 138 n. above.

31. For the 'difficulties of rhyme', see 'Milton' **126, 273** and nn. above.

32. In the dedication to the *Aeneis* Dryden stated that R's translation of Virgil, *Eclogue* VI, in *Miscellany Poems* (1684), 'cannot be too much commended' (Watson, ii. 242).

For Mrs Thrale-Piozzi's report that SJ always wept when reciting the Latin *Dies irae*, see *J. Misc.*, i. 284. As Hill (1905) noted, SJ evidently refers to the resemblance of R's 'And wake the Nations under Ground' ('On the Day of Judgement', l. 9) to Dryden's 'Ode on Mrs. Anne Killigrew' (1686), l. 179 ('To raise the nations under ground'). R had, however, died before the publication of Dryden's poem, and his own apparently did not reach print until 1696.

33. In 'On the Death of a Lady's Dog', 'thou' and 'thee' predominate, with 'you' in fact occurring only in l. 13.

Cf. R's 'How fondly Human Passions turn! | What then we Envy'd, now we Mourn!' (ll. 15–16) with Waller, 'Thyrsis, Galatea', ll. 37–8: 'Under how hard a law are mortals born! | Whom now we envy, we anon must mourn.'

34. R's imitations of Horace's *Odes*, I. xxii, originally prefixed to Katherine Philips's *Poems* (1667), and III. vi, appeared in *Miscellany Poems* (1684). For SJ's own schoolboy versions of *Odes*, I. xxii, see *Poems* (1974), 8–10.

35. For R's *The Ghost of Tom Ross to his Pupil the Duke of Monmouth* (1680) and *The Ghost of the Old House of Commons to the New One Met at Oxford* (1681), see *POAS*,

ii. 249–52, 406–10. For the misprint in 1783 of 'political' as 'poetical', see Textual Notes.

36. SJ refers to R's translation from Guarini's *Pastor fido*, v. ii (cf. 'Gay' 32 and 'A. Philips' 16 below), and his prologue to Katherine Philips's *Pompey. A Tragedy* (from Corneille), performed in Dublin on 10 Feb. 1663. Philips ('The Matchless Orinda') (1632–64) was a friend of R's first wife. Her *Poems* (1667) included 'To the Countess of Roscommon, with a Copy of Pompey': see her *Collected Works*, ed. P. Thomas, i (Cambridge, 1990), 16–18, 223–4, and 'Waller' 147 below. R's connection with Philips was SJ's only significant addition in 1779 to the biographical information he had offered in 1748.

The numerous variants in SJ's quotation from Philips's letter of 19 Oct. 1662 to Sir Charles Cotterel from the text in her *Letters from Orinda to Poliarchus* (1705), 79, suggest that he relied on some intermediary text or transcript (cf. 'Waller' 98 n. below). As Batten, 'Sources', 187–8, pointed out, George Sewell's 'Memoirs' of R in *Works of the Earls* (1731), ii, p.vii, had briefly quoted the same letter (from the 1729 edition of her *Letters*). In 1739 *GD* quoted it from the 1705 edition. SJ describes Philips's *Letters* as 'neglected' in 'Pope' 171 below.

37. As printed, R's translation from Guarini, ll. 1–2, reads: 'Ah happy Grove! dark and secure Retreat | Of sacred Silence, Rest's Eternal Seat.'

38. For *Pompey*, see 36 above. Two letters of 1663–4 from R to Sir Edward Dering survive (British Library). For the 'thought', see R's prologue, ll. 11–13: 'And you alone may boast you never saw | *Caesar* | 'till now, and now can give Him Law. | Great *Pompey* too, comes as a Suppliant here', etc.

39. For SJ's usual faith in the 'judgement of the publick', see 'Smith' 49 and n. below. With his comment that R's 'versification is smooth, but rarely vigorous', cf. 34 above ('not . . . much elegance or vigour'), and contrast 'Rochester' 19 above ('sometimes careless, but . . . sometimes vigorous'). For a similar verdict on another 'correct' poet, see 'Addison' 126–7, 157 below, and for 'rhymes', 'Cowley' 187 and n. above.


## THOMAS OTWAY (1652–1685)

**Composition.** There is no direct evidence for dating 'Otway', but its relationship to 'Duke' (see 'Publication' below and headnote to 'Duke') indicates a date of late 1778 or early 1779.

**Sources.** Although there had been accounts of O in Jacob, i. 193–6, Wood, ii. 781–2, *GD*, viii. 69–71, and Shiels, *Lives*, ii. 324–36, most of SJ's information was available in the unsigned article in *BB*, vi (ii) (1766), Suppl. 137–8, which itself cites Wood and the life of O prefixed to his *Works* (3 vols., 1757). The 1757 biography in fact originally appeared as 'Some Account of the Life and Writings of Mr. Thomas Otway' in his *Works* (2 vols., 1712), i. 7–18, the edition cited here. *BB*'s account, however, provided little information about the dates of O's plays, for which SJ consulted several sources at first hand: Langbaine in 5 (and cf. 11 n.), the 'Life' in O's *Works* in 7, and Shiels in 6 (see n.) and 14. In 1783 he added new material from the Spence MSS in 14. As noted in 15 n. below, he made no use of O's long autobiographical (at times allegorical) poem *The Poet's Complaint of his Muse* (1680) as a source.

**Publication.** In *Prefaces*, vol. iv (31 Mar. 1779). Although separately paginated, it formed a single sheet with 'Duke': see Fleeman (1962), 228 n. The complete proofs are in the Forster Collection.

**Modern Sources:**
(i) Otway

*Works*, ed. J. C. Ghosh (2 vols., Oxford, 1931, repr. 1968)

(ii)

N. Blakiston, 'O's Friend', *TLS* 15 Aug. 1958, 459
J. D. Canfield, 'TO', in *Dictionary of Literary Biography*, lxxx (1989), 146–71
B. Corman, 'J and Profane Authors: The Lives of O and Congreve', in P. J. Korshin (ed.), *J after Two Hundred Years* (Philadelphia, 1986), 225–44
M. M. Duggan, *English Literature and Backgrounds 1660–1700* (New York, 1990), ii. 826–36
R. G. Ham, *O and Lee* (New Haven, 1931)
A. M. Taylor, *Next to Shakespeare: O's 'Venice Preserv'd' and 'The Orphan' and their History on the London Stage* (Durham, NC, 1950)
K. P. Warner, *TO* (Boston, 1982)

1.  This is SJ's most sombre opening to a literary biography.

2.  O was born at Milland, in the parish of Trotton, Sussex, on 3 Mar. 1652, the son of the Revd Humphry Otway (1611–71), Rector of Woolbeding. He wrote about his parents, his childhood, and the unsettling effect of his father's death in *The Poet's Complaint of his Muse* (1680), ll. 47–80 (see **15** and n. below). He attended Winchester 1668–9, matriculated from Christ Church, Oxford, on 27 May 1669, but had withdrawn by 28 Sept. 1671, presumably because of his father's death in Feb. 1671. Although he took no degree at Oxford, O received a Cambridge MA in 1680, perhaps through his friend Richard Duke (q.v. below). The verse epistles he exchanged with Duke at this period mention his visits to Cambridge: see the *Poems* (1717) of Roscommon and Duke, 507–19, and *Works* (1931), ii. 443–6. Jacob, i. 193, referred to some connection of O with St John's College, Cambridge, and to O's 'fast Friendship with Duke'.

3.  O had 'a Probation Part' in Aphra Behn's *The Forc'd Marriage; or, The Jealous Bridegroom* (first performed 20 Sept. 1670): see John Downes, *Roscianus Anglicanus* (1708), 34, cited by Reed in *Lives*, i (1790), 331 n. He later wrote a prologue for Behn's *The City-Heiress* (1682).

4.  According to Downes (see **3** n. above), '*the full House put him to such a Sweat and Tremendous Agony, being dash't, spoilt him for an Actor*'. Earlier biographers did not discuss O's inadequacy as an actor, although Shiels, *Lives*, ii. 325, stated that 'he is said to have failed in want of execution, which is so material to a good player, that a tolerable execution, with advantage of a good person, will often supply the place of judgment, in which it is not to be supposed Otway was deficient'. Boswell believed that SJ 'had thought more upon the subject of acting than might generally be supposed', while acknowledging his 'contempt of tragic acting' (*Life*, iv. 243–4, and cf. iii. 184, iv. 7, v. 38). For another poet and dramatist who failed as an actor, see 'Savage' **56** below.

5. O dedicated *Alcibiades* (performed Sept. 1675; published 1675) to Charles Sackville, Earl of Middlesex (later Earl of Dorset, q.v. below). In 1676 he stated that
Rochester had 'seem'd almost to make it his business to establish it in the good
opinion of the *King*, and his *Royal Highness*' (*Works* (1932), i. 174).

*Palaprat*: there is no *Alcibiade* in the works of the French dramatist Jean de Bigot
Palaprat (1650–1721), who in fact wrote mostly comedies and whose career in the
theatre began later than O's. The reason for SJ's apparently knowing reference to
him remains a mystery. Jean-Galbert de Campistron wrote *Alicibiade* (1686), a
tragedy, but too late for O to have imitated it. SJ had evidently consulted Gerard
Langbaine's *Account of the English Dramatick Poets* (Oxford, 1691): see 11 n. below.
For Langbaine's pursuit of the borrowings of Dryden and others, see 'Dryden' 29
and n. below.

SJ's revision of 'qualify' to 'qualify him' in the proofs was not adopted (see
Textual Notes).

6. *Titus and Berenice*, adapted from Racine's *Bérénice* (1670), and *The Cheats of Scapin*
from Molière's *Les Fourberies de Scapin* (1671), were performed together in Dec.
1676 (published 1677, with a dedication to Rochester).

For SJ's erroneous 'Rapin' instead of 'Racine' in all editions, see Textual Notes.
Although Reed correctly identified Racine as O's source in *Biographica Dramatica*
(1782), ii. 375, the error survived in later editions down to *Lives* (1794). For
confusion of these authors elsewhere in the period, see William Ayre, *Memoirs of
Pope* (1745), ii. 89–90.

*Friendship in Fashion* was 'acted with general Applause' in Apr. 1678 (published
1678), according to Langbaine, *English Dramatick Poets*, 398. A revival at Drury
Lane on 22 Jan. 1750 (not 1749) caused a virtual riot, as SJ, whose *Irene* was
performed there in 1749, may have known at first hand. Shiels, *Lives*, ii. 335, stated
that O's comedy had been 'damned by the audience, on account of the immorality
of the design, and the obscenity of the dialogue'. The account in the *London Stage*
does not confirm that 'immorality' provoked the disturbances. O's prologue in fact
claims disingenuously: 'I'th' next place, Ladies, there's no Bawdy in't, | No not so
much as one well-meaning hint' (ll. 7–8) (*Works*, i. 335).

7. The 'dissolute wits' included Rochester (see 6 above, 8–9 and nn. below, and
'Rochester' 4 and n. above). As O recalled in *The Poet's Complaint of his Muse*, ll.
79–97: 'Gay Coxcombs, Cowards, Knaves, and prating Fools, | Bullies of o're-
grown Bulks, and little Souls, | Gamesters, Half-wits, and Spendthrifts, (such as
think | Mischievous midnight Frollicks bred by Drink | Are Gallantry and Wit, |
Because to their lewd Understandings fit) | Were those wherewith two years at least
I spent, | To all their fulsome Follies most incorrigibly bent.' According to *Les
Soupirs de la Grand Britaigne: or, The Groans of Great Britain* (1713), 67, 'Otway
was more beholding to Capt. *Symonds* the Vintner, in whose Debt he dy'd 400 *l.*
than to all his Patrons of Quality.' 'W.G.' recalled in *Gent. Mag.* (Feb. 1745), 99,
that O 'was of the middle size, about 5 feet 7 inches in height, inclinable to fatness.
He had a thoughtful speaking eye, and that was all. He gave himself up early to
drinking, and like the unhappy wits of that age passed his days between rioting, and
fasting, ranting jollity, and abject penitence, carousing one week with Ld *Pl—th*
[see 8 below], and then starving a month in low company at an alehouse on
*Tower-hill*.'

SJ ends by quoting (loosely) the preface to *Works* (1712), i, sig. A6ᵛ, a passage not in *GD* or *BB*. (For the erroneous 'imminence' for 'innocence' in the last sentence in all editions, see Textual Notes.) Richard Savage also found that 'his friends were only companions, who were willing to share his gaiety, but not to partake of his misfortunes' ('Savage' **307** below). SJ wrote of authors who became dependent on the dissolute in *Rambler* 77 (1750) that 'they saw their protectors hourly drop away, and wondered and stormed to find themselves abandoned . . . debauchery is selfish and negligent, and from virtue the virtuous only can expect regard' (*YW*, iv. 42–3). His 'Sermon 20' also condemned those who follow 'the fashion of a corrupt or licentious age . . . lest they should lose the patronage of villains, and the praise of fools' (*YW*, xiv. 225–6).

8. Through Charles FitzCharles, Earl of Plymouth (1657–80), son of Charles II, O was commissioned as an ensign in the Duke of Monmouth's Regiment of Foot in Feb. 1678. Following the Peace of Nijmegen, O's company returned to England in Jan. 1679 and had disbanded by July 1679 (Ham, *O and Lee*, 92). O described himself as 'a poor Disbanded Souldier' in the epilogue to *Caius Marcius*, l. 27, in Oct. 1679 (see **11** below). SJ's phrase 'whatever was the reason' in effect bypasses such speculations as those of Shiels, *Lives*, ii. 325–6, that cowardice explained his leaving the army.

   Although SJ here ascribes 'A Session of the Poets' (*c*.1677) to Rochester (quoting ll. 53–9), it was not included in Rochester's poems in *Eng. Poets* (1779), as 'Scrutator' (John Loveday) noted in *Gent. Mag.* (1779), 595. It has been attributed to Rochester and to Buckingham, and O himself seems to have believed it was by Elkanah Settle: see *The Poet's Complaint* (1680), ll. 224–32, and *POAS*, i. 352, iii. 304 n., for a story that O challenged Settle to a duel over the poem. O's biographers had regularly quoted these lines: e.g. 'Life' (1712), Wood, *GD*, Shiels, and *BB*. For the 'Session of the Poets' sub-genre, see 'Cowley' **41** n. above.

   Rochester's 'Allusion to Horace' (1675/6), l. 19, describes 'puzzling Otway' labouring in vain to 'divert the Rabble and the Court' (*Works*, ed. H. Love (Oxford, 1999), 71). After patronizing O for some four years, Rochester wrote a contemptuous 'epigram' about him early in 1680 (see *Complete Poems*, ed. D. M. Vieth (New Haven, 1968), 148; Love, *Works*, 91, 424, is more cautious about the identification). According to his 'Love-Letters' in Rochester's *Familiar Letters* (1697), O was in love with Rochester's mistress in these years, Elizabeth Barry, who took leading roles in his plays: see *Works* (1931), ii. 475–81.

9. *Don Carlos* was in fact performed on 8 June 1676 (published 1676). O's preface still boasts of Rochester's patronage. Although Shiels, *Lives*, ii. 335, claimed that 'it had a run of thirty nights', Downes, *Roscius Anglicanus* (1708), 36, stated more convincingly that 'it lasted successively 10 Days; it got more Money than any preceding Modern Tragedy'. For a later comment on the Restoration theatre audience, see 'Dryden' **87** below.

10. *The Orphan* (performed Feb. or Mar. 1680; published 1680) was still being acted in the 1780s. For 'continuance of esteem' as a test of literature, see *YW*, vii. 59–60, and, for other plays described by SJ as still holding the stage in his own day, see 'Rowe' **7**, **15**, 'Hughes' **15**, 'Thomson' **34**, and 'A. Philips' **7** below. Eighteenth-century commentators in fact often condemned *The Orphan*'s immorality: see *Gent.*

*Mag.* (1748), 503, 593, Shiels, *Lives*, ii. 328–9, Francis Gentleman, *The Dramatic Censor* (1770), ii. 40–60, and cf. Corman, 'Profane Authors', 234–5.

*a domestick tragedy*: Addison had already stated of O in *Spectator* 39 (1711) that 'there is something Familiar and Domestick in the Fable of his Tragedy, more than in those of any other Poet'. SJ consistently praises 'domestick' drama, which 'fastens the attention of the reader' (*YW*, viii. 745). Writing to Baretti, 21 Dec. 1762, he stated that 'The good or ill success of battles and embassies extends itself to a very small part of domestic life: we all have good and evil, which we feel more sensibly.' He told Mrs Thrale, 11 July 1770, that 'What is nearest us, touches us most. The passions rise higher at domestick than at imperial tragedies' (*Letters*, i. 213, 345). See also **12** n. below, 'Dryden' **76** and 'Rowe' **7, 15** below. For contemporary discussions of the importance of emotional empathy between audience and characters in the 18th-century theatre, see J. Osborne, 'Drama after 1740', in H. B. Nisbet and C. Rawson (eds.), *Cambridge History of Literary Criticism*, vol. iv (1997), 187–203.

For the appeal of the 'domestick' in other genres, see SJ's exposition of the appeal of biography in *Rambler* 60 (1750), and his preference on 1 May 1783 of the *Odyssey* to the *Aeneid*: 'I like the story of the Odyssey much better...[It] is interesting, as a great part of it is domestick' (*Life*, iv. 218–19). Joseph Warton had preferred the *Odyssey* on similar grounds in *Adventurer* 75 (1753). In his *Essay on Pope* (1756), 276–7, Warton also wrote: 'We have been too long attached to Grecian and Roman stories. In truth, the DOMESTICA FACTA, are more interesting, because we all think ourselves concerned in the actions and fates of our countrymen.' (Cf. Horace, *Ars Poetica*, 285–7: 'Nil intemptatum nostri liquere poetae, | nec minimum meruere decus vestigia Graeca | ausi deserere et celebrare domestica facta' ('Our own poets have left no style untried, nor has least honour been earned when they have dared to leave the footsteps of the Greeks and sing of deeds at home').) In 'Butler' **22** above SJ himself uses 'domestick' to mean '4. Not foreign; intestine', rather than '1. Belonging to the house; not relating to things publick' (*Dict.*). Elsewhere, he states that Pope's *Temple of Fame* had 'little relation to general manners or common life' ('Pope' **317** below), and that tragedies such as Young's *Busuris* were 'too remote from known life to raise either grief, terror, or indignation' ('Young' **162** below). In the higher genres, however, the 'domestick' could be inappropriate or resist 'poetic' rendering: see 'Dryden' **253** and 'Pope' **412** below.

*the affections*: see 'Cowley' **57** n. above. This may be SJ's first acknowledgement of a successful appeal to 'the heart'. Previously he has invoked 'the pathetic' only in its absence, as in 'Cowley' **57–8, 152** and 'Milton' **241, 244** above. Cf. William Guthrie, *An Essay upon English Tragedy* [1747], 27: 'OTWAY succeeded by conversing with the heart alone.'

For 'comprehension' and 'elegance', see 'Cowley' **144** n. above and 'Pope' **350** n. below.

11. Langbaine, *English Dramatick Poets*, 397–8, had noted O's borrowings from *Romeo and Juliet* in *Caius Marius* (performed Oct. 1679; published 1680): cf. **5** above. O's own prologue admitted that 'You'll find h' has rifled him [Shakespeare] of half a Play'.

12. *The Souldiers Fortune*, Pt. I, was in fact performed *c*. June 1680 (published 1681), and Pt. II, as *The Atheist*, *c*. July 1683 (published 1684). Shiels, *Lives*, ii. 336, gave

both dates of publication correctly, and is unlikely to have been responsible for SJ's erroneous date for *Venice Preserved*, in fact performed on 9 Feb. 1682 (published 1682). The most popular non-Shakespearian tragedy of the period, *Venice Preserved* was still regularly acted in London, and was about to enjoy a new lease of life in the 1782/3 season with Mrs Siddons as Belvidera (see *London Stage*). See Taylor, *Next to Shakespeare, passim* and, for changing political interpretations of and reactions to O's play, J. Eglin, *Venice Transfigured: The Myth of Venice in British Culture, 1660–1797* (2001), 139–67.

*want of morality*: Addison complained in *Spectator* 39 (1711) that O had based *Venice Preserved* 'on so wrong a Plot, that the greatest Characters in it are those of Rebels and Traitors'. Such thoughts had not troubled Boswell in Venice in 1765: 'To find myself in the City where Pierre and Jaffeir lived is what my enthusiasm cannot fail to exult in' (*Boswell on the Grand Tour* (1955), 94). Francis Gentleman, *The Dramatic Censor* (1770), i. 333, noted that 'Among fifteen male personages in this play, not one moral character appears—What an unfavourable picture of human nature!'

*scenes of vile comedy*: Gentleman censured 'every scene where Aquilina is concerned, as superfluously prejudical to regularity, offensive to decency, impotently ludicrous, and contemptibly absurd' (*Censor*, i. 313). According to Thomas Davies, *Dramatic Miscellanies* (1784), iii. 230, the 'obscene trash' of one scene between Aquilina and Antonio was omitted in performance. James Boswell Jr. later confirmed that 'The "despicable scenes of vile comedy" can be no bar to its being a favourite of the publick, as they are always omitted in the representation' (*J's Works* (1825), vii. 176 n.). Praising John Hawkesworth's adaptation of Thomas Southerne's *Oroonoko* (1759) in *Critical Review*, 8 (1759), 480–6, SJ had complained that 'scenes of the lowest buffoonery, and the grossest indecency' marred the original 'tragic action'. For similar comments, see 'Dryden' **67** below.

*originally*: 'As the first author', i.e. with originality (*Dict.*). For the importance of originality elsewhere, see 'Milton' **277** and n. above.

*consulting nature in his own breast*: cf. SJ's *Drury-Lane Prologue* (1747), ll. 29–32, on the price which had been paid for modern 'refinement': 'Then crush'd by Rules, and weaken'd as refin'd, | For Years the Pow'r of Tragedy declin'd; | From Bard, to Bard, the frigid Caution crept, | Till Declamation roar'd, while Passion slept'; and *Rambler* 125 (1751), on the loss by recent dramatists of 'almost all that dominion over the passions which was the boast of their predecessors' (*YW*, iv. 305). For Shakespeare as 'the poet of nature', see *YW*, vii. 61–5.

SJ had been anticipated by, among others, Dryden in his preface to Du Fresnoy's *De Arte Graphica* (1695) ('the passions are truly touched in it . . . nature is there, which is the greatest beauty', Watson, ii. 201, but see 'Dryden' **325** below); and by Pope in 1739 ("Tis a talent of nature rather than an effect of judgement to write so movingly', Spence, i. 206). SJ's comment on the 'more energetick' language of *Venice Preserved* also recalls Addison, *Spectator* 39 (1711): '*Otway* has followed Nature in the Language of his Tragedy . . . he has little Pomp, but great Force in his Expressions.' Here and in **15** below SJ comes close to echoing Dick Minim's critical clichés in *Idler* 60 (1759): 'In Otway he found uncommon powers of moving the passions, but was disgusted by his general negligence, and blamed him for making a conspirator his hero; and never concluded his disquisition, without remarking how happily the sound of the clock is made to alarm the audience' (*YW*, ii. 187). For the effect of the 'clock' in *Venice Preserved*, see *Spectator* 44 (1711).

13. O's miscellaneous verse appeared in such collections as *Ovid's Epistles* (1680), *Miscellany Poems* (1684), and Aphra Behn's *Miscellany* (1685).

O is named on the title page of *The History of the Triumvirates* (2 vols., 1686) as the translator from the French of Samuel Citri de La Guette. Although the extent of his contribution is uncertain, such use of his name is evidence of his posthumous reputation.

14. Cf. *Adventurer* 81 (1753) on 'the Admirable Crichton': 'The death of this wonderful man I should be willing to conceal, did I not know that every reader will inquire curiously after that fatal hour which is common to all human beings' (*YW*, ii. 405).

O's death at a public house on Tower Hill is mentioned by Jacob, i. 194, and Wood, ii. 782. Neither *GD* nor *BB* discussed its cause. Shiels, *Lives*, ii. 333–4, apparently first told the story of his choking on bread. SJ inserted most of the penultimate sentence (about O's fever) in 1783 (see Textual Notes) from the Spence MSS, to which he had access from Feb. 1780. By then Joseph Warton had in fact published Spence's account in *Essay*, ii (1782), 47 n. John Dennis (not Pope) told Spence on 11 May 1730 that O had pursued the murderer of his friend Blackston (or Blakiston) towards Dover and subsequently died of a fever after drinking poisoned water (Spence, i. 322). The fact that, as Blakiston, 'O's friend', 549, pointed out, Blackston had died on 7 Apr. 1684, a year before O himself, casts doubt on the story.

Thomas Wilkes, *A General View of the Stage* (1759), 245–7, gave yet another account, reminiscent of Richard Savage's last years (see 'Savage' **259** ff.). O's poverty supposedly prompted Betterton and others to raise money to support him in seclusion in Hampshire, while he wrote another tragedy. After three months O was back in London, borrowing money from Aphra Behn to enable him to complete a tragedy about Iphigenia. A month later Betterton learned that O had died in his lodgings on Tower Hill, and that on the night of his death someone had removed all his papers and books. *Gent. Mag.* (1780), 461, later noted Betterton's advertisement in the *Observator* of 27 Nov. 1686, enquiring about the whereabouts of the MS of four acts of a play by O left incomplete at his death. Prior's lines in 1687 on '*Otway* the Hope, the Sorrow of our Age!' in 'Satyr on the Poets' (published 1694), seem to allude to this: 'He had of's many Wants, much earlier Dy'd, | Had not kind Banker *Betterton* supply'd, | And took for Pawn, the Embrio of a Play' (*Lit. Works*, i. 33).

*indigence, and its concomitants*: O became, with Butler, a much-cited example of impoverished and neglected poetic genius. See 'Butler' **18** and n. above, 'Savage' **274** n. below, and e.g. Dennis, *Remarks upon Mr. Pope's Homer* (1717) in *Works*, ii. 121, and the prefatory apparatus to Pope's *Dunciad* (*TE*, v. 44).

15. *the late collection*: *Eng. Poets* (1779).

*The Poet's Complaint of his Muse; or, A Satyr Against Libells* (1680) is an autobio-graphical poem of 711 lines (cf. **2**, **7–8** and nn. above). The passage SJ failed to understand may have been the allusive political allegory at ll. 465–508. While its Pindaric form alone might explain SJ's dislike of the poem (cf. 'Cowley' **143** n.

above), his lack of interest in its biographical content is surprising (but cf. 'Shenstone' 31 and n. below).

For 'language' and 'versification' see 'Cowley' 181–99 and nn. above, for 'harshness', 'Milton' 177 and n. above, and, for the importance to the poet of 'general knowledge', 'Butler' 37–9 and n. above. O's lack of 'correctness' was something of a commonplace: cf. Pope, *Imit. Horace, Ep. II. i.* (1737), l. 278 ('But Otway fail'd to polish or refine'). Hume described O's genius as 'finely tuned to the pathetic; but he neither observes strictly the rules of the drama, nor the rules, still more essential, of propriety and decorum' (*History of Great Britain*, ii (1757), 453). For Dryden's opinion of O as cited in SJ's note, and for Dick Minim on O's 'negligence', see 12 n. above.

*a zealous royalist*: O dedicated *Don Carlos* to James, Duke of York (mentioning 'the Extream Devotion I owe Your Royal Highness'), and *The Orphan* to his Duchess. He stated in the dedication to *Venice Preserved* that 'a steady Faith, and Loyalty to my Prince, was all the Inheritance my Father left me, and however hardly my ill Fortune deal with me, 'tis what I prize so well that I ne'r pawn'd it yet, and hope I ne'r shall part with it' (*Works* (1932), ii. 200). *Windsor Castle, In A Monument To our Late Sovereign K. Charles II. Of ever Blessed Memory. A Poem* (1685) appeared some two weeks before O's own death. For a time he had been tutor to Nell Gwyn's 10-year-old son by Charles II (Ham, *O and Lee*, 175). For other loyal but disappointed Royalists, see 'Cowley' 35 and n. above.

Although SJ has suggested that O's appeal to 'the heart' and to 'nature' is more important than his defects in 'elegance', 'comprehension', and even morality (see 10, 12 above), Bennet Langton noted that he 'always appeared not to be sufficiently sensible of the merit of Otway' (*Life*, iv. 21). Charles Burney, *History of Music*, iii (1789), 598 n., stated: 'I once asked Dr. Johnson if he did not think Otway a good painter of tender scenes, and he replied, "Sir, he is all tenderness"' (see also *Life*, iv. 21 n.). SJ's cryptic response may have been ironic. James Northcote recalled an argument in which SJ insisted that *Venice Preserved* did not contain 40 good lines and Goldsmith claimed that it was the closest to Shakespeare of all English tragedies (*Memoirs of Sir Joshua Reynolds* (1813), 180–1). Cf. Goldsmith's assertion in 1759 that O was 'next to Shakespeare, the greatest genius England ever produced in tragedy' (*Coll. Works*, i. 500).

## EDMUND WALLER (1606–1687)

**Composition.** Having recently written versions of 'Cowley' and 'Denham' at Ashbourne, SJ may have been looking ahead to 'Waller' when he reminded himself in his diary on 20 Oct. 1777 to write to Percival Stockdale (1736–1811), whose 'Life' of W (1772) he mentions in 61 below (*YW*, i. 279; see 'Sources' below). He presumably started work on it soon after his return to London in early Nov. 1777, completing a version of it in Jan. or Feb. 1778. (For a small clue suggesting that he was working on it in Jan. 1778, see 109 n. below.) Nichols obviously had the MS by c. Mar. 1778, when SJ told him: 'In the Life of Waller Mr. Nichol will find a reference to the *Parliamentary Hist.* from which a long quotation is to be inserted, if Mr. Nichol cannot easily find the book, Mr. Johnson will send it from Streatham. Clarendon is here returned' (*Letters*, iii.

109–10). (For these works, see **25–35, 91–2** and nn. below.) SJ had received the first proofs by 17 Apr. 1778, when Boswell noted that, because it was Good Friday, he 'would not even look at a proof-sheet of his "Life of Waller" ' (*Life*, iii. 313).

SJ had not, however, entirely finished with 'Waller'. On 2 May 1778 he asked Nichols: 'As Waller professed to have imitated Fairfax, do you think a few pages of Fairfax would enrich our edition? Few readers have seen it, and it may please them. But it is not necessary' (*Letters*, iii. 116–17). A long extract from Fairfax's translation (1600) of Tasso was duly appended in **154** below. The surviving proofs also show that the biographical section originally ended at **98**, and that the expansion of the 'character' of W in **99–106** was a still later addition in May or June, inserted after the extract from Fairfax had been printed. Writing to Nichols on 27 July 1778, SJ justified the length of 'Cowley' and 'Waller' on the grounds that these poets 'never had any critical examination before'. Given that Nichols had printed a first version of 'Waller' several months earlier, this explanation may imply that by then SJ had also elaborated his long critical discussion (**107–53**), in accordance with his changing conception of his undertaking (see headnotes to 'Cowley' and 'Butler' above).

In the same note SJ asked Nichols to have 'Waller' bound with 'Denham' and 'Butler' in a pre-publication volume 'to show to my Friends' (*Letters*, iii. 122). In late Sept. 1778 he was rewarded by discovering Fanny Burney reading 'Waller' in this form at Streatham (*Early Journals*, iii. 172). For such a volume in the Hyde Collection, see Fleeman (1962), 215 n.

**Sources.** Although there had been accounts of W in Jacob, i. 265–8, ii. 220–3, Wood, ii. 24–5, *GD*, x. 82–8, and Shiels, *Lives*, ii. 240–57, the evidence indicates that SJ relied primarily on John Campbell's article in *BB*, vi. (ii) (1766), 4099–115, perhaps with some use of its cross-references to earlier articles (see **42** n.).

Both *GD* and *BB* drew extensively on the Earl of Clarendon's *History* and on the anonymous 'Life' in W's *Poems* (1711), evidently based on material made available by W's family, which Joseph Warton suggested had been written by Francis Atterbury (*Essay*, ii (1782), 366). Although there are inevitable similarities in the accounts in *GD* and *BB*, SJ follows *BB* in making more use of Fenton's edition of W's *Works* (1729), and structurally the differences between *GD* and *BB* are striking. *GD*'s main narrative deals with W's political activities in the 1640s, to which SJ devotes **18–60** below, in a mere three sentences, though with elaborate notes drawing on Clarendon, May, and Whitelock (x. 83–7 nn.). In contrast, the emphasis in *BB*, vi (ii). 4103–8, is similar to SJ's, with even more elaborate annotation than *GD*, and a shrewder comparison of the available sources for most of W's career, often echoed exactly by SJ.

Much of SJ's narrative appears in fact to have been guided by *BB*, at times to the point of virtual paraphrase, as in **82–7** below. In **78** he finally refers directly to *BB*, and for other evidence confirming that he relied on it rather than on *GD*, see the notes to **4, 8, 38, 60, 63, 65–71, 72, 96**. It is also clear, however, that SJ at times consulted the sources cited by *BB* at first hand, especially Clarendon and Fenton, and such reference works as the *Parliamentary History* (see 'Composition' above and **25–35, 54–5** below), Burnet's *History* (see **74–5, 97** below), and Rushworth's *Historical Collections* (see **45, 58–9** below).

SJ was also aware of Percival Stockdale's recent 'Life' prefixed to the edition of W's *Works* published by Thomas Davies in 1772 (pp. i–lxv), although resemblances can often be explained by their reliance on the same sources (see headnote above and **61** below, and notes to **14, 19–20, 68, 152, 154** below). Stockdale later recalled in his *Memoirs* (2 vols., 1809), that, before writing his life of W, he had consulted SJ (his neighbour) 'on the materials which were necessary to form it. He immediately mentioned the different authours who had given any account of WALLER; and even the particulars which they recorded of him. I availed myself of his information' (ii. 69–70). SJ later promised to make a friendly reference in 'Waller' to Stockdale, who was in fact dissatisfied with SJ's 'very transient, and anonymous notice' of him in **61** below (ii. 122–3). Encouraged by John Wilkes, Stockdale even took as a personal slight a newspaper report that, in the first *Prefaces* (1779), 'it is the opinion of every good critick' that SJ's 'Waller' was 'supereminently excellent' (ii. 199–201).

SJ's own copy of W's *Poems* (4th edn., 1682), with a few MS notes and corrections, is in the Rothschild Collection at Trinity College, Cambridge: see Fleeman, *Handlist* (1984), 67.

There are 691 quotations from seventy-four different poems by W in the *Dict.* (1755), increased to 693 in 1773.

**Publication.** In *Prefaces*, vol. i (31 Mar. 1779). Pp. 1–6, 11–16, 39–42, and 49–128 of the proofs are in the Forster Collection. Boswell also sent Lord Hailes a set of the proofs on 21 Nov. 1778, presumably by that stage as a gift rather than for correction (*Catalogue* L 611).

**Modern Sources:**
A. W. Allison, *Toward an Augustan Poetic: EW's 'Reform' of English Poetry* (Lexington, Ky., 1962)
P. Beal (ed.), *Index of English Literary Manuscripts*, ii (ii) (1993), 547–619
E. S. de Beer, 'An Uncollected Poem by W', *RES* 8 (1932), 203–8
A. B. Chambers, *Andrew Marvell and EW: Seventeenth-Century Praise and Restoration Satire* (1991)
W. L. Chernaik, *The Poetry of Limitation* (New Haven, 1968)
M. L. Donnelly, 'EW', in *Dictionary of Literary Biography*, cxxvi (1993), 264–85
G. Thorn Drury (ed.), *Poems of EW* (2 vols., 1893; repr. 1901), with a biographical 'Introduction' (i. pp. xiii–lxxiv)
M. M. Duggan, *English Literature and Backgrounds 1660–1700* (New York, 1990), ii. 1003–6
J. W. Gilbert, *EW* (Boston, 1979)
B. D. Hemming (ed.), *The House of Commons 1660–1690*, iii (1983), 653–7
P. Korshin, *From Concord to Dissent* (Menston, 1973), esp. ch. III
C. Lloyd, 'W as a Member of the Royal Society', *PMLA* 43 (1928), 162–5
E. R. Miner, *The Cavalier Mode from Jonson to Cotton* (Princeton, 1971), 24–37
E. T. Riske, 'Dryden and W as Members of the Royal Society', *PMLA* 46 (1931), 951–4
E. T. Riske, 'W in Exile', *TLS* 13 Oct. 1932, 734

1. The son of Robert and Anne Waller, W was in fact born on 3 Mar. 1606 (baptized 9 Mar.) at Coleshill, then in Hertfordshire, though in the parish of Agmondesham (or Amersham), Bucks. His ancestors had moved from Kent as early as the 14th century. His mother was the daughter of Griffith Hampden of Great Hampden, Bucks. Her brother William married Elizabeth Cromwell, Oliver Cromwell's aunt, and was the father of the celebrated parliamentarian John Hampden (1594–1643), who was in fact W's cousin, not his nephew (see also **18, 24, 63** below).

*the zealot of rebellion*: Thomson described Hampden in *Summer* (1730), ll. 1515–17, as 'Wise, strenuous, firm, of unsubmitting Soul, | Who stem'd the Torrent of a downward Age | To Slavery prone, and bade thee [Britain] rise again, | In all thy native Pomp of Freedom bold'. Hume, no Whig, had stated that Hampden 'deservedly acquired, by his spirit and courage, universal popularity thro'out the nation, and has merited great renown with posterity for the bold stand, which he made, in defence of the laws and constitution of his country' (*History of Great Britain*, i (Edinburgh, 1754), 217).

For objections to SJ's reference to 'the zealot of rebellion' (perhaps a response to 'the much famed patriot' in *BB*, vi (ii). 4099 n.), see *Gent. Mag.* (June 1779), 313, and (Oct. 1781), 466, Francis Blackburne, *Remarks on J's Life of Milton* (1780), 20, and Joseph Towers, *An Essay on SJ* (1786), 122. Dr Samuel Beilby, *Remarks on Doctor J's Lives* (York, 1782), 13, denounced SJ's 'malicious and contemptible' description of 'one of the greatest and most virtuous characters that ever existed in this nation', who had been 'the Zealot of the Rights and Liberties of mankind'. SJ illustrated his definition of 'Zealot' as 'One passionately ardent in any cause. Generally used in dispraise' from *Eikon Basilike*: 'The fury of *zealots*, intestine bitterness and division, were the greatest occasion of the destruction of Jerusalem. *King Charles*' (*Dict.*). Cf. 'the meanest zealot for prerogative' in 'Dryden' **116** below and the 'zealots of anarchy', who contested the British right to tax the American colonies in *Taxation No Tyranny* (1775) (*YW*, x. 412).

Boswell's view of 'Waller' was that SJ 'gives a distinct and animated narrative of publick affairs in that variegated period, with strong yet nice touches of character; and having a fair opportunity to display his political principles, does it with an unqualified manly confidence, and satisfies his readers how nobly he might have executed a *Tory History* of his country' (*Life*, iv. 39).

2. Robert Waller died on 26 Aug. 1616, when W was in fact 10. For the fate of the income W inherited, see **103–5** below.

3. W was at Eton *c.*1618–21, and entered King's College, Cambridge, on 22 Mar. 1621, but did not take a degree. He was also admitted to Lincoln's Inn on 3 July 1622. SJ's uncertainty about the age at which W entered Parliament reflects that of 'Life' (1711) and *BB*, vi (ii). 4100. He was in fact almost 18 when he became MP for Ilchester *c.* Feb. 1624, later representing Chipping Wycombe (1628) and Amersham (1628, and Apr. 1640): see Hemming (ed.), *House of Commons*, iii., 653. For Clarendon's comment, see **92** below.

4. *BB*, vi (ii). 4100 n. (but not *GD*), quotes this anecdote about James I, who died on 27 Mar. 1625, from 'Life' (1711), pp. viii–ix. It concerns Dr Lancelot Andrewes (1555–1626), Bishop of Winchester, and Dr Richard Neale or Neile (1562–1640), later Archbishop of York. SJ defines 'To lig' as 'To lie', quoting Spenser (*Dict.*).

5. For 'Of the danger His Majesty (being Prince) escaped in the road at St. Andrews', see also **123** below. The future Charles I escaped drowning at Santander on 12 Sept. 1623 when returning to England from Spain.

SJ quotes Francis Atterbury's anonymous preface to *The Second Part of Mr. Waller's Poems* (1690), sig. A5, which Fenton (1729 edn.), 441–8, had reprinted. (The 1690 text has 'judge barely' for 'judge only' at the beginning of the quotation: see Textual Notes.) Dennis wrote in 1711 that W's 'Language is still good and new' (*Works*, i. 410). For another 'stile which never becomes obsolete', see SJ's discussion in 1765 of Shakespeare's 'comick dialogue' (*YW*, vii. 70). SJ ignores the possibility that W revised his early verse before publishing it in *Poems* (1645): see **7** n. below. For a later comment on the dating of his early poems, see **95** below.

*Tasso*: Dryden wrote in the preface to *Fables* (1700) that 'many besides myself have heard our famous Waller own that he derived the harmony of his numbers from *Godfrey of Bulloign*, which was turned into English by Mr Fairfax' (Watson, ii. 271). For Edward Fairfax's *Godfrey of Bulloigne done into English Heroicall Verse* (1600), see also **81**, **143**, **154** below.

For W's 'smoothness', see **142** ff. below, and cf. 'Denham' **35** above.

6. SJ must have consulted Fenton (1729 edn.), 'Observations', p. xiv, at first hand. He himself is in fact 'mistaken'. Fenton was referring to W's 'To the Queen' (*Poems*, i. 8–10), marking her arrival in England on 12 June 1625, which SJ confuses with the later 'Of the Queen', which mentions her 'fertile womb' (*Poems*, i. 77–9). 'Of His Majesty's Receiving the News of the Duke of Buckingham's Death' was a response to the assassination of George Villiers, 1st Duke of Buckingham, on 23 Aug. 1628, news of which reached Charles I while he was at prayers at Southwick near Portsmouth.

7. W obviously revised both poems before their publication in *Poems* (1645).

8. On 15 July 1631 W married Anne Banks, the daughter and heiress of John Banks (d. 1630), a London mercer, who left her £8,000. She was still a Ward of Court and, until the King intervened, W was threatened with prosecution, as it was intended that she would marry William Crofts, later (1658) Baron Crofts of Saxham (see *Poems*, i, pp. xix–xx, **91** below, and 'Denham' **15** and n. above). Their son died in 1633, but their daughter, Mrs Dormer, was still alive in 1711: see 'Life' (1711), p. xviii. Anne died in Oct. 1634, so that W in fact became a widower at the age of 28: SJ follows *BB*, vi (ii). 4101, in suggesting that he was even younger. For the marriage, see also **94** below.

9. W's poetic courtship of Lady Dorothy Sidney (1617–84), daughter of Robert, 2nd Earl of Leicester, dates from about 1635 (*Poems*, i, p. xxiv). Shiels, *Lives*, ii. 243, stated that 'the Sacharissa of Waller is consigned to immortality, and can never die but with poetry, taste, and politeness'.

SJ implicitly replies here to Fenton's 'Observations' (1729 edn.), p. xxxviii: 'Sacharissa is a name which recalls to mind what is related of the Turks, who in their gallantries think *Sucar Birpara*, i.e. bit of sugar, to be the most polite and endearing compliment they can use to the ladies.' SJ defines 'Saccharine' (from Latin 'saccharum') as 'Having the taste, or any other of the chief qualities of sugar' (*Dict.*).

10. See 'To Amoret', ll. 43–4: 'Sacharissa's beauty's wine, | Which to madness doth incline.' SJ mentioned the poem in conversation in Apr. 1775 (*Life*, ii. 360). For his recurrent contrast of the 'astonishing' and the 'pleasing', see 'Milton' **276** and n. below.

11. SJ comments on 'Dame' that '2. It is still used in poetry for women of rank' (*Dict.*), quoting W's 'To Vandyck' (*Poems*, i. 45). His information about Dorothy Sidney's marriage to Henry Spencer, later Earl of Sunderland, who died at the Battle of Newbury in 1643, ultimately derives from Fenton (1729 edn.), 'Observations',

p. xxxvi. For the story of the meeting with W in old age, see 'Life' (1711), p. xviii, and *BB*, vi (ii). 4102 n.

12. For the character of W by Edward Hyde (1609–74), later Earl of Clarendon, see **90–3** below, and, for W and the 'wits' of the age, **96** below.

13. For the identification of 'Amoret', see Fenton (1729 edn.), 'Observations', p. xlii, cited by *BB*, vi (ii). 4102 n. Lady Sophia Murray or Moray (1624–53), wife of Sir Robert Moray (1608/9–73), was for a time suspected of complicity in W's 'plot' of 1643, along with Lady Aubigny: see **57** below and S. R. Gardiner, *History of the Great Civil War* (1888), i. 158.

14. SJ refers to 'At Penshurst', ll. 37–44, discussed in *BB*, vi (ii). 4102 n., and, for the whales, to 'The Battle of the Summer islands', Cantos II–III. Although the 'Life' (1711), p. xli, was dubious about W's supposed visit to the Bermudas, Fenton (1729 edn.), 'Observations', p. xlviii, *BB*, vi (ii). 4102, and Stockdale, 'Life' (1772), p. xvi, took the possibility seriously. As usual, SJ is sceptical about the use of poetry as biographical evidence. According to Aubrey, *Brief Lives* (1898), ii. 276, W in fact wrote the poem 'upon the information of one that had been there'.

15. W appears to have written all but one of these poems in 1637–42: 'Of Salle' (on the Moroccan pirates at Salle in 1637); 'Upon His Majesty's Repairing of St. Paul's' (written by 1642, since Denham alluded to it in *Cooper's Hill*, ll. 15–20); 'To the King, On His Navy' (*c*.1627?); 'To the Queen-Mother of France, upon her Landing' (1638); 'To my Lord Northumberland, upon the death of his Lady' (1637); and 'To my Lord Admiral, of his late sickness and recovery' (1638).

16. W married Mary Bracey of Thame, Oxfordshire, by 1644. Other biographers give her surname as Brace or Bressy, but SJ follows 'Mary, of the family of Bresse, or Breaux' in *BB*, vi (ii). 4102. She died in 1677 (*Poems*, i, p. lxvii).

    For love poetry, see also **121** below and n. and 'Cowley' **14** and n. above; for women as a cause of 'domestick happiness' (or unhappiness), 'Pope' **340, 412** below; and for SJ's ambivalent attitude to a 'blaze', 'Pope' **310** and n. below.

17. For their children, see **89** and n. below.

18. *exuberant*: '2. Abounding in the utmost degree' (*Dict.*).

    Parliament did not meet between Mar. 1629 and Apr. 1640. SJ follows *BB*, vi (ii). 4102–3, drawing on 'Life' (1711), p. xix: 'his Relation to the *Hampden* Family inducing him to Espouse the Party which was against Ship-Mony, and other Practices in those Times, he never was acceptable to the Reigning Favourites, further than his Muse made him.' Hampden (see **1** above) was prominent in resistance to Charles I's exaction of ship-money in 1636.

19. The Short Parliament of 1640 lasted from 13 Apr. to 5 May. Fenton (1729 edn.), 399–408, gave the full text of W's speech on 22 Apr. 1640, but the passage SJ quotes is in *BB*, vi (ii). 4103 n. The speech was a less disaffected 'exclamation' by a 'patriot' (see 'Pope' **397** and n. below) than SJ suggests. Stockdale had recently described it as 'worthy to have been pronounced in the Roman Forum' for eloquence, wit, and 'irrefragable argument': W's political tenets proved that, while he 'strenuously vindicated the rights of the people', he was 'equally an enemy to despotism and anarchy' (*Works* (1772), p. xxii).

    Dr Samuel Beilby, *Remarks on Doctor J's Lives* (York, 1782), 14–15, detected in SJ's reference to 'imaginary grievances' a provocative allusion to the recent war in

America ('all that wanton effusion of blood and treasure'). He cited SJ's own *Taxation No Tyranny* (1775), which had defended the arbitrary taxation of Americans and urged their submission. Joseph Towers, *Essay on SJ* (1786), 54–5, also objected that W had been motivated by good sense and genuine patriotism, and that 'the grievances of which he complained were real, and not imaginary'. In his early lives of Admiral Blake (1740) and Francis Cheynel (1751), SJ had been more respectful about those who held to their principles at the beginning of the Civil War by declaring for Parliament (*Early Biog. Writings* (1973), 72, 392).

20. Stockdale, 'Life' (1772), pp. xxiii, xxx, had praised W's 'spirited declamations' against the 'pernicious counsels' of the clergy, as well as his moderation 'in times of tumult, fanaticism, and rebellion'.

21–2. W quoted Richard Hooker, *Of the Laws of Ecclesiastical Polity*, i (1593), sect. x. (SJ's own reference to 'B. I sect. 9' was omitted from 22 in 1783, perhaps accidentally, since he made no alteration in the Berg copy, but possibly because it was inaccurate: see Textual Notes.) SJ praised Hooker as a source for 'the language of theology' in his preface to the *Dict.* (1755) (*OASJ*, 319), and used 2,188 quotations from his works (increased to 2,207 in 1773). He told Malone on 15 Mar. 1782 that he had once considered undertaking a new edition of Hooker (Bodleian, MS Malone 30, fo. 64v). See also 'Pope' 44 below.

23. *BB*, vi (ii). 4103 n., defined W's 'great position' similarly, and followed *GD*, x. 83–4 n., in quoting this anecdote from 'Life' (1711), p. xx. It concerns Sir Henry Vane, Secretary of State, Sir Thomas Jermyn, and his son Henry Jermyn, later Earl of St Albans (1660) (see 104 below, and 'Cowley' 12 n., 44 above). On 4 May 1640 Vane told Parliament that Charles I would surrender ship-money in return for subsidies which, according to the anecdote, Vane knew would be refused. Clarendon believed that Vane did so 'to bring all into confusion' (*History of the Rebellion*, ed. W. D. Macray (Oxford, 1888), i. 182), but later historians believe that Vane was not going beyond the King's own wishes.

24. W was MP for Amersham in Apr. 1640, but in fact represented St Ives, Cornwall, *c*. Nov. 1640 to 14 July 1643. He was chosen to carry to the House of Lords the articles of impeachment against Sir Francis Crawley (1584–1649), who had offended the Commons by his judgement in 1636 supporting the King's right to levy ship-money. He was also one of the judges who gave opinion for the Crown against W's cousin (not uncle) John Hampden (see 1 above) at his trial in 1638 for refusing to pay the tax, asserting the incompetence of Parliament to limit the royal prerogative. W's speech of 6 July 1641 was published as *Mr. Waller's Speech in the Painted Chamber* (1641), and reprinted by Fenton (1729 edn.), 408–22. For its popularity see 100 and n. below.

25–35. The debate began on 8 Feb. 1641. As SJ's note explains, he had 'retrieved' W's speech from *The Parliamentary or Constitutional History of England ... to 1660* (24 vols., 1751–62), ix (1753), 347–50. (For his instructions to Nichols about this source, to which SJ had access at Streatham, see 'Composition' above.) SJ no doubt decided to quote the speech at length because, as *Parl. History*, ix. 347 n., itself noted, Fenton (1729 edn.) had omitted it. It had been published as *An Honourable and Learned Speech against Prelates' Innovations* (1641).

27. Hill (1905) suggested an emendation of W's 'the bishops who so answered' to 'the bishops who were so answered', quoting Sir William Blackstone, *Commentaries*

(Oxford, 1775), i. 19, on the earls and barons who replied in these terms to the bishops at the Parliament of Merton in 1236 ('We do not wish to change the laws of England').

29. *Legem rogare . . . Legem ferre*: 'to propose a law . . . to pass a law'.

30. W quotes Cicero, *Tusc. Disp.*, i. ii. 4 ('Public esteem is the nurse of the arts').

36. *BB*, vi (ii). 4104, similarly regretted that 'the fire of this transient love of civil liberty in the public state' had not 'burned with as steady and uniform a flame, as did that of his fixed love for beauty in private life'.

37. The first sentence derives from the 'Life' (1711), pp. xxi–xxii, xxiv, and the second from Clarendon, *History* (1888 edn.), iii. 38–9. *GD*, x. 84–5 nn., and *BB*, vi (ii). 4104 n., both cited these sources.

38. W was nominated as a Commissioner on 1 Feb. 1643. The King's words were reported by Bulstrode Whitelocke, *Memorials of the English Affairs* (1682; 1732 edn. cited), 67. Their implications were discussed by Fenton (1729 edn.), 'Observations', p. xci, *BB*, vi (ii). 4104 and n., and Stockdale, 'Life' (1772), pp. xxxii–xxxiii, but *GD*, x. 84, quoted them without comment.

39–61. SJ's narrative of W's 'plot' in 1643 draws in particular on Clarendon's *History* (1888 edn.), iii. 39–53, the 'Life' (1711), pp. xxiii–xxxvi, and *Parl. History*, xii (1753), 279–97, 317–25, all cited, though not always in the same sequence, in *BB*, vi (ii). 4104–8 and nn. Some details may derive from John Rushworth, *Historical Collections*, ii (ii) (1712), 322–8. Stockdale, 'Life' (1772), pp. xxxiii–xlvi, also gave the plot detailed treatment, drawing mainly on Clarendon's account.

39. Nathaniel Tompkins had married W's sister Cecilia.
    SJ added the last two sentences in 1783, perhaps having noticed this information in Stockdale, 'Life' (1772), p. xxxvii (see Textual Notes). His marginal insertion has been cut out of the Berg copy of *Lives* (1781) which SJ revised for the 1783 edition, perhaps by Nichols for presentation. For a slip of paper bearing these words in SJ's hand, presumably the excision from the Berg copy, see Roy Davids, Cat. VI (Oct. 1999), item 77.

40. Based on Clarendon, *History* (1888 edn.), iii. 40, and 'Life' (1711), p. xxvi, but SJ's note gives *Parl. History*, xii. 287, as the source for John Pym's account.

41. The first sentence is based on Clarendon, *History* (1888 edn.), iii. 40–1, as cited by *BB*, vi (ii). 4105, with a note pointing out that W himself later claimed before the House of Commons that this had been his purpose.

42. *BB*'s cross-reference to its article on Sir Nicholas Crisp (1599?–1666) at iii (1750), 1522–6, probably directed SJ to this information, and to a discussion of the relationship of W's plot to Crisp's plans, previously considered by Clarendon and other historians. Neither Clarendon nor 'Life' (1711) mention the £100,000, but *BB*, iii (1750), 1522 n., cited this sum from David Lloyd, *Memoires* (1668), 617.

43. The Commission of Array, addressed by Charles I to Crisp and other citizens and dated 16 Mar. 1643, was held in Oxford until it could be safely conveyed: see S. R. Gardiner, *History of the Great Civil War* (1888), i. 128, 168, 172. By 19 May it had been carried to London by Katherine, Lady Aubigny, the daughter of Theophilus

Howard, Earl of Suffolk. Her husband had died at Edgehill in 1642, and she herself died in exile at The Hague in 1650 (Cokayne, i. 330).

**44.** 'Life' (1711), p. xxvii, agreed with Clarendon that W and Crisp were engaged in 'distinct Designs', as later did *BB*, vi (ii). 4105, and Stockdale, 'Life' (1772), p. xxxix. In the final sentence, 'they' must refer to Parliament, as in **50** below.

**45.** Cf. 'The discovery of Mr. Waller's plot is variously related' in *BB*, vi (ii). 4105. *GD*, x. 85–6 n., also juxtaposed the differing accounts in Clarendon, *History* (1888 edn.), iii. 44, and 'Life' (1711), p. xxviii, but SJ devotes more space than either to the discrepancies. According to Rushworth, *Historical Collections*, iii (ii). 322, the plot was betrayed by Roe, Tompkins's clerk.

**46.** *terrifick*: 'Dreadful; causing terrour' (*Dict.*).
      Based on 'Life' (1711), p. xxix, and Clarendon, *History* (1888 edn.), iii. 44, as quoted by *BB*, vi (ii). 4105 n. The plot was revealed to Pym during a service at St Margaret's, Westminster (Gardiner, *Civil War*, i. 171).

**47.** Based on Clarendon, *History* (1888 edn.), iii. 44–5, as quoted by *BB*, vi (ii). 4107 n., and 'Life' (1711), p. xxxii.

**49.** Based on Clarendon, *History* (1888 edn.), iii. 45. According to *BB*, iii. (1750), 1524 n., citing Rushworth, the Commission of Array was discovered in Tompkins's cellar.

**50–1.** As in **44** above, 'they' are what SJ calls in **49** 'the rebels', i.e. Parliament.

**51.** *BB*, vi (ii). 4105–7 n., quoted Pym's *A Discovery of the Great Plot* (1643) at length, but not the words SJ cites, which he presumably found in *Parl. History*, xii. 288. The 'day of thanksgiving' was 15 June 1643 (Gardiner, *Civil War*, i. 174).

**53.** *BB*, vi (ii). 4107 n., quoted W's letter to Portland from Fenton (1729 edn.), 430–2.

**54.** Portland's letter is not in *GD* or *BB*, but in *Parl. History*, xii. 317.

**55.** W confronted Portland on 29 June. SJ quotes *Parl. History*, xii. 318.

**57.** Lady Aubigny (see **43** above) had been arrested, but denied any knowledge of the plot and was later allowed to leave for Holland.

**58.** After a court martial, Tompkins and Chaloner were sentenced to death on 3 July 1643 and executed two days later (Gardiner, *Civil War*, i. 184). SJ used more information from the article on Crisp in *BB*, iii (1750). 1524 n., than from its later account of W, but details about the executions and dying speeches may come from Rushworth, *Historical Collections*, iii (ii). 326–8. For Hugh Peters, see also 'Denham' **12** and n. above. SJ added the last sentence in 1783 (see Textual Notes).

**59.** SJ includes more detail from Clarendon, *History* (1888 edn.), iii. 50–1, than *GD* or *BB*. Portland and Conway were released on bail on 31 July 1643 and freed from all restrictions in Aug. 1644. Rushworth, *Historical Collections*, iii (ii). 323, 325, described the part played by Alexander Hampden, who fell ill and later died in confinement (Gardiner, *Civil War*, i. 184).

**60.** Based on Clarendon, *History* (1888 edn.), iii. 51–2, quoted by *BB*, vi (ii). 4108 n., and 'Life' (1711), pp. xxxiii–xxxiv. W's speech of 4 July, arguing that the House of Commons should not allow him to be tried by court martial, was separately printed in 1643, and included in his *Poems* (1645), *Poems* (1711), and Fenton (1729 edn.), 423–9.

*GD*, x. 84 n., 86 n., quoted the accounts by Clarendon and Whitelocke, *Memorials* (1732 edn.), 70, without emphasizing the discrepancies later noted by *BB*, Stockdale, 'Life' (1772), pp. xliv–xlv, and SJ. W was not tried with the other conspirators, but was expelled from the House of Commons on 14 July and removed to the Tower in Sept. 1643. Although plans for a court martial were revived in Aug. 1644, the trial did not proceed, and in Nov. 1644 he was fined £10,000 and banished (Clarendon, *History* (1888 edn.), iii. 52–3; 'Life' (1711), pp. xxxiv–xxxv; Gardiner, *Civil War*, i. 184–5, 490–1). W raised this sum by selling his estate in Bedfordshire. John Aubrey, *Brief Lives* (1898), ii. 276, suggested that this was 'the first time a House of Commons was ever bribed'.

61. SJ quotes Percival Stockdale's 'Life' in W's *Works* (1772), p. lxii (see 'Composition' and 'Sources' above). For SJ's relationship with Stockdale, see 'Pope' headnote below, *Life*, ii. 113 and n., Stockdale's *Memoirs* (1809), ii. 170–201, *J. Misc.*, ii. 330–4, and i. 1–2 n. above.

62. W reached Calais in Aug. 1645, travelled with John Evelyn in Italy in 1646, and was in Rouen 1648–9, where his daughter Margaret was born: see *Poems*, i, pp. lviii–lx, de Beer, 'Uncollected Poem', 203–5, Riske, 'W in Exile', 734, and P. R. Wikelund, 'An Unpublished Letter of Thomas Hobbes', *ELN* 9 (1969), 263–8. From late 1649 W was in Paris: for his 'splendour' there, see 'Life' (1711), p. xl, and 104 below.

As *BB*, vi (ii). 4108 n., noted, both 'To my Lady Morton, on New Year's Day, 1650' and 'Epitaph on Colonel Charles Cavendish' allude to the political situation in England. Oddly, SJ does not refer to the publication of W's *Poems* (1645), mentioned by both *GD* and *BB*, and discussed by Stockdale, 'Life' (1772), pp. xlviii–xlix.

63. SJ's information is in *BB*, vi (ii). 4109 n., deriving from 'Life' (1711), pp. xl, xlii. W was given permission to return to England by the Rump Parliament on 27 Nov. 1651, through his brother-in-law Adrian Scrope, later executed as a regicide in 1660. John Evelyn noted in Paris on 13 Jan. 1652 that W was about to return, 'having now obtain'd leave of the Rebells (who had proscrib'd him)' (*Diary*, iii. 53).

In 1779 SJ named W's house 'Hillburn' (see Textual Notes), but in 1781 altered this to 'Hall-barn', as in 'Life' (1711), pp. xvii, xlii. (*BB*, vi (ii). 4109, had 'Hail Burn'.) For his mother's relationship to Cromwell and John Hampden, see 1 and n. above. The anecdote about Cromwell's visit is in *BB*, vi (ii). 4109 n., from 'Life' (1711), p. vi.

64. Both *GD* and *BB* relate the anecdote from 'Life' (1711), pp. xliii–xliv. SJ does not mention that Cromwell made W a Commissioner for Trade 1655–7.

*enthusiastick*: '1. Persuaded of some communication with the deity. 2. Vehemently hot in any cause. 3. Elevated in fancy; exalted in ideas' (*Dict.*).

65–71. Unlike *BB*, *GD* discussed these poems only briefly.

65. W in fact published his *Panegyrick to My Lord Protector* in 1655: for its reputation see 128 and n. and 'Addison' 128 below. It was not reprinted in later collections of W's poems in his lifetime.

For Cromwell, see also 'Milton' 73 above. In his 'Memoirs of the King of Prussia' in *Literary Mag.*, 1 (1756), 329, SJ wrote: 'I have always thought that what Cromwell had more than our lawful kings, he owed to the private condition in which he first entered the world, in that state he learned his art of secret transaction, and the knowledge by which he was able to oppose zeal to zeal, and make one enthusiast destroy another.' According to William Bowles, SJ considered 'writing the Life of Oliver Cromwell, saying, that he thought it must be highly curious to trace his extraordinary rise to the supreme power, from so obscure a beginning. He at length laid aside his scheme, on discovering that all that can be told of him is already in print' (*Life*, iv. 235–6; cf. Boswell, *Making of the Life*, 247). SJ stated in *Journey* (1985), 20, that Cromwell 'civilized' the Scots 'by conquest, and introduced by violence the arts of peace'. See also J. Gray, 'J, Cromwell, and the Jacobite Cause', *Age of J* 2 (1989), 90–153.

*the detestable band*: the Long Parliament (see **24** above). In *Idler* 45 (1759), SJ evoked an imaginary history painting depicting Cromwell dissolving the Long Parliament ('that hateful assembly') with 'ferocious insolence' on 20 Apr. 1653 (*YW*, ii. 142). Benjamin West exhibited a painting on this subject at the Royal Academy in 1783. See Morris R. Brownell, *SJ's Attitude to the Arts* (Oxford, 1989), 76–8.

**66.** SJ refers to 'Of a war with Spain, and a fight at sea', ll. 103–10.

*the Crown*: *BB*, vi (ii). 4110, cited Whitelocke's *Memorials* (1732 edn.), 548, as the source for Cromwell's conversation on this subject in 1652, also discussed in its article on Cromwell at iii (1750), 1560 and n. Cromwell finally refused the Crown in May 1657.

*fainted in his coach*: SJ no doubt found this story, which is not in standard biographies, in Knightley Chetwood's 'Life' of Virgil in Dryden's *Virgil* (1697): 'his Council, thinking to make their Court by assenting to his judgment, voted unanimously *for him* against *his Inclination*; which surpriz'd and troubled him to such a degree, that as soon as he got into his Coach, he fell into a Swoon' (*Works*, v. 22; later quoted by Malone in *Prose Works of Dryden* (1800), iii. 549–50 n.).

For the 'Debate Between the Committee of the House of Commons and Oliver Cromwell' (*Gent. Mag.* (1741); separate edn., 1742), an abridgement attributed to SJ of a pamphlet of 1660 on the petition by which Cromwell was offered the title of king, see *YW*, x. 74–110, and *Bibliography*, i. 58–9, 67–9.

**67.** W's *Upon the late Storme, and of the Death of His Highnesse* (1658) appeared in *Three Poems upon the Death of his late Highnesse Oliver, Lord Protector* (1659): see also 'Dryden' **7** and 'Sprat' **2** below. Stockdale, 'Life' (1772), p. li, in fact suggested that W was trying to ingratiate himself with Cromwell's son.

**68.** *Restauration*: for this spelling, see 'Milton' **71** n. above.

SJ is less tolerant of W's *To the King, upon his Majesties Happy Return* (1660) than of Dryden's similar conduct: 'The reproach of inconstancy was, on this occasion, shared with such numbers, that it produced neither hatred nor disgrace' ('Dryden' **9** below). Stockdale, 'Life' (1772), p. 1, also expressed 'indignation' at W's 'fulsome praise' of Cromwell, in which 'the tribute which is only due to virtue and piety' was 'prostituted to usurpation, and cruelty'. In contrast, 'Life' (1711), p. xlv, had observed calmly: ''tis an ill Poet that knows not how to *trim*.'

SJ refers to 'To the King, on his Navy', l. 32 ('Dares trust such pow'r with so much piety'), addressed to Charles I (see **15** above), and the *Panegyrick*, l. 124 ('Was so much power and piety in one').

69. Cf. Dryden, Preface to *De Arte Graphica*: 'Fiction is of the essence of poetry' (Watson, ii. 186; quoted under 'Fiction' in the *Dict.*). For SJ's own allegory about Truth and Fiction, see *Rambler* 96 (1751), and for 'truth' and 'fiction' elsewhere, see 'Cowley' **14, 16** and nn. above.

   For flattery as a 'species of prostitution', see *Rambler* 136 (1751) (*YW*, iv. 355), and cf. also **122** below and 'Dryden' **72** and n. below.

70. *BB*, vi (ii). 4110, followed Fenton (1729 edn.), 'Observations', p. lxvii, in citing W's *bon mot* from *Ménagiana* (3rd edn., Paris, 1715), ii. 46–7. Voltaire quoted the anecdote from Bayle's *Dictionnaire* in his *Letters Concerning the English Nation* (1733), 208–9, and it was repeated in *Anecdotes of Polite Literature* (1764), ii. 117, and Goldsmith's *Beauties of English Poesy* (1767) (*Coll. Works*, v. 328).

71. Stockdale, 'Life' (1772), p. liii, considered *To the King* 'certainly far inferior' to the poem on Cromwell.

72. Charles II's first Parliament in fact met on 8 May 1661. W remained MP for Hastings until 1685, when he was returned for Saltash (see also **81** below). Whereas *BB*, vi (ii). 4111 n., discussed W's parliamentary seats at length, *GD* ignored the subject.

   The reference to W's abstemiousness, and the remark by Henry Savile (1642–87), Groom of the Bedchamber to the Duke of York, and later Charles II's Vice-Chamberlain, are in *BB*, vi (ii). 4110, from 'Life' (1711), p. xlvii. Boswell quoted the passage in *BB* about W's sobriety in a note to a discussion by SJ and others of the pros and cons of wine-drinking on 28 Apr. 1778, shortly after he wrote 'Waller' (*Life*, iii. 327 n.). For the wits of the Restoration court, see 'Rochester' **4** and n. and 'Roscommon' **9** above, and, for W's conviviality with the Duke of Buckingham, Christopher Wren, and others, see J. H. Wilson, *A Rake and his Times* (New York, 1954), 152, 155–6.

73. Charles de Saint-Évremond (1613–1703), the French critic, lived in England from the 1660s on a pension from Charles II. For his friendship with W, and praise of his writings in a letter to Corneille, see 'Life' (1711), pp. xlvi–xlvii. *BB*, vi (ii). 4113 n., also quoted his letters about W to La Fontaine.

74. SJ quotes Gilbert Burnet, *History of His Own Times*, i (1724), 388 (cited, but not quoted, by *BB*, vi (ii). 4112 n.). Burnet in fact wrote 'even at eighty' instead of 'though old'.

   SJ also refers to Anchitell Grey, *Debates in the House of Commons, 1667–94* (10 vols., 1763), cited by *BB*, vi (ii). 4110–11 nn. SJ wrote the original proposals for this work for Edward Cave: see *Gent. Mag.* (1745), 135–6. Grey's estimate that W made 189 speeches in this period is confirmed by Hemming (ed.), *House of Commons*, iii (1983), 654.

   For SJ's unusual difficulty with the phrasing of his final sentence, which began in the proofs and continued to 1783, see Textual Notes.

75. SJ quotes Burnet, *History*, i. 583.

76. Although 'Life' (1711), p. xlviii, stated that W 'wou'd never be in the Commission of the Peace or Lieutenancy' (quoted in *BB*, vi (ii). 4111), W was active in public affairs. He was Commissioner for Trade 1660–8, Commissioner for Plantations 1660–72, Commissioner for Irish Accounts 1668, and Commissioner for Trade and

Plantations 1672–4, sitting on some 209 committees after 1660 (Hemming (ed.), *House of Commons*, iii. 653–5).

77. SJ follows *BB*, vi (ii). 4111–12, which cited 'Life' (1711), p. xlviii, and cross-referred to its article on Sir Henry Wotton at vi (ii). 4346–7. Wotton (see 'Milton' 24 and n. above) became Provost of Eton in 1624 and took deacon's orders in 1627. Richard Allestree (1619–81) was Provost from 8 Aug. 1665 to 16 Jan. 1681.

78. This is SJ's first reference to his primary source, *BB*, vi (ii). 4111 and n. (*GD* had no equivalent to 78–82.) In 1667 W helped to draw up the accusations against Clarendon and spoke in the impeachment debates (Hemming (ed.), *House of Commons*, iii. 654). *BB* quoted the passage in W's speech from *State Trials*, ii (1730), 559–61, 567.

79. SJ's misdating of W's second attempt to obtain the Provostship of Eton derives from *BB*, vi (ii). 4111, repeated by Stockdale, 'Life' (1772), p. lv. It may have originated in the account of Cradock's success over W ('who had try'd hard for it') in Wood, ii. 678, who mentions Cradock's appointment as Canon of Chichester in 1669 in the same sentence as the later post at Eton. After Allestree's death on 28 Jan. 1681 (see 77 n. above), Dryden was also rumoured to be a candidate for the Provostship ( J. A. Winn, *John Dryden and his World* (1987), 595 n.). Dr Zachary Cradock was appointed on 24 Feb. 1681, and held the post until 1695. For his 'single sermon' Hill (1905) cited the 'Life' by George Sewell in John Philips's *Poems* (1715), 14: 'I have heard a Story of an eminent Preacher, who, out of an obstinate Modesty, could never be prevail'd on to print but one Sermon, (the best, perhaps, that ever pass'd the Press) to which the Publick gave the Title of Dr. CRADOCK'S WORKS.' Cradock's *Sermon Preached before the King* (1678) was in fact later collected with *The Great End and Design of Christianity* (1706) as *Two Sermons* (1742).

80. W in fact received £1,000 in Jan. 1678 to encourage his support of the government in Parliament. Although never 'a good party man', he remained in high standing at court (Hemming (ed.), *House of Commons*, iii. 656).

81. For W as MP for Saltash, see 72 and n. above.
    SJ refers to W's 'Presage of the Ruin of the Turkish Empire. Presented to His Majesty on his Birthday' (*Poems*, ii. 103–5). For W and Tasso, particularly in Fairfax's translation, see Fenton (1729 edn.), 'Observations', p. xviii, and 5 and n. above, 143, 154 and n. below. For James II's 'holy war at home', see 'Roscommon' 19 and n. above.

82–7. SJ follows closely the narrative in *BB*, vi (ii). 4112 n., drawing on 'Life' (1711), pp. li–lvii. The anecdotes in 82–3 had appeared in *The Tell-Tale* (2 vols., 1756), ii. 364, 398.

82. *Pointed axioms, and acute replies*: for similar scepticism, see 'Rowe' 29 and 'Sheffield' 14 below, and cf. the 'flying Reports and . . . unattested Facts' SJ excluded from his 'Life of Boerhaave' (*Gent. Mag.* (1739), 37).

83. W's daughter Mary married Dr Peter Birch, minister of St James's, the source of some of the family material in 'Life' (1711).

84. For W's son Edmund, see 89 and n. below.

85. W published his *Divine Poems* (1685) at the age of 79. SJ was himself 68 when he wrote this paragraph: cf. 132–3 and nn. below.

SJ adapts 'Of the Last Verses in the Book', l. 1: 'When we for age could neither read nor write' (*Poems*, ii. 144). John Hoole (see **154** and n. below) recorded an anecdote about W told by SJ not long before he died, which 'he said he would record if he lived to revise his life': W 'was accustomed to say that his memory was so bad he would sometimes forget to repeat his grace at table, or the Lord's Prayer, perhaps so that people might wonder at what he did else of great moment' (*J. Misc.*, ii. 153). SJ's source for the story is unclear: Aubrey, *Brief Lives* (1898), ii. 277, 279, noted contradictory reports of W's powers of memory.

**86.** For Coleshill, see **1** above, and for Sir Charles Scarborough, the King's physician, 'Cowley' **22** and n. above.

*tumid*: '1. Swelling; puffed up' (*Dict.*). Boswell mentioned it as one of the few 'uncommon or learned words' in the *Lives* (*Life*, iv. 39). In his last months SJ used the word more than once of his own limbs (*Letters*, iv. 272, 277, 402). For his use of 'tumid' in literary contexts to mean '3. Pompous; boastful; puffy; falsely sublime', see **123** below, 'Milton' **27** above, 'Dryden' **331** and 'Somervile' **8** below, and *YW*, viii. 873.

*some lines of Virgil*: these lines 'about the Condition of Human Life', mentioned in 'Life' (1711), p. lvi, were probably *Georgics*, II. 66–8, translated as: 'In youth alone unhappy mortals live; | But ah! the mighty bliss is fugitive: | Discoloured sickness, anxious labours, come, | And age, and death's inexorable doom' (Dryden).

**88.** For Thomas Rymer's inscription, see 'Life' (1711), pp. lx–lxi, lxxx–lxxxii, and *BB*, vi (ii). 4115 n., and for W's monument see the plate in Fenton (1729 edn.), facing 450. Its dilapidation is not mentioned by *BB*, Stockdale, 'Life' (1772), or the later descriptions of it in *Gent. Mag.* (1790), 806–7, and *The Ambulator...in a Tour round London* (6th edn., 1793), 116. SJ defines 'Dilapidation' only as referring to the 'ruin or decay' of ecclesiastical edifices or property (*Dict.*).

**89.** W had in all five sons and eight daughters (Hemming (ed.), *House of Commons*, iii. 653). SJ's information derives ultimately from 'Life' (1711), pp. lviii–lx, through *BB*, vi (ii). 4113–14 (the sons, in the main text) and 4115 n. (the daughters, consigned to a note). For Mary, who married Dr Birch, see **83** above.

Benjamin was in fact sent to '*Jersey*, a Colony in the *West-Indies*', not New Jersey, according to 'Life' (1711), p. lviii. Edmund (1652–1700), W's heir, was MP for Agmondesham 1689, 1690, and 1695, and joined the Society of Friends in 1698 (Hemming (ed.), *House of Commons*, iii. 657; cf. **99** n. below). Stephen, a lawyer, became a Commissioner of the Union of England and Scotland in 1706. *BB* obtained information from Ralph Waller, a descendant then still living. Edmund Waller, the poet's great-great-grandson, was a student at Aberdeen University when SJ visited it in Aug. 1773 (*Life*, v. 85–6, 493). A recent descendant, Sir John Waller, poet and journalist, died on 22 Jan. 1995.

What was described as W's own library was included in the sale of Hall Barn on 17 Sept. 1832: see A. N. L. Munby (ed.), *Sale Catalogues of Libraries of Eminent Persons*, i (1971), 5–40.

**90–2.** SJ quotes *The Life of Edward Earl of Clarendon* (Oxford, 1759), 24–5. He had discussed its recent publication in *Idler* 65, and later described W in *Idler* 83 as one of Clarendon's 'band of associates'. He had praised Clarendon as a historian, for 'the variety, distinctness, and strength of his characters', while expressing reservations about his style, in *Rambler* 122 (1751) (*YW*, ii. 201–2, 259, iv. 289–90). Joseph Towers, *Essay on SJ* (1786), 56, objected that SJ quotes Clarendon without admitting that his view of W was inevitably prejudiced (cf. 77–8 above). Stockdale later claimed that SJ had told him that he had 'only read parts of my Lord CLARENDON's History' (Thomson, *The Seasons* (1793), unpaginated note to 'Winter' after 222).

90. *familiarly known*: as usual, SJ emphasizes the importance of 'personal knowledge' in biography (see 'Addison' 98 and n. below).

91. For Dr Morley see 96 and n. below.

93–106. SJ's first formal 'character' of a poet begins merely as an examination of Clarendon's account of W: 99–106 were a later addition (see below).

94. See 8 and n. above. W married at the age of 25. As elsewhere, SJ's apparent quotation in fact paraphrases Clarendon's words in 91 above.

95. See 5–7 above for the dating of W's early poems.

96. *BB*, vi (ii). 4101 n. (but not *GD*, x. 83 n.) and Stockdale, 'Life', (1772), pp. xii–xiv, had discussed this discrepancy between Clarendon's account and 'Life' (1711), pp. xi–xii. George Morley (1597–1684), who joined the future Charles II in exile in 1649 and became Bishop of Winchester in 1662, was a cousin of Sir John Denham (q.v.). The 'wits' were probably the circle of Lucius Cary, Vis. Falkland, of which Morley was a member: see 12 above, and 'Cowley' 12 and n. above.

97. For Burnet's account, see 74 and n. above.

98. SJ combines separate phrases from Roger Ascham's account of 'quick wits' in *The Scholemaster* (1570), Bk. I: 'always flattering their betters . . . In youth also they be ready scoffers, privy mockers' (*Whole Works*, ed. J. A. Giles (4 vols., 1864–5), iii. 98–9). SJ had cited Ascham on 'quick wits' in his notes to *Hamlet* (*YW*, viii. 97), and cf. 'Milton' 10 above; see also James Bennet's edition (with SJ's 'Life') of Ascham's *English Works* (1761), 207–11, and, for another quotation from the same passage, *J. Misc.*, i. 314–15.

　　For 'The hunting of the stag' by Margaret Cavendish, Duchess of Newcastle (1623–73), see her *Poems, and Fancies* (1653), 113–16. See also 'Dryden' 43 and n. below. W's remark about the poem appears in Katherine Philips's *Letters from Orinda* (1705), 206: as earlier (see 'Roscommon' 36 and n. above), the freedom of SJ's quotation from this work suggests that he used some intermediary source. See also 147 below.

99–106. These paragraphs are not in the surviving proofs, in which 98 originally ended: 'Such was the life of Waller. Let us now consider his poetry.' SJ wrote in the margin: 'Here I shall put an insertion' (see Textual Notes). The insertion may date from as late as May 1778.

99. Cf. 63 above. Richard Hurd had discussed the 'laxity' of W's 'political principles' in 'Dialogue I. On Sincerity in the Commerce of the World: Between Dr. Henry More and Edmund Waller, Esq.' in his *Moral and Political Dialogues* (1759), 1–38. Stockdale, 'Life' (1772), took a more lenient view of W's attempt to 'adhere to truth' and to a 'just and virtuous medium' in 'times of tumult, fanaticism, and rebellion' (pp. xxx, lxv).

John Hampden, grandson of W's cousin (see 1 above), was fined £40,000 for his part in the Rye House Plot of 1683. W managed to save him from capital punishment. For this episode *BB*, vi (ii). 4111, cited 'Life' (1711), p. xlviii, with a cross-reference to its article on John Hampden at iv. 2529 n. SJ took 'Life' (1711) to refer to the 'safety' of the younger Hampden's son: it was in fact W's own son Edmund (89 above) who was interrogated after the Plot and released on bail. See Thomas Sprat, *A True Account ... of the Horrid Conspiracy* (1685), 21–2, 140 (and 'Sprat' 9 below).

100. See 24 and n. above. W's 'biographer' refers to 'Life' (1711), p. xxi. Stockdale, 'Life' (1772), p. xxvi, believed that W's speech would still stir anyone 'not dead to the impressions of oratory'.

101. In the first sentence 'lost' was corrected to 'left' in 1781 (see Textual Notes). Cf. 'Life' (1711), p. lv: 'He was always inclinable to be passionate, The Fire of his Muse shews he had a share of it in his Temper, and when he was old it was most predominant, but he was soon allay'd by the Interposition of his Friends.'

102. From 'Life' (1711), pp. xlvii–xlix, cited by *BB*, vi (ii). 4114 n.

Fenton (1729 edn.), 377–96, attributed to W Act I of the translation of Corneille's *Pompey the Great: A Tragedy* (1664), to which Charles Buckhurst, later Earl of Dorset (q.v. below), Sir Charles Sedley, and Sidney Godolphin also contributed, according to 'The Session of the Poets' (1668), ll. 109–20 (*POAS*, i. 334). Pope cited this joint translation as evidence that 'the more correct French Poets began to be in reputation' in England soon after the Restoration, in *Imit. Horace, Ep. II. i.* (1737), l. 267 n.: for a rival translation by Katherine Philips, see 147 below and 'Roscommon' 36 and n. above.

For Buckingham's *The Rehearsal* (1671), see 'Dryden' 94 and n. below, where SJ does not mention W's involvement.

103. For W's original 'fortune', see 2, 8 above. SJ's estimate of his final income seems to derive directly from 'Life' (1711), p. xlvii, rather than *BB*.

104. The source for W's 'splendor' at Paris (cf. 63 above) is 'Life' (1711), p. xl, quoted by *BB*, vi (ii). 4108 n. For Henry Jermyn, Earl of St Albans, see 23 and n. above.

105. See 60 above. SJ means that W was forced to sell estates worth £1,000 p.a.: the source is 'Life' (1711), p. xxxvi (and see p. xlii), cited by *BB*, vi (ii). 4108 n.

106. George Chapman finally published his complete translation of the *Iliad* and *Odyssey* as *The Whole Works of Homer* (1616). 'Life' (1711), p. lxvi, noted Dryden's statement in the preface to *Examen Poeticum* (1693) that W told him that he could not read Chapman 'without incredible pleasure and extreme transport' (Watson, ii. 167). For other references to Chapman, see 'Dryden' 207, 344 and 'Pope' 85, 383 below.

Fenton (1729 edn.), 'Observations', p. iii, had quoted the 'Life of Virgil' by Knightley Chetwood in Dryden's translation (1697): 'our excellent Mr Waller ... us'd to say that he wou'd raze any Line out of his Poems which did not imply some Motive to Virtue' (Dryden, *Works*, v. 34). For Pope's approval of W's claim in 1738, see Spence, i. 196, and cf. 'Thomson' 53 and n. below.

107. For SJ's account of how Petrarch filled 'Europe with love and poetry', see 'Cowley' 14 above and cf. 131 below.

'Gothick' (not in the *Dict.*) here means 'medieval': for SJ's use of the word in literary and architectural contexts, see *Journey* (1985), 206 n.

108. 'Life' (1711), p. lxvi, admitted that W 'sometimes trifled...too much, and lavished his Gift on the smaller Poetry'. For 'burlesque', see 'Butler' **52** and n. above, and for the 'familiar', 'Cowley' **138** and n. above.

For the poems SJ cites, in some cases by approximate titles, see *Poems*, i. 80-1, 49, 51, 121, ii. 68, 69. For a familiar couplet from W's 'Upon the Earl of Roscommon's Translation of Horace', ll. 41-2 ('Poets lose half the praise they should have got, | Could it be known what they discreetly blot'), quoted by SJ elsewhere, see 'Pope' **120** and n. below.

109. SJ himself translated 'Anacreon's Dove' (from the *Greek Anthology*) at about the time he was writing 'Waller'. He told Mrs Thrale in Jan. 1778 that, 'as they were the first Greek Verses that had struck him when a Boy; so says he they continue to please me as well as any Greek Verses now I am Threescore'. On 25 Mar. 1778 he said: 'I intended doing it at sixteen, & never did, till I was 68' (*Thraliana*, i. 232-3 and n.). See *Poems* (1974), 213-15. For the '*Sparrow* of Catullus', see his *Carmina* 3, and cf. 'The mistress of Catullus wept for her sparrow many centuries ago' (*Rambler* 129; *YW*, iv. 320).

For what is 'only pretty, the plaything of fashion and the amusement of a day', see also 'West' **14** below.

110. SJ cites 'To Amoret' (see **9** above) and 'Of Love'.

111. In *Idler* 77 (1759) on 'easy poetry', SJ wrote that W 'often attempted, but seldom attained it; for he is too frequently driven into transpositions' (*YW*, ii. 242). Addison wrote of W in *Tatler* 163 (1710): 'that admirable Writer has the best and worse Verses of any among our great *English* Poets.'

112. SJ quotes 'Puerperium', ll. 5-12, originally two four-line stanzas.

113. *the depths of science*: cf. the 'conceits from recesses of learning not very much frequented by common readers of poetry', illustrated in SJ's discussion of 'Metaphysical' poetry in 'Cowley' **65-79** above. For 'To the Sun', see 'Song' ('Stay, Phoebus! stay'), ll. 7-12. Fenton, 'Observations' (1729 edn.), p. xxxv, had compared W's allusion to the 'Copernican' system to the conceits of Donne and Cowley (quoted in *BB*, vi (ii). 4114 n.). SJ also refers to 'Of her passing through a crowd of people', ll. 15-22 (for the printer's problem with SJ's handwriting, see Textual Notes).

*treacle*: the proofs show that SJ originally quoted 'To the King, Upon His Majesty's Happy Return', l. 76 ('Your vipers treacle yield, and scorpions oil' (see Textual Notes). He defines 'Treacle' as '1. A medicine made up of many ingredients' (*Dict.*). 'Theriaca' in Latin was an antidote against the bite of poisonous snakes, the original meaning of 'theriacle' or 'treacle' in Middle English. Cf. the Latin quotation in 'Garth' **11** below.

114. SJ quotes 'At Penshurst', ll. 11-16 (adapting the first line), W's second 'At Penshurst', ll. 1-8, and 'On the Head of a Stag', ll. 11-20. As Hill (1905) noted, Pope condensed the second couplet of the first passage in his *Pastorals*, II. 74 ('Trees, where you sit, shall crowd into a Shade').

115. SJ predictably disliked the mythological 'silver doves...in Cytherea's car' in 'On the Friendship betwixt Two Ladies', ll. 17-24.

116. 'Song' (Chloris! farewell'), ll. 25–8.

117. 'Song' ('Behold the brand of beauty tossed'), ll. 11–16.

118. 'To Chloris', ll. 1–8.

119. 'Of Loving at First Sight', ll. 15–20.

120. See 'To a Lady, from whom he received a Silver Pen', and 'Written on a Card that Her Majesty tore at Ombre'. 'These Verses were written in the Tasso of Her Royal Highness' has only ten lines. Fenton, 'Observations' (1729 edn.), p. lxxxiii, commented: 'I very well remember to have heard the late Duke of *Buckingham-shire* say, that the Author employ'd the greatest part of a summer in composing and correcting them' (quoted in *BB*, vi (ii). 4114 n.).

   *success . . . labour*: cf. 'Pope' **428** below (written by 1756), and his comments on Shakespeare in 1765: 'In tragedy his performance seems constantly to be worse, as his labour is more', and 'success in works of invention is not always proportionate to labour' (*YW*, vii. 72–3, 452).

121. Cf. SJ's remark, reported by Dr Maxwell, on 'the passion of love' that 'its violence and ill effects were much exaggerated' (*Life*, ii. 122). For his objections to 'the romantick omnipotence of Love' in drama, see 'Dryden' **78** and n. below, and for the clichés of 'amorous verses' elsewhere, see 'Cowley' **14** and n. above.

122. SJ quotes (loosely) George Granville, 'To the Immortal Memory of Mr. Edmund Waller', ll. 33–5: see also 'Granville' **3** and n. below. Granville and Aphra Behn were among the contributors to *Poems to the Memory of that Incomparable Poet Edmond Waller By Several Hands* (1688). Rochester, 'An Allusion to Horace' (1675), ll. 56–8, said that W 'In panegyrics does excel mankind. | He best can turn, enforce, and soften things | To praise great conqu'rers, or to flatter Kings.'

123. See **5** above, and 'Of the Danger of His Majesty', ll. 11–12, 157–60. 'Arion' is 'puerile' because mythological, like 'Amphion' in **125**: see **152** below, and 'Butler' **41** and n. above. For 'puerile', see 'Gray' **30** and n. below, and for 'tumid' see **86** n. above.

124. See **6, 15** above.

124*a–b.* Not numbered as separate paragraphs by Hill (1905).

124*a.* For 'the pagan deities', see **152** and n. below. SJ quotes 'Of His Majesty's Receiving the News', ll. 21–2.

124*b.* SJ refers to 'To the King, On his Navy', ll. 19–26, of which ll. 19–20 are: 'Should Nature's self invade the world again, | And o'er the centre spread the liquid main'. Dennis had asked in 1693, 'what does Mr. *Waller* mean, by spreading the Liquid Main o're the Center?', suggesting that 'Center' might mean 'the whole Globe' (*Works*, i. 27). It means 'earth' (i.e. the 'centre' of the universe) in Shakespeare, *Troilus and Cressida*, I. iii. 84, quoted by SJ to illustrate 'Centre' as 'The middle' in the *Dict*.

125. See **15** above for 'Of Salle', and 'Upon His Majesty's Repairing of St. Paul's', from which SJ quotes ll. 11–14, 19–26. As Hill (1905) noted, the 'state-obscuring sheds' were the humble houses built against the nave of St Paul's.

126. SJ paraphrases 'Of the Queen', ll. 25–6 ('She saves the lover, as we gangrenes stay, | By cutting hope, like a lopped limb, away'): see **6** and n. above.

127. See 14 and n. above.

128. See 65–6 above. There are several echoes of W's *Panegyrick* in Pope's first major public poem, *Windsor Forest* (1713), although he wrote in 1738 that, 'When black Ambition stains a Publick Cause, | ... Not *Waller*'s Wreath can hide the Nation's Scar' (*Epilogue to the Satires*, II. 228, 230).

   *a very liberal dividend of praise*: Shiels, *Lives*, ii. 258–64, quoted the *Panegyrick* in full, Hume thought that it 'contains more force than we should expect from the other compositions of this poet' (*History of Great Britain*, ii (1757), 126), and Lyttelton wrote, in his *Dialogues of the Dead* (1760), that it had 'a force and greatness of manner, which give him a rank among the poets of the first class' (*Works* (3rd edn., 1776), ii. 203). Although Goldsmith in 1767 thought its versification would now be considered 'slovenly', it had been in its time 'a prodigy of harmony': 'A modern reader will chiefly be struck with the strength of thinking, and the turn of the compliments bestowed upon the usurper' (*Coll. Works*, v. 327–8). For Stockdale, 'Life' (1772), pp. xlix–l, it was 'A beautiful, and spirited composition, in which the harmony, and delicate graces of Waller are elevated with the dignity of the epick strain'. 'Life' (1711), p. xlii, observed that, 'excepting the bad Title by which *Cromwell* held his Greatness, his personal Qualifications render'd him a fit Subject for so fine a Muse'.

129. SJ refers to or quotes 'Of a War with Spain, and a Fight at Sea', ll. 37–42, 85–6 (see 66 above and 'Dryden' 250 below).

130. See 68–71 above. *BB*, vi (ii). 4111 n., described W's muse as 'fainting on this occasion'.

131. For W's 'Sacred Poems', see 85 above.
   Petrarch's regret for 'the amusements of my youth' had recently been described by Susannah Dobson, *The Life of Petrarch* (1775), ii. 540–1. Cf. his 'Sonnet I' (in traditional arrangements) in e.g. John Nott, *Sonnets and Odes of Petrarch* (1777), 2–3 and n.: 'he reflects on the foolish passion of his youth, which inspired so many love-verses'. For Petrarch, see also 'Cowley' 14 and n. above.

132. Fenton (1729 edn.), 'Observations', p. lxxvii, stated that *To the King, upon his ... Return* (1660) was written in 'the 55th year of Mr. *Waller*'s age: from which time his genius began to decline apace from its meridian' (cited by *BB*, vi (ii). 4110). SJ said in Apr. 1778: 'I value my self upon this, that there is nothing of the old man in my conversation. I am now sixty-eight, and I have no more of it than at twenty-eight.' Elsewhere he objected to 'a wicked inclination in most people to suppose an old man decayed in his intellects' (*Life*, iii. 336, and cf. iv. 181). For other reflections on mental development and decline, see 85 above and 'Young' 161 below, *Letters*, ii. 261, 263–4, iii. 299, where SJ mentions Galen's view that 'life begins to decline from *thirty five*'. Patrick Delany, *Observations upon ... Swift* (1754), 140, had noted that Aristotle 'dates the decline of the human abilities ... in the forty-ninth year'. W in fact published his *Divine Poems* (1685) at the age of 79.

   *Newton*: for SJ's admiration for the great scientist, see *Life*, ii. 125, and for Newton in old age, R. S. Westfall, *Never at Rest: A Biography of Sir Isaac Newton* (Cambridge, 1980), 869, citing as a source Zachary Pearce, whose life SJ published in 1777 (see *Life*, i. 292, iii. 112). Henry Pemberton published Newton's *The*

*Chronology of Ancient Kingdoms Amended* (1728), which blended his interests in astronomy and theology, a year after his death.

133. Although W's sacred poetry had not recently been much discussed, Patrick Delany had praised it warmly in his *Observations upon Swift* (1754), 155–60. Unlike SJ, Stockdale, 'Life' (1772), p. lvii, believed that it showed signs of W's advanced age.

134. See Cowley's preface to his *Poems* (1656) on the importance of recovering the '*Divine Science*' of poetry from 'the *Devil* . . . to restore it to the *Kingdom* of *God*' (*Poems*, ed. A. R. Waller, 12–14). For later attempts to revive elevated religious poetry, and a discussion of SJ's discomfort with 'poetical devotion' (209–21), see D. B. Morris, *The Religious Sublime: Christian Poetry and Critical Tradition in 18th-Century England* (Lexington, Ky., 1972).

135–41. SJ's most extended explanation of his objections to sacred poetry basically elaborates Boileau, *L'Art poétique*, III. 199–200: 'De la foi d'un chrétien les mystères terribles | D'ornements égayés ne sont point susceptibles.' In 1696 John Dennis summarized Boileau's conviction 'That the Terrible Mysteries of the Christian Faith are not capable of delightful ornaments. That the Gospel offers nothing to us but Repentance on the one side, or Eternal Torments on the other, and that the Criminal mixture of Poetical Fictions gives a Fabulous Air, even to its most Sacred Truths' (*Works*, i. 53; see i. 252 ff. for Dennis's reply to Boileau). Henry Felton, *A Dissertation on Reading the Classics* (2nd edn., 1715), 108–14, also argued that 'Nothing is above the Reach of Man, but Heaven; and the same Wit can raise a *Human* Subject, that only debaseth a *Divine*.'

   For SJ's views on sacred poetry elsewhere, see 'Cowley' 147–53, 179 and 'Denham' 18 above, and 'Dryden' 280, 'J. Philips' 7, 'Fenton' 23, 'Yalden' 16, 'Pope' 392, 'Watts' 33, and 'Young' 155 below. Although he considered *Paradise Lost* a special case, he raised some familiar objections in 'Milton' 245–8 above. For his particular hostility to the mingling of sacred truths and profane 'fictions' in poetry, see also 'Milton' 183 and n. above. He did, however, approve of the religious setting of 'Eloisa to Abelard' in 'Pope' 63 below: 'The mixture of religious hope and resignation gives an elevation and dignity to disappointed love, which images merely natural cannot bestow.' Hawkins, *Life* (1787), 46 n., noted that SJ, 'who often expressed his dislike of religious poetry, and who, for the purpose of religious meditation, seemed to think one day as proper as another', read Moses Browne's devotional *Sunday Thoughts* (1752) 'with cold approbation, and said, he had a great mind to write and publish Monday Thoughts'. He wrote most of his own religious verse in old age, in Latin, and without thought of publication. See also D. R. Anderson, 'J and the Problem of Religious Verse', *Age of J* 4 (1991), 41–57.

   Daniel Turner (1710–98) of Abingdon replied in *Devotional Poetry Vindicated. In some remarks on . . . J's . . . Life of Waller* (Oxford, [1785]), commenting that SJ's posthumous *Prayers and Meditations* (1785) contained 'too many things inconsistent with genuine Piety, and that reflect no honour on the Doctor's religious Character' (29 n.). For support for J's views, see e.g. William Enfield on Richard Cumberland's *Calvary; or the Death of Christ . . . In Eight Books* (1792) in *Monthly Review*, NS 9 (1792), 1–7.

135. For 'didactick' and argumentative religious verse, see 'Dryden' **284–6**, 'Black-more' **22–5**, and 'Pope' **363–6** below.

   In *Rambler* 5 (1750) SJ claimed that, since nature offers an 'inexhaustible stock of materials', man 'has always a certain prospect of discovering new reasons for adoring the sovereign author of the universe' (*YW*, iii. 29). His discussion of *The Seasons* in 'Thomson' **46–8** below in fact virtually ignores its religious dimension, which Thomson had stressed in his dedication to *Winter* (2nd edn., 1726). For his similar treatment of the *Night Thoughts*, see 'Young' **160** below, and for 'description' in poetry elsewhere, see 'Cowley' **154** and n. above.

136. SJ's primary objection is to attempts to poeticize and embellish such 'Contemplative piety'. The individual's relationship with God ultimately underlies all his thinking.

137. For 'invention' as an aspect of poetic 'genius', see 'Pope' **373** and n. below. SJ argues that devotional poetry offers no scope for wit, novelty, refined language, or imaginative speculation. Mrs Thrale noted on 30 Oct. 1781 his 'great Aversion to Scripture Allusions as bordering on profane[ne]ss', and he himself said on 11 June 1784: 'I do not approve of figurative expressions in addressing the Supreme Being; and I never use them' (*Thraliana*, i. 516; *Life*, iv. 294–5). For the 'ornaments' and 'allusions' he expects in other kinds of poetry, see 'Cowley' **85, 202** and nn. above.

138. SJ only rarely invokes the pervasive neoclassical assumption that art perfects imperfect nature. Cf. Dryden, 'A Parallel Betwixt Painting and Poetry' (1695): 'a learned painter should form to himself an idea of perfect nature ... thereby correcting nature from what actually she is in individuals, to what she ought to be, and what she was created'; and 'both these arts ... are not only true imitations of nature, but of the best nature, of that which is wrought up to a nobler pitch. They present us with images more perfect than the life in any individual' (Watson, ii. 184, 194; the second passage is quoted in part under 'Imitation' in the *Dict.*). See also Dennis (1704): 'The great Design of Arts is to restore the Decays that happen'd to human Nature by the Fall, by restoring Order' (*Works*, i. 335–6, 514 n., and cf. his quotation from Bacon at i. 326–7); and Addison, *Spectator* 418 (1712): 'it is the part of a Poet to humour the Imagination in its own Notions, by mending and perfecting Nature where he describes a Reality, and by adding greater Beauties than are put together in Nature, where he describes a Fiction.'

   Reynolds invoked the doctrine in *Idler* 82 (1759) (the painter selects 'the most beautiful, that is, the most general form of nature', *YW*, ii. 255), and in 'Discourse XIII' (1786): 'the object and intention of all the Arts is to supply the natural imperfection of things, and often to gratify the mind by realizing and embodying what never existed but in the imagination' (*Discourses*, 299). See also the chapter 'Poetry exhibits a system of nature somewhat different from the reality of things' in Beattie's *Essays* (Edinburgh, 1776), 381–97. SJ himself tends instead to emphasize 'selection' from nature, as in 'Shenstone' **25** below ('the poet's art is selection'), and earlier in *Rambler* 4 (1750): 'It is justly considered as the great excellency of art, to imitate nature; but it is necessary to distinguish those parts of nature, which are most proper for imitation' (*YW*, iii. 2).

139. *the Supreme Being*: SJ conceivably alludes here to the annual Seatonian Prize at Cambridge for poems 'on one or other of the Perfections or Attributes of the Supreme Being'. His friend Christopher Smart won the prize regularly in the

1750s with a series of blank-verse poems on the Eternity, Immensity, Omniscience, Power, and Goodness of the Supreme Being.

140. Mrs Thrale described SJ 'bursting into a flood of tears' when repeating the stanza beginning 'Quarens me sedisti lassus' in the *Dies irae*: 'which sensibility I used to quote against him when he would inveigh against devotional poetry, and protest that all religious verses were cold and feeble, and unworthy the subject, which ought to be treated with higher reverence, he said, than either poets or painters could presume to excite or bestow' (*J. Misc.*, i. 284).

141. According to George Steevens, SJ admitted that, at 'divine service', 'the provocations given by ignorant and affected preachers too often disturb the mental calm which otherwise would succeed to prayer': 'I am apt to whisper to myself on such occasions—How can this illiterate fellow dream of fixing attention, after we have been listening to the sublimest truths, conveyed in the most chaste and exalted language, throughout a Liturgy which must be regarded as the genuine offspring of piety impregnated by wisdom?' (*J. Misc.*, ii. 319).

142. Dryden stated in 1664 that 'the excellence and dignity' of rhyme were 'never fully known till Mr. Waller taught it' (Watson, i. 7); and in 1691 that 'I am desirous of laying hold on his Memory, on all occasions, and thereby acknowledging to the World, that unless he had Written, none of us cou'd Write' (*Works*, xx. 3, and see 307–8 nn. for other references to W). Thomas Rymer, George Granville, Bevil Higgons, Aphra Behn, and others praised W's refinement of English poetry in *Poems to the Memory of that Incomparable Poet Edmond Waller* (1688), Rymer repeating in 1692 that the language 'did not shine and sparkle till Mr. Waller set it running' (*Critical Works* (1956), 127).

In the 'Preface' to *The Second Part of Mr. Waller's Poems* (1690), Francis Atterbury described W as 'the Parent of *English* Verse, and the first that shew'd us our Tongue had Beauty and Numbers in it . . . He undoubtedly stands first in the List of Refiners . . . he sought out, in this flowing Tongue of ours, what parts would last, and be of standing use and ornament' (sigg. A3–A5)'. 'Life' (1711), pp. lxxv–lxxvi, described W as 'certainly the Father of our *English Versification*', who found our poetry 'almost as rude as the Ore in the Mine' but left it 'refin'd and polish'd'. *BB*, vi (ii). 4113, had also emphasized W's contribution to English versification.

143. For W and Fairfax, see **5**, **81** above and **154** below, and for SJ's knowledge of Elizabethan literature, see W. B. C. Watkins, *J and English Poetry before 1660* (Princeton, 1936).

*Davies*: Reed explained SJ's reference to Sir John Davies's *Nosce Teipsum* (1599) in *Lives*, i (1790), 411 n. (For the spelling 'Davis' in 1783, as in 'Dryden' **356** below, see Textual Notes.) SJ had quoted Davies 486 times in the *Dict*. (increased to 508 in 1773), and three times in his notes to Shakespeare. There were several 18th-century editions of *Nosce Teipsum* and his *Poetical Works* had been published in 1773.

144. For Dryden's 'full-resounding line', see Pope, *Imit. Horace, Ep. II. i.* (1737), l. 267, and 'Dryden' **342** and 'Pope' **333** below. Cf. SJ's contrast of Cowley's 'noble lines' with W's 'feeble care' in 'Cowley' **185** above.

The antithesis of W's 'sweetness' and Denham's 'strength' (see 'Denham' **34** above) became a commonplace. Cf. Dryden, *Of Dramatic Poesy* (1668): 'nothing so even, so sweet, and flowing as Mr. Waller; nothing so majestic, so correct as Sir John Denham'; and his earlier reference (1664) to 'This sweetness of Mr. Waller's lyric poesy' (Watson, i. 24, 7). Dennis (1711) referred to 'the Sweetness of *Waller*, or the Force of *Denham*' (*Works*, i. 408). Pope praised 'the *Easie Vigor* of a Line | Where *Denham's* Strength, and *Waller's* Sweetness join' in *Essay on Criticism* (1711), ll. 360–1, and he discussed W's 'sweetness' again in 1730 (Spence, i. 176). Dick Minim predictably described W and Denham as 'the first reformers of English numbers': 'if Waller could have obtained the strength of Denham, or Denham the sweetness of Waller, there had been nothing to complete a poet' (*Idler* 60 (1759); *YW*, ii. 186).

**145.** For 'expletives', see Cowley **189** and n. above.

In the second sentence 'used' (1779–83), echoing 'uses' earlier in the sentence, has been emended to 'lived', a correction suggested by Nichols in the proofs to which SJ did not respond: see Textual Notes.

**146.** For 'rhymes', see 'Cowley' **187** and n. above. W twice rhymed 'know' with 'so' in 'In Answer of Sir John Suckling's Verses', ll. 27–36, and elsewhere used 'so' as a rhyme some twenty times.

Atterbury, *The Second Part of Mr. Waller's Poems* (1690), had claimed that, 'since the stress of our Verse commonly lies upon the last Syllable, you'll hardly ever find him using a word of no force there', and praised his rhymes: 'He had a fine Ear, and knew how quickly that Sense was cloy'd by the same round of chiming Words still returning upon it' (sigg. A6ᵛ–A7).

**147.** For Katherine Philips, see **102** and n. above, and, for her translation of *Pompey*, 'Roscommon' **36–8** and nn. above. Both Fenton (1729 edn.), 'Observations', p. lxxxix, and *BB*, vi (ii). 4114 n., quoted her criticism of W's 'frequent double rhymes in an heroic Poem'. For 'double rhymes', see 'Pope' **377** and n., and for the discussion of 'minute and particular' faults, 'Pope' **384** and n. below.

**148.** *obsolete termination*: see e.g. *Poems*, i.1, 23, 50. Dennis stated in 1693 that W 'was the first who began to contract our Participles which end in *ed*; which being not contracted, exceedingly weaken a Verse' (*Works*, i. 26).

**149.** For triplets and alexandrines, see 'Cowley' **196, 199** and nn. above. Five triplets are signalled by marginal brackets in Fenton (1729 edn.), 85, 89, 243, 249, 365.

**150.** For 'elegance', see also 'Pope' **350** n. below. In contrast, Milton 'sometimes descends to the elegant, but his element is the great' ('Milton' **230** above).

For the 'pathetic' and the 'sublime, see also 'Cowley' **57–8** and nn. above, and the opposition in **107** above of 'grand . . . images' and 'magnanimity' to 'soft images' and 'beauty'. SJ in effect concurs with Hume's opinion that W's poems have 'many faults' and 'but feeble and superficial beauties', and that, for all his 'Gaiety, wit, and ingenuity', 'They aspire not to the sublime; still less to the pathetic' (*History of Great Britain*, ii (1757), 126), a judgement echoed in *Anecdotes of Polite Literature* (1764), ii. 116–17. Stockdale, 'Life' (1772), p. lxiv, had claimed, however, that W's 'music seldom reaches the sublime, tho' frequently plaintive with tenderness'.

*that grace of novelty*: for similar comments on its subsequent disappearance, see 'Dryden' **196** and 'Addison' **160** below.

151. *Alliteration*: see 'Life' (1711), p. lxxix. Erythraeus was a 16th-century Venetian Latinist, cited by William Benson in *Letters Concerning Poetical Translations* (1739), 18–19, 50–7, in an admiring discussion of alliteration in Spenser, Fairfax, and other poets. Defining 'Alliteration' in 1755, SJ had stated: 'Of what the critics call the *alliteration*, or beginning of several words in the same verse with the same letter, there are instances in the oldest and best writers' (*Dict.*), quoting *Paradise Lost*, VII. 471. In 1765 he cited George Gascoigne's 'Certayne Notes of Instruction' in *Posies* (1575), in a note to *Midsummer Night's Dream*, v. i. 145 (*YW*, vii. 158), with a cross-reference to I. ii. 31–8, the passage he has in mind here. He added the reference to Holofernes in *Love's Labour's Lost*, IV. ii. 105–18, in 1783, perhaps prompted by Steevens or Malone (see Textual Notes). SJ's only other reference to alliteration in the *Lives* in 'Gray' **44** below is hostile.

   As well as Benson, 'late critics' who discussed alliteration included Shiels, *Lives*, v. 299–300, who quoted Holofernes, referred to Chaucer, Langland, and Spenser, and described it as an 'affectation' in recent poetry; *The Connoisseur* 83 (1755), which considered it a 'poetical trick'; Goldsmith, who deplored it as a recent fashion in the *Weekly Mag.* (12 Jan. 1760) and the dedication to *The Traveller* (1765) (*Coll. Works*, iii. 53, iv. 247); and Shenstone, who also referred to it as a fashionable device which has 'probably had it's day' in *Works* (1764), ii. 14, 181. Admitting that some critics view alliteration with 'the utmost contempt and abhorrence' as 'finical' and 'offensive', Beattie pointed out that it is found in English poetry as early as Langland and may be 'naturally' pleasing to 'the people' (*Essays* (Edinburgh, 1776), 627 n.). For Thomas Percy's interest in alliteration in medieval, Welsh, and Norse poetry, see his *Reliques* (1765), ii. 260–70, and *Percy Corresp.*, iii (Warton). 12–16, and *Percy Corresp.*, v (Evans). 61–2, 64–8.

152. For SJ's usual dislike of 'old mythology' in modern poetry, see 'Butler' **41** and n. above, and cf. **124a** above.

   Cf. Cowley's preface to *Poems* (1656): 'though those mad stories of the *Gods* and *Heroes*, seem in themselves so ridiculous; yet they were then the *whole Body* (or rather *Chaos*) of the *Theologie* of those times . . . There was no other *Religion*, and therefore *that* was better than *none at all*' (*Poems*, ed. A. R. Waller, 13). Parnell discussed the problem of the ancient 'Theology' in his 'Essay on Homer' in Pope's *Iliad* (1715): 'His Books are now no longer the Scheme of a living Religion, but become the Register of one of former Times' (*TE*, vii. 65). Cf. also *Life*, iii. 10. Stockdale, 'Life' (1772), p. lvii, may have provoked SJ's renewed attack on mythology here by suggesting that the 'gay theology of the heathens' was better suited to poetical imagination than 'our purer religion'.

   SJ alludes finally to 'To the King', appended to 'Instructions to a Painter', ll. 315–16: 'His club Alcides, Phoebus has his bow, | Jove has his thunder, and your navy you' (*Poems*, ii. 59).

153. Although Hill (1905) cited the anecdote of Tasso and Guarini from Giuseppe Baretti's *The Italian Library* (1757), 120, SJ could also have met it in Langbaine, *Account of the English Dramatick Poets* (1691), 193 (see 'Otway' **5** and n. above). For their pastoral dramas, see 'Roscommon' **36** above, and 'Gay' **32** and 'A. Philips' **16** below. Dryden stated in 1697 that Tasso's *Aminta* 'infinitely transcends Guarini's *Pastor Fido* as having more of nature in it, and being almost

wholly clear from the wretched affectation of learning' (Watson, ii. 220). SJ took
the epigraph to *Idler* 71 (1759) from *Aminta* (*YW*, ii. 220).

**154.** SJ wrote against **154** in the proofs: 'This should be more distinguished. It is not a
continuation of what goes before but a preface to what follows' (see Textual
Notes).

For SJ's decision to append this extract from Edward Fairfax's translation from
Tasso, *Godfrey of Bulloigne, or the Recoverie of Jerusalem* (1600), VII. 1–18, see
headnote above, and cf. **5, 81, 143** above. He may have been prompted to do so by
Stockdale's suggestion in W's *Works* (1772), p. lxiv, that comparison with Fairfax
would make clear 'in how rude a state English verse was when Waller began to
write, and what advantage it received from him', even if more elegant language
and more harmonious numbers than W's would now be expected from 'a middling
poet in this age of refinement'. SJ's real purpose may in fact have been to reinforce
his account of the progress of English versification towards 'correctness' in the
hands of Dryden and Pope: see 'Cowley' **185–99** and n. above. Atterbury had in
effect made the same point with reference to Spenser in 1690 (see **142** n. above):
''tis a surprizing Reflection, that between what *Spencer* wrote last, and *Waller* first,
there should not be much above twenty years distance: and yet the one's Language, like the Money of that time, is as currant now as ever; whilst the other's
words are like old Coyns, one must go to an Antiquary to understand their true
meaning and value' (sig. A4ᵛ).

SJ's friend William Collins (q.v. below) was an ardent admirer of Tasso and
Fairfax in the 1740s (see *Poems of Gray, Collins and Goldsmith* (1969), 500, 516–18,
565–6), and SJ himself once planned an edition of Fairfax's translation (*Life*, iv.
381 n.). He included some 250 quotations from it in the *Dict.* (1755) (increased to
258 in 1773). His extract here may have prompted Joseph Warton, *Essay*, ii (1782),
353–4, to assert the superiority of Spenser's 'musical and mellifluous versification'
to that of Fairfax, 'who is so frequently mentioned as the greatest improver of the
harmony of our language'.

SJ wrote the dedication to the translation of *Jerusalem Delivered* (2 vols., 1763)
by John Hoole (1727–1803), whose preface quotes SJ's opinion that a new
translation was 'a work that may very justly merit the attention of the English
reader'. For Hoole's presentation copy to SJ in the Hyde Collection, see Fleeman,
*Handlist* (1984), 23. SJ's good opinion of Hoole's translation was not shared by
Charles Lamb, who told Coleridge, 5 Feb. 1797, that, after reading the 'most
delicious specimen' of Fairfax quoted in SJ's 'Waller', Hoole seemed 'more vapid
than smallest small beer' (*Letters*, ed. E. V. Lucas (1935), i. 93–4). Hoole had been
Principal Auditor of the India House where Lamb also worked: see also **85** n.
above.


## JOHN POMFRET (1667–1702)

**Composition.** SJ does not refer to 'Pomfret', and there is no evidence for dating it. It
was presumably written late in 1778 or early 1779, and evidently printed in the same
sheet as 'King' (*Bibliography*, ii. 1356). P was included in *Eng. Poets* (1779) on SJ's
recommendation (see 'Watts' **1** and n. below).

**Sources.** Most of the information in Jacob, ii. 140–1, was inaccurate, and both *GD* and *BB* ignored P. In 1 below SJ appears to identify his main source as 'Some Account of Mr. Pomfret, and his Writings' by 'Philalethes', added to P's *Poems upon Several Occasions* (6th edn., 1724), but this had also been the source for Shiels, *Lives*, iii. 218–27. P is one of the eight poets (of fifty-two in *Eng. Poets*) not quoted in the *Dict.*

**Publication.** *Prefaces*, vol. iv (31 Mar. 1779). There are no proofs.

**Modern Sources:**
G. Baumann, *Leben und Dichtungen des Rev. JP* (Erlangen, 1931)
D. Hipwell, 'Rev. JP (1667–1702), Poet', *N & Q*, 8th ser. 2 (1892), 27
M. Kallich, 'The Choice by JP: A Modern Criticism', *Enlightenment Essays*, 6 (1975), 12–18

1. P was the son of Thomas and Catherine Pomfret. His father was Vicar of Luton, Bedfordshire, 1666–79, Rector of Maulden, 8 miles south of Bedford, 1683–94, and Prebendary of Lincoln from 1685 until his death in 1705. P was educated at Bedford School, entered Queen's College, Cambridge, 27 Nov. 1680, BA 1684/5, MA 1698 (Venn, *Alumni Cantab. (to 1751)*, iii. 377). He succeeded his father as Curate (1687) and then Rector (1695) of Maulden, and shortly before his death became Rector of Milbrook near Maulden (1702).

   Dr Henry Compton was Bishop of London 1676–1713. The problem arose from P's description of his pleasure in the company of an idealized woman friend in *The Choice*, ll. 98–139, and his later statement that 'I'd have no wife' (l. 157). For replies celebrating the joys of marriage, see *The Virtuous Wife . . . An Answer to The Choice* (1700) ('Reading Good Books, and Needle–work, should be | Her whole Diversion and Felicity', 4), and '*The* CHOICE: *On the Sight of a Poem Call'd* The Choice, *wherein were these Words* [But no Wife]', in *Oxford and Cambridge Miscellany Poems* [1708], 272–4.

2. P married Elizabeth Wingate, 13 Sept. 1692, at Luton. Their only surviving son, John (1702–51), became Rouge Croix Pursuivant of Arms in 1725. SJ's essays often describe 'men who plan schemes of life', and at the end of *Rasselas* the characters are still diverting themselves 'with various schemes of happiness which each of them had formed' (*YW*, xvi. 175).

3. P in fact died in 1702 and was buried at Maulden on 1 Dec. 1702. The incorrect date derives from 'Philalethes' and Shiels.

4. Although many accounts of P (e.g. *NCBEL*, ii. 564) date the first edition of his *Poems* in 1699, such a volume seems to be a 'ghost', its existence perhaps suggested by the date '1699' added to P's 'Preface' in posthumous editions of his *Poems*. The 'Preface' is undated in his *Miscellany Poems* (1702; 2nd edn., 1707), which appears to be his first collection. He had previously published *The Choice. A Poem. By a Person of Quality* (1700 for Dec. 1699), *Reason: A Poem* (1700), and *Two Love Poems* (1701).

4–6. Although he does not invoke here 'the common reader', SJ's references to 'common notions' and 'common expectations' in 5 and the 'many' in 6, indicate that he has in mind such an unaffected but also unambitious reader in his remarks on P's popularity: see 'Cowley' **65** and n. above. Deference to such readers explains his suggestion that P be included in *Eng. Poets* (1779).

5. Ten editions of P's *Poems* had appeared by 1740 (when William Strahan's ledgers record a printing of 3,000 copies of the 10th), as well as numerous piracies. There were at least fourteen further editions by 1800. SJ told Strahan, 20 Jan. 1759, that he had originally intended to entitle *Rasselas* 'The choice of Life or The History of —— Prince of Abissinia' (*Letters*, i. 178).

Jacob, ii. 141, had praised *The Choice*'s 'very easy familiar Style' and described it as already 'universally admir'd for its great Variety and Popularity'. But SJ's remarks recall the description in Shiels, *Lives*, iii. 218, of P's popularity with 'common readers of poetry' and 'people of inferior life', among whom it was as fashionable to own P's *Poems* as for 'persons of taste' to own Pope's works. His topics had wide appeal, his versification was musical, 'and as there is little force of thinking in his writings, they are level to the capacities of those who admire them'. By 1782 John Scott found SJ's respect for 'the Grub–street Pomfret' 'amazing' (to Beattie, 10 May 1782, in Sir William Forbes, *Life and Writings of James Beattie* (Edinburgh, 1806), ii. 111). Hawkins, *J's Works* (1787), ii. 279 n., was also dismissive: 'Of Pomfret's Poems, few have ever been readers but the illiterate, and such as are delighted with trite sentiments and vulgar imagery; and as these are the most numerous of those that can read at all, it is no wonder that by such they have been often perused.' The *Monthly Review*, NS 4 (1791), 340–1, commented that P 'is only esteemed a poet by common capacities, to the level of which his thoughts are expressed'. In 1807 Robert Southey was still asking: 'Why is Pomfret the most popular of the English Poets? the fact is certain and the solution would be useful' (*Specimens of the Later English Poets*, i. 91).

P enjoyed little reputation among sophisticated readers. Unaware that P's popularity was posthumous, Swift wrote in his 'Thoughts on Various Subjects': 'At a Bookseller's Shop, some Time ago, I saw a Book with this Title; *Poems by the Author of the Choice.* Not enduring to read a dozen Lines, I asked the Company with me, whether they had ever seen the Book, or heard of the Poem from whence the Author denominated himself? They were all as ignorant as I. But I find it common with these small Dealers in Wit and Learning, to give themselves a Title from their first Adventure, as *Don Quixot* usually did from his last. This ariseth from that great Importance which every Man supposeth himself to be of' (*Prose Writings*, iv. 249–50). For the text of *The Choice* see *New Oxford Book of C18 Verse* (1984), 1–4.

6. *volubility*: '2. . . . fluency of speech' (*Dict.*).

Cf. 'Milton' **224** above: 'since the end of poetry is pleasure, that cannot be unpoetical with which all are pleased.'

## CHARLES SACKVILLE, EARL OF DORSET (1643–1706)

**Composition.** SJ does not mention 'Dorset', but the fact that it was printed together with 'Halifax', 'Stepney', and 'Walsh', and at about the same time as 'Otway' (see 'Publication' below), suggests that he wrote it in late 1778 or early 1779.

**Sources.** SJ follows closely the information, and sometimes the phrasing, of Philip Nichols's article in *BB*, v (1760), 3557–9, which cites Wood, Burnet, Prior, Shiels, and other sources, and is much superior to both Jacob and Shiels. Although *GD* had included no article on Dorset himself, his public career is summarized in a note to the account of an ancestor at iv (1736), 644 n. For exceptions to SJ's reliance on *BB*, see **4, 6, 12** below. SJ had quoted D some seventeen times in the *Dict*.

**Publication.** In *Prefaces*, vol. iv (31 Mar. 1779). There is a complete set of proofs in the Forster Collection. In the lower margin of p. 1 of the proofs, Nichols has written: 'A Revise directly | Get Otway pulled again'.

**Modern Sources:**

S. Archer, 'The Persons in *An Essay of Dramatic Poesy*', *Papers on Lang. and Lit.* 2 (1966), 305–14

H. A. Bagley, 'A Checklist of the Poems of Charles Sackville, Sixth Earl of Dorset and Middlesex', *MLN* 47 (1932), 454–61

B. Harris, *Charles Sackville, Sixth Earl of Dorset* (Urbana, Ill., 1940)

B. Harris (ed.), *Poems by Charles Sackville, Earl of Dorset* (New York, 1979)

C. J. Phillips, *History of the Sackville Family* (2 vols., 1930), i. 436–93

J. P. Vander Motten, 'The Earl of Dorset and William Killigrew', *N & Q* 222 (1977), 131–3

J. H. Wilson, *The Court Wits of the Restoration* (Princeton, 1948)

1. Prior's 'encomiastick character' (see 'Dryden' **137**, 'Smith' **22**, and 'Prior' **18** below) appeared in the dedication of his *Poems* (1709) to D's son Lionel, Earl of Dorset (*Lit. Works*, i. 248–56). *BB*, v. 3558–9, praised and quoted it, and SJ had cited it in *Rambler* 11 (1750) (*YW*, iii. 61).

   SJ's revision of **1** in 1783 (see Textual Notes) obscured his original explanation that he had not transcribed Prior's 'character', because it could be consulted in his poems in the *Eng. Poets* (1779), vol. xxxii.

2. SJ follows *BB*, but D was in fact born 24 Jan. 1643 and attended Westminster School 1657–8, before travelling to Italy in Dec. 1658. He was MP for East Grinstead, Sussex, 1661–75, and, even in his 'riotous' years, held a number of public appointments traditional in his family (Harris, *Sackville*, 14 n., 20). For the dissolute wits of the Restoration court, see 'Rochester' **4** and n. above.

3. D was styled Lord Buckhurst 1652–75. For this notorious 'frolick' at the Cock Tavern on 16 June 1663, SJ evidently consulted Wood, ii. 1100, at first hand (see **4** below), but is squeamish about his information that the rakes, 'putting down their Breeches . . . excrementiz'd in the Street', before Sir Charles Sedley (1639?–1701) stripped himself naked on a balcony. According to Pepys's *Diary* (1 July 1663), Sedley, 'with a thousand people standing underneath to see and hear him', acted 'all the postures of lust and buggery', preached a mountebank sermon offering for sale 'such a powder as should make all the cunts in town run after him', and 'washed his prick' in a glass of wine 'and then drank it off'. For other versions of the incident, see Harris, *Sackville*, 27–9, and Wilson, *Court Wits*, 40–1.

4. According to accounts of the trial, Sedley was fined 2,000 marks, committed without bail for a week, and bound over for a year (Wilson, *Court Wits*, 40). (Pepys reported that Sedley had been bound over on a recognizance of £5,000.) The sentence about Sedley and Killigrew derives directly from Wood, since *BB* ignored the matter, and Shiels, *Lives*, iii. 96–7 (under 'Sedley'), evidently misunderstood it. Henry Killigrew (1637–1705) was page of honour to Charles II 1661,

and Groom of the Bedchamber to the Duke of York 1662. 'Lisedeius' in Dryden's *Essay on Dramatic Poesy* (1667) has usually been identified as Sedley, to whom Dryden also dedicated *The Assignation* (1673). Jacob, i. 242, later described him as 'deservedly rank'd in the first Class of men of Wit and Gallantry', and as 'every thing that an *English* Gentleman could be'.

5. The English fleet, commanded by James, Duke of York, as Lord High Admiral, the Earl of Sandwich, and Prince Rupert, defeated the Dutch, under Jacob van Opdam, off Lowestoft on 3 June 1665. Pepys at first reported much heavier Dutch losses, describing it as 'A great victory, never known in the world' (8 June 1665).

6. SJ's scepticism about Prior's 'splendid story' that D wrote his 'celebrated song' on the evening before the battle (*Lit. Works*, i. 251: see 1 above) is justified. It had in fact been published by 2 Jan. 1665, five months earlier: see Archer, 'Persons', 306. Cf. 'Milton' **105** and n. above.

   SJ had met John Boyle (1707–62), 5th Earl of Orrery, by 1752: see *Letters*, i. 51 n., 62–3, *Life*, ii. 129, iii. 183, iv. 7–18, v. 237–9 (where SJ describes him as 'a feeble-minded man', whose 'conversation was like his writings, neat and elegant, but without strength'), *Bibliography*, i. 401–2, and P. J. Korshin, 'J and the Earl of Orrery', in W. H. Bond (ed.), *Eighteenth-Century Studies in Honor of Donald F. Hyde*. (New York, 1970), 29–43. SJ's phrase 'hereditary intelligence' refers to the fact that Orrery's great-grandfather, Roger Boyle, 1st Earl of Orrery (1621–79), had been a prominent soldier and dramatist. For other anecdotal information derived from Orrery, see 'Congreve' **2** n., **7** n., 'Fenton' **4, 19**, 'Swift' **65, 123**, and 'Pope' **3** n., **263** below.

   *substract*: under 'Subtract' in the *Dict.* SJ explained that 'They who derive it from the Latin write *subtract*; those who know the French original, write *substract*, which is the common word'.

7. D became a Gentleman of the Bedchamber in Dec. 1669 with a pension of £1,000 p.a. (allegedly on relinquishing Nell Gwyn to Charles II), and visited France on royal business three times in 1669–70 (Harris, *Sackville*, 36–44).

8. D inherited his title and an estate of £3,000 from Lionel (not James) Cranfield, 3rd Earl of Middlesex, in 1674, and succeeded his father as Earl of Dorset in 1677.

9. D in fact married (1) Mary Bagot (d. 1679), widow of the Earl of Falmouth, in June 1674; (2) Mary Compton (d. 1691), daughter of the Earl of Northampton, in 1685; (3) Anne Roche in Oct. 1704.

10. Although D bore the Queen's sceptre at James II's coronation in 1685, he played little part in politics before the King's attempt to repeal the Test Act and Penal Laws. D had been Lord-Lieutenant of Sussex since 1670, but was dismissed in 1688. The seven bishops were tried for seditious libel in June 1688 (Harris, *Sackville*, 114–15). For other references to the turbulent reign of James II, see 'Roscommon' **19** and n. above.

11. D was a member of the Council between James II's flight in Dec. 1688 and Feb. 1689, when the crown was offered to William and Mary. On 26 Nov. 1688 Princess (later Queen) Anne had fled the palace with D and Henry Compton, Bishop of London (Harris, *Sackville*, 116–17; E. Gregg, *Queen Anne* (1980), 65).

12. D became Lord Chamberlain of the Household on 14 Feb. 1689, retaining the post until 1697. He received the Order of the Garter in 1692. He was later criticized for

indolence and for selling places at court (Harris, *Sackville*, 132–5; *POAS*, v. 100–12, 142–3).

In Jan. 1691 fog off the Dutch coast prevented William III's ship from entering harbour, and an attempt to land in an open boat almost led to disaster (Harris, *Sackville*, 149). Both Shiels, *Lives*, iv. 120, and *BB*, v. 3558 n., stated that the ordeal lasted twenty-two hours, on the authority of Burnet. SJ must have checked Burnet, *History*, ii (1734), 71–2, at first hand, and found that he in fact wrote 'above sixteen hours'.

Although SJ's final sentence follows *BB*, v. 3558, there is no evidence that D's health declined soon after this incident. He spent his last years at Bath, where he died on 29 Jan. 1706. When D's family sent Prior to Bath to investigate D's mental state, Prior allegedly reported that he 'is certainly greatly declined in his understanding, but he drivels so much better sense even now than any other man can talk, that you must not call me into court as a witness to prove him an idiot' (Spence, i. 200–1 n.). For Pope's epitaph (*c.*1731) on D, see 'Pope' **387–94** below.

13. Authors patronized by D included Butler, Dryden, Lee, Sprat, Prior, Congreve, Addison, Stepney, and Halifax. There were many tributes to his 'elegance and judgement' (see Harris, *Sackville*, 173–214, 247–51). Literary works dedicated to him included Etherege's *The Comical Revenge* (1664), Thomas D'Urfey's *Don Quixote*, Pt. II (1694) (describing him as 'Wits Dictator and Mecaenas'), Samuel Cobb's *Poetae Britannici* (1700), 6 (as 'Maecenas' again), Congreve's *Love for Love* (1695) (referring to D's *'Monarchy* in *Poetry*' and 'Universal Patronage', a phrase echoed by SJ in 'Halifax' **5** and misapplied in 'A. Philips' **3** below). See also Prior's dedication (1709) to D's son (cf. **1** above), and *Spectator* 85 (7 June 1711), in which Addison attributed to D 'the greatest Wit tempered with the greatest Candour', and described him as 'one of the finest Critics as well as the best Poets of his Age'. Swift believed that D's supposed learning was in fact 'small or none' (*Prose Writings*, v. 258).

*BB* quoted Rochester's remark to the King, reported by Prior in 1709, 'That He did not know how it was, but my Lord DORSET might do any thing, yet was never to Blame' (*Lit. Works*, i. 253).

14. Addison, Dennis, Congreve, and Pope were among those who praised D's satire (Harris, *Sackville*, 230 ff.). For other poetic reputations influenced by extra-literary factors, see 'Halifax' **15**, 'Sheffield' **22**, and 'Granville' **24** below, and cf. 'Savage' **100, 143** below. Under 'Woeful' in the *Dict.* SJ quoted Pope, *Essay on Criticism*, ll. 420–1: 'But let a *Lord* once own the *happy Lines*, | How the *Wit brightens*! How the *Style refines*!' Pope in fact said in 1734 that D was 'the best of all those writers' (the Restoration satirists), and in 1743 that 'Lord Dorset's things are all excellent in their way, for one should consider his pieces as a sort of epigrams. Wit was his talent' (Spence, i. 202, 200).

For D's generosity to Dryden, see 'Dryden' **137** below, Prior, *Lit. Works*, i. 254, and J. Winn, *John Dryden and his World* (1987), 434–5, 457–8; and for Dryden's tendency to flatter D, see 'Dryden' **88, 170, 172** below. SJ's quotation adapts Dryden's 'Discourse of the Original and Progress of Satire' (1693), addressed to D (Watson, ii. 81). Dryden had earlier dedicated *Of Dramatick Poesy: An Essay* (1668) to D, identified by Prior and most later commentators as 'Eugenius' in the dialogue.

In the twenty-five pages of verse by D in *Eng. Poets* (1779), xi. 187–211, the celebrated 'Song' (sixty-six lines) was in fact shorter than 'The Antiquated Coquet' (ninety-six lines). Some more substantial satires have since been attributed to D: see *POAS*, ii. 167–75, iv. 189–214. For a similar reaction to the small output of a titled poet, see 'Roscommon' **23** above.

15. SJ grants D's verse at least some 'vigour' and 'fertility'. He refers to 'To Mr. Edward Howard, on his Incomparable, Incomprehensible Poem called "The British Princes"', and to Pope's imitations of D's 'On the Countess of Dorchester' ('Tell me, Dorinda, why so gay') in his 'Artemisia' and 'Phryne' (published 1727): see Pope, *TE*, vi. 48–5, and, for an earlier imitation of D's style, vi. 15–17.


## GEORGE STEPNEY (1663–1707)

**Composition.** In an undated note, presumably in late 1778 or early 1779, SJ told Nichols: 'I have sent Stepney's Epitaph. Let me have the revises as soon as can be' (*Letters*, iii. 146). By then he had obviously already corrected the first proofs. It was printed at about the same time as 'Dorset', 'Halifax', and 'Walsh' (Fleeman (1962), 228 n.; *Bibliography*, ii. 1355–6). There is an apparent cross-reference in **3** below to 'Smith' (q.v. below), which SJ probably wrote in Feb. 1779.

**Sources.** *GD* and *BB* ignored S. The information in **1–2** and the direct reference in **2** below indicate that SJ's source was Jacob, ii. 205–7, rather than Shiels, *Lives*, iv. 72–6. There are fourteen quotations from S in the *Dict.*

**Publication.** In *Prefaces*, vol. iv (31 Mar. 1779). There are no proofs.

**Modern Sources:**
C. K. Eves, *Matthew Prior: Poet and Diplomatist* (New York, 1939)
W. Graham (ed.), *Letters of Joseph Addison* (Oxford, 1941)
E. K. Halbeisen, 'GS: A Calendar', *N & Q* 159 (1930), 93–6, 114–17
R. Harrison, *Notices of the Stepney Family* (1870), 9, 22–8
D. Hopkins, 'Charles Montague, GS, and Dryden's *Metamorphoses*', *RES* 51 (2000), 83–9
D. B. Horn, *British Diplomatic Representatives 1689–1789* (1932)
S. Spens, *GS, 1663–1707: Diplomat and Poet* (Cambridge, 1997)
H. T. Swedenborg, 'GS, My Lord Dorset's Boy', *HLQ* 10 (1946), 1–33
T. and E. Swedenborg (eds.), *S's Translation of the Eighth Satire of Juvenal* (Berkeley, 1948)

1. S's date of birth and the misspelling of Prendergast derive from Jacob, ii. 205–7. (Shiels, *Lives*, iv. 72, 75, gave instead the wildly inaccurate date of 1693 and 'Pindigrast', but with 'Pendegrast' in the epitaph.) For the Stepneys of Prendergast see Cokayne, *Baronetage*, i. 178–9.

S was the son of George Stepney (d. 1669) and Jane Moseley (d. 1694). His father became Groom of the Chamber to Charles II, purchasing this position in 1664 for £300. Chalmers, *English Poets* (1810), viii. 349 n., noted William Cole's suggestion that S's father had been a grocer, and S. Spens, *GS*, 7, confirms that he had been apprenticed to the Grocers' Company of the City of London, a fact S himself was anxious to conceal (cf. SJ's comments in 'Prior' 1 below).

S entered Westminster School in 1676 and Trinity College, Cambridge, in June 1682 (Scholar 1683, BA 1685/6, MA 1689, Fellow 6 July 1689). He was friendly at both Westminster and Cambridge with Charles Montagu (see 'Halifax' 2 below) and Matthew Prior, whom SJ does not link with S. The contributions of Montagu and S to the Cambridge verses on the death of Charles II in 1685 attracted the attention of the Earl of Dorset: cf. 'Halifax' 5 below. (For SJ's repeated error over Dorset's title, see 'Dryden' 27 n. below.) S at first preferred a 'retir'd life' but, with Montagu and Prior, was later known as one of 'my Lord Dorset's boys'.

2. SJ follows closely Jacob's list (ii. 205) of S's diplomatic appointments at various German courts during the Nine Years War, and from 1701 in Vienna, during the first years of the War of the Spanish Succession. The exhaustive account of S's career by Spens (GS) reveals that his movements round Europe and dates of appointment were even more complicated. His career began as secretary to Sir Peter Wyche, English Resident in Hamburg, 1686–9, followed by a period in Berlin from 1690 as secretary to James Johnston, British Envoy to the Elector of Brandenburg (Spens, GS 32–41). Later in the 1690s S held posts at the imperial court in Vienna, and in Dresden, Frankfurt, and The Hague, and from 1701 was based in Vienna. In 1706–7 he was in the Netherlands. For 'the grand alliance' against Louis XIV, see also 'Prior' 6 below. and for earlier accounts of S's career, see Halbeisen, 'GS' and Horn, *Representatives*. S's voluminous diplomatic correspondence survives in the Public Record Office, the British Library, and the Osborn Collection in the Beinecke Library at Yale, and elsewhere.

For S's own pessimistic view of his career prospects, whether as a diplomat or in England, see his letter to Sir William Trumbull (cf. 'Pope' 23 and n. below) in July 1695, quoted by J. Black, *British Diplomats and Diplomacy 1688–1800* (Exeter, 2001), 49–50. Bernard Connor, *History of Poland* (2 vols., 1698), i. 301, mentioned S's 'Experience in Foreign Affairs, and . . . undoubted Knowledg in Politicks'. John Macky, *Memoirs of Secret Service* (1733), 142, also testified to his diplomatic and linguistic expertise ('No *Englishman* ever understood the Affairs of *Germany* so well, and few *Germans* better'), but Swift mocked Macky's claims for S's verse, which he considered 'Scarse of a third rate' (*Prose Writings*, v. 260). S's appointment as a Commissioner of Trade (1697–1700) brought him £1,000 p.a. (Spens, GS, 178–85).

S died on 15 Sept. 1707. Addison mentioned on 29 Aug. that he had returned to England after being been taken ill in Brussels, on 23 Sept. that he had been 'buried last night in Westminster', and on 26 Sept. that he had left £50 to Prior and 'a Golden Cup and 100. Tomes of his Library' to Lord Halifax: 'His Estate is divided between his two sisters, ye best part of it lies in the Treasury wch owes him Seav'n thousand pound' (i.e. in arrears of salary) (*Letters* (1941), 75–8; see also Spens, GS, 316–19).

As SJ notes, the Latin epitaph derives from Jacob. For S's monument, with a transcription and translation, see John Dart, *Westmonasterium* [1742], ii. 82–4. While helping to amplify SJ's brief biography (of which it occupies more than a third), the elaborate epitaph only underlines S's faded reputation (cf. 'J. Philips' 8 and 'Prior' 44 below).

3. The phrase 'made grey authors blush' in SJ's first sentence alludes to William Oldisworth's comment (1714) on Edmund Smith's 'junior compositions', quoted in 'Smith' 6 below. For SJ's suspicion of 'wonders', see 'Cowley' 5 and n. above.

S's early Latin verse appeared in the Cambridge collections on the marriage of Princess Anne (1683) and the death of Charles II (1685). Elsewhere SJ tends to emphasize the envy and enmity facing a new author, as in *Rambler* 2 (24 Mar. 1750): 'Some are too indolent to read any thing, till its reputation is established; others too envious to promote that fame, which gives them pain by its increase. What is new is opposed, because most are unwilling to be taught' (*YW*, iii. 14). See also *Ramblers* 16 (1750), 146 (1751), and 'Pope' 174–6 below.

4. S contributed 'Satire VIII' to Dryden's *Juvenal* (1693): see 'Dryden' 140, 299 below. S's MS was extensively revised before publication, presumably (as Pope believed) by Dryden himself: see the edition by T. and E. Swedenborg (1948). S subscribed to one of the engraved plates (no. 72) in Dryden's *Works of Virgil* (1697). For his relations with Dryden, see Hopkins, 'Montague', 83–9.

A few of S's poems appeared separately in the 1690s, including *An Epistle to Charles Montagu* (1691) and a *Poem* (1695) on the death of Queen Mary (see 'Prior' 8–9 and n. below); and others in such collections as Tonson's *Miscellany Poems* (1684), *Examen Poeticum* (1693), Gildon's *A New Collection of Poems* (1701), *A New Miscellany* (1701), and *Oxford and Cambridge Miscellany Poems* [1708]. For a revealing letter by S in Feb. 1695 about his dealings with Tonson and Dryden, and the fact that he had written his *Poem* on the death of Queen Mary at the 'command' of Sir William Trumbull, one of the Secretaries of State, see J. Barnard, 'Dryden, Tonson, and *Virgil*', in P. Hammond and D. Hopkins (eds.), *John Dryden: Tercentenary Essays* (Oxford, 2000), 205–6, and cf. 189–90. For an earlier account of this letter and for S's later membership of the Whig Kit-Cat Club, see also K. M. Lynch, *Jacob Tonson, Kit-Cat Publisher* (Knoxville, Tenn., 1971), 42–5, 106–7.

Although S's verse attracted little comment after his death, Pope's mockery in *The Art of Sinking* (1728) provoked a defence of its 'very genteel Air, and handsome Turn of Thinking' in *Characters of the Times* (1728), 32–5. SJ noticeably denies S either 'grace' or 'vigour'. In *Rambler* 106 (23 Mar. 1751) he had mocked regret over the lost authors of the ancient world: 'perhaps, if we could now retrieve them, we should find them only the Granvilles, Montagues, Stepneys, and Sheffields of their time, and wonder by what infatuation or caprice they could be raised to notice' (*YW*, iv. 201). SJ may have had in mind S's recent inclusion in *The Works of the Most Celebrated Minor Poets* (1750), vol. ii.


# JOHN PHILIPS (1676–1709)

**Composition.** This was one of the last of the first series of *Prefaces* to be completed. SJ told Nichols on 1 Mar. 1779: 'I have sent Philips with his epitaphs to be inserted' (see 8 below), adding that 'The fragment of a Preface is hardly worth the impression but that we may seem to do something. It may be added to the life of Phillips' (*Letters*, iii. 152; *Bibliography*, ii. 1356). SJ was referring to Edmund Smith's MS account of P in the Bodleian Library, appended in 18–38 below, of which he may have learned during his visit to Oxford in late July 1777, when he told Henry Thrale, 'I have picked up some little information for my Lives at the library' (*Letters*, iii. 45).

SJ made some rudimentary notes about P's life on a blank page in the notebook in which he had recorded his journey to Wales in July 1774 (British Library, Add. MS 12070, fo. 23 v). This has no clear implications for the date of composition. After the Welsh journal, SJ used a single page for a diary for 5–9 Aug. 1777, but the notes on P appear after a further sixteen blank pages.

**Sources.** Accounts of P appeared in all SJ's usual sources, but the information in **1–9** (except for the two epitaphs) is compressed from Philip Nichols's effusive and wordy article in *BB*, v (1760), 3353–9. (SJ's first MS notes mentioned above may be an outline based on the *BB* article.) Whereas the article in *GD*, viii. 374–6, derived entirely from George Sewell's *Life and Character of Mr. John Philips* (1712), often prefixed to later editions of P's verse, Nichols had obtained further information at first hand from P's contemporaries. For Edmund Smith's incomplete MS account of P in **18–38** below, see 'Composition' above.

**Publication.** In *Prefaces*, vol. iv (31 Mar. 1779). There are no proofs.

**Modern Sources:**
(i) Philips
*Cyder. A Poem in Two Books*, ed. J. Goodridge and J. C. Pellicer (Cheltenham, 2001)
*Poems*, ed. M. G. Lloyd Thomas (Oxford, 1927)

(ii)
J. D. Baird, 'Whig and Tory Panegyrics: Addison's *The Campaign* and P's *Bleinheim*', *Lumen*, 16 (1997), 163–77
J. Chalker, *The English Georgic* (1969), 36–46
K. L. Cope, 'When the Past Presses the Present: Shillings, Cyder, Malts and Wine', in C. R. Kropf (ed.), *Reader Entrapment in 18th-Century Literature* (New York, 1992), 15–43
D. Griffin, 'The Bard of Cyder-Land: JP and Miltonic Imitation', *SEL* 24 (1984), 441–60
C. L. McAlister, 'JP', in *Dictionary of Literary Biography*, xcv (1990), 164–8
C. Mounsey, 'Christopher Smart's *The Hop-Garden* and JP's *Cyder*: A Battle of the Georgics?', in *BJECS* 22 (1999), 67–84
J. C. Pellicer, *JP (1676–1709): Life, Works, and Reception* (Oslo, 2002)
J. C. Pellicer, '*Cerealia* (1706): Elijah Fenton's Burlesque of Milton and Spenser in Critique of JP', *N & Q* 248 (2003), 197–201

1.  P's father (1638–84), Vicar of Bampton, Oxon., from 1669, married Mary Cooke in 1667: after his death she moved with her six sons to Hereford, where she died in 1715 (Thomas (1927 edn.), p. xii). P entered Winchester in 1691. For Sewell's biography of P see 'Sources' above: what follows derives in fact from *BB*, v. 3353, on the authority of William Oldisworth, 'his contemporary at the same school' (see 'Smith' **2** and n. below). The only other poet to whose hair SJ pays much attention is, appropriately, Milton ('the Lady of his college'): see 'Milton' **157** above.

2.  *BB* again cites Oldisworth: 'It was in these intervals chiefly, that he read Milton.'

3.  P in fact matriculated from Christ Church, Oxford, on 16 Aug. 1697. For Dr Busby, headmaster of Westminster School, see 'Dryden' **4** and n. below, and

for the school's connection with Christ Church, 'Smith' 4 and 'King' 2 below. Winchester's traditional tie was with New College: see 'Somervile' 2 below.

John Fell (1625–86), Dean of Christ Church from 1660, was succeeded by Henry Aldrich (1647–1710) in 1689. For P's praise of Aldrich, see *Cyder*, I. 613–20. Like other members of his family, P was a Nonjuror, avoiding the Oath of Allegiance, and accordingly did not obtain the usual university degrees, although Christ Church granted equivalent 'House' degrees which conferred college privileges: see Pellicer, *JP*, 29–43.

For Edmund Smith and his tragedy (1707), see 'Smith' 17 and 46–50 below. In a letter of 29 June 1704, Francis Atterbury reported a rumour from Oxford that P and Smith were the authors of *A Tale of a Tub* (1704): see his *Epistolary Correspondence*, iii (1784), 214, and 'Swift' 26–7 below. *BB*, v. 3354, mentions P's interest in medicine, as does Smith's *Poem* on P's death, l. 12. SJ ignores the long account in *BB*, v. 3359, of P's unsuccessful pursuit of the daughter of Dr Meare, the Principal of Brasenose College.

4. *The Splendid Shilling* in fact first appeared in 1701 in *A Collection of Poems* and in *A New Miscellany of Original Poems*, as 'In Imitation of Milton'. For its separate publication in 1705 see 31 below. According to Smith (see 30 below), P wrote it before the age of 20. Addison praised it in *Tatler* 249 (1710) as 'the finest Burlesque Poem in the *British* Language'.

5. *Bleinheim, A Poem* (Jan. 1705) celebrated Marlborough's victory in 1704. The 'occult opposition' was to Addison's poem on the same subject, *The Campaign* (Dec. 1704), although P is unlikely to have been responding to a poem published only some three weeks before his own: see 'Addison' 25, 130–6 below, and Baird 'Panegyrics', 163–77.

According to Sewell, some 'Great Persons' engaged P to write the poem, which brought him into favour with the Tories Robert Harley (to whom it is dedicated) and Henry St John, later Lord Bolingbroke. Although *BB* stated that P wrote it in St John's London house, *Bleinheim* (1705), 25, itself refers instead to his country seat at Bucklebury near Reading. According to his cousin William Brome in 1731, P once described how Harley had forced him to write *Bleinheim*, adding 'God forgive me also!' (Thomas (1927 edn.), p. xxii and n.). The Secret Service Receipt Books record the payment to P on 10 May 1705 of £100 royal bounty for the poem (Foxon, *English Verse*, P 226). For an anecdote purporting to illustrate Addison's jealousy of P, see Spence, i. 333.

6. For 'greatest', see 'Milton' 194 n. above.

Although P started work on *Cyder* as early as 1706, it did not in fact appear until Jan. 1708, when Jacob Tonson paid him 40 guineas for it (Thomas (1927 edn.), p. xxv). P originally intended to dedicate *Cyder* to his cousin William Brome of Ewithington, Hereford (see *Additions to the Works of Pope* (2 vols., 1776), i. 188–91), whom he mentions at i. 68. Brome recalled in 1731 that Francis Atterbury had helped P 'put [it] together' from 'little Bits of Paper' (Thomas (1927 edn.), p. xxv; see also 119–21 for a MS draft outline of the poem in the Bodleian).

Both Sewell and *BB* discussed *Cyder* as a successful imitation of Virgil's *Georgics*. SJ's use of the past tense ('long continued to be read') implies that its reputation had faded, but he is more positive in 15 below. James Beattie, *Essays*

(Edinburgh, 1776), 674–6, had recently emphasized P's inferiority to Virgil. Although Charles Dunster's elaborate *Cider, A Poem. in Two Books, by John Philips. With Notes, Provincial, Historical, and Classical* (1791) suggests that P still had admirers, the *Monthly Review*, NS 7 (1792), 21–6, questioned its usefulness.

7. Sewell, and Smith in his elegy on P (see 'Smith' **51–2** below), both mention a projected poem on 'The Last Day'. For another poem on this subject, see 'Young' **22, 155** below, and for SJ's objections to sacred poetry elsewhere, 'Waller' **135–41** and n. above.

8. After visiting Bath in search of a cure for his poor health in the summer of 1708, P in fact died on 15 Feb. 1709 at Hereford, where his father had been a Canon-Residentiary of the Cathedral 1675–84, and where his mother still lived. P had addressed the younger Simon Harcourt (1684–1720), son of his patron and an Oxford contemporary, in the opening lines of *Cyder*, Bk. II. See also 'Pope' **401** below.

 *BB* attributed the epitaph in Westminster Abbey to Dr Robert Freind (1667–1751), as, originally, did SJ himself in his MS notes for the biography (see 'Composition' above, and cf. 'Prior' **44** and 'Dyer' **2** below). In 'Milton' **156** above, SJ reported Thomas Sprat's objections to the reference to Milton in Atterbury's epitaph, later restored by Atterbury himself when he became Dean of Westminster. *Gent. Mag.* (1779), 506, described SJ's attribution of the epitaph to Atterbury as 'new'. *BB* did not include the epitaphs, and SJ had to instruct Nichols to insert them, either from Sewell, *Life*, or from Jacob, ii. 138–9 (see 'Composition' above). For an engraving of P's monument in Westminster Abbey, with a translation, see John Dart, *Westmonasterium* [1742], i. 81–3: the quotation from Virgil, *Eclogues*, II. 53, inscribed above P's bust ('honos erit huic quoque pomo'), had been the epigraph to *Cyder*.

9. This 'character' of P derives mostly from *BB*. For SJ's interest in the conversation of poets, see 'Cowley' **220** and n. above. 'I have been told' in the third sentence suggests an unidentified oral source. According to a contributor to *Gent. Mag.* (1780), 280, P was poor company until he was inebriated.

 *BB* listed the various references to tobacco in P's works, also describing Henry Aldrich, Dean of Christ Church, as an incessant smoker whose habit influenced other members of the College (v. 3355 n.). Aldrich in fact composed a musical catch 'to be sung by four men smoking their pipes'. Lord Castle-Durrow, who entered Christ Church in 1701, wrote to Swift, 4 Dec. 1736: 'it greives me to think I was a Favorite of Dean Aldrich, the greatest man who ever presided in that high Post, that over Virgil and Horace Rag [Smith] and Phillips smoaked many a Pipe and drank many a Quart with me, beside the Expence of a Bushel of Nuts, & that now I am scarce able to relish their Beauties' (Swift, *Corresp.*, iv. 548).

 For SJ's opinion of Henry St John, Lord Bolingbroke, as 'a scoundrel and a coward', see *Life*, i. 268 and n., and 'Mallet' **19** and n. below.

10. For SJ's praise elsewhere of 'an original design' in literature, see 'Denham' **28** and n. above. 'The ancient *Centos*' in Greek and Roman literature were poetic compositions based on passages from earlier writers.

 For Milton's readers as 'captives', see 'Milton' **270** above; and for the pleasures of 'novelty', 'Cowley' **55** n. above.

11. Imitations of *The Splendid Shilling* were in fact written at least to the end of the 18th century. They included a rhymed version of P's poem in Giles Jacob's *The Lover's Miscellany* (1719), 53–9, and White Kennett's *Armour* [= Condom] (1723; Foxon, *English Verse*, K 12), which was reprinted in several facetious poetical miscellanies. See also Thomas (1927 edn.), pp. xxxiv–xxxv, and R. P. Bond, *English Burlesque Poetry 1700–1750* (Cambridge, Mass., 1932), 100–10.

*the repeater of a jest*: cf. SJ's discussion of 'burlesque' in 'Butler' **52** above, where 'the reader, learning in time what he is to expect, lays down his book, as the spectator turns away from a second exhibition of those tricks, of which the only use is to shew that they can be played'. For the limited merits of 'originality', see also 'Denham' **28** n. above, and 'Somervile' **8** below. Goldsmith, in *The Beauties of English Poesy* (1767), wrote similarly of P's poem: 'it has been an hundred times imitated, without success. The truth is, the first thing in this way must preclude all future attempts; for nothing is so easy as to burlesque any man's manner, when once we are shewed the way' (*Coll. Works*, v. 324). Yet SJ managed to react politely when shown Thomas Maurice's *The School-Boy, A Poem. In Imitation of Mr. Phillips' Splendid Shilling* (Oxford, [1775]), describing it as 'written in the best blank verse he had read for some time': according i.e. to the elderly Maurice's *Memoirs*, ii (1820), 25–7.

12. SJ quotes (loosely) Charles Gildon, *The Laws of Poetry* (1721), 321. Sir Richard Blackmore, *Advice to the Poets* (1706), ll. 193–8, was one author who denied that *Bleinheim* was 'tolerable': 'No more let *Milton*'s imitator dare | Torture our Language, or torment our Ear | With Numbers harsher than the Din of War. | Let him no more his horrid Muse employ | In uncouth Strains, pure *English* to destroy, | And from its Ruins, yell his hideous Joy.' *A Panegyrick Epistle . . . to S. R— B— on his most Incomparable Incomprehensible Poem* (1706) may be the 'verses against Blackmore' by P, mentioned by Elijah Fenton in a letter of 24 Jan. 1707 (J. Wooll, *Biographical Memoirs of . . . Joseph Warton* (1806), 203), but the attribution has not been generally accepted (see Foxon, *English Verse*, P 31). Thomas Tickell, however, praised P as an imitator of Milton and celebrant of Marlborough in his *Oxford: A Poem* (1707), as did Thomas Couch in his *Poems on Several Occasions* (1708), 46–8.

*all inexpert of war*: quoted from *Bleinheim*, ll. 485–6. For dismissive references to the productions of a 'College', see 'Milton' **182** and n. above, and cf. 'Smith' **49** below for 'a scholar's play . . . of little acquaintance with the course of life'. In contrast, SJ later praises Addison's *Campaign* (see **5** and n. above) as 'the work of man not blinded by the dust of learning: his images are not borrowed merely from books'. Cf. his remarks in 1771 on 'Those that hear of [war] at distance, or read of it in books' (see 'Addison' **130** and n. below), and his quotation from Robert South under 'Army' in the *Dict.*: 'The meanest soldier, that has fought often in an army, has a truer knowledge of war, than he that has writ whole volumes, but never was in any battle.'

*Marlborough*: SJ ends by discussing *Bleinheim*, ll. 178–208. Camille d'Hostun (1652–1728), Comte de Tallard, was captured by Marlborough, brought to England, and released in 1711. For the treatment of Marlborough by other poets, see 'King' **14**, 'Addison' **27**, **131–3**, 'Fenton' **5–6**, 'Somervile' **6**, 'Swift' **46**, and 'Mallet' **11**, **13–14** below. For SJ's own undated Greek epigram on Marlborough, apparently translated from the Latin of Salvini, see *Poems* (1974), 199.

13. For Milton's versification, see **16** n. below and 'Milton' **273–6** above. SJ has not previously considered it in the context of the 'new versification' of the Restoration: see 'Dryden' **340** and n. below. His belief that Milton might have been influenced by Dryden's 'improvements' is surely wishful thinking, given Milton's opinion that Dryden 'was a good rhymist, but no poet' (see 'Milton' **164** above).

*asperities*: SJ defines 'Asperity' as 'Roughness of sound; harshness of pronunciation' (*Dict.*).

14. Thomas (1927 edn.), 112–18, printed two early verse translations (1714–20) of P's *Honoratissimo Viro, Henrico St.-John, Armigero* (1707): cf. **5** and **9** above. For Oldisworth's reference to the poem as 'certainly a masterpiece', see 'Smith' **14** below, and for the admired Latin odes of Edward Hannes (d. 1710), Reader in Chemistry at Oxford and physician to Queen Anne (1702), see also 'Smith' **14** and 'King' **3** n. below. (A Latin poem by a 'John Philips', 'thrown in Dryden's grave' in 1700, according to Shiels, *Lives*, iii. 93–4, was not by P, as J. C. Pellicer has informed me.)

   The emendation proposed in SJ's note is correct: the 1707 text reads 'Ornat! labellis cui Venus insidet!' (l. 50).

15. *grounded in truth*: see 'Cowley' **14** n. above.

   For a brief but negative reference by SJ to P as imitator of Virgil in 1764, see 'Dyer' **11** n. below. He had asserted in *Adventurer* 115 (1753) that 'The first qualification of a writer is a perfect knowledge of the subject which he undertakes to treat' (*YW*, ii. 460); see also 'Dryden' **283** below. P had many connections with Herefordshire (see **1**, **8** above), described as 'Cyder-Land' in *Cyder*, II. 515. For another didactic poet who had 'great intelligence of his subject, which is the first requisite to excellence', see 'Somervile' **7** below.

   SJ described meeting Philip Miller (1691–1771), author of *The Gardener's and Florist's Dictionary* (2 vols., 1724), in conversation on 21 Aug. 1773: 'It does not always follow . . . that a man who has written a good poem on an art, has practised it. Philip Miller told me, that in Philips's CYDER, a poem, all the precepts were just, and indeed better than in books written for the purpose of instructing; yet Philips had never made cyder' (*Life*, v. 78). SJ also refers to this in his early notes for the biography: 'Cyder. Miller' (see 'Composition' above). For SJ's assistance with the botanical terminology in Erasmus Darwin's translation of *A System of Vegetables* (2 vols., 1782–3) from Linnaeus, see *Bibliography*, ii. 1560–2.

16. *disposition . . . precepts . . . transitions*: for SJ's views on didactic poetry, see 'Pope' **328** n. below. Joseph Warton had praised Virgil's 'transitions' in *Works of Virgil* (1753), i, p. viii, in which his 'Reflections on Didactic Poetry' also praise *Cyder* as 'a very close and happy imitation', which gives 'the fullest idea of Virgil's *manner*'. Warton had also anticipated SJ's reservations about P's 'antique expressions, and transpositions' in imitation of Milton, who had used his 'uncommon and unfamiliar phrases' chiefly when writing of hell, chaos, and heaven (i. 432–3). This was conceivably one of the 'most judicious remarks and observations' for which Warton acknowledged that he had been 'obliged' to SJ (i, p. xxx). But Pope had already stated in his 'Postscript' to the *Odyssey* that 'The imitators of *Milton* . . . are not *Copies* but *Caricatura's* of their original; they are a hundred times more obsolete and cramp than he, and equally so in all places' (*TE*, x. 390–1), and elsewhere

said that P had been 'quite wrong' to use Milton's style for such a subject (Spence, i. 197).

*Milton's Sublimity Asserted: In a Poem. Occasion'd by a late Celebrated Piece, Entituled, Cyder, A Poem* (1709), a pamphlet by 'Philo-Milton', had earlier emphasized 'how much he [P] has fallen short of *Milton*', while testifying to the popularity of P's 'idoliz'd piece', which had been 'so much the talk and hopes of the Publick', and had 'raised the Author to the highest Class in the *Muses* School' as Milton's '*Poetical Son*' (pp. iii–vi). Other objections included Tom Brown's 'To the Ingenious Mr. John Philips of Oxon., on the many Scurvy Imitators of Milton' in *Essays Serious and Comical* (1707), 265–6; William Coward, *Licentia Poetica Discuss'd: or, The True Test of Poetry* (1709), 12 n.; a letter in *Spectator* 140 (1711); and *A Letter to a Young Poet* (Dublin, 1721), once attributed to Swift, in his *Prose Writings*, ix. 335: 'Our Celebrated *Milton* has ... spoil'd as many reverend *Rhimers* by his Example, as he has made real *Poets*.' More positively, Thomson, *Autumn*, ll. 645–7, praised 'PHILLIPS, *Pomona*'s Bard, the second thou | Who nobly durst, in Rhyme-unfetter'd Verse, | With BRITISH Freedom sing the BRITISH Song', and see also 'Somervile' 8–9 nn. below.

*blank verse*: see 'Milton' **274** n. above. With SJ's final sentence, cf. also 'Milton' **276**: 'He that thinks himself capable of astonishing, may write blank verse; but those that hope only to please, must condescend to rhyme.' SJ alludes finally to *Cyder*, I. 326 ff., 512 ff., 462 ff.

17. Cf. 'Milton' **252** above: 'But original deficience cannot be supplied'. The decline in P's reputation is suggested by John Langhorne's review of a new edition of his *Poems* in *Monthly Review*, 27 (1762), 227: while *The Splendid Shilling* is still admired, *Bleinheim* is 'turgid and unnatural' and *Cyder* full of 'absurd similes, and impertinent digressions'. P was basically an imitator rather than an original genius.

*Tully*: SJ translates Cicero, *Epist. Ad. Quintum Fratrem*, II. xii. 5 ('multis luminibus ingeni, non multae tamen artis'), but the omission of 'non' in modern texts considerably modifies Cicero's opinion of Lucretius.

SJ does not mention *Cerealia; An Imitation of Milton* (1706), attributed to P by Nichols, *Sel. Collection*, iv. 274, on the authority of Archbishop Tenison's inscription in a copy in Lambeth Library. Although Thomas (1927), p. xxv, accepted this attribution, Foxon, *English Verse*, F 104, ascribed *Cerealia* instead to Elijah Fenton (q.v. below). For further evidence of Fenton's authorship, see Pellicer, '*Cerealia*', 197–201.

18–38. Edmund Smith's account of P (Bodleian, MS Rawl. poet. 113, fos. 32–8, with another copy in MS Rawl. D. 35) was originally intended as a preface to his elegy on P in 1710 (see 'Smith' **51–2** and nn. below). Thomas Rawlins told George Ballard, 26 June 1735, that it was left incomplete at Smith's death: 'I saw the first proof sheet of it wth. several other curious Papers' (Bodleian, MS Ballard 41, fo. 102). For SJ's low opinion of it, see his letter to Nichols, 1 Mar. 1779, quoted in 'Composition' above. Hawkins, *J's Works* (1787), ii. 303–4 n., also thought Smith's 'flimsy discourse ... to the lowest degree contemptible', and, had it not been for P's Oxford connections, unworthy of a place in the Bodleian. SJ's transcription shows only minor variants from the MS, which has been used to correct a few small errors introduced in *Lives* (1783): see Textual Notes to **30, 33, 35** below. Although quotation marks introduce Smith's text, they are not used at its conclusion.

18. For Sprat's 'Life of Cowley', see 'Cowley' **1** above and 'Sprat' **7** below.

19. Smith refers to *The Lives, Opinions, and Remarkable Sayings of the Most Famous Ancient Philosophers. Written in Greek by Diogenes Laertius* (2 vols., 1688, 1696).

20. Smith evidently refers to the *éloges* of the Académie. John Ozell had recently translated Charles Perrault's *Characters Historical and Panegyrical of the Greatest Men that have appear'd in France* (2 vols., 1704). As well as the celebrated dramatists (Molière and Racine) and military figures (Louis II de Bourbon, Prince de Condé, and the Maréchal Vicomte de Turenne), Smith mentions two minor literary figures, the academic Olivier Patru (1604–81) and the poet and grammarian Paul Pellisson-Fontanier (1624–93). For an attack on the French *éloges*, see Voltaire's *Letters Concerning the English Nation* (1733), 237–40.

23–4. Of P's six brothers, Vincent (1691), Robert (1693), and Joseph (1699) were admitted to Oxford, and Vincent entered the Middle Temple in 1695 (Thomas (1927 edn.), pp. xii–xiv).

24. For Grotius, see 'Milton' **25** and n. above. Smith also refers to John Eachard, *Mr. Hobbs's State of Nature Considered* (1672) and *A Second Dialogue* (1673).

26–30. For the debate about 'great' and 'low' burlesque, see 'Butler' **50–2** and n. above.

27. Smith refers to Charles Cotton's *Scarronides, or Virgile Travestie* (1664–5), Garth's *Dispensary* (1699; see 'Garth' **10, 17** below), and Boileau's *Le Lutrin* (Paris, 1674) (see 'Pope' **340** below).

29. Smith quotes (loosely) Juvenal, *Sat.*, X. 166–7 ('race over the Alps, that you may delight schoolboys, and give declaimers a theme').

30. *Galligaskins*: 'Large open hose. Not used but in ludicrous language' (*Dict.*, illustrated from P). Smith quotes *The Splendid Shilling*, ll. 121–3.

31. An advertisement in the *Daily Courant* of 1 Feb. 1705 condemned Bragg's unauthorized edition of *The Splendid Shilling*, published on 29 Jan. 1705. Thomas Bennet's edition, 'Now first correctly publish'd', followed on 8 Feb. (Foxon, *English Verse*, P 246–8). Smith wrote this protest about piracy at about the time the new Copyright Act of 1710 went some way towards securing authors property in their works. See J. Feather, *A History of British Publishing* (1988), 74–7, 81–3.

As Hill (1905) noted, it was Theopompus, an Athenian, who in fact made the reply quoted from Xenophon, *Anabasis*, II. i. 12. See 'Dryden' **136** (for Flecknoe), and 'Blackmore' **41** below. Smith also refers to two popular chapbooks, and to John Tillotson (1630–94), Archbishop of Canterbury, admired for his sermons. For Sir William Temple see 'Swift' **7–19** below.

32. See Virgil, *Eclogues* I, IX.

If 'which is capable … trifling genius' is a quotation, it remains unidentified. 'Scrutator' (John Loveday) in *Gent. Mag.* (1779), 595, interpreted it as a 'slur' on Addison's *The Campaign*.

See Joseph Warton, *Works of Virgil* (1753), i. 29, for the story (from the life attributed to Donatus) of Virgil 'earnestly requesting on his Death-bed, that his Aeneid might be burnt, because it had not received his last Corrections and

Improvements', and of Augustus refusing to allow 'a Poem that was to consecrate his Name to Immortality, to be destroyed'. For an anecdote of Smith himself having to be forced to write his elegy on P, see 'Smith' **51** below.

34. No printed source for this comparison in a 'very polite court' (that of Charles II?) of Milton to 'the rumbling of a wheelbarrow' has been identified. Smith implies that hostility to P's verse was politically motivated: P died before the Tory ministry, in which his patron Henry St John was prominent, came to power in 1710.

35. For Addison's praise of Dominique Bouhours, *La Manière de bien penser dans les ouvrages d'esprit* (1687), translated as *The Art of Criticism* (1705), see *Spectator* 62 (1711). SJ himself recommended Bouhours in his preface to Dodsley's *Preceptor* (1748), and described the work as 'true criticism' on 16 Oct. 1769 (*Life*, ii. 90). Antoine Yart, *Idée de la poësie angloise*, vol. i (Paris, 1749), was the first critic to make a serious case for P's verse to French readers.

38. Smith's MS breaks off just as he is about to discuss the suitability of blank verse for the 'true sublime', an issue which accompanied the rise in Milton's reputation. For Smith's defence of blank verse against rhyme in his elegiac *Poem* on P, see 'Smith' **51** and n. below, and cf. Isaac Watts on Milton in 'The Adventurous Muse' (1709), ll. 48–9: 'The noble hater of degenerate rhyme | Shook off the chains, and built his verse sublime.' For P's imitation of Milton, see **13, 16** above, and 'Milton' **274** and n. above.


# WILLIAM WALSH (1662–1708)

**Composition.** SJ does not refer to 'Walsh', but probably wrote it in late 1778 or early 1779, as it was printed in a single sheet with 'Dorset', 'Halifax', and 'Stepney': see Fleeman (1962), 228 n. and *Bibliography*, ii. 1355–6.

**Sources.** *GD* ignored W, and the unsigned article in *BB*, vi (ii) (1766), Suppl. 185, gave much the same meagre information as Jacob, ii. 223–4 and Shiels, *Lives*, iii. 151–5, some deriving from Wood, ii. 1106 (see **1** below).

There are twenty-eight quotations from W in *Dict.* (1755), increased to twenty-nine in 1773.

**Publication.** In *Prefaces*, vol. iv (31 Mar. 1779). There are no proofs.

**Modern Sources:**
E. Cruickshanks, S. Handley, and D. W. Hayton (eds.), *History of Parliament: The Commons 1690–1715* (Cambridge, 2002), v. 785–8
P. C. Freeman, 'WW: A Survey of his Life and Writings, with a special study of Bodleian MS. Malone 9' (Oxford B. Litt. thesis, 1934)
P. C. Freeman, 'W's Letters and Poems in MS. Malone 9', *Bodleian Quarterly Record*, 7 (1934), 503–7
P. C. Freeman, 'Who was Sir Roger de Coverley?', *Quarterly Review*, 285 (1947), 592–604
P. C. Freeman, 'W and Dryden: Recently Recovered Letters', *RES* 24 (1948), 195–202
P. C. Freeman, 'Two Fragments of W Manuscripts', *RES* 8 (1957), 390–401
R. Lonsdale (ed.), *Eighteenth-Century Women Poets* (Oxford, 1989), 52–3 (for W's sister Octavia Walsh, 1677–1706)

J. M. Osborn, *John Dryden: Some Biographical Facts and Problems*, (1940; rev. edn.,
  Gainesville, Fla., 1965), 226–33
C. E. Ward (ed.), *Letters of John Dryden* (Durham, NC, 1942), 25, 30–48, 52–7, 61–4

1. For Wood see 'Sources' above. W was baptized on 6 Oct. 1662 (Freeman, 'W and
   Dryden', 194 n.), the son of Joseph Walsh (d. 1682), an ardent Royalist in the Civil
   War, and Elizabeth Palmes of Linley, Yorks. He matriculated from Wadham
   College, Oxford, 14 May 1678, and was also entered at the Middle Temple, 6
   Dec. 1679.

2. W's unpublished letters and references to Italy in his *Dialogue* (1691) (see **10** below)
   indicate that he travelled abroad *c*.1682–6. He later tried unsuccessfully to obtain
   diplomatic posts. By the early 1690s he was friendly with Dryden, Congreve,
   Southerne, and other men of letters. Dryden called him 'without flattery, the
   best critick of our nation' in the 'Postscript' to the *Aeneid* (1697) (Watson, ii.
   261). See also **11** n. below.

3. SJ added the references to W as 'a man of fashion' and to John Dennis in 1783
   (see Textual Notes). Cf. the anonymous *The Tryal of Skill* (1704), ll. 505–6: 'His
   Equipage made such a flourishing Shew, | And his Courtly Behaviour so pleas'd'd'
   (*POAS*, vi. 706). In *Reflections on An Essay on Criticism* (1711), Dennis described W
   as 'a learned, candid, judicious Gentleman', who 'lov'd to be well dress'd ... and
   thought it no Disparagement to his understanding' (*Works*, i. 416, 530–1). In the
   *Supplement* (1799) to his *History of Worcestershire*, T. R. Nash reported that W's wig
   cost £80, and would 'employ a barber a fortnight to comb it, and require above
   three pounds of powder' (11).
      W was MP for Worcestershire 1698–1701 and 1702–5, and for Richmond
   1705–8 (see **12** below). He was appointed Gentleman of the Horse on 10 Oct.
   1702. Charles Talbot, Duke of Somerset (1662–1748), was Master of the Horse to
   Queen Anne 1702–12.

4. For W's politics, see e.g. 'The Golden Age Restor'd' (**12** below). Pope called W 'not
   only a Socinian, but ... a Whig' (*Corresp.*, i. 206).
      The author of the 'Preface to the Pastorals' in Dryden's *Virgil* (1697), which ends
   with remarks on French versification, was in fact Knightley Chetwood (1650–1720)
   (Dryden, *Letters*, ed. C. E. Ward (Durham, NC, 1992), 98, 179 n.; *Works*, ed. H. T.
   Swedenborg et al. (Los Angeles, 1956–2000), v. 37–56). For W's friendship with the
   elderly Dryden, see Dryden, *Letters*, and Freeman, 'W and Dryden'. W was one of
   the subscribers who paid 5 guineas for a dedicated full-page engraving in D's *Virgil*.

5. After meeting the youthful Pope through Wycherley, W read his 'Pastorals' in
   1705, although the surviving correspondence begins in 1706. W at first urged Pope
   to write a pastoral comedy (see 'Pope' **30** below, and Pope, *Corresp.*, i. 7, 18–25, 29).
   His marginalia are visible in the surviving MSS of Pope's early poems (Spence,
   i. 31–2). Pope later claimed to have spent 'a good part' of the summer of 1705 with
   W, but his visit to Abberley, Worcs., probably took place in Aug. 1707 (Spence,
   i. 31–2). For the friendship see also M. Mack, *Alexander Pope* (1985), 110–17.

6. SJ quotes *Epistle to Arbuthnot*, ll. 135–6. Cf. his own tribute to Gilbert Walmesley
   in 'Smith' **72–6** below and his statement shortly before his death about his early
   friend, the Hon. Henry Hervey: 'He was a vicious man, but very kind to me. If you
   call a dog HERVEY, I shall love him' (*Life*, i. 106).

7. See *Essay in Criticism*, ll. 729–44. Warburton, *Works of Pope* (1751), i. 208–9 n., expressed doubts about W's stature as a critic, but thought Pope's lines 'a pious offering to the memory of his friend'. The 'learned commentator' may, however, be Joseph Warton, *Essay* (1756), 200: 'If Pope has here given too magnificent an elogy to Walsh, it must pardonably be attributed to friendship, rather than to judgment.' For a rare discussion of W's ideas which is not simply dismissive, see J. M. Levine, *The Battle of the Books* (Ithaca, NY, 1991), 183–90.

8. W in fact died on 16 Mar. 1707/8 at Marlborough on the way from London to Bath (epitaph in Abberley Church, and Nash, i. 4). Shiels and *BB* had suggested 1710.

10. Dryden wrote the preface to W's *A Dialogue concerning Women, Being a Defence of the Sex. Written to Eugenia* (1691). Eugenia was apparently Anne Pierrepont, the recently widowed Countess of Kingston, whom W had hoped to marry: see Freeman, 'W and Dryden', 198–9. Judith Drake, *An Essay in Defence of the Female Sex* (1696), 4–5, was sceptical about W's efforts on behalf of women, claiming that he 'fights under our Colours only for a fairer Opportunity of betraying us'.

10*a–b.* Not numbered as separate paragraphs by Hill (1905).

10*a.* 'Aesculapius' appeared posthumously in *Poems and Translations by Several Hands* (1714).

10*b.* W's *Letters and Poems, Amorous and Gallant* (1692), described by SJ in 'Pope' 171 below as 'mere exercises', was added to *The Annual Miscellany* (2nd edn., 1708), the fourth of the collections later republished by Tonson as *Miscellany Poems... Publish'd by Mr. Dryden* (6 vols., 1716). W was one of the many poets who wrote a *Funeral Elegy* (1695) on the death of Queen Mary: see 'Prior' 8 and n. below.

11. Although SJ quoted W's preface on 'the style of letters' under 'Letter' in the *Dict.*, he had been dismissive about it in *Rambler* 152 (31 Aug. 1751): 'The observations with which Walsh has introduced his pages of inanity are such as give him little claim to the rank assigned him by Dryden among the criticks' (*YW*, v. 44: cf. **2** and n. above). In his *Essay* (1756), 201, Joseph Warton described W, in spite of Pope's admiration, as 'in general a flimsy and frigid writer', noting SJ's judgement in 1751. This fact may have prompted SJ to refer in 1779 to W. 's 'very judicious preface'. It was included in *Eng. Poets*, xii. 301–8: see also 'Cowley' **119** n. above.

12. W's 'The Golden Age Restor'd', a parodic response to a Tory poem, *The Golden Age* (1703), appeared in *Poems on Affairs of State*, ii (1703), 422–5. For the political context of what was once 'a famous State-Poem' (Jacob, ii. 224), including W's involvement in the bitterly contested Worcester elections of 1701 and 1702 (cf. **3** n. above), see *POAS*, vi. 310–12, 487–505. For *Abigail's Lamentation for the Loss of Mr. Harley* (1709), another political poem written shortly before W's death, see *POAS*, vii. 297–305. SJ also refers to W's 'Horace, Ode III. Book III. Imitated, 1705'. (For a possible literary collaboration with Vanbrugh and Congreve in 1704, see 'Congreve' **25** n. below.)

Although SJ finds 'more elegance than vigour' in W's verse, and quoted 'the sublime and pathetick Mr. Walsh' ironically in a letter of 15 June 1780 (*Letters*, iii. 276), he had been known to recite W's poem 'Retirement' 'with great pathos' (*Life*, ii. 133 and n., 491).

## JOHN DRYDEN (1631–1700)

**Composition.** Following his usual custom at Easter, SJ surveyed the preceding year in his diary on 3 Apr. 1779, and noted: 'Little done. Part of the life of Dryden, and the Life of Milton have been written' (*YW*, i. 195). This carefully phrased statement indicates that he had written only part of 'Dryden' since Easter 1778, and had obviously begun it earlier. This is feasible, since by Apr. 1778 he had already received the proofs of 'Waller' (q.v.). Yet it also clear that, even if it is second only to 'Pope' in length, SJ made unusually slow progress with 'Dryden', which on the face of it preoccupied him from, say, Mar. to Aug. 1778. The most likely explanation is that it was in this period that his original plan of providing only 'little lives' evolved into something much more elaborate, and that the completion of 'Dryden' was delayed by, for example, the expansion of 'Cowley', 'Butler', and 'Waller' (see headnotes and i. 26 above).

SJ frequently refers, however, in 'Dryden' itself to his difficulty in establishing the chronology of D's works, and betrays mounting irritation at the 'tedious and troublesome' task of researching 'the minute events of literary history' (see 11, 15, 95, 113, 117, 266 below). In the original 'Advertisement' to *Prefaces* (1779), SJ again complained that 'In this minute kind of History the succession of facts is not easily discovered', and, noticeably, the three tiresome matters he goes on to mention all concern D: the chronology of his plays, the circumstances of his funeral, and his notes on Rymer (see Textual Notes). Even after the publication of 'Dryden', the dating of his plays continued to trouble J: writing to Boswell on 9 Sept. 1779 about a description of D sent by Lord Hailes, which he hoped to use in a later edition, SJ added that, 'as I know his accuracy, [I] wish he would consider the dates, which I could not always settle to my own mind' (*Letters*, iii. 182).

When he wrote to Richard Clark, Sheriff of London, on 17 July 1778 to request information about Elkanah Settle as City Poet, SJ claimed that he had already written 'a great part' of 'Dryden', and it need not be assumed that by this date he had only just reached his discussion of Settle (117–18 below). Clark passed SJ's enquiry to Thomas Whittell, who replied from the Guildhall on 26 Aug. 1778 that he could supply nothing useful about Settle's office (*Letters*, iii. 120–1 and n.). (SJ later presented Clark with a copy of the *Prefaces*, now in the Rothschild Collection in Trinity College, Cambridge.) On 27 July 1778 SJ told Nichols that 'I am very far advanced in *Dryden*, which will be long too', evidently responding to growing concern about the scale on which he was now working. By *c.* mid-Aug. 1778 he could tell Nichols that 'You have now the life of Dryden and you see it is very long', but went on to list further material which was to be appended: a quotation from Milbourne (357), Dryden's notes on Rymer, which had aleady been transcribed (358–405), and a new Dryden letter he had been promised (406) (*Letters*, iii. 122, 124). SJ told the company at Streatham on 27 Aug. 1778 that '*Dryden* is now in the Press' (Burney, *Early Journals*, iii. 105). The phrase 'when Dryden is finished' in his letter to Thomas Cadell on 17 Oct. 1778 (Hyde), explaining his slow progress with his biographies, must refer to its printing rather than its composition (see i. 30–1 above).

John Nichols later printed an undated letter from Isaac Reed, which ends: 'I thank you very heartily for Dryden; it came very seasonably to fill up the taedium of a solitary evening. There are two or three errors in point of fact, which must be rectified' (*Lit. Anec.*, ii. 667 n.). Nichols claimed in a note that Reed was referring to some fugitive poems by Dryden and his son Charles which Nichols was planning to include in his

*Select Collection of Poems* (1780). A different explanation is at least plausible, especially in view of SJ's anxiety about dates: that in the autumn of 1778 Nichols had in fact sent Reed some of the proofs of SJ's 'Dryden' for his comments and corrections, and that some thirty years later he had either forgotten this, or was unwilling to admit it. A section of SJ's biography must seem more likely to 'fill up' Reed's 'solitary evening' than a few pages from the *Select Collection*. (For Reed's contribution to the *Lives*, see i. 72–6 above.)

**Sources.** J. M. Osborn gave a detailed account of the transmission of information about D in the 18th century in *JD: Some Biographical Facts and Problems* (1965), 22–38. Noting the close similarity of the accounts of D by Thomas Birch in *GD*, iv. 676–87, and Thomas Broughton in *BB*, iii (1750), 1749–61, Osborn concluded from three apparently clinching pieces of evidence (23–4) that *GD* had been SJ's primary source: the reference to the supposed origins of the Dryden family in Huntingdonshire (**2** below), the erroneous date of D's death (**152** below), and the text of the 'wild story' about D's funeral (**153** below), all of which appeared to derive from *GD* rather than *BB*. D's death is in fact also misdated by *BB*, but in the other two cases SJ seems clearly to have followed *GD*. Supporting evidence will be found in notes to **26, 32, 50, 85, 94, 140, 148, 159, 163–4** below. Since *BB* had recently been SJ's main source for 'Waller', it would be surprising if he had not at least compared the two accounts, but there is little information in *BB* which is not also in *GD*: for a few possible cases, see notes to **80, 96, 122, 305** below.

SJ recalled in conversation on 15 May 1776 that 'When I was a young fellow I wanted to write the "Life of Dryden"', and went on to describe his interviews with 'the only two persons then alive who had seen him' (*Life*, iii. 71, and cf. iv. 44; for what he learned, see **190** and n. below). In the 1750s he helped Samuel Derrick with the biography prefixed to his edition of D's *Miscellaneous Works* (1760) (see **3** and n. and **188** below). Osborn, *JD*, 15–21, 24–5, discussed the new information brought to light by Derrick, to some of which SJ directed him, as well as SJ's later use of Derrick's biography. Derrick (1760 edn.), i, p. ix, mentions, for example, his attempts to obtain information from D's family. On 22 Sept. 1773 SJ said that 'he had sent Derrick to Dryden's relations to gather materials for his Life; and he believed Derrick had got all that he himself would have got; but it was nothing' (*Life*, v. 240, and cf. i. 455–7 and, for SJ's 'kindness' for Derrick, v. 119). In spite of SJ's proprietorial references to Derrick's biography (for similar claims about Hawkesworth's life of Swift, see headnote to 'Swift' below), Derrick himself thanked David Mallet, Thomas Birch, and Walter Harte for assistance without mentioning SJ (1760 edn., i, pp. viii–ix). (For Mallet's letter to Birch of 26 Dec. 1757, asking him to help Derrick with information about D, see his *Ballads and Songs*, ed. F. T. Dinsdale (1857), 49.)

A source which SJ consulted at first hand was Gerard Langbaine's *Account of the English Dramatick Poets* (1691). As he stated in his 'Advertisement' to *Prefaces* (1779), he considered Langbaine 'the best authority' for dating D's plays, but this reliance explains some of his chronological confusion (see **92** and n. below). (For other direct references to Langbaine, see **25, 29, 62, 65, 90, 180** below.) Several of SJ's scholarly friends could in fact have warned him of the unreliability of Langbaine's dates. In his additions to William Oldys's notes on the *English Dramatick Poets*, Thomas Percy noted Langbaine's 'numberless mistakes', which were 'a perpetual source of confusion' and of 'constant anachronism' in those who relied on his dates (Malone's transcription in the

Bodleian Library, Malone 129, fos. 31–31ᵛ; for Percy's own transcription, made in 1763, now in the University of Edinburgh Library, see B. Davis, *Thomas Percy* (Philadelphia, 1989), 117 n.). Malone later corrected SJ's factual information in his own elaborate biography in D's *Prose Works* (1800), once more blaming the misdating of plays on his reliance on Langbaine (i (i). 1–2).

Another primary source used by SJ may seem to be indicated by his long quotation from Congreve's account of D in his edition of D's *Dramatick Works* (1717), but SJ in fact transcribed it from the paraphrase in *GD* (see **159** and n. below). The difficulty of adding to the limited information available about D no doubt explains the generous space he gives to quotations from contemporary pamphlet attacks on D (see the passages from Clifford, Settle, Burnet, Brown, and Milbourne in **51–2, 54–61, 124, 132–4, 306–8** below), as well the materials appended in **357–406**. Percy provided him with at least some of these relatively unfamiliar pamphlets, such as Martin Clifford's *Notes* (1687) (cf. **112–13, 115**). Percy's MS catalogue of his library lists 'Answers to Dryden & other Pamphlets written on him & his Works in his Life-time (16 in No.)', with a later marginal note, 'Lent to Dr. Sam. Johnson & not returnd. 1784' (Bodleian, MS Percy c. 9, fo. 69: I am grateful to Dr Nick Groom for pointing out this information). On 31 Mar. 1779 Boswell noted Burke's opinion that SJ 'had given too much of Dryden's antagonists' (Boswell, *Laird of Auchinleck*, 63; see also **33** n. below). Hawkins, *Life* (1787), 537, reported, however, that 'Others have assigned to Dryden's life the pre-eminence' among the *Lives*. Malone, who was to add so much new information to SJ's account, asserted in 1800 that 'a more beautiful and judicious piece of criticism perhaps has not appeared since the days of Aristotle' than SJ's 'elaborate and admirable disquisition on his writings' (*Prose Works*, i (i). 549).

D was, after Shakespeare, one of the most frequently quoted authors in the *Dict.* (1755), appearing some 11, 494 times.

**Publication.** In *Prefaces*, vol. iii (31 Mar. 1779). Corrected proofs of pp. 1–16 and 65–80 are in the British Library. SJ's corrections, and other variants between the proofs and the text of *Prefaces* (1779), have been listed and discussed by Fleeman (1962), 219–22. Boswell recorded other variants in *Life*, iv. 45–6. A copy of 'Dryden' as originally published in *Prefaces* (1779), vol. iii, bound without the title page, in which sig. f8 is uncancelled, is in the Rothschild Collection in Trinity College, Cambridge: for its textual significance, see **89** n. below. This copy also contains a few revisions by SJ, none of which were adopted in later editions (see Textual Notes to **89, 146, 154, 187, 282, 305**), and some notes on D's finances on the endpapers (cf. **183–4** below).

**Modern Sources:**
(i) Dryden
*Letters*, ed. C. E. Ward (Durham, NC, 1942)
*Of Dramatic Poesy and Other Critical Essays*, ed. G. Watson (2 vols., 1962)
*Poems*, ed. J. Kinsley (4 vols., Oxford, 1958)
*Poems*, ed. P. Hammond and D. Hopkins (4 vols., 1995–2000)
*Works*, ed. H. T. Swedenborg, Vinton A. Dearing, et al. (20 vols., Los Angeles, 1956–2000)

(ii)
J. E. Adams, 'The Economics of Authorship: Imagination and Trade in J's *Dryden*', *SEL* 30 (1990), 467–86
K. J. H. Berland, 'J's Life-Writing and the *Life of D*', *EC* 23 (1982), 197–218

G. Clingham, 'J's Criticism of D's Odes in Praise of St. Cecilia', *Modern Language Studies*, 18 (1988), 165–80

G. Clingham, 'J, Homeric Scholarship, and "The Passes of the Mind"', *Age of J* 3 (1990), 113–70

L. Damrosch, 'D: The Power of Mind', in *The Uses of J's Criticism* (Charlottesville, Va., 1976), ch. 7

P. Hammond, 'D and Trinity', *RES* 36 (1985), 35–57

P. Hammond and D. Hopkins (eds.), *JD: Tercentenary Essays* (Oxford, 2000)

E. A. Horsman, 'D's French Borrowings', *RES* 1 (1950), 346–51

J. and H. Kinsley (eds.), *D: The Critical Heritage* (1971)

H. Macdonald, *JD: A Bibliography* (Oxford, 1939)

M. E. Novak, 'J, D and the Wild Vicissitudes of Taste', in J. J. Burke and D. Kay (eds.), *The Unknown SJ* (Madison, 1983), 54–75

J. M. Osborn, *JD: Some Biographical Facts and Problems* (New York, 1940; rev. Gainesville, Fla., 1965)

K. Walker, 'Some Notes on the Treatment of D in J's *Dictionary*', *Yearbook of English Studies*, 28 (1998), 106–9

C. E. Ward, *The Life of JD* (Chapel Hill, NC, 1961)

W. K. Wimsatt, 'SJ and D's *Du Fresnoy*', *SP* 48 (1951), 26–39

J. A. Winn, *JD and his World* (New Haven, 1987)

1. Cf. the different tone and emphasis of 'Milton' 1 above.

2. The son of Erasmus and Mary Dryden, D was born at Aldwincle Rectory, the home of his maternal grandfather, the Revd Henry Pickering. His father (*c.*1602–1654) lived a mile away at Titchmarsh. D's paternal grandfather was Sir Erasmus Dryden (1553–1632) of Canons Ashby (Winn, *JD*, 4–8). The Dryden family in fact originated in Cumberland, not Huntingdonshire, an error found in *GD*, iv. 676, but not *BB*.

3. SJ refers to Derrick (1760 edn.), i, p. xiv (see 'Sources' above). At his death on 18 June 1654, D's father left him two-thirds of the rent of £100 p.a. of his farm at Blakesley, and the other third to D's mother in her lifetime (she died 14 Jan. 1671) (Winn, *JD*, 79). For D's later 'complaints of poverty', see **182–9** below.

    For D's upbringing among the 'conservative Puritans' of Northamptonshire, see Winn, *JD*, 8 ff. SJ originally stated that 'Derrick was misinformed' about both D's patrimony and his religious background, but in 1783 added the penultimate sentence and revised the last (see Textual Notes). These changes may have been prompted by Malone, who later noted in D's *Prose Works* (1800), i (i). 37–8 n., that *The Laureate* (1687) described D as 'A bristled baptist bred', and *The Protestant Satire* (1687) as 'bred a saint'. See also Tom Brown in **134** below.

4. D may have entered Westminster School in 1644 (Winn, *JD*, 550 n.). Two of his sons also later attended Westminster (see **157–8** below). Dr Richard Busby (1606–95) was headmaster of Westminster from 1640. Busby, to whom D dedicated his translation of Persius, *Sat.* V, in 1693, was famous for his erudition and for his flogging of miscreants. Cf. D's letter to Montague, [Oct. 1699?]: 'our Master Busby used to whip a boy so long, till he made him a confirmed blockhead' (Watson, ii. 265); and Sir Roger de Coverley's tribute in Addison's *Spectator* 329 (1712): 'Dr. *Busby*, a great Man, he whipp'd my Grandfather, a very great Man. I should

have gone to him my self, if I had not been a Blockhead; a very great Man!' See also
**208** below, and, for other pupils of Busby, 'Dorset' **2** n., 'Stepney' **1**, and 'J.
Philips' **3** above, and 'Smith' **4, 29**, 'Duke' **1**, 'King' **2**, 'Halifax' **2**, 'Rowe' **2**, and
'Prior' **2** below, and *J. Misc.*, ii. 304–5. (For a poet who attended the school before
Busby's regime, see 'Cowley' **4–7** above.)

Bennet Langton reported in 1790 that SJ had once said: 'When I was at Oxford
I allways felt an impulse to insult the Westminster men who were come there, they
appeared to arrogate so much to themselves upon their superficial talent of a
readiness in making latin verses; for I have observed Sir that many of them never
got farther' (Boswell, *Making of the Life*, 365). Boswell did not use this in the *Life*,
perhaps because one of his own sons attended Westminster, and because of SJ's
later respect for such schools (*Life*, iii. 12).

D was admitted at Trinity College, Cambridge, on 13 May 1650, matriculated
on 6 July, and was admitted as a Scholar on 2 Oct. 1650 (Winn, *JD*, 62, 554 n.).

5. Henry Hastings (1630–49), the eldest son of the Earl of Huntington, and perhaps a
schoolfellow of D at Westminster, died on the eve of his wedding in 1649. D's 'On
the Death of Lord Hastings' appeared in a collection of elegies on this occasion,
*Lachrymae Musarum* (1649), and was one of the eight poems added after the volume
had been printed. Other contributors included Denham, Herrick, and Marvell. SJ
quotes the last couplet of a notorious sequence of conceits in D's poem (ll. 53–66).
('Corps' and 'Corpse' are alternative spellings in the *Dict.* Both appeared in **153**
below in *Prefaces* (1779), but were normalized to 'corpse' in 1781.)

For the 'reformation' in versification initated by Denham and Waller, see **217–
22, 340** below, 'Cowley' **185–99** n., 'Denham' **35–42**, and 'Waller' **5, 142–4** above.
In 1693 D described Cowley as 'the darling of my youth' (Watson, ii. 150). For
conceits in his later poetry, see **236, 242, 314** below, and, for conceits elsewhere, see
'Cowley' **58** and n. above.

6. For two short poems D wrote at Cambridge, see *Poems* (1958), i. 4–6; and for
Nichols's 'discovery' of other poems written by D at Cambridge, which turned out
to be by his cousin, see his *Sel. Collection*, ii. 90–1 and n., and *Gent. Mag.* (1781),
515. With 'an author ought first to be a student', cf. J's approval of D's 'acquired
knowledge' in **321** below.

In July 1652 D's College penalized him for disobedience and contumacy to the
Vice-Master (Winn, *JD*, 77). He took his BA early in 1654 and left Cambridge by
23 Apr. 1655. Malone discovered that D later received a MA from Cambridge on
17 June 1668 (*Prose Works* (1800), i (i). 553–4 n.). In his 'Life of Plutarch' (1683),
D referred to Trinity College, 'to which foundation I gratefully acknowledge
a great part of my Education' (*Works*, xvii. 269). SJ goes on to quote 'Prologue to
the University of Oxford' (1676; published 1684), ll. 35–8. D had commented
on 'how grosse flattery the learned will endure' in a letter to Rochester in 1673
(*Letters*, 10).

7. Like Milton and Marvell, D seems to have been employed in Cromwell's government, in his case as a clerk and translator, and he marched in Cromwell's funeral
procession in 1658 (Winn, *JD*, 79–81). His 'Heroique Stanza's, Consecrated to the
Glorious Memory of . . . Oliver, Late Lord Protector' appeared in *Three Poems upon
the Death of his late Highnesse Oliver, Lord Protector* (1659). For the companion
poems, see 'Waller' **67** above (where SJ describes D and Sprat as 'young men,

struggling into notice, and hoping for some favour from the ruling party') and 'Sprat' 2 below.

8. *profession*: '3. The act of declaring oneself of any party or opinion' (*Dict.*) (cf. 119, 125 below). For *Astrea Redux* (1660), see 236–9 below. SJ has added '*most*' to its title.

9. SJ is noticeably more charitable about D's change of 'opinion' than he had been when discussing Waller's panegyrics on both Cromwell and the restored Charles II in 'Waller' 65–70 above. For similarly versatile poets, see H. T. Swedenberg, 'England's Joy: *Astraea Redux* in its Setting', *SP* 50 (1953), 30–44. D's political enemies later reprinted his 'Heroique Stanza's' as *An Elegy on the Usurper O.C. by the Author of Absalom and Achitophel* (1681), and there were other reminders of his changed allegiance: see Tom Brown in 134 below, and Winn, *JD*, 94, 559 n.

10. SJ refers to *To His Sacred Majesty, A Panegyrick on His Coronation* (1661): see also 240–1 below.
   Elkanah Settle, *Notes and Observations on the Empress of Morocco Revised* (1674), 3, and others derided the couplet from *Astraea Redux*, ll. 7–8 (see *Works*, i. 220 n.). Both *GD*, iv. 677 n., and *BB*, iii. 1749 n., quoted Alexander Radcliffe's *News from Hell* (1682) ('Laureat, who was both learn'd and florid, | Was damn'd long since for silence horrid'), *GD* describing it as 'the famous line, which has been treated with great ridicule'. Joseph Spence, *Essay on Pope's Odyssey* (1726–7), i. 142, suggested that it 'has probably been repeated many times more, than the best Line he ever wrote'. Cf. SJ's earlier discussion of 'Nothing' as an 'agent' in 'Rochester' 22 above.

11. This is SJ's first expression of irritation at the problem of dating D's works: see 'Composition' above, 15, 95, 113, 117, 266 below, and his admission in the 'Advertisement' to *Prefaces* (1779) that he had relied on Langbaine 'as the best authority for his plays'. SJ attached great importance to 'a strict attention to truth, even in the most minute particulars' (*Life*, iii. 228), especially to accurate dates: see his 'Preface' to *The Preceptor* (1748) ('*History* can only be made intelligible by some Knowledge of *Chronology*'), his preface to Lenglet Du Fresnoy's *Chronological Tables* (1762) (Hazen, 88, 182), and his letter of 6 Sept. 1777, just before he embarked on the *Lives*: 'Chronology, you know, is the eye of history' (*Letters*, iii. 61). See also his objection in 'Somervile' 5 n. below to neglect of chronology in *Eng. Poets* (1779), and P. A. Alkon, 'J and Chronology', in P. J. Korshin and R. R. Allen (eds.), *Greene Centennial Studies* (Charlottesville, Va., 1984), 143–71.
   Osborn, *JD*, 25, noted that SJ could in fact have 'easily found' first editions of D's plays in the library of his friend David Garrick, but doubted whether he consulted any editions earlier than the collections of Congreve and Derrick. See, however, 12 n. below.

12. SJ refers to *The Wild Gallant* (see 14 below), unaware of an unacted play by D dating from 1660 (Winn, *JD*, 116, 137).
   SJ does not indicate where D's plays are 'said to be printed in the order in which they were written', but may have been referring to one of the variant sets of D's bound-up plays issued by Tonson in the 1690s. To his transcription of Oldys's notes on Langbaine (1691), Thomas Percy (see 'Sources' above, and 50 below) added from the end of *Amphitryon* (1690) a 'Catalogue' of D's plays 'as they are bound in three volumes in Quarto in the order they were written', and later noted

an advertisement on the title page of *Cleomenes* (1692) for sets of the plays 'in the order they were written' (see Malone's retranscription in Bodleian, Malone 130, opp. pp. 145, 157). D signed a similar advertisement to *King Arthur* (1691), 'putting the plays in the Order I wrote them' (Spence, i. 28).

For another poet who, 'having no profession, became by necessity an author', see 'Savage' **24** below. Of the new dramatists of the 1660s only D was a professional writer (Winn, *JD*, 138). In 'A Discourse Concerning Satire' (1693) he referred to 'the stage, to which my genius never much inclined me' (Watson, ii. 91), and see also **91, 264, 329** below.

**13.** D's last play was staged in 1694: see **86–7** below.

**14.** *The Wild Gallant* was performed 5 Feb. 1663. Pepys (23 Feb. 1663) called it 'so poor a thing as I never saw in my life almost'. It was revived in 1667 and revised for publication in 1669, when D admitted in his preface, 'I made the Town my judges; and the greater part condemned it' (Watson, i. 131).

**15.** After 'performances' SJ originally continued in 1779: 'and indeed there is the less, as they do not appear in the collection to which this narrative is to be annexed' (see Textual Notes).

**16.** D dedicated *The Rival Ladies* (acted June 1664; published 1664) to Roger Boyle (1621–79), Earl of Orrery, whose *The General* (Sept. 1664) was performed in London later than *The Rival Ladies*, but had circulated in MS since 1661 and been staged in Dublin in Feb. 1663 (*Works*, viii. 264).

*essay*: '4. First taste of any thing; first experiment' (*Dict.*). D's play is mostly in blank verse, but with rhymed sections. For his defence of rhyme, see Watson i. 5–9.

**17.** The contributions of D and Sir Robert Howard (1626–98) to *The Indian Queen* (acted Jan. 1664; published in Howard's *Four New Plays* in 1665) are still 'not distinguished'.

SJ does not mention here D's marriage on 1 Dec. 1663 to Howard's sister Elizabeth, daughter of Thomas Howard, Earl of Berkshire: see **157** below and Winn, *JD*, 127.

**18.** D prefixed to *The Indian Emperour* (acted spring 1665; published 1667) his 'Connexion of the *Indian Emperour* to the *Indian Queen*'. The 'Key' to 18th-century editions of Buckingham's *The Rehearsal* (see **94** below) explained the allusion (I. ii) by stating that the 'Connexion' was also distributed to the audience of D's tragedy (*Works*, ix. 296–7).

**19.** For the 'description of Night' in *The Indian Emperour*, III. ii. 1 ff., see **265** below, 'Cowley' **98** above, and 'Young' **160** n. below. Rymer (see **200** below) praised it in a discussion of nocturnal descriptions in the preface to Rapin's *Reflections on Aristotle's Treatise of Poesie* (1674) (*Critical Works* (1956), 15). SJ had contrasted it with an admired passage in Shakespeare in his *Observations on . . . Macbeth* (1745) (*YW*, vii. 19–20, and cf. viii. 769–70). His reference to it here may have prompted Wordsworth's dismissal of D's lines in 1815 as 'vague, bombastic, and senseless' (*Prose Works*, iii. 73).

For another famous night scene, introduced incidentally by SJ to illustrate Pope's MS revisions to Homer's *Iliad*, Bk. VIII, see 'Pope' **98** below; and for a comparison of poetic nightpieces from Homer to Collins, see John Gilbert Cooper, *Letters Concerning Taste* (3rd edn., 1757), 41–8.

20. Orrery wrote in a letter of 23 Jan. 1662, 'I found his majty Relish'd rather, the French Fassion of Playes, than the English' (Winn, *JD*, 145–6). D abandoned rhymed heroic drama after *Aureng-Zebe* (1675): see **75–6, 78** n., **203** below.

*he wrote, only to please*: D claimed in the preface to *The Indian Emperour* that the use of rhyme in 'serious' modern plays 'shews that it attained the end, which was to please; and if that cannot be compassed here, I will be the first who shall lay it down. For I confess my chief endeavours are to delight the age in which I live'; and later that 'To please the people ought to be the poet's aim, because plays are made for their delight'.

His later comments on 'pleasing' in the theatre are disillusioned. In the preface to *An Evening's Love* (1671), he complained about his audience, which 'confirms me in my opinion of slighting popular applause, and of contemning that approbation which those very people give, equally with me, to the zany of a mountebank'; and in the preface to *The Spanish Fryar* (1680), claimed to be 'resolved I will settle myself no reputation by the applause of fools' and of 'half-witted judges'. By 1697 he was 'not ambitious of pleasing the lowest or the middle form of readers', but, like Virgil, 'the most judicious: souls of the highest rank, and truest understanding. These are few in number' (Watson, i. 115–16, 120, 145, 276–7, ii. 244). See also **28, 42, 168–70, 334, 399** below, and 'Pope' **304** below. For other comments on 'pleasing' the public, see 'Cowley' **38** and n. above. Cf. also SJ's 'Drury-Lane Prologue' (1747), ll. 53–4: 'The Drama's Laws the Drama's Patrons give, | For we that live to please must please to live'.

21. See Watson, i. 112–18, and, for *The Duke of Lerma*, **25** and n. below.

22. *Annus Mirabilis* (probably published in Jan. 1667) describes the naval campaigns of 1665–6 against the Dutch, and the Great Fire of London in 1666: see **247–63** below.

23. For SJ's loose quotation from D's prefatory letter to Howard, see Watson, i. 97. It refers to Prince Rupert (1619–82) and George Monck (1608–70), Duke of Albemarle, the joint commanders of the English fleet of eighty warships in 1666: see *Annus Mirabilis*, ll. 185 ff., and, for Monck, **237** below.

24. D stated of quatrains: 'I have ever judged then more noble, and of greater dignity, both for the sound and number, than any other verse in use amongst us.' The 'encumbrances' included the fact that the poet must 'bear along in his head the troublesome sense of four lines together. For those who write correctly in this kind must needs acknowledge that the last line of the stanza is to be considered in the composition of the first' (Watson, i. 95–6). John and Anna Laetitia Aikin, in a long discussion of Davenant's *Gondibert* (1651) in *Miscellaneous Pieces, in Prose* (1773), 138–89, suggested that the quatrain had encouraged 'a redundancy of thought, running out into parentheses' in the poem (155).

For later comments on quatrains, see **234–5, 247–8** below, and 'Hammond' **8** below. SJ ignores their use in some elegiac poetry in 'Shenstone' **21–2** and 'Gray' **51** below. (For his own parody in quatrains of Robert Potter in 1779, see *Poems* (1974), 221–3.)

*difficulties*: for the importance of striving with them, see 'Milton' **277** and n. above. Admitting that 'no book was ever spared out of tenderness to the author', SJ had himself in fact represented 'the difficulties that he had encountered' in his preface to the *Dict.* in 1755 (*OASJ*, 327–8).

25. Winn, *JD*, 186–91, 194–8, uncovers political as well as literary aspects of D's quarrel with his brother-in-law, while admitting that the known facts do not fully account for D's 'emotional intensity' (196). See also D. D. Arundell, *Dryden & Howard, 1664–1668* (Cambridge, 1929).

SJ refers here to D's dedication to *The Rival Ladies* (see 16 above); Howard's preface to *Four New Plays* (1665); D's reply in *Of Dramatick Poesie: An Essay* (written 1665–6; published 1667), in which Crites makes Howard's case for rhyme; Howard's preface to *The Great Favourite, or The Duke of Lerma* (1668); and D's preface to *The Indian Emperour* (2nd edn., 1668), although it seems that D withdrew this 'Defence', perhaps under threat of a duel (Winn, *JD*, 198). See also 203 below. SJ also cites Langbaine, *Account of the English Dramatick Poets* (Oxford, 1691), 165.

26. D became Poet Laureate on 13 Apr. 1668, six days after Davenant's death. He was officially paid £100 p.a., with a butt of canary wine, but received nothing before 18 Feb. 1671 (Winn, *JD*, 191–2, 528). For the suggestion that John Sheffield, Earl of Mulgrave, influenced his appointment, see 'Sheffield' 9 and n. below. On 18 Aug. 1670 D was also appointed Historiographer Royal, the combined salary of both posts to be £200 p.a. For SJ's mistaken belief that James II made the second appointment, see 183 below. SJ may have read *GD*, iv. 682, as implying this: *BB*, iii. 1749, and Derrick (1760 edn.), i, p. xvi, came closer to the facts by dating both appointments 1668.

'Laureate' appears only as an adjective in the *Dict.*: 'Decked or invested with a laurel'. For the Laureateship, see also 136 and 'Rowe' 21, 'Savage' 172, 177, 'Pope' 230–1, and 'Gray' 15 below, *Life*, i. 401–2, and Malone, *Prose Works*, i (i). 78–89, 205–11. In 'Savage' 221 below, SJ describes £50 a year as 'a salary which, though by no means equal to the demands of vanity and luxury, is yet found sufficient to support families above want, and . . . undoubtedly more than the necessities of life require'. For the incomes desired by other poets, see 'Cowley' 24 n. above and 'Smith' 68 below.

27. In 1709 Prior identified Eugenius in *Of Dramatick Poesie: An Essay* (1668 for Aug. 1667) as Charles Sackville, later Earl (not Duke) of Dorset (q.v. above) (*Lit. Works*, i. 249). For SJ's repeated error over Dorset's title, see 'Stepney' 1 above, and 'Prior' 18 (although it is correct at 2) and 'A. Philips' 3 below.

Addison stated in 1702 that his *Dialogues* ('Addison' 20, 110 below) were in fact modelled on Fontenelle's *Entretiens sur la pluralité des mondes* (1686) (*Letters*, ed. W. Graham (Oxford, 1941), 35).

28. *Secret Love* was probably acted in Jan. 1667 and published in late 1667 (dated 1668). For the passage in D's preface, see Watson, i. 105.

*whether a poet can judge . . . his own productions*: for the 'causes' which 'may vitiate a writer's judgement of his own works', see 'Milton' 146 and n. above. Addison may have had D in mind in *Guardian* 98 (1713): 'men of the best Sense . . . are always diffident of their private judgment, till it receives a Sanction from the publick. *Provoco ad Populum*, I appeal to the People, was the usual Saying of a very excellent Dramatick Poet, when he had any Disputes with particular Persons about the Justness and Regularity of his Productions.'

For critical 'principles', see **193** below; and for D's intention of writing only 'to please', **20** and n. above.

**29.** *Sir Martin Mar-All* (acted 15 Aug. 1667; published 1668), a collaboration with William Cavendish, Duke of Newcastle (see **43** below), was based on two French comedies (Winn, *JD*, 185, 573 n.). As Langbaine, *English Dramatick Poets*, 170, noted, four of the five stanzas of the song in v. i. ('Blind Love to this hour') derive from Vincent Voiture, *Œuvres* (Paris, 1652), ii. 61–3.

**30.** *The Tempest*, acted Nov. 1667, was published in 1670 after Davenant's death. For SJ's quotation from the preface, see Watson, i. 135, and for the 'Latin proverb', see Cicero, *Philippic*, XII. ii. 5: 'Posteriores cogitationes sapientiores solent esse' ('Second thoughts are usually best').

**31.** D's preface explained that Davenant planned 'the counterpart to Shakespeare's plot, namely that of a man who had never seen a woman, that by this means those two characters of innocence and love might the more illustrate and commend each other' (Watson, i. 135). For a detailed discussion of the adaptation, see *Works*, x. 328–43. After seeing a performance in Brighton in Oct. 1779, Fanny Burney wrote that Dryden had turned the 'beautiful improbabilities' of Shakespeare's play into 'a childish Chaos of absurdity & obscurity' (*Early Journals*, iii. 393).

Although Hill (1905) quoted Hawkins's praise of Purcell's music for *The Tempest*, the music in question was for a production in about 1695 and was probably by John Weldon (1676–1736).

**32.** SJ's uncertainty about dates leads him at this point to jump ahead some five years, the correct sequence resuming at **43** below. *The Empress of Morocco* (acted Mar. or Apr. 1673), a heroic play by Elkanah Settle (1648–1724), was published in Nov. 1673 with (unusually) engraved plates of scenes from the play (see **40** below), and a dedicatory epistle (not preface) to Henry Howard, later Duke of Norfolk. For a performance at court by a cast of noble amateurs, and for Rochester's prologue to the play, see **101** and n. below and Winn, *JD*, 245. Dennis discussed D's quarrel with Settle in *Remarks upon Pope's Homer* (1717) (*Works*, ii. 118). *GD*, iv. 680 n., summarized it, while leaving scope for SJ to provide more detailed illustration (see **37** below). *BB* virtually ignored it. For Settle's later career, see **115–16** below.

*sculptures*: SJ defines 'Sculpture' as 'The art of engraving on copper' (*Dict.*). *inflammation*: '1. The act of setting on flame' (*Dict.*).

**33.** D probably wrote only the preface and postscript to *Notes and Observations on the Empress of Morocco* (1674), which was mostly by the dramatist John Crowne (Winn, *JD*, 582 n.), as SJ should have known. Dennis (see **32** above) made it clear that Crowne and perhaps Thomas Shadwell were involved, and Jacob, i. 220–1, Wood, ii. 1076, and Shiels, *Lives*, iii. 350–1, also mentioned the joint authorship, later explained again by Malone in *Prose Works* (1800), i (i). 272–3 n. See M. E. Novak (ed.), *The Empress of Morocco and its Critics* (Los Angeles, 1968).

**34–41.** *Notes and Observations* is cited from *Works*, xvii. 83–184.

*Gent. Mag.* (July 1779), 363, commented on SJ's use of such material, whether or not by D himself, that the 'illiberal abuse of Settle, now obsolete, and ever disgusting, we could well have spared. Dabbling in a puddle is never pleasing.' See also Burke's remark quoted in 'Sources' above.

**34.** *Works*, xvii. 84–5.

**35.** *Works*, xvii. 85.

**36.** *Works*, xvii. 112–13 (probably not by D).

**37–9.** *Works*, xvii. 104–6 (probably not by D).

**40.** For 'sculptures', see **32** and n. above. Dennis wrote in 1717 that Settle's play was 'the First that ever was printed with Cuts' (*Works*, ii. 118).

*poor Dryden*: for other poets described by SJ as 'poor', see 'Lyttelton' **17** and n. below.

**41.** *Works*, xvii. 118–19. Malone, *Prose Works* (1800), ii. 273–4 n., and others accept the attribution to D of this parody of the opening speech of Act II of Settle's play.

**42.** For the inevitable envy of greatness, see 'Denham' **11** and n. above.

*the claps of multitudes*: cf. 'the claps of a playhouse' in **175** below, D's 'servile submission to an injudicious audience' in **326** below, and, for pleasing 'the multitude', see 'Cowley' **38** and n. above. Rochester referred in 'An Allusion to Horace', ll. 13–14, to 'the false judgment of an audience | Of clapping fools'. Cf. also Congreve's resolution 'to commit his quiet and his fame no more to the caprices of an audience' in 'Congreve' **25** below. Pope later refused to write for theatre, because 'everybody that did write for the stage was obliged to subject themselves to the players and the town' (Spence, i. 15; 'Pope' **70** n. below), and stated in his 'Preface' to Shakespeare (1725) that 'Stage-Poetry of all other, is more particularly levell'd to please the *Populace*, and its success more immediately depending upon the *Common Suffrage*' (*Prose Works*, ii. 15). Reynolds warned the students of the Royal Academy in 1772 to be 'select in those whom you endeavour to please', since 'the lowest style will be the most popular, as it falls within the compass of ignorance itself' (*Discourses*, 149).

**43.** D dedicated *An Evening's Love, or The Mock Astrologer* (acted 12 June 1668; published 13 Feb. 1671) to William Cavendish, Duke of Newcastle (see **29** and n. above), who wrote plays and verse as well as *A New Method and Extraordinary Invention to Dress Horses* (1667), which had first appeared in French (Antwerp, 1658).

The literary works and personality of 'his lady', Margaret Cavendish (1623–74), Duchess of Newcastle, have recently received much more attention: see 'Waller' **98** above, and G. Greer et al. (eds.), *Kissing the Rod* (1988), 163–74. D described her as 'a Lady whom our Age may justly equal with the *Sappho* of the *Greeks*, or the *Sulpitia* of the *Romans*' (*Works*, x. 199), and Langbaine, *Account of the English Dramatick Poets* (Oxford, 1691), 390–4, as 'worthy the Mention and Esteem of all Lovers of Poetry and Learning'. For her subsequent treatment in the biographical reference works consulted by SJ, see R. Terry, *Poetry and the Making of the English Literary Past* (Oxford, 2001), 262–5.

**44.** For D's remarks in his preface on the sources of the early 17th-century dramatists Ben Jonson, Francis Beaumont, and John Fletcher, his discussion of tragedy, comedy, and farce, his defence of his own 'immorality' (cf. **170–1, 204** below), and Charles II's comment on D's 'thefts', see Watson, i. 154, 145–50, 151–2, 153. SJ had encouraged Charlotte Lennox's demonstration of Shakespeare's use of Giambattista Giraldi Cinthio (1504–73) as a source in her *Shakespear Illustrated*, i (1753), 27–37: see *YW*, vii. 48 n. and 215.

**45.** Maximin's extravagant speeches in *Tyrannick Love, or the Royal Martyr* (acted 24 June 1669; published 1670) were notorious. D professed penitence for such 'sins' in the dedication to *The Spanish Fryar* (1681) (Watson, i. 276): see **334** below.

**46.** For the 'seven weeks', see Watson, i. 140–1. For similar claims, see **64, 264** below.

**47.** SJ was misled in his first sentence by the misdating of *Tyrannick Love* in 1677 by Langbaine, *English Dramatick Poets*, 173–4. For SJ's quotation from the preface, see Watson, i. 138, and for D's 'malice to the parsons', see also **179** below.

**48.** The two parts of *The Conquest of Granada* were acted in Dec. 1670 and Jan. 1671 (published 1672). Contemptuous of 'wonders' in most other contexts (see 'Cowley' **5** n. above), SJ here admits that they can be 'delightful' in the theatre. In 1765 he contrasted Shakespeare with dramatists who 'can only gain attention by hyperbol-ical or aggravated characters, by fabulous and unexampled excellence or depravity' (*YW*, vii. 64).

**49.** D's epilogue contrasts Jonson's 'mechanic humour' with 'an age more gallant': 'Wit's now arrived to a more high degree; | Our native language more refin'd and free. | Our ladies and our men now speak more wit | In conversation than those poets writ' (Watson, i. 167–8). The 'postscript' is D's 'Defence of the Epilogue' (Watson, i. 169–83). D had promised a 'second dialogue' on these matters in *Of Dramatick Poesy* (1667) (Watson, i. 17).

**50.** For 'probability', see 'Butler' **49** and n. above, and for attacks on D by Edward Howard, Richard Flecknoe, and Thomas Shadwell, see Winn, *JD*, 222–4.

    Martin Clifford (d. 1677) was secretary to the Duke of Buckingham and Master of the Charterhouse (1671): see also **94** below and 'Cowley' **1** n. above. His letters criticizing D circulated in MS at this time (Winn, *JD*, 231, 236) and were later published as *Notes upon Mr. Dryden's Poems, in Four Letters* (1687). GD, iv. 682 n., may have drawn SJ's attention to this pamphlet (*BB* ignored it). For pamphlets about D lent to SJ by Thomas Percy (1729–1811), Dean of Carlisle (1778), see headnote above.

**51.** SJ quotes Clifford, *Notes*, 3–4.

**52.** Clifford, *Notes*, 6–7, referred to D's statement that 'The first image I had [of Almanzor] was from the Achilles of Homer' (Watson, i. 163). For Ancient Pistol, see Shakespeare's *1 Henry IV* and *Henry V*.

**53–61.** For Settle, see **32–41** above. His reply to D (and his collaborators) in *Notes and Observations on the Empress of Morocco Revised* (1674) aimed to show that he was no more guilty of extravagant metaphor than D himself. Charles Gildon, *Lives and Characters of the English Dramatick Poets* [1699], 122, believed that, 'in his Dispute with Mr. *Dryden*, he had evidently the better of him; tho', being a modest Man, he suffer'd himself to be run down by his Antagonist in his Interest in the Town'.

**53.** From Settle, *Notes*, 23–5, on *The Indian Emperour*, 1. ii. 93 ff. As usual, there is some mistranscription in SJ's quotations.

**54.** Settle, *Notes*, 53.

**55a, 57a, 58a–b, 59a.** Not numbered as separate paragraphs by Hill (1905).

**55–55a.** Settle, *Notes*, 70 (adapted), quoting *Conquest of Granada I*, III. i. 261–7.

**56.** Settle, *Notes*, 74–5, quoting *Annus Mirabilis*, ll. 601–12.

*in his altitudes*: J. P. Hardy (ed.), *Johnson's Lives of the Poets: A Selection* (Oxford, 1971), 127 n., glossed 'altitudes' as 'lofty mood, ways, airs, phrases' (*OED*), but Settle seems in fact to mean '4. Height of excellence; superiority' (*Dict.*). Thomas Gray referred in 1748 to 'nonsense in all her altitudes' (*Corresp.*, i. 296), and SJ himself in 1782 to Queeney Thrale 'in all your altitudes, at the opera' (*Letters*, iv. 99). *Gent. Mag.* (1775), 559–60, in fact included the phrase in a list of euphemisms for drunkenness.

**57–59a.** Settle, *Notes*, 77–8.

**57.** *Conquest of Granada I*, II. i. 130, 226–7, and IV. ii. 287–8.

**58.** *Conquest of Granada II*, V. iii. 339–40, quoted again by SJ in **330** below and in a letter of 21 Jan. 1784 (*Letters*, iv. 275).

**58b.** Hill (1905) noted the allusion to *Poor Robin's Almanack*, published from 1664.

**59.** *Conquest of Granada I*, III. i. 510–14.

**60.** Settle, *Notes*, 80–1, quoting *Conquest of Granada I*, IV. i. 11–14, and IV. i. 4.

**61.** Settle, *Notes*, 82–4, citing *Annus Mirabilis*, ll. 925–8, Cowley, *Davideis*, Bk. I (*Poems*, ed. Waller (1905), 248), and *Conquest of Granada I*, III. i. 43–4 and II. i. 22–3.

**62.** *Marriage A-La-Mode* was acted in late 1671 (published 1673). SJ cites Langbaine, *English Dramatick Poets*, 166.

D's dedication thanked Rochester (q.v. above) for correcting the MS and for showing the comedy to Charles II (*Works*, xi. 221–4). Rochester did not in fact turn against D until 1676 (see **93, 101** below). D attacked him in the preface to *All for Love* (1678) and referred disapprovingly to him in 'A Discourse Concerning Satire' (1693) (Watson, i. 225–9, ii. 75). For the relationship, see Winn, *JD*, 244–55, 286–8, 307–9. The tone of SJ's references to Rochester suggests that he had not yet written his biography of him: see 'Rochester' headnote above.

**63.** D dedicated *The Assignation* (acted autumn 1672; published 1673) to Sir Charles Sedley (1639?–1701). For SJ's quotation, see Watson, i. 184; and for D's 'usual complaint', see **102, 137, 173, 182** below.

**64.** D himself claimed that *Amboyna, or The Cruelties of the Dutch to the English Merchants* (acted May 1673; published 1673) was 'contriv'd and written' in a month (*Works*, xii. 5). A few scenes are in blank verse. (By *The Virgin Martyr*, SJ means *Tyrannick Love, or the Royal Martyr*: see **45–6** above.) Based on the Dutch massacre of the English at Amboyna in 1623, *Amboyna* was primarily propaganda during the Anglo-Dutch War. D's epilogue, ll. 1–4, invokes Tyrtaeus and the Spartans.

**65–70.** At this point SJ's chronological survey jumps from 1673 to plays D wrote between 1679 and 1685. Osborn, *JD*, 26, pointed out that all these 'misplaced' plays appeared in vol. iv of Congreve's edition (1717), and suggested that either SJ accidentally picked up vol. v before vol. iv, or that 'his manuscript was disarranged when it reached the printer. The mistake was a simple mechanical one, and Johnson's use of source books is not involved.'

If **65–70** were moved to follow **81** below, SJ's chronology of the plays would be roughly correct. The likelihood that a leaf of SJ's MS was misplaced at some stage is strengthened by the fact that the text of **65–70** would have fitted neatly into the two sides of a leaf of the MS. SJ wrote on average 215 words per quarto page in the MS of 'Pope' (cf. *Journey* (1985), p. lii), and **65–70** contain some 400 words, slightly fewer than average because of the number of short paragraphs. This would also explain SJ's apparent reference in **68** to *Oedipus* as if he had already discussed this play, although he does not in fact mention it until **81**. See also **68** n. below.

**65.** *Troilus and Cressida* was acted by Apr. 1679 (published 1679). Langbaine, *English Dramadick Poets*, 173, praised the confrontation between Hector and Troilus in III. ii. D prefixed to the play 'The Grounds of Criticism in Tragedy', a more restrained version of his reply to Rymer's *Tragedies of the Last Age* (1678) in 'Heads of an Answer to Rymer' (see **358–405** below).

**66.** *The Spanish Fryar* (acted Nov. 1680; published 1681) combines a comic plot exposing a corrupt Catholic friar with a serious plot in favour of legitimate succession. In the context of the Popish Plot, D tried to defuse the explosive issue of Catholicism by attaching it to a figure of fun. The play was banned under James II, but revived by Queen Mary in 1689 (*Prose Works* (1800), i (i). 214–17 n.; Winn, *JD*, 332–6, 437).

D's dedication to Lord Haughton, 'recommending a Protestant play to a Protestant patron', boasted about the double plot (Watson, i. 274, 279), later praised by Addison in *Spectator* 267 (1712). SJ mentioned D's satisfaction with his double plot in 1765, but considered *The Merchant of Venice* superior in this respect (*YW*, vii. 241, and cf. 351).

**67.** For the quotation, in which D in fact wrote 'half a poet for the stage', see Watson, i. 279. For SJ's views on tragicomedy elsewhere, see 'Otway' **12** and n. above, *Rambler* 156 (1751), and *YW*, vii. 67.

**68.** *The Duke of Guise* (acted 28 Nov. 1682; published 1683) was an uncompromising and controversial anti-Whig collaboration with Nathaniel Lee (1653?–92). D gave a detailed account of his contribution, quoted by SJ from his *Vindication* of the play (see **69** below), because he was originally thought to be the sole author. For the full political context, see P. Kewes, 'D and the Staging of Popular Politics', in Hammond and Hopkins (eds.), *JD*, esp. 74–89.

SJ refers to D's earlier collaboration with Lee in *Oedipus* (1678) (see **81** below), as if he had already discussed it: for the probable accidental misplacing of these paragraphs, see **65–70** n. above. In the second sentence SJ originally wrote 'writing another play', which he revised in proof to 'writing a play', as if sensing that something had gone wrong (see Textual Notes).

**69.** *The Duke of Guise* drew a parallel between the French Holy League of the 16th century and the recent Protestant Association in England. The Duke of Monmouth, who was allegedly denigrated as the Duke of Guise in the play (and finally assassinated), succeeded in banning it for some months (Winn, *JD*, 381–6). D denied the identification with Monmouth and replied to other Whig attacks in a long and evasive pamphlet, *The Vindication of the Duke of Guise* (1683).

**70.** The correct title of D's opera is *Albion and Albanius* (acted 3 June 1685; published 1685). An allegory of the Restoration, with music by Louis Grabu, it grew out of D's plans for *King Arthur* in 1684 (see **85** below). It was in rehearsal when Charles II died in Feb. 1685. The Duke of Monmouth's invasion ten days after its first performance in June 1685 ended a run of six nights, as SJ could have learned from Downes, *Roscius Anglicanus* (1708), 40, or (as 'Scrutator' noted in *Gent. Mag.* (1779), 594) from D. E. Baker's *Companion to the Play-House* (1764). For SJ's misapplication of this information to *King Arthur* in 1783, see **85** and n. below. What may have been the first revival of *Albion and Albanius* after 312 years took place at the Dartington International Summer School, Devon, in Aug. 1997.

71. Returning to 1674, SJ resumes the chronological sequence of D's plays accidentally interrupted by **65–70** above.
    *The State of Innocence* (written by 1674, but not acted; published 1677) is a rhymed condensation (in about 1,400 lines) of Milton's *Paradise Lost*: see N. von Maltzahn, 'D's Milton and the Theatre of Imagination', in Hammond and Hopkins (eds.), *JD*, 32–56. For D's visits to the elderly Milton, who died in Nov. 1674, to seek permission to adapt his epic, see Winn, *JD*, 164–5, and for Milton's opinion of D, see 'Milton' **164** above. Dennis stated in 1721 that D admitted to him that, at the time of his meetings with M, he 'knew not half the Extent of his Excellence' (*Works*, ii. 169). For the suggestion that in 1675 D made use of Milton's *Samson Agonistes* in *Aureng-Zebe* (see **75–7** below), see *St. James's Magazine*, (1762), 144–52.
    SJ no doubt felt that Satan and the angel Raphael, quite apart from the unfallen Adam and Eve, could not 'decently be exhibited' in a public theatre. *The State of Innocence* may also have remained unacted because of the elaborate and expensive stage effects D visualized. (For two different stage versions of *Paradise Lost* performed in Bristol and Northampton in Feb. 2004, see Fergus Allen in *TLS*, 20 Feb. 2004, 20.)
    SJ quotes Marvell's 'On Mr. Milton's Paradise Lost', ll. 17–24, prefixed to the revised 1674 edition of the poem. For D's claim in 1677 to have written *The State of Innocence* in a month, see Watson, i. 196.

72. See D's dedication of *The State of Innocence* to Mary of Modena, Duchess of York: 'We think not the Day is long enough when we behold you . . . Our sight is so intent on the Object of its Admiration, that our Tongues have not leisure even to praise you; for Language seems too low a thing to express your Excellence; and our Souls are speaking so much within, that they despise all foreign conversation.' D compares his admiration to 'the rapture which Anchorites find in Prayer, when a Beam of the Divinity shines upon them' (*Works*, xii. 82–3).
    Discussing flattery in *Rambler* 104 (1751), SJ complained that 'the terms peculiar to the praise and worship of the Supreme Being, have been applied to wretches whom it was the reproach of humanity to number among men' (*YW*, iv. 193). For D as a flatterer, see also **88, 170, 172** below, and 'Waller' **69** and n. above. For objections to the mingling of sacred and profane, see also **238, 276, 295, 335** below, and 'Milton' **183** and n. above.

73. In 'The Author's Apology for Heroic Poetry and Poetic Licence' D states that 'Poetic licence I take to be the liberty, which poets have assumed to themselves in all ages, of speaking things in verse which are beyond the severity of prose', and that 'sublime subjects ought to be adorned with the sublimest, and (consequently often) with the most figurative expressions' (Watson, i. 205–7).

74. SJ quotes 'The Author's Apology' (Watson, i. 196 and n.). At least three transcripts of *The State of Innocence* have survived. For SJ's later comments on authors 'forced

to publish' by the supposed threat of a faulty 'surreptitious edition', see 'Pope' **53**
and n. below. D's friend John Oldham justified the publication of his 'Satyr against
Vertue' on such grounds in the 'Advertisement' to *Satyrs upon the Jesuits* (1681):
see *Poems*, ed. H. F. Brooks and R. Selden (Oxford, 1986), 4.

75. The hero of *Aureng-Zebe* (acted 17 Nov. 1675; published 1676) was an Indian
Muslim prince who obtained his throne somewhat deviously at the time of the
Restoration and was still alive. Adapting the story from François Bernier's *Voyages*
(1673), D in fact represented him as a model of filial piety and inner fortitude
(Winn, *JD*, 272–4). SJ refers to Racine's preface to *Bajazet* (1672): 'L'éloignement
des païs répare en quelque sorte la trop grande proximité des temps.'

76. In the prologue to *Aureng-Zebe* D 'presumes' that the play is the 'most correct of
his', but admits that he 'Grows weary of his long-loved mistress Rhyme' (ll. 8, 12).
As Hill (1905) noted, a letter in Addison's *Guardian* 110 (1713) criticized the
speeches of D's 'imperial' characters for the impropriety and coarseness beneath
their 'shining Dress of Words'. In *Rambler* 125 (1751) SJ later argued that in
*Aureng-Zebe*, III. i., 'every circumstance concurs to turn tragedy to farce' (*YW*, iv.
304). For the appeal of the 'domestick', see 'Otway' **10** and n. above.
    The 'complaint of life' is the famous speech of the imprisoned Aureng-Zebe in
IV. i. 33 ff. ('When I consider life, 'tis all a cheat'), which SJ had echoed in his *Irene*
(1749), III. ii. 19–33, and quoted at least three times in the *Dict.* (at some length
under 'Life'), as well as in conversation (*Life*, ii. 124–5, and cf. iv. 303). Thomas
Davies, *Dramatic Miscellanies* (1784), ii. 159–60, stated that it was 'still repeated by
all lovers of poetry', but that he had only ever heard SJ refer to Nourmahal's reply
to it.

77. SJ repeats his opinion that John Sheffield, Duke of Buckinghamshire, lacked 'the
fire and fancy of a poet' in 'Sheffield' **28** below. (For distinctions elsewhere between
the poet and the writer of verses, see 'Cowley' **51** above and 'Addison' **14** below.)
For Sheffield's patronage of D, see **26** n. above, and cf. Dennis in 1701: "Tis
known to all the observing World, that you generously began to espouse him, when
he was more than half oppress'd, by a very formidable Party in the Court of King
*Charles* II' (*Works*, i. 198).
    D mentions his plan for a heroic poem, which Sheffield had already related to
Charles II, in the dedication to *Aureng-Zebe*, here loosely quoted by SJ (*Works*, xii.
154–5). For the projected epic on King Arthur, and his accusation in 1700 that
Richard Blackmore had stolen the plan, see Watson, ii. 91–2, 292–3, and i. 191, and
**140, 145, 176** below.

78. *All for Love: or The World Well Lost* (acted 12 Dec. 1677; published 1678) was
adapted from Shakespeare. In 'A Parallel betwixt Painting and Poetry' (1695), D
said that *The Spanish Fryar* 'was given to the people: and I never writ anything for
myself but *Anthony and Cleopatra*' (Watson, ii. 207).
    SJ does not mention that *All for Love* was 'Written in Imitation of Shakespeare's
Stile' (cf. his objections to another imitator in 'Rowe' **15** below), or that, the better
to imitate 'the divine Shakespeare', D now 'disencumbered' himself 'from rhyme'
(Watson, i. 231): cf. **20** above and **203** below. Atterbury later stated that, as 'the
living Glory of our English Poetry', D 'has disclaim'd the use of [rhyme] upon the
Stage, tho no man ever employ'd it there so happily as He. 'Twas the strength of his
Genius that first brought it into Credit in Plays; and 'tis the force of his Example

that has thrown it out agen' (*The Second Part of Mr. Waller's Poems* (1690), sigg. A8–A8ᵛ).

*the romantick omnipotence of Love*: Corneille had made the conflict of love and honour central to French tragedy in the mid-17th century. As early as 1739 SJ had referred, in his notes to Crousaz, to the fashionable 'infection' of gallantry 'filling the stage with amorous sadness, or refined obscenity' (*OASJ*, 94). Joseph Warton also objected to this 'epedemical effeminacy' in *Adventurer* 113 (1753) and *Essay on Pope* (1756), 262–5, and SJ complained again in 1765 about love as 'the universal agent' in drama ('love is only one of many passions, and . . . has no great influence upon the sum of life'): see *YW*, vi. 62–3, and cf. also 'Waller' 121 above, and *Life*, ii. 460. Writing about *All for Love* in 1721, Dennis asked whether there 'was ever any thing so pernicious, so immoral, so criminal, as the Design of that Play?' (*Works*, ii. 163; for the place of love in tragedy, see also i. 438–9, 473).

Yet SJ also found it hard to envisage a tragedy without at least some love interest, which he had provided in his own *Irene* (1749), and see also his remarks in 'Addison' **66, 87** below. In **323–4** below he comments on D's insensibility to 'Love, as it subsists in itself, with no tendency but to the person loved'. In conversation he could assert of 'the passion of love' that 'its violence and ill effects were much exaggerated' (*Life*, ii. 122), but also insisted that 'we must not ridicule a passion which he who never felt never was happy, and he who laughs at never deserves to feel—a passion which has caused the change of empires, and the loss of worlds—a passion which has inspired heroism and subdued avarice' (*J. Misc.*, i. 290). See also J. Gray, '"A Native of the Rocks": J's Handling of the Theme of Love', in P. Nath (ed.), *Fresh Reflections on SJ* (Troy, NY, 1987), 106–22.

*romantick*: '1. Resembling the tales of romances; wild. 2. Improbable; false. 3. Fanciful; full of wild scenery' (*Dict.*). Cf. **137** below, and 'Swift' **53** and 'Pope' **141, 199** below.

80. *The Kind Keeper, or Mr. Limberham* (acted 11 Mar. 1678; published 1679), a bawdy farce about 'our crying sin of keeping', was suppressed after three performances. D's dedication states that he 'alter'd or omitted in the Press' passages which gave offence, perhaps to identifiable and influential 'keepers' of mistresses (*Works*, xiv. 5–6). *BB*, iii. 1752 n. (but not *GD*), quoted Langbaine, *English Dramatick Poets*, 164, on this matter.

81. In *Oedipus* (acted late 1678; published 1679) D collaborated again with Nathaniel Lee (see **68** and n. above). He specified his contribution in his *Vindication of the Duke of Guise* (1683), 42. For earlier treatments of the subject, including Corneille's *Œdipe* (1659), see *Works*, xiii. 50–69; and, for SJ's discussion of Sophocles' *Oedipus*, see his preface to Maurice's *Poems* (1779) (*OASJ*, 588–90).

82. Having inadvertently dealt with D's plays between 1679 and 1685 in **65–70** above, SJ now abruptly moves forward more than a decade from 1678 to *Don Sebastian* (see also **139** below). D's preface explained that it had proved 'insupportably too long' and that he had cut 1,200 lines from 'the most poetical parts' in performance (Watson, ii. 44–5). For Dorax and Sebastian, see *Don Sebastian*, IV. iii. 381–669, and for SJ's earlier demonstration that another scene 'degenerates too much towards buffoonery and farce', see *Rambler* 125 (1751) (*YW*, iv. 302–3).

**82a.** Not numbered as a separate paragraph by Hill (1905). *Don Sebastian* (acted 4 Dec. 1689; published 1690) was D's first play since 1685.

**83.** D acknowledged his debt to Plautus and Molière in the dedication to *Amphitryon* (acted Oct. 1690, with music by Henry Purcell; published 1690). In the 18th century, it was second in popularity only to *The Spanish Fryar* among D's plays (*Works*, xv. 224–5, 462). For Cibber's account of D reading it to the actors, see 'Congreve' **7** n. below.

**84.** D's preface to *Cleomenes, The Spartan Hero* (acted Apr. 1692; published 1692) mentioned the 'foolish' objection 'rais'd against me by the Sparks, for *Cleomenes* not accepting the Favours of *Cassandra*' (*Works*, xvi. 78). SJ quotes (loosely) Steele's anecdote from *Guardian* 45 (1713). *Cleomenes* was in fact also 'remarkable' in that it was temporarily prohibited by Queen Mary for political reasons, as Oldys noted in his annotated Langbaine (ii, opp. 157). Cf. Winn, *JD*, 453.

**85.** *King Arthur* (acted by June 1691, with music by Purcell; published 1691) was a revision of the original 'opera' D planned in 1684 (Winn, *JD*, 393–4). His dedication to George Savile, Marquis of Halifax, explains that he wrote it for Charles II, whose clemency, moderation, and good sense he praises (*Works*, xvi. 3–4). The political sensitivity of some of SJ's readers is clear from Dr Samuel Beilby's reaction, in *Remarks on Doctor J's Lives* (York, 1782), 15–17, to his reference to D's 'pleasing account' of Charles II's 'latter life': 'What more could have been said by the meanest zealot for papacy and despotism?' (Beilby echoes the last words of **116** below.)

   In 1783 SJ contradicted his initial statement that *King Arthur* was never acted by carelessly adding the final sentence about Monmouth's invasion, which in fact concerned *Albion and Albanius* (see **70** and n. above, and Textual Notes). Hawkins, *J's Works* (1787), ii. 339 n., noted that *King Arthur* was in fact 'well received, and is yet a favourite entertainment', and Malone, *Prose Works*, i (i). 212 n., pointed out SJ's confusion. SJ obviously relied on *GD*, iv. 678 n., which merely listed the play, rather than *BB*, iii. 1752 n., which confirmed that it had been acted.

**86.** D dedicated *Love Triumphant* (acted Jan. 1694; published 1694) to James Cecil, Earl of Salisbury, a prominent Catholic and Jacobite, who had died in Oct. 1693. For SJ's (adapted) quotation, see *Works*, xvi. 169, and for D's 'lowness of fortune' after the Revolution, see **136–7** below.

**86a.** Not numbered as a separate paragraph by Hill (1905). For D's admission that '*Aristotle*... has declar'd, that the Catastrophe which is made from the change of Will is not of the first Order of Beauty', see *Works*, xvi. 169. A critic described the play as 'one of the worst he ever writt, if not the very worst' (Winn, *JD*, 473). In his prologue D bade farewell to the stage: for his first play, see **14** above.

**87.** For D's finances, see also **183–4** below.

   Outside court circles, antagonism to the theatre lingered from the Common-wealth period and resurfaced in the later attacks on the stage by Jeremy Collier in 1698 (see **175** below and 'Congreve' **18–23** below) and others. John Evelyn wrote on 18 Sept. 1666 that he was 'very seldom at any time, going to the publique *Theaters*, for many reasons, now as they were abused, to an atheistical liberty, fowle + undecent; Women now (& never 'til now) permitted to appear & act, which inflaming severall young noble-men, & gallants, became their whores, & to some their Wives' (*Diary*, iii. 465–6). But SJ may overstate the narrowness of theatre audiences in the later Restoration period: cf. 'Otway' **9** above. For 'dissolute licentiousness', see also **170** below.

*The first that had two nights*: for the origins of the practice of awarding the dramatist the third night's takings (less house expenses), see *The London Stage*, i (1965), pp. lxxx–lxxxiii. Thomas Southerne's dedication to *Sir Anthony Love* (1690) contains the first clear reference to a second benefit on the sixth night, as Warton, *Essay*, ii (1782), 401, noted: for Southerne, see **90, 177** below, and 'Fenton' **7** and n. below. This practice later became fairly common, as did a third benefit night after 1700. Mrs Thrale recorded in Aug./Sept. 1777: 'Mrs Porter the famous Actress told Johnson who told me that Southern was the first Poet who had two Benefit Nights, and that Rowe was the first who had three' (*Thraliana*, i. 132; for Mary Porter, see 'Addison' **61** n. below). Shiels, *Lives*, v. 328–9, described Southerne as the first author to enjoy second and third benefits, stating that he received £700 for his last play, whereas Dryden never made more than £100. According to Malone, *Supplement to Shakespeare* (1780), i. 43, Farquhar had a third benefit for *The Constant Couple* (1700). For Dennis's complaint that he was denied a second benefit for a tragedy in 1719, see his *Works*, i. 176–80.

*The London Stage* mentions several authors in the 1680s and 1690s who solicited attendance at benefit nights to increase their profits. Shiels, *Lives*, v. 328–9, claimed that D disdained the 'degree of servility' involved in such 'drudgery of solicitation' of 'persons of distinction'. SJ's estimate of D's £100 includes the benefit performance, the patron's reward for the dedication of the printed text, and the sale of the copyright. Warton, *Essay*, ii (1782), 248 n., estimated that D usually received £25 for the copyright of his plays, and £70 from benefit nights. For Reed's estimate of SJ's own profits from *Irene* (1749), see *Life*, i. 198 n.

88. For 'flattery', see **72** above, and **170, 172** below.

89. Fleeman (1962), 223, noted a curious textual feature of the first sentence. In a cancel found in almost all copies of *Prefaces* (1779), vol. iii, sig. f8, the text of the proofs was revised to 'a kind of learning then little known, and therefore welcome as a novelty, and of that flexile and applicable kind, that it might be always introduced without apparent violence or affectation' (see Textual Notes). Perhaps by accidentally working from unbound sheets of 'Dryden', the compositor printed the uncancelled text in *Lives* (1781), followed by all later editions. (The uncancelled text survived in a copy of *Prefaces*, vol. iii, in the Rothschild Collection in Trinity College, Cambridge.) Since SJ acquiesced in this reversion to the unrevised text in *Lives* (1781) (when a small, possibly authorial, revision was made) and, more significantly, in 1783, it is retained here. 'Scrutator' in *Gent. Mag.* (1783), 47, noted this apparent 'revision' of the text in 1781.

    SJ here takes at face value what the 'hack author' in Swift's *A Tale of a Tub* (1704) claimed D had told him 'in Confidence' about his critical prefaces: 'I much fear, his Instructions have edify'd out of their Place, and taught Men to grow wiser on certain Points, where he never intended they should' (ed. A. C. Guthkelch and D. N. Smith (Oxford, 1958), 131). For Swift and D, see 'Swift' **18** below.

90. Most new plays had a specially written prologue and epilogue: Colley Cibber received two guineas for a prologue in 1695. It was probably in 1682, however, that D asked Southerne for six guineas for both prologue and epilogue for *The*

*Loyal Brother* (*London Stage*, i, p. cxxxvi). SJ's anecdote may derive from Warburton's note on 'To Mr. Thomas Southern, on his Birth-day, 1742' (which describes him as 'sent down to raise | The price of prologues and of plays') in Pope's *Works* (1751), vi. 82 n.; or from Warton's *Essay on Pope* (1756), 260, both sources stating that D asked for six rather than four guineas for writing both prologue and epilogue. Shiels, *Lives*, v. 328 and n., repeated the story, but gave the figures as five and ten guineas ('From the information of a gentleman personally acquainted with Mr. Southern, who desires to have his name conceal'd'). For Malone's reconsideration of the evidence, see D's *Prose Works* (1800), i (i). 453–6.

For comparative purposes, it is worth noting that SJ received two guineas for each *Rambler* in the 1750s; and when, early in his career, he supplied clergymen with sermons, 'his price, I am informed, was a moderate one, a guinea' (Hawkins, *Life* (1787), 391). He was probably not paid for the few theatrical prologues he wrote.

91. For D's self-confessed lack of dramatic genius, see **12** and n. above, and **264, 329** below.

For D's contract in 1668 with the King's Company to produce three (not four) plays a year in return for a share in the company's profits, see Osborn, *JD*, 202–7, and Winn, *JD*, 191. D freed himself from the contract, estimated as originally worth over £300 p.a., by about 1675. Malone, *Supplement to Shakespeare* (1780), i. 395–6, printed a document in which the shareholders complained of D's failure to deliver the promised three plays a year. SJ may have learned about it from Isaac Reed, who then owned the document. Reed described the contract itself in *Biographia Dramatica* (1782), i. 134, as involving four plays, but Malone corrected this in his supplementary notes to vol. i.

92. Cf. Mrs Thrale-Piozzi's later marginal comment on the six plays D supposedly wrote in 1678: 'Impossible!!! The man, veins, and bowels, must have been left wholly *empty*, writing as he did six plays in one year—what nonsense!' (Lobban, 137). As Malone, *Prose Works* (1800), i (i). 75–6, showed, SJ was misled into this wildly inaccurate statement by the misdating of these plays by Langbaine, *English Dramatick Poets*, 152, 154, 157, 170, 172, repeated by Jacob, i. 80–2: for the correct dates, see **78, 63, 48, 29, 71** above, and cf. SJ's remarks on the difficulty of dating such plays in his 'Advertisement'. Isaac Reed had corrected the dates in *Lives*, ii (1790), 53–4 nn.

One of Langbaine's purposes had been to demonstrate the extent of D's borrowings (cf. **28** above and **103** below). Lope Felix de Vega Carpio (1562–1635), the Spanish dramatist, claimed to have written 1,500 plays, of which about 470 are extant.

93. For D and Rochester, see **62** and n. above and **101** below.

94. *The Rehearsal* (acted 7 Dec. 1671; published 1672) was originally written by George Villiers, Duke of Buckingham (1628–87), and others before 1665, when the plague closed the London theatres. For Buckingham's assistants, see **50–2** above, 'Butler' **13** above, and 'Sprat' **4** below. SJ also mentions Waller and Cowley as collaborators in 'Waller' **102** above. Wood, ii. 804, and *GD*, iv. 679 n. (but not *BB*), stated that Sprat, Clifford, and Butler were involved as early as 1664. By the time it was performed, D was Poet Laureate (**26** above).

For D's explanation in 1693 of his decision not to respond to *The Rehearsal*, see Watson, ii. 77–8. 'On the Duke of Bucks', quoted by Malone, *Prose Works* (1800), i (i). 95–7 n., from *Poems on Affairs of State*, ii (1703), 216, mocked the time taken to write the play ('Troy was not longer before it was won'): cf. 'Butler' **15** n. above. For performances of *The Rehearsal* in 1717, see 'Pope' **233** and n. below. Garrick acted in it in 1741 and it had been staged in London as recently as 1777 and 1778.

**95.** For similar complaints, see **11** and n. above. In *Rambler* 103 (1751) SJ wrote about 'the cobwebs of petty inquisitiveness', which entangle some minds in 'trivial employments and minute studies' (*YW*, iv. 187). Cf. Pope's hope of persuading the world that he had 'a mind too great for such minute employment' as 'verbal criticism' ('Pope' **127** below).

**96.** As Malone, *Prose Works*, i (i). 100, noted, SJ was confused here by his misdating of *The Conquest of Granada* (acted 1670–1), *Tyrannick Love* (published 1670), and *Marriage A-La-Mode* (acted late 1671). *The Assignation* (1672) was parodied in the additions to *The Rehearsal* (3rd edn., 1675).

Like Langbaine, *GD*, iv. 679 n., named only three of these plays (omitting *Marriage A-La-Mode*), whereas *BB*, iii. 1754 n., quoted the parodies of *Conquest of Granada* and *Tyrannick Love*, and added *The Wild Gallant* and *Marriage A-La-Mode* as additional targets. SJ here seems closer to *BB* than to *GD*. The *Rehearsal* in fact glances at even more plays by D and other dramatists.

**97.** Bilboa, originally the leading character, was modelled first on Sir Robert Howard (see **17–18, 23, 25** above), and only later on Sir William Davenant (see **26, 30** above), after Howard became Buckingham's political ally (Winn, *JD*, 178–9).

**98.** For Bayes's nose, see II. v and III. i. The damage to Davenant's nose from venereal disease was notorious, but the Earl of Arlington, Buckingham's political enemy, also wore a patch on his nose: see M. Stocker, 'Political Allusion in *The Rehearsal*', *PQ* 67 (1988), 11–35.

**98a.** Not numbered as a separate paragraph by Hill (1905).

**99.** SJ has evidently changed his mind since doubting on 31 Mar. 1772 that Bayes ('a mighty silly character') 'was meant for Dryden' (*Life*, ii. 168). In July 1773 Mrs Thrale noted that he had said of *The Rehearsal* that 'the greatness of Dryden's Character is even now the only principle of Vitality which preserves that Play from a State of Putrefaction' (*Thraliana*, i. 172, and cf. *Life*, iv. 320).

For biographical inferences from the depiction of Bayes the poet in *The Rehearsal*, including D's addiction to snuff and his spectacles, see Winn, *JD*, 44, 219, 220, 230–1, 579 nn.; and for Bayes's blooding and purging, see *The Rehearsal*, II. i. 114–20. Osborn, *JD*, 29, noted that SJ was the first biographer of D to cite Charles Lamotte, *An Essay on Poetry and Painting* (1730), 103.

**100.** *The Rehearsal*, III. v, included parody of Davenant's *Love and Honour* (1649; revived 1661). No printed source has so far been found for SJ's suggestion that this scene also alluded to James Butler, Duke of Ormond (1610–88), the Royalist commander in Ireland. As elsewhere, SJ's 'is said' points to an oral source, probably his friend Thomas Percy, who for many years planned an edition of *The Rehearsal*: see *Percy Corresp.*, iii (Warton). 148–67. Although Ormond is not mentioned in the surviving proofsheets of Percy's 'New Key' to the play (Bodleian Library), an autograph note on a copy of *The Rehearsal* which he collated with other editions reads: 'The dispute of Love & Honour referred to the Marquis of Ormond being supposed engaged with a Mistress, while his army was defeated before Dublin in 1649.' Percy tantalizingly added 'See . . .', but fading and fraying have made the reference illegible.

In 1730 Jacob Tonson had a 'key' to *The Rehearsal*, which he 'refuses to print . . . because he had been so much obliged to Dryden' (Spence, i. 277).

**101.** For Settle's *Empress of Morocco*, see **32** and n. above. Rochester wrote a prologue for the performance at court which followed the public production on 3 July 1673. Hill (1905) traced the phrase quoted by SJ to the life of Rochester attributed to Saint-Évremond in *The Works of the Earls of Rochester and Roscommon* (3rd edn., 1709), sig. b8, but it in fact refers to Rochester's patronage of John Crowne, not Settle: 'his Lordship withdrew his Favours, as if he would be still in Contradiction to the Town.'

*town*: '5. The court end of London' (*Dict.*).

**102.** For D's 'complaints', see **63** above, and **137, 162, 173** and 'Prior' **5** below; and for authorial self-confidence, 'Milton' **26** and n. above.

**103.** Bayes boasts of his plagiarism in *The Rehearsal*, I. i. Langbaine, *English Dramatick Poets*, was the most assiduous, but not the only, detector of D's borrowings (see **92** above): see **229, 329** below and Osborn, *JD*, 177, 237–40. D tried to justify his methods of composition in the preface to *An Evening's Love* (1671) (Watson, i. 152–5).

For 'generality' as making 'no impression on the reader', see **283** and n. below.

**104.** The estimate of twenty-eight plays is correct, if D's *Secular Masque* (1700) is excluded.

**105.** It was widely believed that D at least assisted John Sheffield, Earl of Mulgrave (later Duke of Buckinghamshire), with 'An Essay on Satire', which circulated in MS in 1679. The poem satirized both Rochester and the Duchess of Portsmouth, mistress of Charles II, who were suspected of responsibility for the attack on D in Rose Alley on 18 Dec. 1679: see e.g. Wood, ii. 804–5. For Mulgrave's statement that D was 'intirely innocent of the whole matter', see 'Sheffield' **23** and n. below, and Winn, *JD*, 325–9, 593–4.

As 'Scrutator' (John Loveday) noted in *Gent. Mag.* (1783), 47, the couplet SJ quotes from *Essay on Poetry* was added to the poem in 1691 and did not appear in the text in *Eng. Poets* (1779): it should in any case read 'deserve' for 'deserves'.

**106.** SJ refers to D's 'Character of Polybius and his Writings' in Sir Henry Sheeres's translation of Polybius' *History* (2 vols., 1693); the 'Life of Lucian' (written *c.*1696), published in *Works of Lucian* (1711); the 'Life of Plutarch' in *Plutarch's Lives* (5 vols., 1683–6), vol. i; and Bk. I of the *Annals and History of Cornelius Tacitus* (3 vols., 1698), which Thomas Gordon, *Works of Tacitus* (1728), 1–2, accused D of translating from the French of Amelot de la Houssaye rather than the Latin.

**107.** Rymer, Settle, Otway (q.v.), Tate, and Duke (q.v.) were among the contributors to *Ovid's Epistles, Translated by Several Hands* (1680). D in fact translated two epistles (VII and XI) and collaborated with Mulgrave on XVII.

D's preface (Watson, i. 268–73) cites Ben Jonson's translation of Horace's *Ars Poetica* (1640) as an example of literal translation or 'metaphrase' (see **223** below);

Waller's *The Passion of Dido* (1658) from *Aeneid*, Bk. IV (not mentioned in 'Waller' above), as an example of free translation or 'paraphrase'; and Cowley and Denham as pioneers of 'imitation', when the translator writes 'as he supposes that author would have done, had he lived in our age, and in our country'. SJ had quoted D under 'Imitation', 'Metaphrase', and 'Paraphrase' in the *Dict*.

SJ also refers to George Sandys, *Ovid's Metamorphoses* (1621–6) (see **223** below, 'Cowley' **197** above, and 'Pope' **5** below), Barten Holyday (and William Dewey), *Juvenal and Persius Translated* (Oxford, 1673) (see **223**, **299** below), and Sir Richard Fanshawe's translation of Guarini's *Pastor fido* (1647) (see 'Denham' **24** and 'Roscommon' **36** above). See also **223–6**, **267**, **299–300**, **304**, **356** below, and, for SJ's views on translation elsewhere, 'Cowley' **125** and 'Denham' **32** and n. above.

108. D wrote *Absalom and Achitophel* (1681) during the Exclusion Crisis of 1681, when Anthony Ashley Cowper (1621–83), Earl of Shaftesbury, tried to secure the succession to the throne of James Scott (1649–85), Duke of Monmouth, Charles II's illegitimate but Protestant son, in preference to the Catholic James, Duke of York. D's satire appeared a week before Shaftesbury's trial for treason.

109. SJ's father Michael Johnson (1656–1731), bookseller in Lichfield, was described as a bookbinder in the town by 29 Jan. 1683 (*Life*, i. 35 n.). For another reference to him, see 'Sprat' **19** below. For the story that he took the infant SJ to hear Henry Sacheverell preach at Lichfield in 1710, see *Life*, i. 38–9 and n., and for Sacheverell's trial, see 'Addison' **14** and n. below. G. Holmes, *The Trial of Doctor Sacheverell* (1973), 74–5, estimated that some 100,000 copies of his seditious sermon (1709) were sold.

110. See *Spectator* 512 (1712): 'in Writings of this kind, the Reader comes in for half of the Performance ... The Poetry is indeed very fine, but had it been much finer it would not have so much pleased, without a Plan which gave the Reader an Opportunity of exerting his own Talents.' SJ himself wrote in *Rambler* 106 (1751): 'It is not difficult to obtain readers, when we discuss a question which every one is desirous to understand, which is debated in every assembly, and has divided the nation into parties' (*YW*, iv. 201–2). For *Absalom and Achitophel*, see also **268–72** below.

111. Winn, *JD*, 363, discusses four such responses to *Absalom and Achitophel*. For the pamphlet attacks on D lent to SJ by Thomas Percy, see headnote above.

112. Rochester's *Works* (3rd edn., 1709), 111, and Jacob, ii. 193, attributed *Satyr, To His Muse. By the Author of Absalom & Achitophel* (1682) (see also **157** and **166** below) to John, Lord Somers (1651–1716). Pope rejected the attribution in *Epistle to Dr. Arbuthnot* (1734), l. 141 n. The author may have been Thomas Shadwell.

113. *Azaria and Hushai* (1682), ascribed to Elkanah Settle (see **32** ff. above) by Wood, ii. 1077–8, is now thought to be by Samuel Pordage (1633–1691?). For D's attribution of *Absalom Senior, or Achitophel Transprosed* (1682) to Settle, see *The Second Part of Absalom and Achitophel*, l. 446. For SJ's impatience with minute 'poetical transactions', see **11**, **95** and nn. above.

114. *The Medall* (published 16 Mar. 1682) responded to the medal struck by the Whigs to mark the Grand Jury's verdict in Shaftesbury's trial on 24 Nov. 1681. SJ's defines 'Ignoramus' by means of a long legal quotation, which notes that its

meaning is in effect 'that all farther inquiry upon that party, for that fault, is thereby stopped' (*Dict.*). For SJ's later MS note, derived from Spence, about the poem's origins, see **183** n. below.

115. *The Medal Revers'd* (1682), attributed to Settle by Wood (1721), ii. 1077, is also now thought to be by Samuel Pordage (cf. **113** n. above).

   SJ's account of Settle derives from Pope's notes to *Dunciad* (1729), I. 88, III. 16, 281 (*TE*, v. 69–70, 151, 183). He had described Settle's all-purpose elegy and epithalamium in *Idler* 12 (1758) (*YW*, ii. 42). For Settle's numerous poems on funerals and marriages after 1700, often found in distinctive presentation bindings, see Foxon, *English Verse*, S 226–349. Foxon noted that 'Between 1714 and 1723 the same basic poem *Thalia triumphans* was issued with alternative additions applying it to various persons' (i. 713).

   Dennis had described Settle as a once 'formidable Rival' to D in *Remarks on Pope's Homer* (1717) (*Works*, ii. 118). Leonard Welsted also noted that Settle was 'formerly the mighty rival' of D in his *Epistles, Odes, &c.* (2nd edn., 1725), pp. xl–xli.

116. D wrote the character of Doeg in Nahum Tate's *The Second Part of Absalom and Achitophel* (1682), ll. 412–56, as well as the character of Shadwell as Og (see **136** and n. below).

   On 17 July 1778, while writing 'Dryden', SJ tried to obtain information about Settle as the last of the 'City Poets': see headnote above. He asked Richard Clark for details of 'The history of that office—when or how it began—the succession of City Laureats—their salary—their employment—when Settle obtained it—how long he held it', and for information about the elderly Settle's admission to the Charterhouse. He explained that 'The account of the City Poet will be a great addition to my Work' (*Letters*, iii. 120–1). SJ no doubt recalled his conversation with John Wilkes about Settle as City Poet on 15 May 1776 (*Life*, iii. 75–6). Pope's note to *Dunciad*, I. 90, describing Settle as 'Poet to the City of *London*. His office was to compose yearly panegyrics upon the Lord Mayor', probably influenced a satiric reference to Settle in SJ's own early poem 'The Young Author' (*c.*1729), l. 24 (*Poems* (1974), 33). For Settle's later career, see F. C. Brown, *Elkanah Settle: His Life and Works* (Chicago, 1910), and P. Rogers, 'Pope, Settle and the Fall of Troy', in *Literature and Popular Culture in Eighteenth-Century England* (1985), 87–101.

   As noted by Wood, ii. 1078, Settle's *Panegyrick* (1683) praised George Jeffreys (1644–89), Baron Jeffreys, the notoriously brutal Lord Chief Justice.

117. Cf. **11** and n. above. SJ's impatience with the 'tedious' problem of dating D's miscellaneous verse, such as his contributions to Tonson's *Miscellany Poems* (1684) and *Sylvae* (1685), may help to explain his failure to refer here to *Religio Laici* (1682) (see **118**, **284–5** below), which would have been relevant to the following discussion of D's conversion.

118. Charles II died on 6 Feb. 1685. For James II's Catholicism, see 'Roscommon' **19** and n. above.

   Sir Kenelm Digby (1603–65) (see 'Cowley' **9** above) was apparently brought up as a Roman Catholic after his father's conversion. Hawkins, *J's Works* (1787), ii. 349 n., traced the apocryphal story about the brothers John (1549–1607) and William (1544?–94) Rainolds or Reynolds to Thomas Fuller's *Church-History*

(1655), Bk. X, 47. The theologian William Chillingworth (1602–44) converted temporarily in 1630–4: see *Rambler* 29 (1750) (*YW*, iii. 150–1). For SJ's comments on 30 Mar. 1778 on the conversion to, and reconversion from, Roman Catholicism of Sir Robert Sibbald (1641–1722), see *Life*, iii. 227–8.

D had certainly 'enquired why he was a protestant' in *Religio Laici* (cf. **117** n. above). On 15 Apr. 1778, while writing 'Dryden', SJ condemned a young woman who had become a Quaker: 'She could not have any proper conviction that it was her duty to change her religion, which is the most important of all subjects . . . we ought not, without very strong conviction indeed, to desert the religion in which we have been educated. That is the religion given you, the religion in which it may be said that Providence has placed you. If you live conscientiously in that religion, you may be safe.' SJ 'rose again into passion, and attacked the young proselyte in the severest terms of reproach' (*Life*, iii. 298–9). SJ told Hester Thrale, 2 July 1784: 'If you have abandoned your children and your religion, God forgive your wickedness' (*Letters*, iv. 338). For other reflections on conversion to Roman Catholicism, see 'Garth' **16** and n. below.

119. D's warrant as Poet Laureate and Historiographer Royal was renewed on 27 Apr. 1685, some two months after James II's accession (Winn, *JD*, 412). For 'profession', see **8** n. above and **125** below. Derrick (1760 edn.), i, pp.xxii–xxiii, defended D against the charge of being 'a time-server and hypocrite in religion'. Joseph Towers, *Essay on SJ* (1786), commented that SJ's own account 'dextrously palliated' D's 'turning Papist, on the accession of a Popish king' (*Early Biographies* (1974), 210). Although D's conversion has often been seen as opportunistic, it involved some disadvantages (see Winn, *JD*, 413, 610 n.). See also **158** below, and the conclusion of D's letter in **406** below.

SJ said a few months before his death, 'I would be a Papist if I could. I have fear enough; but an obstinate rationality prevents me. I shall never be a Papist, unless on the near approach of death, of which I have a great terrour' (*Life*, iv. 289; and cf. ii. 103, 255, and Boswell, *Making of the Life*, 134). For his usually hostile attitude to Roman Catholicism, see M. Suarez, SJ, 'J's Christian Thought', in G. Clingham (ed.), *Cambridge Companion to SJ* (Cambridge, 1997), 196. SJ's allusion to 'my late conversion' not long before his death (*YW*, i. 417–18) probably refers to a new state of repentance rather than conversion into a new faith. See J. M. Osborn, 'Dr. J and the Contrary Converts', in F. W. Hilles (ed.), *New Light on J* (New Haven, 1959), 297–317; D. J. Greene, 'Dr. J's "Late Conversion": A Reconsideration', in M. Wahbi (ed.), *Johnsonian Studies* (Cairo, 1962), 61–92; M. Quinlan, *SJ: A Layman's Religion* (Madison, 1964), 163–72; and C. F. Chapin, *The Religious Thought of SJ* (Ann Arbor, 1968), 32–51.

120. Elsewhere, but perhaps not here, 'I am willing to believe' usually implies some scepticism, as in 'Gray' **22** below.

SJ's last sentence may echo D's 'To the Reader' prefixed to *The Hind and the Panther* (1687): 'I may safely say, that Conscience is the Royalty and Prerogative of every Private man. He is absolute in his own Breast, and accountable to no Earthly Power, for that which passes only betwixt God and Him.' But cf. also 'actions are visible, though motives are secret' ('Cowley' **44** above); 'The fact is certain; the motives we must guess' ('Addison' **57** below); 'The heart cannot be completely known', in SJ's 'Life' in Zachary Pearce, *A Commentary on the Four Evangelists*

(1777), i, p.xxxvii; and 'Sermon 16': 'To determine the degrees of virtue and wickedness in particular men, is the prerogative only of that Being that searches the secrets of the heart' (*YW*, xiv. 178). SJ may also echo Gray's *Elegy*, ll. 125–8: 'No farther seek his merits to disclose, | Or draw his frailties from their dread abode, | (There they alike in trembling hope repose) | The bosom of his Father and his God.' For the difficulty of understanding human motives, see also Folkenflik, 74–7.

121. James II ordered the publication of *Copies of Two Papers Written by the Late King Charles II; together with a Copy of a Paper written by the Late Dutchess of York* (1686), which related Charles II's deathbed conversion to Catholicism. When Edward Stillingfleet, Bishop of Worcester, Charles II's former Chaplain, replied in *An Answer to Some Papers Lately Printed* (1686), D was engaged to publish *A Defence of the Papers* (1686), although the extent of his contribution is unclear (Winn, *JD*, 420, 612 n.). Stillingfleet replied with *A Vindication of the Answer* (1687).

122. D in fact translated *The History of the League* by the French Jesuit Louis Maimbourg (Paris, 1683) in 1684, before his conversion, by order of Charles II, to whom it is dedicated.

D's name appears not merely on the title page, but at the end of the dedication, of *The Life of St. Francis Xavier* (1688), translated from the French of Dominic Bouhours. SJ may mean that D did not acknowledge it as his work elsewhere. As Osborn, *JD*, 14, noted, *BB*, iii. 1755–6, 1757, devoted more space to these two works than *GD*, iv. 682, 687, which merely listed the Maimbourg translation among D's miscellaneous publications.

*pious fraud*: Hill (1905) suggested that SJ alludes to '*pious* frauds and *holy* shifts' in Butler's *Hudibras*, i. iii. 1145 (repeated at iii. ii. 63). SJ had in fact quoted 'pious frauds' from 'King Charles' (i.e. *Eikon Basilike*) under 'Pious' in the *Dict*.

123. See Tom Brown, *The Late Converts Exposed...With Reflections on the Life of St. Xavier* (1690), 33 (and cf. 128 and n. below). D's dedication to the Queen, whose son was born a few days after the publication of the *Life* on 10 June 1688 (see 135 and n. below), refers to the efficacy of prayers to St Francis in inducing pregnancy (*Works*, xix. 3, 449–50).

124. D's translation of Antoine Varillas, *Histoire des revolutions arrivées dans l'Europe en matière de religion* (6 vols., 1686–9), was entered in the Stationers' Register but not published (Winn, *JD*, 421, 612 n.). Gilbert Burnet published *Reflections on Mr. Varillas' History* (1686), and a *Continuation* and a *Defence* of the *Reflections* in 1687. The *Answer* to Burnet was not in fact by D but by Varillas himself: as Malone, *Prose Works* (1800), i (i). 194–6, later noted, SJ seems to have misunderstood *GD*, iv. 682 n. For another reply to Varillas, see 'King' 3 below.

Both *GD*, iv. 682–3 n., and *BB*, iii. 1757 n., quoted this passage from Burnet's *Defence* (Amsterdam, 1687), 138–40, which alludes to D's portrayal of Burnet as the Buzzard in *The Hind and the Panther* (1687), III. 1121–288.

125. For 'argument' in verse, see 285 and n., 327 below, and for 'truth', 'Cowley' 14 n. above.

126. D published *The Hind and the Panther* in Apr. 1687.

127. For *The Hind and the Panther Transvers'd to the Story of the Country-Mouse and the City-Mouse* (1687), see also **288** below, and 'Halifax' **5** and 'Prior' **5** below (where the title is correctly italicized).

128. Thomas or Tom Brown (1663–1704), humorist and miscellaneous writer, published *The Reasons of Mr. Bays Changing his Religion* (1688), *The Late Converts Exposed* (1690), and *The Reasons of Mr. Joseph Hains the Player's Conversion and Re-Conversion* (1691). *GD*, iv. 680 n., drew attention to these pamphlets, which Thomas Percy may once again have lent SJ (see headnote above). Joseph Haines (1648–1701), actor and author, notoriously reconverted from Catholicism in 1689.

129. Crites (Sir Robert Howard) and Eugenius (Charles Sackville, Lord Buckhurst) appeared in D's *Of Dramatick Poesy* (see **27** and n. above).

130. For a poet who also aspired to be a 'merry fellow', see 'Denham' **22** above. Tom Brown's *Works* (3 vols., 1707; 4 vols., 1711–12) were in fact often reprinted, most recently in 1778–9 in Dublin.

   Although SJ has little taste for 'low' humour, Jacob, ii. 15–19, stated that Brown 'for Humour excell'd all of his Time . . . he was a Facetious and Excellent Companion, tho' withal sometimes very Satirical . . . The first piece which made him known to the Town, was an Account of the Conversion of Mr. *Bayes*, in a Dialogue, which met with very great Applause.' Shiels, *Lives*, iii. 204–17, stated that Brown's satire of D 'discovered no small erudition, but managed with a great deal of humour, in a burlesque way; which make both the reasoning and the extensive reading, which are abundantly shewn in it, extremely surprizing and agreeable'.

131. For language as 'the dress of thought', particularly as a 'garb' which can degrade and obscure, see 'Cowley' **181** above. For 'little Bayes', see *The Reasons of Mr. Bays* (1688), 1. Prior and Montagu also used the phrase in *The Hind and the Panther Transvers'd* (1687) (Prior, *Lit. Works*, i. 41). For Ajax's shield, see *The Late Converts* (1690), 2.

132. SJ quotes *The Late Converts* (1690), 1, alluding to Henry Peacham, *The Worth of a Peny: or A Caution to Keep Money* (1641; 7 later edns. by 1695).

133. *The Late Converts* (1690), 9, refers to John Wilson's popular *The Cheats* (acted 1663; published 1664), which satirizes Scruple, a nonconformist minister; Sir Robert Howard, *The Committee* (acted 1662; published 1665), a savage anti-Puritan satire; and Edward Ravenscroft, *The London Cuckolds* (acted 1681; published 1682), which ridiculed City Whigs, and was staged annually on Lord Mayor's Day, 'in contempt and to the disgrace of the city . . . it being not only a very immoral, but a very ill-written piece' (*Biographia Dramatica* (1782), ii. 191). Garrick ended the custom in 1751.

134. *The Late Converts* (1690), 4. For D's 'first religion', and his early poem on Cromwell, see **3, 7–9** and nn. above.

135. *Britannia Rediviva. A Poem on the Birth of the Prince* (23 June 1688) celebrated the birth of Prince James Francis Edward (1688–1766) some two weeks earlier: see **123** above, and **298** below. For defeated expectations of happiness, see 'Denham' **19** and n. above.

136. James II left England on 23 Dec. 1688. As elsewhere (cf. **298** below), SJ expresses little sympathy for D's predicament as a Catholic and Jacobite after 1688. For the

impact of these events on other poets, see 'Dorset' 11–12 above and 'Sprat' 12–13, 'Halifax' 6, 'Sheffield' 15, and 'Granville' 4–6 below; and cf. *Life*, ii. 341–2, iv. 170–1.

In Mar. 1689 Thomas Shadwell replaced D as Poet Laureate and Historiographer Royal. D had satirized Shadwell as Og in *The Second Part of Absalom and Achitophel* (1682), ll. 408–11, 457–509 (see 116 and n. above). SJ may have deduced from *GD*, iv. 682, and *BB*, iii. 1757, that Shadwell's appointment provoked D's attack on Shadwell in *Mac Flecknoe*, and Shiels, *Lives*, iii. 76, and Derrick (1760 edn.), i, p. xxv, said so explicitly, Derrick dating the satire 1689. Langbaine, *Account of the English Dramatick Poets* (Oxford, 1691), 443, had, however, implied an earlier date: 'Mr. *Dryden*, I dare presume, little imagined, when he writ that Satyr of *Mack-Flecknoe*, that the Subject he *there* so much exposes and ridicules, should have ever lived to have succeeded him in wearing the *Bays*.' *Mac Flecknoe* was in fact written as early as 1676 and (as noted by Malone, *Prose Works*, i (i). 169–70) published on 4 Oct. 1682. D did not acknowledge his authorship until 1692 (Watson, ii. 115). After Shadwell's death of an opium dose on 20 Nov. 1692, Nahum Tate became Laureate and Thomas Rymer Historiographer (Winn, *JD*, 461).

Pope acknowledged his debt to *Mac Flecknoe* in *Dunciad*, II. 2 n. (see 'Pope' 356 below). SJ does not return to this 'exquisitely satirical' poem in his later critical survey.

137. For Prior's account, see 'Dorset' 1, 12, 14 above, and Prior, *Lit. Works*, i. 254.

In 'A Discourse Concerning Satire' (1692), addressed to Dorset, William III's Lord Chamberlain, D stated that he had 'patiently suffered the ruin of my small fortune, and the loss of that poor subsistence which I had from two kings . . . And now age has overtaken me; and want, a more insufferable evil, through the change of the times, has wholly disenabled me.' D then mentioned 'a most bountiful present' he had received from Dorset (Watson, ii. 92, and cf. ii. 217). For a story of D finding a banknote for £100 under his plate at a Christmas dinner given by Dorset, see Jacob, ii. 16 (under 'Thomas Brown'). See also 182 below and, for 'romantick', 78 n. above.

139. In the preface to *Don Sebastian* (see 82 and n. above), his first play since 1683 apart from the opera *Albion and Albanius* (1685), D stated that 'misfortunes have once more brought him against his will upon the stage' (Watson, ii. 44). In the preface to *Cleomenes* (1692), he said: 'No body can imagine, that in my declining Age I write willingly, or that I am desirous of exposing, at this time of day, the small Reputation which I have gotten on the *Theatre*' (*Works*, xvi. 79). For the 'four dramas more', see 83–6 above.

140. For *The Satires of Decimus Junius Juvenalis . . . Together with the Satires of Aulius Persius Flaccus* (1693 for Oct. 1692), see also 'Stepney' 4 above, and 'Duke' 2 and 'Congreve' 40 below. Other contributors included Nahum Tate and Thomas Creech, and D's sons John and Charles (see 157–8 and nn. below). See also 299–302 below.

D's dedication ('A Discourse Concerning Satire') discussed his epic plans and the possibility of a new version of the supernatural 'machinery' required by epic theory (Watson, ii. 91–2, 86–91; cf. 82 above). *GD*, iv. 687 n., but not *BB*, had quoted the passage. For Milton's projected epic on King Arthur, see 'Milton' 86 above.

**141–2.** For the debate at this period about the use of pagan or Christian 'machinery' in epic, see Dennis, *Works*, i. 460–2, and cf. 'Milton' 222 above, and 'Pope' **55, 59, 336–7, 341** below.

**141.** For SJ's ambivalent responses to 'enchantments', see Henson.

D cited Boileau's opinion from *L'Art poétique* (1674), III. 205–16 (Watson, ii. 86). For other references to Boileau's critical views, see 'Addison' **38** and 'Pope' **375** below, and for Mrs Thrale's report that SJ 'delighted exceedingly in Boileau's works', see *J. Misc.*, i. 334 and cf. i. 416.

For Rinaldo in the 'enchanted wood', see Tasso, *Gerusalemme liberata*, Canto XVIII.

**143.** SJ's brief account of what might be expected from a modern English epic, even from D's pen, is polite but noticeably cool.

**144.** After outlining his epic plans, D said that he had been 'discouraged in the beginning of my attempt' by having 'no prospect of a future subsistence' (Watson, ii. 92). In 1687 he had expected to become President of Magdalen College or Warden of All Souls College, Oxford, and was still hoping in 1699 for some kind of pension to enable him to translate Homer (Winn, *JD*, 508, 613 n.).

SJ's final sentence may allude distantly to his own pension. He said on 14 July 1763 that 'the pleasure of cursing the House of Hanover, and drinking King James's health, are amply overbalanced by three hundred pounds a year' (*Life*, i. 429).

**145.** D made this accusation in the preface to *Fables* (1700) (Watson, ii. 292–3): see **77** and n. above and **176** below, and 'Blackmore' **7, 11** below.

**146.** Although D mentioned the Virgil translation in a letter of 12 Dec. 1693, when he had already completed *Georgic* III (*Letters*, 64), and Evelyn described him as 'intent upon' it on 11 Jan. 1694 (*Diary*, v. 164), the contract with Jacob Tonson is dated 15 June 1694 (Winn, *JD*, 475).

In 'A Parallel of Poetry and Painting', prefixed to his translation of C. A. Du Fresnoy's *De Arte Graphica* (1695), D said that he took two months from Virgil for the task, and wrote the preface in twelve mornings (Watson, ii. 183, 207–8). For SJ's use of the 'Parallel' in the *Dict.*, see DeMaria (1986), 218–19, and for his own brief 'parallel' of poetry and painting, see *Idler* 34 (1758) (*YW*, ii. 106). He had stated in his 'Account of the Harleian Library' in *Gent. Mag.* (1742), 639: 'PAINTING is so nearly allied to Poetry, that it cannot be wondered that those who have so much esteemed the one have paid an equal Regard to the other.'

**147.** D's *Works of Virgil* was delivered to subscribers early in July 1697. A different interpretation of his 'oeconomy of flattery' is possible. Winn, *JD*, 484–6, points out that, instead of dedicating the *Virgil* to William III (cf. D's letter in **406** below), D instead dedicated its various sections to Hugh, Lord Clifford (1663–1730), more than once imprisoned for Catholic conspiracy, whose father had been a patron of D; and to Philip Stanhope, Earl of Chesterfield (1633–1713), and John Sheffield, Earl of Mulgrave (see 'Sheffield' **16** and n. below), both of whom, though Anglicans, had recently refused the loyalty oaths to King William demanded of freeholders. D told Chesterfield in 1697 that he had hoped to dedicate the translation to James II (*Letters*, 85–6). Swift mocked the work's 'Multiplicity of *God-fathers*' in *A Tale of a Tub* (1704) (ed. Guthkelch and

Smith, 72). For the political implications of the dedications and subscription lists, see also J. Barnard, 'D, Tonson, and the Patrons of *The Works of Virgil* (1697)', in Hammond and Hopkins (eds.), *JD*, 174–239.

Pope estimated in Apr. 1742 that D 'cleared every way about £1,200 by his *Virgil*'. A modern estimate would be closer to £1,400 (Spence, i. 27).

148. SJ refers to Luke Milbourne's *Notes on Dryden's Virgil* (1698), mentioned by *GD*, iv. 683 n., but not apparently by *BB*. For Milbourne's objections, an example of his translation, and D's reply in *Fables* (1700), see **178, 306–8, 357** below.

Pope ironically praised Milbourne in *Dunciad*, II. 349 n., for quoting his own translation of Virgil (1688), and so allowing comparison with D's. Pope cited Milbourne again in an appended parallel of his own career with D's (*TE*, v. 230–5). See also *Essay on Criticism* (1711), l. 463: 'New *Blackmores* and new *Milbourns* must arise.'

149. SJ indicates in **184–5** below that his own enquiries had brought to light the agreement and receipt for *Fables Ancient and Modern* (published in fact in Mar. 1700). According to the contract of 20 Mar. 1699, Tonson agreed to pay D 250 guineas for 10,000 lines of verse, of which he had already received some 7,500.

150. SJ refers not to *A Song for St. Cecilia's Day* (1687: see **279–80** below), but to D's more famous *Alexander's Feast, or The Power of Musique* (1697), set to music by Jeremiah Clarke for the annual St Cecilia's Feast (see **318–20** and, for the more familiar title, **188** below). For other odes for music at this period, see 'Addison' **128**, 'Hughes' **6**, 'Congreve' **39**, and 'Pope' **320** below. For the lost letter cited by Birch in *GD*, iv. 685, see Osborn, *JD*, 13 and n.; and for the story of Boileau's 'Equivoque' (*Sat.* XII), see his *Œuvres* (Paris, 1747), i. 233 n. SJ uses other anecdotes about Boileau in 'Prior' **11** and 'Congreve' **3** below.

151. D twice referred in 1699 to his translation of *Iliad*, Bk. I, as a specimen of the whole (*Letters*, 121, 132), and did so again in the preface to *Fables* (1700), where he claimed a closer kinship with Homer than with Virgil (Watson, ii. 270, 274). He had translated 'the last parting of *Hector* and *Andromache*' from *Iliad*, Bk. VI, in *Examen Poeticum* (1693).

Pope stated in his preface to the *Iliad* (1715) that, had D 'translated the whole work, I would no more have attempted *Homer* after him than *Virgil*' (*TE*, vii. 22). James Beattie, *Essays* (Edinburgh, 1776), 359 n., criticized 'a vulgarity, and even meanness, of expression' in D's translations of both Homer and Virgil. For a recent view that what survives of D's *Iliad* is 'more Homeric' than Pope's 'paler, more *neo*-classical version of heroic struggle', see J. A. Winn, 'D's Translation of "The First Book of Homer's *Ilias*" ', in Hammond and Hopkins (eds.), *JD*, 264–81.

152. D in fact died on 1 May 1700 at the house in Gerrard St., Soho, in which he had lived since the winter of 1688–9 (Winn, *JD*, 436). Although Jacob, i. 86, had the correct year, *GD*, iv. 676, Shiels, *Lives*, iii. 82, and *BB*, iii. 1759, all gave 1701, perhaps because Pope misdated D's death in a note to his epitaph on Rowe in 1726 (see *TE*, vi. 208–9). SJ repeats the error in 'Pope' **14** below.

D complained of 'St Anthony's Fire in one of my legs' on 29 Dec. 1699 (*Letters*, 132, and cf. 135–6), and described himself as crippled in the preface to *Fables* (1700) (Watson, ii. 272). Unlike some other early accounts, SJ's omits the unpleasant details of D's death after his swollen leg developed gangrene.

**153.** This 'wild story' appeared originally in the *Memoirs of William Congreve* (1730 for Aug. 1729), published by Curll and edited by a dubious 'Charles Wilson', who may have been John Oldmixon: see P. Rogers, 'Congreve's First Biographer: The Identity of "Charles Wilson" ', *MLQ*, 31 (1970), 330–44. Thomas Davies, *Dramatic Miscellanies* (1784), iii. 340, later claimed that John Arbuthnot and the actress Mrs Bracegirdle tried to suppress or censor it before publication.

The author of this account of D's funeral was the much maligned Elizabeth Thomas (1675–1731), who wrote it while imprisoned for debt. For a few months before his death, she had corresponded with D about her poetry: see **170–1** n. below, 'Pope' **29, 142** and nn. below, and R. Lonsdale, *Eighteenth-Century Women Poets* (Oxford, 1989), 32–3. For her poems to or concerning D, see her *Miscellany Poems on Several Subjects* (1722), 18–25, 87–97, 112–14. The 'biographical dictionary' from which (unusually) SJ admits to quoting her account must be *GD*, iv. 683–4 n., since the versions in *BB*, iii. 1759 n., and Shiels, iii. 83–5, were abridged.

Malone, *Prose Works* (1800), i (i). 347–67, later analysed and discredited Thomas's narrative, commenting on 'The audacity of this woman in publishing this false and ridiculous account', when many who had attended the funeral were still alive (362 n.). (Malone also appended 'Mr. Russel's Bill for Mr. Dryden's Funeralls', 562–3.) Unaware of its author, P. Fussell, *SJ and the Life of Writing* (1971), 267–9, discussed the story as evidence of SJ's interest in 'the mode of ghoulish farce'.

The facts appear to be that D was buried on 2 May 1700 in St Anne's, Soho, but that, after the intervention of the Earl of Dorset, the corpse was disinterred and embalmed, lay in state at the College of Physicians, and was finally buried in Chaucer's grave in Westminster Abbey on 13 May, when Dr Samuel Garth (q.v. below) spoke an unusual funeral oration. Charles Montagu contributed to the funeral expenses: see F. H. Ellis, in *POAS*, vi. 206–8, and Winn, *JD*, 512. 'Lord Jefferies' in Thomas's story was John Jeffreys (1670?–1702), 2nd Baron Jeffreys. Coincidentally, while SJ's 'Dryden' was in the press, the *Gazetteer* of 8 Sept. 1778 quoted *BB*'s account of D's funeral to contradict a claim in the same paper on 5 Sept. that it had been a dignified and elaborate occasion.

**154.** SJ's uncertainties about the story are betrayed by his various revisions. After 'evidence;' the text in *Prefaces* (1779) continued, 'but having been since informed that there is in the register of the College of Physicians an order relating to Dryden's funeral, I can doubt its truth no longer'. He had changed his mind by the time he wrote the 'Advertisement' to *Prefaces*, dated 15 Mar. 1779: 'I had been told that in the College of Physicians there is some memorial of Dryden's funeral, but my intelligence was not true; the story therefore wants the credit which such a testimony would have given it. There is in Farquhar's *Letters* an indistinct mention of it as irregular and disorderly, and of the oration which was then spoken. More than this I have not discovered.' In the Rothschild copy of *Prefaces*, vol. iii, SJ redrafted the beginning and end of his original assertion in **154** as quoted above to 'I understood for a time that... funeral, but further enquiry cannot discover it', but this retraction did not appear in *Lives* (1781). In 1783 SJ omitted his earlier statement on the matter from the 'Advertisement', transferred a compressed version of the reference to Farquhar to **154**, and made no further mention of the College of Physicians. For these revisions, see Textual Notes.

It is possible that SJ had been confused by Isaac Reed's attempts to obtain accurate information. In *Lives* (1790), ii. 87 n., Reed noted an entry in the Register of the College of Physicians, 3 May 1700: 'At the request of several persons of quality that Mr. Dryden might be carried from the College of Physicians to be interred at Westminster, it was unanimously granted by the President and Censors.' Reed commented: 'This entry is not calculated to afford any credit to the Narrator concerning Lord Jefferies. R.' (See also Malone, *Prose Works* (1800), i (i). 372.) *Gent. Mag.* (July 1779), 364, criticized SJ's original vagueness in **154** about the contents of the Register: 'More than hearsay evidence should surely have been had before so much was said'. The same writer referred drily to SJ's change of mind about his hearsay evidence in his 'Advertisement': 'On this we shall comment no further'.

Oldys's MS notes on Langbaine, *English Dramatick Poets*, referred to 'Farquar's Letter about the confusion at his [D's] funeral', as SJ may have learned from Percy, Steevens, or Malone, who had transcribed Oldys's notes: see e.g. Malone's transcription in the Bodleian, i, fo. 182. For Farquhar's account, printed by Malone in *Prose Works* (1800), i (i). 363, see his *Works*, ed. S. S. Kenny (Oxford, 1988), ii. 358–9, 585. Edward Ward's account of the funeral in his *London Spy*, 2 (Apr. 1700), 5–8, was quoted by *Gent. Mag.* (1786), 291–3, and by Hawkins, *J's Works* (1787), ii. 362 n. John Tutchin's poem, *A Description of Mr. Dryden's Funeral* (1700), expanded in *Poems on Affairs of State* (1703), ii. 229–35, has also been attributed to Tom Brown. By contrast, Alexander Oldys's *An Ode, By way of Elegy, on The Universally lamented Death of the incomparable Mr. Dryden* (1700) envisaged D being welcomed to heaven by Waller, a repentant Milton, Cowley, Rochester ('a Happy Convert'), Shakespeare, Chaucer, 'Spritely Afra [Behn]', Herbert, and others.

**156.** SJ quoted under 'Deposite' in the *Dict.* a comment in Garth's preface to *Ovid's Metamorphoses* (1717) on the absence of a monument for D. Congreve mentioned a plan to erect one in his dedication of D's *Dramatick Works* (1717) to the Duke of Newcastle (i, sigg. al–al$^v$), but Pope later complained about the continuing delay in his epitaph on Rowe (see 'Pope' **409** and n. below).

The monument was finally erected in 1721 by John Sheffield, Duke of Buckinghamshire. The inscription in fact gave D's dates as well as his name: SJ may have been misled by Atterbury's reference in a letter of 23 Sept. 1720 to Pope's 'design ... of giving Dryden's Name only below, and his Bust above' (Pope, *Corresp.*, ii. 55). John Dart, *Westmonasterium* [1742], i. 90 and plate, described the monument as 'Plain, majestick, and just, equal to the great Imagination of the Patron who erected it, and the Merits of the Poet whose Name it bears ... The Epitaph is a silent Reproach to abundance of others in this Church, by showing how few Words are necessary to express real Merit, and how many are requisite to set off none'.

**157.** SJ has not previously referred to D's marriage in Dec. 1663 (see **17** n. above), although his widow is mentioned in the account of D's funeral in **153** above. The author of *Satyr, To His Muse* (1682) (see **112** above) claimed that D was forced to marry her ('After two children and a third Miscarriage, | By Brawny Brother's hector'd into Marriage'), and Samuel Pordage, in *Azaria and Hushei* (1682) (see **113** above), that she was 'a teeming Matron ere she was a Wife': see Winn, *JD*, 125, 564 n.

Charles Dryden (1666–1704) was educated at Westminster and Cambridge, leaving without a degree, and had a place under Lord Middleton, one of the Secretaries of State. By 1692 he was in Italy and employed in the Papal Guards, but returned to England in 1698 (see Winn, *JD*, 415, 421, 436, 453, 550–1, 620 n.). Hill (1905) silently emended 'cross' in SJ's last sentence to 'across', but SJ defines 'Cross' as '2. Over; from side to side' (*Dict.*).

158. John Dryden (1668–1703) was also educated at Westminster, and entered Christ Church, Oxford, in 1685, but did not matriculate. In 1688 he was one of the Catholic Fellows imposed on Magdalen College by James II, only to be removed a few months later. After joining a Catholic regiment to resist William III which never saw action, he was in Rome by 1692, and was employed by Cardinal Howard. He dedicated *The Husband His Own Cuckold* (1696), with a prologue by Congreve and an epilogue by his father, to his uncle Sir Robert Howard, who revised the play for the stage. D's preface reveals that his son had sent the play from Rome 'some years since' and that he himself doubted its suitability for the stage (*Works*, iv. 471–3). Although D also expressed his hopes for his son's return to England, John died in Rome in 1703 (see Winn, *JD*, 415, 433, 436, 453). For Charles and John as translators of Juvenal, see **140** above.

Erasmus-Henry Dryden (1669–1710), educated at Charterhouse and the Catholic College at Douai, later entered the English College at Rome (1690) and the Dominican monastery (1691). He was ordained as Father Thomas Dryden in 1703, returned to England by 1706, and in 1710 inherited a baronetcy from Sir Robert Dryden, the poet's cousin (see Winn, *JD*, 366, 415, 436, 473, 492, 506, 626 n.).

For D's 'sincerity in his second religion', see his letter of 7 Nov. 1699, when he was still hoping for a pension. Though willing to 'forbear satire' on the government, 'I can neither take the Oaths, nor forsake my Religion, because I know not what Church to go to, if I leave the Catholique ... Truth is but one; & they who have once heard of it, can plead no Excuse, if they do not embrace it' (*Letters*, 123).

159. Malone commented: 'on the contrary, there are few English poets, of whose external appearance more particulars have been recorded' (*Prose Works* (1800), i (i). 430–8 and nn.). For other evidence about D's appearance, see Osborn, *JD*, 141, 159, 162–3.

SJ quotes the 'Dedication' to D's *Dramatick Works* (1717), I. sigg. a6ᵛ–a8ᵛ, so freely that Hill (1905), i. 483–4, appended what Congreve actually wrote. The explanation is that SJ followed the paraphrase of Congreve's 'portrait' in *GD*, iv. 685 n., rather than the direct quotation in *BB*, iii. 1760 n. For Congreve's original text, see *D: The Critical Heritage* (1971), 263–6. Earlier in the dedication Congreve stated: 'I had the happiness to be very Conversant, and as intimately acquainted, with Mr. *Dryden*, as the great Disproportion in our Years could allow me to be' (sig. A3ᵛ).

160. For the 'fondness of friendship' in other biographical accounts, see 'Smith' **2** and n. below. D asked Congreve to defend his reputation in 'To My Dear Friend Mr. Congreve' (1694), ll. 70–5. For D's collaboration with Congreve in the 1690s, see J. Brady in Hammond and Hopkins (eds.), *JD*, 113–39.

161. D stated in the dedication of *Troilus and Cressida* (1679): 'for my own part, I never cou'd shake off the rustique bashfulness which hangs upon my nature' (*Works*,

xiii. 220). For the 'modesty' of another poet who also had 'a very high opinion of his own merit', see 'Addison' **109** below; and for other references to 'the usual concomitant of great abilities, a lofty and steady confidence in himself', see **102** above and 'Milton' **26** and n. above. SJ was himself notoriously unwilling to initiate a subject in conversation: see *Life*, iii. 307 and n.

**162.** Cf. **214** below.

**163.** Jacob Tonson believed that D 'was very suspicious of rivals' (Spence, i. 319). SJ was rightly sceptical about the accusation concerning D and Thomas Creech (1659–1700), which apparently originated in Tom Brown's *The Late Converts Exposed* (1690), 53–4 (see **128** above). (It is mentioned by *GD*, iv. 687 n., but not by *BB*.) Creech, who successfully translated Lucretius in 1682, and later contributed to D's Juvenal translation in 1693 (see **140** n. above and **300** below), praised D's 'helping hand' in the preface to *The Odes, Satyrs and Epistles of Horace, Done into English* (1684). The inferiority of the Horace translation was often noted, as by William Coward, *Licentia Poetica Discuss'd* (1709), 25 n. Charles Gildon, *The Laws of Poetry* (1721), 318–20, dismissed Brown's story, while admitting that Creech was 'the most unfit man in the World' to translate Horace. Thomas Southerne claimed to have been present when D in fact tried to dissuade Creech from the undertaking, 'an attempt which his genius was not adapted to': see George Russel, *Works* (Cork, 1769), ii. 338, and Malone, *Prose Works*, i (i). 505–11.

**165.** Dennis described D in 1694 as one who 'with a breath can bestow or confirm reputation' (*Letters*, 69), and cf. **190, 199** below.

**166.** For the conversation of other poets, see 'Cowley' **200** n. above. D said that 'My conversation is slow and dull, my humour saturnine and reserved' in 'A Defence of An Essay of Dramatic Poesy' (1668) (Watson, i. 116). SJ quotes *Satyr, To His Muse* (1682), sig. B2ᵛ (see **112** above). Pope said *c.*1728 that D 'was not a very genteel man. He was intimate with none but poetical men ... and not very conversible' (Spence, i 25).

**168.** SJ quotes D's preface to *Fables* (1700) (Watson, ii. 272), and refers to Thomas Carte, *History of the Life of James, Duke of Ormonde* (1736), ii. 554, and Horace, *Epist.*, I. xvii. 35.

For the attitude of other poets to 'familiarity with the great', see 'Swift' **52, 134** and 'Pope' **23** below.

**169.** Rochester charged D with attempting obscene wit in 'An Allusion to Horace' (1676), ll. 71–6; *Satyr, To His Muse* (1682), sigg. B2–B2ᵛ, said that D 'set up for wit and awkwardly was lewd'; and Shadwell, *The Medal of John Bayes* (1682), 3–4, accused D of obscenity when in rakish court circles. D himself told Dennis in Mar. 1694: 'I appeal to the World if I have Deceiv'd or defrauded any Man: And for my private Conversation, they who see me every day can be the best Witnesses, whether or no it be Blameless and Inoffensive. Hitherto I have no reason to complain that Men of either Party shun my Company' (*Letters*, 73).

**170–1.** See **44** above and **269** below, and, for Jeremy Collier's denunciation of D's plays in 1698, **175** below. SJ has already used the phrase 'dissolute licentiousness' in **87** above.

SJ described the obscenity of the Restoration stage in his *Drury-Lane Prologue* (1747), ll. 17–28. In *Rambler* 77 (1750) he condemned the author who 'tortures his fancy, and ransacks his memory, only that he may leave the world less virtuous than he found it' (*YW*, i. 44). For his disapproval of Fielding's *Tom Jones*, see *Life*, ii. 173–4 and nn. In 1765 he remarked that the 'great fault' of *The Merry Wives of Windsor* 'is the frequency of expressions so profane, that no necessity of preserving character can justify them. There are laws of higher authority than those of criticism' (*YW*, vii. 339, and cf. viii. 546). See also 'Congreve' **22**, 'Granville' **18**, 'Savage' **193**, 'Swift' **137**, and 'Pope' **360** below, and 'Rochester' headnote and **11** n. above (for the omission of Rochester's obscene verse from *Eng. Poets*). In 'Addison' **123** below he praises Addison for having 'separated mirth from indecency, and wit from licentiousness'.

**170.** For Rochester's disdain for D's attempted mimicry of aristocratic libertinism, see 'An Allusion to Horace', ll. 71 ff: 'Dryden in vain tryd this nice way of Witt, | For he to be a roaring Blade thought fitt. | But when he would be sharp he still was blunt: | To frisk his frolick fancy hee'd cry Cunt', etc. For another poet who, SJ hopes, 'rather talked than lived viciously', see 'Duke' **4** below.

Hume believed, less leniently, that the 'immeasurable licentiousness' of the Restoration court was 'more destructive to the refined arts than even the cant, nonsense, and enthusiasm of the preceding period'. The genius of D's *Alexander's Feast* and *Absalom and Achitophel* produces only 'regret and indignation, on account of the inferiority or rather great absurdity of his other writings' (*History of Great Britain*, ii (1757), 453).

**171.** Cf. Rymer's translation of Rapin's *Reflections on Aristotle's Treatise* (1674), 143: 'All *Poetry* that tends to the Corruption of Manners, is Irregular and Vicious; and *Poets* are to be look'd on as a publick Contagion, whose Morals are not pure.' In *Spectator* 166 (1711) Addison described 'vicious Writers' as spreading an 'Infection' in society.

*ideal*: 'Mental; intellectual; not perceived by the senses' (*Dict.*). Cf. 'Milton' **257** above, and 'Addison' **44**, 'Prior' **49**, and 'Savage' **169** below, and for SJ's coinage 'unideal', 'Milton' **173** and n. above.

*his repentance*: see **175** below. In 'To the Pious Memory of ... Mrs. Anne Killigrew' (1686), ll. 56–66, D regretted 'the steaming Ordures of the Stage'. Elsewhere he wrote that 'it will be scarcely admitted that either a poet or a painter can be chaste, who give us the contrary examples in their writings and their pictures', and admitted to Elizabeth Thomas (see **153** n. above) in 1700 that he had been 'too much a libertine in most of my poems' (Watson, ii. 187, 267–8). James Beattie had recently described D's translation of Virgil's 'Georgic III' as 'in one place exeedingly filthy, and in another shockingly obscene' (*Essays* (Edinburgh, 1776), 534–5).

**172.** *hyperbolical adulation*: Aphra Behn (*c*.1640–1689) dedicated *The Feigned Curtezans* (1679) to Nell Gwyn. Malone, *Prose Works* (1800), i (i). 243–5, claimed other dedications in the period 'sometimes far surpassed any of Dryden's for extravagance of praise'. As noted in **147** n. above, D's panegyrics could have political as well as financial motives. For D and patronage, see D. Griffin, *Literary Patronage in England, 1650–1800* (Cambridge, 1996), ch. 4. SJ can in fact argue at times that 'unmerited praise' does not in itself prove that 'the encomiast always knows and feels the falseness of his assertions': see 'Halifax' **12** and 'Prior' **13** below.

*the prostitution of his judgement*: Pope, later praised by SJ because he 'never set his genius to sale' ('Pope' **270** below), attacked such 'Prostitution of Praise' in *Guardian* 4 (1713). For 'the prostitutes of praise', for lavish dedications as degrading 'literature from its natural rank', and for SJ's own refusal to degrade 'the dignity of virtue' by 'the meanness of a dedication', see *Ramblers* 104, 136 (1751), 208 (1752) (*YW*, iv. 193, 356, v. 317). In 1755 he defined 'Dedication' as '2. A servile address to a patron', and 'Dedicator' as 'One who inscribes his work to a patron with compliment and servility' (*Dict.*). Although he omitted 'servile' from the first definition in 1773, he often associates the word and its cognates with dedications, as here and in 'Addison' **27** and 'Thomson' **8** below.

SJ's only dedication was of the *Plan of a Dictionary* (1747) to Lord Chesterfield, but he supplied many friends with dedications addressed to members of the royal family and potential patrons: see Hazen, *passim*. In 1773 he stated that 'The known style of a dedication is flattery: it professes to flatter' (*Life*, v. 285), and in Sept. 1781 advised a scholar to dedicate his work to 'some powerful and popular neighbour, who can give him more than a name', rather than to SJ himself (*Letters*, iii. 357). At least twelve works were dedicated to SJ himself: see *NCBEL*, ii (1971), 1150–1. See also **88** above, 'Savage' **63** below, and *Life*, i. 257, ii. 1–2, v. 285–6. For a wider context, see P. Rogers, 'Book Dedications in Britain 1700–1799: A Preliminary Survey', *BJECS* 16 (1993), 213–33.

173. *a strain of discontent*: see also **63, 102, 137** above and **182** below. SJ quotes D's dedication to *Eleonora* (1692) (Watson, ii. 63).

D claimed in the 'Discourse Concerning Satire' (1693): 'More libels have been written against me than almost any man now living; and I had reason on my side to have defended my own innocence . . . I have seldom answered any scurrilous lampoon, when it was in my power to have exposed my enemies: and being naturally vindicative, have suffered in silence, and possessed my soul in quiet' (Watson, ii. 126, and see also ii. 77–8). For his 'controversy with Settle', see **32–42** above.

*pollutes*: SJ defines 'Pollute' as '3. To corrupt by mixtures of ill, either moral or physical' (*Dict.*): cf. 'Pope' **254** below.

From his early years in London, when his Latin ode 'Ad Urbanum' advised Edward Cave to treat attacks on his periodical with 'haughty silence' ('Superbo . . . Silentio') (*Gent. Mag.* (Mar. 1738), 156), SJ's own recommended policy was to ignore literary hostility (*Life*, i. 314, ii. 61 and n., v. 174, 274 and n.). See also 'Addison' **70**, 'Prior' **5**, 'Blackmore' **42**, and 'Pope' **146–7, 235–6** below, and his letters to Charlotte Lennox, 30 July 1756, and Hester Thrale, 1 May 1780, 5 July 1783 (*Letters*, i. 136, iii. 249, iv. 169). In *Rambler* 176 (1751), which attributed this doctrine of forbearance to Vida, SJ unusually contemplated replying to attacks with 'firmness and spirit' (*YW*, v. 166), and later admitted to Thomas Warton, 1 Feb. 1755, on the publication of the *Dict.*: 'I hope however the criticks will let me be at peace for though I do not much fear their skill or strength, I am a little afraid of myself, and would not willingly feel so much illwill in my bosom as literary quarrels are apt to excite' (*Letters*, i. 92).

174. Cf. **136** above on *Mac Flecknoe*.

175. For the passage in the preface to *Fables* (1700), quoted with some freedom by SJ, see Watson, ii. 293–4. For a fuller account of Collier's *A Short View of the*

*Immorality and Profaneness of the English Stage* (1698), see 'Congreve' **18–24** below. With 'the claps of a playhouse' cf. 'the claps of multitudes' in **42** above. SJ later applies D's comment on Collier's *'horse-play'* to Dennis in 'Addison' **153**.

*a reflection . . . of great asperity*: presumably D's earlier complaint that his sense has been 'wire-drawn into blasphemy or bawdry, as it has often been by a religious lawyer, in a late pleading against the stage' (Watson, ii. 279), although he also referred to Collier in a verse epistle to Peter Motteux (1698), ll. 1–22, and the epilogue to *The Pilgrim* (1700).

**176.** For the Whig poet Sir Richard Blackmore (q.v. below), see Watson, ii. 292–3, and **77, 140** and nn., **145** above.

**177.** SJ quotes Blackmore's *A Satyr against Wit* (1700 for Nov. 1699) from the text in his *Collection of Poems* (1718), 89, which omitted the original mollifying couplet. By 'exuberance' SJ means 'Over-growth . . . useless abundance' (*Dict.*): see 'Thomson' **50** and n. below.

Blackmore had already attacked D's obscenity and ridiculed his complaints of poverty in the preface to *King Arthur* (1697), to which D replied in the 'Prologue' to *The Pilgrim* (1700): see also 'Blackmore' **14–19** and nn. below.

**178.** For Luke Milbourne (1649–1720), see Watson, ii. 291, 294, **148** above, and **306–8, 357** below.

**179.** Ch. III of Collier's *Short View* (1698) discussed abuse of the clergy on the stage, quoting several examples from D's plays: although not all concerned Christian priests, Collier believed that D knew that 'the transition from one Religion to the other is natural'. Milbourne, *Notes on Dryden's Virgil* (1698), 9, also criticized D's hostility to the clergy. For such 'malignity' elsewhere, see **47** above, Watson, i. 138–9, 179, ii. 282–4, and *Poems* (1958), iii. 1012, and see also Winn, *JD*, 497–9. D's 'The Character of a Good Parson', expanded from Chaucer, in *Fables* (1700) may have been an attempt to counter such accusations. SJ cites Joseph Trapp's preface to his *Aeneis of Virgil*, i (1718) p.lii, referring to D's *Georgics*, iii. 737.

For the importance of distinguishing 'the follies of paganism' from Christian truth, see 'Milton' **236** n. above.

**180.** Langbaine, *English Dramatick Poets*, 171, Tom Brown, *The Late Converts* (1690), sig. 2A, and Milbourne, *Notes on Dryden's Virgil* (1698), 9, 19, all made this suggestion. For D's denial, see Watson, ii. 292.

**181.** See e.g. **269, 276, 286–8** below. For SJ's praise of the speeches of Comus and Satan for lacking 'any such expressions as might taint the reader's imagination', see 'Milton' **199, 216** above, and for the 'corruption of the times', 'Rochester' **4** and n. above.

**182.** For D's 'complaints of poverty', see **3, 86, 137** and n. above and **227–8** below. In a 'Discourse Concerning Satire' (1693) he claimed to have 'patiently suffered the ruin of my small fortune, and the loss of that poor subsistence which I had from two kings'. In the dedication of *Examen Poeticum* (1693) he asked: 'Why am I grown old, in seeking so barren a reward as fame? The same parts and application which have made me a poet might have raised me to any honours of the gown, which are often given to men of as little learning and less honesty than myself.' Dedicating Virgil's *Pastorals* to Lord Clifford in 1697, he described himself as 'worn out with study and oppressed by fortune: without other support than the constancy and patience of a Christian'; and in the 'Postscript' to the *Aeneid* as 'struggling with wants, oppressed with sickness, curbed in my genius, liable to be misconstrued in all I write' (Watson, ii. 92, 156–7, 217, 258; see also i. 190–1, ii. 44–5). In contrast, SJ wrote in 1765 that 'The genius of Shakespeare was not to be depressed by the weight of poverty . . . the incumbrances of his fortune were shaken from his mind, "as dewdrops from a lion's mane"' (*YW*, vii. 89).

183. For D's 'emoluments', see the appendix, 'Official Payments to Dryden and his Family', in Winn, *JD*, 525–31. For some details of D's finances noted by SJ in a copy of *Prefaces* (1779), vol. iii (1779), see *The Rothschild Library* (2 vols., 1969), i. 320. This information derived from the Spence MSS (i. 26–8), which became available to him in Feb. 1780.

It was in fact Charles II who made D Historiographer Royal in 1670, in succession to James Howell (see **26** n. above). James II renewed the appointment in Apr. 1685 (see **118** n. above) and increased the notional stipend to £300 p.a., although payments were usually in arrears.

*he seldom lives frugally who lives by chance*: cf. 'Savage' **229** below.

184. For D's theatrical profits, see **87** above.

For SJ's earlier enquiries of Jacob Tonson (1714–67) about D's dealings with his great-uncle Jacob Tonson (1656?–1736), see **149** and n. above. The agreement (now in the British Library) is in fact dated 20 Mar. 1699, and was printed by Derrick (1760 edn.), i, pp.xxvii–xxviii. Tonson itemized the exact currency in which D was paid on 23 Mar. 1699, ending with the calculation about the guineas at £1 1s. 6d. SJ defines a guinea as 'A gold coin valued at one and twenty shillings' (*Dict.*).

185. Hill (1905) estimated that the *Fables* contain 11,924 lines. Malone, *Prose Works* (1800), i (i). 320, 561–2, later showed that SJ misunderstood the agreement: Tonson did not in fact pay for the extra verses supplied by D, and the balance of £31 5s., making the total up to the agreed £300, was finally paid to D's estate in 1713, when Tonson published a new edition of *Fables*.

186. For this letter, first printed by Malone in 1800, see *Letters*, 82–3. During the crisis over debased coinage in 1696, Tompion the watchmaker asked D for payment in silver, which had a fixed value, rather than gold.

187. Although D mentioned Tonson's 'kindnesses' in the early 1690s, he was later irritated by the terms of the contract for his *Virgil* (Winn, *JD*, 475–7, 480–4).

According to Malone, *Prose Works* (1800), i (i). 524, SJ heard the anecdote about D and Henry St John, later Lord Bolingbroke, from Dr William King (1685–1763), Principal of St Mary Hall, Oxford, whom SJ met in 1755 and who brought him the diploma for his Oxford MA (*Life*, i. 279 and n.; *Letters*, i. 98). Malone also told another story about D and Tonson (i (i). 525–8). See also K. M. Lynch, *Jacob Tonson, Kit-Cat Publisher* (Knoxville, Tenn., 1971), ch. II ('D and Tonson'), and J. Barnard, 'D, Tonson and *Virgil*', in Hammond and Hopkins (eds.), *JD*, 174–239. For D and St John, who contributed a commendatory poem to the *Virgil* (*Works*, v. 61–2), see also **319** n. below.

*mercantile ruggedness*: SJ referred to the 'avarice' of booksellers in 'Savage' **128** below, and to 'the ruggedness of the commercial race' in *Rasselas*, ch. XV (*YW*, xvi. 62), defining 'Ruggedness' as '2. Roughness; asperity' (*Dict.*). Later he usually did them 'ample justice' as 'generous liberal-minded men' and as 'the patrons of literature' (*Life*, i. 304–5 and cf. 438, and cf. 'Collins' 4 n. below). In his letter of 12 Mar. 1776 about the book trade, he accepted that it was unrealistic to expect booksellers to 'buy and sell under the influence of a disinterested zeal for the promotion of Learning' (*Letters*, ii. 306).

188. See Derrick (1760 edn.), i, pp. ix, xxviii. Malone, *Prose Works* (1800), i (i). 327–8, doubted the sums mentioned by Derrick. For SJ's claim that he sent Derrick to consult Tonson's relations, see headnote and *Life*, v. 240. *Fables* (1700) includes a verse dedication to Mary Somerset, wife of James Butler, Duke of Ormond.

Walter Moyle (1672–1721), politician and author, helped D with his translation of Du Fresnoy (1695) (see Watson, ii. 194). In Sept. 1697 D described the writing of *Alexander's Feast* as 'no way beneficial' to him, and as undertaken as a favour to friends (see 406 below).

189. SJ refers to 'A Discourse Concerning Satire' (Watson, ii. 92). For delayed payments to D, see 26 n., 183 n. above.

190. For some of D's 'petty habits', see SJ's discussion of *The Rehearsal* in 99 above.

In May 1776 SJ identified 'the only two persons then alive' (i.e. *c*.1750) who had known D as Colley Cibber (1671–1757) and Owen Swiny (or MacSwinny) (1676–1754): 'Swinney's information was no more than this, "That at Will's coffee-house Dryden had a particular chair for himself, which was set by the fire in winter, and was then called his winter-chair; and that it was carried out for him to the balcony in summer, and was then called his summer-chair." Cibber said only "That he remembered him a decent old man, arbiter of critical disputes at Will's." You are to consider that Cibber was then at a great distance from Dryden, had perhaps one leg only in the room, and durst not draw in the other' (*Life*, iii. 71–2). As Damrosch (1976), 171, noted, the pun on 'seat' as '3. Mansion; residence' (*Dict.*) disappeared in Boswell's version. SJ told Malone that 'he had not lived in any intimacy with Colley Cibber, but that he had been sometimes in company with him: and that he was much more ignorant than he could well have conceived any man to be, who had lived for near sixty years with authors, criticks, and some of the most celebrated characters of the age' (Dryden, *Works* (1800), i. 486 n.). For Cibber, see also 'Pope' 230 n. below.

*Will's Coffee-house*: owned by William Urwin, it was a famous resort of the 'wits' in Covent Garden. See 'Pope' 31 below, *Prose Works* (1800), i (i). 485–93, and B. Lillywhite, *London Coffee Houses* (1963), 655–9. Cf. Swift's derisive account of '*Will*'s Coffee-house, where the Wits (as they were called) used formerly to assemble; that is to say, five or six Men, who had writ Plays, or at least Prologues, or had Share in a Miscellany, came thither, and entertained one another with their trifling Composures, in so important an Air, as if they had been the noblest Efforts of human Nature, or that the Fate of Kingdoms depended on them' (*Prose Writings*, iv. 90).

191. *judicial astrology*: see 'Butler' 47–8 above, and 'Congreve' 14 and 'Swift' 30 below. The material (by Elizabeth Thomas) in *Memoirs of Congreve* (1730), i. 24–31, attributed to 'C. Wilson' and published by Edmund Curll, is unreliable (see 153 and n. above).

SJ quotes *Annus Mirabilis* (1667), ll. 1161, 1165–8. Hill (1905) noted other references to the 'planetary powers' in *Absalom and Achitophel* (1681), ll. 230–1, and 'To the Memory of Anne Killigrew' (1686), ll. 41–3. In the dedication to the *Aeneid* (1697), D stated that Horace, Persius, and Augustus believed in astrology (*Works*, v. 290), and, in the preface to *Fables* (1700), that 'Chaucer was likewise an astrologer, as were Virgil, Persius and Manilius' (Watson, ii. 277).

SJ did not add his reference to D's letter in **406** below, about casting a horoscope for his son Charles, until 1783. Other revisions in 1783 suggest that the letter was belatedly appended in 1779 (see headnote and Textual Notes), and SJ may not have had a chance to read it closely.

**193.** Cf. SJ's reference to Aristotle as 'the father of criticism' in 'Cowley' **52** above. For the metaphor of 'literary paternity' at this period, see R. Terry, *Poetry and the Making of the English Literary Past* (Oxford, 2001), 145–51. SJ listed D's 'Essays and Prefaces' among the English works from which 'the Art of Poetry will be best learned' in the preface to Dodsley's *Preceptor* (1748): see Hazen, 184. In the *Dict.* he quoted his first definition of 'Criticism' itself directly from D ('*Criticism*, as it was first instituted by Aristotle, was meant a standard of judging well').

*principles*: SJ quotes in the *Dict.* (under 'Door') D's assertion in 1695 that 'without rules there can be no art, any more than there can be a house without a door to conduct you into it' (Watson, ii. 194). He asserted in *Rambler* 92 (1751) that it was 'the task of criticism to establish principles; to improve opinion into knowledge', while opposing 'rational deduction' and 'the dominion of science' to 'the tyranny of prescription'. *Rambler* 156 (1751) admitted that 'Criticism has sometimes permitted fancy to dictate the laws by which fancy ought to be restrained, and fallacy to perplex the principles by which fallacy is to be detected.' In *Rambler* 208 (1752) SJ claimed to have established 'all my principles of judgment on unalterable and evident truth' (*YW*, iv. 122, v. 66, 319). In **28** above SJ differentiates between 'all that can be reduced to principles of science' in literature and 'those parts where fancy predominates', and in **201–2** below between D's 'general precepts' and his more erratic 'occasional and particular positions' (and cf. his comment on D in 'Butler' **50** above).

For the 'principles' of writing, see also **89, 201** above, and cf. 'Addison' **159** (where SJ opposes 'taste' to 'principles'), **164** below, where Addison 'draws the principles of invention from dispositions inherent in the mind of man'. However attractive the idea of definitive critical 'principles' may have been, SJ's sceptical and anti-authoritarian temperament tended in practice to resist prescriptive or dogmatic principles. In 'Milton' **225** above he disapproves of 'such readers as draw their principles of judgement rather from books than from reason', and he refers in 'Pope' **374** below to 'the cant of those who judge by principles rather than perception'; cf. also the 'dull collection of theorems' in **199** below.

*the greatest dramatist*: in 1765 SJ stated that Shakespeare's 'adherence to general nature has exposed him to the censure of criticks, who form their judgments upon narrower principles'; and that he wrote 'with the world open before him; the rules of the ancients were yet known to few, the publick judgment was unformed; he had no example of such fame as might force him upon imitation, nor criticks of such authority as might restrain his extravagance' (*YW*, vii. 65, 69). D himself wrote in 1692 that Shakespeare 'had rather written happily, than knowingly and justly', and that, though Ben Jonson knew 'the rules', he 'seemed to envy posterity that knowledge' (Watson, ii. 73).

194. SJ refers to William Webbe, *A Discourse of English Poetrie* (1586), George Puttenham, *The Arte of English Poesie* (1589), and Ben Jonson, *Timber* (1640). For
Cowley's critical prefaces and notes, see 'Cowley' **110** and n. above, and for D's
*Of Dramatick Poesy* (1667), **27** above. Malone later gave a much fuller account of
early literary criticism, mentioning Gascoigne, Sidney, Campion, Daniel, and
Bolton, as well as the French critics Hédelin and Corneille (*Prose Works* (1800), i
(i). 58–60).

195. Cf. D's own account in 1692 of his critical uncertainty when writing *Of Dramatick
Poesie* in the 1660s: 'I have the right of a first discoverer ... I was drawing the
outlines of an art without any living master to instruct me in it ... I was sailing in a
vast ocean, without other help than the polestar of the Ancients, and the rules of
the French stage among the Moderns' (Watson, ii. 73–4). Bolingbroke claimed
*c*.1728 that D 'assured me that he got more from the Spanish critics alone than
from the Italian and French and all other critics put together' (Spence, i. 317).

196. For the same point, see 'Waller' **150** above and 'Addison' **160** below, and cf.
*Rambler* 106 (1751): 'it often happens that the general reception of a doctrine
obscures the books in which it was delivered. When any tenet is generally received
and adopted as an incontrovertible principle, we seldom look back to the arguments upon which it was first established' (*YW*, iv. 203).

197. SJ discussed the importance of understanding the historical context of Shakespeare and 16th-century literature in a letter to Thomas Warton, 16 July 1754
(*Letters*, i. 81), and see also *YW*, vii. 3, 56, 81, and 'Hughes' **4** n. below. For the
relevance of context to later literature, see 'Addison' **160–2** and 'Pope' **349** below.

198. In *Of Dramatick Poesie* (see **27** above) D discussed Shakespeare, Jonson, and
Beaumont and Fletcher. SJ had quoted D's encomium of Shakespeare (Watson,
i. 67) in the preface to his own edition of 1765, commenting: 'It is not very grateful
to consider how little the succession of editors has added to this authour's power
of pleasing' (*YW*, vii. 112). In 'Pope' **128** below he states that Pope's preface to his
own edition 'expanded with great skill and elegance' D's character of Shakespeare.

*exact without minuteness, and lofty without exaggeration*: cf. SJ's praise of Goldsmith
in 'Parnell' **1** below for 'the art of being minute without tediousness, and general
without confusion'. For Longinus' praise of Demosthenes, see *On the Sublime*,
ch. XVI.

199. Following Horace, it was often asserted that poets (rather than those preoccupied
with 'rules' and 'faults') made the best critics: see Dennis, *Works*, i. 398, 527–
8 nn., and ii. 486 n.; Pope, *Essay on Criticism*, ll. 15–16: 'Let such teach others
who themselves excell, | And *censure freely* who have *written well*' (quoted under
'Excel' in the *Dict.*); Addison, *Spectator* 291 (1712): 'there is not a *Greek* or *Latin*
Critick who has not shewn, even in the stile of his Criticisms, that he was a Master
of all the Elegance and Delicacy of his Native Tongue' (quoted under 'Criticism'
in the *Dict.*); and Henry Felton, *A Dissertation on Reading the Classics* (2nd edn.,
1715), p. xi: 'The best Performers are the best Judges in every Art.' Cf. also **165**
above, and 'Blackmore' **29** below ('Blackmore's prose is not the prose of a poet, for
it is languid, sluggish, and lifeless').

200. *a dispute between two mathematicians*: SJ refers to the dispute between Joseph
Justus Scaliger and Christopher Clavius concerning the corrections to the Gre-

gorian Calendar in the 16th century. See the letter from Isaac Casaubon to Jacques-Auguste de Thou quoted in W. C. Waterhouse, 'A Source for J's "Malim Cum Scaligero Errare"', *N & Q* 248 (2003), 222–3. SJ had applied this saying, adapting Cicero, *Tusculan Disputationes*, I. xvii. 39, to commentators on Horace in Mar. 1776: 'You will admire Bentley more when wrong than Jason when right' (*Life*, ii. 444).

Thomas Rymer (1641–1713), a dogmatic admirer of French neoclassical criticism, was best known for *The Tragedies of the Last Age* (1678) and *A Short View of Tragedy* (1693). For D's unpublished reply to him, see **358–405** below. He later told Dennis: 'For my own part I reverence Mr. Rym[er']s Learning, but I detest his Ill Nature and his Arrogance' (*Letters*, 71– 2). Pope said in 1736 that Rymer 'is generally right, though rather too severe in his opinions of the particular plays he speaks of, and is on the whole one of the best critics we ever had' (Spence, i. 205). SJ included twenty-one quotations from Rymer in the *Dict.*, increased to twenty-two in 1773, and replied to some of his criticism of Shakespeare in 1765 (*YW*, vii. 65–6, 68).

*Truth*: for its importance, see 'Cowley' **14** and n. above. In 'Sermon 20' SJ asserts that 'We cannot make truth; it is our business only to find it' (*YW*, xiv. 223). With SJ's allegory here cf. *Rambler* 96 (1751), in which Truth is coldly received until she disguises herself in Fiction, and *Rambler* 168 (1751), in which Truth 'loses much of her power over the soul, when she appears disgraced by a dress uncouth or ill-adjusted' (*YW*, iv. 152, v. 126). See also **131** and n. above.

201. SJ originally wrote in the first sentence in 1779 that D poured out his knowledge with 'great liberality, and seldom published any work without a critical dissertation, by which he encreased the book and the price, with little labour to himself', but omitted this in 1783 (see Textual Notes). In *Rambler* 93 (1751) he stated that D 'was known to have written most of his critical disquisitions only to recommend the work upon which he then happened to be employed' (*YW*, iv. 132), and in **89** above that they were intended to 'increase the value of his copies'. Cf. Swift's claim that D wrote his prefaces only 'for filling, | To raise the volume's price a shilling' ('On Poetry: A Rapsody' (1733), ll. 253–4).

*To write con amore*: a reviewer suggested that SJ himself wrote 'Pope', 'Addison', and 'Thomson' '*con amore*' (*Critical Review*, 52 (1781), 83), and Boswell later said the same of 'Pope' (*Life*, iv. 46).

For D as 'no lover of labour', and for the 'pursuit of unattainable perfection', see also **340–1** and nn. below, and 'Pope' **298, 304** below.

202. *the structure of the human mind*: cf. 'Cowley' **49** and n. above, and 'Addison' **110, 164** below.

*sometimes capricious*: cf. SJ's earlier comment on D's 'precipitate' and 'immature' critical opinions in 'Butler' **50** above.

SJ quotes (with silent omissions) Joseph Trapp's lectures as Professor of Poetry at Oxford, *Praelectiones Poeticae* (3 vols., Oxford, 1711–19), iii. 122, listed among the works from which 'the Art of Poetry will be best learned' in SJ's preface to Dodsley's *Preceptor* (1748) (Hazen, 184). For Trapp see also **179** above and **310** below. The passage was translated in Trapp's *Lectures on Poetry* (1742), 348: 'We know our Countryman, Mr. *Dryden*'s Judgment, about a Poem of *Chaucer*'s, truly beautiful, and worthy of Praise; namely, that it was not only equal, but even superior to the *Iliad* and *Aeneid*: But we know, likewise, that his Opinion was not always the most accurate, nor form'd upon the severest Rules of Criticism. What was in Hand, was generally most in Esteem; if it was uppermost in his Thoughts, it was so in his Judgment too.' SJ omits Trapp's next sentence: 'I am sure, the Opinion is too monstrous to deserve a serious Refutation.'

D in fact wrote in the preface to *Fables* (1700) that Chaucer's *Knight's Tale* was 'perhaps not much inferior to the *Ilias* or the *Aeneis*: the story is more pleasing than either of them, the manners as perfect, the diction as poetical, the learning as deep and various, and the disposition full as artful: only it includes a greater length of time, as taking up seven years at least' (Watson, ii. 290–1; quoted in part in the *Dict.* under 'To take up'). For this 'hyperbolical commendation', see also **314** below.

**203.** Hawkins, *Life* (1787), 535, describing SJ's 'fondness for rhyme' as 'one of the blemishes in his judgment', claimed to have heard him accuse D of 'want of principle in this respect, and of veering about in his opinion on the subject'.

For D's views on rhymed drama, see **20, 25, 78** and nn. above. He referred as early as 1664 to 'the pains of continual rhyming', and the natural tendency of the English tongue to 'slide' into blank verse (Watson, i. 5), and finally 'disencumbered' himself from rhyme in *All for Love* (1677): 'Not that I condemn my former way, but that this is more proper to my present purpose' (Watson, i. 231). In 'To the Earl of Roscommon' (1684), he dismissed rhyme as 'At best a pleasing sound, and fair barbarity' (Watson, ii. 15).

Spence, *Essay on Pope's Odyssey*, i (1726), 121–2, quoted D's statement in 1697 that 'he who can write well in rhyme may write better in blank verse. Rhyme is certainly a constraint even to the best poets' (Watson, ii. 240). Given his dislike of blank verse (see 'Milton' **274** and n. above), SJ is quietly triumphant about the fact that D 'departed from his own decision' when translating *Iliad*, Bk. I. For his projected translation of the whole *Iliad*, see **151** and n. above; and for anecdotal evidence for his supposed preference for blank verse, see *Prose Works* (1800), i (i). 113, 314–18.

By 1711 Addison in *Spectator* 39 claimed to be 'very much offended when I see a Play in Rhyme, which is as absurd in *English*, as a Tragedy of *Hexameters* would have been in *Greek* or *Latin*'. Poets already felt under pressure by the 1690s to use blank verse rather than rhyme when translating 'Heroic' verse, as Thomas Fletcher, of New College, Oxford, explained in the 'Preface' to his *Poems on Several Occasions, And Translations* (1692), sigg. A5$^v$–A7: 'Methinks blank Verse carries in it somewhat of the Majesty of *Virgil*; when Rhimes, even the most happy of them (after tedious pumping for them, and having good Expressions balk'd for want of them) do but emasculate Heroick Verse, and give it an unnatural Softness . . . an Heroe drest up in them looks like *Hercules* with a Distaff.' Fletcher added that, 'if a *Dryden* (a Master of our Language and Poetry) would undertake to Translate *Virgil* in blank Verse, we might hope to read him with as great pleasure in our Language, as his own'. SJ would not have been gratified to find that Fletcher offered not merely blank-verse translations of Virgil, but a blank-verse Pindaric ode (53–66). For blank-verse translations of Virgil by Brady (1714–17) and Trapp (1718), see **309–10** below.

**204.** Cf. D's preface to *An Evening's Love* (1671): 'I know no such law to have been constantly observed in comedy, either by the ancient or modern poets' (Watson, i. 150). For his 'grossness', see also **44, 170–1** above.

**205.** For Ovid and Claudian, see D's preface to *Sylvae* (1685) (Watson, ii. 21–2). SJ's note cites George Sewell's censure in his preface to Ovid's *Metamorphoses* (1717), i, pp. viii–ix.

SJ merges here two separate statements by D about Statius. Although he compared the first line of Statius, *Sylvae*, quoted here ('A mound doubled by a Colossus on its top') with the first line of Virgil's *Eclogues* in the dedication to *The Spanish Fryar* (1681), SJ refers primarily to D's comment in 'A Parallel Betwixt Poetry and Painting' (1695) that 'Virgil would have thought Statius mad' had he seen the opening lines of *Sylvae*. D then compared *Aeneid*, I. 1, with the opening of Statius' unfinished epic *Achilleis* (Watson, i. 277, ii. 204–5).

**206.** *condemned him to straw*: following his reference in **205** to Virgil thinking Statius 'mad', SJ alludes to the straw proverbially provided as bedding in Bedlam (cf. *Life*, ii. 374 and n.). This usage is not in the *Dict*.

**207.** Langbaine, *Account of the English Dramatick Poets* (Oxford, 1691), 168–9, noted D's blunder in referring to 'the tragedy of Queen Gorboduc, in English verse' in the dedication to *The Rival Ladies* (1664) (Watson, i. 5–6), also mentioned facetiously by Pope in a letter in 1717 (*Corresp.*, i. 408). *The Tragedy of Gorboduc* (1563) by Thomas Sackville and Thomas Norton was in blank verse, and Gorboduc was a king.

In the preface to *Annus Mirabilis* (1667), D described George Chapman's translation of Homer (see 'Waller' **106** and n. above) as in 'verses of six feet', whereas the *Iliad* (1598–1611) was in verse of seven feet and the *Odyssey* (1615?) of five feet (Watson, i. 96).

For D's vagueness in 1700 about the contents of *Iliad*, Bk. II, see Watson, ii. 276 and n.

**208.** *literature*: here and in **210**, SJ means 'Learning; skill in letters' (*Dict.*) (cf. 'Milton' **4** and n. above).

For Dr Busby, Westminster School, and Cambridge, see **4** and n. above, and for Cowley and Milton as Latinists, 'Cowley' **33–4** and n. above.

**209.** See *Of Dramatick Poesie* (Watson, i. 41). For the attribution of the Latin *Medea* to Seneca, and the single line of Ovid's play, see Quintilian, *Institutio Oratoria*, IX. ii. 9, VIII. v. 6.

**210.** In his 'Life of Plutarch' (1683), D confessed 'to my shame that I never read any thing but for pleasure', with history as 'the most delightful entertainment of my life' (Watson, ii. 4). Malone, *Prose Works* (1800), i(i). 511–12, believed that SJ and others underestimated the range of D's reading.

**211.** *knowledge*: in his extended comparison of the 'genius' of D and Pope in 'Pope' **308–10** below, SJ admits the superiority of D's 'acquired knowledge'. The contrast between D's 'great stores of intellectual wealth' here, later described as 'treasure' and 'large materials' (see **233, 321** below), and the literal poverty of which he so frequently complains (see **182** above) is seen as central to SJ's biography by Adams, 'Economics', 467–86.

Cf. Mrs Thrale-Piozzi's later marginal note on this paragraph: 'This is a portrait of Doctor Johnson's *own* mind and manners; I told him so, and he was not ill pleased' (Lobban, 140). Hill (1905) thought the passage one of those which prompted Boswell's comment that, in drawing D's character, SJ 'has given some touches of his own' (*Life*, iv. 45). William Hayley, *Two Dialogues* (1787), 120, had suggested that, 'in the general cast of his mind, as well as in his political and religious notions', SJ resembled D more than any other poet in the *Lives*. For SJ's 'partial fondness' for D, see 'Pope' **311** below.

212. SJ quotes *Threnodia Augustalis*, ll. 337-45.

213. SJ's words provided the text for a discussion of 'probable reasoning' in 18th-century thought by H. Trowbridge, 'Scattered Atoms of Probability', *ECS* 5 (1971-2), 1-30.

214. For other discussions of prose style, see 'Cowley' **200** and n. above, and for the 'easy' style, see 'Rochester' **18** and n. above. SJ characterizes D's prose again in 'Pope' **309** below. Damrosch (1976), 182-3, suggested that SJ has his own prose in mind in his comments on 'the formality of settled style' in **214-15**.

For D's tendency to 'self-commendation', see **162** above, and with the list of virtues and avoidance of concomitant defects in SJ's final sentence, cf. 'Parnell' **1** and n. below.

215. SJ said on 13 Apr. 1778, while writing 'Dryden': 'Those who have a style of eminent excellence, such as Dryden and Milton, can always be distinguished ... I think every man whatever has a peculiar style, which may be discovered by nice examination and comparison with others: but a man must write a great deal to make his style obviously discernible' (*Life*, iii. 280). For the characteristics by which an author will 'make himself known', see also 'Addison' **33** below.

*another and the same*: although Hill (1905) suggested that SJ alludes to Pope, *Dunciad*, III. 40 ('another yet the same'), SJ is in fact quoting D himself on the phoenix, in 'Of the Pythagorean Philosophy', ll. 580-1: 'Self-born, begotten by the Parent Flame | In which he burn'd, another and the same' (noted by G. F. Parker, *J's Shakespeare* (Oxford, 1989), 46, and by J. A. Winn in 'Dr. Johnson Reads Mr. Dryden', a paper at the ASECS conference, Nashville, Tenn., Apr. 1997). Cf. William Mudford, *Critical Enquiry into the Moral Writings of Dr. SJ* (1802), on the *Rambler*: 'In him there is no variation; he is for ever one and the same. All his pictures are alike, and in all we trace the reflection of a cynic' (J. T. Boulton (ed.), *J: The Critical Heritage* (1971), 77).

*beauty who*: Hill's suggested emendation to 'beauty which' is unnecessary. By 'beauty' SJ means '4. A beautiful person' (*Dict.*), i.e. who cannot be caricatured.

216. Cf. e.g. James Granger, *Biographical History of England* (3rd edn., 1779), iv. 37: 'Dryden was the father of true English poetry, and the most universal of poets ... He was the great improver of our language, and versification', which 'became harmonious' only in the age of D and Waller. D himself claimed that 'the language, wit, and conversation of our age are improved and refined above the last' in 'A Defence of the Epilogue' (1672) (Watson, i. 170-83). See also **356** below.

SJ will in fact assert later that Pope's translation of Homer 'may be said to have tuned the English tongue' ('Pope' **348**).

**217.** *forced thoughts, and rugged metre*: see 'Cowley' **65–101** above, and for the progress towards 'correctness', 'Cowley' **185–99** and n. above. For Waller and Denham, see **5** above and **222, 340** below (and cf. **290** below), and 'Denham' **35, 37** and 'Waller' **142** ff. above. D himself described Denham's *Cooper's Hill* as 'the exact standard of good writing' as early as 1664, and later stated that 'our numbers were in their nonage' before Denham and Waller (Watson, i. 7, ii. 281, and cf. ii. 150).

**218.** SJ here qualifies the crucial contribution often attributed to Denham and Waller.

For 'comprehension', see 'Cowley' **144** and n. above; and for 'regularity' and 'propriety', **263** below, and 'Roscommon' **24** and n. above.

**219–21.** For 'poetical diction', see also 'Cowley' **181–4** and n. above. In the preface to *Troilus and Cressida* (1679), D described the task of rescuing Shakespeare's genius from 'that heap of rubbish under which many excellent thoughts lay wholly buried'. He discussed the difficulty of finding an adequate modern language for epic translation in the dedication to the *Aeneid* (1697), claiming in his 'Postscript' to have contributed to 'the choice of words, and harmony of numbers, which were wanting, especially the last, in all our poets, even in those who, being endued with genius, yet have not cultivated their mother-tongue with sufficient care; or, relying on the beauty of their thoughts, have judged the ornament of words, and sweetnesss of sound, unnecessary' (Watson, i. 239–40, ii. 251–2, 258–9).

Cf. SJ's description of the 'neglected' state of the language in his 'Preface' to the *Dict.*: 'I found our speech copious without order, and energetic without rules: wherever I turned my view, there was perplexity to be disentangled, and confusion to be regulated' (*OASJ*, 307–8). He also described the 'unformed', fluctuating, and experimental poetical language of Shakespeare's day in the *Proposals* (1756) for his edition (*YW*, vii. 53).

**219.** Cf. SJ's preface to Baretti's *Easy Phraseology* (1775): 'Of every learned and elegant people the language is divided into two parts: the one lax and cursory, used on slight occasions with extemporary negligence; the other rigorous and solemn, the effect of deliberate choice and grammatical accuracy. When books are multiplied and style is cultivated, the colloquial and written diction separate by degrees, till there is one language of the tongue, and another of the pen' (Hazen, 10).

With the 'original rectitude' of some early writers, cf. the 'instinctive elegance . . . a particular provision made by Nature for literary politeness' envisaged in 'Cowley' **5** above.

**220.** For 'harshness', see 'Milton' **177** and n. above, and for 'terms of art' in poetry, see also **255–6** and n. below.

In the *Plan of a Dictionary* (1747), **22–4**, SJ announced his intention of including definitions of the 'poetical' meaning of words, 'where it differs from that which is in common use', but in practice did so only intermittently.

**221.** For the difference between poetry and prose (or the 'prosaic'), see also **285** below, 'Cowley' **129, 142** above, and 'Roscommon' **30**, 'Fenton' **24**, 'Somervile' **8**, 'Pope' **399, 441**, 'Collins' **17**, and 'Akenside' **19** below, and *Ramblers* 86, 88 (1751). Although SJ later derided the view that language was 'more poetical as it was more remote from common use' (see 'Gray' **30** below), Addison had argued in *Spectator* 285 (1712) that the language of the higher kinds of poetry must 'deviate from the common Forms and ordinary Phrases of Speech', to avoid familiar and vulgar associations. See also Beattie's recent discussion 'Of the Language of

Poetry' in his *Essays* (Edinburgh, 1776), 498–580, and Erasmus Darwin's dialogue on 'the essential difference between Poetry and Prose' in *The Botanic Garden. Part II* (Lichfield, 1789), 40–50.

For 'colours of diction', see 'Milton' **193** and n. above.

222. *The new versification*: see **5, 217** and n. above and **343** below. Langbaine, *English Dramatick Poets*, 131, stated that D 'has with success practic'd the new way of Versifying introduc'd by his Predecessor, Mr. *Waller*, and follow'd since with success, by Sr. *John Denham*, and others'. For 'the new turn of Verse' introduced by Waller, see also Francis Atterbury's preface to *The Second Part of Mr. Waller's Poems* (1690), sigg. A5$^v$–A8$^v$: 'Before his time, men Rhym'd indeed, and that was all: as for the harmony of measure, and that dance of words, which good ears are so much pleas'd with, they knew nothing of it . . . So that really verse in those days was but down-right Prose, tagg'd with Rhymes.'

D discussed versification in 'A Discourse Concerning Satire' (1692); the dedication to *Examen Poeticum* (1694), where he described his own age as 'much better' than the last 'for versification, and the art of numbers'; and the dedication to the *Aeneid* (1697), where he claimed to be 'the first Englishman' to have imitated Virgil 'in his numbers, his choice of words, and his placing them for the sweetness of the sound'. See also the postscript to the *Aeneid*, already quoted in **219–21** n. above (Watson, ii. 147–8, 164–5, 167–8, 234–8, 258).

According to Joseph Trapp, *Lectures on Poetry* (1742), 61, Cowley and his contemporaries studied only 'the Beauty of Thought' and neglected 'the melody of Verse', until D 'added to English Poetry what it only wanted, Numbers, Harmony, and Accuracy'. Cf. also the preface to *Poems and Translations by Several Hands* (1714): 'Ill Poets make better Verses now, than Good Ones did Fifty Years ago. Versification was so highly improv'd by Mr. Dryden, and has been of late so well study'd, that one may expect it even from those from whom we expect little else.'

223. For the principles of translation, see **107** and n. above and **299–300** below, and 'Denham' **32** and n. above. Walker, 'Some Notes', 106–9, has pointed out that most of SJ's quotations from D in the *Dict.* come from his translations, especially of Virgil and Ovid.

D discussed the inadequacy of the French language for heroic poetry in the dedication to the *Aeneid* (1697) (Watson, ii. 238–40), having alluded briefly in 'To the Earl of Roscommon', ll. 24–9, to Roscommon's assertion of French inferiority to English translation in his *Essay on Translated Verse* (1684), ll. 39–58. For the doubts of such critics as Rapin and Bouhours about the adequacy of French versification and language for epic poetry, see Clingham, 'Homeric Scholarship', 140. Voltaire conceded the superiority of the English language and 'Genius' for poetry and translation in *Essay upon . . . Epick Poetry* (1727), 122–3.

Étienne de Silhouette, in the preface to *Essai sur la critique. Par M. Pope* (Paris, 1736), pp. x–xvii, also attributed the superiority of English translation to the richness and flexibility of the language. Thomas Newton, in Milton's *Paradise Lost* (1749), i, p. xli, wrote of the French that 'nothing sheweth the weakness and imperfection of their language more, than that they have few or no good poetical translations of the greatest poets; they are forced to translate Homer, Virgil, and Milton into prose'. SJ returns to the subject in 'Pope' **347** below.

D discussed Jonson, Cowley, and Denham in his influential statement about translation in the preface to *Ovid's Epistles* (1680) (Watson, i. 262–73) (see **107** above). SJ refers to Owen Feltham's *Resolves Or, Excogitations. A Second Centurie* (1628), sig. A2ᵛ: 'In my opinion, they disgrace our *Language*, that will not giue a *Latine* Verse his *English*, under two for one.' SJ had already cited this passage in his earlier account in *Idler* 69 (1759) of how poetic translators 'shook off their constraint' after the Restoration (*YW*, ii. 216). Feltham (1602?–68) was an 'adversary' because he attacked Jonson in an ode in the 'Lusoria' appended to his *Resolves* (8th edn., 1661), although he had earlier contributed an elegy in his memory to *Jonsonus Virbius* (1638). (Langbaine, *English Dramatick Poets*, 302–4, reprinted both poems.)

D described George Sandys as 'the best versifier of the former age' in the preface to *Fables* (1700), but had earlier written less favourably about him (Watson, ii. 270, 164). D respected Barten Holyday's learning, but thought 'the verse of his translation and his English are lame and pitiful' (Watson, ii. 136): see **107** and n. above and **299** and n. below. See also 'Cowley' **124** ff. and **202** above, and the preface to his Pindaric odes (*Poems*, ed. Waller (1905), 155–6).

**224.** SJ quotes the dedication to the *Aeneid* (1697): 'The way I have taken is not so strait as metaphrase, nor so loose as paraphrase' (Watson, ii. 246). For these terms, see **107** n. above.

*divaricate*: 'To divide into two' (*Dict*.).

**225.** SJ is paraphrasing D in Watson, ii. 247, 136. For other comments on levels of style, see **285, 292–5** below, 'Addison' **46, 167–8**, and 'Swift' **113** below. Cf. SJ's approval of D's ideas about translation with his contempt for the banality of Roscommon's notions ('Roscommon' **27** above).

See also 'Pope' **349–52** below for SJ's later defence of the 'elegance' of Pope's Homer translation, on grounds which depart somewhat from D's prescriptions here.

**226.** SJ refers to Sir Edward Sherburne (1618–1702), 'A Brief Discourse concerning Translation', in *The Tragedies of L. Annaeus Seneca* (1702), pp. xxxvi–xxxix, discussed earlier in *Idler* 69 (1759) (*YW*, ii. 217). Sherburne rejected interpretations of Horace, *Ars Poetica*, l. 133 ('don't try to render word for word like a faithful translator'), as condemning 'Verbal' translation. For SJ's copy of Sherburne, see Fleeman, *Handlist* (1984), 57. He added a quotation from Sherburne on translation to the *Dict*. (4th edn., 1773) under 'Interpreter'.

**227.** Pope stated in his preface to the *Iliad* that flaws in D's translation from Homer 'ought to be excused on account of the Haste he was obliged to write in'. In *Iliad*, I. 41 n., he attributed an error in D's translation to his 'extreme haste in writing', the fault of 'those who suffer'd so noble a Genius to lie under the necessity of it' (*TE*, vii. 22, 88). Dennis in 1717 deplored the lack of 'Encouragement' D suffered and his supposed death in poverty (*Works*, ii. 121). This was a common topic: in *Idler* 60 (1759) Dick Minim 'often expressed his commiseration of Dryden's poverty, and his indignation at the age which suffered him to write for bread' (*YW*, ii. 186).

**228.** SJ may have in mind Voltaire's assertion in *Letters Concerning the English Nation* (1733), 175, that D should have written only a tenth of what he produced (quoted by *GD*, iv. 687). Cf. SJ's well-known statement that 'No man but a blockhead ever wrote, except for money' (*Life*, iii. 19), and see also 'Pope' **304** below.

**229.** SJ quotes *Don Sebastian*, II. iii. 586. For D's borrowings, see **29**, **103** above.

**230–3.** For D's own mockery of 'occasional' poets in *Of Dramatick Poesy*, see Watson, i. 20. He did not in fact dedicate his major original poems to patrons, stating that *Religio Laici* was 'a Confession of my own' and that *The Hind and the Panther* was 'neither impos'd on me, nor so much as the Subject given me by any man': see D. Griffin, *Literary Patronage in England, 1660–1800* (Cambridge, 1996), 91–2.

SJ described the unfortunate author who is unable to choose his own subject in *Rambler* 21 (1750), and his own problems as an essayist committed 'to compose on a stated day' in *Rambler* 208 (1752) (*YW*, iii. 119, v. 318). For 'occasional poetry', see also **284** and n. below, 'Waller' **69** above, and 'Rowe' **6**, 'Addison' **77**, 'Prior' **13**, **20**, **58**, 'Savage' **64**, **179**, **249**, and (as a contrast to D) 'Pope' **301** below.

**230.** The anecdote about Virgil is ultimately from Donatus' life of Virgil. Cf. Joseph Warton's *Works of Virgil* (1753), i. 32: 'He used to revise his Verses with a prodigious Severity, to dictate a great Number of Lines in the Morning, and to spend the rest of the Day in correcting them, and reducing them to a less Number.' SJ cites this passage again in 'Pope' **299** below, and cf. 'Milton' **125** above.

**231.** Cf. *Rambler* 143 (1751): 'Bruyere declares that we are come into the world too late to produce any thing new, that nature and life are preoccupied, and that description and sentiment have been long exhausted. It is indeed certain that whoever attempts any common topick, will find unexpected coincidences of his thoughts with those of other writers... There is likewise a common stock of images'; and *Adventurer* 95 (1753): 'Writers of all ages have had the same sentiments, because they have in all ages had the same objects and passions' (*YW*, iv. 394, ii. 425).

**232.** Cf. *Rambler* 145 (1751) for a contrast of modern hack writers with traditional notions of the author, who 'must feel in himself some peculiar impulse of genius... must watch the happy minute in which his natural fire is excited... must carefully select his thought and polish his expressions' (*YW*, v. 10).

**234.** For D's 'Heroique Stanza's' on Cromwell (1659), see **7** above.

**235.** For Sir William Davenant, see **24** and n., **30** above. For poems by Waller and Cowley praising Davenant's *Gondibert* (1651), and a collection of *Certain Verses Written By Some of the Authors Friends* (1653) mocking it, see *Gondibert*, ed. D. F. Gladish (Oxford, 1971), 269–86. For his quatrains, see **247** and n. below.

**236.** For the 'ruggedness' of Donne and Jonson, see 'Cowley' **62** and n. above, and, for D's conceits, see **5** above. SJ praises D's 'rejection of unnatural thoughts and rugged numbers' in 'Pope' **304** below.

SJ quotes *Astraea Redux* (1660), ll. 51, 53–4, 93–6.

**237.** *Astraea Redux*, ll. 151–78. For George Monck, Duke of Albemarle, see **23** and n. above.

**238.** SJ quotes *Astraea Redux*, ll. 119–22, 143–4, and refers to 262–5, alluding to Exodus 33: 18–23, 34: 5–6.

For SJ's hostility to modern use of ancient mythology, see 'Butler' **41** and n. above, and for the mingling of sacred and profane, **72** and n. above and **335** below, and 'Milton' **183** and n. above.

**239.** SJ quotes *Astraea Redux*, ll. 207–8, 242–5, 252–5.

J. P. Hardy (ed.), *Johnson's Lives of the Poets: A Selection* (Oxford, 1971), 171 n., traced the anecdote about François de Malherbe (1555–1628) to A. H. de Sallengre, *Mémoires de littérature* (The Hague, 1715–17), ii. 72–3. For the suggestion that Malherbe had a serious influence on *Astraea Redux*, see Winn, *JD*, 560–1.

**240.** SJ quotes *To His Sacred Majesty* (1661), ll. 79–84: see **10** above.

**241.** *To His Sacred Majesty*, ll. 69–70.

*one particle of that old versification*: the pronunciation of 'fruition' with four syllables.

**242–6.** SJ quotes *To My Lord Chancellor Presented on New-years-day* (1662), ll. 31–42, 73–8, 105–18, 119–22, 147–56.

**244.** *obscurity*: see also **332** below, and 'Pope' **45**, 'Thomson' **4**, 'A. Philips' **36**, and 'Collins' **9** below, and, for earlier discussions, *Rambler* 169 (1751), *Adventurer* 58 (1753), *Idlers* 36 (1758), 70 (1759).

**246.** *unsociable matter*: cf. the 'very incongruous and unsociable ideas' in 'Cowley' **194** and n. above.

**247.** For *Annus Mirabilis* (1667), and for D's comments on the quatrain and its 'inconvenience', see **22–4** and nn. above. SJ added 'for he complains of its difficulty' in the first sentence in 1783 (see Textual Notes).

*greatest*: SJ evidently means 'most elaborate' as in **22** above (cf. 'Milton' **194** and n. above).

For poets who 'borrow every thing from their predecessors', see 'Cowley' **60–1** and n. above, and cf. **329** below.

See Boileau, 'Epître IV' (1672), ll. 119–24, in his *Oeuvres* (Paris, 1747), i. 315–16; and see also v. 52–3 n., for a note on earlier references to gunpowder in French poetry. SJ refers to Waller, 'Of a War with Spain, and a Fight at Sea' (see 'Waller' **66, 129** above), and Milton, *Paradise Lost*, VI. 469–520, 571–607. Precedents for Milton's 'war in heaven' (see 'Milton' **255** above) have been found in Ariosto, Spenser, and Samuel Daniel. *Annus Mirabilis* probably appeared in Jan. 1667, and *Paradise Lost* in Aug. 1667.

**248.** For Davenant's quatrain, see **24** and n. and **235** above.

**249.** *more sentiment than description*: SJ defines 'Sentiment' as '1. Thought; notion; opinion. 2. The sense considered distinctly from the language or things; a striking sentence in a composition' (*Dict.*). At **270** below he complains again that there is more sentiment than description in *Absalom and Achitophel*. See also **327** below ('sentences were readier at his call than images'), and 'Cowley' **168** above ('Tasso affords images, and Cowley sentiments'). For a complaint about description with insufficient sentiment, see 'Collins' **9** below, and for description in poetry, 'Cowley' **154** and n. above.

**250.** For Waller's poem, see **247** n. above. SJ also refers to a poem in Petronius, *Satyricon*, 119, l. 1 ('[The conquering Roman] now held the whole world').

**251.** SJ quotes *Annus Mirabilis*, ll. 57–60.

**251*a*.** Not numbered as a separate paragraph by Hill (1905). SJ quotes *Annus Mirabilis*, ll. 61–4. For 'burlesque', see 'Butler' **52** and n. above.

**252.** SJ quotes *Annus Mirabilis*, ll. 93–120, describing the English attack on the Dutch East India fleet at Bergen.

**253.** For 'the sublime', see 'Cowley' **58** and n. above, and for the 'domestick', 'Otway' **10** and n. above.

SJ defines a 'castor' (l. 97) as '1. A beaver' (*Dict.*, quoting this line).

**254.** SJ quotes *Annus Mirabilis*, ll. 269–84.

**255–6*a*.** *terms of art*: although D's preface to *Annus Mirabilis* defended his use of 'the proper terms which are used at sea', he explained in the dedication to the *Aeneid* (1697) that he had avoided 'the cant of any profession', because Virgil 'writ not to mariners, soldiers, astronomers, gardeners, peasants, etc., but to all in general, and in particular to men and ladies of the first quality' (Watson, i. 96, ii. 254). Pope censured some surviving 'sea-terms' in D's translation in 1710, 'because no Terms of Art, or Cant-Words, suit with the Majesty & dignity of Style [which] Epic Poetry requires' (*Corresp.*, i. 101), and Addison similarly criticized '*Technical Words*, or Terms of Art' in *Paradise Lost* in *Spectator* 297 (1712). D's sea-terms had recently been criticized by George Campbell, *The Philosophy of Rhetoric* (1776), ii. 24.

In *Rambler* 99 (1751) SJ condemned the 'jargon of a particular profession', and wrote in *Rambler* 173 (1751): 'Every art has its dialect, uncouth and ungrateful to all whom custom has not reconciled to its sound, and which therefore becomes ridiculous by a slight misapplication, or unnecesary repetition' (*YW*, iv. 168, v. 151). Reviewing Thomas Blackwell's *Memoirs of the Court of Augustus* (1756), SJ deplored his 'delight' in 'terms of art . . . words that every other polite writer has avoided and despised' (*OASJ*, 498).

His comment on 'Mackerel-Gale' in the *Dict.* indicates his opinion of such terms in poetry: 'Mackerel-Gale seems to be, in *Dryden*'s cant, a strong breeze; such I suppose, as is desired to bring *mackerel* fresh to market' (quoting *The Hind and the Panther*, III. 455–6). For other comments on 'the harshness of terms appropriated to particular arts' in poetry, see **220** above, and **279, 336** below, and 'Milton' **234, 263** above. SJ did, of course, include 'terms of art' in the *Dict.*: see his *Plan* (1747), 5, and his preface (*OASJ*, 313). In *Rambler* 86 (1751) he explained that, while he avoided 'the dialect of grammarians' when addressing general readers, it was difficult to convey 'the precepts of an art without the terms by which the peculiar ideas of that art are expressed' (*YW*, iv. 89). *Idler* 70 (1759) later makes clear that, in non-literary contexts, they can be essential: 'Every hour produces instances of the necessity of terms of art . . . it is not but by necessity that every science and every trade has its peculiar language' (*YW*, ii. 219).

**256.** SJ quoted *Annus Mirabilis*. ll. 581–92, to illustrate 'Oakum', 'Calk', 'Mallet', 'Instop', 'Marline', and 'Tarpawling' in the *Dict.*

**256*a*.** Not numbered as a separate paragraph by Hill (1905).

**257.** See *Annus Mirabilis*, ll. 617–64. SJ in fact criticizes the 'absurdities' of ll. 653–6 in **330** below.

For the Royal Society, see 'Cowley' **31** and n. above. D was elected on 19 Nov. and admitted on 26 Nov. 1662 (Winn, *JD*, 129).

**258.** SJ quotes *Annus Mirabilis*, ll. 649–50, and the revised text of D's note, which originally read 'knowledge of Longitudes'. In 1755 SJ helped Zachariah Williams to publicize his supposed discovery of a method of determining longitude at sea (*Life*, i. 301–2 and n.).

**259.** See *Annus Mirabilis*, ll. 833–1164, with Charles II's speech at ll. 1045–80.
For 'reason' and 'emotion' in D's poetry, see also **322–5** below.

**260.** SJ quotes *Annus Mirabilis*, ll. 861–5.

**260a.** Not numbered as a separate paragraph by Hill (1905). The Latin ('All things were laid to rest in the calm quiet of night') is not in fact by Virgil, but was cited by Seneca, *Controversiae*, VII. i. 27, from a fragment of Varro.

**261.** *Annus Mirabilis*, ll. 889–92, refer to the heads of traitors impaled on London Bridge.

**262.** *Annus Mirabilis*, ll. 1165–216, predict the rebuilding of London and its mercantile expansion. The final simile is: 'Thus to the Eastern wealth through storms we go; | But now, the Cape once doubled, fear no more: | A constant Trade-wind will securely blow, | And gently lay us on the Spicy shore.'

**263.** *propriety*: see **218** above, and 'Roscommon' **24** and n. above.

**264.** For SJ's quotation from 'A Discourse Concerning Satire', see Watson, ii. 91, and **12, 91** above. D did not publish another major poem until 1681 (**108** above).

SJ defines 'Addict' as '1. To devote; to dedicate, in a good sense; which is rarely used. 2. It is commonly taken in a bad sense; as, *he addicted himself to vice*' (*Dict.*). In 1773 he added: '3. To devote one's self to any person, party, or persuasion. A Latinism.'

*the opinion of Harte*: SJ no doubt heard this directly from the poet and historian Walter Harte (1709–74), an Oxford tutor, friend of Pope, and later a Canon of Windsor, of whose scholarship and 'companionable talents' SJ thought highly (*Life*, ii. 120; see also 'Pope' **70** and n. below). Derrick acknowledged Harte's help in his edition of Dryden (1760), i, p. viii. SJ added 130 quotations from Harte to the *Dict.* in 1773, notably from his volume of religious verse, *The Amaranth* (1767): for SJ's copy, marked for use in the *Dict.*, see Fleeman, *Handlist* (1984), 21.

SJ is once more troubled by dates, evidently believing that *The State of Innocence* (written by 1674; published 1677) and *Tyrannick Love* (acted 1669; published 1670) were later than *Aureng-Zebe* (acted 1675; published 1676): see **92, 96** above, and, for the rapid composition of the first two plays, **46, 71** above, and cf. 'Milton' **178** above.

**265.** SJ is reluctant to concede the superiority of blank verse to the couplet even in drama, although he used it in his own tragedy *Irene* (1749): see **20, 203** above and 'Milton' **274** and n. above.

For 'the description of Night', see **19** and n. above, and, for 'the rise and fall of empire', *Conquest of Granada II*, I. i. 1–16.

**266.** See **11** and n. above.

**267.** For D's preface and other contributions to *Ovid's Epistles* (1680), see **107** and n. and **223** above.

268. For *Absalom and Achitophel*, see **108–10** above. SJ gave 'great applause to the character of Zimri' (ll. 543–68) on 16 Oct. 1769 (*Life*, ii. 85). Joseph Warton commented (posthumously) on SJ's 'exaggerated panegyric': 'if this poem is of a nature purely and merely political and controversial, it does not partake of the essence of real poetry' (Dryden, *Poetical Works*, ed. H. J. Todd (1811), i. 266 n.). Warton claimed that *Absalom* was 'in the present age but little read' (i. 272 n.).

269. Although his comment on 'irreligiously licentious' lines in *Absalom and Achitophel* (cf. **170–1** and n. above) may allude to it, SJ seems less troubled by D's famous opening description of Charles II as David than Joseph Warton (see **268** n. above), who found it 'very filthy and abominable' (i. 210 n.). For allegory, see 'Cowley' **151** and n. above.

270. For the imbalance of sentiment and description, see **249** and n. above and **326** below.

    For 'admiration' as wearisome, see 'Cowley' **58** and n. above.

271. For the 'action' in epic theory, see 'Milton' **225** and n. above.

    When D published *Absalom and Achitophel*, the crisis caused by the Whig attempt, led by the Earl of Shaftesbury and the Duke of Monmouth, to exclude the Catholic James, Duke of York, from the throne was still unresolved. Cf. 'To the Reader': 'The conclusion of the Story, I purposely forebore to prosecute . . . Were I the Inventour, who am only the Historian, I should certainly conclude the Piece, with the Reconcilement of *Absalom* [Monmouth] to *David* [Charles II]. And, who knows but this may come to pass? Things were not brought to an Extremity where I left the Story' (*Poems* (1958), i. 216). For Charles II's concluding speech, see ll. 933–1025. SJ quotes l. 1028 (with 'times' for 'time').

272. *enchanted castle*: for a suggested source, see J. Hardy, 'J and *Don Bellianis*', *RES* 17 (1966), 297–9, referring to the 16th-century Spanish romance *Don Bellianis de Grecia* by Geronimo Fernandez (1547–79). Henson, 32–5, also compared Granville's 'Concerning Unnatural Flights in Poetry', 71–2, quoted under 'Magick' in the *Dict*.: 'Like castles built by *magick* art in air, | That vanish at approach, such thoughts appear' (see 'Granville' **30** below). For SJ's fondness for old romances, see *Life*, i. 48–9, and *Percy Corresp*., vii (Shenstone). 9–10; and for a poet who 'diligently perused . . . the old romances of knight errantry', see 'Smith' **69** below.

273. D contributed at least ll. 310–509 (and perhaps ll. 79–102, 522–55) to Nahum Tate's *The Second Part of Absalom and Achitophel* (1682), including the satirical characters of Elkanah Settle as Doeg and Thomas Shadwell as Og: see **116, 136** above, and for Tate, 'Rowe' **21** and n. below. For a later comment on 'personal satire', see 'Pope' **356** below.

274. *The Medall* (see **114** and n. above) is a more direct satiric attack on Shaftesbury, from which SJ quotes ll. 50–64.

275. For *Threnodia Augustalis. A Funeral-Pindarique Poem* (1685), on the death of Charles II on 6 Feb. 1685, see **212** above. SJ objects to the coupling of Latin and Greek words in its title. For a reply to SJ's objection, see *Works*, iii. 303–4.

    For SJ's dislike of 'irregularity of . . . metre', see 'Cowley' **141** and n. above, and for the 'pathetick', 'Cowley' **57** and n. above. SJ adapts l. 8 ('And Petrifie with grief', quoted under 'Petrify' in the *Dict*.), and quotes ll. 160–4.

276. SJ quotes *Threnodia Augustalis*, ll. 97–106. For the mingling of pagan fable with Christianity, see also 72 and n. above and 'Milton' 183 and n. above.

277. *Threnodia Augustalis*, ll. 429–517, celebrate the accession of James II. Hill (1905) noted D's hints in ll. 377–82 that Charles II had failed to reward him adequately.
    For 'sincerity', see 'Cowley' 108 and n. above.

278. SJ refers to 'To the Pious Memory of the Accomplisht Young Lady Mrs. Anne Killigrew, Excellent in the two Sister-Arts of Poesie, and Painting. An Ode' (1686). He quotes Horace, *Odes*, IV. ii. 7 ('[so does Pindar] seethe and, brooking no restraint, rush on').
    SJ's praise of D's ode, with its 'torrent of enthusiasm', as the 'noblest' in the language, is unexpected, given his usual dislike of irregular odes (cf. 275). If his intention was to disconcert admirers of Thomas Gray, whose *The Bard* was often described in similar terms (see 'Gray' 32 ff. below), he succeeded. There was an early protest in the *London Review* in Nov. 1779 (see iv. 526 below). Adam Smith was reportedly baffled by SJ's praise of D's 'Killigrew' ode: 'The criticism had induced him to read it over, and with attention, twice, and he could not discover even a spark of merit. At the same time, he mentioned Gray's odes' (*Lectures on Rhetoric and Belles Lettres*, ed. J. C. Bryce (Oxford, 1983), 229–30). John Scott of Amwell (to Beattie, 10 May 1782) asked: 'what must one think of the critic's taste, who could prefer Dryden's wretched, conceited "Ode on Mrs. Killigrew," to the "British Bard" of our English Pindar?' (Sir William Forbes, *Life and Writings of James Beattie* (Edinburgh, 1806), ii. 111).
    J. T. Callender, *Deformities of Dr. SJ* (Edinburgh, 1782), 6, thought D's 'verses on Mrs Killigrew are below all criticism'. Robert Potter, *Inquiry* (1783), 11–12, was astounded by SJ's judgement, and Gilbert Wakefield, *Poems of Mr. Gray* (1786), 121, protested at SJ's 'extravagant encomiums' on D's ode ('sentiments at once puerile, low, and turgid; and debased by meanness of expression'), when defending Gray's *The Bard* against SJ's criticism. Joseph Warton derided SJ's praise of D's ode here and in 318 below in his *Works of Pope* (1797), i, pp. xix, 159 n. (the first stanza was 'really unintelligible, and full of absurd bombast'), and in his posthumously published notes on D (see 268 n. above) linked this 'unaccountable perversity of judgement' to SJ's attacks on Milton's *Lycidas* and Gray's *The Bard* (ii. 259–60 n.).

279. SJ quotes *A Song for St. Cecilia's Day* (1687), ll. 1–15. The 'second' ode is *Alexander's Feast*, also written for St Cecilia (see 150 and n. above and 318–20 below).
    *too technical*: for SJ's objection to 'technical' terms in poetry, see 225 and n. above. D had a precedent for 'diapason' ('concord') in Milton, 'At A Solemn Music', l. 23: SJ had in fact quoted both passages under 'Diapason' in the *Dict*.
    For 'remote' rhymes, see also 'Akenside' 23 below. Shenstone made the same point with reference to Milton's *Lycidas* in 1748, and in his 'Essay on Elegy' (*Letters* (1939), 133; *Works* (1764), i. 9).

280. SJ quotes *Song for St. Cecilia's Day*, ll. 55–63. He is uneasy about D's reference to the Last Day (cf. 'Young' 155 below) but had quoted this passage under 'Untune' ('To make incapable of harmony') in the *Dict*. For sacred poetry, see 'Waller' 135 and n. above.

**281.** SJ quotes *Eleonora: A Panegyrical Poem* (1692), ll. 270–90, on the death of Eleanor Bertie, Countess of Abingdon.

**282.** SJ quotes *Eleonora*, ll. 1–11. For the difference between a true simile and mere 'exemplification', see 'Addison' **132** and n. below.

**282a.** Not numbered as a separate paragraph by Hill (1905).

**283.** D's dedication to James Bertie, Earl of Abingdon, admits that he had not met the Countess, citing as a precedent the fact that Donne had never met Elizabeth Drury, memorialized in his *Anniversaries* (1612) (Watson, ii. 61–2).

*general*: see Cowley **58** and n. above. Here the word means merely 'generalized', when precise 'Knowledge of the subject' was desirable, a point SJ made about another commemorative poem in 'Pope' **415** below. Cf. 'that perplexity which generality produces' in **103** above.

**284.** This is SJ's first reference to *Religio Laici or A Laymans Faith* (1682) (cf. **117** n. above), from which he quotes ll. 453–4. He had quoted its opening lines under 'Reason' in the *Dict*.

Precedents for D's title include not only Sir Thomas Browne's *Religio Medici* (1642), but Lord Herbert of Cherbury's *De Religione Laici* (1645), imitated in Charles Blount's *Religio Laici* (1683) in reply to D, Sir George Mackenzie's *Religio Stoici* (1663), and the anonymous *Religio Clerici* (1681).

*a voluntary effusion*: described as a 'Confession of my own' (see **230–3** n. above), D's poem was a response to Henry Dickinson's translation (1682) of Richard Simon's *Histoire critique du Vieux Testament* (1678). D in fact also said of *The Hind and the Panther* (1687) that 'it was neither impos'd on me, nor so much as the Subject given me by any man' (*Poems* (1958), ii. 468).

**285.** Although disappointed in **284** that *Religio Laici* is 'rather argumentative than poetical', SJ later mentions the fact that D 'was the first who joined argument with poetry' among his achievements in **356** below. For argument and ratiocination in poetry, see also **125** above and **295, 297, 327–8** below, 'Waller' **135** above ('the happy power of arguing in verse'), and 'Blackmore' **46** and 'Pope' **179** below.

*this middle kind of writing*: for SJ's usual distinctions beween the 'poetic' and the 'prosaic' or 'familiar', see **221** above and **295** below, and 'Cowley' **138** and n., **142** above. Only *Religio Laici* and parts of *The Hind and Panther* seem to exemplify the 'middle kind of writing' he describes here, since he ignores its presence in Pope's later verse. He may, however, echo 'The Design' prefixed to *An Essay on Man*, in which Pope stated that he had been unable to treat his subject 'more *poetically*, without sacrificing perspicuity to ornament' (*TE*, iii (i). 8). D's own preface explained that 'the Smoothness, the Numbers and the Turn of Heroick Poetry' would have been inappropriate: 'The Expressions of a Poem, design'd purely for Instruction, ought to be Plain and Natural, and yet Majestick' (*Poems* (1958), i. 311). For different stylistic levels in *The Hind and the Panther*, see **292–5** below, and cf. **225** and n. above.

**286.** For *The Hind and the Panther* (1687), see **126–7** above. SJ refers to II. 80 ff., II. 64–76.

*incommodious*: 'Inconvenient; vexatious without great mischief' (*Dict.*).

287. See *The Hind and the Panther*, I. 528–30, II. 156 ff., 394–662. For 'allegory', see 'Cowley' **151** and n. above.

*worried*: SJ defines 'To Worry' as '2. To harass, or persecute brutally' (*Dict.*).

288. For *The Hind and the Panther Transvers'd* (1687), see **127** above and 'Halifax' **5** and 'Prior' **5** below. Cf. D's opening lines (quoted in **290** below) with the parody: 'A milk-white *Mouse* immortal and unchang'd, | Fed on soft Cheese, and o're the *Dairy* rang'd; | Without, unspotted; innocent within, | She fear'd no danger, for she knew no *Ginn*' (p. 4).

   Joseph Spence, *An Essay on Pope's Odyssey* (1726), 32, commented on the absurdity in D's poem 'of mixing *Fable* and *Reality* together . . . so grossly', and the 'infinite humour and good sense' of the parody. For the appeal to 'temporary passions', see 'Butler' **41–3** above.

289. Pope's comment on the versification of *The Hind and the Panther* (whether or not influenced by his Roman Catholicism) has not been found in his letters or conversation as recorded by Spence. SJ may have heard it from Savage or Walter Harte (see **264** and n. above).

290. SJ quotes *The Hind and the Panther*, I. 1–8.

   Cf. his statement in **217** above that 'Waller and Denham . . . had shewn that long discourses in rhyme grew more pleasing when they were broken into couplets.' D himself wrote in *Of Dramatick Poesie* that 'most commonly, the sense is to be confined to the couplet', but that 'nothing that does . . . run in the same channel, can please always', and that 'many times the close of the sense falls into the middle of the next verse' (Watson, i. 82). For the closed couplet, see also 'Denham' **37** and n. above, and for the negative sense of 'uniformity' as monotonous, see 'Butler' **35** and n. above.

291. *the interruption of the pause*: SJ's comment on *The Hind and the Panther*, I. 7, reveals his sensitivity to the 'ruggedness' (2. 'Roughness; asperity', *Dict.*) of an emphatic caesura after the fourth syllable of a line. For a detailed discussion of metrical pauses, see *Rambler* 90 (1751), and for metrical 'variety', see also **349, 351** and nn. below.

292. SJ quotes 'To the Reader' (*Poems* (1958), ii. 469), and *The Hind and the Panther*, I. 160–5.

293–4. SJ quotes *The Hind and the Panther*, I. 308–26, 554–72.

295. For D's discussion of these stylistic levels, see 'To the Reader' (*Poems* (1958), ii. 469), and cf. **225** and n. above; for SJ's examples of 'incongruity' (see **286** above), see iii. 60, i. 531, ii. 711; and for the confusion of the sacred and profane, see also **72** and n. above and 'Milton' **183** and n. above.

296. With SJ's final sentence, cf. the fate of *Hudibras* in 'Butler' **41** and n. above.

297. For 'poetical ratiocination' and the effect of 'metre' on 'argument', see **285** and n. above.

298. For *Britannia Rediviva* (1688), and the impact of the events of 1688–9 on D, see **135–9** above.

299. For the translation by D and others of the *Satires* of Juvenal and Persius, see **140** and n. above. SJ refers to Sir Robert Stapylton's *Juvenal's Sixteen Satyrs* (1647)

and Barten Holyday's *Juvenal and Persius Translated and Illustrated* (1673) (see also **107, 223** and nn. above).

**300.** Comparing him with Horace, D wrote of Juvenal: 'His expressions are sonorous and more noble; his verse more numerous, and his words are suitable to his thoughts, sublime and lofty' (Watson, ii. 130). Cf. SJ's reference to Juvenal's 'massiness and vigour' in 'Congreve' **40** below. His comment on the translation's failure in 'dignity' and 'grandeur' has often been contrasted with his own success in imitating Juvenal's *Satires* III and X in *London* (1738) and *The Vanity of Human Wishes* (1749). SJ once said of Juvenal's satires that he 'probably should give more, for he had them all in his head', although some 'were too gross for imitation' (*Life*, i. 193). For Thomas Creech, see **163** and n. above.

**302.** In the 'Argument' to Persius' 'Third Satyr', D said merely that he had translated it at Westminster School, where, with similar verse exercises, he believed it was 'still in the Hands of my *Learned Master*, the Reverend Doctor *Busby*' (see **4** and n. above) (*Poems* (1958), ii. 758). *GD*, iv. 676, had explained this clearly, and SJ may be replying here to Derrick (1760 edn.), i, p. xiv.

**303.** D had translated the '*Pollio*' (Virgil, 'Eclogue IV') in *Miscellany Poems* (1684), and the two episodes from *Aeneid*, Bks. V and X, in *Sylvae* (1685). He revised all three translations for inclusion in the *Works of Virgil* (1697).

**304.** See D's own extended comparison of Homer and Virgil in the preface to *Fables* (1700) (Watson, ii. 274–7). For similar comparisons of the two poets, see Sir William Temple, *Of Poetry* (1690) (in Spingarn, iii. 82–3), Dennis in *The Advancement and Reformation of Modern Poetry* (1701) (in *Works*, i. 265–6), Addison, *Spectator* 160 (1711), and Pope's preface to the *Iliad* (1715) (vii. 3–16). SJ himself compared them in conversation on 22 Sept. 1777 (*Life*, iii. 193–4 and n.). For his later discussion of Homer, see 'Pope' **83** below.

*elocution*: '3. The power of expression or diction; eloquence; beauty of words' (*Dict.*), illustrated by two quotations from D (see Watson, i. 97, 98).

In comparing 'the author' and 'the translator', SJ echoes D's dedication to the *Aeneid*: 'He who invents is master of his thoughts and words: he can turn and vary them as he pleases, till he renders them harmonious; but the wretched translator has no such privilege: for being tied to the thoughts, he must make what music he can in the expression' (Watson, ii. 251).

**305.** Analysis of the subscription lists to D's *Virgil* confirms SJ's belief that the nation considered its 'honour', irrespective of party, as 'interested in the event' (see J. Barnard, cited in **147** n. above). In his dedication to the *Aeneid* D argued — 'for the honour of my country' — for English superiority to the French or Italian in 'heroic poetry', and in the 'Postscript' hoped that the translation 'will be judged in after-ages, and possibly in the present, to be no dishonour to my native country, whose language and poetry would be more esteemed abroad, if they were better understood' (Watson, ii. 239–40, 258). Cf. SJ's own preface to the *Dict.*: 'I have devoted this book, the labour of years, to the honour of my country' (*OASJ*, 327).

Lady Mary Chudleigh stated that D had made Virgil 'the welcome Native of our Isle' (*Poems* (1703), 25–8), and Dennis (1704) that Virgil 'is now, by Mr. *Dryden*'s Translation, to be reckon'd among our own Poets' (*Works*, i. 331). Addison, 'as a *British* free-holder', later praised 'the Labours of those who have improved our Language with the Translation of old *Latin* and *Greek* Authors . . . what is still more for the Honour of our Language, it has been taught to express with Elegance, the greatest of their Poets in each Nation'. Addison's examples included Dryden's *Virgil*, and what had so far appeared of Pope's *Iliad* and Rowe's *Lucan* (*Freeholder* 40, 1716).

D's 'Postscript' acknowledged the editions of, and commentaries on, Virgil lent to him by Gilbert (later Sir Gilbert) Dolben (1658–1722), MP and barrister (Watson, ii. 260). The unnamed friends mentioned in his dedication were the youthful Addison, who contributed the preface to the *Georgics* (described by SJ as 'juvenile, superficial, and uninstructive' in 'Addison' **13** below), and the prose 'arguments'; and Knightley Chetwood (1650–1720), Dean of Gloucester, who supplied the preface to the *Pastorals* and the 'Life of Virgil' (Watson, ii. 254). D's 'Postscript' also complimented Addison by name on his translation of part of *Georgic IV* (Watson, ii. 161–2). Unusually, *BB*, iii. 1758 n., but apparently not *GD*, mentions the assistance of Dolben and Addison.

**306.** SJ quotes Pope's preface to the *Iliad* (1715) (*TE*, vii. 22), echoed again in 'Pope' **93** below.

For Luke Milbourne's *Notes on Dryden's Virgil* (1698), see also **148, 178** above and **357** below. Malone, *Prose Works* (1800), i (i). 315–17 n., printed a letter from Milbourne to Tonson, 24 Nov. 1690, with a laudatory poem about D, which contrasts with his later 'outrageous insolence and contempt'. SJ ignores Swift's ridicule of D's pretensions in competing with Virgil in 'The Battel of the Books' in *A Tale of a Tub* (1704), ed. A. C. Guthkelch and D. N. Smith (2nd edn., Oxford, 1958), 246–7, and see also 36.

**307.** SJ quotes Milbourne, *Notes*, 108–11.

Under 'Ver. 3.' the second quoted line is Milbourne's joke: D actually wrote 'And how to raise on Elms the teeming Vine'. Milbourne quotes John Ogilby's translation of the *Works* of Virgil (1649), as revised in 1654, and refers at the end of the extract to John Vicars, *The XII Aeneids of Virgil Translated* (1632). D replied in the preface to *Fables* (1700), stating that if Milbourne 'prefers the version of Ogilby to mine . . . 'tis agreed on all hands that he writes even below Ogilby' (Watson, ii. 292).

**308.** For a later 'abettor', see William Benson's preface and notes to *Virgil's Husbandry, or an Essay on the Georgics: Being the First Book Translated into English Verse . . . With Notes Critical, and Rustic* (1725).

**309.** According to his *Proposals* (1713), Nicholas Brady (1659–1726) planned to publish his blank-verse translation of *Virgil's Aeneis* by subscription in three-monthly instalments, but only Bk. I (1714) appeared by these means (Bks. I–VI followed in 2 vols. in 1716–17). For the translation of the Psalms by Brady and Nahum Tate, see 'Blackmore' **35** below.

**310.** For Joseph Trapp (1679–1747), author of *Abra-Mule, or Love and Empire: A Tragedy* (1704), *Praelectiones Poeticae* (3 vols., 1711–19), *The Aeneis of Virgil Translated* (2 vols., 1718–20), and *The Works of Virgil* (3 vols., 1731; 4th edn., 1737), see **179, 202** and n. above. After meeting him on 17 Mar. 1712, Swift noted, 'Trap is a coxcomb' (*Jnl. to Stella*, ii. 516).

Trapp used blank verse for his translation because it was 'not only more Majestick, and Sublime, but more Musical, and Harmonious' (i, pp. xl–xlix).

His preface also explained his aim of remaining close to Virgil's sense without sacrificing elegance, sublimity, and spirit: 'I should not be sorry, nay I should be glad, if at the same time it served as a Construing-Book to a School-Boy' (i, pp. xxxvi–xxxvii). Trapp succeeded, according to the author of *The Rights of Precedence between Physicians and Civilians* (1720): 'I will own, he has taught me, and I believe some other Gentlemen who had lost their *Latin*, the true grammatical construction of Virgil, and deserves not our acknowledgements only, but those of *Eaton* and *Westminster*' (quoted in John Nichols, *Supplement to Swift*, (1779), ii. 169). After discussing Trapp's criticism of D's translation and describing Trapp's own as 'the dullest that ever was written', Shiels, *Lives*, ii. 78, commented that it 'conveys the author's meaning literally, so consequently may be fitter for a school-boy'. Vicesimus Knox noted: 'it has been observed of his Virgil, that he had done wisely to have stopped at his preface' (*Essays Moral and Literary* (new edn., 1782), ii. 379). James Beresford published yet another blank-verse translation of *The Aeneid of Virgil* (1794).

311. *mellifluence*: 'A honied flow; a flow of sweetness' (*Dict.*). For Pope's 'sweetness', see 'Pope' 348 below.

SJ no doubt has in mind Joseph Warton's decision to include Christopher Pitt's translation of the *Aeneid* (1728–40), rather than D's, in his edition of Virgil's *Works* (4 vols., 1753). In his dedication to Lord Lyttelton, Warton referred to D's 'numerous' and sometimes 'unaccountably gross' errors as noted in Joseph Spence's *Polymetis* (1747), and he himself illustrated in detail Pitt's greater fidelity to Virgil (i, pp. xvii–xxv). For other comparisons of the two translations, see 'Pitt' 10 and n. below, and for further comments on D's faults and negligences, mainly by Spence, see Malone, *Prose Works* (1800), ii. 566–70.

312. SJ's evocation of the power of 'Works of imagination' to attract and captivate the reader's attention echoes such earlier critics as Jean-Baptiste Du Bos in his *Réflexions critiques* (1719): 'the best poem is that which engages us most; that which bewitches us [*qui nous séduit*] so far, as to conceal from us the greatest part of its faults, and to make us even willingly forget those we have seen, and with which we have been offended' (*Critical Reflections* (1748), trans. Thomas Nugent, i. 242). Cf. also Joseph Spence, *Essay on Pope's Odyssey*, ii (1727), 4–5: 'A Noble natural Genius, however irregular and unconfin'd, delights us in a much higher degree, than the most uniform and correct ... The very Negligencies of *Homer* shew the Greatness of his Spirit ... Nothing can be plainer than that our Judgments ought to be form'd upon the Whole, and not upon Particulars.'

*attracting and detaining the attention*: under 'Attention' in the *Dict.* SJ chose illustrations from Locke ('By attention the ideas, that offer themselves, are taken notice of, and, as it were, registered in the memory') and Watts ('Attention is a very necessary thing; truth does not always strike the soul at first sight'). For the success or failure of authors in drawing (or 'seducing' or 'enchanting') the reader's 'attention' into 'captivity', see 270 above and 326 below, 'Cowley' 39, 123 and 'Milton' 202–3, 252, 267, 270, 277 above, 'Butler' 34, 'Rowe' 11, 'Addison' 166, 'Prior' 65–6, 'Congreve' 11, 16, 'Gay' 29, 'Swift' 114, 'Pope' 365–6, and 'Gray' 45 below. Some poetry can, however, demand too much from the reader, as when SJ complains that 'Attention has no relief' in 'Cowley' 170 above. For an instance of 'the power of continuity of attention' in SJ's youth, which 'I have seldom in my whole life obtained', see *YW*, i. 20–1. SJ was describing, however, not the voluntary reader but the diligent student, for whom discipline is essential.

*pleasing captivity*: *Rambler* 60 (1750) states that biography can 'enchain the heart by irresistible interest', and *Rambler* 92 (1751) refers to the 'inexplicable elegancies' which are 'the enchantresses of the soul' (*YW*, iii. 319, iv. 122). Damrosch (1976), 46, notes that Watts used the phrase 'pleasing captivity' of the power of oratory, in his *Logick* (1725), 518: cf. 'Watts' **24** and n. below. SJ's own usage often reflects his definition of 'Captive' (3) as 'One charmed or ensnared by beauty or excellence' (*Dict.*). The language of seduction and captivity can, however, be associated with dangerous indulgence of the imagination, as in *Rambler* 89 (1751).

For other references to the book as a physical object laid down, or even thrown away, by the weary reader, see 'Milton' **252** and n. above. In Aberdeen in 1773 SJ glanced at a theological work before 'he threw it down again' (*Life*, v. 88).

*in hope of new pleasure are perused again*: for poetry whose power is 'exhausted by a single perusal', see 'Young' **157** below.

313. For Ariosto, see also 'Milton' **237** above. Charles Gildon, *The Laws of Poetry* (1721), 23, stated that Shakespeare and Ariosto had exuberant imaginations but no art; Thomas Blackwell, *Enquiry into the Life and Writings of Homer* (1735), 32, wrote of 'the high Spirit and secret Force which bewitches a Reader, and dazzles his Eyes, that he can see no Faults in *Dante* and *Ariosto*'; and Elizabeth Cooper, *The Muse's Library* (1737), 255, claimed that Spenser 'debauch'd his Taste with the Extravagances of *Ariosto*'. Yet Boileau preferred Ariosto to 'cold authors' in his *Art poétique*, III. 291–2 ('J'aime mieux Arioste et ses fables comiques, | Que ces auteurs toujours froids et melancholiques'); and Hume, in his *Four Dissertations* (1757), 212, wrote of Ariosto's 'faults' that, 'If they are found to please, they cannot be faults; let that pleasure which they produce, be ever so unexpected and unaccountable' (cited by Warton, *Essay*, i (2nd edn., 1762), 240 n.). After discussing Ariosto's 'maze of indigestion and incoherence', Thomas Warton claimed that 'it is absurd to think of judging either Ariosto or Spenser by precepts which they did not attend to ... Spenser, and the same may be said of Ariosto, did not live in an age of planning ... The various and the marvellous were the chief sources of delight' (*Observations on the Fairy Queen* (2nd edn., 1762), i. 12–15). For a positive allusion to *Orlando furioso* in SJ's letter to Warton, 1 Feb. 1755, see *Letters*, i. 92.

In 1765 SJ defended Shakespeare's 'practice contrary to the rules of criticism' against the objections of Rymer, Dennis, and Voltaire, arguing that his 'violations of rules' only confirmed his 'comprehensive genius'. The 'first purpose of a writer' is 'exciting restless and unquenchable curiosity, and compelling him that reads his work to read it through'. A new reader of Shakespeare should keep 'his attention ... strongly engaged', and ignore commentators: 'The mind is refrigerated by interruption ... Parts are not to be examined till the whole has been surveyed.'

After noting the defects of *The Merry Wives of Windsor*, SJ concluded that 'its general power, that power by which all works of genius shall finally be tried, is such, that perhaps it never yet had reader or spectator, who did not think it too soon at an end'. He wrote of *King Lear* that 'There is perhaps no play which keeps the attention so strongly fixed' (*YW*, vii. 65–7, 79, 83, 111, 341, viii. 702). For suspicion of 'critics', see also 'Pomfret' **4** above and 'Smith' **47**, 'Addison' **15, 81**, 'Blackmore' **9**, 'Pitt' **10**, and 'Gray' **51** below.

**314.** For *Fables* (1700), see **149** above.

*refaccimento*: SJ's friend Giuseppe Baretti translated 'rifacimento' as 'restauration, reparation, re-establishment' in his *Dictionary of the English and Italian Languages* (1760), vol. i, but SJ's source may have been John Hoole's preface to his transla-tion of Ariosto's *Orlando furioso* (vol. i. 1773; 5 vols., 1783). Hoole refers to Berni's 'Rifacimento' of Boiardo, and discusses the works SJ mentions here: the modern-izations of Matteo Maria Boiardo's *Orlando innamorato* (1480) by Lodovico Domenichi (1545) and Francesco Berni (1541). (*Gent. Mag.* (1773), 134, quoted the relevant passage.)

SJ refers to D's modernizations of 'The Cock and the Fox: or, The Tale of the Nun's Priest' and 'Palamon and Arcite, or, The Knight's Tale'. Warton, who believed that D would 'owe his immortality' to the *Fables*, replied sternly to SJ in *Essay*, ii (1782), 17. Admitting the absurdity of ancient heroes engaging 'at the lists and a modern combat', Warton continued: 'Frigid and phlegmatic must be the critic, who could have leisure dully and soberly to attend to the anachronism on so striking an occasion. The mind is whirled away by a torrent of rapid imagery, and propriety is forgot.'

For D's 'hyperbolical commendation' of 'Palamon and Arcite' and Trapp's objection to it, see **202** and n. above. SJ in fact quoted the poem several times in the *Dict.*; see Henson, 79. In 'To the Dutchess of Ormonde', prefixed to *Fables* (1700), D also referred to Chaucer's 'ancient Song: | Which *Homer* might without a Blush reherse, | And leaves a doubtful Palm in *Virgil*'s Verse: | He match'd their Beauties, where they most excell; | Of Love sung better, and of Arms as well' (ll. 2–6). For the poem's 'remote conceits', see e.g. ll. 21–9, 70–9, and cf. **5, 236, 242** above.

**315.** *Fables* (1700) includes 'Sigismunda and Guiscardo', 'Theodore and Honoria', and 'Cymon and Iphigenia' from Boccaccio, *Decameron*, IV. 1, V. 8, V. 1. For Thomas Gray's admiration for 'Theodore and Honoria', see his *Corresp.*, iii. 1290–1. Filippo Beraldo the elder (1453–1505) translated 'Cymon' into Latin in 1505: SJ came across it in Paris on 25 Oct. 1775 (*YW*, i. 248).

**316.** Cf. **216** above.

**317.** See Congreve's dedication to D's *Dramatick Works* (1717), i. sig. a11. For SJ's brief comparison of D's prologues with those of Garrick in conversation in Mar. 1775, see *Life*, ii. 325.

**318.** For *Alexander's Feast; Or The Power of Musique. An Ode, In Honour of St. Cecilia's Day* (1697), see also **150, 188** above, and, for 'the Ode on *Killigrew*', **278** above. D in fact wrote the prologue, epilogue, song, and 'Secular Masque' for *The Pilgrim* later. He wrote to Tonson in Dec. 1697: 'I am glad to heare from all Hands, that my Ode is esteemed the best of all my poetry, by all the Town: I thought so my self when I writ it but being old, I mistrusted my own Judgment' (*Letters*, 98). For an anecdote of D telling a young admirer of the poem, 'You are right . . . a nobler Ode never *was* produced, nor ever *will*', see Malone (1800), i. (i). 476–7.

SJ praises *Alexander's Feast* even more decisively when comparing it to Pope's 'St. Cecilia Ode' in 'Pope' **320** below. Mrs Thrale heard him recite lines from it in

Jan. 1779 (*Thraliana*, i. 361). Pope had admired it in *Essay on Criticism* (1711), ll.
374–83 and *Corresp.*, i. 22–3. Shiels, *Lives*, iii. 78, stated: 'We cannot be too lavish
in praise of this Ode.' Warton, *Essay* (1756), 52, placed it 'at the head of modern
lyric compositions', and praised it again in his posthumously published notes on D
(see **268** n. above), while linking it with Gray's *The Bard* (1757): 'If Dryden had
never written anything but this Ode, his name would have been immortal, as
would that of Gray, if he had never written anything but his *Bard*' (ii. 345–6).
*Anecdotes of Polite Literature* (5 vols., 1764), i. 173–4, similarly described it as 'the
best modern lyric composition'. According to Gray in 1768, it was the only
English ode 'of the sublime kind' (*Poems* (1969), 175 n.).

Goldsmith's reservations in 1767 were therefore unusual: 'This ode has been
more applauded, perhaps, than it has been felt; however, it is a very fine one, and
gives its beauties rather at a third, or fourth, than at a first, perusal' (*Coll. Works*, v.
322). See also James Beattie, *Essays* (Edinburgh, 1776), 360 n., James Granger,
*Biographical History of England* (3rd edn., 1779), iv. 38, John Pinkerton, *Letters of
Literature* (1785), 34. For recent discussions, see Clingham 'J's Criticism', 165–80,
and T. Mason and A. Rounce, '*Alexander's Feast; or The Power of Musique*: The
Poem and its Readers', in Hammond and Hopkins (eds.), *JD*, 140–73. Handel's
*Alexander's Feast* (1736) is a setting of Newburgh Hamilton's adapted and en-
larged version of D's ode: see R. Smith, *Handel's Oratorios and Eighteenth-Century
Thought* (Cambridge, 1995), 17, 32, 82, 192, 367 n.

**319.** For the 'fortnight's labour', see **150** and n. above. Warton, *Essay*, ii (1782), 19–21,
told a story of Henry St John (later Lord Bolingbroke) calling on D and finding
that he had stayed up all night to write the poem 'at one sitting'. The anecdote,
transmitted from Pope to Gilbert West to Richard Berenger and finally to Warton,
did not convince Malone (*Prose Works* (1800), i (i). 285).

Lines 77, 112, 143 are unrhymed, while other unrhymed lines are repeated, e.g.
13–14, 17–18.

**320.** SJ refers to *Alexander's Feast*, ll. 169–70, 168 (repeated at 179–80, 178). He
evidently means that its 'last stanza' has 'less emotion' than the 'striking' conclusion to D's earlier *Ode for St. Cecilia* (see **280** above). He had objected briefly to the
poem's ending in his review of Warton's *Essay on Pope* in 1756 (*OASJ*, 490).

*vicious*: this spelling replaced 'vitious' in 1783 (see Textual Notes). Both spellings
appear in the *Dict.*, with 'vitious' as the main entry.

For objections to 'broken metaphors' which confuse the literal and the figurative, see also 'Cowley' **120–1, 133** and 'Denham' **31** above, and 'Addison' **129, 131**,
'Pope' **326, 419**, and 'Gray' **29, 33** below, and *Idler* 34 (1758).

**321.** Cf. SJ's comment in **218** above that the minds of Waller and Denham were not 'of
very ample comprehension', and see also 'Cowley' **144** and n. above, and 'Pope'
**308** below. For D's 'acquired knowledge', see **211** above.

**322.** Cf. SJ's comments on *Annus Mirabilis* in **259** above.

**323.** SJ quotes (loosely) *Tyrannick Love*, II. i. 292–7, which he had recited in conversation on 16 Oct. 1769 (*Life*, ii. 85 and n.).

**324.** *the Love of the Golden Age*: cf. SJ's scepticism about the 'simple friendships of the
*Golden Age*' in 'Pope' **273** below. For his objections to 'the romantick omnipotence
of Love' in drama, see **78** and n. above.

325. For the 'pathetick', see **209, 259, 275** above, and 'Cowley' **57** and n. above, and for 'sensibility', 'Pope' **67** and n. below. James Beattie, *Essays* (Edinburgh, 1776), 359 n., had recently written that D's 'genius did not lead him to the sublime or pathetic. Good strokes of both may doubtless be found in him; but they are momentary, and seem to be accidental. He is too witty for the one, and too familiar for the other.'

SJ's appeals to 'simplicity' are infrequent, but see 'Swift' **112**, 'Pope' **83, 349**, and 'Shenstone' **33** below. For Dennis's 'Of Simplicity in Poetical Compositions' (1711), see 'Addison' **163** and n. below.

For Otway's tenderness and pathos, and for D's opinion of him, see 'Otway' **15** and n. above. Charles Gildon, *The Laws of Poetry* (1721), 211, wrote that D rarely touched 'the Passions' and 'commonly expressed a very mean, if not contemptible opinion, of Otway' (quoted by *GD*, iv. 679 n. and *BB*, iii. 1753 n.). For a story of D speaking dismissively of Otway's *Don Carlos*, see Macdonald, *Bibliography*, 211–12, which notes, however, that he wrote prologues for special performances of *Venice Preserved* in 1682. SJ finally adapts 'A Parallel betwixt Poetry and Painting' (1695): 'but nature is there, which is the greatest beauty' (Watson, ii. 201).

326. For ignorance of our own motives, see e.g. *Ramblers* 28 (1750) ('it is not easy for a man to know himself') and 87 (1751) ('We are sometimes not ourselves conscious of the original motives of our actions') (*YW*, iii. 152, iv. 95). Cf. **120** above on the difficulty of reading the motives of others.

For D's dependence on 'the claps of multitudes', see **42** and n. above; for 'false magnificence' in his plays, see **45, 48** above; for the importance of 'captivating' the 'attention', see **312** and n. above; and for 'sentiment' rather than 'description' in D's poetry, see **249** above.

SJ's revision in 1783 of 'reviving former thoughts, or impressing new' to 'reviving natural sentiments, or impressing new appearances of things' (see Textual Notes) reinforces his appeal to the ideal blend of the 'natural' and the 'new': see 'Cowley' **55** and n. above.

327. *ratiocination*: see **125, 285** and n., **297** above and **356** below. D wrote in 'A Defence of an Essay of Dramatic Poesy' (1668) that 'they cannot be good poets who are not accustomed to argue well . . . moral truth is the mistress of the poet as much as of the philosopher' (Watson, i. 120). In Buckingham's *The Rehearsal*, IV. ii, Bayes says: 'Reasoning! 'Y gad, I love reasoning in verse.'

*liberty and necessity*: SJ commented cryptically to Mrs Thrale on 12 May 1778, while writing 'Dryden', that D 'puzzled himself about predestination' (*Life*, iii. 347). He probably had in mind such passages as the discussion of free will and necessity in *The State of Innocence*, IV. i, and the digression on free will in 'The Cock and the Fox', ll. 507–52 (quoted under 'Conditional' in the *Dict.*). Tom Brown, *The Reason of Mr. Bays Changing his Religion* (1688), 19–20, described Adam in *The State of Innocence* as acquainted 'with all the arguments of the Supralapsarians . . . in the Mysterious Controversie about Freewill' (quoted by N. von Maltzahn, 'D's Milton', in Hammond and Hopkins (eds.), *JD*, 48–9). In *A Tale of A Tub* (1704) Swift described *The Hind and the Panther* as 'the Masterpiece of a famous Writer now living [in 1698], intended for a compleat Abstract of sixteen thousand Schoolmen from *Scotus* to *Bellarmin*' (ed. A. C. Guthkelch and D. N. Smith (Oxford, 1958), 69).

328. Cf. 'Butler' 33 above: 'Every position makes way for an argument, and every objection dictates an answer.'

SJ quotes Horace, *Ars Poetica*, l. 311 ('Once that is provided, words [will readily follow']).

329. Cf. D's preface to *The Indian Emperour* (1668): 'If the humour of this [age] be for low comedy, small accidents, and raillery, I will force my genius to obey it ... I know I am not so fitted by nature to write comedy: I want that gaiety of humour which is required to it. My conversation is slow and dull; my humour saturnine and reserved.' In the preface to *An Evening's Love* (1671) he wrote: 'I am sometimes ready to imagine that my disgust of low comedy proceeds not so much from my judgment as from my temper; which is the reason why I so seldom write it ... That I admire not any comedy equally with tragedy is, perhaps, from the sullenness of my humour.' See also the dedication to *Aureng-Zebe* (1676): 'I never thought myself very fit for an employment where many of my predecessors have excelled me in all kinds; and some of my contemporaries, even in my own partial judgment, have outdone me in comedy' (Watson, i. 116, 145, 191). In 1765 SJ wrote that D's 'genius was not very fertile of merriment, nor ductile to humour, but acute, argumentative, comprehensive, and sublime' (*YW*, vii. 957).

For 'discrimination' of characters, see 'Milton' 268 and n. above, for the imitation of other poets rather than of nature, see 247 above, and for the charge of plagiarism, see 103, 229 above.

330. SJ wrote in *Rambler* 31 (1750) that D 'sometimes slipped into errors by the tumult of his imagination, and the multitude of his ideas' (*YW*, iii. 171).

The spelling 'Excentrick' (all editions) is not in the *Dict.*: SJ defines 'Eccentrick' as '4. Irregular; anomalous; deviating from stated and constant methods'. For 'wit', see 'Cowley' 54–6, 104 and nn. above, and for 'unideal', 'Milton' 173 and n. above.

SJ quotes *Conquest of Granada II*, v. iii. 339–40 (mocked by Settle at 58 above), *Tyrannick Love*, iv. i. 151, 154–6, and *Annus Mirabilis*, ll. 653–6 (cf. 257 and n. above), which he had quoted on 30 Apr. 1773 as an example of poetic 'nonsense' (*Life*, ii. 241). For his use of D's heroic plays in the *Dict.*, see Henson, 148, 235 n. 2.

SJ finally adapts Cowley, 'To Mr. Hobbes' (with '*sense*' for 'Truth') (*Poems*, ed. Waller (1905), 188). For D's attempts to defend his own 'nonsense', see e.g. Watson, i. 142–3.

331. SJ quotes *Conquest of Granada I*, i. i. 207–9, *Tyrannick Love*, v. i. 238–41, i. i. 245–50, and *Don Sebastian*, i. i. 361–7.

For 'tumid' as 'falsely sublime' (*Dict.*), see also 'Waller' 123 above.

332. SJ quotes *Conquest of Granada I*, iv. ii. 455–61. For 'obscurity', see 244 and n. above.

333. SJ quotes *Conquest of Granada II*, iii. i. 59–61, iii. iii. 86, 92–5.

334. SJ quotes the preface to *The Spanish Fryar* (1681) (Watson, i. 276), referring to characters in *Tyrannick Love* and *The Conquest of Granada*: see 45, 48 above. Cf. Granville, 'Concerning Unnatural Flights in Poetry' (1701), ll. 81–4: 'To a wild Audience, he conform'd his voice, | Comply'd to Cust[om ...] Choice: | Deem then the P[...] Rage, and

For 'pleasing' the audience, see **20, 28, 42, 326** above, and 'Cowley' **38** and n. above; and cf. *Rambler* 188 (1752): 'we have all, at one time or another, been content to love those whom we could not esteem' (*YW*, v. 221).

**335.** *mythology*: see **238, 276** above, and 'Butler' **41** and n. above. For objections to the confusion of 'religion and fable', see **72** and n., **295** above, and 'Milton' **183** and n. above.

**336.** SJ refers to *Aeneid*, III. 526–7 (quoted under 'Larboard' in the *Dict.*), and *The Hind and the Panther*, III. 96 (quoted under 'To Spoom' in the *Dict.*), I. 57–8. For 'terms of art' in poetry, see **255** and n. above.

SJ's interest in optical phenomena is reflected in the many quotations from Newton's *Opticks* in the *Dict.*

**337.** SJ quotes *Annus Mirabilis*, ll. 1121–4, and 'To the Memory of Mrs. Anne Killigrew', ll. 184–5.

For 'mean' diction, see **220** above.

**338.** SJ quotes 'Heroique Stanza's', ll. 89–91.

**339.** *the use of French words*: for French usages, which reflected the influence of the newly returned court, see *To His Sacred Majesty*, l. 102, and *Astraea Redux*, l. 203. As Hill (1905) noted, *The Rehearsal* (1671), I. ii, mocked Bayes for this affectation. In his 'Defence of the Epilogue' (1672) D himself objected to 'their way of refining, who corrupt our English idiom by mixing it too much with French', but later pleaded the necessity of enriching English by 'trading' with other modern languages (see Watson, i. 45–6 n., 176–7, 239 n., ii. 46, 252). SJ included 'Fraischeur' in the *Dict.*, but censured it as 'a word foolishly innovated by *Dryden*', and omitted 'fougue'. He also condemned D for 'a mere Gallicism' under 'To Renounce'. Horsman, 'Borrowings', 346–51, noted that many such French words, not all introduced by D, were later naturalized (e.g. bizarre, fatigue, naïveté, coquette). For hostility to French linguistic influence see e.g. Addison, *Spectator* 165 *(1711)* and Henry Felton, *A Dissertation on Reading the Classics* (2nd edn., 1715), 85–90.

In *Rambler* 208 (1752), SJ claimed to have tried 'to refine our language to grammatical purity', asserting that it needed no 'help from other nations' (*YW*, v. 318–19). See also his preface to the *Dict.* (e.g. *OASJ*, 319, 326), his description in 1756 of Fulke Greville's *Maxims, Characters, and Reflections* as 'too Gallick', and his objection in 1763 to the 'French structure' of Hume's style (*Letters*, i. 129–30, *Life*, i. 463; *J. Misc.*, ii. 10). See also T. B. Gilmore, 'J's Attitude towards French Influence on the English Language', *MP* 78 (1981), 243–60, and DeMaria (1986), 171–2, 178–9, and cf. 'Milton' **270** above, 'Pope' **378** and n. below, and (for his 'genuine Anglicism') 'Addison' **168** below. For Gallicisms in the age of Shakespeare, see *YW*, viii. 820, and for 'innovators', see 'Milton' **58** and n. above.

**340.** SJ wrote in *Rambler* 31 (1750) that D's 'warmth of fancy, and haste of composition very frequently hurried him into inaccuracies' (*YW*, iii. 170). Mrs Thrale heard him challenge Garrick to produce from D's verse 'twenty lines in a series that would not disgrace the poet' (*J. Misc.*, i. 185; SJ said much the same about Shakespeare, *Life*, ii. 96). For the contrast of D's negligence with Pope's fastidious 'correctness', see 'Pope' **294, 298, 304–5** below. As Beattie had recently pointed out, 'as the public ear becomes more delicate, the negligence will be more glaring, and the disappointment more intensely felt; and correctness of rhime and of measure will of course be the more indispensable' (*Essays* (Edinburgh, 1776), 566).

*an idea of pure perfection*: writing in *Rambler* 169 (1751) that 'No vanity can more justly incur contempt and indignation than that which boasts of negligence and hurry', SJ pointed out that such an author has been afforded 'no glimpse of perfection, of that sublime idea which human industry has from the first ages been vainly toiling to produce' (*YW*, v. 130–1). For the pursuit of 'perfection', see also **201** above, 'Blackmore' **44** below on 'that ideal perfection which every genius born to excel is condemned always to pursue, and never overtake', and the preface to Shakespeare, on 'that superiority of mind, which despised its own performances, when it compared them with its powers' (*YW*, vii. 91, 112). For the religious aspect of the pursuit of perfection, see Addison, *Spectator* 111 (1711); and for another account of the 'ideal beauty' and 'images of perfection' in the author's mind, see William Melmoth, *Letters on Several Subjects*, ii (1749), 231–6.

SJ tends to be more sceptical about 'perfectionism' when writing about his *Dict.* In his *Plan of a Dictionary* (1747), 24–5, he described 'perfection' as 'of little use among human beings'. While compiling the *Dict.*, he often emphasized the burden placed on an author by unattainable conceptions, as in *Rambler* 74 (1750) on the danger of 'a too rigorous habit of examining every thing by the standard of perfection . . . Knowledge and genius are often enemies to quiet, by suggesting ideas of excellence, which men and the performances of men cannot attain.' In *Rambler* 207 (1752) he wrote: 'so frequent is the necessity of resting below that perfection which we imagined within our reach, that seldom any man obtains more from his endeavours than a painful conviction of his defects' (*YW*, iv. 27, v. 311). See also *Ramblers* 14, 70 (1750); 134, 169 (1751).

In *Adventurer* 85 (1753) SJ concluded that 'it is, however, reasonable, to have perfection in our eye; that we may always advance towards it, though we know it never can be reached' (*YW*, ii. 416–17). In the preface to the *Dict.* itself, he admitted that 'to pursue perfection was, like the first inhabitants of Arcadia, to chase the sun, which . . . was still beheld at the same distance from them', claiming that 'no dictionary of a living tongue ever can be perfect', and that 'I may surely be contented without the praise of perfection' (*OASJ*, 322, 327, 328). In his 'Advertisement' to the revised edition of 1773, he asserted again that 'Perfection is unattainable, but nearer and nearer approaches may be made'. Cf. also Reynolds's 'Discourse IX' (16 Oct. 1780): 'The mind is constantly labouring to advance, step by step, through successive gradations of excellence, towards perfection, which is dimly seen, at a great though not hopeless distance, and which we must always follow because we never can attain' (*Discourses*, 230).

SJ's comparison of D with Waller, Denham, and Cowley (see **5, 217, 222** above and **342–3** below) prompted Joseph Warton's enquiry in 1797: 'Where then was Milton?' (*Works of Pope*, iv. 37 n., and cf. **342** n. below). SJ's later attempt to place Milton in this context in 'J. Philips' **13** above is unconvincing: 'Milton's verse was harmonious, in proportion to the general state of our metre in Milton's age, and, if he had written after the improvements made by Dryden, it is reasonable to believe that he would have admitted a more pleasing modulation of numbers into his work.'

With SJ's final sentence, cf. his statement in 1765 that most authors 'who find themselves exalted into fame, are willing to credit their encomiasts, and to spare the labour of contending with themselves' (*YW*, vii. 91).

341. *He was no lover of labour*: see **201** above, and for the 'effect of necessity' on D's writing, **227–8** above. In the preface to *The Indian Emperour* (1668), he admitted that he lacked time for revision: '''Tis enough for those who make one poem the business of their lives to leave that correct' (Watson, i. 110–11). A much less obsessive reviser of his works than Pope (see 'Pope' **307** below), D in fact corrected *Of Dramatick Poesie* with some care (Watson, i. 10), and later took trouble with his *Virgil* (*Letters*, 97–8). For a dramatist who 'never wrote in distress' or 'haste', and whose 'works were finished to his own approbation, and bear few marks of negligence and hurry', see 'Rowe' **17** below; and for the importance of 'diligence', 'Milton' **118** and n. above.

342. *dilatation*: '1. The act of extending into greater space; opposed to *contraction*' (*Dict.*).

SJ had quoted these lines from Pope, *Imit. Horace, Ep. II. i.* (1737), ll. 267–9, in the 'Prosody' prefixed to the *Dict.* (see **348** n. below) and under 'March' in the *Dict.* itself, and does so again in 'Pope' **333** below. In *Essay*, ii (1782), 351–2, Warton complained that they ignore Milton's contribution to 'the harmony and extent of our language': cf. **340** n. above.

343. For the development of English versification, see **5, 217–22** and nn. above and **356** below, and 'Cowley' **185–99** n. and 'Roscommon' **24** and n. above. SJ refers to Waller's 'feeble care' in 'Cowley' **185** above.

Shiels, *Lives*, v. 248–9, conceivably influenced by SJ himself, wrote that D 'found poetry in a very imperfect state; its numbers were unpolished; its cadences rough, and there was nothing of harmony or mellifluence to give it a graceful flow. In this harsh, unmusical situation, Dryden found it (for the refinements of Waller were but puerile and unsubstantial) he polished the rough diamond, he taught it to shine, and connected beauty, elegance, and strength, in all his poetical compositions. Though Dryden thus polished our English numbers, and thus harmonized versification, it cannot he said, that he carried his art to perfection.' Shiels went on to describe Pope's 'additional harmony'.

Under the spelling 'To Chuse' in the *Dict.*, SJ merely cross-refers to 'To Choose'.

344. For 'triplets', see **345** n. below and 'Cowley' **199** and n. above. SJ refers to Thomas Phaer, *The Seven First Bookes of the Eneidos of Virgill, Converted in Englishe* (1558), *The Nine Fyrst Bookes* (1562), and *The Whole XII Bookes* (completed by Thomas Twyne, 1573); and Joseph Hall, *Virgidemiarum* (1597–8) (see also 'Pope' **380** below). Thomas Warton, *History of English Poetry*, iii (1781), 395–9, discussed Phaer's translation in some detail. For George Chapman, see **345** n. below.

345. For alexandrines, see 'Cowley' **196** and n. above. In the dedication to the *Aeneid* (1697), D stated that the precedents for his use of alexandrines and triplets ('these privileges of English verse ... the Magna Charta of heroic poetry') were Spenser (who has 'given me the boldness to make use sometimes of his alexandrine line'), Chapman, who in fact uses triplets but not alexandrines in his translation of Homer, and Cowley (cf. **207** and n. above and **348** below): see Watson, ii. 237–8,

247 and n. In the 'Prosody' prefixed to the *Dict.* SJ quotes Chapman to illustrate the fourteen-syllable line.

**346.** For Phaer, see **344** above.

**347.** SJ quotes Thomas Parnell, 'An Imitation of Some French Verses', ll. 1–4.

**348.** SJ refers to Michael Drayton, *Polyolbion* (1612–22). He owned a copy of William Oldys's edition of Drayton's *Works* (1748), which he marked for use in the *Dict.* In the 'Prosody' prefixed to the *Dict.* he quoted *Polyolbion* to illustrate his statement that 'Our ancient poets wrote verses sometimes of twelve syllables.' His later statement that 'The verse of twelve syllables, called an *Alexandrine*, is now only used to diversify heroick lines' is illustrated by the lines by Pope quoted in **342** above.

In 1697 D cited Cowley as a precedent for his use of the alexandrine, although Cowley in fact used it sparingly (see **345** n. and 'Cowley' **196** and n. above). Warton, *Essay* (1756), 150, described D as 'the first who introduced it into our English heroic', but later lost confidence in this assertion: see W. D. MacClintock, *Warton's Essay on Pope: A History of the Five Editions* (Chapel Hill, NC, 1933), 64–5. James Boswell Jr. later noted that the alexandrine appeared as a variant in pentameter verse as early as Joseph Hall's *Virgidemiarum* (1597–8) (*J's Works* (1825), vii. 346 n.).

**349.** See Swift, 'A Description of a City Shower' (1710), ll. 61–3. He explained his dislike of triplets and alexandrines in a note to these lines in 1735, and in a letter of 12 Apr. 1735 (*Corresp.*, iv. 321).

*regularity . . . variety*: for the interplay of 'variety' and 'uniformity', see also 'Butler' **35** and n. above. Although SJ admitted in *Rambler* 86 (1751) that 'we are soon wearied with the perpetual recurrence of the same cadence' (*YW*, iv. 90), he usually tolerates only limited metrical variety, at times hankering for a 'lawful' and almost scientific 'regularity' and disliking any 'surprise' (cf. **290–1** above and **350–1** below). After illustrating various metres in the 'Prosody' prefixed to the *Dict.* (1755), he stated: 'In all these measures the accents are to be placed on even syllables; and every line considered by itself is more harmonious, as this rule is more strictly observed.' In 1773, however, he added: 'The variations necessary to pleasure belong to the art of poetry, not the rules of grammar.'

On this matter SJ would have agreed in principle with Reynolds in 'Discourse VIII' (1778): 'When variety entirely destroys the pleasure proceeding from uniformity and repetition, and when novelty counteracts and shuts out the pleasure arising from old habits and customs, they oppose too much the indolence of our disposition: the mind therefore can bear with pleasure but a small portion of novelty at a time' (*Discourses*, 206). Cf. Beattie, *Essays* (Edinburgh, 1776), 566: 'in poetry, as in music, Rhythm is the source of much pleasing variety; of variety tempered with uniformity, and regulated by art.'

SJ defines 'Acute accent' as 'that which raises or sharpens the verse', and 'Grave' as 'Not sharp of sound; not acute' (*Dict.*), corresponding to 'stressed' and 'unstressed' (cf. **354** below, where 'grave' clearly means 'weak').

**350.** *the braces of the margins*: the printer's marginal 'braces' or 'brackets' conventionally indicated triplets.

**351.** *casualty*: '1. Accident; a thing happening by chance, not design' (*Dict.*). Cf. 'Pope' **59** and n. below.

**352.** In his *Essay*, i (2nd edn., 1762), 147, Warton suggested that Pope had made his *Iliad* monotonous by avoiding alexandrines, later attributing this opinion to Elijah Fenton (Pope's *Works* (1797), vii. 69 n.). Warton may have heard this from his father, the elder Thomas Warton, a friend of Fenton, and related it to SJ, who repeats it in 'Pope' **376** below. For Pope's early objections to alexandrines and triplets, see *Corresp.*, i. 24.

**353.** *rhymes*: see also 'Cowley' **187** and n. above. SJ refers to D's dedication to the *Aeneid* (1697): 'Rhyme is certainly a constraint even to the best of poets, and those who make it with most ease; though perhaps I have as little reason to complain of that hardship as any man' (Watson, ii. 240).

**354.** SJ quotes (loosely) Pope, 'Epistle to Mr. Jervas', ll. 25–6 (with 'Fill'd' for 'Fir'd'), and D's 'Palamon and Arcite', III. 671–2.

**354a.** Not numbered as a separate paragraph by Hill (1905). For a verse paragraph ending with the first line of a couplet, see 'Palamon and Arcite', II. 308–9, and, for French practice, see e.g. Boileau, *Épitres*, I. 115–16.

**355.** SJ quotes *The Hind and the Panther*, II. 537 (with 'throne' for 'crown').

**356.** SJ's source for Pope's words has not been identified. He may be reporting what such friends of Pope as Savage or Walter Harte had told him, or misattributing a version of what Congreve wrote in D's *Dramatick Works* (1717), sig. a9: 'no Man hath written in our Language so much, and so various Matter, and in so various Measures, so well.' Pope did, however, say that he 'learned versification wholly from Dryden's works, who had improved it much beyond any of our former poets' (Spence, i. 24). Warburton stated in Pope's *Works* (1751), iv. 18, that, 'On the first sight of Dryden, he found he had what he wanted. His Poems were never out of his hands; they became his model; and from them alone he learnt the whole magic of his versification.' See also Ruffhead, *Life of Pope* (1769), 22–3.

Late in life D told Mrs Steward, 7 Nov. 1699, that his aim had been to 'improve the Language, & Especially the Poetry', of the nation (*Letters*, 123). SJ summarizes his earlier discussions of D's achievements in versification (**216**), poetical argument (**125, 297, 327–8**), and translation (**223–5**), quoting 'sapere et fari' from Horace, *Epist.*, I. iv. 9. He originally wrote: 'He taught us that it was possible to reason in rhyme,' but added the reference to Sir John Davies, *Nosce Teipsum* (1599), in 1783 (see Textual Notes and 'Waller' **143** and n. above). He finally quotes Suetonius, *Divus Augustus*, 29.

**357.** For Luke Milbourne see **148** and n. and **306–8** above. SJ quotes his *Notes on Dryden's Virgil* (1698), 206–9.

**358–405.** D wrote these notes on the endpapers of a copy of Thomas Rymer's *The Tragedies of the Last Age* (1678 for Aug. 1677), probably in the winter of 1677/8 (*Works*, xvii. 412 n.). They were first published in Tonson's *Works of Beaumont and Fletcher* (1711), i, pp. xii–xxvi, and were reprinted in a new edition of their *Works* (1778), i, pp. xix–xxvi, while SJ was writing 'Dryden'. He was only vaguely aware of this, stating in his 'Advertisement' to *Prefaces* (1779) that 'I have been told that Dryden's Remarks on Rymer have been printed before'. His revision of this statement in 1781 is no more decisive: 'Dryden's Remarks on Rymer have been somewhere printed before' (see Textual Notes).

When SJ transcribed D's notes, or, more probably, had them transcribed, they were owned by David Garrick, who died in Jan. 1779, shortly before the publication of *Prefaces*, vols. i–iv. The volume containing them was lost in the fire which destroyed Sir John Hawkins's library in 1785. Surprisingly, its fate was unknown to Malone, who failed to trace it through Garrick's widow and in 1800 appealed for its recovery (*Prose Works*, i (i). 569–70).

The major problem posed by D's 'Heads of an Answer to Rymer' (Malone's title in 1800) is that Tonson and SJ printed them in very different sequences. Malone himself, *Prose Works*, i (ii). 300–14, loyally followed SJ's arrangement, 'though I have some doubt whether it be correct'. Osborn, *JD*, 283, summarized this puzzling divergence as follows: if the paragraphs in Tonson's text are numbered 1–52, they appear in SJ's version in the order 34, 51–2, 35–8, 1–6, 29–33, 39–50, 7–28. For speculation about the reasons for this disparity and for preferences of one text to the other, see Watson, i. 210–11, and his 'D's First Answer to Rymer', *RES* 14 (1963), 17–23; Osborn, *JD*, 283–5; and *Works*, xvii (1971), 185–93, 411–76, 501–4. Tonson's text is preferred by both Watson and *Works*.

Damrosch (1976), 181, noted that SJ 'does not ask himself why Dryden never published his answer to Rymer or whether it differs from the criticism he did publish'. A possible explanation of SJ's lack of curiosity could be that this appended material became available to him only after he had completed 'Dryden'. D's notes on Rymer were in fact a more informal and franker version of the views he later expressed in 'The Grounds of Criticism in Tragedy' (1679) (Watson, i. 243–61: see **65** above). DeMaria (1986), 209, has suggested that the quotation from Rymer SJ used to illustrate 'Cut out' in the *Dict.* indicated his opinion of the critic (cf. **200** above): 'You know I am not cut out for writing a treatise, nor have a genius to pen any thing exactly.'

Citations of 'Rymer' below refer to *The Tragedies of the Last Age* in *Critical Works* (1956), 17–76.

**359.** For the 'tenderness' of French poets, see René Rapin, *Réflexions sur la poétique d'Aristote*, ii, p. xx.

**360.** See Rapin, *Réflexions*, ii, p. xxi.

**363.** See Aristotle, *Poetics*, VII, and 'Milton' **224** and n. above.

**365a.** Not numbered as a separate paragraph by Hill (1905).

**366.** D refers to *Poetics*, VI. 12 ('[not] on account of its dignity, but its priority'); and Rymer, 18.

**380.** The reference to '*Rapin.*' (i.e. *Réflexions*, i, p. ix) is not in Tonson's text.

**382.** Cf. Rymer, 22: '*Sophocles* adding a *third* Actor, and *painted* Scenes, gave (in *Aristotle*'s opinion,) the utmost *perfection* to Tragedy.'

**383a.** Not numbered as a separate paragraph by Hill (1905).

**387–8.** Cf. 'The Grounds of Criticism in Tragedy': 'Shakespeare writ better betwixt man and man; Fletcher, betwixt man and woman: consequently, the one described friendship better; the other love' (Watson, i. 260).

**392.** Rymer discussed three plays by Beaumont and Fletcher: *A King and No King* (1619), *The Maides Tragedy* (1619), and *The Bloody Brother* (1639; entitled *The Tragedy of Rollo Duke of Normandy*, Oxford, 1640). See **402–3** below.

**394.** Cf. Rymer, 19, on the actor Hart: 'what he *delivers*, every one takes upon *content*; their *eyes* are prepossest and charm'd by his *action*, before ought of the *Poets* can approach their *ears*'.

**397.** Cf. Rymer, 19: 'But were it to be suppos'd that *Nature* with us is a *corrupt* and deprav'd *Nature*, that we are *Barbarians*, and *humanity* dwells not amongst us; shall our *Poet* therefore pamper this *corrupt* nature, and indulge our barbarity?'

**398.** Cf. Rymer, 19, on Athens and London: 'Certain it is, that *Nature* is the same, and *Man* is the same, he *loves*, *grieves*, *hates*, *envies*, has the same *affections* and *passions* in both places.'

**400.** Cf. Rymer, 20: 'Lastly, (though *Tragedy* is a Poem for *men* of *sense*,) yet I cannot be perswaded that the people are so very mad of *Acorns*, but that they could be well content to eat the *Bread* of civil persons.'

**402.** The initial '2.', omitted by Hill (1905), is printed as 'Secondly,' in Watson, i. 215.

**403.** For Rollo's murders, see Rymer, 32.

**406.** Dr William Vyse (1742–1816), Canon Residentiary of Lichfield (1772) and Rector of St Mary's, Lambeth (1777), provided SJ with the text of D's letter of 3 Sept. 1697 to his sons John and Charles in Rome. Boswell described Vyse as 'son of the respectable clergyman [Archdeacon William Vyse] at Lichfield, who was contemporary with Johnson, and in whose father's family Johnson had the happiness of being kindly received in his early years'. The elder Vyse was a contemporary of SJ at Pembroke College, Oxford (*Life*, iii. 124–5; see also *Letters*, i. 317 and n., iii. 38–9). For some less 'respectable' aspects of the younger Vyse, see Fanny Burney, *Early Journals*, iii. 304 n., 374.

Although SJ mentioned 'Drydens letter from lambeth, which is promised me' to Nichols in mid-Aug. 1778 (*Letters*, iii. 124), it may have been appended to the biography at a late stage (see **191** n. above). For a full text of the letter, with a postscript by D's wife omitted by SJ, see *Letters*, 92–6, 178–9.

D was staying with Sir William Bowyer (1639–1722) of Denham Court, Uxbridge, a relative of his wife. For Tonson's efforts to make the depiction of Aeneas in the plates in D's *Virgil* resemble William III, see Winn, *JD*, 484, 624–5 nn. The plan to alter Sir Robert Howard's *The Conquest of China* was abandoned, perhaps because of Collier's attack on D in 1698 (Winn, *JD*, 492, 499). For 'a song for St. Cecilia's Feast' ('Alexander's Feast'), see **150**, **318** above. For D's interest in astrology (here casting Charles Dryden's nativity), see **191** and n. above, where SJ added a cross-reference to this letter in 1783. Orlando Bridgeman, one of the Stewards of the St Cecilia's Feast in 1697, subscribed to D's *Virgil* (*Letters*, 178 n.).

## EDMUND SMITH (1672?–1710)

**Composition.** SJ refers in **76** to the death of David Garrick on 20 Jan. 1779. He may still have been working on 'Smith' at Streatham when he told Frances Reynolds on 15 Feb. 1779, 'I have about a week's work to do, and then I shall come to live in town' (*Letters*, iii. 151). On 1 Mar. 1779 he told Nichols about the Latin text which was to be appended to it (*Letters*, iii. 152: see **77** below). At about the time of its publication at the end of Mar. a note (presumably by Nichols) to 'Biographical Anecdotes of the Late Mr. Garrick' (*Gent. Mag.* (1779), 117 n.) mentioned that a character of Gilbert Walmesley 'is given by Dr. Johnson, in his elegant Life of Edmund Smith' accompanying the *Eng. Poets.*

**Sources.** Jacob's account, i. 243–5, is rudimentary, *GD* ignored S, and both Shiels, *Lives*, iv. 303–12, and Philip Nichols in *BB*, vi (ii) (1766), Suppl. 162–3, relied heavily on William Oldisworth's 'Character' prefixed to S's *Works* (1714). SJ accordingly took the unusual step of excerpting the whole of Oldisworth's account (of which he had no high opinion, as **27** reveals) in **3–26** below. (SJ's text follows the first edition of 1714, ignoring small corrections in the 3rd edition of 1719: see **5** n. below.)

SJ had, however, a significant additional source for S's years at Oxford, ignored by earlier biographers, in Dr John Burton's *The Genuineness of Lord Clarendon's History . . . Vindicated* (Oxford, 1744). He also used anecdotes about S he had heard as a young man in Lichfield from Gilbert Walmesley (**61–76** below), and later from Thomas Clark (see **45** below). In **77** he quotes a MS in the Bodleian Library, which he may have come across in Oxford in late July 1777, when he told Henry Thrale, 'I have picked up some little information for my Lives at the library' (*Letters*, iii. 45): cf. headnote to 'J. Philips' above. For these reasons, *Gent. Mag.* (Sept. 1779), 453–6, reprinted virtually the whole of SJ's own section of 'Smith' as the most 'original' of the first series of *Prefaces*.

**Publication.** In *Prefaces*, vol. iv (31 Mar. 1779). No proofs have survived.

**Modern Sources:**
J. A. W. Bennet, 'Oxford in 1699', *Oxoniensia*, 4 (1939), 147–52
E. M. Geffen, 'The Expulsion from Oxford of E ("Rag") S', *N & Q* 170 (1936), 398–401
E. M. Geffen, 'The Parentage of E ("Rag") S', *RES* 14 (1938), 72–8
I. Green, 'The Publication of Clarendon's Autobiography', *BLR* 10 (1982), 349–67
D. Nichol Smith (ed.), *The Letters of Thomas Burnet to George Duckett 1712–22* (Oxford, 1914)
M. G. Lloyd Thomas (ed.), *The Poems of John Philips* (Oxford, 1927)
K. E. Wheatley, 'The Relation of ES's *Phaedra and Hippolitus* to Racine's *Phèdre* and *Bajazet*', *Romanic Review*, 37 (1946), 306–28

> **2.** For Oldisworth and Burton, see headnote above. SJ no doubt enjoyed exposing the reader to Oldisworth's 'indistinct' panegyric before offering his own 'plainer' and more sceptical narrative.
>
> William Oldisworth (1680–1734) entered Hart Hall, Oxford, in 1698. Swift described him on 12 Mar. 1713 as 'an ingenious fellow, but the most confounded vain Coxcomb in the World; so that I dare not let him see me, nor am acquainted with him' (*Jnl. to Stella*, ii. 637). In Nov. 1716 Pope quoted Bernard Lintot's opinion that Oldisworth 'translates an Ode of *Horace* the *quickest* of any man in *England*' (*Corresp.*, i. 373). Gilbert Walmesley (see **71–6** below) wrote to George Duckett, 1 Jan. 1715: 'I see Captn. Ragg's works are Printed together; yt. is, Those yt. Lintot had a Property in the Printing of wth. a hasty imperfect Account of the Author, wrote by Oldisworth' (Bodleian, MS Firth c. 13, fo. 50ᵛ). For S as 'Captain Rag', see **44** and n. below, and for a later reference to Oldisworth, see 'Broome' **3** below.

*all the partiality of friendship*: cf. 'the fondness of friendship' in Congreve's account of Dryden ('Dryden' **160** above), 'the fondness of a friend' in the accounts by Welwood and Steele quoted in 'Rowe' **27** and 'Addison' **108** below, and see also 'the fondness of friendship' in 'Addison' **14** below. Shiels, *Lives*, iv. 312, praised the 'laudable fondness' of Oldisworth's account of S. SJ quotes John Burton (1744), 40 (see **59** below).

**3–26.** Additional information about S has normally been used in the notes to SJ's own narrative in **27** ff. below.

**4.** Oldisworth quotes Horace, *Ars Poetica*, ll. 409–11 ('I fail, myself, to see the good either of study without a spark of genius or of untutored talent. Each requires the other's help in a common cause').

**5.** *curious felicity*: the studied felicity attributed to Horace by Petronius, *Satyricon*, 118, l. 18. For the Latin form, see 'Pope' **343** below and, for Dryden's use of the phrase, see Watson, ii. 31, 93, 206.

Although all SJ's editions (1779–83) have '*curious felicity chiefly*', the erroneous italicization of 'chiefly' had been corrected in S's *Works* (3rd edn., 1719): see Textual Notes.

**6.** *they may make grey authors blush*: SJ uses this phrase in 'Stepney' **3** above. For precocious compositions, see 'Cowley' **6** and n. above. Oldisworth ends by quoting Horace, *Sat.* I. v. 44 ('for me there is nothing in life to compare with the joy of friendship').

*Gent. Mag.* (Nov. 1779), 549, pointed out that 'diligent enquiry' in Oxford might unearth some of S's university verses. This suggestion may have come from Nichols, who printed such material in *Sel. Collection*, iv. 62, vii. 105–12: see also **29** n. below. S contributed to the Oxford collections of 1688 ('On the Birth of the Prince of Wales'), 1689 ('On the Inauguration of King William and Queen Mary'), and 1690 ('On the Return of the King from Ireland'). Two of the three MS poems by S in the Bodleian, in praise of 'Marlborough's arms', were performed at university ceremonies with settings attributed to Richard Goodson, Professor of Music, and have recently been recorded by the New Chamber Opera Ensemble (*Music from Ceremonial Oxford*, 2001).

**9.** For university exercises, see also 'Yalden' **2** below. William Jane was the Regius Professor of Divinity 1680–1707.

*sciolists*: SJ defines 'Sciolist' as 'One who knows many things superficially' (*Dict.*). Oldisworth's last sentence may allude to Richard Steele's *The Christian Hero* (1701).

**10.** Cf. SJ's scepticism about Milton's reading of the classics in 'Milton' **20** above. Authors' fear of criticism is a recurrent theme in the Earl of Shaftesbury's writings, e.g.: 'The CRITICKS, it seems are formidable to 'em . . . the dreadful *Specters*, the *Giants*, the *Enchanters*, who traverse and disturb 'em in their Works.' Whereas modern authors 'save their illacquir'd Reputation, by the Decrial of an *Art*, on which the Cause and Interest of *Wit* and *Letters* absolutely depend', Boileau and Corneille 'apply'd their *Criticism* with just Severity, even to their own Works' (*Characteristicks* (5th edn., 1732), i. 231, iii. 280, 266).

Oldisworth also refers to François Hédelin, Abbé d'Aubignac (1604–76), *Pratique du théâtre* (1657; trans. 1684), and René Le Bossu, *Traité du poème épique* (1675; trans. 1695): see 'Milton' **209** and n. above.

11. Oldisworth adapts Ben Jonson, *Timber, or Discoveries*: 'They write a verse as smooth, as soft, as cream, | In which there is not torrent, nor scarce stream' (*Ben Jonson*, ed. I. Donaldson (Oxford, 1985), 541).

13. In 1701 S delivered the annual *Oratio* by a MA of Christ Church in honour of Sir Thomas Bodley. It was printed in 1711 and included in his *Works* (1714), 95–101. Three MSS of the speech are in the Bodleian.

14. Translations from Horace by Sir William Temple (see 'Swift' **7** ff. below) appeared in his *Miscellanea. The Third Part* (1701), 345–50, 357–60. See also 'Roscommon' **34** above. For Philips's Latin ode to Henry St John, and the Latin verse of Dr (later Sir) Edward Hannes, see 'J. Philips' **14** above. Poems by Hannes and Dr Ralph Bathurst appeared in *Musarum Anglicanarum Analecta* (Oxford, 1692), 20–40, 90–3, 292–4. For S's 'Pocockius', see **31** below, and for Waller on Cromwell, 'Waller' **65, 128** above. 'Thuanus' refers to Jacques de Thou, *Historiae suae Temporis* (Paris, 1604–20).

For the 'great men' who suggested that S 'write a history', see **43** below. Oldisworth quotes Lucretius I. 26–7 ('whom you, goddess, have willed at all times to excel, endowed with all gifts').

15. S made only occasional appearances in the miscellanies of the period. 'A Description of the Battel and Victory...at Blenheim' by 'Mr. *Smith*, of *Oxford*' in *Miscellaneous Works of the Earls of Rochester and Roscommon* (1707), ii. 36–9, is presumably his, and his elegy on Philips (see **51–2** below) was reprinted in Lintot's *Miscellaneous Poems and Translations* (1712), 149–63. For a poem 'To Mr. Edmund Smith', see *Oxford and Cambridge Miscellany Poems* [1708], 329–31.

*condolance* (third sentence): included only as the French origin of 'Condolence' in the *Dict.*

16. *enameled*: SJ defines 'Enamel' as 'To inlay; to variegate with colours, properly with colours fixed by fire' (*Dict.*).

17. For *Phaedra and Hippolitus* (1707) and Addison's prologue, see **46–50** below. Euripides and Seneca wrote tragedies on the subject, but S's play was based on Racine's *Phèdre* (1677): see Wheatley, 'Relation', 306–28.

18. See *Tatler* 9 (1709), quoting William Wycherley: '*That*, said he, *among these Fellows is call'd* Easy Writing, *which any one may easily Write.*'

19. *Julio*: Giulio Romano (1499–1546), follower of Raphael.

21. Oldisworth quotes Horace, *Epist.*, II. ii. 12 ('though poor, I am in nobody's debt').

22. All SJ's editions (1779–83) misprint '*grand monde*' as '*grande monde*': see Textual Notes.

In his recent dedication to his *Poems on Several Occasions* (1709), Prior wrote of the Earl of Halifax that 'His Faults brought their Excuse with them, and his very Failings had their Beauties' (*Lit. Works*, i. 252–3).

24. For S's projected translation of Pindar, see **53** and n. below, and for the tragedy on Lady Jane Grey, see **66** and 'Rowe' **16** and n. below.

25. Richard Parker (*c.*1671–1728), Fellow of Merton College from 1693, later held several livings. There had been earlier translations of Boileau's *Traité du sublime* (1674) in 1680 and 1698. Two years after S's death, Leonard Welsted published *The Works of Dionysius Longinus, On the Sublime...With Some Remarks on the*

*English Poets* (1712). Later enquiries did not bring the MS of S's unpublished translation to light: see *Gent. Mag.* (1777), 110, 371.

26. The 'Advertisement' of *Thales. A Monody, Sacred to the Memory of Dr. Pococke... From an authentic Manuscript of Mr. Edmund Smith* (1751) claimed that the 'editor' possessed other MSS of S, but the authenticity of *Thales* itself is uncertain.

27. Cf. SJ's comments on the 'mist of panegyrick' in Sprat's biography of Cowley ('Cowley' 1 above), and his praise of Dryden's account of Shakespeare as 'a perpetual model of encomiastick criticism; exact without minuteness, and lofty without exaggeration' ('Dryden' **198** above).

28. Cf. **3** above. S was the son of Edmund Neale, a merchant, who in 1670 married Margaret, daughter of Sir Nicholas Lechmere of Hanley Castle, near Upton, Worcestershire, later Baron of the Exchequer. Lechmere's will (1697) condemned Neale's dissolute life and desertion of his wife twenty years earlier. S was brought up by Lechmere's sister and her husband, Matthew Smith of London, whose name he adopted: see Geffen, 'Parentage'.

A memorial inscription, stating that S died in 1710 'Aetat. 42', followed Oldisworth's 'Character' in *Works* (1714), and also appeared in Jacob. Shiels, *Lives*, iv. 311, repeated this information, and *BB* accordingly stated that he was born in 1668, as did Reed in *Lives* (1790), ii. 244 n. SJ himself suggests in **29** that S was 20 in 1689. As Geffen, 'Parentage', pointed out, if born in 1668, S would have been illegitimate. At his admission to Oxford (see **29** below), he was said to be aged 16 and therefore born in 1672, the date now usually accepted.

29. S was a King's Scholar at Westminster School 1684–8. For Dr Busby, the headmaster, see 'Dryden' **4** and n. above. S matriculated from Christ Church, Oxford, 25 June 1688; BA 1692, MA 8 July 1696. For his preference of Christ Church to Trinity College, Cambridge, see **4** above, and for Swift's comments in Apr. 1711 on the elections at Westminster School in the post-Busby era, see *Jnl. to Stella*, ii. 257–8 ('they say 'tis a sight, and a great trial of wits').

In a note to S's three Latin poems of 1688–90 (see **6** n. above) in his *Sel. Collection*, vii. 105–12, Nichols pointed out that their dates settled the question of when he entered Oxford, but SJ did not revise his second sentence in 1783.

30. SJ's source for S's behaviour at Oxford is John Burton, *The Genuineness of Lord Clarendon's History* (Oxford, 1744), 42 n. For S's 'scandalous and profligate misbehaviour', see also Bodleian, MS Tanner 314, fo. 205.

The subject of S's 'Pocockius' was Dr Edward Pococke (1604–91), Canon of Christ Church and Professor of Hebrew at Oxford since 1660. For an anecdote about the writing of the ode, see **51** n. below. SJ said after receiving his pension: 'Had this happened twenty years ago, I should have gone to Constantinople to learn Arabick, as Pococke did' (*Life*, iv. 28). 'Orientalist' is not in the *Dict*.

31. 'Pocockius' appeared in *Musarum Anglicanarum Analecta*, ii (Oxford, 1699), 303–6 (see 'Addison' **10** below). On 10 Apr. 1778 SJ repeated some lines from the ode, 'and said they were Smith's best verses' (*Life*, iii. 269). Joseph Trapp (see 'Dryden' **310** and n. above) collected his lectures as Professor of Poetry at Oxford as *Praelectiones Poeticae* (3 vols., 1711–19). For his praise of S's ode, see the English

translation as *Lectures on Poetry* (1742), 207–9. For earlier comments on modern Latin poetry, see 'Cowley' **33–4** and 'Milton' **10, 176** above.

32. SJ quotes 'Pocockius', ll. 37–40.

33. For a similar objection involving 'colours', see 'Addison' **131** and n. below. SJ slightly misquotes Cowley, 'On the Death of Sir Henry Wotton', ll. 3–4.

34. See Cowley, 'To Mr. Hobbes', st. vi, and 'Pocockius', ll. 57 ff. SJ himself used the secret flames beneath Etna's flowery side as an image in *Irene* (1749), v. ii. 33–7.

35. See **29** n. above.

36. SJ's source is Burton, *Genuineness*, 42 n. S was rebuked for 'riotous Misbehaviour', together with Samuel Beane, who had followed him from Westminster to Christ Church (Bodleian, MS Tanner 314, fo. 205).

38. Burton, *Genuineness*, 41, related that in 1703 'it was remark'd as something very singular in his behaviour that he shew'd an occasional conformity to his College-rules, which by way of ridicule he call'd *whitening* himself'. Peter Foulkes (1676–1747) became Censor in 1703. In 1696, while still an undergraduate, he had published two texts of Demosthenes with John Freind (1675–1728), also of West-minster and Christ Church.

   William Brome's letter to Richard Rawlinson, 9 May 1732, makes clear why S was unlikely to become Censor: 'Next as to Captain Rag: perhaps there was no person in any Society so irregular & unconformable to Rules as he was: he scarce ever came to Prayers; & such behaviour could never recommend him to an intimacy with his Governour . . . the Dean had an aversion to him . . . Rag could never have any office in the College . . . if the Dean did speak to the Captain 'twas only to chide him' (Bodleian, MS Rawl. J 405, fos. 88–9, quoted by Geffen, 'Expulsion', 398–401). For S as 'Captain Rag' see **44** below.

39. Henry Aldrich (1647–1710) was Dean of Christ Church from 1689 (see 'J. Philips' **3** above).

   *The Town Display'd. In a Letter to Amintor in the Country* (1701) (anonymous in Foxon, *English Verse*, T 433) has been attributed to S by W. G. Hiscock, *A Christ Church Miscellany* (Oxford, 1946), 21–2. The line 'too gross to be repeated' is presumably the last of the following about 'drunken *A[ldric]h*': 'No Rakish Priest in Country, or in Town, | Is more a Scandal to the Clergy's Gown | . . . *S[tratfor]d* he hugs, his Dear Lov'd Natural Child, | So oft Defiling, and so oft Defil'd: | With what aversion we behold the Sot, | Bugger the Bastard which he once begot!' (14–15).

40. See Burton, *Genuineness*, 42, and, for a modern account, Geffen, 'Expulsion', 398–401. The earlier threat of expulsion in 1700 (see **36** above) was carried out, as S had 'not amended his behaviour nor conformed to the discipline of this House' (Bodleian, MS Tanner 314, fo. 205). The 'Canons' are members of the governing body of Christ Church, which is a cathedral as well as a college.

41. The friend was no doubt Gilbert Walmesley (see **71** below).

42. *the Tories had expelled him*: a reference to Christ Church's Tory and High Church reputation (see also **57** and n. below). S had been admitted to the Inner Temple as early as 1690, so may have considered a legal career. At this period he met the youthful Pope, according to Spence: ' "Igad that young fellow will either be a madman or make a very great poet" (Rag Smith, after being in Mr. Pope's company

when about fourteen).' Pope's supposed age would date the meeting in 1702, but it probably occurred later (Spence, i. 13 and n.).

43. For Oldisworth's 'hint', see **14** above and, for the source of the anecdote, **45** below. As Hill (1905) suggested, S was presumably disconcerted by the prospect of describing—in a Whig history of the events of 1688—the complex and discredited role of Robert Spencer, 2nd Earl of Sunderland (1640–1702), whose son Charles Spencer, the 3rd Earl (1674–1722), was currently Secretary of State. Addison became Sunderland's under-secretary in Dec. 1706 (see 'Addison' **26, 79** n., **90, 93** below). Mrs Thrale gave a less reliable version of the story in Aug./Sept. 1777 (*Thraliana*, i. 132).

Byron quoted Addison's words in the last sentence in a letter to John Cam Hobhouse from Pisa, 23 Nov. 1821 (*Letters and Journals*, ed. L. A. Marchand, ix (1979), 69).

44. *Captain Rag*: according to Burton, *Genuineness*, 40, S 'was an immoral man in some points...commonly known by the name of Captain *Rag*, distinguish'd by...the affectation of a rakish slovenly appearance in dress'. For the nickname see also **2** n., **38** n. above and **51** n. below. Anne Finch, Countess of Winchilsea, referred to S as 'Poet RAG' and to his friend John Philips in 'A Tale of the Miser, and the Poet' (written 1709) in her *Miscellany Poems* (1713), 148. A contributor to *Gent. Mag.* (1780), 280, attributed the nickname to 'the tattered condition of his *gown*, which was always flying in rags about him; and to conceal which, he wore one end of it in his pocket; a practice still common enough at Oxford, among the young *Rags* of the present days'. Joseph Warton stated in *Adventurer* 59 (1753) that later poets 'neglect to change their linnen, because SMITH was a sloven'.

45. SJ twice referred to 'the late learned and ingenious' Thomas Clark (d. 1761) in notes to *Othello* in 1765 (*YW*, viii. 1017, 1034).

46. The prologue and epilogue to S's *Phaedra and Hippolitus*, one of the few plays included in *Eng. Poets* (1779), xxi. 87–189, were written by the Whig Addison and the Tory Prior respectively: see **70** below. Addison's prologue ridiculed Italian opera ('Addison' **27** n. below).

Prior commented on S's changing allegiance in a letter to Sir Thomas Hanmer, 24 June 1707, shortly after the play's publication: 'Phaedra is a prostitute, and Smith's dedication [see **48** below] is nonsense—people do me a great deal of honour, they say when you and I had lookt over this piece for six months, the man could write verse; but when we had forsaken him, and he went over to St[eele] and Ad[dison] he could not write prose' (*Lit. Works*, ii. 899).

47. For Addison's remarks, see **49** and n. below. S's tragedy was in fact performed on 21, 22, 25, 26 Apr. 1707 (published 19 June 1707), the cast including Betterton, Mrs Barry, and Mrs Oldfield. In Mar. 1707 Oldmixon's *The Muses Mercury* had warned S's friends against raising excessive expectations, and in May reported the play's short run. It enjoyed later revivals, including two performances in 1780. Tom Davies attributed its cold reception to English distaste for the theme of incest (*Dramatic Miscellanies* (1784), ii. 44–5). For plays supported by a 'band of applauders', see 'Addison' **59** and 'A. Philips' **6** below.

48. Lintot in fact gave S only £50 for the play (Nichols, *Lit. Anec.*, viii. 301). According to Fielding's *Covent-Garden Journal* 19 (7 Mar. 1752), 'the late learned Bernard

Lintott the Bookseller ... having purchased the Copy of a Tragedy called Phædra and Hypolitus, lamented that the Author had not put a little more Humour in it; for that, he said, was the only thing it wanted' (ed. B. A. Goldgar (Oxford, 1988), 131).

Although S dedicated his tragedy to the Earl of Halifax (see 'Halifax' 11 below), he presumably failed to present it in person to his prospective patron. This anecdote probably derived from Gilbert Walmesley (see 71 below). For similar negligence, see 'Thomson' 27 below. Among the possible reasons for S's conduct, SJ appears not to take 'pride' very seriously, but cf. Pope's later dealings with Lord Halifax, when 'the poet fed his own pride with the dignity of independence' ('Pope' 102 below); and SJ's comment to Reynolds, 19 Aug. 1784, on 'that sullen pride which expects to be solicited to its own advantage' (*Letters*, iv. 375).

49. In *Spectator* 18 (1711), Addison asked: 'Would one think it was possible (at a Time when an Author lived that was able to write the *Phaedra* and *Hippolitus*) for a People to be so stupidly fond of the *Italian* Opera, as scarce to give a Third Days Hearing to that admirable Tragedy?' Revealingly, Dick Minim in *Idler* 60 (1759) 'often lamented the neglect of *Phaedra and Hippolitus*' (*YW*, ii. 187).

*the voice of the people*: for SJ's usual confidence in popular judgement, which he shared with Boileau, see 'Cowley' 38 and n., 'Roscommon' 39, and 'Otway' 12 above, and 'Addison' 136, 'Gay' 31, 'Savage' 121, 164, 219–20, 'Pope' 280, 'Thomson' 25, and 'Gray' 51 below. Boswell stated that SJ had, 'upon all occasions, a great deference for the general opinion', believing that 'the publick' must be the judges of an author's 'pretensions' (*Life*, i. 200; and cf. ii. 238, iii. 26). See also *J. Misc.*, ii. 7, 19; *Ramblers* 23 ('the publick, which is never corrupted, nor often deceived, is to pass the last sentence upon literary claims'), 25, 52 (1750); and *Adventurer* 138 (1754) ('If mankind were left to judge for themselves, it is reasonable to imagine, that of such writings, at least, as describe the movement of the human passions, and of which every man carries the archetype within him, a just opinion would be formed' (*YW*, iii. 128, 136, 280, ii. 496).

SJ explained in Nov. 1756 that he disliked reading literary MSS, 'nor do I think an author just to himself who rests in any opinion but that of the publick' (*Letters*, i. 149). On 12 Aug. 1784 he told Queeney Thrale: 'In matters of human judgement, and prudential consideration, consider the publick voice of general opinion as always worthy of great attention' (*Letters*, iv. 367). His opinion was hardly unorthodox. Owen Ruffhead wrote in the *Monthly Review*, 24 (1761), 181–2: 'When Pliny was dissatisfied with the Judgment of his Critical Friends, to whom he submitted his compositions, he used to say, *Ad populum provoco*. In all cases, whatever, the last resort is undoubtedly to the people, from whose decree no appeal can be made to any superior tribunal.'

As in *Rambler* 23 above, SJ sometimes conceded that the public could be temporarily 'deceived': see 'Granville' 24 and 'Gray' 14, 32 below, and *Ramblers* 2, 21 (1750). In 'Pope' 304 below he criticizes Dryden for writing 'merely for the people; and when he pleased others, he contented himself'. Yet he did not simply endorse Imlac's lofty view that the poet 'must contemn the applause of his own time, and commit his claims to the justice of posterity' (*Rasselas*, ch. X, *YW*, xvi. 45; cf. 'Milton' 138 and n. above). For ideas in the period about the 'consensus gentium', and the notion, usually resisted by SJ, that true taste is the possession of the few, see Dennis, *Works*, i. 458–9 n.

*The fable is mythological*: for SJ's dislike of mythology, see **54** below and 'Butler' **41** and n., above, and for our lack of interest in manners and sentiments 'remote from life', see 'Milton' **244** above.

*a scholar's play*: Robert Potter (as 'W.B.') in *Gent. Mag.* (1781), 507, suggested that SJ's various assertions that S's tragedy pleased 'the criticks only' (**47** above), and here that 'the learned reject it as a school-boy's tale' and that 'it is a scholar's play', are contradictory. Cf. SJ's description of *Bleinheim* by S's friend John Philips as 'the poem of a scholar . . . a man who writes books from books, and studies the world in a college' ('J. Philips' **12** above).

SJ quotes '*incredulus odi*' from Horace, *Ars Poetica*, l. 188 ('I disbelieve and detest'). For his later use of the phrase, and the assertion that 'we are affected only as we believe', see 'Gray' **40–1** below. Boswell said of SJ: 'I never knew any person who upon hearing an extraordinary circumstance told, discovered more of the *incredulus odi*' (*Life*, iii. 229). Cf. 'Cowley' **5** and n. above.

For diction, see 'Cowley' **181–4** and n. above; for 'luxuriant' language, 'Thomson' **50** and n. below; and for dialogue, 'Butler' **34** and n. above. Shiels, *Lives*, iv. 312, said similarly that S's 'language, however luxuriously poetical, yet is far from being proper for the drama, and there is too much of the poet in every speech he puts in the mouths of his characters', and that S needed 'a more general knowledge of real life and characters'.

50. In *Remarks on Prince Arthur* (1696), Dennis explained that he had abandoned an adaptation of Euripides' *Hippolytus* for 'the *English* Stage' because 'its Subject appears to depend too much on the fabulous History' (*Works*, i. 78).

51. For Philips's death on 15 Feb. 1709, see 'J. Philips' **8** and n. above. S in fact published his *Poem on the Death of Mr. John Philips* in May 1710 (Foxon, *English Verse*, S 516) and it was later reprinted in Lintot's *Miscellaneous Poems and Translations* (1712), 149–63. The *Poem* included a notable defence of blank verse against 'Tyrannic Rhyme' (cf. 'J. Philips' **38** and n. above). One of the passages SJ found 'too ludicrous' may have been S's mockery of Blackmore, who had attacked Philips as '*Milton*'s imitator' in *Advice to the Poets* (1706) (see 'J. Philips' **12** n. above). Leonard Welsted also published *A Poem to the Memory of the Incomparable Mr. Philips* in July 1710 (Foxon, *English Verse*, W 308).

In its article on Philips, *BB*, v (1760), 3354 n., told a story (from a relative of the poet) that S was locked for three days in a room in the lodgings of Dr Robert Shippen, the Principal of Brasenose College, until he finished the poem. A contributor to *Gent. Mag.* (1780), 280, pointed out a suspiciously similar anecdote of John Urry (see **77** below) locking S in a room until he had written his Latin 'Pocockius', in Thomas Warton, *Life of Sir Thomas Pope* (2nd edn., 1780), 449. Since S left Oxford several years before writing the *Poem* on Philips, this is more likely.

For S's unfinished account of Philips, originally intended as a preface to the *Poem*, see **52** n. below and 'J. Philips' **18–38** above. Thomas Newcomb referred to their friendship in *Bibliotheca, or The Modern Library* (1712): 'See Rag on Phillips still attends; | In life, in death, harmonious friends; | Pleas'd his lov'd Isis to forego, | To meet the darling shade below.' Newcomb also recalled S's slovenly appearance (**44** above): 'No longer now the modish gown | In ropy shreds hangs quivering down, | Tuck'd close, but gently, round the side, | Some dismal breach beneath to hide; | Or else protecting from the air | Some parts, as nature form'd them, bare'

(Nichols, *Sel. Collection*, iii. 56–7). In a later account, S and Philips were 'such intimate chronies, that whoever invited one, always had the company of the other of course. The consequence was not disagreeable. Philips was never good company till he was drunk, Smith never but while he was sober' (*Gent. Mag.* (June 1780), 280).

52. Walmesley (see 71 below) may have been SJ's source. William Brome, Philips's cousin, told Rawlinson in a letter of 9 May 1732 that S had sent him copies of his elegy for distribution, and that he had delivered the money collected to S in London in May 1710, when S showed him part of his intended 'Prefatory Discourse' to the poem. This money enabled S to visit George Duckett (see 56 below), and he died a few weeks later (Bodleian, MS Rawl. J 405, fos. 88–9).

53. See 24–6 above. Nothing further is known of S's Pindar. For Longinus, see 'Cowley' 58 and n. above. S's intended translation anticipated the satire on the false sublime, and ridicule of Blackmore's epics, in Pope's *Art of Sinking in Poetry* (1728) (see 'Pope' 143 below). Pope conceived the idea in about 1714, when Oldisworth's 'Character' of S was published: for his possible indebtedness, see *The Art of Sinking in Poetry*, ed. E. L. Steeves (New York, 1952), pp. xxiv, lvi and n.

54. For S's 'Lady Jane Grey', see 24 above and 66 and n. below.
    For the fate of *Phaedra and Hippolitus*, see 49 above.

55. For a contemporary poetic treatment of this subject, see 'Young' 28 and 156 below (where SJ comments that Young's '*Jane* is too heroick to be pitied'). For the 'passions', see 'Cowley' 57 and n. above.

56. George Duckett (1684–1732) of Hartham, near Chippenham, Wilts., was a MP and a Commissioner of the Excise, and later an enemy of Pope (see 'Pope' 122, 153 and nn. below). SJ's account of S's last days probably derives from Gilbert Walmesley (see 71 below), Duckett's friend and correspondent. S was commemorated in *On the Death of Mr. Edmund Smith, late Student of Christ-Church, Oxon. A Poem, in Miltonic Verse* (1712) (Foxon, *English Verse*, O 197–8).
    The misspelling of 'Hartham' as 'Gartham' (see Textual Notes) occurs in all SJ's editions (1779–83), although 'Hartham' appears in the article on Smith in Reed's *Biographia Dramatica* (1782), i. 422–3.
    *avocations*: SJ defines 'Avocation' as '1. The act of calling aside' and '2. The business that calls; or the call that summons away' (*Dict.*).

57. *The History of the Rebellion and Civil Wars in England*, by Edward Hyde, Earl of Clarendon (1609–74), was published at Oxford in 1702–4. Although there were Whig accusations as early as 1711 of pre-publication interference with Clarendon's text, the most persistent and prominent charges were made by John Oldmixon, especially in his *History of England* (1730 for 1729), pp. viii–ix, 227. Oldmixon cited a letter from George Duckett claiming that S had told him in June 1710, shortly before his death, that he had been employed to alter Clarendon's text by the Tory clerics Henry Aldrich (see 39 above), George Smalridge (1663–1719), later Bishop of Bristol (see 'Swift' 27 below), and Francis Atterbury (1662–1732), later Bishop of Rochester (see 'Yalden' 11–12 and 'Pope' 131–2 below). Like S, all three were products of Westminster and Christ Church.
    For a recent account, and for the complex state of Clarendon's text, see Green, 'Publication', esp. 353–6; and for Pope's attack on Oldmixon in a note on the controversy in the *Dunciad*, see *TE*, v. 125–6 and n.

58. Oldmixon's accusation was translated in the *Bibliothèque raisonnée des ouvrages des savans de l'Europe* in July–Sept. 1731, Atterbury's reply appearing in Oct.–Dec. 1731 (*BB*, i (2nd edn., 1778), 343 n.). Atterbury's *Vindication* also appeared separately in England, and was reprinted in *The Clarendon-Family Vindicated* (1732) and elsewhere. Other pamphlet contributions included a reply by Oldmixon in 1732. See Atterbury's *Epistolary Corresp.*, ed. J. Nichols, i (1783), 278–92, his letter to Pope, 23 Nov. 1731 (Pope, *Corresp.*, iii. 245–6 and n.), and, for his 'exile', 'Pope' **131–2** below.

59. Dr John Burton (see headnote above) originally entered the controversy with a series of articles in the *Weekly Mag.* in Mar. 1733, reprinted in *Gent. Mag.* (1733), 117–18, 129–30, 140–1, 146–7, and see 335–6. In *The Genuineness of Lord Clarendon's History . . . Vindicated* (Oxford, 1744), he collected all the evidence (including Oldmixon's accusations and Atterbury's reply), and demonstrated the falsity of the charge. Although Burton's text suggests Whiggish sympathies (103, 113), SJ's comment on his political views was questioned in *Gent. Mag.* (1779), 455 n.: 'This, we are well assured, is a mistake. Dr. Burton always avowed himself a Tory.'

   SJ had referred to the parts played by Oldmixon and Duckett in *Idler* 65 (1759): 'the authenticity of Clarendon's history, tho' printed with the sanction of one of the first universities of the world, had not an unexpected manuscript been happily discovered, would, with the help of factious credulity, have been brought into question by the two lowest of all human beings, a scribbler for a party, and a commissioner of excise.' (For SJ's view of excise collectors, see 'Excise' in the *Dict.* and *Life*, i. 294–5 and n.) In 1761 he added a note suggesting that the Bodleian Library should exhibit the MS of Clarendon's *Life* (1759), the authenticity of which had also been questioned (*YW*, ii. 203 and n.).

60. SJ refers to Burton's revelations about S's erratic career at Oxford: see **30, 36, 40** above.

61–70. For Gilbert Walmesley as SJ's source in these paragraphs, see **71** below; and, for anecdotes which may have the same origin, **41, 48, 52, 56** above. SJ is recalling conversations which took place some forty years earlier.

61. SJ refers to the younger Scaliger, Joseph Justus (1540–1609): see *Scaligeriana, sive Excerpta ex Ore Josephi Scaligeri* (1666), of which SJ himself owned a later edition. SJ had praised his 'wonderful sagacity and erudition' in 1765 (*YW*, vii. 110), and in his Latin verses on the theme of 'Know Thyself', written while he was revising the *Dict.* (4th edn., 1773), compared his own achievements unfavourably with those of Scaliger: see *Poems* (1974), 188.

65. Cf. 'Pope' **297** below: 'If conversation offered any thing that could be improved, he committed it to paper.'

66. For S's 'Lady Jane Grey', see **24** above and 'Rowe' **16** and n. below. Thomas Burnet asked Duckett to send S's MS for Rowe's inspection in Mar. 1714: see *Burnet–Duckett Letters* (1914), 57, 62–3.

67. For another poet's 'scholastick rust', see 'Broome' **2** and n. below.

   Dr John Jortin told a curious anecdote about S wearing a nightgown covered with printed ballads at a masquerade, to save the expense of a costume. The company at first followed S around, reading the ballads, but eventually began removing them until he was 'deplumed' (Hawkins, *Life* (1787), i. 471–2 n.).

68. Addison (q.v. below) had been a contemporary at Oxford until 1699: for his subsequent career during S's lifetime, see 'Addison' **19, 25–6, 29** below. For other poetic 'murmurers at Fortune', see 'Dryden' **173** and n. above and 'Savage' **336** below. For Cowley's desire for £500 p.a., see 'Cowley' **24** n. above, and for SJ's belief that £100 p.a. was 'a revenue in those days not inadequate to the conveniencies of life', see 'Dryden' **26** and n. above.

69. For SJ's own interest in 'the old romances of knight errantry', see 'Dryden' **272** and n. above.

70. For SJ's comments elsewhere on authorial self-confidence, see 'Milton' **26** and n. above; and, for Addison, Prior, Halifax, and Oldisworth, **46, 48, 27** above.

71–6. Gilbert Walmesley (1680–1751), Registrar of the Ecclesiastical Court in Lichfield, had been a friend of the young SJ from about 1727. (This may explain why SJ's undergraduate collection of books included 'Smith's Works': see *Gleanings*, v. 227.) He had entered Trinity College, Oxford, in 1698, and been called to the Bar in 1707: see *Life*, i. 81, 102, and ii. 466–7, and Clifford (1955), 92–104. His letters to Duckett 1711–15 are in the Bodleian (MS Firth c. 13, fos. 36–53). Boswell told SJ in 1780: 'All that you have said in grateful praise of Mr Walmsley, I have long thought of you; but we are both Tories, which has a very general influence upon our sentiments' (*Life*, iii. 439).

72. Walmesley's early friendship with SJ and Garrick was already public knowledge: see *Gent. Mag.* (1765), 450–1, and (1779), 117 n. Walmesley revealed his opinion of SJ's early career in London in a letter to Garrick, 3 Nov. 1746: 'When you see Mr. Johnson, pray [give] my compliments, and tell him I esteem him as a great genius—quite lost both to himself and the world' (Garrick, *Private Corresp.*, ed. J. Boaden (1831–2), i. 45).
    For the meaning of 'literature', see 'Milton' **4** and n. above.

73. SJ said on 10 Nov. 1773 that 'difference in political principles' was 'much increased by opposition. There was a violent Whig, with whom I used to contend with great eagerness. After his death I felt my Toryism much abated.' Boswell believed that SJ was referring to Walmesley (*Life*, v. 386). For Walmesley as a Whig, see also D. J. Greene, *The Politics of SJ* (2nd edn., Athens, Ga., 1990), 62–4, and 'Addison' **51** and n. below. For an earlier reference to the 'virulence' of political faction, see 'Garth' **15** below, and cf. Addison, *Freeholder* 53 (1716): 'Our Children... no sooner begin to speak but Whig and Tory are the first Words they learn. They are taught in their Infancy to hate one half of the Nation; and contract all the Virulence and Passion of a Party, before they come to the Use of their Reason.'
    SJ's reference to Whig 'virulence and malevolence' was provocative. A contributor to the *Westminster Mag.*, 7 (Nov. 1779), 591–2, was shocked to see SJ 'vomiting out *anathemas* and damnation against the assertors of religious and civil liberty; against men to whom we are indebted for every blessing of life, and enabled by them, even in these dark and perilous times, to contemplate with the most exquisite pleasure the noble fabric of British freedom'. For Dr Samuel Beilby, *Remarks on Doctor J's Lives* (York, 1782), 24–5, a Whig is one who 'uniformly resists illegal power' and 'steadily supports our present happy establishment in Church and State, as it was marked out at the Revolution... The Whig principle is the principle of humanity.'

74. For other poets who preserved their principles in spite of exposure to vice and folly, see 'King' **17**, 'Prior' **52** (only just), and 'Collins' **10** below.

76. Dr Robert James (1705–76), physician and inventor of Dr James's Powder (which may have hastened Goldsmith's death in 1774), had been a schoolfellow of SJ in Lichfield: see 'Akenside' **11** n. below, and *Life*, i. 159, iii. 4.

    David Garrick (1717–79), actor and theatrical manager, also a native of Lichfield and once SJ's pupil at Edial (*Life*, i. 97–101), died on 20 Jan. 1779, not long before SJ wrote 'Smith'. Mrs Thrale noted on 27 Jan. 1779 that Garrick's death 'has crushed the Spirits of many People among whom I now live—Johnson, Murphy — Burney' (*Thraliana*, i. 363–4). According to Arthur Murphy, SJ told Mrs Garrick that he was willing, with her approval, to be 'the editor of his works, and the historian of his life' (*J's Works* (1792), i, p. lxvii). Thomas Davies, *Memoirs of Garrick* (1780), acknowledged SJ's assistance and quoted his tribute to the actor here (i. 392). Mrs Garrick had part of SJ's last sentence engraved on her husband's momument at Lichfield (*Letters*, iii. 150 n.).

    Boswell asked SJ on 24 Apr. 1779 about the precise meaning of his eulogy of Garrick, which John Wilkes had already questioned. SJ defended the 'tame' phrase 'harmless pleasure' as high praise, on the grounds that 'pleasure is in general dangerous, and pernicious to virtue'. Boswell thought SJ's words 'hyperbolically untrue' and 'was not satisfied' by his explanation: see *Life*, iii. 387–8, and Boswell, *Laird of Auchinleck*, 98–9, and, for the dangers of pleasure, *Rasselas*, ch. XLVII (*YW*, xvi. 166–7). George Steevens stated that SJ's tribute 'sounds to my ear like the chill though elegant praise of one who lamented the actor, but not the man' (Boswell, *Making of the Life*, 150). On the death of Samuel Foote, the comic actor, SJ had told Hester Thrale, 3 Nov. 1777: 'the world is really impoverished by his sinking glories' (*Letters*, iii. 92–3).

77. SJ instructed Nichols on 1 Mar. 1779 to append this material from Bodleian, MS Rawl. poet. 113, fo. 47: see headnote above and *Letters*, iii. 152. SJ may have learned of it in Oxford in July 1777. Nichols noted in *Sel. Collection*, iv. 63, that it had already appeared in *The Student*, i (1750), 383–4, as '*Mr.* EDMUND SMITH's *Burlesque on his own* ODE *on the Death of Dr.* POCOCKE'. For S's Latin 'Pocockius', see **14** and **30–4** above.

    Dr John Urry (1666–1715) of Christ Church, editor of Chaucer's *Works* (1721), had been a sergeant 'with a halberd' in the university regiment during Monmouth's rebellion, hence 'Halberdiae': see Thomas Warton, *Life of Sir Thomas Pope* (2nd edn., 1780), 449 (and cf. **51** n. above).


## RICHARD DUKE (1658–1711)

**Composition.** SJ wrote it in late 1778 or early 1779, when he sought help from John Nichols (see below).

**Sources.** *GD*, *BB*, and Shiels ignored D, and SJ's brief first version relied on Jacob, ii (1720), 50, as the proofs reveal (see Textual Notes and **1** below). Nichols eventually came to SJ's rescue. SJ wrote to him, *c*. Dec. 1778: 'By some accident I laid your note upon Duke, up so safely that I cannot find it. Your informations have been of great use to me. I must beg it again, with another list of our authours, for I have laid that with the other' (*Letters*, iii. 146). SJ's request for the 'list of our authours' suggests that, after completing 'Milton', he was just starting to compile the shorter lives in *Prefaces*, vol. iv.

Although Hart (1950), 1089–90, reasonably assumed that SJ's letter refers to the notes on D in Nichols's edition of William King's *Original Works* (1776), iii. 138, 307 (see headnote to 'King' below), Nichols may well have shown SJ the updated information on D he was about to publish in his *Supplement to Swift's Works* (1779), ii. 467, in a note on Swift's reference to D in his *Jnl. to Stella* (see **2, 7** below). One of these sources enabled SJ to revise **1** in particular and to add most of **5–7**: see Textual Notes. D's inclusion in *Eng. Poets* (1779) aroused some surprised comment, and relatively little has been written about him since. Although he is not quoted by name in the *Dict.*, see **2** n. below.

**Publication.** In *Prefaces*, vol. iv (31 Mar. 1779). The first proofs are in the Forster Collection, but SJ revised them so extensively that a further set must have been printed before publication. Though separately paginated, 'Duke' formed a single sheet with 'Otway': see Fleeman (1962), 228 n.

**Modern Sources:**
R. G. Ham, *Otway and Lee* (New Haven, 1931)
E. Hart, 'Some New Sources of J's *Lives*', *PMLA* 65 (1950), 1089–90
S. R. Maitland, 'D the Poet', *N & Q* 2nd ser. 2 (1856), 4–5
*Poems on Affairs of State*, ii (1965), 127–34, 360–3 (three political poems)
J. Yeowell, 'RD the Poet', *N & Q*, 3rd ser. 12 (1867), 21–2, 69

1. D was born 13 June 1658, the son of Richard Duke, a scrivener, and his second wife Anne Pierce. He inherited property in London and some books at his father's death in 1679 (Maitland, 'D the Poet', 4–5, and Yeowell, 'RD the Poet', 21). He was educated at Westminster (1670) and entered Trinity College, Cambridge, 25 June 1675; BA 1678/9, MA 1682, Fellow 1683. (Venn, *Alumni Cantab.*, incorrectly dates his Fellowship 1688: see **5** below.)

   Charles Lennox, Duke of Richmond (1672–1723), was the natural son of Charles II and the Duchess of Portsmouth. Pope later stated that, until his secret marriage to the Countess of Drogheda in 1679, William Wycherley the dramatist was to have been the Duke's tutor (Spence, i. 35). D may have replaced him at this time.

2. Swift described D in 1711 as 'one of the wits when we were children, but turned parson, and left it, and never writ further than a prologue or recommendatory copy of verses' (*Jnl. to Stella*, i. 192). D was friendly with Thomas Otway (q.v. above) and exchanged verse epistles with him: see Ham, *Otway*, 176–9, 204–5. For a time he belonged to a circle of younger poets associated with Dryden, contributing to such projects as *Ovid's Epistles, Translated by Several Hands* (1680) (see 'Dryden' **107** above), *Miscellany Poems* (1684), and *Examen Poeticum* (1693). He wrote commendatory verses for Thomas Creech's *Lucretius* (2nd edn., 1683) and Henry Dickinson's *Critical History of the Old Testament* (2nd edn., 1682), the ostensible occasion of Dryden's *Religio Laici*. D also contributed to Plutarch's *Lives* (1683) and translated 'Satire IV' in Dryden's *Juvenal* (1693) (see 'Dryden' **106–7, 140** above). SJ twice quotes this satire in the *Dict.* (under 'Fisherman' and 'Obsequiously'), but attributes it to Dryden.

   'The Review. Never before Printed', in which SJ finds 'some vigorous lines', appeared in *Poems By the Earl of Roscommon . . . Together with Poems By Mr. Richard*

*Duke* (1717), 323–40. According to the prefatory 'To the Reader' (sig. A2ᵛ), D wrote it 'a little after the publishing Mr. *Dryden's Absalom* and *Achitophel*; he was persuaded to undertake it by Mr. [Thomas] *Sheridan*, then Secretary to the Duke of *York*; but Mr. *Duke* finding Mr. *Sheridan* design'd to make use of his Pen to vent his Spleen against several Persons at Court that were of another Party, than that he was engaged in, broke off proceeding in it, and left it as it is now printed'. He had earlier published *Floriana. A Pastoral* (1681).

3–4. For the 'dissoluteness' of the Restoration wits, see 'Rochester' 4 and n. above.

3. D published separate sermons in 1703–4. His *Fifteen Sermons* (1714; 3rd edn., 1730) appeared posthumously. In his *Dissertation on Reading the Classics* (2nd edn., 1715), 212–13, Henry Felton praised D 'under the Double Capacity of a *Poet* and a *Divine*', especially for the '*Classic Learning*' and '*Christian Spirit*' of his sermons.

4. SJ suggested that Dryden's 'dissolute licentiousness' was similarly 'artificial and constrained' in 'Dryden' 170 above.

5. 'On the Marriage of George Prince of *Denmark* and the Lady Anne', by 'R. Duke, *Fellow of* Trin. Coll.' appeared in *Hymenaeus Cantabrigiensis* (1683), sigg. P1–2. According to Narcissus Luttrell, *Brief Historical Relation* (Oxford, 1857), i. 130, D had made a speech 'in English verse' at Trinity College before Charles II on 27 Sept. 1681. Luttrell noted erroneously on 18 Apr. 1693 (iii. 81): 'Mr. Duke, the poet, is made bishop of Man.'

6. D was ordained by 1685, Prebendary of Gloucester 1688–1711, and Rector of Blaby, Leics., 1688–1708. The title page of his *Sermons* describes him as Chaplain to Queen Anne.

7. D became Chaplain to Sir Jonathan Trelawney, Bishop of Winchester, in 1707 and, according to Luttrell, *Brief Historical Relation* (Oxford, 1857), vi. 332, obtained the living of Witney, Oxon., worth £700 p.a., in July 1708. (At vi. 690, Luttrell revised the figure to £500 p.a.)

SJ's reference to D's death after an 'entertainment' glosses over the facts supplied by Nichols: 'Returning home from liberal drinking on *Saturday* night, *Feb.* 10, he was found dead the next morning' (*Supplement to Swift*, ii. 467). Swift noted on 14 Feb. 1711 that 'Dr. Duke died suddenly two or three nights ago . . . He had a fine living given him by the bishop of Winchester about three months ago; he got his living suddenly, and he got his dying so too.' (Swift's 'three months' must be a mistake for 'three years'.) On 16 Feb. he noted that 'Atterbury and Prior went to bury poor Dr. Duke' (*Jnl. to Stella*, i. 191–3). Like D, they had both been at Westminster and Trinity College, Cambridge.

# WILLIAM KING (1663–1712)

**Composition.** SJ presumably wrote it in late 1778 or early 1779. It was printed at the same time as 'Pomfret' (*Bibliography*, ii. 1356).

**Sources.** Wood, ii. 1063, and Jacob, ii. 87–8, gave brief accounts of K. *GD*, vi. 529–30, and Shiels, *Lives*, did little more than summarize Dr Joseph Browne's memoir in K's *Remains* (1732) (reissued as *Posthumous Works* in 1734). Although much of SJ's information was available in Philip Nichols's article in *BB*, iv (1757), 2850–6, he was in fact

able, as Hart (1950), 1101–10, showed, to make use of the ampler and better documen-
ted 'Memoirs of Dr. King' in John Nichols's edition of his *Original Works in Verse and
Prose* (3 vols., 1776), i, pp. ix–xxix, with which Isaac Reed had assisted him. Nichols did
not hesitate to draw attention to this unacknowledged debt, by noting in his *Sel.
Collection*, iii. 3 n., that SJ had 'elegantly epitomized' his 'Memoirs' of K. Alexander
Chalmers's later comment that SJ made 'little use' of Nichols's account meant only that
SJ might have included even more detail from it (*J's Works* (1806), x. 35 n.). Nichols
had recycled some of his notes on K's poems in *Works* (1776) (signed 'N.') in *Eng. Poets*
(1779), vol. xx.

K is not to be confused with William King (1650–1729), Archbishop of Dublin (see
'Parnell' 3 and 'Swift' 36 and nn. below), or William King (1685–1763), Principal of St
Mary Hall, Oxford (see 'Dryden' 187 and n. above).

There were 108 quotations from K in the *Dict.* (1755), increased to 111 in 1773.

**Publication.** In *Prefaces*, vol. iv (31 Mar. 1779). There are no proofs.

**Modern Sources:**

J. Fuller, *Carving Trifles: WK's Imitation of Horace* (Chatterton Lecture, British
    Academy, 1976; repr. in *English Poets* (Oxford, 1988), 80–104)
E. L. Hart, 'Some New Sources of J's *Lives*', *PMLA* 65 (1950), 101–10
C. J. Horne, 'The Life and Works of Dr. WK of Christ Church' (B.Litt. thesis, Oxford,
    1940)
C. J. Horne, 'Dr. WK's *Miscellanies in Verse and Prose*', *Library*, 4th ser. 25 (1944), 37–
    45
C. J. Horne, 'The Phalaris Controversy: K *versus* Bentley', *RES* 22 (1946), 289–303
C. J. Horne, 'The Learned and Ingenious Dr. WK and *A Tale of a Tub*', in E. Maslen
    (ed.), *Comedy: Essays in Honour of Peter Dixon* (1993), 134–52
F. M. Keener, *English Dialogues of the Dead* (New York, 1973), 38–48
R. D. Lund, '*Rufinus* and the *Dunciad*: Pope's Debt to WK', *Papers in Lang. and Lit.* 20
    (1984), 293–300
R. D. Lund, ' "More Strange than True": Sir Hans Sloane, K's *Transactioneer*, and the
    Deformation of English Prose', *SEC* 14 (1985), 213–30

1. Edward Hyde, 3rd Earl of Clarendon (1661–1723), looked after K in his final illness
   and arranged his burial in Westminster Abbey (Nichols, *Original Works*, i, p. xxvi).
   For K's family connections, see also 9 n. below, and for a later reference to
   Clarendon, see 'Gay' 7 below.

2. K was a King's Scholar at Westminster, 1678: for Dr Busby, the school's notorious
   headmaster, see 'Dryden' 4 and n. above. He matriculated from Christ Church,
   Oxford, 26 Dec. 1681; BA 8 Dec. 1685; MA 6 July 1688. He continued using the
   privileges of his Studentship at Christ Church when visiting Oxford for the rest of
   his life.

   The account of K's remarkable reading derives ultimately from *Remains* (1732),
   16. Nichols, *Original Works*, i, p. xxvii, had taken it at face value, printing examples
   of K's notes on books (not all early) as 'Adversaria' (i. 223–80). For SJ's similar
   scepticism about Barretier's precocious childhood reading ('my Incredulity may,
   perhaps, be the Product rather of Prejudice than Reason, as Envy may beget a
   Disinclination to admit so immense a Superiority'), see *Early Biog. Writings* (1973),
   173; and for his doubts about 'rigid adherence to a particular plan of study', *Life*,

i. 428. Recommending arithmetic to Sophia Thrale, 24 July 1783, SJ wrote: 'A thousand stories which the ignorant tell, and believe, dye away at once, when the computist takes them in his gripe' (*Letters*, iv. 176).

A 'grand compounder' was a student of independent income who paid extra fees, usually to obtain privileges from the University, such as a more rapid degree. See Wood, ii (Fasti). 226, 231, and Deane Swift, *An Essay upon the Life of . . . Swift* (1755), 47 n.

3. K was assisted by Edward Hannes of Christ Church (see 'Smith' 14 and n. above) in *Reflections upon Mr. Varillas his History of Heresy* (1688), a response to Antoine Varillas's *Histoire des revolutions arivées dans l'Europe en matière de religion* (6 vols., Paris, 1686–9), which included an attack on John Wyclif. See also 'Dryden' 124 and n. above.

K became DCL on 7 July 1692, and, through John Tillotson, Archbishop of Canterbury, an advocate at Doctors' Commons, 12 Nov. 1692. This enabled him to plead in the Courts of Civil and Ecclesiastical Law.

4. Robert Molesworth (1656–1725), later Viscount Molesworth (1716), became envoy to Denmark in 1689 and criticized the Danish monarchy in his *Account of Denmark, As It was in the Year 1692* (1694). In 1724 Swift addressed the fifth of his *Drapier's Letters* to Molesworth, invoking him as as one of the dangerous writers for whom Liberty is a blessing and who propose 'a *new Set* of Principles in Government' (*Prose Writings*, x. 93–4).

*wild principles*: Joseph Towers, *Essay on SJ* (1786), objected to SJ's dismissive reference to the convictions of Algernon Sydney, Locke, and 'the best and ablest writers that have appeared upon the subject' of government (*Early Biographies* (1974), 211). For SJ's scepticism elsewhere about 'liberty', see 'Milton' 169 and n. above, and for 'subordination' 'Swift' 52 and n. below.

5. Prince George of Denmark was the consort of Princess (later Queen) Anne. Nichols, *Original Works*, i, p.xi, followed Wood, ii. 914, 1064, in stating that K became Princess Anne's secretary in Jan. 1694, but no more is known of this appointment, which may have been short-lived. In his preface to *Miscellanies* [1709], K stated that he wrote his *Animadversions on a Pretended Account of Danmark* (1694) at the request of the Revd Brink, minister of the Danish Church in London, basing it on a 'memorial' presented to William III by Edmund Scheel, the Danish envoy. There were German and Dutch editions of K's reply to Molesworth, and it was translated into French to enable the King of Denmark to read it.

6. For K's part in the quarrels of Francis Atterbury, Charles Boyle, later Earl of Orrery, and other Christ Church men, with Dr Richard Bentley over the genuineness of the 'Epistles of Phalaris' in the 1690s, see Horne, 'Phalaris', 289–303, and J. M. Levine, *The Battle of the Books* (Ithaca, NY, 1991), 102–5, and cf. 'Swift' 28 below. K's intervention in his *Dialogues of the Dead* (1699) provoked a further attack from Bentley: see *Works* (1776), i. 133–86. For K's contribution to the subgenre of 'Dialogues of the Dead', see Keener, *Dialogues*, 38–48.

Nichols and Bowyer had recently reissued Bentley's *Dissertation upon the Epistles of Phalaris* (1777). A reviewer in *Gent. Mag.* (1777), 35, commented on the original controversy that 'wit and judgment, as it often happens, were here at variance, each of them occasionally assisted by learning'. SJ's verdict is predictably more trenchant. Cf. *Rambler* 154 (1751): 'The laurels which superficial acuteness gains in triumphs over ignorance unsupported by vivacity, are observed by Locke to be lost whenever real learning and rational diligence appear against her' (*YW*, v. 56). SJ in fact 'thought very highly of Bentley; that no man now went so far in the kinds of learning that he cultivated; that the many attacks on him were owing to envy, and to a desire of being known, by being in competition with such a man' (*Life*, v. 174, and cf. 274).

7. K's *A Journey to London in the Year 1698* (1698) parodied *A Journey to Paris in 1698* (1698) by Dr Martin Lister (1638?–1712), a member of the Royal Society.

   *The Transactioneer, with Some of his Philosophical Fancies* (1700) satirized Hans Sloane (1660–1753), editor of the *Philosophical Transactions of the Royal Society* 1695–1713: see also **12** n. below, Lund, 'More Strange', 213–30, and *Sir Hans Sloane, Collector, Scientist, Antiquary, Founding Father of the British Museum*, ed. A. Macgregor (1994), 19–20, 39 n. As 'Scrutator' (John Loveday) noted in *Gent. Mag.* (1779), 595, Sloane became Secretary of the Royal Society in 1693, but did not succeed Newton as President until 1727. For the Royal Society, see 'Cowley' **31** and n. above. SJ ignores K's early mock-heroic exercise, *The Furmetary. A Very Innocent and Harmless Poem* (1699).

8. Jacob, ii. 87, stated of K that 'the natural Gaity of his Temper, and the Love of Company led him too much into those Pleasures and Freedoms that are inconsistent with the Practise of a Profession'. Although SJ is already making K's 'poverty, his idleness, and his wit' (**12**) a prominent theme, Horne, 'Life', 26–7 and 47, showed that K worked seriously as an Advocate of Doctors' Commons between 1694 and 1700, and suggested that 'voluptuary dreams' and 'indulgence' came later in his career. Nichols explained that 'All appeals from the Ecclesiastical and Admiralty Courts are . . . determined by a Court of Delegates, consisting of three Common Law Judges, and five Civilians', and claimed that K 'made an excellent Judge . . . as often as he was called to that Bench' (*Works* (1776), i, p. xiv and n.).

   Lady Katherine Darnley, natural daughter of James II and later Duchess of Buckinghamshire (see 'Sheffield' **20** below), in fact won her case against James, Earl of Anglesey, on 12 June 1701, after a marriage of less than two years. (For SJ's date see Nichols, *Original Works*, i, pp. xv–xvii.) This notorious case involved the unusual intervention of Parliament in a marital dispute about cruelty and maintenance, in spite of the Earl's claims of privilege as a peer: see L. Stone, *Road to Divorce: England 1530–1987* (Oxford, 1990), 317–18.

9. Horne, 'Life', 5, 104, noted that, at the time of K's appointment, the Lord-Lieutenant of Ireland was Laurence Hyde, Earl of Rochester (1642–1711), a member of the Hyde family to which K was distantly related (cf. **1** above). K was in Ireland by 13 Nov. 1701 as Judge of the High Court of Admiralty. He subsequently became Commissioner of the Prizes, Keeper of the Records in Dublin Castle (cf. 'Addison' **29** below), and Vicar-General to Archbishop Narcissus Marsh.

10. Mountown or Monkstown, south of Dublin, was the country villa of Anthony Upton, Justice of the Common Pleas of Ireland 1702–14, who committed suicide in 1718.

11. *Mully of Mountown. A Poem* (1704), a celebration of an amiable cow, was reprinted in *A New Collection of Poems Relating to State Affairs* (1705), 584–7, and *Poems*

*on Affairs of State*, iv (1707), 38–41. In the preface to his *Miscellanies* [1709], K claimed that, although *Mully* 'was taken for a State Poem, and to have many Mysteries in it', he wrote it only 'for a Country Diversion'. SJ follows Nichols, *Original Works*, i, p. xix: 'the Critics would have imposed [*Mully*] upon the world for a *political allegory*', when it was 'no more than a grateful expression of the happiness he felt in his sequestered situation, buried alive, as it were, with his beloved Mully.' For a time Swift's *A Tale of a Tub* (1704) was attributed to K, who disowned it as profane and coarse in *Some Remarks on the Tale of a Tub* (1704): see Horne, 'Life', 115.

12. For the Earl of Wharton as Lord-Lieutenant of Ireland from Dec. 1708, see 'Addison' **29** below. K had in fact probably returned to England by late 1707, applying himself thereafter to writing rather than the law.

   *Useful Transactions in Philosophy and other Sorts of Learning* (3 pts., Feb.–Sept. 1709), Pt. III, included 'A Voyage to the Island of Cajamai in America', a satire on Hans Sloane's *Voyage to Jamaica* (1707) (see *Original Works*, ii. 132–78). For the possible influence of K's satirical works on the 'Scriblerian' writings of Swift, Pope, and others, see J. M. Levine, *Dr. Woodward's Shield* (Berkeley, 1977), 247–50. In *The Present State of Wit* (1711) John Gay said of the *Useful Transactions* that, although K 'has a World of Wit, yet as it lies in one particular way of Raillery, the Town soon grew weary of his Writings'. Gay's assertion that K was later confined in the Fleet Prison for debt is unconfirmed: see *Poetry and Prose*, ed. V. A. Dearing (Oxford, 1974), ii. 449.

   SJ also refers to *The Art of Love* (1707) and *The Art of Cookery* (1708), the latter alluding to Martin Lister's recent edition (1705) of *De Opsoniis et Condimentis* by Epicius Coelius ('The Soups and Sauces of the Ancients'). SJ ignores K's *Miscellanies in Prose and Verse* [1709].

13. For Henry Sacheverell's trial in 1710, see 'Dryden' **109** above and 'Addison' **14** and n. below, and, for another 'lover of the Church' in this crisis, 'Sprat' **17** below. K's *Vindication of Dr. Sacheverell* (1710), probably a collaboration with Charles Lambe, replied to William Bisset's *A Modern Fanatick* (1710): see *Works* (1776), ii. 179–279.

   K probably wrote only Nos. 11 and 12 of the Tory *Examiner* before Swift took over in Nov. 1710: see 'Prior' **22** and 'Swift' **39** and n. below, and *Swift vs. Manwaring*, ed. F. H. Ellis (Oxford, 1985), pp. xxv, 253–4 n. For K's 'strictures' on the 'adulatory sermon' delivered at the funeral of the profligate Duke of Devonshire in 1708 by the Whig cleric White Kennett (1660–1728), later Bishop of Peterborough, see *Works* (1776), iii. 37–40, and cf. Pope, *Imit. Horace, Ep. II. ii* (1737), ll. 220–3. For Kennett, see also 'Pope' **107** below.

14. Bernard Lintot paid K £50 for *An Historical Account of the Heathen Gods and Heroes* (1711), the largest sum he received for a literary work between 1708 and 1712 (Nichols, *Lit. Anec.*, viii. 297). It remained in use as a schoolbook to the end of the century. SJ is more positive elsewhere about such 'condescensions of learning': see 'Milton' **106** and n. For SJ's own projected 'History of the Heathen Mythology ... with references to the poets', see *Life*, iv. 381 n.

   *Rufinus, or an Historical Essay on the Favourite Ministry* (1712), with *Rufinus, or The Favourite. Imitated from Claudian* annexed, is an attack on Marlborough.

15. The *Gazette* was the official government newspaper. SJ's definition of 'Gazetteer' in the *Dict.* ('2. It was lately a term of the utmost infamy, being usually applied to wretches who were hired to vindicate the court') no doubt alluded to Walpole's use of the *Daily Gazetteer* from 1735 as his 'sole propaganda organ' (B. Goldgar, *Walpole and the Wits* (Lincoln, Nebr., 1976), 134). SJ revised the definition in 1773 to 'An officer appointed to publish news by authority, whom *Steele* calls the lowest minister of state'.

Richard Steele was Gazetteer between Apr. or May 1707 and Oct. 1710, under Lord Sunderland, Secretary of State for the Southern Department, at £300 p.a. (Steele, *Corresp.* (1941), 21–4 and nn.). Swift wrote on 31 Dec. 1711: 'I have settled Dr. King in the *Gazette*; it will be worth two hundred pounds a year to him . . . I shall know to-morrow, when I am to carry Dr. King to dine with the secretary [Boling-broke]' (*Jnl. to Stella*, ii. 452; see also ii. 543, for the duties and perquisites of 'the prettyest Employmt in Engd of its bigness'). On 8 Jan. 1712 he described the post as worth £250 p.a. (*Corresp.*, i. 286). SJ also refers to Dr John Freind (1675–1728), physician and politician, one of Bentley's Christ Church opponents in the Phalaris controversy (see **6** above), and Matthew Prior (q.v. below).

Thomas Hearne wrote after K's death: 'About a Year since he was Gazeteer; but he did not hold it above two Months, being extremely negligent in yt Affair' (see **18** n. below). The Act of Insolvency of 1712 meant that the names of thousands of discharged prisoners had to be advertised in the *Gazette*, and the unexpectedly laborious post involved correcting proofs in the small hours of the morning. K had resigned and been replaced by 1 July 1712 (Nichols, *Original Works*, i, pp. xxiv–xxv, from *Remains* (1732), 162; Swift, *Jnl. to Stella*, ii. 543).

16. From 1712 K lived with a friend between Lambeth and Vauxhall (Nichols, *Original Works*, i, p. xxv), near Lambeth Palace, the residence of Thomas Tension (1636–1715), the Archbishop of Canterbury, described by Swift as 'the most good for nothing Prelate I ever knew' (*Prose Writings*, v. 260, 271). The Whig Archbishop would not have shared K's pleasure at the 'surrender' of Dunkirk to Major-General John Hill on 8 July 1712, as part of the preliminaries to the Peace of Utrecht. For disagreements with the French over Dunkirk, see P. Hyland, 'A Breach of the Peace: The Controversy over the Ninth Article of the Treaty of Utrecht', *BJECS* 22 (1999), 51–66.

SJ's source for K's 'honest merriment' is *Works* (1776), i, p. xxv, which related from *Remains* (1732), 164, that K 'invited the watermen and his poor neighbours of Lambeth in general to partake of some barrels of ale, at a house near his little cot . . . in honour of his Queen and Country', and that the company 'returned to their respective homes, neither mad, drunk, nor disappointed'. In Nov. 1716 Pope reported Lintot's claim that 'Dr. King would write verses in a tavern three hours after he couldn't speak' (*Corresp.*, i. 373).

17. K died on 25 Dec. 1712 and was buried two days later in Westminster Abbey without a monument: see John Dart, *Westmonasterium* [1742], ii. 139. Memorial poems included 'Upon the late Learned and Ingenious Dr. William King' in *The Poetical Entertainer*, 4 (1713), 17–23, and William Oldisworth, *A Pindarick Ode, to the Memory of Dr. William King* (1713) (Foxon, *English Verse*, O 156).

Nichols, *Original Works*, i, pp. xxvi–xxviii, and all earlier accounts, follow *Remains* (1732), 165, in emphasizing K's pure principles and pious death, in spite

of his irregular habits: he died 'with all the Patience and Resignation of a Philosopher, and the true Devotion of a Christian Hero'. For others who preserved their
'principles' in spite of their irregularities, see 'Smith' **74** and n. above.

18. For contrasts of the 'diverting' and the 'astonishing', see 'Milton' **276** and n. above;
for 'sublimity', see 'Cowley' **58** and n. above; for the 'familiar', see 'Cowley' **138**
and n. above; and for other writers who aspired to be 'merry', see 'Denham' **22** and
n. above.

   Horace Walpole misleadingly reported to Mason, 19 Feb. 1781, that SJ admired
'that wretched buffoon Dr. King, who is but a Tom Brown in rhyme' (*Corresp.*,
xxix. 110–11). SJ does not in fact allow any sympathy he may have felt for K's
spirited anti-Whiggism (see **4, 13, 16** above) to affect his literary judgement. With
his obvious disapproval of K's 'voluptuary dreams' and 'indulgence' (**8**), 'neglect of
business' (**9**), and 'idle and thoughtless' character (**10**), cf. Hearne's description of
K in 1712 as 'a Man of excellent Natural Parts, wch he imploy'd in writing little,
trivial Things, to his dying Day . . . he was so addicted to ye Buffooning way, that he
neglected his proper Business, grew very poor, & so dyed in a sort of contemptible
manner' (*Remarks and Collections*, ed. C. E. Doble, iv (1898), 44).

   K's prose and verse can be more inventive and amusing than SJ suggests.
Nichols praised K's 'peculiar vein of humour and exquisite raillery' in his *Supplement to Swift* (1779), i. 144 n., and Chalmers agreed: 'His talent for humour ought
to be praised in the highest terms. In that at least he yielded to none of his
contemporaries' (*J's Works* (1806), x. 35 n.).


# THOMAS SPRAT (1635–1713)

**Composition.** SJ does not refer to 'Sprat', but probably wrote it in late 1778 or early
1779.

**Sources.** Almost all SJ's information was available in Philip Morant's article in *BB*,
vi (i) (1763), 3814–20, which drew on Wood, ii. 1096–8, and *Some Account of the Life and
Writings of . . . Thomas Sprat* (1715). The notes to **13–17** below confirm his dependence
on *BB* rather than *GD*, ix (1739), 379–82. He appears to have made no use of Jacob, ii.
194–5, or Shiels, *Lives*, iii. 236–42. In **18–19** SJ draws on his father's memories.

   There are some 185 quotations from S's prose (only) in *Dict.* (1755), increased to 187
in 1773.

**Publication.** In *Prefaces*, vol. iv (31 Mar. 1779). The complete proofs are in the
Forster Collection.

**Modern Sources:**
J. I. Cope and H. W. Jones (eds.), TS's *History of the Royal Society* (St Louis, 1958)
H. W. Jones, 'TS (1635–1713)', *N & Q* 197 (1952), 10–14, 118–23
H. W. Jones and A. Whitworth, *TS: A Check List of his Works* (1952)

   1. S was in fact born at Beaminster, Dorset, in 1635 (Jones and Whitworth, *TS*,
   11–12). His father, also Thomas, later moved to Talaton near Exeter. S's will
   (1711) referred to his 'obscure Birth, and Education, in a far distant Country,

where I was the Son of a private Minister' (*Life* (1715), 8), but not to Eton and Westminster, whose products dominated the ecclesiastical hierarchy. This may have been a later elaboration by Warburton, *Works of Pope* (1751), iv. 160 n. S's son Thomas (d. 1720) was educated at Westminster (Jones and Whitworth, *TS*, 13). S matriculated from Wadham College, Oxford, on 12 Nov. 1652; Scholar 25 Sept. 1652, BA 1655, MA 1657, Fellow of Wadham 1657–70, BD and DD 1669.

2. For *Three Poems upon the Death of his Late Highnesse Oliver, Lord Protector* (1659), see 'Waller' **67** and 'Dryden' **7** above. SJ quotes S's poem in **22** below. The collection's title may explain SJ's unusual reference to Cromwell as 'Oliver'.

   The passages quoted by SJ (with such variants as 'sublime' for 'lofty' and 'equal and proportioned' for 'proportion'd and equall') from S's dedication of his ode to John Wilkins (1614–72), Warden of Wadham, had appeared in *BB*. The 'excellent poet' was Cowley: for his Pindaric 'way of writing', see **3**, **22** below, and 'Cowley' **143** and n. above. SJ shows restraint, in view of S's later association with the Stuart court, in leaving S's flattery of Cromwell to speak for itself. For SJ's interest in John Wilkins, see *Letters*, iv. 176 and 273 n.: the 209 quotations from his prose works in the *Dict.* were increased to 304 in 1773.

3. S stated that *The Plague of Athens* (1659) was 'attempted in English after the incomparable Dr. Cowley's Pindarick Way'. He did not in fact write specifically on Cowley's death, but 'Upon the Poems of Abraham Cowley, in Imitation of his own Pindarick Odes', in Cowley's *Works* (1668).

4. S became Prebendary of Carlton-cum-Thurlby, Lincs., on 20 Oct. 1660, perhaps while still a deacon, since he was apparently not ordained until 10 Mar. 1661 (Jones and Whitworth, *TS*, 119). He did not become a Chaplain to Charles II until Aug. 1676.

   For S's collaboration on the Duke of Buckingham's *The Rehearsal* (1671), work on which began as early as 1664, see 'Dryden' **94** and n. above, and for S and Buckingham at a later period, 'Butler' **13–14** n. above. SJ's obvious sources seem not to mention 'Cowley's recommendation', but Oldys stated, in his annotated Langbaine, *Account of the English Dramatick Poets* (Oxford, 1691), iv, opp. p. 546 (see 'Cowley' **17–20** n. above), that Cowley and Martin Clifford recommended S to Buckingham, 'their old acquaintance'. Steevens, Percy, or Malone could have pointed this out to SJ.

5. For Wilkins, see **2** above. For the Royal Society, of which S became a Fellow in 1663, see also 'Cowley' **31** and n. above. His *History of the Royal-Society of London* (1667) included Cowley's prefatory poem 'To the Royal Society'. For SJ's recommendation of S's *History* to a student, see *Life*, iv. 311.

   *flux* (adjective): 'Unconstant; not durable; maintained by a constant succession of parts' (*Dict.*).

6. Wood, ii. 1097, described Samuel Sorbière's *Relation d'un voyage en Angleterre* (Paris, 1664) as 'an insolent Libel on our Nation'. S addressed his *Observations on Monsieur de Sorbier's Voyage into England* (1665) to Christopher Wren. His defence of English drama against Sorbière's criticism of its irregularities anticipated Dryden's *Of Dramatick Poesie* (1668) (see 'Dryden' **27** above). Addison in *The Freeholder* 30 (2 Apr. 1716) praised the *Observations* for 'just Satyr and Ingenuity'.

7. In his will Cowley, who died in 1667, asked S to edit his *Works* (see 'Cowley' 1, **46** above). S's edition (1668) included his admired prefatory biography, of which a shorter Latin version appeared in Cowley's *Poemata Latina* (1668).

8. S became Prebendary of Westminster 1668 and Cannon 1669; Rector of Uffington, Lincs., 1670 (presented by the Duke of Buckingham); Curate and Lecturer of St Margaret's, Westminster, 1679; Canon of Windsor 1680; Dean of Westminster 1683 (see 'Milton' **156** and 'J. Philips' **8** above); and Bishop of Rochester 1684.

Like his sources, SJ ignores S's marriage in 1676 to Helen, Lady Wolseley (d. 1726), of Ravenstone, Staffs.

9. The alleged Rye House Plot of June 1683 against the King and James, Duke of York, led to the execution on dubious evidence of, among others, Lord William Russell and Algernon Sidney, who subsequently became celebrated Whig 'martyrs'.

In his *Second Letter to the Earl of Dorset* (1689) (see **11** n. below), S claimed that Charles II had commanded him to write the *True Account* in condemnation of the supposed conspirators, admitted Russell's 'great probity', and apologized for what *BB*, vi (i). 3817 n., described as 'a most odious task', which exposed S to 'the *Resentment* of persons of great titles and high stations, and indeed of the bulk of the nation'.

SJ has added the second '*present*' to the title of the *True Account*.

10. *BB*, vi (i). 3817 n. corrected the statement in *GD*, ix. 380, that S became Dean of the Chapel-Royal. SJ was probably misled by Wood, ii. 1096, who dated the supposed appointment 29 Dec. 1685, rather than by *GD*. S instead became Clerk of the Closet at this time.

S was appointed to James II's Commission for Ecclesiastical Affairs in 1686, 'for which he incurr'd the censure of many good Men, that were accounted true Sons of the Church of *England*' (Wood, ii. 1096). Evelyn stated that the Commission 'had not only faculty to Inspect + Visite all Bishops diocesses, but to change what lawes + statutes they shold think fit to alter, among the Colledges; to punish fine + give Oathes, call witnesses, but the main drift was to suppresse zealous preachers &c' (14 July 1686; *Diary* (1955), iv. 519–20). For another member of the Commission, appointed 'without knowledge . . . of its illegality', see 'Sheffield' **13** below.

On 20 May 1688 ('the critical day') S allowed James II's Declaration of Indulgence suspending the penal laws and Test Acts against Roman Catholics to be read in Westminster Abbey, although it was 'almost universaly forborne throughout all London' (Evelyn, *Diary*, iv. 584). According to William Legge, later Earl of Dartmouth, S could hardly 'hold the proclamation in his hands for trembling' (*DNB*). Henry Compton (1632–1713), Bishop of London, already disciplined by the Ecclesiastical Commission in 1686, was one of the seven bishops prosecuted by James II for petitioning against the Declaration.

11. As in **10** above, SJ's narrative compresses S's two self-exculpatory letters to the Earl of Dorset (1688–9), reprinted as *Two Letters . . . to . . . the late Earl of Dorset* (1711), and quoted at length in *BB*.

12. S at first opposed the resolution declaring the throne vacant after the departure of James II. SJ's 'manfully' conveys some sympathy with S's dilemma. Cf. 'Halifax' **5** and n., 'Sheffield' **15**, and 'Granville' **6–7** below.

**13–16.** SJ's account is based on S's *A Relation of the Late Wicked Contrivance of Stephen Blackhead and Robert Young, against the Lives of Several Persons* (2 pts., 1692–3), quoted at length by *BB*, but dealt with in a single sentence by *GD*, ix. 381. Together with Archbishop Sancroft and the earls of Marlborough and Salisbury, S was implicated as a Jacobite conspirator, arrested on 7 May, and released on 13 June 1692. As S's *Relation* revealed, Robert Young (1656?–1700) had had a notable career as an impostor and forger since the 1670s.

**13.** S 'complied... with the new establishment' to the extent of assisting at the coronation of William III and Mary in Apr. 1689. Abel Boyer, *History of Queen Anne* (1735), ii. 60, later wrote that S 'bore a dubious Character as to his Principles in Divinity and Politicks, being said to accommodate one to the other, and both to the Times and Persons in Power'.

The *Dict.* does not include the precise meaning of 'Association' here: 'A document setting forth the common purpose of a number of persons, and signed by them as a pledge that they will carry it into execution' (*OED*).

**17.** For Henry Sacheverell, see 'King' 13 above, and 'Halifax' 10 and 'Addison' 14 n. below. S voted 'honestly' (i.e. as a Tory and High Churchman) for Sacheverell at his trial in 1710.

*seventy-ninth year*: derived from *BB*, whereas *GD* has 'seventy-seventh'. For S's monument in Westminster Abbey, with a translation of the Latin inscription, see John Dart, *Westmonasterium* [1742], i. 144 and plate.

**18.** Cf. Burnet, *History* ii (1734), 629, as quoted by *BB*, vi (i). 3820 n.: 'his Parts were very bright in his Youth, and gave great Hopes; but these were blasted by a lazy libertine Course of Life, to which his Temper and Good Nature carried him, without considering the Duties or even the Decencies of his Profession.'

Evelyn heard 'an incomparable sermon' by 'that greate *Wit* Dr. *Sprat*' in St Paul's on 23 Nov. 1679: 'his talent was, a great memorie, never making use of notes, a readinesse of Expression, in a most pure and plaine style, for words & full of matter, easily delivered' (*Diary*, iv. 188).

**19.** SJ originally attributed the anecdote about the preachers only to 'an old man'. In 1783 he identified him as his own father, Michael Johnson (1656–1731), bookseller of Lichfield (see Textual Notes). Speculation in *Gent. Mag.* (1779), 453 n. that the 'old man' was Gilbert Walmesley (see 'Smith' 71–6 and n. above) may have prompted him to do so. For an earlier reference to his father, see 'Dryden' 109 and n. above.

**20.** SJ cites Thomas Salmon, *An Impartial Examination of Bishop Burnet's History of his Own Times* (1724), ii. 852. The sermons were preached before the Commons on 22 Dec. 1680, a fast day. On 26 Dec. S became Prebendary and, on 27 Dec., Canon, of the Chapel-Royal, Windsor (Jones, 'TS', 120).

**21.** S collected his *Sermons* in 1697. For the other works, see 5, 6–7, 9, 15 above.

*I have heard it observed*: Malone noted that this 'observation' was made to SJ 'by the right hon. Wm. Gerard Hamilton [1729–96], as he told me, at Tunbridge, August, 1792' (*J.'s Works* (1825), vii. 392 n.). SJ earlier described S in 'Cowley' 1 above as 'an author whose pregnancy of imagination and elegance of language have deservedly set him high in the ranks of literature'.

In a brief account of S in *Lives of the Most Famous English Poets* (1687), 217, William Winstanley praised 'the Smoothness of the Stile, and exactness of the Method' in his *History of the Royal-Society* rather than his verse, referring to 'a very applauded, tho little Poem, entitled *The Plague of Athens*'. Henry Felton, *Dissertation on Reading the Classics* (2nd edn., 1715), 210–12, described S as 'the correctest Writer of the Age', and Wood, ii. 1096–7, as 'an excellent Poet, Orator, and one who hath arrived to a great Mastery of the English Language'. In 1744 Pope listed S among the prose authorities for a projected English dictionary (Spence, i. 170). Lord Orrery, *Remarks on . . . Swift* (1752), 152–3, later questioned S's reputation for 'elegance and correctness', and Hawkins, discussing SJ's attitude to 17th-century prose writers, claimed that in fact 'the tinsel of Sprat disgusted him' (*Life* (1787), 271).

22. For similar statements by SJ that his primary concern was with the poet and his poetry, see 'Halifax' **1**, 'Prior' **28**, and 'Akenside' **15** below.

   For S's admiration for Cowley see **2** above, and for SJ's hostility to 'Pindarick liberty', 'Cowley' **143** and n. above. According to Wood, ii. 1097, S was known as '*Pindarick Sprat*'. Pope described him in 1736 as 'a worse Cowley' (Spence, i. 193). For 'conceits' elsewhere, see 'Cowley' **58** and n. above. SJ paraphrases S's 'To the Happy Memory of the Late Lord Protector', ll. 4–5 (also quoted in *BB*, vi (i). 3814 n.): 'Thy fame, like men, the elder it doth grow, | Will of itself turn whiter too' ('whiter' meaning 'more auspicious').


## CHARLES MONTAGU, EARL OF HALIFAX (1661–1715)

**Composition.** SJ does not refer to 'Halifax', but probably wrote it in late 1778 or early 1779. It was printed together with 'Dorset', 'Stepney' (q.v.), and 'Walsh'.

**Sources.** SJ's account compresses the heavily annotated article by Philip Nichols in *BB*, v (1760), 3149–57, which made use of the prefatory memoir in *The Works and Life of the Right Honourable Charles, Late Earl of Halifax* (1715), probably by William Pittis (see P. Rogers, 'Two Notes on John Oldmixon', *N & Q* 215 (1970), 298–9). There had been brief earlier accounts of H in Jacob, ii. 109–14, *GD*, vii. 629–31 (less detailed than *BB*), and Shiels, *Lives*, iii. 243–7.

   There are nine quotations from H in the *Dict.* (1755), increased to ten in 1773.

**Publication.** In *Prefaces*, vol. iv (31 Mar. 1779). Pp. 1–6 (of 12) of the proofs are in the Forster Collection.

**Modern Sources:**
G. L. Anderson, 'Lord H in Gildon's *New Rehearsal*', *PQ* 33 (1954), 423–6
B. D. Henning (ed.), *The House of Commons 1660–1690* (1983), iii. 81–2, and E. Cruickshanks, S. Handley, and D. W. Hayton (eds.), *1690–1715* (2002), iv. 850–80
H. M. Hooker, 'Charles Montagu's Reply to *The Hind and the Panther*', *ELH* 8 (1941), 51–73
D. Hopkins, 'Charles Montagu, George Stepney, and Dryden's *Metamorphoses*', *RES* 51 (2000), 83–9
J. D. Kern, 'An Unpublished MS. of Charles Montagu, Earl of H', *JEGP* 32 (1933), 66–9
*Poems on Affairs of State*, iv (1968), 116–45, 152, 159–63, 233–4

1. SJ is reacting to *BB*'s inevitable emphasis on H's political career: cf. 'Sprat' 22 and n. above.

   *in this collection*: in *Lives* (1781) SJ's original references to *Eng. Poets* (1779) as 'this collection' were revised to 'the late collection' or a similar formulation. This case may have been overlooked, or revision struck SJ or Nichols as more complicated than usual.

2. H was the son of George Montagu of Horton (*c*.1622–1681) and grandson of Sir Henry Montagu, 1st Earl of Manchester (*c*.1563–1642). He was baptized 12 May 1661 at St Margaret's, Westminster, and entered Westminster School in 1675. For Dr Busby see 'Dryden' 4 n. above.

   The 'extemporary epigrams', and the inaccurate details of H's relationship with George Stepney, derive from *BB*, following *Life* (1715), 4–5. Stepney entered Trinity College, Cambridge, in 1682 (see 'Stepney' 1 above), but H had in fact preceded him on 8 Nov. 1679; MA 1682, Fellow 1683–8.

3. H was in fact 18 when he entered Trinity (see 2 n. above).

4. H's cousin Dr John Montagu was Master of Trinity College 1683–1700. SJ defines 'Fellow-Commoner' as '2. A commoner at Cambridge of the higher order, who dines with the fellows' (*Dict.*).

   *BB* related that Isaac Newton and H planned to form a philosophical society at Cambridge, and noted that H left Newton £100 in his will. The fact that H also left £5,000 and the lifetime use of a valuable estate to Newton's niece Catherine Barton prompted speculation about their relationship, as in Mrs Manley's *Memoirs of Europe* (1710), 252, 268. Swift referred to her regularly in *Jnl. to Stella* in 1710–11. Through H, Newton became Warden of the Mint in 1696. In 1717 she married John Conduitt, his successor as Warden. See R. S. Westfall, *Never at Rest: A Biography of Sir Isaac Newton* (Cambridge, 1980), 596–601.

5. Like Stepney, H contributed to *Hymenaeus Cantabrigiensis* (1683) on the marriage of Princess Anne, and *Moestissimae ac Laetissimae Academiae Cantabrigiensis affectus* (1685) on the death of Charles II. For the Earl of Dorset as 'universal patron', see 'Dorset' 13 and n. above.

   For *The Hind and the Panther Transvers'd to the Story of the Country-Mouse and the City-Mouse* (1687), see 'Dryden' 127, 288 above and 'Prior' 5 below. In spite of early scepticism about the extent of H's contribution (see Spence, i. 279 n., 330), it is likely that H wrote the preface and Prior the verse, and that they collaborated on the remaining prose content (Prior, *Lit. Works*, ii. 831–4). For another reply to Dryden by H, see Hooker, 'Reply'. H was later satirized in an elaboration of his own joke, *The Mouse Grown A Rat: or The Story of the City and Country Mouse newly Transpros'd* (1702), an attack on his political career and financial policies sometimes attributed to John Tutchin.

   The convention to declare the throne vacant after the flight of James II met in Jan. 1689 (cf. 'Sprat' 12 above). H had married Anne, widow of Robert Montagu, 3rd Earl of Manchester, in 1688. Described by some sources as a sexagenarian with a jointure of £1,500, she died in 1698 (Cokayne, viii. 372; Henning (ed.), *House of Commons*, iii. 81; *POAS*, iv. 229 n.). H was a Clerk of the Privy Council 1689–92.

6. SJ refers to H's *An Epistle to the Earl of Dorset Occasion'd by his Majesty's Victory in Ireland* (1690).

The anecdote in *BB* about William III derives from *Life* (1715), 17, and turns on the proverbial expression 'man or mouse' (cf. 'today a man, tomorrow a mouse') (F. P. Wilson (ed.), *Oxford Dictionary of Proverbs* (3rd edn., Oxford, 1970), 506, 827). The King spoke both Dutch and French and, in spite of SJ's doubts about his knowledge of English idiom, had been well grounded in English from childhood, as Lord Hailes noted *c.*1782: see Carnie (1956), 175, and N. A. Robb, *William of Orange*, i (1962), 79, 86, 126.

7. H was MP for Maldon 1689, 1690, and for Westminster 1695, 1698–1700.

SJ paraphrases the anecdote about H's speech in *BB*, which derived from *Life* (1715), 30. From as early as 1703 it was in fact repeatedly, and more convincingly, told of Anthony Ashley, 3rd Earl of Shaftesbury (1671–1713), in a parliamentary debate in Nov. 1695: see Abel Boyer, *The History of William III* (3 vols., 1702–3), iii. 117, and *GD*, ix. 179. This was pointed out by Lord Hailes *c.*1782 (see Carnie (1956), 175), Joseph Towers, *Essay on SJ* (1786) (*Early Biographies* (1974), 211), Hawkins, *J's Works* (1787), iii. 14 n., and Reed in *Lives*, ii (1790), 286 n. It was also related of Shaftesbury by his own son: see R. A. Voitle, *The Third Earl of Shaftesbury* (Baton Rouge, La., 1984), 74–5.

8–10. In *Prefaces* (1779), vol. iv, sig. c1 (pp. 7–8; from the end of **8** to the beginning of **10**) is a cancel (not noted by Fleeman, *Bibliography*, i. 1355–6). No uncancelled state of the leaf appears to have survived.

8. H was one of the Lords of the Treasury 1692–4, Privy Counsellor 1694–1702, and Chancellor of the Exchequer 1694–9. As Chancellor, H undertook a recoinage in Feb. 1694 after a collapse of confidence in silver coins due to counterfeiters and clippers. The Bank of England was also incorporated in 1694: H issued the first exchequer bills and formed a consolidated fund to meet the interest on government loans.

The vote commending H occurred on 16 Feb. 1698. He became First Lord of the Treasury 1697–9, one of the Lord Justices (or Regents) in July–Dec. 1698 and June–Oct. 1699, and Auditor of the Exchequer 1699–1714, a post worth some £4,000 a year. He received a peerage in Dec. 1700. On 14 Apr. 1701 he was impeached for obtaining grants for the King in the name of others and for his share in the Second Partition Treaty (see 'Prior' **16** and 'Swift' **25** n. below), but the House of Lords dismissed the resolution on 24 June 1701.

9. H was one of the Whig leaders dismissed from the Privy Council on 21 Apr. 1702. Although he was accused in the House of Commons on 19 Jan. 1703 of neglect of his duties as Auditor of the Exchequer, the Lords again protected him (5 Feb. 1703).

H successfully moved the rejection in the Lords of the Occasional Conformity Bill in Dec. 1703, and published *An Answer to Mr. B———'s Speech* (1704), in reply to William Bromley, a supporter of the bill, which was intended to prevent nonconformists qualifying as officeholders by taking communion in an Anglican church. A modified version of the bill was passed in 1711 (see 'Granville' **18** n. below). H headed the Enquiry into the danger of the Church 1705, and was a Commissioner for the Union of Scotland 1706–7.

In June 1706 H was appointed a special envoy to convey the insignia of the Order of the Garter to the Elector of Hanover (the future George I), when he was accompanied by Joseph Addison (see 'Addison' **26** below). For the trial of Henry

Sacheverell before the House of Lords in Mar. 1710, see 'Addison' 14 and n. below, and G. Holmes, *The Trial of Doctor Sacheverell* (1973). The writ for summoning the Electoral Prince (the future George II), obtained in Apr. 1714, was opposed by Queen Anne.

10. After the Queen's death, H was one of the Lord Justices of the Realm, 1 Aug.–18 Sept. 1714. In Oct. 1714 he became Earl of Halifax, and once more First Lord of the Treasury and a Privy Counsellor.

His nephew George Montagu inherited the title at H's death from pneumonia on 19 May 1715. For H's monument in Westminster Abbey, with a translation of the Latin inscription, see John Dart, *Westmonasterium* [1742], i. 174–5 and plate. For SJ's comments elsewhere on defeated expectations of happiness, see 'Denham' 19 and n. above.

11–15. SJ's definition of 'Patron' in the *Dict.* is well known: '1. One who countenances, supports, or protects. Commonly a wretch who supports with insolence, and is paid with flattery.' Equally familiar is his letter to his own 'patron' Lord Chesterfield, 7 Feb. 1755 (*Letters*, i. 94–7, and cf. i. 203–4). In the same year he substituted 'patron' for 'garret' in *The Vanity of Human Wishes*, l. 160, on the pains of the scholarly life ('Toil, Envy, Want, the Patron, and the Jail'). Less familiar are the attitudes to patronage reflected in his quotations under other words in the *Dict.*: see DeMaria (1986), 211–14. For SJ's views on patronage in his essays (usually hostile, though occasionally sympathetic to the patron's dilemmas), see *Ramblers* 21, 27, 91, 104–5, 136, 160, 163, 166, 190, 193, *Adventurer* 61, *Idlers* 14, 55, 102. For the perversions and dangers of the patronage system, see J. Leed, 'Patronage in the Rambler', *Studies in Burke and his Time*, 14 (1972–3), 5–21.

In conversation on 19 Aug. 1773, SJ said: 'We have done with patronage . . . With patronage, what flattery! what falsehood! . . . [the author] must say what pleases his patron, and it is an equal chance whether that be truth or falsehood' (*Life*, v. 59). He would have no doubt have shared the view of his friend Charles Burney, the historian of music: 'If a work has real merit, the PUBLIC does more for it, by enabling the booksellers to give a price for the copy-right, than, in times when a Mecaenas could be found, any author could ever expect from *individual patronage*' (*Monthly Review*, NS 28 (1799), 225–7).

For the argument that, in practice, SJ was 'no enemy of private patronage' in his biographies, see D. Griffin, 'J's *Lives of the Poets* and the Patronage System', *Age of J* 5 (1992), 1–33, revised in his *Literary Patronage in England, 1650–1800* (Cambridge, 1996), 220–45. See also 'Dorset' 13 above, and 'Pope' 100–3 and 'Dyer' 6 below. For SJ's own patronage of authors through encouragement and practical help rather than financial support, see G. Holladay and O. M. Brack Jr., 'J as Patron', in P. J. Korshin and R. R. Allen (eds.), *Greene Centennial Studies* (Charlottesville, Va., 1984), 172–99.

11. Addison had praised H at the end of his 'Account of the Greatest English Poets' (1694) and addressed 'A Letter from Italy' (1704) to him (see 'Addison' 14–16, 21 below). Poets who praised H included Stepney, Smith, Rowe, Hughes (see 'Hughes' 4 below), Congreve, Tickell, Somervile, Steele, Gay, and Dennis. Steele dedicated *Tatler*, vol. iv (1711) and *Spectator*, vol. ii (1712) to him. Rowe sought his

patronage in 1705 ('Rowe' 19 n. below), and, after George I's accession, published *Mecænas* (1714), a poem on the honours conferred on H.

Even Swift hoped for his 'Favors' and 'Protection' in two letters to H in 1709, although he later described one of H's replies as 'a most admirable original of Court promises and professions' (*Corresp.*, i. 142–3, 150, 157–60, iv. 345 and n.). Elsewhere he wrote of H that 'His encouragements were onely good words and dinners—I never heard him say one good thing or seem to tast what was said by another' (*Prose Writings*, v. 258). He also criticized him in 'A Libel on Doctor Delany' (1730), ll. 33–40 (*Poems*, ii. 481). For Mrs Manley's scepticism about H as politician, financier, and patron in 1709, see *The New Atlantis*, ed. R. Ballaster (1991), 99–100, 207, 263–5.

H was an early reader of the youthful Pope's *Pastorals* (Spence, ii. 616) and, shortly before his death, subscribed for ten sets of his *Iliad* translation. But Pope declined the offer of a pension from H after the accession of George I, and told an elaborate anecdote to prove that H was 'rather a pretender to taste than possessed of it' (*Corresp.*, i. 271; Spence, i. 87–8; see 'Pope' 100–3 below). The character of 'Bufo' in Pope's *Epistle to Arbuthnot*, ll. 231–48, is now usually taken to be a conflation of H and Bubb Dodington (see 'Thomson' 15 and n. below).

12. SJ adapts *Epistle to Arbuthnot*, l. 233 ('Fed with soft Dedication all day long'). Thomas Tickell's dedication to *The First Book of Homer's Iliad* (1715), published shortly after H's death, stated that the work would be 'perhaps the only one inscribed to his Lordship, that will escape being Rewarded by him' (sig. A2ᵛ; see 'Tickell' 8 below).

Resistance to facile interpetations of human behaviour here balances SJ's usual dislike of flattery (see 'Dryden' 172 and n. above): cf. 'Prior' 13 below. For 'comparison', see 'Cowley' 38 and n. above.

13. Cf. 'Savage' 100 below: 'So powerful is genius, when it is invested with the glitter of affluence! Men willingly pay to fortune that regard which they owe to merit' (and see also 143).

Hill (1905) compared SJ's remarks here with his pleasure at hearing the Italian ambassador in London praise the *Rambler* (*Life*, iii. 411).

15. In *Rambler* 106 (1751), H is one of the poets of a previous age of whom we 'wonder by what infatuation or caprice they could be raised to notice', their 'artifical fame' the result of 'the prejudice of faction, the stratagem of intrigue, or the servility of adulation' (*YW*, iv. 201). For transient literary fame, see also *Idler* 59 (1759) (*YW*, ii. 183), and for other reputations based on non-literary factors, see 'Dorset' 14–15 above, and 'Walsh' 9, 'Sheffield' 22, and 'Granville' 24 below.

*the monthly bundles of verses*: the poetry sections of such monthly periodicals as the *Gent. Mag.*

# THOMAS PARNELL (1679–1718)

**Composition.** SJ does not refer to 'Parnell'. Although McCarthy, 57, suggested that he might have written it in the autumn of 1779, when, instead of joining the Thrales at Brighton, he stayed at home, supposedly to work (*Thraliana*, i. 409), there is in fact no certain evidence that SJ returned to his *Prefaces* before Feb. 1780. Given P's much later place in the sequence in *Eng. Poets* (1779) and *Prefaces* (1781) than in the reordered *Lives* (1781), when he was brought forward from 37th to 20th place, it is not obvious why SJ should have given it particular priority. Another factor is SJ's apparent use of the Spence MSS, to which he had access from early Feb. 1780, although Goldsmith had already made use of them (see 'Sources' below). 'Parnell' seems to have been printed on the same sheet as 'Pitt' (*Bibliography*, ii. 1363), to which SJ referred as recently completed in early May 1780 (see headnote to 'Pitt' below), and he probably wrote it at about the same time.

Sources. Jacob, ii (1720), 132–3, offered only a thin account of P, and *GD*, Shiels, and *BB* ignored him. SJ therefore relied on Oliver Goldsmith's recent short biography, prefixed to an edition of P's *Poems on Several Occasions* (1770), pp. i–xxxv: for his earlier opinion of it, see 1 and n. below. Goldsmith used information from the poet's nephew Sir John Parnell and other relatives, from his own father and uncle who had known P, and from SJ's friend George Steevens, and twice referred to Joseph Spence's MS anecdotes (*Coll. Works*, iii. 409, 420, 426, 428 n.). Goldsmith also printed letters addressed to P by Pope and members of his circle. To this SJ can add only a passage from Ruffhead (see 6 below) and some Swift-related material, probably provided by Nichols (see 5 n. below).

The three quotations from P in the *Dict.* (1755) were increased to eighteen in 1773, perhaps in response to Goldsmith's edition of 1770.

Publication. In *Prefaces*, vol. viii (15 May 1781). Pp. 1–8 (of 12) of the proofs are in the Forster Collection. Boswell recorded a variant from proofs which have not survived in *Life*, iv. 54.

Modern Sources:

C. Gerrard, 'P, Pope and Pastoral', in A. Ribeiro and J. G. Basker (eds.), *Tradition in Transition: Women Writers, Marginal Texts and the Eighteenth-Century Canon* (Oxford, 1996), 221–40

R. L. Green, 'Notes on TP and his Chester Relations', *N & Q* 185 (1943), 308–11

R. D. Havens, 'P's "Hymn to Contentment"', *MLN* 59 (1944), 329–31

C. J. Rawson, 'Some Unpublished Letters of Pope and Gay; and Some Manuscript Sources of Goldsmith's *Life of TP*', *RES* 10 (1959), 371–87

C. J. Rawson, 'New Parnell Manuscripts', *Scriblerian*, 1 (1969) 1–2

C. J. Rawson and F. P. Lock, 'Scriblerian Epigrams by TP', *RES* 33 (1982), 148–57

C. J. Rawson and F. P. Lock (eds.), *Collected Poems of TP* (Newark, Del., 1989)

M. M. Smith (ed.), *Index of English Literary Manuscripts*, iii (ii) (1989), 235–51

T. M. Woodman, 'P, Politeness and "Pre-Romanticism"', *EC* 33 (1983), 205–19

T. M. Woodman, *TP* (Boston, 1985)

T. M. Woodman, ' "Softest Manners, Gentlest Arts": The Polite Verse of TP', in *Politeness and Poetry in the Age of Pope* (1989)

T. M. Woodman, 'TP', in *Dictionary of Literary Biography*, xcv (1990), 159–63

   1. Goldsmith's biography of 1770 (see headnote) is cited from his *Coll. Works*, iii. 407–28.

      The *Critical Review*, 30 (1770), 44–50, had lamented the 'poverty of essential facts' in Goldsmith's biography, and SJ agreed in conversation on 31 Mar. 1772: 'Goldsmith's Life of Parnell is poor; not that it is poorly written, but that he had poor materials; for nobody can write the life of a man, but those who have eat and drunk and lived in social intercourse with him' (*Life*, ii. 166). Goldsmith admitted that he could provide only 'Some dates, and a few facts scarce more interesting than those that make the ornaments of a country tomb-stone', and had conveyed little sense of P's 'peculiarities' (iii. 408–9).

According to Mrs Thrale, SJ expressed further doubts about Goldsmith as biographer in July 1773: 'I wonder said he who will be my Biographer? Goldsmith to be sure I replied if you should go first—and he would do it better than any body. —but then he would do [it?] maliciously says Johnson' (*Thraliana*, i. 173, entry dated 16 Nov. 1777). In 1786 she claimed that SJ had gone on to explain that 'his particular malice towards me, and general disregard for truth, would make the book useless to all, and injurious to my character' (*J. Misc.*, i. 166).

As well as providing the Latin epitaph for Goldsmith's monument in Westminster Abbey (*Life*, iii. 81–5), SJ in fact often praised his friend generously: 'Whether, indeed, we take him as a poet,—as a comick writer,—or as an historian, he stands in the first class'; he 'was a man, who, whatever he wrote, did it better than any other man could do' (*Life*, ii. 166, iii. 253); he 'was the best writer he ever knew upon every subject he wrote upon' (Thomas Campbell, *Diary of a Visit to England in 1775*, ed. J. L. Clifford (Cambridge, 1947), 77). SJ wrote to Bennet Langton, 5 July 1774, after the death of 'poor Goldsmith': 'But let not his frailties be remembred. He was a very great Man' (*Letters*, ii. 147). According to Fanny Burney, SJ said in Aug. 1778 that Goldsmith 'would have been a great man, had he known the real value of his internal resources', but also described him in the following month as his last literary 'Hero' (*Early Journals*, iii. 95, 168). For other comments, see *Life*, ii. 235–7, iii. 84–5 n. In late 1776 SJ considered replacing Percy as Goldsmith's biographer: see K. C. Balderston, *The History and Sources of Percy's Memoir of Goldsmith* (Cambridge, 1926), 20–3.

In his dedication of *She Stoops to Conquer* (1773) to SJ, with whom he had 'lived many years in intimacy', Goldsmith had praised his wit and 'unaffected piety' (*Coll. Works*, v. 101). SJ's own tribute may have been prompted not merely by affectionate respect. Copyright problems had prevented the inclusion of Goldsmith in *Eng. Poets* (1779), and SJ here reminds his readers not merely of this omission but of qualities missing in many of the poets he was dutifully discussing: see i. 164–5 above. SJ in fact echoes his praise of Dryden's character of Shakespeare as 'exact without minuteness, and lofty without exaggeration' in 'Dryden' 198 above. The 'without . . . without' figure also recalls his earlier praise of Denham's famous quatrain in *Cooper's Hill* for the way that 'every mode of excellence' is 'separated from its adjacent fault by so nice a line of limitation' ('Denham' 30–1 above). For other versions of the device, see 'Cowley' 200, 'Dryden' 214 above, and 'Addison' 167–8, 'Prior' 55, and 'Pope' 367 below; and for another writer who 'at once comprehends the vast, and attends to the minute', see 'Thomson' 46 and n. below.

2. SJ's biography closely follows Goldsmith's narrative. He quotes Homer, *Odyssey*, XXIV. 190 ('That is what is due to the dead').

3. See Goldsmith, *Coll. Works*, iii. 407–8. P was the son of Thomas Parnell, a supporter of Cromwell, and his wife Anna. For P's Chester relatives, see Green, 'Notes'. He was baptized at St Catherine's Church, Dublin, on 14 Sept. 1679, was taught at school by a Dr Jones, and entered Trinity College, Dublin, on 25 Nov.

1692; BA 1697, MA 1700. Goldsmith, who also entered Trinity College at the age of 13, commented that this 'is much sooner than usual, as at that university they are a great deal stricter in their examination for entrance, than either at Oxford or Cambridge'. He also noted that P was ordained by dispensation, 'as being under twenty-three years of age' (iii. 408 and n.). William King, Bishop of Derry, and later Archbishop of Dublin (see 7 below and 'Swift' 64 below), is said to have been the guardian of P and his brother John (Swift, *Corresp.*, i. 345 n.).

4. See Goldsmith, *Coll. Works*, iii. 408. P was ordained deacon in 1700 and priest in 1704. It was in fact through William King that he became Archdeacon of Clogher on 9 Feb. 1706. For St George Ashe, see also 'Congreve' 4 n. and 'Swift' 70 below.

   P married in 1706. Goldsmith referred to 'Miss Anne Minchin': the revision of 'Miss' to 'Mrs.' may reflect SJ's uneasiness about 'Miss', which he defines not merely as '1. The term of honour to a young girl', but '2. A strumpet; a concubine; a whore; a prostitute' (*Dict.*).

5. By comparison with SJ, Goldsmith, *Coll. Works*, iii. 409–10, had played down Swift's role and described P as 'a friend to both sides', although his 'Tory connexions... gave his friends in Ireland great offence'. Pope recalled in 1735 that P 'had come over... when Lord Oxford was at the head of affairs partly for preferment in Lord Oxford's ministry' (Spence, i. 62). Although Swift described Robert Harley, Earl of Oxford, welcoming P in 1712 (*Jnl. to Stella*, ii. 543, 611–12), SJ's account seems closer here to Patrick Delany, *Observations on Swift* (1755), 28–9. In Dec. 1712 Swift went to some trouble to introduce P to Bolingbroke, whom he complimented in his *Essay on the Different Stiles of Poetry* (1713) (*Jnl. to Stella*, ii. 586, 588, 591, 612, 623). Pope's 'dedication' is the 'Epistle to Robert Earl of Oxford' prefixed to P's *Poems* (1722): for Oxford and P see ll. 7–12, and 9 below. For Oxford as an inadequate patron, see also 'Rowe' 19 and 'Pope' 91 below. Goldsmith stated that P's 'fortune (for a poet) was very considerable', but that 'his expences were greater than his income' (iii. 416).

   SJ ignores P's membership of the Scriblerus Club, and his prefatory 'Essay on Homer' in Pope's *Iliad*, vol. i (1715), both of which Goldsmith had emphasized (iii. 412, 419–21). For SJ's later (and still cursory) treatment of these matters, see 'Pope' 88 (from Spence, i. 83–4) and 222 below. See also *The Memoirs of Martinus Scriblerus*, ed. C. Kerby-Miller (New Haven, 1950), esp. 12–14, 37–40, 46–7, 57–60. P later contributed an effusive commendatory poem to Pope's *Works* (1717).

6. SJ's source here is Owen Ruffhead, *Life of Pope* (1769), 492 n.: Pope told Warburton that P had ambitions as a popular preacher, 'and began to be distinguished in the mob-places of Southwark and London, when the Queen's sudden death destroyed all his prospects, and at a juncture when famed preaching was the readiest road to preferment. This fatal stroke broke his spirits: he took to drinking, became a sot, and soon finished his course.' (For Swift's early 'hope to excel in preaching', see 'Swift' 120 below.) Pope stated in 1735 that P was 'a great drinker, and strangely open and scandalous in his debaucheries', and in 1743 that he 'took to dramming (on the loss of a wife or a mistress)' (Spence, i. 210, 220). Mrs Thrale-Piozzi later claimed in a marginal note to have heard SJ 'say—what 'tis plain he would not *write*,—how Parnell could not get thro' a sermon without turning his head (even in the pulpit) to drink a dram' (Lobban, 141–2).

In conversation in Edinburgh in 1773 SJ justified such biographical information as an 'instructive caution to avoid drinking, when it was seen, that even the learning and genius of Parnell could be debased by it'. On 17 Sept. 1777, about to embark on his biographies, he was less certain 'whether it should be mentioned that Addison and Parnell drank too freely: for people will probably more easily indulge in drinking from knowing this; so that more ill may be done by the example, than good by telling the whole truth' (*Life*, iii. 155; cf. 'Addison' 117 and n. below).

Swift mentioned the death of P's wife in Aug. 1711: 'she seemed to be an excellent good-natured young woman, and I believe the poor lad is much afflicted; they appeared to live perfectly well together.' In July 1712 he reported that P 'has been ill for grief of his Wives death, and has been 2 Months at the Bath' (*Jnl. to Stella*, i. 340-1, ii.543, and cf. ii. 623). Goldsmith believed that this loss 'made so great an impression on his spirits, that it served to hasten his own', driving him 'to seek from wine, if not relief, at least insensibility' (*Coll. Works*, iii. 408, 422). For SJ's deletion of a sentence on this subject, see 8 n. below; and for P's 'almost manic-depressive temperament', see Woodman, *TP*, 10-11.

7. Goldsmith, *Coll. Works*, iii. 408, did not mention Swift or the prebend, which P in fact failed to obtain. Nichols inserted this information in the proofs (see Textual Notes), and used it again in his *Sel. Collection*, iii. 209-10 n.: see Swift, *Corresp.*, i. 344-5, 356. P returned to Ireland in late 1714 (Pope, *Corresp.*, i. 269). He was presented by Archbishop King to the vicarage of Finglass in May 1716.

8. After spending the summer in England, P in fact died in Chester at the age of 39 on 24 Oct. 1718 (Pope, *Corresp.*, i. 415). Both Goldsmith, *Coll. Works*, iii. 408, 422, and Nichols, *Sel. Collection*, iii. 210 n., stated that he died in July 1718. For other cases of defeated expectations, see 'Denham' 19 and n. above.

SJ deleted in proof most of an eloquent sentence on P's grief for his wife: 'But his prosperity was clouded by that which took away all his powers of enjoying either profit or pleasure, the death of his wife, whom he is said to have lamented with such sorrow as hastened his end' (see Textual Notes). Boswell commented: 'I should have thought that Johnson, who had felt the severe affliction from which Parnell never recovered, would have preserved this passage' (*Life*, iv. 54). For SJ's conviction that 'all unnecessary grief is unwise', see *Life*, iii. 136 and n. and *J. Misc.*, i. 205-6, 230-1.

For SJ's Latin epitaph on P (1773), which emphasizes the sweetness and piety of his writings, see *Life*, iv. 54, v. 404; and for Goldsmith's English epitaph, see *Poems of Gray, Collins and Goldsmith* (1969), 695.

9. P wrote *Spectators* 460, 501 (1712) and *Guardians* 56, 66 (1713): with a fifth essay, they were collected as 'Visions' in his *Poems On Several Occasions* (1722 for Dec. 1721), 183-221.

Pope edited this posthumous collection at P's request, receiving £15 from Lintot for the copyright (Pope, *Corresp.*, i. 415-16; Nichols, *Lit. Ill*, viii. 300; cf. 'Pope' 124 below). Pope told Jervas, 12 Dec. 1718: 'What he gave me to publish, was but a small part of what he left behind him, but it was the best, and I will not make it worse by enlarging it' (*Corresp.*, ii. 24). In 1720 he referred in an endnote to the *Iliad* to P's recent death and to 'those beautiful Pieces of Poetry the Publication of which he left to my Charge, almost with his dying Breath' (*TE*, viii. 578). For the possibility that he 'edited' P's texts, see Woodman, *TP*, 48-50, and Rawson and

Lock, *Poems*, 20–3, 27–9. SJ later notes that Pope found P's 'Essay on Homer', written for the *Iliad* translation, 'so harsh that he took great pains in correcting it' ('Pope' 88). For Pope's dedicatory poem to the Earl of Oxford, see 5 above and Pope to Oxford, 21 Oct. 1721 (*Corresp.*, ii. 90). The volume also contains 'To Mr. Pope', a survey of Pope's poetry, and a Latin translation of Belinda's toilet-scene from *The Rape of the Lock* (105–15).

Only nine of the twenty poems printed by Pope had been published in P's lifetime: these included some lyrics in Steele's *Poetical Miscellanies* (1714), and the *Essay on Different Stiles of Poetry* (1713) and *Homer's Battle of the Frogs and Mice. With the Remarks of Zoilus* (1717), which Swift and Pope respectively had encouraged him to publish (Rawson and Lock, *Poems*, 16–17). Pope later printed P's version of Donne's *Satire III* with his own imitations of Donne in his *Works*, ii (ii) (1738).

SJ ignores P's *Essay on Different Stiles*, which Pope omitted from *Poems* (1722), perhaps because it praised the exiled Bolingbroke (cf. 5 and n. above, and Swift's letter of 26 Mar. 1722, *Corresp.* ii. 424). Nichols failed to find a copy in time for inclusion in *Eng. Poets* (1779), but printed it in his *Sel. Collection*, iii. 217–36.

For Goldsmith's 'just praise' of P's poems, see *Coll. Works*, iii. 424–5. After expressing reluctance to disagree with his friend, SJ goes on to do just that in **10–11** below.

P had given English explanations of the 'Greek names' in his translation from Homer.

10. See Goldsmith, *Coll. Works*, iii. 424–6. The *Poemata* of Théodore de Bèze (1519–1605) had been reprinted in London in 1713. P's debt to Aurelius Augurellus (*c*.1440–1524) was noted in the *Literary Mag.* (Jan. 1758), shortly after SJ's association with it (Rawson and Lock, *Poems*, 486–8, 516–18). Goldsmith's suggested source for 'When Spring comes on' ('a French poet, whose name I forget') has not been identified. For the 'description of Barrenness', see P's 'To Mr. Pope', originally prefixed to Pope's *Works* (1717): Goldsmith thought it 'one of the finest compliments that ever was paid to any poet'. P's source was Joannes Secundus, *Elegies*, III. xii (Rawson and Lock, *Poems*, 491–2).

Goldsmith had 'indirectly preferred' the 'Night-Piece' to Gray's *Elegy* ('Gray' 51 below) by stating that P's poem, 'with very little amendment, might be made to surpass all those night pieces and church yard scenes that have since appeared'. One reviewer took this as an allusion to Gray (*Coll. Works*, iii. 426 and n.), and Vicesimus Knox, in his *Essays Moral and Literary* (1782), ii. 186, read it as betraying 'a little jealousy' of Gray, and cited Goldsmith's earlier reservations about the *Elegy* in 1767 (*Coll. Works*, v. 320). Knox also claimed to have heard Goldsmith 'make some oblique and severe reflections on the fashionable poetry' (i.e. of Gray). For Goldsmith's earlier objections to P's use of octosyllabics for so solemn a subject, see *Coll. Works*, v. 325.

Rawson and Lock, *Poems*, 527–9, concluded that, in spite of its antiquity, the story in P's 'The Hermit' need be traced no further back than to Sir Percy Herbert's *Certaine Conceptions* (1650), James Howell's source in his *Epistolae Ho-Elianae*, IV. iv (1655). Pope suggested in 1735 that the poem had a Spanish source, as Goldsmith mentioned (while partly garbling his quotation from Spence, i. 209–10). Goldsmith also cited Henry More's *Divine Dialogues* (1668), 321. A. P.

Hudson discussed different versions of the story in 'The Hermit and Divine Providence', *SP* 28 (1931), 218–34.

In response to SJ's apparent preference of the 'Allegory on Man' (see 11 below) to 'The Hermit', a contributor to *Gent. Mag.* (Feb. 1783), 130, commented that 'without doubt the Hermit is the most popular of Parnell's productions', and that SJ 'might have pronounced a judgment less subversive of the agreement he would establish between criticism and common sense', but went on himself to criticize 'The Hermit' for over-elaboration. For Frances Reynolds's account of an 'eloquent oration' by SJ on the ways of providence prompted by 'The Hermit', see *J. Misc.*, ii. 255–6; and for a debate between SJ, Boswell, and, later, Malone in 1778 and 1779 about an 'inconsistency' in the poem, see *Life*, iii. 220, 392–3 and n.

11. For the 'Allegory of Man', see 10 n. above. SJ has in mind as a source for P's 'Hymn to Contentment' a poem entitled 'Content', once attributed to John Cleveland. For other early parallels, see Woodman, *TP*, 67–71.

12. For 'comprehension', see 'Cowley' 144 and n. above; for 'easy' writing, 'Rochester' 18 and n. above; and for 'diction', 'Cowley' 181–4 and n. above. SJ adapts Pope's 'Epistle to Mr. Jervas', l. 67: 'And finish'd more through happiness than pains.' Goldsmith, *Coll. Works*, iii. 420, 423, also praised 'that ease and sweetness for which his poetry is so much admired', contrasting P's refined 'poetical language' with the 'follies and affectations' of the 'misguided innovators', who were returning English to its 'pristine barbarity'. Opposite the title page of P's *Poems* (1770), Goldsmith quoted Hume's 'Of Simplicity and Refinement in Writing': ''Tis sufficient to run over Cowley once: But Parnel, after the fiftieth reading, is as fresh as at the first' (iii. 422 n.).

With SJ's final sentence on Nature and Art in P's verse, cf. the similar comment on the interplay of 'life' and 'invention' in 'Addison' 165 below, and 'Pope' 388 below (originally 1756): 'nature cannot be properly opposed to *art*; nature being, in this sense, only the best effect of *art*.' SJ's view was echoed into the next century, e.g. by Thomas Campbell, *Specimens of the British Poets* (1819): P's 'poetry is like a flower that has been trained and planted by the skill of the gardener, but which preserves in its cultured state the natural fragrance of its wilder air' (quoted by Woodman, *TP*, 111). For SJ's earlier association of P's verse with scenes of 'pastoral virtue', see his diary for 25 July 1774 (*YW*, i. 175). See also 'Dryden' 347 above for a quotation from P illustrating 'the most soft and pleasing of our lyric measures'.

13. SJ implies that P's later reputation depended at least partly on Pope's 'corrections' (see 9 above).

Not long before he died, Pope ordered that P's unpublished MSS should be burned, but a copy evidently survived (Spence, i. 58). Later published as P's *Posthumous Works* (1758), these devotional verses and scriptural paraphrases are now accepted as early apprentice-work (Woodman, *TP*, 13–24; Rawson and Lock, *Poems*, 29 ff.). Their authenticity was questioned by *Gent. Mag.* (1758), 282–4, which considered them despicable doggerel, and by *Critical Review*, 6 (1758), 118–21, but accepted, in spite of their lack of P's usual elegance, by *Monthly Review*, 19 (1758), 380–5. Thomas Gray described the volume to Mason, 11 Aug. 1758, as 'the dunghill of Irish-Grub-street' (*Corresp.*, ii. 579–80). Goldsmith excluded these poems, which did 'very litle credit to his reputation' (iii. 424).

Both *Eng. Poets* (1779) and Bell's *British Poets* (1778) reprinted the *Posthumous Works* (1758). SJ's dismissive comment was implicitly aimed at Nichols, the 'compiler' of *Eng. Poets* ('the last edition'), who admitted responsibility for their inclusion, 'with several additional poems which I had formerly collected', in his *Sel. Collection*, iii. 210 n. The reviewer of *Eng. Poets* in *Gent. Mag.* (1779), 599 (presumably Nichols's friend John Duncombe) believed that this new material had been 'too severely censured', and was genuine ('the first effusions of the author's pen'), but lacked the 'friendly embellishments' enjoyed by 'the poems which passed through Mr. Pope's hands'.


## SIR SAMUEL GARTH (1661–1719)

**Composition.** Although SJ does not refer to 'Garth', he probably wrote it in late 1778 or early 1779. The booksellers' optimistic announcement in the *Gazetteer* on 20 Oct. 1778 that vols. i–xx of the *Eng. Poets*, with the relevant biographies, would be published by Christmas must have put SJ under some pressure, since G appeared in vol. xx.

**Sources.** SJ's main source was John Campbell's article in *BB*, iii (1750), 2129–37, mentioned in **11** below. *BB* was ampler than Jacob, ii. 58–9, *GD*, v. 395–8, and Shiels, *Lives*, iii. 263–72 (itself based on *BB*). In 1783 SJ was able to add further information from the Spence MSS (see **16** below).

In SJ's copy of the *Works of the Most Celebrated Minor Poets*, vol. i (1749) (Hyde Collection), G's verse is marked for use in the *Dict.*: see Fleeman, *Handlist* (1984), 50. One hundred and fifty-four quotations from G duly appeared in 1755.

**Publication.** In *Prefaces*, vol. iv (31 Mar. 1779). There are no proofs.

**Modern Sources:**
S. J. Ackerman, 'The "Infant Atoms" of G's Dispensary', *MLR* 74 (1979), 513–23
R. I. Cook, *Sir SG* (Boston, 1980)
P. J. Daly, 'Monarchy, the Disbanding Crisis, and SG's *Dispensary*', *Restoration*, 25 (2001), 35–52
F. H. Ellis (ed.), *Poems on Affairs of State*, vi (1970), 58–128 (for *The Dispensary*)
D. Hopkins, 'Dryden and the Garth–Tonson *Metamorphoses*', *RES* 38 (1987), 64–74
P. Rogers, 'The Publishing History of G's *Dispensary*', *Trans. of the Cambridge Bibl. Soc.* 5 (1971), 167–77
J. F. Sena, 'The Letters of SG', *BNYPL* 78 (1974), 69–94
J. F. Sena, *The Best-Natured Man: Sir SG, Physician and Poet* (New York, 1986)

1.  G was in fact born in 1661 at Bolam, Durham, the son of William Garth, and educated at a school at Ingleton, near Staindrop (Sena, *Sir SG*, 1). He entered Peterhouse, Cambridge, 6 July 1676; BA 1679, MA 1684, MD 7 July 1691 (incorporated at All Souls, Oxford, 14 July 1694). He studied at Leiden 1687–8 and was in France in 1688 (Sena, *Sir SG*, 7). It was in fact on 26 June 1693 that he became a Fellow of the Royal College of Physicians. For the studies of other medical poets, see 'Blackmore' **2** and 'Akenside' **5** below.

    Dr John Radcliffe (1650–1714), a notable benefactor of the University of Oxford, was the most prominent Tory physician. For John Arbuthnot's portrayal in 1712 of

Radcliffe and G as representatively Tory and Whig, see A. W. Bower and R. A. Erickson (eds.), *The History of John Bull* (Oxford, 1976), 208, and cf. William Pittis, *Some Memoirs of the Life of John Radcliffe, M.D.* (1715), and J. B. Nias, *Dr. John Radcliffe* (Oxford, 1918). G gave medical advice to the young Pope (see Spence, i. 29–30), who told Martha Blount on Radcliffe's death: 'your Doctor is gone the way of all his patients, & was hard put to it how to dispose of an Estate miserably unwieldy, and splendidly unuseful to him. Sir Sam. Garth says, that for Ratcliffe to leave a Library was as if an Eunuch should found a Seraglio' (*Corresp.*, i. 269).

SJ did not correct the spelling of Radcliffe's name in 1783, in spite of an objection in *Gent. Mag.* (Jan. 1783), 47.

2–9. Most early editions of G's poem included prefatory accounts of the animosities aroused by the Dispensary project, as did *Eng. Poets* (1779), xx. 3–12, but SJ's narrative summarizes *BB*'s long footnote on the subject (iii. 2129–31 n.), including the 'edict' discussed in 3–4. For a modern account, see Sena, *Sir SG*, 17–37.

2. Cf. Jonathan Richardson the Younger, *Richardsoniana* (1776), 333: 'it was a fine character of *Garth*, that "No physician knew his art more, nor his trade less".'

3. SJ refers to Sir William Temple, *Miscellanea. The Third Part* (1701), 152: 'the Divines seem to have had the most Honour, the Lawyers the most Money, and the Physicians the most Learning.' Boswell quoted this paragraph when consulting three eminent Scottish physicians about SJ's ill health in Mar. 1784. Elsewhere he mentions SJ's 'peculiar pleasure in the company of physicians' and his 'esteem for physicians' (*Life*, iv. 263, 293, v. 183). See also 'Akenside' 11 below and, for a denial that physicians' fees were exorbitant, *J. Misc.*, i. 223.

5. The 'laboratory' did not become fully operational until the spring of 1698 (Sena, *Sir SG*, 34).

6. Although the apothecaries had a monopoly on the sale of medicines, they were barred from medical practice, and were ultimately subordinate to the College of Physicians. They seem, however, often to have given medical advice, particularly to the poor. At stake in the quarrel between the College and the Society of Apothecaries was not simply the benevolent provision of a free medical service, but the authority of the College of Physicians on the one hand (see 10 below), and the highly profitable monopoly enjoyed by the apothecaries on the other. The Apothecaries Bill of 1695 raised their status.

9. The subscription raised about £500. For the 'agreement', see *BB*, iii. 2131. The 'medicinal charity' had come to an end by Apr. 1726 (Sena, *Sir SG*, 34–7).

10. *The Dispensary* appeared in 1699. For the influence of the 'passions and prejudices then prevalent' on a poem's reputation, see also 'Butler' 41 and n. above. Dryden praised G and criticized the apothecaries in 'To my Honour'd Kinsman, John Driden', ll. 107–8, in *Fables* (1700): '*Garth*, gen'rous as his Muse, prescribes and gives; | The Shop-man sells; and by Destruction lives', etc. Pope compared the dispute between physicians and apothecaries to the relationship of authors and critics in *Essay on Criticism* (1711), ll. 108–11. SJ does not refer to the accusation that '*Garth* did not write his own *Dispensary*' mentioned later in Pope's *Essay*, l. 619. For what Pope called a 'common slander at that time', see *TE*, i. 309 n.

11. This Latin lecture was endowed by William Harvey (1578–1657). G had earlier delivered the Gulstonian Lecture, founded by Theodore Gulston or Goulston

(d. 1632), to the College of Physicians in 1694 (Sena, *Sir SG*, 9–10, and cf. 'Akenside' **12** below). He became one of the Censors (i.e. the governing body) of the College, 3 Oct. 1702, and FRS 1706.

G's *Oratio Laudatorio* (1697) included a eulogy of William III and an attack on charlatans which inevitably linked it to the Dispensary quarrel. Although SJ here makes one of his few direct references to *BB* as a source, Rogers (1980), 161, claimed that variants in SJ's quotation from G's *Oratio* show that it did not derive from the text in *BB*, iii. 2131–2 n. There is in fact only one variant ('autem' for 'tamen'), which could have been a slip in transcription. *BB* translates G's Latin as: 'Yet not with weapons do these swarms of mountebanks inflict wounds, but with some nostrum more dangerous than any weapon; not with plain gunpowder, but with some strange foreign dust they charge their packets; not with leaden bullets, but with pills as mortal, they do their business.'

SJ does not refer here to G's oration at Dryden's funeral in 1700 (see 'Dryden' **153** above). Thomas Hearne reported that G 'did not mention one word of Jesus Christ, but made an oration as an apostrophe to the great god Apollo … and, as a conclusion, instead of a psalm of David, repeated the 30th ode of the third book of Horace, beginning *Exegi monumentum*. He made a great many blunders in the pronunciation' (*Remains* (1869), ii. 267). See also Malone, *Prose Works of Dryden* (1800), i (i). 363 n., 373–80 and nn., and Sena, *Sir SG*, 69–76.

SJ also ignores G's involvement in the quarrel between Blackmore and the Wits in 1699–1700, in which the Dispensary issue played some part (see 'Blackmore' **17** below, and Sena, *Sir SG*, 69–760). *The Dispensary* includes a parody of Blackmore's poetry (IV. 178–92). Sena, *Sir SG*, 122–5, has shown, however, that G and Blackmore later acted as medical colleagues. Like his sources, SJ does not mention G's marriage in 1705 to Martha Beaufoy (d. 1717), daughter of Sir Henry Beaufoy of Emscote, Warwicks. (Sena, *Sir SG*, 117).

**12.** For G's political affiliations, especially after 1710, see Sena, *Sir SG*, 101–15. The Whig Kit-Cat Club included such prominent politicians and patrons of the arts as Lords Halifax, Somers, Sunderland, and Dorset, and such authors as Addison, Steele, Vanbrugh, Congreve, and Walsh: see also 'Blackmore' **21** below, and K. M. Lynch, *Jacob Tonson, Kit-Cat Publisher* (Knoxville, Tenn., 1971), 37–66. Pope and Tonson remembered in 1730 that 'Garth, Vanbrugh, and Congreve were the three most honest-hearted, real good men of the poetical members of the Kit-Cat Club' (Spence, i 50).

G wrote 'To the Earl of Godolphin' when Queen Anne dismissed the Whig Lord Treasurer on 8 Aug. 1710. Prior criticized it in *Examiner* 6 (7 Sept. 1710), and Addison replied in *Whig Examiner* 1 (14 Sept. 1710) and again in *Tatler* 239 (19 Oct. 1710): see 'Addison' **77** and 'Prior' **22** below, and Prior, *Lit. Works*, i. 389–94. Unlike *GD*, *BB*, iii. 2133 n., discussed this episode at some length.

**13.** G visited the Duke of Marlborough in the Netherlands on behalf of the Whigs in 1711 and, when the Marlboroughs were banished in 1712, the Duchess gave G a diamond worth £200 (Sena, *Sir SG*, 105, 108–9). After the accession of George I, G was knighted on 11 Oct. 1714: for the use of Marlborough's sword, *BB*, iii. 2133, cited the *Chronological Diary* (1714–15), 12.

**14.** Eighteen poets contributed, over a period of some twenty-four years, to the translation of Ovid's *Metamorphoses* eventually published by Tonson in 1717, which in effect made the Latin poet 'a Whig apologist': see Sena, *Sir SG*, 90, 182 n.; Hopkins, 'Dryden', 64–74. G himself translated Bk. XIV and part of XV.

SJ's censure of G's preface may react to the claim in *BB*, iii. 2135, that it 'would have been sufficient to have raised him an immortal reputation, if it had been the only product of his pen'. Although SJ had already cited G's preface as an example of 'absurdity of pride' arising from lack of self-knowledge in *Rambler* 24 (1750) (*YW*, iii. 134), he quoted it in the *Dict.* (see e.g. 'Dissonance' and 'Irreparable'). Warton, *Essay on Pope* (1782), ii. 27, described it as 'written in a flowing and lively style, but full of strange opinions'.

G in fact died on 18 Jan. 1719, as all SJ's sources stated. For his ill health in his last years, and for what amounted to an attempted suicide, see Spence, i. 325–6.

15. Both Pope and Lady Mary Wortley Montagu testified to G's good nature (Spence, i. 44, 50, 304). For the 'virulence and malevolence' of the Whigs at this period, see 'Smith' **73** above, and for SJ's approval of those whose 'zeal of party' did not extinguish 'kindness' for opponents, see also 'Addison' **105** and n. below.

G read the MS of the youthful Pope's *Pastorals* in 1706 (Spence, i. 32, ii. 616). Pope dedicated 'Summer' to G, and later praised him at the end of the Preface to the *Iliad* (1715), in *Dunciad*, II. 140 n., and in *Epistle to Arbuthnot*, l. 137. In spite of Pope's basically Tory sympathies, the anecdote in 'Pope' **100** below conveys the relaxed nature of his friendship with G (and cf. 'Pope' **74** below). Swift was on sociable terms with G in 1710–11 (*Jnl. to Stella*, i. 48, 75, 337). G would know Addison through the Whig Kit-Cat Club and the club at Button's (see **12** above and 'Addison' **116** below). He wrote the epilogue to *Cato* (1713) and became Addison's physician (Sena, *Sir SG*, 132). Steele complimented G in *Tatler* 78 (1709) and later dedicated *The Lover* (1714) to him, praising his benevolence and charity. The Tory George Granville, Lord Lansdowne (q.v. below), addressed a poem 'To my Friend Dr. Garth in his Sickness' (quoted in *BB*, iii. 2137 n.).

For reports of G's religious heterodoxy, see *BB*, iii. 2137 n., and Sena, *Sir SG*, 58, 77, 81–3. According to Edward Young, G 'sent to Addison (of whom he had a very high opinion) when on his death-bed, to tell him whether the Christian religion was true' (Spence, i. 344). SJ follows *BB* in quoting Pope's letter to Jervas in 1720: 'His death was very Heroical, and yet unaffected enough to have made a Saint, or a Philosopher famous: But ill Tongues, and worse Hearts have branded even his last Moments, as wrongfully as they did his Life, with Irreligion. You must have heard many Tales on this Subject; but if ever there was a good Christian, without knowing himself to be so, it was Dr. *Garth*' (*Corresp.*, ii. 25). Pope had similarly described G as 'the best good Christian he, | Altho' he knows it not', in 'A Farewell to London. In the Year 1715', ll. 15–16. John Barber told Swift, 22 Apr. 1735: 'You may remember Dr. *Garth* said he was glad when he was dying; for he was weary of having his shoes pulled off and on' (Swift, *Corresp.*, iv. 325).

16. SJ added this paragraph in 1783 from the Spence MSS. For reports by Pope and others that G died a Catholic, see Spence, i. 209 and n., and Sena, *Sir SG*, 137–41.

SJ refers to William Lowth's preface to *Directions for the Profitable Reading of the Holy Scriptures* (1708): '*Superstition* and *Profaneness* are not so far asunder as some may imagine: One Extreme doth usually produce another; and when Men have for some times bewilder'd themselves in the *Maze* of *Scepticism* and *Infidelity*, and can find nothing whereon to fix, they will be ready to hearken to the *Popish* Pleas for the

*Infallibility* of the *Church,* or to any thing else that may put a stop to their endless Wand'rings, and give rest to their weary Souls' (sig. A4ᵛ). For SJ's reflections on Dryden's conversion, see 'Dryden' 118 above. A few months before he died, SJ told Boswell: 'A good man, of a timorous disposition, in great doubt of his acceptance with GOD, and pretty credulous, might be glad to be of a church where there are so many helps to get to Heaven' (*Life,* iv. 289).

17. SJ may react here to praise of *The Dispensary* in *BB,* iii. 2129 n., as 'a most beautiful and elegant composition . . . one of the best poems in our language'. Although G exerted 'his full vigour', SJ allows the satire only limited 'elegance' or 'poetical ardour'. SJ shows no interest in it as a mock-heroic precursor of *The Rape of the Lock,* a matter emphasized in Warton's *Essay* (1756), 216–18. In his review of Warton, SJ had commented that G 'is mentioned with perhaps too much honour' as anticipating Pope (*OASJ,* 492).

SJ's reference to J. F. Du Resnel Du Bellay is puzzling, since the preface to his translation of Pope's *Essay on Man* (Paris, 1737) does not mention G, and the opinion SJ attributes to him here is not found in the long note about G in *Les Principes de la morale et du gout* (Amsterdam, 1739), 206 n. SJ had appended Du Resnel's preface to his own translation of Crousaz's *Commentary* on Pope's *Essay* (1739, 1742): see 'Pope' 181–3 below. For 'discrimination of characters', see 'Milton' 268 and n. above.

G added 430 lines to *The Dispensary* in the course of the eight authorized editions in his lifetime. For Pope's praise of G's improvements, see Jonathan Richardson the Younger, *Richardsoniana* (1776), 195–6 n. Richardson Pack, *Miscellanies in Verse and Prose* (1719), 96–7, wrote: 'Almost every Thing he left out was a Robbery from the Publick: Every Thing he added hath been an Embellishment to his *Poem.*' For a modern discussion of his revisions, see F. H. Ellis in *POAS,* vi. 723.

For the fate of poetry written on temporary subjects, see 'Butler' 41 and n. above. Goldsmith wrote of *The Dispensary* in his *Beauties of English Poesy* (1767), that 'our approbation, at present, is cooler, for it owed part of its fame to party' (*Coll. Works,* v. 324). Although SJ implies that G's poem was no longer remembered, it inspired Bonnell Thornton's topical *The Battle of the Wigs. An Additional Canto to Dr. Garth's Poem of the Dispensary. Occasioned by the Disputes between the Fellows and Licentiates of the College of Physicians, in London* (1768). Walpole suggested that 'the inimitable compliments in that harmonious Satire to our Heroic Deliverer [William III] made the monkish Pedant [SJ] attempt to obliterate so deathless a Chef d'oeuvre' (William Mason, *Satirical Poems . . . With Notes by Horace Walpole,* ed. P. Toynbee (Oxford, 1926), 33).

SJ ignores here G's *Claremont* (1715), a substantial topographical poem celebrating the Duke of Newcastle's country estate, which he had mentioned with apparent approval in 'Denham' 28 above, and quoted in the *Dict.* (under 'Woad').

# NICHOLAS ROWE (1674–1718)

**Composition.** SJ told Mrs Thrale on 6 Apr. 1780: 'I am upon Rowe, who cannot fill much paper' (by comparison i.e. with the recently completed 'Addison' and 'Prior'). On 15 Apr. he reported: 'I thought to have finished Rowe's life to day, but I have five or six visitors who hindred me, and I have not been quite well.' By 9 May 1780 he could list it among the lives already 'done' (*Letters*, iii. 228, 238, 254). It was no doubt while working on it in Apr. that SJ noticed the attribution to R in *Eng. Poets* (1779) of an 'Epigram on a Lady who shed her Water at seeing the Tragedy of *Cato*', 'a little piece unnaturally and odiously obscene' about which he protested to Nichols: 'I was offended, but was still more offended when I could not find it in Rowe's genuine volumes. To admit it had been wrong, to interpolate it is surely worse. If I had known of such a piece in the whole collection I should have been angry.—What can be done?' (*Letters*, iii. 226–7). Whether or not he tried to mollify SJ at the time, Nichols was unrepentant after his death about the inclusion of the epigram (which in fact appeared in some early editions of R's *Works*): see *Gent. Mag.* (1785), 10 n. (It is now usually attributed to Pope, or to Pope and R jointly: see *TE*, vi. 99–100.) Mrs Thrale had read proofs of 'Rowe' (bound with 'Prior') by 6 Aug. 1780, presumably in one of the prepublication volumes SJ had promised her on 27 July (*Thraliana*, i. 448; *Letters*, iii. 289).

Nichols later recalled: 'The life of Rowe is a very remarkable instance of the uncommon strength of Dr. Johnson's memory. When I received from him the MS. he complacently observed, "that the criticism was tolerably well done, considering that he had not seen Rowe's Works for thirty years"' (*J's Works*, ed. A. Chalmers (1806), x. 72 n.; cf. 'Congreve' 33 below). (The comment is placed in perspective by the fact that, when Mrs Thrale made him read out some passages from his own *Irene* (1749) in Aug. 1778, he said that 'he had not ever Read so much of it before since it was first printed': see Burney, *Early Journals*, iii. 110.) SJ had no doubt read R's plays carefully in the early 1750s for the *Dict.*, in which 235 quotations appeared (increased to 241 in 1773). For his ability to recite passages from them, see 7 n. below. His memory did not extend to dates for the plays, which do not appear in his MS (see Textual Notes to 5, 10–11, 14–16 below) and may have been supplied by Isaac Reed.

Apart from 'Pope', 'Rowe' is the only biography to survive in MS (Hyde Collection). For a facsimile, see the *R. B. Adam Library* (1929), vol. i (after 159), and for a discussion of some of its features, see Introduction, i. 176–7 above.

**Sources.** Much of SJ's information (but with little critical discussion of the plays apart from *Tamerlane*) was available in Philip Nichols's article in *BB*, v (1760), 3520–31. For once SJ might just as well have relied on *GD*, viii (1739), 786–9, since both sources made much use of the memoir of R by the Whig physician Dr James Welwood (1652–1727) prefixed to *Lucan's Pharsalia* (1718), pp. xviii–xxv. SJ did, however, also consult Welwood at first hand (see 22–6 below). The entries in Jacob, i. 212–13, and Shiels, *Lives*, iii. 272–84, have little relevance, unless SJ glances at Shiels in 7 below. In his notes to 19–20 SJ acknowledges his use of the Spence MSS, to which he had access from early Feb. 1780.

For use of R in the *Dict.*, see above.

**Publication.** In *Prefaces*, vol. vi (15 May 1781). There are no proofs.

**Modern Sources:**
N. Ault, 'Pope and R', in *New Light on Pope* (1949), 128–55
J. D. Canfield, *NR and Christian Tragedy* (Gainesville, Fla., 1977)
J. D. Canfield and A. W. Hesse, in *Dictionary of Literary Biography*, lxxxiv (1989), 262–89
J. A. Dussinger, 'Richardson and J: Critical Agreement on R's *The Fair Penitent*', *ES* 49 (1968), 45–7

A. W. Hesse, 'Some Neglected Life Records of NR', *N & Q* 220 (1975), 348–53, 484–8

A. W. Hesse, 'Pope's Role in Tonson's "Loss of R"', *N & Q* 222 (1977), 234–5

A. W. Hesse, 'Who was Bit by R's Comedy *The Biter?*', *PQ* 62 (1983), 477–85

A. Jenkins, *NR* (Boston, 1977)

J. Sutherland (ed.), *Three Plays by NR* (1929)

1. R was in fact born at Little Berkford, now Little Barford, near Bedford. (SJ's 'Berkford' in the MS, following Welwood and other sources, was misprinted as 'Beckford' in 1781–3: see Textual Notes.) He was baptized 30 June 1674. His father John Rowe entered the Middle Temple on 7 May 1669 and was called to the Bar on 29 May 1674. His mother Elizabeth died in 1679.

   *dispensing power*: the monarch's privilege of exercising exemption from the operation of statutes, used recently by James II to appoint Catholics to offices. SJ's source is the statement in Welwood, *Pharsalia*, p. xix, that John Rowe 'durst do this in the late King *James's* Reign, at a time when a *Dispensing Power* was set up, as inherent in the Crown'. It was in fact after James II's flight that John Rowe published *Les Reports de G. Benloe et G. Dalison des divers pleadings* (1689), on Elizabethan legal cases. He died on 30 Apr. 1692, shortly after becoming a sergeant-at-law, and was buried in the Middle Temple Church.

1 note. *the Villare*: the list of English cities, towns, and villages in Sir Henry Spelman, *Villare Anglicanum* (1656) (cf. 'Gay' 1 n. below). The modern spelling is Lamerton (near Tavistock).

2. SJ rarely uses the first names of his poets, but cf. 'Swift' 7, 'Thomson' 1, and 'Watts' 3 below.

   After the 'Free School' founded by Sir Roger Chomondeley in Highgate (*J's Works* (1787), iii. 28 n.), R attended Westminster School 1688–91: for Dr Richard Busby, the famous headmaster, see 'Dryden' 4 and n. above.

3. R in fact entered the Middle Temple, 4 Aug. 1691, at the age of 17, when his father was described as one of the Masters of the Utter Bar. SJ's comments on R's understanding of the law derive directly or indirectly from Welwood.

4. At his death in 1692, R's father left him £300 p.a. and his chambers in the Middle Temple (Spence, i. 349). R was called to the Bar 22 May 1696, but relinquished his chambers in the Middle Temple by May 1700. For earlier depictions of students who left 'the drudgery of the law' for 'the more airy and elegant parts of learning', see *Rambler* 26 (1750), and *Idler* 71 (1759), in which Dick Shifter 'made a copious collection of plays, poems, and romances, to which he has recourse when he fancies himself tired with statutes and reports' (*YW*, iii. 142, ii. 220). Steele had described the 'Templar', who preferred wit and the theatre to his legal studies, in *Spectator* 2 (1711). Cf. also the 'Clerk', 'Who pens a Stanza when he should *engross*' in Pope, *Epistle to Arbuthnot*, ll. 17–18, Tom Riot in the *Connoisseur* 133 (1756), and 'Congreve' 4–5 below.

   R was in fact 26 when *The Ambitious Step-Mother* was acted in Dec. 1700 (published 1701). It was praised by Congreve, by the anonymous *A Comparison between the Two Stages* (1702), 180–1, and by Downes, *Roscius Anglicanus* (1708), 45.

5. *Tamerlane* was acted Dec. 1701 with Thomas Betterton in the title role (published 1702). *BB*, v. 3520 n., discussed at length the identifications of Tamerlane and

Bajazet as William III and Louis XIV: for a modern discussion, see J. Loftis, *The Politics of Drama in Augustan England* (Oxford, 1963), 31–4. R's praise of Tamerlane's 'piety, moderation, fatherly love of his people, and hatred of tyranny and oppression' in his dedication encouraged the association with King William, as did Garth's prologue. Welwood, *Pharsalia*, p. xx, enlarged on R's 'noble' characterization of Tamerlane, which derived from Richard Knolles's *General History of the Turkes* (1603): see Canfield, *NR*, 47. For SJ's attitude to William III elsewhere, see 'Prior' 13 and n. below.

6. For 'occasional poetry', see 'Dryden' **230–3** and nn. above.

    After Apr. 1710, *Tamerlane* was not acted again till 1715, i.e. during the years of Tory ascendancy. It was later acted annually on 4 and 5 Nov., the anniversaries of William III's birthday and landing in England, often with a new prologue or epilogue expressing loyalty to the government. R wrote such a prologue in 1716, and Horace Walpole produced a new epilogue for performances on 4 and 5 Nov. 1746, to mark the suppression of the recent Jacobite rising (Walpole, *Corresp.*, xiii. 16 n.). Garrick wrote to John Home from Drury Lane Theatre, 5 Nov. 1757: 'I sit down to write you in the midst of drums, trumpets, and, above all, the roarings of the mighty Bajazet; we are celebrating the glorious and immortal memory as loudly as we can' (*Letters*, ed. D. M. Little and G. M. Kahrl (1963), i. 269). Within a few years a writer in the *St. James's Chronicle*, 12 Nov. 1761, claimed that the origin of the custom was no longer remembered.

    *a Saracen upon a sign*: in Addison's *Spectator* 121 (1711), the depiction of Sir Roger de Coverley on an inn sign is changed 'by a little Aggravation of the Features... into the *Saracen's Head*'.

7. *The Fair Penitent* was acted in May 1703 (published 1703). It had been performed in London annually between 1776 and 1783, notably in 1782 when Mrs Siddons played Calista. After meeting SJ at the Bishop of Chester's in 1782, Hannah More wrote: 'You would have enjoyed seeing him take me by the hand in the middle of dinner, and repeat with no small enthusiasm, many passages from the "Fair Penitent"' (*J. Misc.*, ii. 197).

    For the appeal of the 'domestick', see **15** below and 'Otway' **10** and n. above, and for 'diction', 'Cowley' **181–4** and n. above.

    *The Fair Penitent* was in fact an adaptation of Philip Massinger's *The Fatal Dowry* (1632), one reason why Hester Thrale believed in July 1780 that SJ here overpraises R's play (*Thraliana*, i. 448). For an extended comparison of the two plays, see *Gent. Mag.* (1782), 603–6. Richard Cumberland in *The Observer*, Nos. 77–9 (1785), later replied to SJ by arguing that Massinger's play was superior (see S. Elledge (ed.), *Eighteenth-Century Critical Essays* (Ithaca, NY, 1961), ii. 948–70). According to 'The Bookseller to the Reader', prefixed to Massinger's *The Bond-Man; or, Love and Liberty* (1719), all fourteen of his plays had been 'revised by Mr. *Rowe* before his Death, and design'd by him for the Press'.

8. Lovelace is the villain of Samuel Richardson's *Clarissa* (1747–8). Introducing Richardson's *Rambler* 97 (1751), SJ described him as an author who 'has enlarged the knowledge of human nature, and taught the passions to move at the command of virtue' (*YW*, iv. 153). In a chapter he either wrote or influenced in Charlotte Lennox's *The Female Quixote* (1752), IX. xi, Richardson is again praised for conveying 'the most solid Instructions, the noblest Sentiments, and the most

exalted Piety, in the pleasing Dress of a Novel'. See also *Life*, ii. 49, 174–5, *J. Misc.*, ii. 190, and Dussinger, 'Richardson', 45–7.

Some anxious discussions of the propriety of exhibiting vicious characters on the stage followed Collier's attack on the theatre in 1698: see Dennis, *Works*, i. 185, 477–8 n. Francis Gentleman, *The Dramatic Censor* (1770), i. 273, later considered R's Lothario 'the most reproachable character our moral author ever drew, and indeed as dangerous a one as we know . . . this licentious gallant, gilds his pernicious principles with very delusive qualifications, especially for the fair sex'.

For the dangerous attraction of vicious characters, see also *Rambler* 4 (1750): 'Vice, for vice is necessary to be shewn, should always disgust; nor should the graces of gaiety, or the dignity of courage, be so united with it, as to reconcile it to the mind' (*YW*, iii. 24). In 1765 he wrote: 'There is always danger lest wickedness conjoined with abilities should steal upon esteem, though it misses of approbation; but the character of Iago is so conducted, that he is from the first scene to the last hated and despised' (*YW*, viii. 1047, and cf. vii. 375, 523–4, viii. 938). The problem arises primarily from sexual glamour, since SJ is more tolerant of Rhodegune's heroic wickedness in 11 below, as earlier of Almanzor's 'illustrious depravity' in *The Conquest of Granada* ('Dryden' 48 above). See also 'Savage' 198 below.

Richardson had in fact revised *Clarissa* to make Lovelace's villainy more obvious to susceptible women readers. Beattie, *Essays* (Edinburgh, 1776), 403–4, had recently discussed the need to depict a character's faults and accomplishments so as to 'engage our esteem, pity, or admiration, without weakening our hatred of vice, or love of virtue'.

9. John Downes, *Roscius Anglicanus* (1708), 46, thought *The Fair Penitent* 'a very good Play for three *Acts*' only. Horace Walpole stated in 1775 that 'the four first acts . . . are very good' (*Corresp.*, xli. 297). SJ noted in 1765 of Shakespeare that, 'When he found himself near the end of his work, and in view of his reward, he shortened the labour, to snatch the profit' (*YW*, vii. 71–2; and cf. vii. 400, viii 566, 1011).

Shiels, *Lives*, iii. 276–7, also stated that Calista 'has not the least claim to be called the Fair Penitent, which would be better changed to the Fair Wanton'. Her final remorse arose from 'external distress' rather than 'any compunctions of conscience . . . he has not drawn a Penitent'. For a modern discussion, see Canfield, *NR*, 129–30, 145 n. SJ had decided to reduce his own heroine's repentance for treachery and apostasy in his *Irene* (1749): see K. H. Adams, 'A Critic Formed: SJ's Apprenticeship with *Irene*, 1736–1749', in P. Nath (ed.), *Fresh Reflections on SJ* (Troy, NY, 1987), 192–4.

10. *Ulysses*, in fact acted on 22 Nov. 1705 (published 1706), had ten performances by 15 Dec.

*mythological stories*: for SJ's dislike of them, see 'Butler' 41 n. above. Hume observed of such 'repetition': 'We have become so much accustom'd to the names of MARS, JUPITER, VENUS, that . . . the constant repetition of these ideas makes them enter into the mind with facility, and prevail upon the fancy, without influencing the judgment' (*Treatise of Human Nature*, ed. L. A. Selby-Bigge (2nd edn., Oxford, 1978), 121).

11. *The Royal Convert*, in fact acted 25 Nov. 1707 (published 1708), is set in a pseudo-Saxon England. SJ may allude to Burke's discussion of the 'reasons in nature why

the obscure idea, when properly conveyed, should be more affecting than the clear'
(*A Philosophical Enquiry into the Sublime and Beautiful* (1958), 61). For the importance of holding the 'attention', see 'Dryden' **312** and n. above.

Dryden translated the play's motto, 'Laudatur et alget' (Juvenal, *Sat.*, I. 74) as
'[For virtue is but drily] prais'd, and starves'.

12. Cf. *Tamerlane*, II. i: 'Now mourn, thou God of Love, since Honour triumphs.' SJ
had made this point in *Rambler* 140 (1751): 'The god of love is mentioned in
*Tamerlane* with all the familiarity of a Roman epigrammatist' (*YW*, iv. 377).
Rhodegune talks of Venus and Jupiter's thunder in *The Royal Convert*, III. i and
IV. i *ad fin.* In May 1780, shortly after completing 'Rowe', SJ stated in conversation
that the Saxon Rhodegune 'could never have heard about Jupiter' (*Thraliana*, i. 384).

In *Rambler* 140 SJ noted the 'frequent outrages of local or chronological propriety' in Milton's *Samson Agonistes*, while referring wryly to his own *Irene* (1749), I.
ii. 58–9: 'a late writer has put Harvey's doctrine of the circulation of the blood into
the mouth of a Turkish statesman' i.e. 200 years before its discovery (*YW*, iv. 377).
For Shakespeare's carelessness about 'distinctions of time or place', see *YW*, vii.
72, viii. 663, 703, 908. Addison noted similar lapses in Dryden's tragedies in
*Guardian* 110 (1713). For such anachronisms see also 'Roscommon' **28** above and
'Granville' **32** and 'Pope' **241** below.

13. The closing lines of *The Royal Convert* allude to the recent Union of England and
Scotland (1707), imitating Cranmer's prophecy at the end of Shakespeare's *Henry
VIII*, v. v.

14. *The Biter*, acted in fact on 4 Dec. 1704 (published 1705), satirized an East India
merchant: see Hesse, 'Who was Bit', 477–85 and **30** below. SJ defines 'Biter' as 'A
tricker; a deceiver', quoting Steele, *Spectator* 504 (1712) (*Dict.*).

Congreve described *The Biter* on 9 Dec. as 'a foolish farce ... which was damned'
(*Letters and Documents*, ed. J. C. Hodges (1964), 34). According to Downes, *Roscius
Anglicanus* (1708), 46, 'it had a six Days run; the six Days running it out of Breath,
it Sicken'd and Expir'd'. Thomas Davies also told the story of R laughing at his
own jests in 1784: 'Did not the tragic Rowe write The Biter, a comedy; and was he
not the only person of the audience that laughed during the acting of it?' (*Dramatic
Miscellanies* (1784), i. 167–8). Although SJ's 'He is said' often implies a source in
oral tradition, he himself may have been Davies's source.

15. R dedicated *Jane Shore*, acted 2 Feb. 1714 (published 1714), to the youthful Duke
of Queensbury, with a eulogy of his father (see **19** below). The play was performed
annually in London between 1776 and 1783.

R's title page announced his professed imitation of Shakespeare. For an immediate complaint about its perfunctoriness, see Charles Gildon, *A New Rehearsal, Or
Bays the Younger* (1714), 77, expanded as *Remarks on Mr. Rowe's Tragedy of the
Lady Jane Grey, and All his Other Plays* (1715). Pope said in 1736: 'It was mighty
simple in Rowe to write a play now, professedly in Shakespeare's style, that is,
professedly in the style of a bad age' (Spence, i. 183). In *Peri Bathous* (1728) Pope
had mocked 'a Play professedly writ in the style of Shakespear', but in fact quoted
a line from *Lady Jane Grey* (Pope, *Prose Works*, ii. 204). See also Shiels, *Lives*,
iii. 278, and, for an account of R's pseudo-Shakespearian effects, Sutherland,
*Three Plays*, 33–5. SJ had not reacted to Dryden's earlier claim to have imitated
Shakespeare in *All for Love* (1678): see 'Dryden' **78** n. above.

Mrs Thrale noted that the only 'particularly tender' passage SJ ever praised was Jane Shore's 'Forgive me! *but* forgive me' in Act V, also admired by Warton, *Essay* (1756), 275–6. In 1782 Hannah More heard SJ condemn whining about 'metaphysical distresses, when there was so much want and hunger in the world. I told him I supposed that he never wept at any tragedy but Jane Shore, who had died for want of a loaf. He called me a saucy girl, but did not deny the inference' (*J. Misc.*, i. 283–4, ii. 196–7). See also **32** below and, for the 'domestick', **7** above and 'Otway' **10** and n. above.

16. R explained in the preface to *Lady Jane Grey*, acted 20 Apr. 1715 (published 1715), that Edmund Smith's MS, which he obtained through Thomas Burnet and George Duckett in Apr. 1714, contained only one 'near perfect' scene, of which he could use 'some thirty lines at the most' after 'some alteration': see 'Smith' **24, 54–5** (where SJ is more positive about the play's subject), **66** above.

Although SJ claims that R's tragedy 'has sunk into oblivion', Reed, *Biographia Dramatica* (1782), ii. 183, stated: 'This is an admirable play, and is frequently performed with success to this day, though not absolutely on the acting list of plays.' It had been acted at Covent Garden as recently as 9 Dec. 1774.

According to *BB*, v. 3522 n., citing William Ayre, *Memoirs of Pope* (1745), i. 210–11, R discussed with Pope in 1716 the possibility of a play about Charles I, and before his death began a tragedy about the Rape of Lucretia, a subject he preferred to Pope's suggestion of Mary Queen of Scots.

17. See **4** n. above. For an account of the financial arrangements in 1706 which secured R a steady income for the rest of his life, see Hesse, 'Life Records', 348–53.

*negligence or hurry*: cf. SJ's comments on Dryden, who also wrote prologues and epilogues to order for others, in 'Dryden' **90, 340–1** above. Pope in fact provided a jaunty 'Epilogue to *Jane Shore* Design'd for Mrs. Oldfield', which was not spoken or printed with the play, perhaps because she disliked it: see N. Ault, *New Light on Pope* (1949), 133–8. R wrote a new epilogue for Congreve's *Love for Love* on Thomas Betterton's retirement from the stage (1709); a prologue for Susanna Centlivre's *The Gamester* (1704), and an epilogue for her *The Cruel Gift* (1716); and a prologue to Cibber's *The Non-Juror* (1717). For a poem addressed by Mrs Centlivre to R in 1718, see *Eighteenth Century Women Poets* (Oxford, 1989), 77–8.

18. In the MS this paragraph is marked for insertion from the appended materials, presumably as an afterthought: see Textual Notes.

R's edition of Shakespeare's *Works* (6 vols., 1709; 9 vols., 1714) added biographical information from Thomas Betterton, made some progress in correction of the text, and for the first time made the plays widely accessible in octavo format. R received £36 10s. for the edition (*Gent. Mag.* (1787), 76). As in 1765 (*YW*, vii. 93), SJ mistakenly suggests that R's preface and biography were distinct, as Reed noted in *Lives*, ii (1790), 315 n.

*boasts of criticism*: SJ echoes his statement in 1765 that, although R 'seems to have thought very little on correction or explanation', later editors have silently adopted his textual emendations, which, had they been their own, would have been introduced with 'ostentatious expositions' and 'self congratulations'. Although it was 'not written with much elegance or spirit', R's life of Shakespeare had been put to similar use (*YW*, vii. 93–4). SJ made several references to R in 1765, but later attaches more importance to Pope's edition in popularizing Shakespeare ('Pope' **128** below).

19. Although R applied to the Earl of Halifax for a public post as early as Oct. 1705 (Sutherland, *Three Plays*, 7), it was apparently through the Duke of Somerset that he became under-secretary to James Douglas, Duke of Queensberry, Secretary of State (primarily for Scotland), from 5 Feb. 1709 until the Duke's death on 6 July 1711 (see **25** below). Swift wrote on 8 Mar. 1709: 'Nic Row is with great difficulty coming in to be Secretary to the Duke of Queensberry, much against his Grace's Inclination' (*Corresp.*, i. 129). For Welwood's comment on the relationship, see **25** below.

Pope told the anecdote about R and Robert Harley, Earl of Oxford, in 1736 (Spence, i. 96). It is also found in John Ozell's translation of Mayans y Siscár's *Life of Cervantes* (1738), 67, Shiels, *Lives*, iii. 280, *The Tell-Tale* (2 vols., 1756), ii. 384–5, and *BB*, v. 3521 n. George Harris recorded a version supposedly told by R himself in his diary on 4 Dec. 1744 (D. Burrows and R. Dunhill, *Music and Theatre in Handel's World* (Oxford, 2002), 209). Another early version is related of 'ane English gentleman . . . very much noticed for his wit and poetry, and withall a man of no fortune': see *The Lockhart Papers*, ed. A. Aufrere (2 vols., 1817), i. 372. For another story involving a poet and *Don Quixote*, see 'Blackmore' **4** below.

Although Hill (1905) stated that R owned *Don Quixote* only in French, the sale catalogue of his library (26 Aug. 1719) listed a Spanish edition, as well as a Spanish grammar and dictionary: see Canfield, *NR*, 184, 189, and A. W. Hesse, 'NR's Knowledge of Spanish', *PBSA* 69 (1975), 546–52, and **23** below. SJ himself took Spanish lessons from Baretti, as he told Mrs Thrale, 2 Apr. 1773, but could already read the language and owned a Spanish edition of *Don Quixote* (*Letters*, ii. 26 and n.; *Life*, i. 49, 526).

*consolation*: so SJ's MS, although 'congratulation' later appeared in all editions (see Textual Notes).

20. Although Shiels, *Lives*, iii. 280, later referred to his 'wanton cruelty' to R, Pope believed that Oxford had not meant to be 'cruel': 'it was more like his odd way' (Spence, i. 96). Lord Hailes commented *c*.1782: 'I believe that Rowe *took* a hint which the Minister did not mean to give, & that what Ld O. said, was merely in ye style of levee conversation': see Carnie (1956), 176. For Oxford's inadequacy as a patron, see 'Parnell' **5** above and 'Pope' **91** below, and for Pope's friendship with R, **27** and n. below.

Pope was also the source for R's reluctance to converse with Tories (Spence, i. 93). Swift in fact claimed to have pressed Oxford for favours for R and other Whig authors (*Corresp.*, ii. 369; *Jnl. to Stella*, 27 Dec. 1712, ii. 589). For a Tory poet who disliked conversing with Whigs, see 'Prior' **45** below. In 1773 SJ condemned Burke's 'maxim of sticking to a certain set of *men* on all occasions' for political reasons (*Life*, v. 36).

21. With SJ's first sentence, cf. Welwood's final sentence in **25** below.

*poet laureat*: Nahum Tate, who had succeeded Shadwell in Dec. 1692, was not 'ejected', but died on 30 July 1715 in The Mint (the asylum for debtors: cf. 'Pope' **269** below). R became Laureate to George I on 1 Aug. 1715. Thomas Gray, who declined the Laureateship in Dec. 1757 ('Gray' **15** below), told Mason that 'Rowe was, I think, the last Man of character that had it' (*Corresp.*, ii. 544). Although R produced his *Ode for the New Year MDCCXVI* (1716), he wrote on 22 Oct. 1716 to ask John Hughes for assistance with his next official ode (J. Duncombe (ed.), *Letters, By Several Eminent Persons Deceased*, i (1772), 106–7 and n.).

R's salary as Land-Surveyor of the Customs (Sept. 1716) was £200 p.a. Gay mentions his appointment as Clerk of the Prince of Wales' Council on 30 Dec. 1714 (*Letters* (1966), 16). Seven months before he died, he became Clerk of the Presentations in Chancery on 5 May 1718. For the fortunes of other poets after the Hanoverian accession, see 'Addison' 81 and n. below.

22. Passages from the translation of Lucan had appeared in Tonson's *Poetical Miscellanies*, v (1704), 93–101, and vi (1709), 49–161, volumes which R may in effect have edited. Anthony Collins, *A Discourse of Free-Thinking* (1713), 141–7, also quoted part of Book IX as by 'an *Ingenious Author*'. For Pope's 'good opinion' of R's translation in 1710, see *Corresp.*, i. 104. Addison also praised it in *Freeholder* 40 (1716). Welwood published the full translation after R's death (dated 1718 for Mar. 1719: see Foxon, *English Verse*, R 292), 391 subscribers taking 431 copies. Cf. 'Hughes' 11 below.

23–6. SJ quotes James Welwood's 'Preface. Giving some Account of Lucan and his Works, and of Mr. Rowe' in *Lucan's Pharsalia*, pp. xxiv–xxv (but omitting the preferments already listed in 21 above). The passage is marked for insertion in the MS (see Textual Notes). SJ quotes more from Welwood than *BB*, *GD*, or Shiels *Lives*, iii. 282–3.

23. R 'was a pretty personage, and a very pretty sort of man' ([Erasmus?] Lewis, in Spence, i. 349).

26. R married Antonia, daughter of Anthony Parsons, Auditor of the Revenue, on 6 July 1693. After her death in Feb. 1712, he married Anne, daughter of Joseph Devenish of Buckham, Dorset. She signed the dedication of *Lucan's Pharsalia* to George I, who rewarded her with a pension of £40 p.a. (Cunningham, *Lives* (1854), ii. 113–14 n.). Lord Hailes believed that Pope, *Epilogue to the Satires* (1738), II. 108–9, alludes to her later marriage to a Col. Deane or Deanes, but this has not been generally accepted (see Dryden, *Prose Works*, ed. Malone (1800), i (i). 386 n.). She published R's *Works* (2 vols., 1747).

Unusually, SJ leaves it to Welwood to describe R's death. Charles Beckingham dedicated *Musarum Lachrymae: or Miscellany Poems to the Memory of Nicholas Rowe, by Several Hands* (1719) to Congreve. For Pope's epitaphs on R, see 'Pope' 408–10 and n. below.

27. *the fondness of a friend*: see also 'Smith' 2 and n. above and 'Addison' 14 below.

SJ quotes Pope's letter to John Caryll, 20 Sept. 1713, which he readdressed to Edward Blount, 10 Feb. 1716, in print (*Corresp.*, i. 190, 329–30, and cf. i. 186–7). *GD*, viii. 792, gave part of this passage, but *BB*, v. 3522 n., had merely summarized it. In 1743 Pope remembered R laughing 'all day long! he would do nothing else but laugh' (Spence, i. 109). For an account of R's good nature and affability, see William Ayre, *Memoirs of Pope* (1745), i. 209–19, and for R's friendship with Pope, Ault, 'Pope and R', 128–55.

28. SJ quotes Warburton from Owen Ruffhead, *Life of Pope* (1769), 493 n. Insertion of the passage is called for in the MS: see Textual Notes. With Pope's alleged opinion that R 'had no heart', cf. his 'Epitaph on Mr. Rowe', l. 4: 'For never Heart felt Passion more sincere.'

29. For SJ's scepticism about 'pointed sentences', see also 'Sheffield' 14 below, and 'pointed axioms' in 'Waller' 82 above.

30. Shiels, *Lives*, iii. 284, stated that R's poems 'are but little read', while 'the most celebrated speeches in his plays . . . are repeated by every body who reads poetry, or attends plays'. For *The Biter*, see 14 above. SJ surprisingly ignores R's popular 'Colin's Complaint': see 'Addison' 85 and 'Shenstone' 25 below, and the references to it in his review of Warton's *Essay on Pope* in 1756 (*OASJ*, 490), and in letters of 15 Sept. 1777 and 11 Apr. 1780 (*Letters*, iii. 67, 235, 237). In 1767 Goldsmith described it as 'better than any thing of the kind in our language' (*Coll. Works*, v. 329).

For SJ's protests at the bawdy 'Epigram' attributed to R in *Eng. Poets* (1779), see headnote above.

31. *the Unities*: although SJ defended Shakespeare's failure to observe the Unities of Time and Place in 1765, he did not consider them an irrelevance (cf. *YW*, vii. 76–7, 216, and viii. 1037, 1048). He defines 'Drama' as 'A poem accomodated to action; a poem in which the action is not related, but represented; and in which therefore such rules are to be observed as make the representation probable' (*Dict.*). See also 'Addison' 144 below, introducing Dennis's discussion of the absurder consequences of 'rigorous unity'. In 1765 SJ stated: 'He that can take the stage at one time for the palace of the Ptolemies, may take it in half an hour for the promontory of Actium . . . where is the absurdity of allowing that space to represent first Athens, and then Sicily, which was always known to be neither Sicily nor Athens, but a modern theatre' (*YW*, vii. 77).

*an act*: in *Rambler* 156 (1751), which also questioned the Unities, SJ stated that 'Whenever the scene is shifted the act ceases' (*YW*, v. 68), and later defines 'Act' as '7. A part of a play, during which the action proceeds without interruption' (*Dict.*).

After the abrupt ending of the execution scene in *Lady Jane Grey*, Act. V, Pembroke and Gardiner speak the final nineteen lines.

32. For 'discrimination of characters', see 'Milton' 268 and n. above, and for the 'general', 'Cowley' 58 and n. above.

SJ's summary comments here and in 33 hardly explain his praise of *The Fair Penitent* in 7 above as 'one of the most pleasing tragedies on the stage'. For *Jane Shore*, see 15 and n. above. Alicia's mad-scene in Act V impressed others more: for Warton, *Essay* (1756), 276, 'the madness of Alicia is well painted', and Charles Churchill praised Susannah Cibber in the role in *The Rosciad* (1761), ll. 787–92.

33. Cf. SJ's statement in 1765 that Shakespeare 'has speeches, perhaps sometimes scenes, which have all the delicacy of Rowe, without his effeminacy' (*YW*, vii. 91; for other references to R's plays, see vii. 416, viii. 966). Warton, *Essay on Pope* (1756), 272–3, had similarly described R's failure, for all his elegant diction and 'versification highly melodious', to 'cleave the heart with pangs of commiseration': his plays are 'musical and pleasing poems', but 'inactive and unmoving tragedies'.

One of Dick Minim's critical commonplaces in *Idler* 60 (1759) may glance at Warton: 'The versification of Rowe he thought too melodious for the stage, and too little varied in different passions' (*YW*, ii. 187). Others, however, had said much the same: see Shiels, *Lives*, iii. 74–5, 278, and Robert Dodsley's reference in a letter of 2 Apr. 1757 to the 'smooth & flowing harmony of numbers (which I always look'd upon in Rowe as a fault)' (*Corresp.* (Cambridge, 1988), 271). For 'diction', see 7 above and 'Cowley' 181–4 and n. above.

34. SJ refers to *The Life of Pythagoras [by Dacier], with . . . The Golden Verses Translated from the Greek* (1707, for Oct. 1706), quoted in *Rambler* 129 (1751) (*YW*, iv. 324).

R translated Bk. I of Claude Quillet's *Callipaedia* (1712), George Sewell, Samuel Cobb, and William Diaper contributing the other books. SJ himself owned Latin and English versions of the *Callipaedia* when at Oxford, but *Eng. Poets* (1779) omitted this elegantly versified sex-manual. See also R. DeMaria, *SJ and the Life of Reading* (Baltimore, 1997), 109–11.

35. *Lucan's Pharsalia* (see **22** above) appeared in *Eng. Poets* (1779), vols. xxvii–xxviii. After his emphasis in **32–3** on the limitations of R's 'reasonableness and propriety', 'elegance', and 'suavity', and the absence of 'any deep search into nature', the importance SJ attaches to this verse translation is striking. Placed at the service of an ancient author, R's 'vigorous and animated versification', which 'seldom wants either melody or force', produced 'one of the greatest productions of English poetry'. SJ noticeably does not share Welwood's Whiggish enthusiasm for the way in which R's translation placed 'the Cause of Liberty . . . in such a Shining Light' (p. xxi).

In contrast, Shiels, *Lives*, iii. 283–4, while noting its 'musical' versification and fidelity, reported that R's *Pharsalia* was 'little read, and he is only distinguished as a dramatist'. *Gent. Mag.* (1781), 225, was also sceptical: 'it is rather a paraphrase than a translation, two lines of the original being often expanded into ten or twelve'. For translation, see also 'Denham' **32** and n. above.

For Quintilian on Lucan, see *Institutes*, x. i. 90. Dryden wrote in 1672 that Lucan 'treats you more like a philosopher than a poet, and instructs you in verse, with what he had been taught by his uncle Seneca in prose. In one word, he walks soberly afoot, when he might fly' (Watson, i. 60).

*senatorial*: so SJ's MS, although 'dictatorial' later appeared in all editions (see Textual Notes).